THE

WORKS

OF

DANIEL WEBSTER.

VOLUME V.

ELEVENTH EDITION.

BOSTON:
LITTLE, BROWN AND COMPANY.
1858.

DEDICATION

OF THE FIFTH VOLUME

TO

J. W. PAIGE, Esq.

My dear Sir:

The friendship which has subsisted so long between us, springs not more from our close family connection, than from similarity of opinions and sentiments.

I count it among the advantages and pleasures of my life; and I pray you to allow me, as a slight, but grateful token of my estimate of it, to dedicate to you this volume of my Speeches.

DANIEL WEBSTER

CONTENTS

OF THE FIFTH VOLUME.

SPEECHES IN CONGRESS.

LEGAL ARGUMENTS AND SPEECHES TO THE JURY.

SPEECHES IN CONGRESS.

(CONTINUED.)

A UNIFORM SYSTEM OF BANKRUPTCY.*

On the 1st of April, 1840, Mr. Webster obtained leave of the Senate to introduce a bill to establish a uniform system of bankruptcy, which was referred to the Standing Committee on the Judiciary. On the 3d of April, another bill for the same purpose was introduced, on leave, by Mr. Tallmadge of New York, and referred in like manner to the Judiciary Committee. These bills on the 18th of the same month were reported back to the Senate, without amendment. On the 22d of April, Mr. Clayton of Delaware, a member of the Judiciary Committee, reported a bill on the same subject; and on the same day, Mr. Wall of New Jersey, chairman of the committee, and on behalf of a minority, submitted an amendment intended to be proposed to the original bill introduced by Mr. Webster. The subject thus brought before the Senate was discussed for many successive days, principally in reference to the amendment proposed by the minority of the committee to Mr. Webster's bill. The character of the bill and of the amendment will sufficiently appear from the following speech.

I feel a deep and anxious concern for the success of this bill, and, in rising to address the Senate, my only motive is a sincere desire to answer objections which have been made to it, so far as I may be able, and to urge the necessity and importance of its passage. Fortunately, it is a subject which does not connect itself with any of the party contests of the day; and although it would not become me to admonish others, yet I have prescribed it as a rule to myself, that, in attempting to forward the measure, and to bring it to a successful termination, I shall seek no party ends, no party influence, no party advancement. The

* A Speech delivered in the Senate of the United States, on the 18th of May, 1840, on the proposed Amendment to the Bill establishing a Uniform System of Bankruptcy.

subject, so far as I am concerned, shall be sacred from the intrusion of all such objects and purposes. I wish to treat this occasion, and this highly important question, as a green spot in the midst of the fiery deserts of party strife, on which all may meet harmoniously and amicably, and hold common counsel for the common good.

The power of Congress over the subject of bankruptcies, the most useful mode of exercising the power under the present circumstances of the country, and the duty of exercising it, are the points to which attention is naturally called by every one who addresses the Senate.

In the first place, as to the power. It is fortunately not an inferred or constructive power, but one of the express grants of the Constitution. "Congress shall have power to establish uniform laws on the subject of bankruptcies throughout the United States." These are the words of the grant; there may be questions about the extent of the power, but there can be none of its existence.

The bill which has been reported by the committee provides for voluntary bankruptcies only. It contains no provisions by which creditors, on an alleged act of bankruptcy, may proceed against their debtors, with a view to subject them and their property to the operation of the law. It looks to no coercion by a creditor to make his debtor a subject of the law against his will. This is the first characteristic of the bill, and in this respect it certainly differs from the former bankrupt laws of the United States, and from the English bankrupt laws.

The bill, too, extends its provisions, not only to those who, either in fact or in contemplation of law, are traders, but to all persons who declare themselves insolvent, or unable to pay their debts and meet their engagements, and who desire to assign their property for the benefit of their creditors. In this respect, also, it differs from the former law, and from the law of England.

The questions, then, are two: 1st. Can Congress constitutionally pass a bankrupt law which shall include other persons besides traders? 2d. Can it pass a law providing for voluntary cases only, that is, cases in which the proceedings originate only with the debtor himself?

The consideration of both these questions is necessarily involved in the discussion of the present bill, inasmuch as it has been denied that Congress has power to extend bankrupt laws farther than to merchants and traders, or to make them applicable to voluntary cases only. This limitation of the power of Congress is asserted on the idea that the framers of the Constitution, in conferring the power of establishing bankrupt laws, must be presumed to have had reference to the bankrupt laws of England, as then existing; and that the laws of England then existing embraced none but merchants and traders, and provided only for involuntary or coercive bankruptcies.

Now, Sir, in the first place, allow me to remark, that the power is granted to Congress in the most general and comprehensive terms. It has one limitation only, which is, that laws on the subject of bankruptcies shall be uniform throughout the United States. With this qualification, the whole subject is placed within the discretion and under the legislation of Congress. The Constitution does not say that Congress shall have power to pass *a* bankrupt law, nor to introduce *the* system of bankruptcies. It declares that Congress shall have power to "establish uniform laws on the subject of bankruptcies throughout the United States." This is the whole clause; nor is there any limitation or restriction imposed by any other clause.

What, then, is "the subject of bankruptcies"? or, in other words, what are "bankruptcies"? It is to be remembered that the Constitution grants powers to Congress by particular or specific enumeration; and, in making this enumeration, it mentions bankruptcies as a head of legislation, or as one of the subjects over which Congress is to possess authority. Bankruptcies are the subject, and the word is most certainly to be taken in its common and popular sense; in that sense in which the people may be supposed to have understood it, when they ratified the Constitution. This is the true rule of interpretation. And I may remark, that it is always a little dangerous, in construing the Constitution, to search for the opinions or understanding of members of the Convention in any other sources than the Constitution itself, because the Constitution owes its whole force and authority to its ratification by the people, and the people judged of it by the meaning most apparent on its face. How particular members may have understood its provisions, if it could be ascertained, would not be conclusive. The question would still be, How did the people understand it? And this can be decided only by giving their usual acceptation to all words not evidently used in a technical sense, and by inquiring, in any case, what was the interpretation or exposition presented to the people when the subject was under consideration.

Bankruptcies, in the general use and acceptation of the term, mean no more than failures. A bankruptcy is a fact. It is an occurrence in the life and fortunes of an individual. When a man cannot pay his debts, we say he has become a bankrupt, or has failed. Bankruptcy is not merely the condition of a man who is insolvent, and on whom a bankrupt law is already acting. This would be quite too technical an interpretation. According to this, there never could be bankrupt laws, because every law, if this were the meaning, would suppose the existence of a previous law. Whenever a man's means are insufficient to meet his engagements and pay his debts, the fact of bankruptcy has taken place; a case of bankruptcy has arisen, whether there be a law providing for it or not.

There may be bankruptcies, or cases of bankruptcy, where there are no bankrupt laws existing. Or bankrupt laws may exist, which shall extend to some bankruptcies, or some cases of bankruptcy, and not to others. We constantly speak of bankruptcies happening among individuals, without reference to existing laws. Bankruptcies, as facts, or occurrences, or cases for which Congress is authorized to make provision, are failures. A learned judge has said that a law on the subject of bankruptcies, in the sense of the Constitution, is a law making provision for persons failing to pay their debts. Over the whole subject of these bankruptcies, or these failures, the power of Congress, as it stands on the face of the Constitution, is full and complete.

And now, let us see how it is that this broad and general power is, or can be, limited by a supposed reference to the English system. The argument is this. The members of the Convention which framed the Constitution, in conferring this power on Congress, must be supposed to have had reference to the bankrupt laws of England; and the bankrupt laws of England, as then existing, embraced only merchants and traders, and were only applied to debtors at the instance of their creditors; therefore the inference is said to be, that traders only should be regarded as subjects of any bankrupt law to be passed by Congress, and that no such law should give the debtor himself a right to become bankrupt, at his own request; or at least, that every such law should give a right to the creditor to proceed against his debtor. But is this the just analogy? Is this the point of view in which a general resemblance of our system and the English system may be supposed to have been contemplated? Clearly not, in my opinion. Let it be admitted that the framers of the Constitution looked to England for a general example; they must be supposed, nevertheless, to have looked to the power of Parliament, and not to the particular mode in which that power had been exercised, or the particular law then actually existing. The true analogy is, as it seems to me, between power and power; the power of Parliament and the power of Congress; and not between the power of Congress and any actually existing British statute, which might be, perhaps, in many respects, quite unsuitable to our condition.

The members of the Convention did not study the British statutes, nor examine judicial decisions, to ascertain the precise nature of the actually existing system of bankruptcy in England. Still less did the people of the United States trouble themselves with such inquiries. All saw that Parliament possessed and exercised a power of passing bankrupt laws, and of altering and amending them, from time to time, according to its own discretion, and the necessities of the case. This power they intended to confer on Congress, as largely, for aught that appears, as they saw it held by Parliament. The early British statutes were not confined to traders; later statutes were so confined; and more recently, again, changes have been made, which bring in very numerous classes of persons who were not esteemed traders, in England, at the time of the adoption of the Constitution of the United States. I may add that bankrupt laws, properly so called, or laws providing for the *cessio bonorum*, on the continent of Europe, and in Scotland, were never confined to traders; and while the members of the Convention may be supposed to have looked to the example of England, it is by no means improbable that they contemplated also the example and institutions of other countries. There is no reason to suppose that it was intended to tie up the hands of Congress to the establishment of that particular bankrupt system which existed in England in 1789, and to deny to it all power of future modification and amendment. It would be just as reasonable to say that the United States laws of copyright, of patents for inventions, and many others, could only be mere transcripts of such British statutes on the same subjects as existed in 1789.

The great object was to authorize Congress to establish a uniform system throughout all the States. No State could of itself establish such a system; it could only establish a system for itself; and the diversities, inconsistencies, and interferences of the several State systems had been subjects of much well-grounded complaint. It was intended to give Congress the power to establish uniformity in this respect; and if the English example was regarded, it was regarded in its general character of a power in Parliament to pass laws on the subject, to repeal them, and pass others, in its discretion, and to deal with the whole subject, from time to time, as experience of the exigencies of the public should suggest or require. The bankrupt system of England, as it existed in 1789, was not the same which had previously existed, nor the same as that which afterwards existed, or that which now exists. At first, the system was coercive, and the law a sort of criminal law, extending to all persons, as well as traders. But changes had taken place before 1789, and other changes, and very important changes, have taken place since. The system is now greatly simplified and improved, and it is also made much more extensive as to those whom it embraces. It is hardly too much to say, that it is preposterous to contend, not only that we are to refuse to ourselves the light of our own experience, and all regard to our own peculiar situation, but that we are also to exclude from our regard and notice all modern English improvements, and confine ourselves to the English bankrupt laws as they existed in 1789. The power of Congress is given in the fullest manner, and by the largest and most comprehensive terms and forms of expression; and it cannot be limited by vague presumptions of a reference to other existing codes, or loose conjectures about the intents of its framers, nowhere expressed or intimated in the instrument itself, or any contemporaneous exposition.

I think, then, that Congress may pass a law which shall include persons not traders, and which shall include voluntary cases only. And I think, further, that the amendment proposed by the honorable member from New Jersey is, in effect, exactly against his own argument. I think it admits all that he contends against. In the first place, he admits voluntary bankruptcies, and there were none such in England in 1789. This is clear. And in the next place, he admits any one who will say that he has been concerned in trade; and he maintains, and has asserted, that in this country any body may say that. Any body, then, may come in under the bill. The only difference is, unless he is *bonâ fide* a trader, he must come in under a disguise, or in an assumed character. Whatever be his employment, occupation, or pursuit, he must come in as a trader, or as one who has been concerned or engaged in trade. The honorable member attempts a distinction between the traders and those who can say that they have been engaged in trade. I cannot see the difference. It is too fine for me. A trader is one concerned in trade, and to be concerned in trade is to be a trader. What is the difference? But if persons may be concerned in trade, and yet not be traders, still such persons were not embraced in the English statutes, which apply to traders by name; and therefore the gentleman's bill would embrace persons not within those statutes as they stood in 1789.

The gentleman's real object is, not to confine the bill to traders, but to embrace every body; and yet he deems it necessary for every person applying to state, and to swear, that he has been engaged in trade. This seems to me to be both superfluous and objectionable; superfluous, because, if we have a right to bring in persons under one name, we may bring in the same persons under another name, or by a general description; objectionable, because it requires men to state what may very much resemble a falsehood, and to make oath to it. Suppose a farmer or mechanic to fail; can he take an oath that he has been engaged in trade? If the objection to bring in others than traders is well founded in the Constitution, surely mere form cannot remove it. Words cannot alter things. The Constitution says nothing about traders. Yet the honorable gentleman's amendment requires all applicants to declare themselves traders; and if they will but say so, and swear so, it shall be so received, and nobody shall contradict it. In other words, a fiction, not very innocent, shall be allowed to overcome an unconstitutional objection. The gentleman has been misled by a false analogy.

He has adopted an example which does not apply to the case, and which he yet does not follow out. The British statutes are confined to traders. But then they contain a long list of persons who, it is declared, shall be deemed and taken to be traders within the acts. This list they extend, from time to time; and whenever any one included within the list becomes a voluntary bankrupt, he avers, in substance, that he is a trader, within the act of Parliament. If it had been necessary, as it is not, to follow this example at all, the gentleman's bill should have declared all persons traders for the purposes of this act, and then every body could have made the declaration without impropriety, as in England the applicant only states that which the law has made true. He declares himself a trader, because the law has already declared that he shall be considered a trader. His conscience, therefore, is protected. He swears only according to the act of Parliament, if he swear at all. But as the provision stands here, it calls on every one to declare himself a trader, or that he has been engaged in trade, not within the particular meaning or sense of any act of Congress, but in the usual and popular acceptation of the word.

Suppose, Sir, a cotton-planter, by inevitable misfortune, by fire or flood, or by mortal epidemics among his hands, is ruined in his affairs. Suppose he desires to make a surrender of his property, and be discharged from his debts. He will be told, You cannot have the benefit of the law as a cotton-planter; it is made only for traders, or persons engaged in trade. Are you not a trader? No. I am no trader, and was never engaged in trade. I bought my land here, bought my hands from Carolina, have bought my stock from Kentucky, and raised cotton and sold it. But I never bought an article to sell again. I am no trader. But you must swear that you have been engaged in trade; you must apply, not as John Jones, Esquire, cotton-planter, on the Red River, but as Mr. John Jones, trader, at his storehouse, at or near the plantation of John Jones, Esquire. And so John Jones, the cotton-planter, must either remain as he is, excluded from the provisions of the law altogether, or sneak into them under a disingenuous fiction, if it be not something worse.

This attempt, therefore, Sir, to avoid a supposed difficulty, encounters two decisive objections. In the first place, there is no difficulty to be avoided; in the second place, if there were, this manner of avoiding it would be mere evasion.

But now, Sir, I come to a very important inquiry. The Constitution requires us to establish *uniform* laws on the subject of bankruptcy, if we establish any. What is this uniformity, or in what is it to consist? The honorable gentleman says that the meaning is, that the law must give a coercive power to creditors, as well as a voluntary power to debtors; that this is the constitutional uniformity. I deny this altogether. No idea of uniformity arises from any such consideration. The uniformity which the Constitution requires is merely a uniformity throughout all the States. It is a local uniformity, and nothing more. The words are perfectly plain, and the sense cannot be doubted. The authority is, to establish uniform laws on the subject of bankruptcies throughout the United States. Can any thing be clearer? To be uniform is to have one shape, one fashion, one form; and our bankrupt laws, if we pass them, are to have one shape, one fashion, and one form in every State. If this be not so, what is the sense of the concluding words of the clause, "throughout the United States"? My honorable friend from Kentucky* has disposed of this whole question, if there ever could be a question about it, by asking the honorable gentleman from New Jersey what *uniform* means, in the very same clause of the Constitution, where the word is applied to rules of naturalization; and what it means in a previous clause, where it declares that all duties of impost shall be *uniform* throughout the United States.

It can hardly be necessary to discuss this point further. If it were, the whole history of the Constitution would show the object of the provision. Bankrupt laws were supposed to be closely connected with commercial regulations. They were considered to be laws nearly affecting the intercourse, trade, and dealing between citizens of different States; and for this reason it was thought wise to enable Congress to make them uniform. The Constitution provided that there should be but one coinage, and but one power to fix the value of foreign coins. The legal medium of payment, therefore, in fulfilment of contracts, was to be ascertained and fixed, for all the States, by Congress,

* Mr. Crittenden.

and by Congress alone; and Congress, and Congress alone, was to have the power of providing a uniform mode in which contracts might be discharged without payment. Look to the discussion of the times; to the expositions of the Constitution by its friends when they urged its adoption; look to all within the Constitution, and all without it; look anywhere, or everywhere, and you will see one and the same purpose, one and the same meaning; and that meaning cannot be more clearly expressed than the words of the clause themselves express it, that laws to be established by Congress on the subject of bankruptcies *shall be uniform throughout the United States.*

Now, Sir, the gentleman's bill is not uniform. It proposes that there may be one law in Massachusetts, and another in New Jersey. The gentleman's bill includes corporations; but then it gives each State a power to exempt its own corporations, or any of them, from the operation of the law, if it shall so choose. It decides what shall be, in the case of banks, an act of bankruptcy; but then it provides that any State may say, nevertheless, that, in regard to its own banks, or any of them, this shall not be an act of bankruptcy.

Here is the provision: —

> "*Provided, however*, That nothing herein contained shall apply to, or in any wise affect, any corporation or association of persons, incorporated or acting under a law of any State of the Union, or any Territory of the United States, where such corporation or association shall be authorized by their charter, or any express law of such State or Territory, to do or commit the act herein declared to be an act of bankruptcy, or where, by any such law of any such State or Territory, the said incorporation or association of persons shall or may be exempted from the provisions of this act."

Pray, Sir, what sort of uniformity is this? A uniformity which consists in the authorized multiplication of varieties. Who will undertake to defend legislation of this kind, under our power to establish uniform laws on the subject of bankruptcies throughout the United States? Not only is it in direct violation of the plain text of the Constitution, but it leaves the very evils, every one of them, which a provision in the Constitution intended to shut out. The Constitution says that Congress may *establish* uniform laws; the gentleman's bill says that Congress may *propose* a law, at least so far as corporations are concerned, but that still each State may take what it likes, and reject the rest; and this, he contends, is establishing a uniform law.

I pray, Sir, where is this power of exemption to stop? If we may authorize States to exempt their corporations, may we not, with equal propriety, authorize them to exempt their individual citizens? May we not say that each State may decide for itself whether it will have any thing to do with the law, when we have passed it, or what parts it will adopt, and what parts it will refuse to adopt?

But, Sir, I must wait till some attempt is made to defend this part of the gentleman's bill. I must see some show of propriety, some plausibility, before I reason against it further. In the view I take of it at present, it appears to me utterly repugnant to the plain requirements of the Constitution, and destitute, not only of all argument for its support, but of all apology also. I see nothing in it but naked unconstitutionality.

But, Mr. President, if these provisions were constitutional, they would still be in the highest degree unjust, inexpedient, and inadmissible. What is the object of bringing the banks into the bill at all? Certainly there can be no just object other than to insure the constant and punctual discharge of their duties, by always paying their notes on presentment. Clearly there can be no object but to prevent their suspensions of payment. And it might be said that this object was kept in view, if the law were uniform, peremptory, inflexible, and applying to all banks. But when you give the power of exemption to the States, you sanction the very evil which you propose to remedy. You profess to prescribe a general rule, and yet authorize and justify its violation. Do not the States now exempt their banks, and is not that the very evil from which we suffer? Is not suspension, under the authority of State exemption, the topic, the discussion of which every day nearly stuns us by its reverberation from the walls of this chamber? The charters of the banks are, in general, well enough. They require punctual specie payments, under severe penalties, and, in some cases, under the penalty of forfeiture. But under the pressure of circumstances, and from a real or supposed necessity, the States relieve the banks from these penalties, and forbear to enforce the forfeitures. And will they not, most assuredly, also relieve the banks in the same manner, and for the same reasons, if they have the power, from the penalties of our bankrupt law? State permission, State indulgence, State exemption, is the very ground on which suspension now stands, and on which it is justified. And it is now proposed that Congress shall give its authority and sanction to all this. It is proposed that Congress shall solemnly recognize the principle, and approve and sanction the practice, of State exemption, of the suspension of specie payments by State authority. If the States will not enforce their own laws against the banks, can any one imagine that they will see the equally or still more severe penalties of our bankrupt law enforced, while they have the power to prevent it?

Some weeks ago, the honorable member from Pennsylvania* moved for a committee to inquire into the propriety of amending the Constitution, so as to insert a provision giving Congress power to restrain the circulation of small bank-notes. I did not concur in his measure, not thinking the Constitution needed amendment in that respect; but his argument was quite intelligible. He said that this abolition of small bills could not now be accomplished, because the States could not be brought to act in concert; yet they might all be brought to consent that Congress should establish a uniform rule upon the subject. That was a fair reasoning towards a proper object. It went for uniformity on a point of great commercial importance. But how is it here? We do not propose uniformity; we do not require that one rule may extend over all. Far otherwise; for we propose to authorize difference, according to the discretion and circumstances of the State. Having the power to establish uniformity, we delegate an authority to create variety. Charged by the Constitution to establish one rule, we ourselves, instead of performing that duty, call upon others to establish different and varying rules. All must see to what this leads, or rather, what this is; for it is a measure which would be perfect in its beginning; it would reach its destiny at its commencement, its mischievous tendencies would be accomplished at its birth. The passage of this bill would add the solemn sanction of Congress to the sanction by the States of the suspension of specie payments by the banks. That is the practical sum and substance, the long and the short of the whole matter. If our constitu-

* Mr. Buchanan.

tional power enables us to embrace the banks in this bill, and if we see no insuperable or greatly formidable practical objections, then, I think, we ought to include them all, without any power of escape.

Suppose the bill should be made uniform, then, and include all banks; have we the power, and is it expedient, to pass it in that shape?

On the motion for a committee, made some time ago by the member from Pennsylvania, to which I have already referred, I suggested the opinions which I entertain on one branch of the power of Congress connected with this subject. The constitutional point now arising I do not mean to treat, nor to decide; it is open to others, and will, no doubt, be discussed by them. But upon the expediency or propriety of including banks and other corporations in this bill, I will say a few words. The State with which I am connected can have as little objection to including banks in the bankrupt bill as any other State. Many persons in Massachusetts, quite respectable and well informed, are in favor of the measure. But it appears to me they have not well considered the practical difficulties. Let us look at what is proposed to be done.

There are eight hundred or a thousand State banks in the country, each with its charter conferring its rights, prescribing its duties, and enjoining penalties. They are banks of deposit, banks of discount, and banks of circulation. It is now generally admitted that they are lawfully created. Their legal existence is established. They possess in the aggregate, I suppose, two hundred millions of capital. Some of them are founded entirely on private ownership, while in some others the States creating them are proprietors, and in some others, again, the States are sole proprietors. Some of them have a right to suspend specie payments for a limited time; others have not this right, the charter of each being its own constitution.

Such being the general state of things, it is now proposed to subject all these banks to the operation of a bankrupt law, so that, when they stop payment for a day or an hour, their property and effects may be seized for distribution among their creditors, and their operations broken up. It is proposed to do this, although the charters of the banks may expressly authorize them to do that very thing which is an act of bankruptcy under this bill, and for which their property is to be thus seized. Heıc is certainly a direct collision between State authority and the authority of the United States, which ought to be avoided whenever it can be. The act of Congress in this case would be made to repeal or annul *pro tanto* the law of the State. I do not say that this can in no case be done; but I say that all such collisions ought to be avoided, if possible.

It is proposed that Congress shall prescribe duties to the banks not prescribed by their own charters; and for the violation of those duties thus prescribed by Congress, it is proposed to proceed against them as bankrupts, to sequestrate their effects, and virtually annul their franchises. If this can be done, should it be done without clear and cogent necessity? Without wishing to represent the proposition as extravagant, or speaking of it with disrespect, it seems to me to be bold, if not rash, until a case of absolute necessity is made out. What would become of the bank stock in case of such seizure and sequestration? What extent of depression and fluctuation would attach to it, when such a law should be passed? What would become of the entire circulation of the country, if a general suspension should happen, and all the banks should be thus seized? What would become of the country, creditors and debtors, and of all business, if a general suspension should happen, and all the banks should be placed in the hands of the federal courts, their paper entirely disgraced, and an immediate collection of all their debts attempted to be enforced? What would become of some of the States who own the banks, and of others who derive revenues from them? And how could such immense affairs be administered by the courts of the United States? These difficulties appear to me to be startling. If, indeed, we were quite confident that such a provision would hereafter prevent all general suspensions, we might venture upon the measure. We might expect to be able to deal with here and there an individual case. But this provision is not certain to prevent general suspension in great emergencies or great commercial revolutions. Twice within a few years the banks have suspended, notwithstanding the penalties of their own charters and the laws of their own States. The real truth is, that, in the absence of all regu'ation or control by Congress, the banks have attempted, and do attempt, regulation by their own concert of action. They make a law for themselves.

A general suspension is the result of a general concurrence, or of a general conviction of the necessity of suspension, on the part of all the banks, or many of them. This has happened, and, in the present state of affairs, may happen again, notwithstanding a bankrupt law. In my opinion, indeed, it is certain to happen, notwithstanding all the bankrupt laws we can pass, until Congress shall do its duty by enacting prospective and preventive remedies; and if it should happen, one of two things must ensue; either Congress would be called together to repeal the law, or an utter and dead stop would take place in the payment of debts, in the concerns of commerce, and, indeed, in all the business of life.

In addition to the charters, it is to be remembered that several of the States have provisions of their own, founded on their own statutes, for proceeding against failing banks. Such banks are put into commission, or under sequestration, by the State courts, and a judicial administration and settlement of their affairs take place. Is our bankrupt law expected to supersede these State bankrupt laws? Are our courts to dispossess the State courts?

Sir, I will not pursue this subject further. I repeat, that, in the part of the country to which I belong, I believe there is a pretty strong disposition to include the banks in the bankrupt law. The people in that quarter apprehend from it no danger to themselves or their own institutions, and they wish to see banks elsewhere coerced, by the most effectual means, to resume and to maintain specie payments. I need not say, that they are among the greatest sufferers by the present most ruinous state of things. They pay, and others do not pay them. They cannot long stand the present state of the currency, and, like them, I am ready to adopt any practical measure, any thing short of convulsive shocks between State authority and the authority of the United States, to relieve it. But I confess, that, for myself, to say nothing of the constitutional points, I see formidable difficulties in subjecting State banks to forfeiture and destruction by an act of bankruptcy. At any rate, if the banks are to be dealt with in bankruptcy at all, their case would require, obviously, very many peculiar provisions, and they should constitute the subject of a bill by themselves. Such a bill should be prospective, the commencement of its operation deferred, the act of bankruptcy more clearly determined, provision made to avoid, as far as possible, collision with State authorities, and provision also for superseding the commission, on resumption of payment, or security given. Various provisions of this kind, as it seems to me, would be essentially necessary.

Leaving this very important part of the case, another question arises upon the proposed amendment. Shall the bankruptcy act, in its application to individuals, be voluntary only, or both voluntary and compulsory? It is well known that I prefer that it should be both. I think all insolvent and failing persons should have power to come in under its provisions, and be voluntary bankrupts; and I think, too, that, as to those who are strictly merchants and traders, creditors ought to have a right to proceed against them, on the commission of the usual acts of bankruptcy, and subject them to the provisions of the act. But the committee think otherwise. They find many objections to this from many parts of the country, and especially from the West. In a country so extensive, with a people so various, with such different ideas and habits in regard to punctuality in commercial dealings, great opposition is anticipated to any measure so strict and so penal as a coercive bankruptcy. I content myself, therefore, with what I can get. I content myself with the voluntary bankruptcy. I am free to confess my leading object to be, to relieve those who are at present bankrupts, hopeless bankrupts, and who cannot be discharged or set free but by a bankrupt act passed by Congress. I confess that their case forms the great motive of my conduct. It is their case which has created the general cry for the measure. Not that their interest is opposed to the interest of creditors; still less that it is opposed to the general good of the country. On the contrary, I believe that the interest of creditors would be greatly benefited even by a system of voluntary bankruptcy alone, and I am quite confident that the public good would be eminently promoted. In my judgment, all interests concur; and it is the duty of providing for these unfortunate insolvents, in a manner thus favorable to all interests, which I feel urging me forward on this occasion.

And now, Sir, whence does this duty arise which appears to me so pressing and imperative? How has it become so incumbent upon us? What are the considerations, what the reasons, which have so covered our tables with petitions from all classes and all quarters, and which have loaded the air with such loud and unanimous invocations to Congress to pass a bankrupt law?

Let me remind you, then, in the first place, Sir, that, commercial as the country is, and having experienced as it has done, and experiencing as it now does, great vicissitudes of trade and business, it is almost forty years since any law has been in force by which any honest man, failing in business, could be effectually discharged from debt by surrendering his property. The former bankrupt law was repealed on the 19th of December, 1803. From that day to this, the condition of an insolvent, however honest and worthy, has been utterly hopeless, so far as he depended on any legal mode of relief. This state of things has arisen from the peculiar provisions of the Constitution of the United States, and from the omission by Congress to exercise this branch of its constitutional power. By the Constitution, the States are prohibited from passing laws impairing the obligation of contracts. Bankrupt laws impair the obligation of contracts, if they discharge the bankrupt from his debts without payment. The States, therefore, cannot pass such laws. The power, then, is taken from the States, and placed in our hands. It is true that it has been decided, that, in regard to contracts entered into after the passage of any State bankrupt law, between the citizens of the State having such law, and sued in the State courts, a State discharge may prevail. So far, effect has been given to State laws. I have great respect, habitually, for judicial decisions; but it has, nevertheless, I must say, always appeared to me that the distinctions on which these decisions are founded are slender, and that they evade, without answering, the objections founded on the great political and commercial objects intended to be secured by this part of the Constitution. But these decisions, whether right or wrong, afford no effectual relief. The qualifications and limitations which I have stated render them useless, as to the purpose of a general discharge. So much of the concerns of every man of business is with citizens of other States than his own, and with foreigners, that the partial extent to which the validity of State discharges reaches is of little benefit.

The States, then, cannot pass effectual bankrupt laws; that

is, effectual for the discharge of the debtor. There is no doubt that most, if not all, the States would now pass such laws, if they had the power; although their legislation would be various, interfering, and full of all the evils which the Constitution of the United States intended to provide against. But they have not the power; Congress, which has the power, does not exercise it. This is the peculiarity of our condition. The States would pass bankrupt laws, but they cannot; we can, but we will not. And between this want of power in the States and want of will in Congress, unfortunate insolvents are left to hopeless bondage. There are probably one or two hundred thousand debtors, honest, sober, and industrious, who drag out lives useless to themselves, useless to their families, and useless to their country, for no reason but that they cannot be legally discharged from debts in which misfortunes have involved them, and which there is no possibility of their ever paying. I repeat, again, that these cases have now been accumulating for a whole generation.

It is true they are not imprisoned; but there may be, and there are, restraint and bondage outside the walls of the jail, as well as in. Their power of earning is, in truth, taken away· their faculty of useful employment is paralyzed, and hope itself become extinguished. Creditors, generally, are not inhuman or unkind; but there will be found some who hold on, and the more a debtor struggles to free himself, the more they feel encouraged to hold on. The mode of reasoning is, that, the more honest the debtor may be, the more industrious, the more disposed to struggle and bear up against his misfortunes, the greater the chance is, that, in the end, especially if the humanity of others shall have led them to release him, their own debts may be finally recovered.

Now, in this state of our constitutional powers and duties, in this state of our laws, and with this actually existing condition of so many insolvents before us, it is not too serious to ask every member of the Senate to put it to his own conscience to say, whether we are not bound to exercise our constitutional duty. Can we abstain from exercising it? The States give to their own laws all the effect they can. This shows that they desire the power to be exercised. Several States have, in the most solemn manner, made known their earnest wishes to Congress. If we still refuse, what is to be done? Many of these insolvent persons are young men with young families. Like other men, they have capacities both for action and enjoyment. Are we to stifle all these for ever? Are we to suffer all these persons, many of them meritorious and respectable, to be pressed to the earth for ever, by a load of hopeless debt? The existing diversities and contradictions of State laws on the subject admirably illustrate the objects of this part of the Constitution, as stated by Mr. Madison; and they form that precise case for which the clause was inserted. The very evil intended to be provided against is before us, and around us, and pressing us on all sides. How can we, how dare we, make a perfect dead letter of this part of the Constitution, which we have sworn to support? The insolvent persons have not the power of locomotion. They cannot travel from State to State. They are prisoners. To my certain knowledge, there are many who cannot even come here to the seat of government, to present their petitions to Congress, so great is their fear that some creditor will dog their heels, and arrest them in some intervening State, or in this District, in the hope that friends will appear to save them, by payment of the debt, from imprisonment. These are truths; not creditable to the country, but they are truths. I am sorry for their existence. Sir, there is one crime, quite too common, which the laws of man do not punish, but which cannot escape the justice of God; and that is, the arrest and confinement of a debtor by his creditor, with no motive on earth but the hope that some friend, or some relative, perhaps almost as poor as himself, his mother it may be, or his sisters, or his daughters, will give up all their own little pittance, and make beggars of themselves, to save him from the horrors of a loathsome jail. Human retribution cannot reach this guilt; human feeling may not penetrate the flinty heart that perpetrates it; but an hour is surely coming, with more than human retribution on its wings, when that flint shall be melted, either by the power of penitence and grace, or in the fires of remorse.

Sir, I verily believe tha the power of perpetuating debts against debtors, for no substantial good to the creditor himself, and the power of imprisonment for debt, at least as it existed in this country ten years ago, have imposed more restraint on personal liberty than the law of debtor and creditor imposes in any other Christian and commercial country. If any public good were attained, any high political object answered, by such laws, there might be some reason for counselling submission and sufferance to individuals. But the result is bad, every way. It is bad to the public and to the country, which loses the efforts and the industry of so many useful and capable citizens. It is bad to creditors, because there is no security against preferences, no principle of equality, and no encouragement for honest, fair, and seasonable assignments of effects. As to the debtor, however good his intentions or earnest his endeavors, it subdues his spirit, and degrades him in his own esteem; and if he attempts any thing for the purpose of obtaining food and clothing for his family, he is driven to unworthy shifts and disguises, to the use of other persons' names, to the adoption of the character of agent, and various other contrivances, to keep the little earnings of the day from the reach of his creditors. Fathers act in the name of their sons, sons act in the name of their fathers; all constantly exposed to the greatest temptation to misrepresent facts and to evade the law, if creditors should strike. All this is evil, unmixed evil. And what is it all for? Of what benefit to any body? Who likes it? Who wishes it? What class of creditors desire it? What consideration of public good demands it?

Sir, we talk much, and talk warmly, of political liberty; and well we may, for it is among the chief of public blessings. But who can enjoy political liberty if he is deprived, permanently, of personal liberty, and the exercise of his own industry and his own faculties? To those unfortunate individuals, doomed to the everlasting bondage of debt, what is it that we have free institutions of government? What is it that we have public and popular assemblies? What is even this Constitution itself to them, in its actual operation, and as we now administer it? What is its aspect to them, but an aspect of stern, implacable severity? an aspect of refusal, denial, and frowning rebuke? nay, more than that, an aspect not only of austerity and rebuke, but, as they must think it, of plain injustice also, since it will not relieve them, nor suffer others to give them relief? What love can they feel towards the Constitution of their country, which has taken the power of striking off their bonds from their own paternal State governments, and yet, inexorable to all the cries of justice and of mercy, holds it unexercised in its own fast and unrelenting grasp? They find themselves bondsmen, because we will not execute the commands of the Constitution; bondsmen to debts they cannot pay, and which all know they cannot pay, and which take away the power of supporting themselves. Other slaves have masters, charged with the duty of support and protection; but their masters neither clothe, nor feed, nor shelter; they only bind.

But, Sir, the fault is not in the Constitution. The Constitution is beneficent as well as wise in all its provisions on this subject. The fault, I must be allowed to say, is in us, who have suffered ourselves quite too long to neglect the duty incumbent upon us. The time will come, Sir, when we shall look back and wonder at the long delay of this just and salutary measure. We shall then feel as we now feel when we reflect on that progress of opinion which has already done so much on another connected subject; I mean the abolition of imprisonment for debt. What should we say at this day, if it were proposed to reëstablish arrest and imprisonment for debt, as it existed in most of the States even so late as twenty years ago? I mean for debt alone, for mere, pure debt, without charge or suspicion of fraud or falsehood.

Sir, it is about that length of time, I think, since you,* who now preside over our deliberations, began here your efforts for the abolition of imprisonment for debt; and a better work was never begun in the Capitol. Ever remembered and ever honored be that noble effort! You drew the attention of the public to the question, whether, in a civilized and Christian country, debt incurred without fraud, and remaining unpaid without fault, is a crime, and a crime fit to be punished by denying to the offender the enjoyment of the light of heaven, and shutting him up within four walls. Your own good sense, and that instinct of right feeling which often outruns sagacity, carried you at once to a result to which others were more slowly brought, but to which nearly all have at length been brought, by reason, reflection, and argument. Your movement led the way; it became an example, and has had a powerful effect on both sides of the Atlantic. Imprisonment for debt, or even arrest and hold-

* Hon. Richard M. Johnson, Vice-President of the United States.

ing to bail for mere debt, no longer exists in England; and former laws on the subject have been greatly modified and mitigated, as we all know, in our States. "Abolition of imprisonment for debt," your own words in the title of your own bill, has become the title of an act of Parliament.

Sir, I am glad of an occasion to pay you the tribute of my sincere respect for these your labors in the cause of humanity and enlightened policy. For these labors thousands of grateful hearts have thanked you; and other thousands of hearts, not yet full of joy for the accomplishment of their hopes, full, rather, at the present moment, of deep and distressing anxiety, have yet the pleasure to know that your advice, your counsel, and your influence will all be given in favor of what is intended for their relief in the bill before us.

Mr. President, let us atone for the omissions of the past by a prompt and efficient discharge of present duty. The demand for this measure is not partial or local. It comes to us, earnest and loud, from all classes and all quarters. The time is come when we must answer it to our own consciences, if we suffer longer delay or postponement. High hopes, high duties, and high responsibilities concentrate themselves on this measure and this moment. With a power to pass a bankrupt law, which no other legislature in the country possesses, with a power of giving relief to many, doing injustice to none, I again ask every man who hears me, if he can content himself without an honest attempt to exercise that power? We may think it would be better to leave the power with the States; but it was not left with the States; they have it not, and we cannot give it to them. It is in our hands, to be exercised by us, or to be for ever useless and lifeless. Under these circumstances, does not every man's heart tell him that he has a duty to discharge? If the final vote shall be given this day, and if that vote shall leave thousands of our fellow-citizens and their families, in hopeless and helpless distress, to everlasting subjection to irredeemable debt, can we go to our beds with satisfied consciences? Can we lay our heads upon our pillows, and, without self-reproach, supplicate the Almighty Mercy to forgive us our debts as we forgive our debtors? Sir, let us meet the unanimous wishes of the country, and proclaim relief to the unfortunate throughout the land. What should hinder? What should stay our hands from this good work? Creditors do not oppose it; they apply for it; debtors solicit it, with an importunity, earnestness, and anxiety not to be described; the Constitution enjoins it; and all the considerations of justice, policy, and propriety, which are wrapped up in the phrase Public Duty, demand it, as I think, and demand it loudly and imperatively, at our hands. Sir, let us gratify the whole country, for once, with the joyous clang of chains, joyous because heard falling from the limbs of men. The wisest among those whom I address can desire nothing more beneficial than this measure, or more universally desired; and he who is youngest may not expect to live long enough to see a better opportunity of causing new pleasures and a happiness long untasted to spring up in the hearts of the poor and the humble. How many husbands and fathers are looking with hopes which they cannot suppress, and yet hardly dare to cherish, for the result of this debate! How many wives and mothers will pass sleepless and feverish nights, until they know whether they and their families shall be raised from poverty, despondency, and despair, and restored again to the circles of industrious, independent, and happy life!

Sir, let it be to the honor of Congress that, in these days of political strife and controversy, we have laid aside for once the sin that most easily besets us, and, with unanimity of counsel, and with singleness of heart and of purpose, have accomplished for our country one measure of unquestionable good.

A UNIFORM SYSTEM OF BANKRUPTCY.*

Mr. President, — The commendable temper in which the discussion has been so far conducted leads me to hope that now, when we are in the midst of the difficulties of the question, the Senate will indulge me in a few remarks. That there are difficulties I freely acknowledge. The subject of bankruptcies is a difficult subject everywhere, and perhaps particularly difficult here, as one of the results of a division of legislative powers between Congress and the States. But these difficulties are not insurmountable, and their only influence, therefore, should be to stimulate our efforts, and to increase at once our caution and our zeal.

It seems to be agreed, by all the friends of any bankrupt bill, that there shall be a provision for voluntary bankruptcy. The question now is, whether there ought to be also a compulsory power, or a power on the part of creditors to subject their debtors, in certain cases, to the operation of the law.

It is well known that the bill introduced by me contained such a power, and I should still prefer to retain it. But I do not think this of so much importance as some other gentlemen, and I should cheerfully support a bill which did not contain it, if by so doing I could contribute to the success of the general measure. In truth, on this question, and on many others, my vote will be governed by a desire to make the bill acceptable to others.

Now, Sir, the argument for the compulsory clause is, that, without this power, the creditors have no security; that the bill

* A Speech delivered in the Senate of the United States, on the 5th of June, 1840, on Mr. Clay's Motion to strike out the Compulsory Part of the Bankrupt Bill.

is a one-sided measure, a measure for the benefit and relief of debtors only, quite regardless of the just rights of creditors. All this I deny. I maintain, on the contrary, not only that there is just security for the rights of creditors under the voluntary part of the bill, but that that part, of itself, and by itself, is of the highest value and importance to creditors. This proposition takes for granted, what I have no doubt will be found true, that persons in insolvent circumstances will generally become voluntary bankrupts. And, in the second place, I maintain that very little value is added to the security of creditors by the compulsory part of the bill. These are points on which I propose now particularly to address the Senate, and, with its patience, I hope to make them clear.

When I speak of creditors, I mean the class of creditors generally, or all who, in the course of business, give trust for merchandise, or other things sold, or for money loaned. When I speak of the creditors of insolvents, I mean the creditors, in the mass, of such persons as are actually and really insolvent, that is, unable to pay their debts, whether their insolvency be known and acknowledged or not. And to creditors, and the rights of creditors, in both these senses and uses of the word, I maintain that the provisions contained in the voluntary part of this bill are of great value.

The rights of creditors are the means which the laws furnish for the enforcement and collection of their debts. In the case of an insolvent debtor, the laws at present give to the creditor, among other things, a right to pursue and demand his future earnings. This right the present bill proposes to take away. The question is, therefore, whether, in taking away this right, the bill provides for the creditor any just equivalent.

I do not admit, indeed, that by a bankrupt law we might not take away some of the existing rights or remedies of creditors, if it should appear just and proper to do so, without providing any new right or remedy as an equivalent. The relation of debtor and creditor forms a general subject of legislation. The proper law-making power may act upon this relation, and alter and modify it, upon principles of general policy, justice, and utility, whenever it sees fit. But I am willing to occupy a narrower ground, and to undertake to show, that, by the provisions of this bill, we leave creditors in a better condition than we found them; in other words, that, as a voluntary system alone, it is beneficial to creditors.

The law, it is proposed, shall last some few years, that Congress and the country may see what is its actual operation. It will act immediately on its passage; and this operation, as I maintain, will be favorable to creditors. In other words, the law will be useful to creditors, in reference to the creation of debts. It will, I insist, increase the probability that he who parts with his money or his merchandise on credit will be paid for his merchandise, or repaid his money. Sir, we live in a highly commercial country, and a highly commercial and enterprising age. The system of credit, which I hold to be very useful, and, indeed, essential to our general prosperity, may, no doubt, be carried to excess. There is such a thing as over-trading, and such a thing as false credit; and both these things are public evils. All admit this; and many think the evils so great, that they seem to be enemies to the credit system altogether. I am not one of these; but still I desire to keep credit within bounds, and to avoid over-trading.

Now, Sir, what is it that upholds so much false credit? What is it that enables men to extend their transactions so far beyond their capital? What is it that enables them, also, to go on, often for a long time, after they become really insolvent? It is the practice of indorsement and suretyship, a practice, I venture to say, more extensive in the United States than in any other country. Men get trust upon the strength of other men's names. I do not speak of the discount of notes and bills taken in the common operations of sale and purchase, but I speak of pure accommodation, of the discount of paper representing no transaction of sale or purchase, but made for borrowing money merely, and indorsed for the sole accommodation of the borrower. That great excesses have been committed in operations of this kind, no man who has attended to the transactions of trade can doubt; nor can any one doubt that great evils arise from this source. Indorsement and suretyship, therefore, are the means by which excessive and false credit is upheld. And how is this indorsement obtained? This leads us one step farther in the inquiry. How is it that persons, continuing to carry on business after they are really insolvent, and are suspected, if not known to be so, can procure others to indorse their paper? Sir, we all know how it is. It is by promising to secure indorsers at all events. It is by giving an assurance that, if the party stops payment, a preference shall be made, and the indorsers shall be favored creditors. Hence it is quite general, perhaps universal, that, when an insolvent assigns his property for the benefit of his creditors, he classifies his creditors, and puts indorsers into the first class. This has become a sort of law of honor. A man that disregards it is, in some measure, disgraced. We hear daily of honorary debts, and we hear reproaches against those who, being insolvent, have yet pushed on, in the hope of retrieving their affairs, until, when failure comes, and come it does, sooner or later, they have not enough left to discharge these honorary obligations.

Now, at the bottom of all this is preference. The preference of one creditor to another, both debts being honest, is allowed by the general rules of law, but is not allowed by bankrupt laws. And this right of preference is the foundation on which the structure rests. On the legal right or power of preference lies the promise of preference. On the promise of preference lies indorsement. On indorsement lies extensive and false credit. On excessive and false credit lies over-trading. This, Sir, is the regular stratification. If we strike out preference, we shall knock away the foundation-stone. And this bill will strike it out.

If this bill shall pass, every indorser who shall not take previous security will see that, in case of failure, he can no longer be protected or preferred, but must come in for his share, and his share only, with other creditors. And this is right. For one, I have always thought that, if any difference were to be made, indorsers should be paid last, because they come in as volunteers; they profess to run a risk. They are not giving credit in the common way, as other persons do, who sell on trust, in the ordinary way of business, and in order to earn their livelihood; but they assume a voluntary responsibility. And why should they be preferred to the grocer, the tailor, or the butcher, who has only dealt in the common way of his trade, and has not volunteered to give any trust or credit whatever? Well, Sir, will not indorsement stay its hand when this bill shall have taken away all power of preference? Will not men hesitate, more than they now do, about lending their names, when they find that, in case of failure, they must come in for neighbor's fare with all other creditors? I think they will.

And, Sir, if there be less of indorsement, there will be less of fictitious credit, and less of over-trading. Every man's business will be brought down so much the nearer to his own property, his own capital, and his own means. And if every trading man's business be brought down to some nearer proportion to his own capital and his own means, does not this diminish the probability of his failure? Certainly it does; and therefore whoever deals with him, and trusts him, is not so likely to lose his debt. There will be more general security in giving credits. And therefore I say, that, if you take away the power and practice of preference, you affect, to some extent, false credit and over-trading; and by these means you give a security to the creditor, even in the creation of his debt; and this is one advantage, to the whole class of creditors, to be expected from this bill. It is a general advantage, and its precise amount cannot be stated; but it is a clear advantage nevertheless.

But there is a second, and a still greater advantage. Mr. President, allow me to ask, What is that feature, the capital feature, which we most often see in the insolvencies which take place among the trading classes? What is that which there is the more frequent occasion to regret and to reprehend? Is it not that the party has gone on too long? Is it not that, after he knew himself to be really insolvent, that is, after he knew he had not property enough left to pay his debts, instead of stopping, and winding up his concerns, he has ventured still deeper, and made his ultimate case thereby still more desperate? Under the present state of law, this happens quite too often. I am afraid it would be found, on inquiry, that failures are generally worse in this country than elsewhere; that is to say, that generally the amount of assets is less in proportion to the amount of debts. And, in my opinion, the present state of the law encourages and produces this result. For, Sir, let me ask, What will a man naturally do who has been unfortunate, and has sustained such losses as to bring his property below his debts, while this is known to himself, and not known to others? If he stops and surrenders, however honestly and fairly, he cannot be sure of a discharge, and the unpaid balance may keep him a pauper for life. On the other hand, he sees that another voyage, another speculation, some new turn of fortune, may possibly relieve him, and bring him out a man of property. On one side, poverty for life is his only prospect, and only destiny, so far at least as the law allows him any ground of hope; and on the other, there is some chance of escape. Now, Sir, I will ask any sensible man, if a state of law could be devised more likely to encourage headlong enterprise and rash speculation. Can you place a man in a condition where he will be more likely to throw himself upon desperate chances, and to plunge deeper and deeper?

We are not without experience on this point, and much instruction may be gathered from one memorable instance. The great fire in New York is supposed to have destroyed property to the amount of twenty or twenty-five millions of dollars, in houses, warehouses, and merchandise. But nobody failed. This is a fact full of admonition. I ask attention to it. Nobody failed, notwithstanding this immense loss of property; and what was the reason? No one doubts that hundreds were rendered deeply insolvent by this so extensive calamity. Why, then, did they not stop? The answer is, that the extent of their losses was, in many cases, known only to themselves, and they concealed their own true condition. And they had strong motives for so doing. If they announced themselves insolvent, and stopped, nothing was before them and their families, for their whole lives, but poverty and distress. On the other hand, there was a hope that, if they could maintain their credit, they might, by extreme exertion and extreme good-fortune, extricate themselves. On the strength of that hope, slight as it was, they buoyed themselves up, and tried to stem the current which was carrying them, notwithstanding all their struggles, to utter and desperate bankruptcy. They paid exorbitant interest for money; they suffered themselves to be jewed in every dark alley in the city; they sacrificed every thing to maintain their credit, and in the end, when every thing else was gone, credit went also. And when they finally failed, where was the fund for dividends to creditors? Why, Sir, it had gone to the pocket of the capitalist; it had been devoured by the voracity of usury. I know of one instance in which a merchant paid more than fifty thousand dollars extra and unlawful interest, for the purpose of upholding his credit, and failed after all. And there are well-authenticated cases of payment of still larger sums. Boundless extras and gross exorbitancy were thus suffered to eat up what belonged to creditors.

Now, Sir, would it not have been better for all parties, and for the public, that these unfortunate persons should have stopped payment the morning after the fire, assigned all that was left of their property, and received a discharge? And this, be assured, many of them would have done, if the law had provided that by so doing they should obtain that discharge. But there was no such legal provision; they had no hope on that side, but from the consent of *all* their creditors, and they believed that *all* would not consent; and therefore there was no way left to them but to keep on, wading into deeper water at every step, and stopping at last with nothing to divide except among indorsers.

Mr. President, we hear it frequently said, that honest debtors may always obtain discharges from their creditors upon an honest assignment of their effects. This is the language of the memorial of the Board of Trade, and this is the language, especially, of the letter to the honorable member from New York, which has been read. Sir, such is not my opinion, nor the fruit of my experience. I believe that creditors are generally humane and just; but there will always, or often, be some who are selfish, unjust, or indifferent. There will be some who will not compound. The man, therefore, who would stop, since he knows he is insolvent, if he could be sure of a discharge, cannot be sure of it. He may be as honest as possible; he may strip himself of the last farthing; but yet he cannot promise himself any release. It is notorious that some creditors will and do hold on; and as to the debtor, this is as decisive as if all did so. Now, Sir, this bill proposes an object to a man whose circumstances have become insolvent, and makes that object sure. It tells him, by way of inducing him to stop in season, and before he has wasted his property, that by assigning it, and acting honestly in all things, he shall have a discharge; that no unreasonable creditor shall be able to prevent it; and with this certainty before him he will stop in season, or, at least, he will be much more likely to stop in season than he is at present.

This, then, Sir, is the second benefit which this bill confers on creditors. And who will deny that it is a clear and a great benefit? It holds out a strong inducement to debtors to stop in season, and to distribute their property honestly, while they have yet property to distribute, and before they have wasted it all in useless sacrifices to retrieve their affairs.

But there is a third benefit which this bill confers on creditors. It takes away the power and the motive of concealment. Under the present state of things, the motives of an insolvent man lead in the opposite direction of his duties. Every thing is brought to bear against his honesty and integrity. He has every temptation to conceal his property; and there are many ways in which he may conceal it. If he surrenders all, he cannot be discharged, and therefore will be in no condition to earn any thing more. He may, therefore, not choose to surrender, and may set his creditors at defiance. I have heard of an instance in which a man failed for one hundred and fifty thousand dollars. He showed assets to the amount of eighty thousand, and there was no reason to suppose that he had any more, or had acted dishonestly in any way. He offered to give up all for a discharge; but while most of his creditors were willing to discharge him on such a surrender, some were not. A year afterwards he renewed his offer of giving up all, but his property had by this time become diminished by ten thousand dollars, so that he had but seventy thousand to offer; and the obstinate creditors of last year were now willing to take what was then offered, but would not take less; and so the process of offer and refusal went on; and the last I heard of the case, this proceeding was likely to result in the creditors' getting nothing, and the debtor's becoming a beggar. If there be not many cases exactly like this, or quite so strong in all their circumstances, there are still very many which much resemble it; and this bill will put an end to them all.

Sir, the great motive by which the debtor is to be brought to act honestly and fairly is his hope of a discharge. This is to him every thing. Hardly any earthly object, in his view, can be greater. It is this which is to reinstate him in a condition of effort and action. Creditors can obtain a benefit, by means of this, far superior to any good which they can ever get by holding on to his future earnings. Generally, this last right is good for nothing to the mass of creditors, though sometimes an individual may profit by it. In some cases, it is true, where the amount of debt is small, the bankrupt will struggle hard to earn the means of payment, that he may afterwards work for himself. But if the amount be large, he will make no such effort. He will not work altogether for his creditors. Not only will he not do that, but, as I have already said, he is under strong temptation to retain and conceal what he already possesses. I need not say of what evil consequence all this is. I need not say what ill-will naturally grows up between debtors and creditors standing in this relation. The creditor thinks his debtor unjust and roguish; the debtor regards his creditor as remorseless and cruel; and mutual reproaches and deep bitterness of feeling are often the result. How much better, Sir, every way, that the law, by its timely interference, should give the debtor's property to whom it belongs, and set him free to begin a new career of industry and usefulness!

And, in the fourth place, Sir, this bill gives the creditors an *equal* distribution of the debtor's effects. In the present state of things, a bankrupt may pay one creditor all, and another nothing; and he who gets nothing may, perhaps, fail himself, when, if he could have received his just proportion, he might have been saved. The great interest of the mass of creditors is, that the debtor's effects shall be *equally* divided among them all. At present, there is no security for such equal division, and this bill proposes to give such security. And I repeat, that, if any thing ever comes of the power of a creditor to hold on upon his debt, in the hope of getting something out of the future earnings of a notoriously insolvent debtor, it is usually not the mass of creditors, but only some one of them, who gets any thing; and that one, very likely, may be he who deserves least.

These, Mr. President, are the securities, the new securities, the important securities, which this bill furnishes to the creditors. If there be nothing in them, let that be shown; but until it is shown, let it not be said that there is nothing in this bill for the creditors' benefit.

And, Mr. President, these provisions belong to the voluntary, as well as the involuntary, parts of the bill. The real reciprocity, the real equivalent, must be looked for in the provisions made for conducting the proceedings, and not in the source in which the proceedings originate. Suppose creditors to have ever so full a power of declaring their debtors bankrupts; this would not avail them, unless proper provision were made for a full assignment and fair distribution of the property. On the other hand, if such provision be made, the creditor is secured, although the proceedings originate with the debtor himself. It may be wise, or it may be unwise, to retain the coercive clauses; but whether retained or not, they do not constitute the true equivalent or reciprocal benefit of the creditor.

The real state of the case stands thus. The benefit of a debtor consists in obtaining a discharge; this he shall have, but, in order to obtain it, he shall give the creditors the benefit of a full and honest surrender of all his property; he shall show, if a merchant, that he has kept proper and regular books of account; it must appear that there has been no false swearing on his part, or the concealment of any part of his property; that he has not admitted any false or fictitious debt against his estate; that he has not applied any trust money to his own use; and that he has not paid any debt by way of preferring one creditor to another, in contemplation of bankruptcy. And the Senate, if they see fit, may insert that the consent of creditors shall be necessary to his discharge, though, for one, I should never agree to that, without reserving a right to the debtor to summon dissenting creditors to appear before the proper tribunal, and show some just reason for withholding a discharge.

I have now, Sir, gone through with all that I proposed to say upon the voluntary part of this bill. My undertaking was, to show that that part of the bill does, by itself, and of and in itself alone, contain provisions of the highest importance to creditors and the security of creditors; and, on the various points which I have noticed, I am ready to meet any gentleman who may choose to contest the matter. The opinions which I have expressed I hold with confidence, and am willing to defend them, and to submit them to the judgment of all men of experience.

My second general proposition is, that, whether it were advisable, on the whole, or not, to retain the compulsory part, yet that part does not give any important addition to the security of creditors; and that therefore it is not of great consequence whether it be retained or not.

In the first place, let us remember that the form of proceeding is the same, after its commencement, whether it be begun by the debtor or his creditor. If there be any benefit to the creditor at all in the compulsory part, it must be in the mere power of declaring his debtor a bankrupt under certain circumstances, and of causing him, willing or unwilling, to go through the bankrupt process. Now, the difficulty is, that, though this power might sometimes be beneficial to the creditor, yet it is next to impossible so to describe the circumstances which shall constitute a just occasion for the exercise of the power, as not to leave it still, in a great measure, a voluntary matter with the debtor when he will subject himself to the provisions of the law. This has been found the difficulty in all systems; and most bankruptcies are, therefore, now substantially voluntary. Those acts which are in this bill called acts of bankruptcy, and which, if committed, shall enable a creditor to sue out a commission against his debtor, are nearly all of them voluntary acts, which the debtor may perform or not at his pleasure, and which, of course, he will not perform, if he wishes to avoid the process of bankruptcy.

These acts, as stated in the bill, are, secretly departing from the State with intent to defraud his creditors; fraudulently procuring himself to be arrested, or his lands and goods attached or taken in execution; removing or concealing his goods to prevent their being levied upon or taken by legal process; making any fraudulent conveyance of his lands or goods; lying in jail twenty days for want of bail, or escaping from jail, or not giving security according to law when his lands or effects shall be attached by process.

An insolvent may avoid the commission of most of these acts if he chooses, especially as there are now few instances of imprisonment for debt. The acts of bankruptcy, according to the British statute, are very much like those in this bill. But a trader may declare himself insolvent, and thereupon a commission may issue against him; and that is supposed to be now the common course. Creditors will seldom, if ever, use this power. A creditor desirous of proceeding against his debtor for payment or security, naturally acts for himself alone. He arrests his person, attaches his property, if the law allows that to be done, or gets security for his own debt the best way he can, leaving others to look out for themselves. Concert among creditors, in such cases, is not necessary, and is uncommon; and a single creditor, acting for himself only, is much more likely to take other means for the security of his debt than that of putting his debtor into bankruptcy. Nevertheless, I admit there are possible cases in which the power might be useful. I admit it would be well if creditors could sometimes stop the career of their debtors; and if the honorable member from New York,* or any other gentleman, can frame a clause for that purpose, at once efficient and safe, I shall vote for it. Even as these clauses now stand, I should prefer to have them in the bill; my original proposition having been, as is well known, that there should be both compulsory and voluntary bankruptcy; and I vote now to strike the provision out, only because others, I find, object to it, and because I do not think it of any great importance.

I proceed, Sir, to take some notice of the remarks of the honorable member from New York; and what I have first to say is, that his speech appeared to me to be a speech against the whole bill, rather than a speech in favor of retaining the compulsory clause. He pointed out the evils that might arise from the voluntary part of the bill; but every one of them might arise, too, under the other part. He spoke of the hardship to creditors in New York; that they should be obliged to take notice of the insolvency of their debtors in the Western States, and to go thither to prove their debts, or resist the discharge. But this hardship, certainly, is no greater when the Western debtor declares himself bankrupt, than when he commits an act of bankruptcy, on which some Western creditor sues out a commission against him.

All the other inconveniences, dangers, or hardships to creditors, which the honorable gentleman enumerated, were, in like manner, as far as I recollect, as likely to arise when a creditor puts the debtor into bankruptcy, as when he puts himself in. The gentleman's argument, therefore, is an argument against the whole bill. He thinks Eastern creditors of Western debtors will be endangered, because State legislatures, in States where debtors live, as well as commissioners, assignees, and so forth, will have all their sympathies on the side of the debtors. Why, Sir, State legislatures will have nothing to do with the matter, under this bill; and as to the rest, how is it now? Are not creditors now in the power of local administrations affected, in

* Mr. Tallmadge.

all respects, by these same sympathies? Are there no instances, indeed, and is there no danger, of laws staying process, embarrassing remedies, or otherwise interrupting the regular course of legal collection? For my own part, I cannot doubt that a New York merchant, learning that his debtor in the South or West is in insolvent or failing circumstances, would rather that his affairs should be settled in bankruptcy, in the courts of the United States, than that his debtor should settle them himself, paying whom he pleased, and disposing of his property according to his own will, or under the administration of the insolvent laws of the State.

The gentleman seemed to fear that, if Western traders may make themselves bankrupts, New York merchants will be shy of them, and that Western credit will be impaired or checked. Perhaps there would be no great harm if this should be so. A little more caution might not be unprofitable; but the answer to all such suggestions is, that the bill applies only to cases of insolvents, actual, real insolvents; and when traders are actually insolvent, the sooner it is known the better, nine times out of ten. Nor do I feel any alarm for our mercantile credit abroad, which has awakened the fears of the gentleman. What can foreign merchants suppose better for them than such an administration of the effects of debtors here, as that, if there be foreign creditors, they shall be sure of a just and equal dividend, without preference either to creditors at home or indorsers? It is not long since, in some of the States, (I hope it is not so anywhere now,) that creditors within the State had preference over creditors out of it. And, if we look to other countries, do we find that well-administered systems of bankruptcy enfeeble or impair mercantile credit? Is it so in regard to England, or to France?

The honorable member feels alarm, too, lest the banks should be great sufferers under the operation of this bill. He is apprehensive that, if it shall pass, very many debtors of the banks will become bankrupts, pay other creditors more or less, and pay the banks nothing. Sir, this is not according to my observation. Bank debts are usually preferred debts, because they are debts secured by indorsement. But, by mentioning the case of the banks, the gentleman has suggested ideas which I have long entertained, and which I am glad of this opportunity to express briefly, though I shall not dwell on them.

Sir, a great part of the credit of the country is bank credit. A great part of all indorsement and suretyship is bank indorsement and bank suretyship. I do not speak particularly of the great cities; I speak of the country generally. Now, indorsement, as I have already said, rests on the idea of preference. And if we take away preference, do we not diminish bank indorsement and bank accommodation? And do we not in this way act directly on the quantity of bank paper issued for circulation? Do we not keep the issues of paper nearer to the real wants of society? This view of the case might be much pressed and amplified. There is much in it, if I am not mistaken. For the present, I only suggest it; but he who shall consider the subject longest and deepest will be most thoroughly convinced that in this respect, as well as others, the abolition of preference to indorsers will act beneficially to the public.

The immediate motion before the Senate, Mr. President, does not justify a further extension of my observations on this part of the case. My object has been to prove that this bill is not one-sided, is not a bill for debtors only, but is what it ought to be, a bill making just, honest, and reasonable provisions for the distribution of the effects of insolvents among their creditors; and that the voluntary part of the bill alone secures all these principal objects, because, in the great and overruling motives of obtaining a discharge, it holds out an inducement to debtors who know themselves to be insolvent to stop, to stop seasonably, to assign honestly, and to conform in good faith to all the provisions intended for the security of their debtors.

STATE OF THE FINANCES IN 1840.*

A MOTION was submitted in the Senate, on the 14th of December, 1840, to refer so much of the President's message at the beginning of the session as relates to the finances to the Standing Committee on Finance. This question coming up for discussion on the 16th, Mr. Webster addressed the Senate substantially as follows: —

MR. PRESIDENT, — It has not been without great reluctance that I have risen to offer any remarks on the message of the President, especially at this early period of the session. I have no wish to cause, or to witness, a prolonged, and angry, and exciting discussion on the topics it contains. The message is, mainly, devoted to an elaborate and plausible defence of the course of the existing administration; it dwells on the subjects which have been so long discussed among us; on banks and banking, on the excess of commerce and speculation, on the State debts, and the dangers arising from them, on the Sub-treasury, as it has been called, or the Independent Treasury, as others have denominated it. I propose now to deal with none of these points. So far as they may be supposed to affect the merits or character of the administration, they have, as I understand it, been passed upon by the country; and I have no disposition to reargue any of them. Nor do I wish to enter upon an inquiry as to what, in relation to all these things, is supposed to have been approved or disapproved by the people of the United States, by their decision in the late election. It appears, however, thus far, to be the disposition of the nation to change the administration of the government. All I propose at this

* Remarks upon that part of the President's Message which relates to the Revenue and Finances, delivered in the Senate of the United States, on the 16th and 17th of December, 1840.

time to do is, to present some remarks on the subject of the finances, speaking on the present state of things only, without recurring to the past, or speculating as to the future. Yet I suppose that some proper forecast, some disposition to provide for what is before us, naturally mixes itself up, in a greater or less degree, with all inquiries of this sort.

In this view, I shall submit a few thoughts upon the message of the President; but I deem it necessary to preface what I shall say with one or two preliminary remarks.

And, first, I will say a word or two on the question, whether or not unfounded or erroneous impressions are communicated to the people by that document, in several respects. In this point of view I first notice what the President says on the eighth page. He there represents it as the great distinctive principle, the grand difference in the characters of our public men, that of one class of them it has been the constant object to create and to maintain a public debt, and of another to prevent and to discharge it. This I consider as an unfounded imputation on those who have conducted the government of this country. The President says, "I have deemed this brief summary of our fiscal affairs necessary to the due performance of a duty specially enjoined upon me by the Constitution. It will serve also to illustrate more fully the principles by which I have been guided in reference to two contested points in our public policy, which were earliest in their development, and have been more important in their consequences than any that have arisen under our system of government; I allude to a national debt and a national bank." About a national bank I have nothing at present to say; but here it is officially announced to us, that it has been a great contested question in the country, whether there shall or shall not be a national debt, as if there were public men who wished a national debt, to be created and perpetuated for its own sake! Now I submit it to the Senate, whether there has ever existed in the country any party, at any time, which avowed itself in favor of a national debt, *per se*, as a thing desirable? Does the history of the past debts contracted by the government lay the least foundation for any such assertion? The first national debt we have had was the loan negotiated in Holland, by John Adams. None, I presume, ever doubted the policy of such a loan, in the then existing circumstances of the country.

Then there came the debt contracted for the pay of the Revolutionary army, by the Continental Congress, or rather by the country through that Congress. Next were the debts incurred during the war, by the States, for the purpose of carrying on the war. Provision was made for discharging these debts as the cost of our Revolution; can any body object to a debt like this? Of the same character were the loans made by government to carry on the late war with Great Britain. These are the principal national debts we have ever contracted, and I cannot but think it singularly unfortunate that what looks so much like an imputation on those who authorized these loans should come from the head of an administration which, so far as I know, *is the first that has ever commenced a national debt in a time of profound peace.*

And now to proceed to the actual state of the finances. The message, though it does not call the obligations of the government a national debt, but, on the contrary, speaks in the strongest terms against a national debt, yet admits that there are treasury-notes outstanding, and bearing interest, to the amount of four and a half millions; and I see, connected with this, other important and leading facts, very necessary to be considered by those who would look out beforehand that they may provide for the future.

Of these, the first in importance is, that the expenditures of the government, during the term of the present administration, have greatly exceeded its income. I shall not now argue the question whether these expenditures have been reasonable or unreasonable, necessary or unnecessary. I am looking at the facts in a financial view, purely; and I say that during the last four years *the public expenditure has exceeded the public income at the rate of* SEVEN MILLIONS OF DOLLARS PER ANNUM. This is easily demonstrated.

At the commencement of the first year of this presidential term, in January, 1837, there was in the treasury a balance of six millions of dollars, which was reserved from distribution by what has usually been called the Deposit Act. The intention of Congress was to reserve five millions only; but, in consequence of an uncertainty which attended the mode of effecting this result, the Secretary wishing to be in his calculations, at least, on the safe side, it turned out that the sum actually reserved was six millions. Here, then, was this amount in the treasury on the 1st of January, 1837. Events occurred during that year which induced Congress to modify the deposit act, so as to retain in the treasury the fourth instalment of the sum to be deposited with the States, which amounted to nine millions. I find, further, from the communications of the Secretary of the Treasury now submitted to the Senate, that, for the stock belonging to the public in the Bank of the United States, for which bonds had been given to the treasury by the Bank of the United States of Pennsylvania, which bonds are now paid, there have been received eight millions. Now, Sir, these are all items of a preëxisting fund, no part of which has accrued since January, 1837.

To these I may add the outstanding treasury-notes running on interest (four and a half millions), and the whole forms an aggregate of *twenty-seven and a half millions of dollars*, in addition to the current revenue, which have been expended in *three and a half* or four years, excepting, of course, what may remain in the treasury at the end of that term. Here, then, has the government been expending money at the rate of nearly eight millions per annum beyond its income. What state of things is that? Suppose it should go on. Does not every man see that we have a vast debt immediately before us?

But is this all? I am inclined to think that, in one respect at least, it is not all. The treasury, I think, has not duly distinguished, in reference to one important branch of its administration, between treasury funds proper and a trust fund, set apart by treaty stipulation, to be invested for the benefit of certain Indian tribes. I say the treasury has taken, as belonging to the government, that which properly belongs to a trust fund, which the government engaged to invest in permanent stocks for the benefit of certain Indian tribes. This makes it necessary to look a little into these trust funds. By our treaty with the Chickasaws, the proceeds of the sales of the lands ceded to the United States by that tribe were to be invested in permanent stocks, for the use of the members of that tribe. At the date of the last communication which I find from the treasury, the amount received on these sales was $ 2,498,000.06. Bonds had been purchased to the amount of $ 1,994,141.03; but as some of these bonds were purchased at rates above par, the sums vested in them amounted to $ 2,028,678.54. This would leave a balance of $ 369,000 uninvested at that time; and the Secretary informs us that the portion of it which had been received from the land offices had been "mixed up in the general fund." Here, then, is one item of trust money, money not our own, which has been mixed up with our own money, and received as part of the available funds of the treasury. The stocks purchased for the Chickasaws appear to be as follows:—

Number of Bonds.	Interest, where payable.	Interest, when payable.	Times redeemable.	Rate per cent.	Am'nt of each.	Total.
125 Ten.	Philadelphia, . . .	1st January and July,	1848	5	$ 1,000	$ 125,000.00
125 do.	do. . .	do. do.	1853	5	. .	125,000.00
65 do.	Treasurer's office, Tenn.,	25th January and July,	1861	$5\frac{1}{4}$	. .	65,000.00
1 do.	do. do. do.	do. do.	. .	$5\frac{1}{4}$	. .	1,666.66
65 Ala.	Phœnix Bank, N. Y., .	1st Monday May and Nov.	1852	5	1,000	65,000.00
250 do.	do. do. do. .	do. do.	1865	5	. .	250,000.00
500 do.	Union Bank, N. Orleans,	1st Monday June and Dec.	. .	5	. .	500,000.00
500 do.	Commercial Bank, do.	do. do.	1866	5	. .	500,000.00
161 Ind.	New York, . . .	1st January and 1st July,	1857	5	. .	161,000.00
41 do.	. . . . . .	. . . .	. .	5	. .	41,000.00
3 Ohio	. . . . .	. . . .	1856	6	35,000 15,000 50,000	100,000.00
1 Md.	Baltimore, . . .	8th February and August,	Ad libitum	5	. .	30,091.80
1 do.	do. . . .	do. do.	1849	5	. .	13,000.00
1 do.	do. . . .	do. do.	1844	5	. .	11,233.00
1 do.	do. . .	1st January and quarterly,	1870	6	. .	6,149.57
	Amount of stock for Chickasaws,	. . . .				$ 1,994,141.03

As a matter of account and book-keeping, this might be thought correct, or it might not; but I think it would have been better to keep a separate account for funds thus held in trust, as every private individual does, who is made a trustee for the interests of others. If the facts are as I have gathered from the report submitted to Congress, here are three or four hundred thousand dollars of the trust fund not invested, and which remain yet to be invested for the benefit of these Indian tribes. As to the rates at which these bonds were purchased, I find it stated that one "lot" of Alabama bonds was taken on the 31st of March, 1836, at $4\frac{1}{2}$ per cent. premium; others, immediately after, at 4; others, in May, at $3\frac{1}{2}$; and others, in March, 1837, at 1 per cent. off. Tennessee bonds were purchased at par; Ohio bonds at $11\frac{7}{10}$ advance; part of the Maryland bonds at 3 per cent. off, part at 1 per cent. off, and part at $14\frac{4}{10}$ advance.

So much for the investment under the treaty with the Chickasaws. But we have other treaties presenting a more important case. We have treaties with eight tribes of Indians, by which the United States stipulated to invest the amounts agreed to be paid for the lands ceded by them in State stocks. Take, for example, the stipulation in the treaty with the Sioux of the Mississippi. The article of the treaty is in these words: —

"Art. 2. In consideration of the cession contained in the preceding article, the United States agree to the following stipulations on their part: First, to invest the sum of $300,000 in such safe and profitable State stocks as the President may direct, and to pay to the chiefs and braves as aforesaid, annually, for ever, an income of not less than five per cent. thereon."

The stipulations in the other treaties are substantially the same. The whole amount thus agreed to be invested for the eight tribes, by treaties mostly entered into in the years 1837 and 1838, is $2,580,100. This appears from the following statement, which I find in the documents.

Statement exhibiting the Amount of Interest appropriated by Congress to pay the following Tribes, in lieu of investing the Sums, provided by the Treaties, in Stocks.

Names of Tribes.	Amount provided by Treaties to be invested in safe Stocks.	Annual Interest appropriated by Congress.	Treaties.
Ottawas and Chippewas,	$200,000	$12,000	Resolution of Senate.
Osages, ...	69,120	3,456	Resolution of Senate, Jan. 19, 1838.
Delawares, ...	46,080	2,304	Treaty, 1832.
Sioux of Mississippi, .	300,000	15,000	Treaty, Sept. 29, 1837.
Sacs and Foxes of Mississippi,	200,000	10,000	Treaty, Oct. 21, 1837.
Sacs and Foxes of Missouri,	157,400	7,870	Treaty, Oct. 21, 1837.
Winnebagoes, ...	1,100,000	55,000	Treaty, Nov. 1, 1837.
Creeks, ...	350,000	17,500	Treaty, Nov. 23, 1838.
Iowas, ...	157,500	7,875	Treaty, 1837.
	$2,580,100	$131,005	

Now, Sir, not one dollar of all this has been invested. The very statement which I have quoted shows this. The statement declares, that, instead of investing this large sum, according to contract, the United States pays interest upon it, as upon a debt.

We are indebted, therefore, to these Indians in the whole amount we agreed to pay for these lands, which have been transferred to us, surveyed, put in market, and large portions of them, I suppose, before this, been disposed of. We promised to invest the proceeds for their benefit, which has not been done. Instead of asking for money wherewith to purchase these stocks, the treasury has been contented to ask for the amount of interest only, holding the United States debtors to the Indians, whereby a debt, to all intents and purposes, to the whole amount of this trust fund, is created, and is to be added to the amount of debt due by the government. I do not say it must be paid to-day, or to-morrow; but it is an outstanding debt. The government is under an undischarged treaty obligation to raise the money, and with it to buy stock for the benefit of the Indians.

In addition to all this, there will be found, I have no doubt, a heavy amount of outstanding debts due for public works, expenses growing out of army operations in Florida, indemnities for Indian spoliations in the South and West, and for a variety of other objects.

Now, Sir, I agree with all that is said in the message as to the great impolicy, in time of peace, of commencing a public debt; but it seems to me rather extraordinary and inappropriate in the President to admonish others against such a measure, with all these facts immediately before him. In principle, there is no difference, as to the creation of a public debt, whether it be by issuing stock, redeemable after a certain period, or by issuing treasury-notes, which are renewable, and constantly renewed; and if there be any difference in point of expediency, none can entertain any great doubt which of the two forms is best. Treasury-notes are certainly not the cheaper of the two.

Now, we find the existence of this public debt as early as the existence of the present administration itself. It began at the extra session, in September, 1837. From the date of the first treasury-note bill, in October, 1837, there has been no moment in which the government has not been in debt for borrowed money. The Secretary says it is not expected that the treasury-notes now out can be paid off earlier than in March, 1842. In whatever soft words he chooses to clothe the matter, the sum and substance is this, that there must be a new issue of treasury-notes before the government can be freed from embarrassment.

I must confess that it seems to me that the scope and tendency of the remarks in the message are to produce an erroneous impression. Here is a series of very strong sentiments against a public debt, against *beginning* a public debt, and all said in face of a debt already begun, existing now, and under such circumstances as to create the fear that it will turn out to be a very large one. We know that these various outstanding charges cannot, or at least will not, be brought together, and presented in one aggregate sum, for some months to come. Is it intended by this document to forestall public opinion, so as, when it shall appear that there is a public debt, to give to it a date posterior to the 4th of March next? I hope not. I do not impute such a design. So far, however, as I am concerned, I shall take special good care to prevent any such result. I shall certainly recommend that there be a new set of books opened; that there be what merchants call "a rest"; that what is collected prior to March, 1841, and what is expended prior to March, 1841, stand against each other; so that, if there shall appear a balance in favor of this administration, it may be stated; and if the result shall be that the administration is left in debt, let that debt appear, and let it be denominated "the debt of 1841," which it will be the duty of Congress, as such, to provide for.

In one or two other respects, the message is calculated to create quite an erroneous impression. On the fifth page, the President speaks on the subject of the treasury-notes in as mitigated a tone as possible, and tells us, first, that "this small amount still outstanding" is "composed of such as are not yet due." I suppose we all knew that. And then he adds that they are "less by twenty-three millions than the United States have on deposit with the States." I ask the Senate, and I would ask the President if I could, whether he means to recommend to Congress to withdraw the deposits now in the hands of the States, in order to discharge this debt on treasury-notes? Do the administration look to these deposits as a fund out of which to discharge any of the debts of the treasury? I find no recommendation of such a measure. Why, then, were these two things connected? There is nothing in the fact that the amount of treasury-notes is less by twenty-three millions than the amount deposited with the States, unless the President means to recommend that the latter sum shall be looked to as a means of discharging the former. Does he mean merely to inform Congress that twenty-three are less than twenty-eight? If not, why are the two thus placed in juxtaposition, and their amounts compared?

The Secretary of the Treasury treats the matter in much the same way. He speaks of the deposits with the States as of funds in the treasury. Look at his report. In stating the resources of the treasury, he mentions the twenty-eight millions on deposit with the States. What can be the purpose of such a statement? When a Secretary of the Treasury presents to the world a statement of the means of his department, it is universally supposed that his statement is confined to what either exists in the treasury, or is likely to accrue under the operation of existing laws. But this deposit with the States is no more under the control of the treasury, than any other money in the country. He knows full well that an act of Congress is as necessary to his disposal of any part of that sum, as it is to augment the rate of duties at the custom-house. The treasury can no more use the deposits with the States, than it can lay a direct tax. What can be the purpose, the fair purpose, of presenting sums as funds in the treasury, when they are not in the treasury? Or what can be the fair purpose of referring to a fund as a means of payment, when it cannot be touched unless the President means to recommend to Congress to recall the deposits made with the States? That Congress can do, and so it can augment the rate of duties; but till it does, those deposits are no more means in the treasury than if they belonged to another nation. The day, I hope, will come, I have long desired it, when we shall see plain fact plainly stated; when the reports of our fiscal officers will deal less in guesses at the future, and will no longer use forms and phrases, I will not say which are designed to mislead or to mystify, but the result of which is to mislead the nation, by mystifying the subject.

I said that, though the honorable Secretary pretty clearly intimates that we must resort to a new issue of treasury-notes, yet the result of all is, that, if Congress wishes to avoid the necessity either of increasing the duties or of issuing new treasury-notes, he has a resource ready for it; namely, to reduce its appropriations below even his own estimates. This is much like what he told us last year; and yet, though we did reduce our appropriations within even his estimates, still the treasury is in want of money.

One other remark is suggested by what the President says to us on the sixth page of his message. He tells us that it is possible to avoid the "creation of a permanent debt by the general government," and then goes on to observe: "But, to accomplish so desirable an object, two things are indispensable; first, that the action of the federal government be kept within the bounds prescribed by its founders." Now, I did suppose that this duty of keeping the action of the federal government within the bounds of the Constitution was absolute; that it was not affected by times, circumstances, or condition, but was always peremptory and mandatory. What is the inference to be drawn from the President's language? If the treasury is empty, you must keep within the Constitution. And what if it is full? Are you to break its bounds? to transcend the Constitution? I have always thought we should neither be tempted to do this by an overflowing treasury, nor deterred by an empty one from taking such a course as the exigencies of the country might require in the discharge of our duties. The duty of keeping within our constitutional limits is an absolute duty, existing at all times and in all conditions of things. If the treasury be full to overflowing, we are still to undertake nothing, to expend money for nothing, which is not fairly within our power. And if the treasury be empty, and the public service demand expenditures, such as it is our province to make, we are to replenish the treasury.

There is also an important omission in the message, to which I would call the notice of the Senate and of the country. The President says the revenue has fallen off two and a half millions of dollars under two biennial reductions of the rate of duties at the custom-houses under the law of 1833. Be it so. But do we not all know that there is before us, within a year, a much greater "relinquishment" (if that is the term to be applied to it), and within a year and a half more another, and the last of these reductions? Do we not see, then, from the present existence of a large debt, and from this further reduction of duties, (that is, if nothing shall be done to change the law as it now stands,) that a case is presented which will call for the deliberate consideration of Congress, and that some effort will be required to relieve the country?

But here is no recommendation at all on the subject of revenue. No increase is recommended of the duties on articles of luxury, such as wines and silks, nor any other way suggested of providing for the discharge of the existing debt. The result of the whole is, that the experience of the President has shown that the revenue of the country is not equal to its expenditure; that the government is spending seven millions a year beyond its income; and that we are in the process of running right into the jaws of debt. And yet there is not one practical recommendation as to the reduction of the debt, or its extinguishment; but the message contents itself with general and ardent recommendations not to create a debt.

I know not what will be done to meet the deficiency of the next quarter. I suppose the Secretary's recommendation to issue treasury-notes will be followed. I should myself have greatly preferred a tax on wines and silks. It is obvious that, if this or something like it is not done, the time approaches, and is not far off, when provision must be made by another Congress.

I have thus stated my views of this portion of the message. I think it leads to what may render an extra session necessary, a result I greatly deprecate on many accounts, especially on account of the great expenditure with which it will unavoidably be attended. I hope, therefore, that those who now have the power in their hands will make such reasonable and adequate provision for the public exigency as may render the occurrence of an extra session unnecessary.

Mr. Wright having on the 17th instant spoken in answer to Mr. Webster's remarks of the day before, Mr. Webster replied, to the following effect:—

I shall detain the Senate but a short time in answer to some of the honorable member's remarks, as he has really not met the argument which I had the honor yesterday to submit to the Senate. To begin with the subject of Indian treaties. The honorable member has said, that the fund arising from the sale of the Chickasaw lands has all been invested to within some forty or fifty thousand dollars. I founded what I said in relation to this fund on the returns furnished to the Senate, and, according to that document, the balance uninvested amounts to three hundred and sixty thousand dollars. I added, that I had heard that ninety thousand dollars had been invested since the date of the returns. I made no complaint of the mode in which this fund has been invested, so far as it has been invested; and if the whole of it has been invested, so much the better. But in regard to the two and a half millions of the fund belonging to the Winnebagoes and other tribes, and which, according to the treaty, was to be invested for the benefit of those tribes, I ask of the Senate whether the gentleman from New York has fairly met the force of the argument advanced by me. I have not complained of the treaty, nor charged the administration with any extravagance or want of providence in entering into it. That is not the point. The point is, that this amount constitutes a *debt*, for the payment of which it is incumbent on the government to provide; and that, as such, it ought to be kept before the view of Congress, whereas it has been kept entirely out of sight. That is my point. The honorable member admits that it is a debt, but contends that it is not to be reckoned as a portion of the public national debt. If by this the honorable member means to say, that this amount forms no part of the debt arising from borrowed money, unquestionably he is right. But still it is a national debt; the nation owes this money; and it enters necessarily, as one important item or element, into a statement of the financial condition of the government.

The honorable member has asked, if this were so, why such a statement ought not, in like manner, to include the Indian annuities. They are included in effect. Does not the annual report from the department always state the amount of those annuities as part of the expenditures for which Congress is to provide? Are they not always in the estimates? So the member asks why the pensions are not to be included. The same answer might be made. The amount of that expenditure, also, is annually laid before Congress, and it is provided for as other demands on the government. I have not complained of this amount of two and a half millions of Indian debt; I have never opposed these treaties. All I have contended for is, that, as an amount to be provided for, it is as much a part of the public debt as if it consisted of borrowed money; it is a demand which Congress is bound to meet. In any general view, therefore, of the liabilities of the government, is there one of those liabilities which could with more truth and justice be inserted than this?

I have said that I commend the argument of the President, in opposition to a national debt; and I should be quite unwilling to have it supposed that any thing I said could be wrested (I do not charge that it has been intentionally so wrested) to favor the idea of a public debt at all. But I must still insist that the language employed by the President on the eighth page of his message does refer to past political contests in this country, and does hold out the idea that, from the beginning of the government, in the political contests which have agitated the country, there have been some men or some parties who were in favor of the creation and continuance of a public debt, as part of their policy; and this I have denied. The idea in the message is not that there are certain great *interests* in the country which are always, from the nature of things, in favor of such a debt, on account of the advantages derivable from it to themselves, as the honorable member has argued to-day. If the President had stated this, as it has now been stated in the speech of the honorable member, nobody could have taken any exception to it. But that is not the language of the message. The point of objection is, that the message charges this fondness for a national debt upon some one of the parties which have engaged in the past political strifes of the country, and has represented it as a broad and general ground of distinction between parties, that one was the advocate of a national debt, as of itself a good, and the other the opponent of the existence of a debt. This I regard as an imputation wholly unfounded; and it is on this ground that I have objected to that portion of the executive communication. No facts in our history warrant the allegation. It is mere assumption.

When up before, I omitted one important item, in stating the amount of expenditures under the existing administration beyond the accruing revenue, which ought to be brought to the public view. If I am in error, the honorable member will put me right. In March, 1836, a law passed, postponing the payment of certain revenue bonds, in consequence of the great fire in New York, for three, four, and five years. The great mass of these postponed bonds have fallen due, and been received into the treasury, since the present administration came into power. The total amount is about six millions of dollars. This being so, the whole amount of expenditure over and above the accruing revenue amounts to thirty-four millions, or thereabouts, and thus gives an annual excess of expenditures over receipts of *eight and a half millions* a year; and I insist again, looking at the matter in a purely financial view, looking at the comparative proportion of liabilities and of means to discharge them, that when the President finds an excess of the former continuing for four years, at the rate of *eight and a half millions per annum*, and does not particularize any one branch of expenditure in which a considerable practical reduction can be made, (unless so far as it may take place in the pension list, by the gradual decease of the pensioners,) and when he proposes no new measure as a means of replenishing the exhausted treasury, the question for Congress and for the nation to consider is, whether this is a safe course to be pursued in relation to our fiscal concerns. Is it wise, provident, and statesmanlike?

There is another point in which the honorable member from New York has entirely misapprehended me. He says that I appeared to desire to avoid, as a critical and delicate subject, the question of the tariff; or rather, had complained that this administration had not taken it up. Now, I did not say a word about the tariff, further than to state that another great reduction was immediately approaching in the rate of duties, of which the message takes no notice whatever; though it does not fail to refer to two reductions which have heretofore taken place. What I said on the subject of imposing new duties for revenue had reference solely to *silks and wines*. This has been a delicate point with me at no time. I have, for a long period, been desirous to lay such a duty on silks and wines; and it does appear to me the strangest thing imaginable, the strangest phase of the existing system of revenue, that we should import so many millions of dollars worth of silks and wines entirely free of duty, at the very time when the government has been compelled, by temporary loans, to keep itself in constant debt for four years past. So far from considering this a matter of any delicacy, had the Senate the constitutional power of originating revenue bills, the very first thing I should move, in my place, would be to lay a tax on both these articles of luxury.

Were I to draw an inference from the speech of the honorable member, it would be that it rather seemed to be his own opinion, and certainly seemed also to be that of the President, that it would be wiser to withdraw the whole or a part of the money deposited with the States, than to lay taxes on silks and wines. In this opinion I do not at all concur. If the question were between such a withdrawal and the imposition of such a tax, I should, without hesitation, say, lay the tax, and leave the money with the States where it is. I am greatly mistaken if such a preference would not meet the public approbation. I am for taxing this enormous amount of twenty or thirty millions of foreign products imported in a single year, and all consumed in the country, and consumed as articles of luxury, by the rich alone, and for leaving the deposits in possession of the States with whom they have been placed.

I believe I have now noticed so much of the honorable Senator's speech as requires a reply; and I shall resume my seat with again repeating that it has been no part of my purpose to ascribe either extravagance, or the opposite virtue, to the administration, in the purchase of Indian lands or other transactions. That is not my object, or my point, on this occasion. I wish only to present a true financial view of the condition of our affairs, and to show that our national debt is much greater and more serious than a hasty reader of the message might be led to conclude; and however warmly it admonishes the country against a national debt, yet these admonitions are all uttered at a moment when a national debt has already been begun, begun in time of peace, begun under the administration of the President himself.

THE ADMISSION OF TEXAS.*

At a very early period of the session of 1845–46, a joint resolution for the admission of the State of Texas into the Union, was introduced into the House of Representatives by Mr. Douglass of Illinois, from the Committee on the Territories. This resolution, having rapidly passed through all the stages of legislation in the House, was referred in the Senate to the Committee on the Territories, and promptly reported back by Mr. Ashley of Arkansas, without amendment. On the 22d of December the resolution came up, on the question of a third reading, and was opposed by Mr. Webster as follows:—

I am quite aware, Mr. President, that this resolution will pass the Senate. It has passed the other house of Congress by a large majority, and it is quite well known that there is a decided majority in this house also in favor of its passage. There are members of this body, Sir, who opposed the measures for the annexation of Texas which came before Congress at its last session, who, nevertheless, will very probably feel themselves now, in consequence of the resolutions of the last session, and in consequence of the proceedings of Texas upon those resolutions, bound to vote for her admission into the Union. I do not intend, Mr. President, to argue either of the questions which were discussed in Congress at that time, and which have been so much discussed throughout the country within the last three years.

Mr. President, there is no citizen of this country who has been more kindly disposed towards the people of Texas than myself, from the time they achieved, in so very extraordinary a

* Remarks in the Senate of the United States, on the 22d of December, 1845, on the Admission of the State of Texas into the Union.

manner, their independence of the Mexican government. I have shown, I hope, in another place, and shall show in all situations, and under all circumstances, a just and proper regard for the people of that country; but with respect to its annexation to this Union it is well known that, from the first announcement of any such idea, I have felt it my duty steadily, uniformly, and zealously to oppose it. I have expressed opinions and urged arguments against it everywhere, and on all occasions on which the subject came under consideration. I could not now, if I were to go over the whole topic again, adduce any new views, or support old views, as far as I am aware, by any new arguments or illustrations. My efforts have been constant and unwearied; but, like those of others in the same cause, they have failed of success. I will therefore, Sir, in very few words, acting under the unanimous resolution and instructions of both branches of the legislature of Massachusetts, as well as in conformity to my own settled judgment and full conviction, recapitulate before the Senate and before the community the objections which have prevailed, and must always prevail, with me against this measure of annexation.

In the first place, I have, on the deepest reflection, long ago come to the conclusion, that it is of very dangerous tendency and doubtful consequences to enlarge the boundaries of this country, or the territories over which our laws are now established. There must be some limit to the extent of our territory, if we would make our institutions permanent. And this permanency forms the great subject of all my political efforts, the paramount object of my political regard. The government is very likely to be endangered, in my opinion, by a further enlargement of the territorial surface, already so vast, over which it is extended.

In the next place, I have always wished that this country should exhibit to the nations of the earth the example of a great, rich, and powerful republic, which is not possessed by a spirit of aggrandizement. It is an example, I think, due from us to the world, in favor of the character of republican government.

In the next place, Sir, I have to say, that while I hold, with as much integrity, I trust, and faithfulness, as any citizen of this country, to all the original arrangements and compromises under which the Constitution under which we now live was adopted, I never could, and never can, persuade myself to be in favor of the admission of other States into the Union as slave States, with the inequalities which were allowed and accorded by the Constitution to the slave-holding States then in existence. I do not think that the free States ever expected, or could expect, that they would be called on to admit more slave States, having the unequal advantages arising to them from the mode of apportioning representation under the existing Constitution.

Sir, I have never made an effort, and never propose to make an effort; I have never countenanced an effort, and never mean to countenance an effort, to disturb the arrangements, as originally made, by which the various States came into the Union. But I cannot avoid considering it quite a different question, when a proposition is made to admit new States, and that they be allowed to come in with the same advantages and inequalities which were agreed to in regard to the old. It may be said, that, according to the provisions of the Constitution, new States are to be admitted upon the same footing as the old States. It may be so; but it does not follow at all from that provision, that every territory or portion of country may at pleasure establish slavery, and then say we will become a portion of the Union, and will bring with us the principles which we have thus adopted, and must be received on the same footing as the old States. It will always be a question whether the other States have not a right (and I think they have the clearest right) to require that the State coming into the Union should come in upon an equality; and if the existence of slavery be an impediment to coming in on an equality, then the State proposing to come in should be required to remove that inequality by abolishing slavery, or take the alternative of being excluded.

Now, I suppose that I should be very safe in saying, that if a proposition were made to introduce from the North or the Northwest territories into this Union, under circumstances which would give them an equivalent to that enjoyed by slave States, — advantage and inequality, that is to say, over the South, such as this admission gives to the South over the North, — I take it for granted that there is not a gentleman in this body from a slave-holding State that would listen for one moment to such a proposition. I therefore put my opposition, as well as on other grounds, on the political ground that it deranges the balance of the Constitution, and creates inequality and unjust advantage against the North, and in favor of the slave-holding country of the South. I repeat, that if a proposition were now made for annexations from the North, and that proposition contained such a preference, such a manifest inequality, as that now before us, no one could hope that any gentleman from the Southern States would hearken to it for a moment.

It is not a subject that I mean to discuss at length. I am quite aware that there are in this chamber gentlemen representing free States, gentlemen from the North and East, who have manifested a disposition to add Texas to the Union as a slave State, with the common inequality belonging to slave States. This is a matter for their own discretion, and judgment, and responsibility. They are in no way responsible to me for the exercise of the duties assigned them here; but I must say that I cannot but think that the time will come when they will very much doubt both the propriety and the justice of the present proceeding. I cannot but think the time will come when all will be convinced that there is no reason, political or moral, for increasing the number of the States, and increasing, at the same time, the obvious inequality which exists in the representation of the people in Congress by extending slavery and slave representation.

On looking at the proposition further, I find that it imposes restraints upon the legislature of the State as to the manner in which it shall proceed (in case of a desire to proceed at all) in order to the abolition of slavery. I have perused that part of the constitution of Texas, and, if I understand it, the legislature is restrained from abolishing slavery at any time, except on two conditions; one, the consent of every master, and the other, the payment of compensation. Now I think that a constitution thus formed ties up the hands of the legislature effectually against any movement, under any state of circumstances, with a view to abolish slavery; because, if any thing is to be done, it must be done within the State by general law, and such a thing as the consent of every master cannot be obtained; though I do not say that there may not be an inherent power in the people of Texas to alter the constitution, if they should be inclined to relieve themselves hereafter from the restraint under which they labor. But I speak of the constitution now presented to us.

Mr. President, I was not in Congress at the last session, and of course I had no opportunity to take part in the debates upon this question; nor have I before been called upon to discharge a public trust in regard to it. I certainly did, as a private citizen, entertain a strong feeling that, if Texas were to be brought into the Union at all, she ought to be brought in by diplomatic arrangement, sanctioned by treaty. But it has been decided otherwise by both houses of Congress; and, whatever my own opinions may be, I know that many who coincided with me feel themselves, nevertheless, bound by the decision of all branches of the government. My own opinion and judgment have not been at all shaken by any thing I have heard. And now, not having been a member of the government, and having, of course, taken no official part in the measure, and as it has now come to be completed, I have believed that I should best discharge my own duty, and fulfil the expectations of those who placed me here, by giving this expression of their most decided, unequivocal, and unanimous dissent and protest; and stating, as I have now stated, the reasons which have impelled me to withhold my vote.

I agree with the unanimous opinion of the legislature of Massachusetts; I agree with the great mass of her people; I reaffirm what I have said and written during the last eight years, at various times, against this annexation. I here record my own dissent and opposition; and I here express and place on record, also, the dissent and protest of the State of Massachusetts.

OREGON.*

Very early in the first session of the Twenty-ninth Congress, General Cass, one of the Senators from Michigan, introduced resolutions directing the Committees on Military Affairs, the Militia, and Naval Affairs, respectively, to inquire into the condition of the national fortifications and their armaments; into the present condition of the militia and the state of the militia laws; and into the condition of the navy of the United States, and the quantity and condition of the naval supplies on hand. These resolutions were supported by General Cass in a short speech, in which he pointed to the relations of the United States and Great Britain in reference to the Oregon Territory, as making these inquiries into the state of the military defences of the country both prudent and necessary. On these resolutions Mr. Webster made the following remarks: —

I do not propose to offer any opposition whatever to the passage of the resolutions, though I cannot perceive that there is any very great necessity for their adoption. It does not appear to me that they charge the committees with any especial new duty. Inquiry into the matters here suggested is the ordinary duty of the committees, and I do not think there are any extraordinary circumstances existing which render it necessary, on this occasion, to instruct them by a resolution of the Senate, or to stimulate them in the performance of an established duty. Nevertheless, I regret the introduction of these resolutions, combined, as they are, with the remarks which the Senator from Michigan has thought proper to address to the Senate, because I agree with the Senator from Kentucky,† that their introduc-

* Remarks on the Resolutions moved by General Cass in the Senate of the United States, on the 15th of December, 1845, directing Inquiry into the Condition of the Military Defences of the Country.

† Mr. Crittenden

tion in that manner appears to give something to them of significance, which will create unnecessary alarm. Every member of the Senate knows, and every man of intelligence knows, that unnecessary alarm and apprehension about the preservation of the public peace is a great evil. It disturbs the affairs of the country, it disturbs the calculations of men, it deranges the pursuits of life, and even, to a great extent, changes the circumstances of the whole business of the community. This truth will be felt more especially by every gentleman acquainted or connected with the seaboard. They all know what an immense amount of property is afloat upon the ocean, carried there by our citizens in the prosecution of their maritime pursuits. They all know that a rumor of war, or the breath of a rumor of war, will affect the value of that property. They all know what effect it will have upon insurances. They all know what immense amounts of property on shore will be affected by the agitation of public opinion upon an intimation of the disturbance of the pacific relations existing between this country and foreign states.

Sir, there are two ways, in either of which a government may proceed; and, when I have stated them, I think it will be obvious to every one which is the wisest. We may, if we choose, create alarm and apprehension. We may, if we are wiser, cause no unnecessary alarm, but make quiet, thorough, just, politic, statesmanlike provision for the future.

Mr. President, I am entirely of the opinion of the Senator from Kentucky. I have not been able to bring myself to believe that war will grow out of this matter, certainly not immediately; and I think I cannot be mistaken when I say, that the recommendations which the chief magistrate has made to Congress do not show that he expects war. I think it impossible to mistake the meaning of the President. He does not expect war. Looking at the state of things around us, and at what is stated by the executive, I cannot believe that he apprehends any danger.

Sir, I abstain cautiously from offering any remark upon that portion of the message which refers to the negotiation. I abstain with equal care from any remark upon a correspondence which has been published. I do not wish to say whether it appears from that correspondence that negotiation is so completely and entirely at an end, that no amicable disposition of the question may be looked for hereafter from a diplomatic source. It is enough for me, in order to accomplish all the purposes of these few remarks, to say, that, while I am incapable of bringing myself to the belief that the President apprehends any immediate danger of war, I may be allowed to suppose, or to imagine, that he may entertain an opinion similar to that which has been expressed this morning by the Senator from Connecticut.* He may possibly, having communicated the ultimatum of this government, look for propositions to come from the other side. Whether it be in this view or upon other grounds that the expectation is entertained, it is enough for me to deprecate any false alarm that may disturb the tranquillity of the country.

The President may feel, as I am bound to suppose he does feel, the full weight of the responsibility which attaches to him in relation to every public interest, and the greatest of all interests, the peace of the country. I am bound to suppose that he understands the position in which he is placed, and that he judges wisely as to the extent to which he should go in submitting propositions to Congress. Therefore, I entirely concur in the opinion which has been expressed, that he cannot regard the present position of affairs as leading to any immediate danger of war.

Acting upon these conclusions, and entertaining these views, all the regret I feel at the introduction of these resolutions is, as I have said, that, accompanied with the remarks which fell from the honorable Senator when he called them up, they may have a tendency to create unnecessary alarm. I trust that every member of the community will perceive that it is expedient to prevent all alarm; at the same time, as far as I am concerned, if gentlemen think that the time has come for enlarging the defences of the country, for augmenting the army and the navy, I am ready to coöperate with them.

* Mr. Niles.

OREGON.*

At the first session of the Twenty-ninth Congress, the President in his annual message recommended to the two houses that the United States should give notice to Great Britain of their intention to terminate the Convention between the two countries, concluded in 1827, for the joint occupation of the Oregon Territory; in pursuance of the right reserved to either party by that Convention on notice duly given to the other party. A joint resolution to carry this recommendation into effect was introduced into the Senate by Mr. Allen of Ohio, and referred to the Committee on Foreign Relations. It was reported back to the Senate with amendments proposed by the committee, and other amendments were moved by individual Senators. Among other amendments the following, preceded by a preamble, was moved by Mr. Crittenden of Kentucky: —

"That the President of the United States be, and he hereby is, authorized, at his discretion, to give to the British government the notice required by its said second article for the abrogation of the said Convention of the 6th of August, 1827: *Provided however*, that, in order to afford ampler time and opportunity for the amicable settlement and adjustment of all their differences and disputes in respect to said territory, said notice ought not to be given till after the close of the present session of Congress."

This amendment to the proposition of the committee was discussed on several successive days; and on the 26th of February, Mr. Colquitt of Georgia brought forward two resolutions, as a substitute for the resolution of Mr. Crittenden. The first was substantially a repetition of Mr. Crittenden's proposition. The second was in the following terms: —

* Remarks made in the Senate of the United States, on the 26th of February, 1846, on the various propositions before the Senate relative to giving notice to the British Government of the intention of the Government of the United States to put an end to the Convention for the Joint Occupation of the Oregon Territory.

"And be it further resolved, that it is earnestly desired that the long standing controversy, respecting limits in the Oregon Territory, be speedily settled by negotiation and compromise, in order to tranquillize the public mind and to preserve the friendly relations of the two countries."

The question being on the adoption of Mr. Crittenden's substitute for the committee's amendment, Mr. Webster spoke as follows: —

Mr. President, — I concur most cordially in the sentiments so beautifully expressed by the honorable Senator* who has just taken his seat. I do not differ with him a hair's breadth in the principles he has laid down, nor in his sense of propriety in regard to the present debate. My purpose has merely been, to ascertain whether the question to be debated cannot be put in a more convenient form than that which it assumes at present. The Senator from Kentucky moved an amendment to the amendment reported from the Committee on Foreign Relations. The Senator from Georgia then suggested another, slightly differing in form, which he intends to move, when it shall be in order, as a substitute for that of the Senator from Kentucky. To facilitate the action of the Senate, it has been proposed to the gentleman from Kentucky to accept the amendment of the Senator from Georgia; and he has now declared, that, in regard to the first part of the proposition of the gentleman from Georgia, he has no difficulty in accepting it in place of his own, or as a modification of his own. In regard to the latter part of that proposition, he considers it as in its nature distinct and substantive; he understands it as going further than his own proposition, and as not being, therefore, a natural substitute for it. Now, if it is the disposition of the Senate to act on this subject further than has been proposed by the honorable Senator from Kentucky, the only question will be, whether the Senator will not consent wholly to withdraw his own amendment, and suffer that of the Senator from Georgia to be moved in its place.

I do not, however, think it of particular importance that the Senate should express an opinion on this matter to-day or to-morrow, or this week or the next. I suppose, indeed, that the proceedings of the Senate on this subject are regarded with extreme interest at home, and looked upon with great respect abroad; and I feel more strongly, perhaps, than the Senator from

* Mr. Crittenden.

Kentucky the evils to which he has referred, because I live in the very midst of them, and witness from day to day the great injury sustained by the commercial interests of this country from the present uncertain and anxious posture of affairs.

Let me add a few words more. I shall vote for both portions of the amendment suggested by the Senator from Georgia. I am prepared to do so. At the opening of the present session of Congress, the President, not called upon by the Senate, sent to the two houses the correspondence which had taken place between the Secretary of State and the representative of the British government here, recommending at the same time the giving of notice to that government of the termination of the Convention of 1827. The correspondence thus submitted has very properly been made a subject of remark in both houses. I will say nothing in regard to the propriety of sending that correspondence here. I suppose such a step could hardly be justified, save on the ground that the negotiation was ended by the rejection of the President's offer of the parallel of forty-nine degrees of north latitude as the boundary, and the immediate withdrawal of that offer; because, in the general practice of governments, it has been found very inconvenient to publish the letters which may pass between negotiators before the negotiation is ended. But as the President has sent us this correspondence, and as the Senate is called upon to act on the proposition of notice, I thought it would expedite our decision to have before us also any further correspondence which might have taken place subsequently to that first sent. I accordingly moved the call, and, in response to it, the more recent correspondence has been laid before us, from which we learn the offer by the British envoy to submit the question to arbitration, and the rejection of that offer by the executive.

Now, without meaning at this time to go into any sort of examination of the course of the President in this matter, or indulging in any remark expressive of an unfriendly feeling towards the administration, or any disposition to embarrass the government, for I feel nothing of the kind, and nothing is further from my intention, I must still be permitted to say, that the existing posture of affairs is such as to render it quite desirable that we should know what is the opinion of the executive in regard to this measure and its consequences. Nobody doubts that the two houses of Congress have a perfect authority to terminate the Oregon Convention, without offence to any body. This is our specified right, and its exercise can present no just cause of complaint in any quarter. But, though this is an undoubted truth, yet it must be considered in connection with the circumstances which have been made to surround it. The resolution of notice has passed the other house of Congress with a qualification, or addition, or whatever else it should be called, which prevents it in some respects from being a mere naked notice of termination. It comes with that qualification or condition for adoption here. Other propositions are offered in the Senate, and are entertained as fit subjects of consideration.

The Senator from Kentucky, in one part of his speech, says that he will leave the entire responsibility of this controversy where the Constitution has placed it, and contends that those who have the power to conduct the foreign diplomacy of the country are responsible to the country and to the world for the manner in which they shall exercise that power. This is certainly very just, but it raises a doubt whether we ought to do more than simply to give, or to refuse to give, the naked notice. But some modification of the mere naked notice has been already attached to it in the other house; and there is, as I believe, a conviction on the part of a large majority of the Senate, that it should, to a certain extent, be qualified. Now, I hold that, under these circumstances, we have a right to know in what point of view the executive himself regards this notice; what are the ends he has in view, and what are the consequences to which, in his judgment, the notice is to lead.

When speaking on this subject some weeks ago, I said it was most obvious that the President could not expect war; because he did not act as the chief magistrate of such a nation as this must be expected to act, if, charged as he is with the defence of the country, he expected any danger of its being assaulted by the most formidable power upon earth. I still say there is nothing in the executive communications to show us that the President does expect a war. He must, then, expect nothing but a continuance of the present controversy, or a settlement of it by negotiation. But how is it to be settled? On what terms? On what basis? All that we hear is, "The whole of Oregon or none." And yet there is to be negotiation. We cannot conceal from ourselves or the world the gross inconsistency of such conduct. It is the spirit of the whole negotiation, on our part, that Oregon is ours; there is nothing like admitting even a doubt, on the part of ourselves or others, as to that position; and yet we are to negotiate! What is negotiation? Does any gentleman expect that the administration are, by negotiation, to persuade Great Britain to surrender the whole of what she holds in Oregon? They may do this; I cannot say they will not. If that is their expectation, let them try their hand at it; I wish them success. That is, I wish that we may get "all Oregon" if we can; but let our arguments be fair, and let our demands be reasonable.

But I do not understand the position we are placed in. The executive seems to be for negotiation, and yet is against taking any thing but the whole of Oregon. What, then, is to be the ground of negotiation? What is the basis on which it is to proceed? If the President has made up his mind not to treat for less than the whole, he should say so, and throw himself at once on the two houses of Congress.

I am entitled to make this remark, because it cannot be disguised that the probable effect of this notice is viewed very differently by very intelligent gentlemen, all friends of the administration, on this floor. The Senator from Georgia regards it as a measure tending to peace. He hopes, he expects, peace from it, and he thinks the expression of such opinions as he avows will enable the administration to secure the peace of the country. There are certain other gentlemen, and among them the honorable Senator from Michigan,* who are much less ardent in their hopes of peace. That Senator's impression has been, that, if we pass this notice, there is a possibility and a prospect of war; and so, against the gentleman's own declarations and disavowals, his speeches generally terminate in the expression that war is inevitable.

After an explanation from Mr. Cass, Mr. Webster proceeded as follows: —

The gentleman thinks we shall not recede, and that England will not recede; and then what more likely to happen than a

* Mr. Cass.

war? It was the Senator's argument, and not any particular expression he employed, which gave me the idea that such was his impression. I do not charge the gentleman with saying that "war is inevitable"; but what he did say yet rings in my ears, and on every return of the like language I am reminded of the sentence with which the Roman Senator ended all his speeches, "Delenda est Carthago."

I am desirous of expressing the sentiment (without wishing to embarrass the administration: if negotiations are pending I will hold my tongue; my tongue shall be blistered before I will say any thing against our own title so long as negotiations are pending; but the President must see the embarrassment under which we stand; I am willing to aid the administration, and will aid it to obtain all to which we are justly entitled) that I must know something of the views, expectations, end, and objects of the President in recommending this notice. I cannot much longer be quiet in the existing posture of affairs, when no measures of defence are recommended to us, but negotiation is held out as likely to bring the question to a settlement by England's giving up the whole matter in dispute. My doubt of that is as strong as that expressed by the Senator from Michigan. I say here, so far as my own knowledge goes, that it is not the judgment of this country, that it is not the judgment of this Senate, that the government of the United States shall run the hazard of a war for Oregon, by renouncing as no longer fit for consideration propositions made by ourselves to Great Britain thirty years ago, and repeated again and again before the world. I do not speak of any specific propositions, but of the general idea, of the general plan, so justly suggested by the Senator from Missouri,* of separating the interests of British subjects and American citizens beyond the Rocky Mountains. I repeat the assertion, that it is not the judgment of this country that we are bound to reject our own propositions, made over and over again, twenty and thirty years ago. I do not believe that such is the judgment of this Senate. I have the fullest belief that the propositions proposed by the gentleman from Georgia concur with the views of a large majority of this body.

(A Voice. Yes, of two thirds.)

* Mr. Benton.

A gentleman near me says of two thirds of it; and I am willing to try that question immediately. I am ready now to take the question, whether this difficulty shall or shall not be settled by compromise. Compromise I can understand; but negotiation, with a fixed resolution to take and not to give, with a predetermination not to take less than the whole, is what I do not and cannot understand in diplomacy. I wish we could take that question now; not for the purpose of giving information in any quarter, but in order to put an end to the present distressing, distracting state of things. There are many subjects which we should attend to, all of which are greatly and materially embarrassed by the present position of this affair. It is proposed, for example, to remodel the tariff. But with what view? To augment revenue, or reduce revenue? If it is to augment the revenue, then, I ask, is that with a view to war? If it is to reduce revenue, then, I ask, is that with a view to peace? How can we possibly know how to act, without the least knowledge whether there is a likelihood of the continuance of peace, or whether we are on the eve of a war?

The embarrassment in the private affairs of men is equally pressing. The nation possesses a great commerce. Now it is easy for a gentleman to say, "I disregard commerce on a question of the national honor." So do I, when that is the question. If the honor of my country is attacked, I will say, in the memorable language once used by a member of the other house, "Perish commerce!" But there are interests not to be trifled with. Those great interests of this country, in which is involved the daily bread of thousands and millions of men, are not to be put in jeopardy for objects not in reality connected either with the honor or the substantial interests of the country. I wish, therefore, so soon as it is practicable, to obtain an expression of the opinion of the Senate. If it shall be the opinion of this body that it is best to give the naked notice recommended in the President's message, that will throw the responsibility upon the executive to the fullest extent. I am for taking a question either on the naked notice, or on notice in some modified form, such as shall express what I believe to be the judgment both of the Senate and of the country.

OREGON.*

Mr. President, — I shall advise my honorable friend, the member from Delaware, to forbear from pressing this resolution for a few days. There is no doubt that there are letters from Mr. McLane; but as the chairman of the Committee on Foreign Relations opposes this motion, I am to presume that the executive government finds it inconvenient to communicate those letters to the Senate at the present moment. Yet it is obvious, as the Senate is called upon to perform a legislative act, that it ought, before the hour of its decision comes, to be put in possession of every thing likely to influence its judgment; otherwise, it would be required to perform high legislative functions on mere confidence.

There is certainly some embarrassment in the case. If the executive government deems the communication of the correspondence inconvenient, it can only be because negotiation is still going on, or, if suspended, is expected to be resumed. So far as negotiation is concerned, the communication, or publication, of the correspondence may very properly be thought inconvenient. But then the President has recommended the passage of a law, or resolution, by the two houses of Congress. In support of this recommendation, he himself sent us, unasked, at the commencement of the session, the correspondence up to that time. Now, if that was necessary, the rest is necessary. If we are entitled to a part, we are entitled to the whole. In my opinion, the mistake was in calling on Congress to authorize notice

* Remarks made in the Senate of the United States, on the 30th of March, 1846, on a Resolution moved by Mr. Clayton of Delaware, on the 3d instant calling upon the President for such portions of the Correspondence between the Governments of the United States and Great Britain, as had not already been communicated.

to be given England of the discontinuance of what has been called the joint occupation, until negotiation had been exhausted. Negotiation should have been tried first, and when that had failed, and finally failed, then, and not till then, should Congress have been called upon.

I now go on the ground, of course, that the notice for discontinuing the joint occupancy is properly to be given by authority of Congress, a point which I do not now discuss. It is said, indeed, that notice is to be used as a weapon, or an instrument, in negotiation. I hardly understand this. It is a metaphor of not very obvious application. A weapon seems to imply not a facility, or mere aid, but the means, either of defence against attack, or of making an attack. It sounds not altogether friendly and pacific. I doubt exceedingly whether, under present circumstances, notice would hasten negotiation; and yet such are those circumstances, that there may be as much inconvenience in standing still as in going forward. The truth is, that great embarrassment arises from the extreme pretensions and opinions put forward by the President in his inaugural address a year ago, and in his message last December. But for these, notice would have been harmless, and perhaps would have been authorized by both houses without much opposition, and received by England without dissatisfaction. But the recommendation of the notice, coupled with the President's repeated declarations, that he held our title to the whole territory to be "clear and unquestionable," alarmed the country. And well it might. And if notice were required, in order to enable the President to push these extreme claims to any and every result, then notice ought to be refused by Congress, unless Congress is ready to support these pretensions at all hazards.

Here lies the difficulty. Congress is not prepared, and the country is not prepared, as I believe, to make the President's opinion of a clear and unquestionable right to the whole territory an ultimatum. If he wants notice for such a purpose, he certainly must see that it becomes a grave question whether Congress will grant it. It was a great, a very great mistake, to accompany the recommendation of notice with so positive an assertion of our right to the whole territory. Did the President mean to adhere to that, even to the extremity of war? If so, he should have known that, after what has happened in years past, the country was not likely to sustain him. Did he mean to say this, and afterwards recede from it? If so, why say it at all? Surely, the President could not be guilty of playing so small a part, as to endeavor to show himself to possess spirit, and boldness, and fearlessness of England greater than his predecessors, or his countrymen, and yet do all this in the confident hope that no serious collision would arise between the two countries. So low an ambition, such paltry motives, ought not to be imputed to him. When the President declared that, in his judgment, our title to the whole of Oregon was "clear and unquestionable," did he mean to express an official, or a mere personal opinion? If the latter, it certainly had no place in an official communication. If the former, if he intended a solemn official opinion, upon which he was resolved to act officially, then it is a very grave question how far he is justified, without new lights, or any change of circumstances, in placing the claims of the country, in this respect, on other grounds than those upon which they had stood under his predecessors, and with the concurrence of all branches of the government for so many years; for it is not to be doubted that the United States government has admitted, through a long series of years, that England has rights in the northwestern parts of this continent which are entitled to be respected.

Mr. President, one who has observed attentively what has taken place here and in England within the last three months must, I think, perceive that public opinion, in both countries, is coming to a conclusion that this controversy ought to be settled, and is not very diverse in the two countries as to the general basis of such a settlement. That basis is the offer made by the United States to England in 1826. There is no room to doubt, I think, that this country is ready to stand by that offer, substantially and in effect. Such is my opinion, at least; and circumstances certainly indicate that Great Britain would not, in all probability, regard such a proposition as unfit to be considered.

I said, some weeks ago, that I did not intend to discuss titles at length, and certainly not to adduce arguments against our own claim. But it appears to me that there is a concurrence of arguments and considerations in favor of regarding the forty-ninth parallel as the just line of demarcation, which both countries might well respect. It has for many years been the extent of our claim. We have claimed up to forty-nine degrees, and nothing beyond it. We have offered to yield every thing north of it. It is the boundary between the two countries on this side of the Rocky Mountains, and has been since the purchase of Louisiana from France. I do not think it important either to prove or disprove the fact, that commissioners under the treaty of Utrecht established the forty-ninth parallel as the boundary between the English and French possessions in America. Ancient maps and descriptions so represent it; some saying that this line of boundary is to run "indefinitely west," others saying, in terms, that it extends "to the northwestern ocean." But what is more important, we have considered this boundary as established by the treaty of Utrecht, at least on this side of the Rocky Mountains. It was on the strength of this that we drove back the British pretensions, after we had obtained Louisiana, north, from the head-waters of the Mississippi to this parallel of forty-nine. This is indubitable. We have acted, therefore, and induced others to act, on the idea that this boundary is actually established. It now so stands in the treaty between the United States and England. If, on the general notion of *contiguity* or *continuity*, this line be continued "indefinitely west," or is allowed to run to the "northwestern ocean," then it leaves on our side the valley of the Columbia, to which, in my judgment, our title is maintainable on the ground of Gray's discovery. The government of the United States has never offered any line south of forty-nine, (with the navigation of the Columbia,) and it never will. It behooves all concerned to regard this as a settled point. With respect to the navigation of the Columbia, permanently or for a term of years, that is all matter for just, reasonable, and friendly negotiation. But the forty-ninth parallel must be regarded as the general line of boundary, and not to be departed from for any line farther south. As to all straits, and sounds, and islands in the neighboring sea, all these are fair subjects for treaty stipulation. If the general basis be agreed to, all the rest, it may be presumed, may be accomplished by the exercise of a spirit of fairness and amity.

And now, Mr. President, if this be so, why should this settlement be longer delayed? Why should either government hold back longer from doing that which both, I think, can see must be done, if they would avoid a rupture? Every hour's delay is injurious to the interests of both countries. It agitates both, disturbs their business, interrupts their intercourse, and may, in time, seriously affect their friendly and respectful feeling towards each other. Having said this, Mr. President, my purpose is fulfilled. It would be needless, even if it were proper, to say more. I consider the general sentiment of both countries as almost entirely concentrated on this line as the general basis of a line of demarcation. As yet nothing has happened to touch the point of honor of either government. Why, then, should not the propitious moment be seized? It is not humiliation, it is not condescension even, in either government, to do that now which it sees it must do at some time, if it would avoid serious and calamitous collision. Now, while there is no point of honor raised, in correspondence or otherwise, between the two governments, why should not both seize the auspicious moment? Let fairness and candor, and, I will add, prudence and foresight, rule the hour. Let this controversy be settled, the sooner the better, substantially, according to my judgment, in the manner in which it must eventually be settled, and let the vast and useful intercourse between the two nations be set free from all alarm and disturbance.

It would suit my views of what this occasion calls for, that the measure under consideration* should be postponed for a month, because I desire, if it can be done, that the negotiation should close, and close favorably; and so put an end to the question of notice. I desire that more especially, because every one must see that, if forced to act here upon this notice, we must, as a matter of course, call for all information not yet transmitted to Congress similar in character to that which the President has already sent us. I do not propose that, however. I would not divide the Senate on such a proposition, but I would suggest to those who have the conduct of this affair, whether it is not every way better now to postpone this joint resolution for some time, till some correspondence may take place between the two governments, till there is opportunity for the transmission of letters and despatches, and until it be seen whether it will be necessary to give the notice at all. I say

* The notice to the British government that it is the intention of the government of the United States to terminate the Convention.

this because I have the fullest persuasion that notice will be no aid to negotiation in the present circumstances of the country; and yet I am sorry to say that, if no agreement be come to, and the matter is not speedily settled, there are strong considerations arising at home which may render it proper, in my judgment, to pass the notice. If I had the control of this measure, or the conduct of it here, I should lay it on the table for a month. But I have not that power of control. Gentlemen must judge of the propriety of this suggestion according to their own discretion. Of this, however, I suppose there is no doubt, that, in the present circumstances of the case, the executive government may feel that it is at this peculiar moment inconvenient to make this communication; and I must presume inconvenient only because negotiations are resumed, or are expected to be resumed. Inasmuch as that is the case, I hope my honorable friend from Delaware will let his resolution lie informally on the table.

After some remarks from Mr. Allen of Ohio, Mr. Webster said in reply: —

One word, Sir. It is very true that I have expressed myself on this occasion with premeditated precision. It is an important question, respecting the intercourse of nations, in a considerable emergency between these two nations. It is of importance to be precise, and I really do not think that it would be far but of the way if other gentlemen sometimes would take the same care to make their expressions precise. The gentleman sees fit to consider that this will be regarded as humiliation abroad, humiliation on our part. I fancy not. I am quite apprehensive that, if any countenance in Great Britain, be it high or low, for any thing that has occurred here at this session, puts on a pout, or a sarcastic smile, it is not more likely to be originated by what has taken place on our side of this question than by what may take place on the other.

One word upon a more important part of the case. The gentleman says that I offer now the boundary of the Columbia. Pray, Sir, let me be understood; and such misapprehension of my offer certainly shows that I was not far out of the road of reason and propriety in stating what I intended to say to the Senate in writing. What I have said, and took care to say with precision, was this: First, that in my opinion, — I lay down no law, I say nothing *ex cathedrâ*, — that, in my opinion, public sentiment in both countries is strongly tending to a union upon a settlement on the general basis of our offer of 1826. Now I ask the Senator from Ohio if he does not think just so himself?

Mr. Allen having made one or two remarks expressive of dissent, Mr. Webster resumed as follows: —

If my opinion be so wide of the truth, and the opinion of the country is not tending, as the gentleman says it is not, as I represented it, then my opinion goes for nothing. Let him, however, hear what I said, which I said with care and premeditation; it is, that the line of the forty-ninth degree is the line of demarcation on which, as a general basis, public opinion is settling. I do not say the precise basis, because I immediately added, that, looking to the line of the forty-ninth degree as the line of demarcation, the use of the Columbia River by England, permanently or for a number of years, and the use of the straits and sounds in the adjacent sea, and the islands along the coast, would all be matter of friendly negotiation. I have not recommended to our government one thing or another about allowing England, for a term of years, the use of the Columbia River; not at all. If the line of the forty-ninth degree be established as the general line of demarcation, giving us a straight track from the Lake of the Woods to the Pacific, I am satisfied that the government negotiate about what remains. But the Senator and Senate will do me the justice to admit, that I said as plainly as I could, and in as short a sentence as I could frame, that England must not expect any thing south of the forty-ninth degree. I may be mistaken, but it seems to me as clear as the sun at noonday, that there is a tendency of opinion, moved by a great necessity to settle this question, a strong tendency of opinion, in this country, that we ought to stand by our offer of 1826 in its substance. Is not that just what was argued by the gentleman from South Carolina* the other day? Is not that the result of the discussion in which my friend from New Jersey† took part, to prove that that was the extent of our claim, and that the whole country knows it? Now I think there are rea-

* Mr. Calhoun. † Mr. Dayton.

sons for that. But I rose merely to explain. I mean then to say, for the sake of perfect distinctness I repeat it, that I am of opinion that this matter must be settled upon the forty-ninth parallel. Then as to the use of the Columbia River permanently or for a term of years, and also in regard to all that respects straits, and sounds, and islands in the neighboring seas, they are fit subjects for negotiation. But that England must not expect any thing south of the forty-ninth degree, and that the people of the United States, by a great majority, are content now to abide by what this government offered to England in 1826.

DEFENCE OF THE TREATY OF WASHINGTON.*

In the course of the debates in Congress in the session of 1845-46 on the resolution for terminating the Convention for the joint occupancy of the Oregon Territory, the treaty of Washington and the negotiation which led to it were subjects of comment and animadversion in both houses. The general principles upon which the negotiation had been conducted on the part of the United States, as well as the particular provisions of the treaty were found fault with. The American negotiator (Mr. Webster) was charged with having failed, in several respects, to assert the rights and protect the interests of the country. He was accused of having unconstitutionally surrendered a portion of the State of Maine to a foreign power, and of having accepted a line of boundary between the United States and the British Provinces unfavorable to the former. The mode was condemned in which the subject of the search of vessels suspected of being engaged in the slave trade on the coast of Africa was disposed of; and it was insisted, that no redress had been obtained for the violation of the territorial rights of the United States in the destruction of the "Caroline."

Not having been a member of the last Congress, Mr. Webster had as yet had no favorable opportunity to undertake a vindication of the treaty, which had been the subject of attack upon the grounds just indicated, from the time of its negotiation. The debate upon the Oregon question furnished the occasion for such a defence. Mr. Dickinson, a Senator from New York, in the publication of his speech on that subject, referred to a speech of Mr. Charles J. Ingersoll, a member of the House of Representatives from Pennsylvania, and quoted his words, as his authority for certain injurious statements in reference to the affair of the Caroline. Mr. Webster felt called upon to repel the charge thus made and vouched for, and availed himself of the opportunity to enter, in

* A Speech delivered in the Senate of the United States, on the 6th and 7th of April, 1846.

the following speech, into a general history and defence of the negotiation and the treaty.

It is altogether unexpected to me, Mr. President, to find it to be my duty, here, and at this time, to defend the treaty of Washington of 1842, and the correspondence accompanying the negotiation of that treaty. It is a past transaction. Four years almost have elapsed since the treaty received the sanction of the Senate, and became the law of the land. While before the Senate, it was discussed with much earnestness and very great ability. For its ratification it received the votes of five sixths of the whole Senate, a greater majority, I believe I may say, than was ever before found for any disputed treaty. From that day to this, although I had taken a part in the negotiation of the treaty, and felt it to be a transaction with which my own reputation was intimately connected, I have been willing to leave it to the judgment of the nation. Some things, it is true, had taken place, of which I have not complained, and do not complain, but which, nevertheless, were subjects of regret. The papers accompanying the treaty were voluminous. Their publication was long delayed, waiting for the exchange of ratifications; and, when finally published, they were not distributed to any great extent, or in large numbers. The treaty, meantime, got before the public surreptitiously, and, with the documents, came out by piecemeal. We know that it is unhappily true, that, away from the large commercial cities of the Atlantic coast, there are few of the public prints of the country which publish official papers on such an occasion at length. I might have felt a natural desire, that the treaty and the correspondence should be known and read by every one of my fellow-citizens, from East to West, and from North to South. Indeed, I did feel such a desire. But it was impossible. Nevertheless, in returning to the Senate again, nothing was further from my purpose than to renew the discussion of any of the topics debated and settled at that time; and nothing further from my expectation than to be called upon by any sense of duty to my own reputation, and to truth, to make now any observations upon the treaty, or the correspondence.

But it has so happened, that, in the debate on the Oregon question, the treaty, and I believe every article of it, and the correspondence accompanying the negotiation of that treaty, and I believe every part of it, have been the subject of disparaging, disapproving, sometimes contumelious remarks, in one or the other of the houses of Congress. Now, with all my indisposition to revive past transactions and make them the subjects of debate here, and satisfied, and indeed highly gratified, with the approbation of the treaty so very generally expressed by the country, at the time and ever since, I suppose that it could hardly be expected, nevertheless, by any body, that I should sit here from day to day, through the debate, and through the session, hearing statements entirely erroneous as to matters of fact, and deductions from these supposed facts quite as erroneous, all tending to produce unfavorable impressions respecting the treaty, and the correspondence, and every body who had a hand in it, — I say it could hardly be expected by any body that I should sit here and hear all this, and keep my peace. The country knows that I am here. It knows what I have heard, again and again, from day to day; and if statements wholly incorrect are made here, and in my presence, without reply or answer from me, why, shall we not hear in all the contests of party and elections hereafter, that this is a fact, and that is a fact, because it has been stated where and when an answer could be given, and no answer was given? It is my purpose, therefore, to give an answer here, and now, to whatever has been alleged against the treaty, or the correspondence.

Mr. President, in the negotiation of 1842, and in the correspondence, I acted as Secretary of State, under the direction, of course, of the President of the United States. But, Sir, in matters of high importance, I shrink not from the responsibility of any thing I have ever done under any man's direction. Where-ever my name stands I am ready to answer it, and to defend that with which it is connected. I am here to-day to take upon myself, without disrespect to the chief magistrate under whose direction I acted, and for the purposes of this discussion, the whole responsibility of every thing that has my name connected with it, in the negotiation and correspondence.

Sir, the treaty of Washington was not entered into to settle any, or altogether for the purpose of settling any, new questions The matter embraced in that treaty, and in the correspondence accompanying it, had been interesting subjects in our foreign relations for fifty years, unsettled for fifty years, agitating and annoying the counsels of the country, and threatening to disturb its peace for fifty years. My first duty, therefore, in entering upon such remarks as I think the occasion calls for in regard to one and all of these topics, will be, to treat the subjects historically, to show when each arose what has been its progress in the diplomatic history of the country, and especially to show in what posture each of those important subjects stood at the time when General Harrison acceded to the office of President of the United States. This is my purpose. I do not intend to enter upon any crimination of gentlemen who have filled important situations in the executive government in the earlier, or in the more recent, history of the country. But I intend to show, in the progress of this discussion, the actual position in which things were left in regard to the topics embraced by the treaty, and the correspondence attending its negotiation, when the executive government devolved upon General Harrison, and his immediate successor, Mr. Tyler.

Now, Sir, the first of these topics is the question of the northeastern boundary of the United States. The general history of that question, from the peace of 1783 to this time, is known to all public men, of course, and pretty well understood by the great mass of well-informed persons throughout the country. I shall therefore state it quite briefly.

In the treaty of peace of September, 1783, the northern and eastern, or perhaps, more properly speaking, the northeastern boundary of the United States, is described as follows: —

"From the northwest angle of Nova Scotia, namely, that angle which is formed by a line drawn due north from the source of St. Croix River to the Highlands; along the said Highlands, which divide those rivers that empty themselves into the River St. Lawrence from those which fall into the Atlantic Ocean, to the northwesternmost head of Connecticut River; thence, along the middle of that river, to the forty-fifth degree of north latitude; from thence, by a line due west on said latitude, until it strikes the River Iroquois or Cataraquy. . . . . .

"East, by a line to be drawn along the middle of the River St. Croix, from its mouth in the Bay of Fundy, to its source, and from its source directly north to the aforesaid Highlands."

Such is the description of the northeastern boundary of the United States, according to the treaty of peace of 1783. And it is quite remarkable that so many embarrassing questions should have arisen from these few lines, and have been matters of controversy for more than half a century.

The first disputed question was, "Which, of the several rivers running into the Bay of Fundy, is the St. Croix, mentioned in the treaty?" It is singular that this should be matter of dispute, but so it was. England insisted that the true St. Croix was one river; the United States insisted it was another.

The second controverted question was, "Where is the northwest angle of Nova Scotia to be found?"

The third, "What and where are the highlands, along which the line is to run, from the northwest angle of Nova Scotia to the northwesternmost head of Connecticut River?"

The fourth, "Of the several streams which, flowing together make up Connecticut River, which is that stream which ought to be regarded as its northwesternmost head?"

The fifth was, "Are the rivers which discharge their waters into the Bay of Fundy rivers 'which fall into the Atlantic Ocean,' in the sense of the terms used in the treaty?"

The fifth article of the treaty between the United States and Great Britain of the 19th of November, 1794, after reciting, that doubts had "arisen what river was truly intended under the name of the River St. Croix," proceeded to provide for the decision of that question, by creating three commissioners, one to be appointed by each government, and these two to choose a third; or, if they could not agree, then each to make his nomination, and decide the choice by lot. The two commissioners agreed on a third; the three executed the duty assigned them, decided what river was the true St. Croix, traced it to its source, and there established a monument. So much, then, on the eastern line was settled; and all the other questions remained wholly unsettled down to the year 1842.

But the two governments continued to pursue the important and necessary purpose of adjusting boundary difficulties; and a convention was negotiated in London, by Mr. Rufus King and Lord Hawkesbury, and signed on the 12th day of May, 1803, by the second and third articles of which it was agreed, that a commission should be appointed in the same manner as that provided for under the treaty of 1794; to wit, one commissioner to be appointed by England, and one by the United States, and these two to make choice of a third; or, if they could not agree, each to name the person he proposed, and the choice to be decided by lot; this third commissioner, whether appointed by choice or by lot, would, of course, be umpire or ultimate arbiter.

Governments, at that day, in disputes concerning territorial boundaries, did not set out each with the declaration that the whole of its own claim was "clear and unquestionable." Whatever was seriously disputed they regarded as in some degree, at least, doubtful or disputable; and when they could not agree, they saw no indignity or impropriety in referring the dispute to arbitration, even though the arbitrator were to be appointed by chance from among respectable persons named severally by the parties.

The commission thus constituted was authorized to ascertain and determine the northwest angle of Nova Scotia; to run and mark the line from the monument, at the source of the St. Croix, to that northwest angle of Nova Scotia; and also to determine the northwesternmost head of Connecticut River; and then to run and mark the boundary line between the northwest angle of Nova Scotia and the said northwesternmost head of Connecticut River; and the decision and proceedings of the said commissioners, or a majority of them, were to be final and conclusive.

No objection was made by either government to this agreement and stipulation; but an incident arose to prevent the final ratification of this treaty, and it arose in this way. Its fifth article contained an agreement between the parties settling the line of boundary between them beyond the Lake of the Woods. In coming to this agreement they proceeded, exclusively, on the grounds of their respective rights under the treaty of 1783; but it so happened that, twelve days before the convention was signed in London, France, by a treaty signed in Paris, had ceded Louisiana to the United States. This cession was at once regarded as giving to the United States new rights, or new limits, in this part of the continent. The Senate, therefore, struck this fifth article out of the convention; and as England did not incline to agree to this alteration, the whole convention fell.

Here, Sir, the whole matter rested till it was revived by the treaty of Ghent, in the year 1814. By the fifth article of that treaty it was provided, that each party should appoint a commissioner, and that those two should have power to ascertain and determine the boundary line, from the source of the St. Croix to the St. Lawrence River, according to the treaty of 1783; and if these commissioners could not agree, they were to state their grounds of difference, and the subject was to be referred to the arbitration of some friendly sovereign or state, to be afterwards agreed upon by the two governments. The two commissioners were appointed, explored the country, and examined the boundary, but could not agree.

In the year 1823, under the administration of Mr. Monroe, negotiations were commenced with the view of agreeing on an arbitration, and these negotiations terminated in a convention, which was signed in London, on the 29th of September, 1827, under the administration of Mr. Adams. By this time, collisions had already begun on the borders, notwithstanding it had been understood that neither party should exercise exclusive possession pending the negotiation. Mr. Adams, in his message of the 8th of December, 1827, after stating the conclusion of the convention for arbitration, adds:—

> "While these conventions have been pending, incidents have occurred of conflicting pretensions, and of a dangerous character, upon the territory itself in dispute between the two nations. By a common understanding between the governments, it was agreed that no exercise of exclusive jurisdiction by either party, while the negotiation was pending, should change the state of the question of right to be definitely settled. Such collision has, nevertheless, recently taken place, by occurrences the precise character of which has not yet been ascertained."

The King of the Netherlands was appointed arbitrator under this convention, and he made his award on the 10th of January, 1831. This award was satisfactory to neither party; it was rejected by both, and so the whole matter was thrown back upon its original condition.

This happened during the first term of General Jackson's administration. He immediately addressed himself to new efforts for the adjustment of the controversy. His energy and diligence have both been much commended by his friends; and they have not been disparaged by his opponents. He called to his aid, in the Department of State, successively, Mr. Van Buren, Mr. Livingston, Mr. McLane, and Mr. Forsyth.

Now, Mr. President, let us see what progress General Jackson made, with the assistance of these able and skilful negotiators, in this highly important business. Why, Sir, the whole story is told by reference to his several annual messages. In his fourth annual message, of December, 1832, he says: "The question of our northeastern boundary still remains unsettled." In December, 1833, he says: "The interesting question of our northeastern boundary remains still undecided. A negotiation, however, upon that subject, has been renewed since the close of the last Congress." In December, 1834, he says: "The question of the northeastern boundary is still pending with Great Britain, and the proposition made, in accordance with the resolution of the Senate, for the establishment of a line according to the treaty of 1783, has not been accepted by that government. Believing that every disposition is felt on both sides to adjust this perplexing question to the satisfaction of all the parties interested in it, the hope is yet indulged that it may be effected on the basis of that proposition." In December, 1835, a similar story is rehearsed. "In the settlement of the question of the northeastern boundary," says President Jackson, "little progress has been made. Great Britain has declined acceding to the proposition of the United States, presented in accordance with the resolution of the Senate, unless certain preliminary conditions are admitted, which I deemed incompatible with a satisfactory and rightful adjustment of the controversy." And in his last message the President gives an account of all his efforts, and all his success, in regard to this most important point in our foreign relations, in these words: "I regret to say, that many questions of an interesting nature, at issue with other powers, are yet unadjusted; among the most prominent of these is that of the northeastern boundary. With an undiminished confidence in the sincere desire of his Britannic Majesty's government to adjust that question, I am not yet in possession of the precise grounds upon which it proposes a satisfactory adjustment."

With all his confidence, so often repeated, in the sincere desire of England to adjust the dispute, with all the talents and industry of his successive cabinets, this question, admitted to be the most prominent of all those on which we were at issue with foreign powers, had not advanced one step since the rejection of the award of the King of the Netherlands, nor did General Jackson know the grounds upon which a satisfactory adjustment was to be expected. All this is undeniably true; and it was all admitted to be true by Mr. Van Buren when he came into office; for in his first annual message he says:—

"Of pending questions the most important is that which exists with the government of Great Britain in respect to our northeastern boundary. It is with unfeigned regret that the people of the United States must look back upon the abortive efforts made by the executive for a period of more than half a century to determine what no nation should suffer long to remain in dispute, the true line which divides its possessions from those of other powers. The nature of the settlements on the borders of the United States, and of the neighboring territory, was for a season such, that this, perhaps, was not indispensable to a faithful performance of the duties of the federal government.

"Time has, however, changed this state of things, and has brought about a condition of affairs in which the true interests of both countries imperatively require that this question should be put at rest. It is not to be disguised, that, with full confidence, often expressed, in the desire of the British government to terminate it, we are apparently as far from its adjustment as we were at the time of signing the treaty of peace in 1783. . . . . . The conviction, which must be common to all, of the injurious consequences that result from keeping open this irritating question, and the certainty that its final settlement cannot be much longer deferred, will, I trust, lead to an early and satisfactory adjustment. At your last session, I laid before you the recent communications between the two governments, and between this government and that of the State of Maine, in whose solicitude concerning a subject in which she has so deep an interest every portion of the Union participates."

Now, Sir, let us pause and consider this. Here we are, fifty-three years from the date of the treaty of peace, and the boundary not yet settled. General Jackson has tried his hand at the business for five years, and has done nothing. He cannot make the thing move. And why not? Do he and his advisers want skill and energy, or are there difficulties in the nature of the case not to be overcome till some wiser course of proceeding shall be adopted? Up to this time not one step of progress has been made. This is admitted, and is, indeed, undeniable.

Well, Sir, Mr. Van Buren then began his administration, under the deepest conviction of the importance of the question, in the fullest confidence in the sincerity of the British government, and with the consciousness that the solicitude of Maine concerning the subject was a solicitude in which every portion of the Union participated.

And now, Sir, what did he acccomplish? What progress did he make? What step forward did he take, in the whole course of his administration? Seeing the full importance of the subject, addressing himself to it, and not doubting the just disposition of England, I ask again, What did he do? What advance did he make? Sir, not one step, in his whole four years. Or rather, if he made any advance at all, it was an advance backward; for, undoubtedly, he left the question in a much worse condition than he found it, not only on account of the disturbances and outbreaks which had taken place on the border, for the want of an adjustment, and which disturbances themselves had raised new and difficult questions, but on account of the intricacies, and complexities, and perplexities, in which the correspondence had become involved. The subject was entangled in meshes, which rendered it far more difficult to proceed with the question than if it had been fresh and unembarrassed.

I must now ask the Senate to indulge me in something of a more extended and particular reference to proofs and papers, than is in accordance with my general habits in debate; because I wish to present to the Senate, and to the country, the grounds of what I have just said.

Let us, accordingly, follow the administration of Mr. Van Buren, from his first message, and see how this important matter fared in his hands.

On the 20th of March, 1838, he sent a message to the Senate, with a correspondence between Mr. Fox and Mr. Forsyth. In this correspondence Mr. Fox says:—

"The United States government have proposed two modes in which such a commission might be constituted; first, that it might consist of commissioners, named in equal numbers by each of the two governments, with an umpire to be selected by some friendly European power. Secondly, that it might be entirely composed of scientific Europeans, to be selected by a friendly sovereign, and might be accompanied, in its operations, by agents of the two different parties, in order that such agents might give to the commissioners assistance and information.

. . . . .

"Her Majesty's government have themselves already stated that they have little expectation that such a commission could lead to any useful result, and that they would, on that account, be disposed to object to it; and if her Majesty's government were now to agree to appoint such a commission, it would only be in compliance with the desire so strongly expressed by the government of the United States, and in spite of doubts, which her Majesty's government still continue to entertain, of the efficacy of the measure."

To this Mr. Forsyth replies, that he perceives, with feelings of deep disappointment, that the answer to the propositions of the United States is so indefinite, as to render it impracticable to ascertain, without further discussion, what are the real wishes and intentions of her Majesty's government. Here, then, a new discussion arises, to find out, if it can be found out, what the parties mean. Meantime, Mr. Forsyth writes a letter of twenty or thirty pages to the Governor of Maine, concluding with a suggestion that his Excellency should take measures to ascertain the sense of the State of Maine with respect to the expediency of a conventional line. This correspondence repeats the proposition of a joint exploration, by commissioners, and Mr. Fox accedes to it, in deference to the wishes of the United States, but with very little hope that any good will come of it.

This is the result of one whole year's work. Mr. Van Buren sums it up thus, in his message of December, 1838: —

"With respect to the northeastern boundary of the United States, no official correspondence between this government and that of Great Britain has passed since that communicated to Congress towards the close of their last session. The offer to negotiate a convention for the appointment of a joint commission of survey and exploration, I am, however, assured, will be met by her Majesty's government in a conciliatory and friendly spirit, and instructions to enable the British minister here to conclude such an arrangement will be transmitted to him without needless delay."

We may now look for instructions to Mr. Fox, to conclude an arrangement for a joint commission of survey and exploration. Survey and exploration! As if there had not already been enough of both! But thus terminates 1838, witn a hope of coming to an agreement for a survey! Great progress this, surely!

And now we come to 1839. And what, Sir, think you, was the product of diplomatic fertility and cultivation in the year 1839? Sir, the harvest was one *project*, and one *counter-project*. On the 20th of May, Mr. Fox sent to Mr. Forsyth a draft of a convention for a joint exploration, by commissioners, the commissioners to make report to their respective governments. This was the British *project*.

On the 29th of July, Mr. Forsyth sent to Mr. Fox a *counter-project*, embracing the principle of arbitration. By this, if the commissioners did not agree, a reference was to be had to three persons, selected by three friendly sovereigns or states; and these arbitrators might order another survey. Here the parties, apparently fatigued with their efforts, paused; and the labors of the year are thus rehearsed and recapitulated by Mr. Van Buren at the end of the season:—

"For the settlement of our northeastern boundary, the proposition promised by Great Britain, for a commission of exploration and survey, has been received, and a counter-project, including also a provision for the certain and final adjustment of the limits in dispute, is now before the British government for its consideration. A just regard to the delicate state of this question, and a proper respect for the natural impatience of the State of Maine, not less than a conviction that the negotiation has been already protracted longer than is prudent on the part of either government, have led me to believe that the present favorable moment should on no account be suffered to pass without putting the question for ever at rest. I feel confident that the government of her Britannic Majesty will take the same view of this subject, as I am persuaded it is governed by desires equally strong and sincere for the amicable termination of the controversy."

Here, Sir, in this "delicate state of the question," all things rested till the next year.

Early after the commencement of the warm weather, in 1840, the industrious diplomatists resumed their severe and rigorous labors, and on the 22d of June, 1840, Mr. Fox writes thus to Mr. Forsyth:—

"The British government and the government of the United States agreed, two years ago, that a survey of the disputed territory, by a joint commission, would be the measure best calculated to elucidate and solve the questions at issue. The President proposed such a commission, and her Majesty's government consented to it; and it was believed by her Majesty's government, that the general principles upon which the commission was to be guided in its local operations had been settled by mutual agreement, arrived at by means of a correspondence which took place between the two governments in 1837 and 1838. Her Majesty's government accordingly transmitted, in April of last year, for the consideration of the President, a draft of the convention, to regulate the proceedings of the proposed convention.

"The preamble of that draft recited, textually, the agreement that had been come to by means of notes which had been exchanged between the two governments; and the articles of the draft were framed, as her Majesty's government considered, in strict conformity with that agreement.

"But the government of the United States did not think proper to assent to the convention so proposed.

"The United States government did not, indeed, allege that the proposed convention was at variance with the result of the previous correspondence between the two governments; but it thought that the convention would establish a commission of 'mere exploration and survey'; and the President was of opinion, that the step next to be taken by the two governments should be to contract stipulations, bearing upon the face of them the promise of a final settlement, under some form or other, and within a reasonable time.

"The United States government accordingly transmitted to the undersigned, for communication to her Majesty's government, in the month of July last, a counter-draft of a convention, varying considerably in some parts (as the Secretary of State of the United States admitted, in his letter to the undersigned of the 29th of July last) from the draft proposed by Great Britain.

. . . . .

"There was, undoubtedly, one essential difference between the British draft and the American counter-draft. The British draft contained no provision embodying the principle of arbitration. The American counter-draft did contain such a provision. The British draft contained no provision for arbitration, because the principle of arbitration had not been proposed on either side during the negotiations upon which that draft was founded; and because, moreover, it was understood, at that time, that the principle of arbitration would be decidedly objected to by the United States. But as the United States government have now expressed a wish to embody the principle of arbitration in the proposed convention, her Majesty's government are perfectly willing to accede to that wish.

"The undersigned is accordingly instructed to state officially to Mr.

Forsyth, that her Majesty's government consent to the two principles which form the main foundation of the American counter-draft; namely, first, that the commission to be appointed shall be so constituted as necessarily to lead to a final settlement of the questions of boundary at issue between the two countries; and secondly, that, in order to secure such a result, the convention by which the commission is to be created shall contain a provision for arbitration upon points as to which the British and American commission may not be able to agree.

"The undersigned is, however, instructed to add, that there are many matters of detail in the American counter-draft which her Majesty's government cannot adopt.

"The undersigned will be furnished from his government, by an early opportunity, with an amended draft, in conformity with the principles above stated, to be submitted to the consideration of the President. And the undersigned expects to be at the same time furnished with instructions to propose to the government of the United States a fresh, local, and temporary convention, for the better prevention of incidental border collisions within the disputed territory during the time that may be occupied in carrying through the operations of survey or arbitration."

And on the 26th of June, Mr. Forsyth replies, and says: —

"That he derives great satisfaction from the announcement that her Majesty's government do not relinquish the hope, that the sincere desire which is felt by both parties to arrive at an amicable settlement will at length be attended with success; and from the prospect held out by Mr. Fox of his being accordingly furnished, by an early opportunity, with the draft of a proposition amended in conformity with the principles to which her Majesty's government has acceded, to be submitted to the consideration of this government."

On the 28th of July, 1840, the British amended draft came. This draft proposed that commissioners should be appointed, as before, to make exploration; that umpires or arbitrators should be appointed by three friendly sovereigns, and that the arbitration should sit in Germany, at Frankfort on the Maine. And the draft contains many articles of arrangement and detail, for carrying the exploration and arbitration into effect.

At the same time, Mr. Fox sends to Mr. Forsyth the report of two British commissioners, Messrs. Mudge and Featherstonhaugh, who had made an *ex parte* survey in 1839. And a most extraordinary report it was. These gentlemen had discovered, that, up to that time, nobody had been right. They invented a new line of highlands, cutting across the waters of the Aroostook and other streams emptying into the St. John, which, in every previous examination and exploration, had escaped all mortal eyes.

Here, then, we had one *project* more for exploration and arbitration, together with a report from the British commissioners of survey, placing the British claim where it had never been placed before. And on the 13th of August, there comes again, as a matter of course, from Mr. Forsyth, another *counter-project*. Lord Palmerston is not richer in projects than Mr. Forsyth is in counter-projects. There is always a Roland for an Oliver. This counter-project of the 13th of August, 1840, was drawn in the retirement of Albany. It consists of eighteen articles, which it is hardly necessary to describe particularly. Of course, it proceeds on the two principles already agreed on, of exploration and arbitration; but in all matters of arrangement and detail it was quite different from Lord Palmerston's draft, communicated by Mr. Fox.

And here the rapid march of diplomacy came to a dead halt. Mr. Fox found so many and such great changes proposed to the British draft, that he did not incline to discuss them. He did not believe the British government would ever agree to Mr. Forsyth's plan, but he would send it home, and see what could be done with it.

Thus stood matters at the end of 1840, and in his message, at the meeting of Congress in December of that year, his valedictory message, Mr. Van Buren thus describes the condition of things which he found to be the result of his four years of negotiation.

"In my last annual message you were informed that a proposition for a commission of exploration and survey, promised by Great Britain, had been received, and that a counter-project, including also a provision for the certain and final adjustment of the limits in dispute, was then before the British government for its consideration. The answer of that government, accompanied by additional propositions of its own, was received through its minister here, since your separation. These were promptly considered; such as were deemed correct in principle, and consistent with a due regard to the just rights of the United States and of the State of Maine, concurred in; and the reasons for dissenting from the residue, with an additional suggestion on our part, communicated by the Secretary of State to Mr. Fox. That minister, not feeling himself sufficiently instructed upon some of the points raised in the discussion, felt it to be his duty to refer the matter to his own government for its further decision."

And now, Sir, who will deny that this is a very promising condition of things, to exist FIFTY-SEVEN years after the conclusion of the treaty!

Here is the British project for exploration; then the American counter-project for exploration, to be the foundation of arbitration. Next, the answer of Great Britain to our counter-project, stating divers exceptions and objections to it, and with sundry new and additional propositions of her own. Some of these were concurred in, but others dissented from, and other additional suggestions on our part were proposed; and all these concurrences, dissents, and new suggestions were brought together and incorporated into Mr. Forsyth's last labor of diplomacy, at least his last labor in regard to this subject, his counter-project of the 13th of August, 1840. That counter-project was sent to England, to see what Lord Palmerston could make of it. It fared in the foreign office just as Mr. Fox had foretold. Lord Palmerston would have nothing to do with it. He would not answer it; he would not touch it; he gave up the negotiation in apparent despair. Two years before, the parties had agreed on the principle of joint exploration, and the principle of arbitration. But in their subsequent correspondence, on matters of detail, modes of proceeding, and subordinate arrangements, they had, through the whole two years, constantly receded farther, and farther, and farther from each other. They were flying apart; and, like two orbs moving in opposite directions, could only meet after they should have traversed the whole circle.

But this exposition of the case does not describe, by any means, all the difficulties and embarrassments arising from the unsettled state of the controversy. We all remember the troubles of 1839. Something like a border war had broken out. Maine had raised an armed *civil posse;* she fortified the line, or points on the line, of territory, to keep off intruders and to defend possession. There was Fort Fairfield, Fort Kent, and I know not what other fortresses, all memorable in history. The legislature of Maine had placed eight hundred thousand dollars at the discretion of the Governor, to be used for the military defence of the State. Major-General Scott had repaired to the frontier, and under his mediation an agreement, a sort of treaty, respecting the temporary possession by the two parties of the territory in dispute, was entered into between the Governors of Maine and New Brunswick. But as it could not be foreseen how long the principal dispute would be protracted, Mr. Fox, as has already been seen, wrote home for instructions for another treaty, a treaty of less dignity, a collateral treaty, a treaty to regulate the terms of possession, and the means of keeping the peace of the frontier, while the number of years should roll away, necessary, first, to spin out the whole thread of diplomacy in framing a convention; next, for three or four years of joint exploration of seven hundred miles of disputed boundary in the wilderness of North America; and, finally, to learn the results of an arbitration which was to sit at Frankfort on the Maine, composed of learned doctors from the German universities.

Really, Sir, is not this a most delightful prospect? Is there not here as beautiful a labyrinth of diplomacy as one could wish to look at, of a summer's day? Would not Castlereagh and Talleyrand, Nesselrode and Metternich, find it an entanglement worthy the labor of their own hands to unravel? Is it not apparent, Mr. President, that at this time the adjustment of the question, by this kind of diplomacy, if to be reached by any vision, required telescopic sight? The country was settling; individual rights were getting into collision; it was impossible to prevent disputes and disturbances; every consideration required that whatever was to be done should be done quickly; and yet every thing, thus far, had waited the sluggish flow of the current of diplomacy. *Labitur et labetur.*

I have already stated, that on the receipt of Mr. Forsyth's last counter-plan, or counter-project, Lord Palmerston, at last, paused. The British government appears to have made up its mind that nothing was to be expected, at that time, from pursuing further this battledore play of *projets* and *contre-projets.* What occurred in England we collect from the published debates of the House of Commons. From these we learn, that after General Harrison's election, and, indeed, after his death, and in the first year of Mr. Tyler's Presidency, Lord Palmerston wrote to Mr. Fox as follows: —

"Her Majesty's government received, with very great regret, the sec ond American counter-draft of a convention for determining the boundary between the United States and the British North American Provinces, which you transmitted to me last autumn, in your despatch of the 15th of August, 1840, because the counter-draft contained so many inadmissible propositions, that it plainly showed that her Majesty's government could entertain no hope of concluding any arrangement on this subject with the government of Mr. Van Buren, and that there was no use in taking any further steps in the negotiations till the new President should come into power. Her Majesty's government had certainly been persuaded that a draft which, in pursuance of your instructions, you presented to Mr. Forsyth, on the 28th of July, 1840, was so fair in its provisions, and so well calculated to bring the differences between the two governments about the boundary to a just and satisfactory conclusion, that it would have been at once accepted by the government of the United States; or that, if the American government had proposed to make any alterations in it, those alterations would have related merely to matters of detail, and would not have borne upon any essential points of the arrangement; and her Majesty's government were the more confirmed in this hope, because almost all the main principles of the arrangement which that draft was intended to carry into execution had, as her Majesty's government conceived, been either suggested, or agreed to, by the United States government itself."

Lord Palmerston is represented to have said, in this despatch, of Mr. Forsyth's counter-project, that he "cannot agree" to the preamble; that he "cannot consent" to the second article; that he "must object to the fourth article"; that the "seventh article imposed incompatible duties"; and to every article there was an objection, stated in a different form, until he reached the tenth, and as to that, "none could be more inadmissible."

This was the state of the negotiation a few days before Lord Palmerston's retirement. But, nevertheless, his Lordship would make one more attempt, now that there was a new administration here, and he would submit "new proposals." And what were they?

"And what does the House think," said Sir Robert Peel, in the House of Commons, "were the noble Lord's proposals in that desperate state of circumstances? The proposal of the noble Lord, after fifty-eight years of controversy, submitted by him to the American government for the purpose of a speedy settlement, was that commissioners should be nominated on both sides; that they should attempt to make settlement of this long disputed question; and then, if that failed, that the king of Prussia, the king of Sardinia, and the king of Saxony were to be called in, not to act as umpires, but they were each to be requested to name a scientific man, and that these three members of a scientific commission should proceed to arbitrate. Was there ever a proposition like this suggested for the arrangement of a question on which two countries had differed for fifty-eight years? And this, too, was proposed after the failure of the arbitration on the part of the king of Holland, and when they had had their commission of exploration in vain. And yet, with all this, there were to be three scientific men, foreign professors, one from Prussia, one from Sardinia, and one from Saxony! To do what? And where were they to meet; or how were they to come to a satisfactory adjustment?"

It was asked in the House of Commons, not inaptly, ,What would the people of Maine think, when they should read that they were to be visited by three learned foreigners, one from Prussia, one from Saxony, and one from Sardinia? To be sure, what would they think, when they should see three learned foreign professors, each speaking a different language, and none of them the English or American tongue, among the swamps and morasses of Maine in summer, or wading through its snows in winter, — on the Allegash, the Maguadavic, or among the moose deer, on the precipitous and lofty shores of Lake Pohenagamook, — and for what? To find where the division was, between Maine and New Brunswick! Instructing themselves by these labors, that they might repair to Frankfort on the Maine, and there hold solemn and scientific arbitration on the question of a boundary line, in one of the deepest wildernesses of North America!

Sir, I do not know what might have happened, if this project had gone on. Possibly, Sir, but that your country has called you to higher duties, you might now have been at Frankfort on the Maine, the advocate of our cause before the scientific arbitration. If not yourself, some one of the honorable members here very probably would have been employed in attempting to utter in the heart of Germany the almost unspeakable names bestowed by the Northeastern Indians on American lakes and streams. Mr. Fox, it is said, on reading his despatch, replied, with characteristic promptitude and good sense, "For Heaven's sake, save us from the philosophers! Have sovereigns, if you please, but no professional men."

But Mr. Fox was instructed, as it now appears, to renew his exertions to carry forward the arbitration. "Let us," said Lord Palmerston, in writing to him, "let us consider the American *contre projet* as unreasonable, undeserving of answer, as withdrawn from consideration, and now submit my original *projet* to Mr. Webster, the new Secretary of State, and persuade him it is reasonable."

But with all respect, Sir, to Lord Palmerston, Mr. Webster was not to be so persuaded; that is to say, he was not to be persuaded that it was reasonable, or wise, or prudent, to pursue the negotiation in this form further. He hoped to live long enough to see the northeastern boundary settled; but that hope was faint, unless he could rescue the question from the labyrinth of projects and counter-projects, explorations and arbitrations, in which it was involved. He could not reasonably expect that he had another half-century of life before him.

Mr. President, it is true that I viewed the case as hopeless, without an entire change in the manner of proceeding. I found the parties already "in wandering mazes lost." I found it quite as tedious and difficult to trace the thread of this intricate negotiation, as it would be to run out the line of the Highlands itself. One was quite as full as the other of deviations, abruptnesses, and perplexities. And having received the President's* authority, I did say to Mr. Fox, as has been stated in the British Parliament, that I was willing to attempt to settle the dispute by agreeing on a conventional line, or line by compromise.

Mr. President, I was fully aware of the difficulty of the undertaking. I saw it was a serious affair to call on Maine to come into an agreement, by which she might subject herself to the loss of territory which she regarded as clearly her own. The question touched her proprietary interests, and, what was more delicate, it touched the extent of her jurisdiction. I knew well her extreme jealousy and high feeling on this point.† But I be-

* Mr. Tyler.

† It is now well known, that in 1832 an agreement was entered into between some of the heads of department at Washington, namely, Messrs. Livingston, McLane, and Woodbury, under the direction of President Jackson, on the part of the United States, and Messrs. Preble, Williams, and Emery, on the part of the government of Maine, by which it was stipulated that Maine should surrender to the United States the territory which she claimed beyond the line designated by the King of the Netherlands, and receive, as an indemnity, ONE MILLION of acres of the public lands, to be selected by herself, in Michigan The

lieved in her patriotism, and in her willingness to make sacrifices for the good of the country. I trusted, too, that her own good sense would lead her, while she doubtless preferred the strict execution of the treaty, as she understood it, to any line by compromise, to see, nevertheless, that the government of the United States was already pledged to arbitration, by its own proposition and the agreement of Great Britain; that this arbitration might not be concluded and finished for many years, and that, after all, the result might be doubtful. With this reliance on the patriotism and good sense of Maine, and with the sanction of the President, I was willing to make an effort to establish a boundary by direct compromise and agreement, by acts of the parties themselves, which they could understand and judge of for themselves, by a proceeding which left nothing to the future judgment of others, and by which the controversy could be settled in six months. And, Sir, I leave it to the Senate to-day, and the country always, to say how far this offer and this effort were wise or unwise, statesmanlike or unstatesmanlike, beneficial or injurious.

Well, Sir, in the autumn of 1841 it was known in England to be the opinion of the American government, that it was not advisable to prosecute further the scheme of arbitration; that that government was ready to open a negotiation for a conventional line of boundary; and a letter from Mr. Everett, dated on the 31st of December, announced the determination of the British government to send a special minister to the United States, authorized to settle all matters in difference, and the selection of Lord Ashburton for that trust.* This letter was answered, on the 29th of January, by an assurance that Lord Ashburton would be received with the respect due to his government and to himself.† Lord Ashburton arrived in Washington on the 4th of April, 1842, and was presented to the President on the 6th.

On the 11th, a letter was written from the Department of State to the Governor of Maine, announcing his arrival, and his declaration that he had authority to treat for a conventional

existence of this *treaty* was not known for some time, and it was never ratified by the high contracting parties.

* The letter of Mr. Everett referred to will be found among the Diplomatic Papers, in the sixth volume.

† See the letter, in the sixth volume.

line of boundary, or line by agreement, on mutual conditions, considerations, and equivalents.*

The Governor of Maine was informed, that,

> "Under these circumstances, the President has felt it to be his duty to call the serious attention of the governments of Maine and Massachusetts to the subject, and to submit to those governments the propriety of their coöperation, to a certain extent and in a certain form, in an endeavor to terminate a controversy already of so long duration, and which seems very likely to be still considerably further protracted before the desired end of a final adjustment shall be attained, unless a shorter course of arriving at that end be adopted than such as has heretofore been pursued, and as the two governments are still pursuing. . . . . .
>
> "The opinion of this government upon the justice and validity of the American claim has been expressed at so many times, and in so many forms, that a repetition of that opinion is not necessary. But the subject is a subject in dispute. The government has agreed to make it matter of reference and arbitration; and it must fulfil that agreement, unless another mode of settling the controversy should be resorted to with the hope of producing a speedier decision. The President proposes, then, that the governments of Maine and Massachusetts should severally appoint a commissioner or commissioners, empowered to confer with the authorities of this government upon a conventional line, or line by agreement, with its terms, conditions, considerations, and equivalents, with an understanding that no such line will be agreed upon without the assent of such commissioners.
>
> "This mode of proceeding, or some other which shall express assent beforehand, seems indispensable, if any negotiation for a conventional line is to be attempted; since, if happily a treaty should be the result of the negotiation, it can only be submitted to the Senate of the United States for ratification."

A similar letter was addressed to the Governor of Massachusetts. The Governor of Maine, now an honorable member of this house,† immediately convoked the legislature of Maine, by proclamation. In Massachusetts the probable exigency had been anticipated, and the legislature had authorized the Governor, now my honorable colleague here,‡ to appoint commissioners on behalf of the Commonwealth. The legislature of Maine adopted resolutions to the same effect, and duly elected four commissioners from among the most eminent persons in the

* See the letter, in the sixth volume.

† Mr. Fairfield.

‡ Mr. John Davis.

State, of all parties; and their unanimous consent to any proposed line of boundary was made indispensable. Three distinguished public men, known to all parties, and having the confidence of all parties in any question of this kind, were appointed commissioners by the Governor of Massachusetts.

Now, Sir, I ask, Could any thing have been devised fairer, safer, and better for all parties than this? The States were here by their commissioners; Great Britain was here by her special minister, and the Canadian and New Brunswick authorities within reach of the means of consultation; and the government of the United States was ready to proceed with the important duties it had assumed. I put the question to any man of sense, whether, supposing the real object to be a fair, just, convenient, prompt settlement of the boundary dispute, this state of things was not more promising than all the schemes of exploration and arbitration, and all the tissue of projects and counter-projects, with which the two governments had been making themselves strenuously idle for so many years. Nor was the promise not fulfilled.

It has been said, absurdly enough, that Maine was coerced into a consent to this line of boundary. What was the coercion? Where was the coercion? On the one hand, she saw an immediate and reasonable settlement; on the other hand, a proceeding sure to be long, and its result seen to be doubtful. Sir, the coercion was none other than the coercion of duty, good sense, and manifest interest. The right and the expedient united, to compel her to give up the wrong, the useless, the inexpedient.

Maine was asked to judge for herself, to decide on her own interests, not unmindful, nevertheless, of those patriotic considerations which should lead her to regard the peace and prosperity of the whole country. Maine, it has been said, was persuaded to part with a portion of territory by this agreement. Persuaded! Why, Sir, she was invited here to make a compromise, to give and to take, to surrender territory of very little value for equivalent advantages, of which advantages she was herself to be the uncontrolled judge. Her commissioners needed no guardians. They knew her interest. They knew what they were called on to part with, and the value of what they could obtain in exchange. They knew, especially, that on the one hand was immediate settlement, on the other, ten or fifteen years more of delay and vexation. Sir, the piteous tears shed for Maine, in this respect, are not her own tears. They are the crocodile tears of pretended friendship and party sentimentality. Lamentations and griefs have been uttered in this Capitol about the losses and sacrifices of Maine, which nine tenths of the people of Maine laugh at. Nine tenths of her people, to this day, heartily approve the treaty. It is my full belief, that there are not, at this moment, fifty respectable persons in Maine who would now wish to see the treaty annulled, and the State replaced in the condition in which it was, with Mr. Van Buren's arbitration before it, and inextricably fixed upon it, by the plighted faith of this government, on the 4th of March, 1841.

Sir, the occasion called for the revision of a very long line of boundary; and what complicated the case, and rendered it more difficult, was, that the territory on the side of the United States belonged to no less than four different States. The establishment of the boundary was to affect Maine, New Hampshire, Vermont, and New York. All these States were to be satisfied, if properly they could be. Maine, it is true, was principally concerned. But she did not expect to retain all that she called her own, and yet get more, and still call it compromise and an exchange of equivalents. She was not so absurd. I regret some things which occurred; particularly, that, while the commissioners of Maine assented, unanimously, to the boundary proposed, on the equivalents proposed, yet, in the paper in which they express that assent, they seem to argue against the act which they were about to perform. This, I think, was a mistake. It had an awkward appearance, and probably gave rise to whatever of dissatisfaction has been expressed in any quarter.

And now, Sir, I am prepared to ask whether the proceeding adopted, that is, an attempt to settle this long controversy by the assent of the States concerned, was not wise and discreet, under the circumstances of the case? Sir, the attempt succeeded, and it put an end to a controversy which had subsisted, with no little inconvenience to the country and danger to its peace, through every administration from that of General Washington to that of Mr. Van Buren. It is due to truth and to the occasion to say, that there were difficulties and obstacles in the way of this settlement, which had not been overcome under the administration of Washington, or the elder Adams, or Mr. Jefferson, or Mr. Madison, or Mr. Monroe, or Mr. John Quincy Adams, or General Jackson, or Mr. Van Buren. In 1842, in the administration of Mr. Tyler, the dispute was settled, and settled satisfactorily.

Sir, whatever may be said to the contrary, Maine was no loser, but an evident gainer, by this adjustment of boundary. She parted with some portion of territory; this I would not undervalue; but certainly most of it was intrinsically worthless. Captain Talcott's report, and other evidence, sufficiently establish that fact.*

Maine having, by her own free consent, agreed to part with this portion of territory, received, in the first place, from the treasury of the United States, one hundred and fifty thousand dollars, for her half of the land, a sum which I suppose to be much greater than she would have realized from the sale of it in fifty years. No person, well informed on the subject, can doubt this. In the next place, the United States government paid her for the expenses of her *civil posse* to defend the State, and also for the surveys. On this account she has already received two hundred thousand dollars, and hopes to receive eighty or one hundred thousand dollars more. If this hope shall be realized, she will have received four hundred and fifty thousand dollars in cash.

But Maine, I admit, did not look, and ought not to have looked, to the treaty as a mere pecuniary bargain. She looked at other things than money. She took into consideration that she was to enjoy the free navigation of the River St. John. I thought this a great object at the time the treaty was made; but I had then no adequate conception of its real importance. Circumstances which have since taken place show that its advantages to the State are far greater than I then supposed. That river is to be free to the citizens of Maine for the transportation down its stream of all unmanufactured articles whatever. Now what is this River St. John? We have heard a vast deal lately of the immense value and importance of the River Columbia and its navigation; but I will undertake to say, that, for all purposes of human use, the St. John is worth a

* See the letter of Captain Talcott, in the sixth volume.

hundred times as much as the Columbia is, or ever will be. In point of magnitude, it is one of the most respectable rivers on the eastern side of this part of America. It is longer than the Hudson, and as large as the Delaware. And, moreover, it is a river which has a mouth to it, and that, in the opinion of the member from Arkansas,* is a thing of some importance in the matter of rivers. It is navigable from the sea, and by steamboats, to a greater distance than the Columbia. It runs through a good country, and its tributaries afford a communication with the Aroostook valley. I will leave it to the member from Maine to say whether that valley is not one of the finest and most fertile parts of the State. I will leave it not only to him, but to any man at all acquainted with the facts, whether this free navigation of the St. John has not, at once, greatly raised the value of the lands on Fish River, on the Allegash, the Madawaska, and the St. Francis. That whole region has no other outlet, and the value of the lumber which has, during this very year, been floated down that river, is far greater than that of all the furs which have descended from Fort Vancouver to the Pacific.

On this subject I am enabled to speak with authority, for it has so happened that, since the last adjournment of the Senate, I have looked at an official return of the Hudson's Bay Company, showing the actual extent of the fur trade in Oregon, and I find it to be much less than I had supposed. An intelligent gentleman from Missouri estimated the value of that trade, west of the Rocky Mountains, at three hundred thousand dollars annually; but I find it stated in the last publication by Mr. McGregor, of the Board of Trade in England, (a very accurate authority,) that the receipts of the Hudson's Bay Company for furs west of the Rocky Mountains, in 1828, is placed at one hundred and thirty-eight thousand dollars. I do not know, though the member from Missouri is likely to know, whether all these furs are brought to Fort Vancouver; or whether some of them are not sent through the passes in the mountains to Hudson's Bay; or to Montreal, by the way of the north shore of Lake Superior. I suppose this last to be the case. It is stated, however, by the same authority, that the amount of goods

* Mr. Sevier.

received at Fort Vancouver, and disposed of in payment for furs, is twenty thousand dollars annually, and no more.

Now, Sir, this right to carry lumber and grain and cattle to the mouth of the River St. John, on equal terms with the British, is a matter of great importance; it brings lands lying on its upper branches, far in the interior, into direct communication with the sea. Those lands are valuable for timber now, and a portion of them are the best in the State for agriculture. The fact has been stated to me, on the best authority, that in the Aroostook valley land is to be found which has yielded more than forty bushels of wheat to the acre, even under the common cultivation of new countries. I must, therefore, think that the commissioners from Maine were quite right in believing that this was an important acquisition for their State, and one worth the surrender of some acres of barren mountains and impenetrable swamps.

But, Mr. President, there is another class of objections to this treaty boundary, on which I wish to submit a few remarks. It has been alleged, that the treaty of Washington ceded very important military advantages on this continent to the British government. One of these is said to be a military road between the two Provinces of New Brunswick and Lower Canada; and the other is the possession of certain heights, well adapted, as is alleged, to military defence. I think the honorable member from New York, farthest from the chair,* said, that by the treaty of Washington a military road was surrendered to England, which she considered as of vital importance to her possessions in America.

Mr. Dix explained that he had not spoken of a "military *road*," but of a portion of territory affording a means of military communication between two of her Provinces.

Well, it is the same thing, and we will see how the matter stands. The honorable member says, that he said a means of military communication, and not a military road. I am not a military man, and therefore may not so clearly comprehend, as that member does, the difference between a military road and a means of military communication; but I will read from the hon-

* Mr. Dix.

orable member's speech, which I have before me, understood to have been revised by himself. The honorable member says:—

"The settlement of the northeastern boundary, one of the most delicate and difficult that has ever arisen between us, affords a striking evidence of our desire to maintain with her the most friendly understanding. We ceded to her a portion of territory which she deemed of vital importance as a means of military communication between the Canadas and her Atlantic Provinces, and which will give her a great advantage in a contest with us. The measure was sustained by the constituted authorities of the country, and I have no desire or intention to call its wisdom in question. But it proves that we were not unwilling to afford Great Britain any facility she required for consolidating her North American possessions, acting in peace as though war was not to be expected between the two countries. If we had cherished any ambitious designs in respect to them, if we had had any other wish than that of continuing on terms of amity with her and them, this great military advantage would never have been conceded to her.

"On the other hand, I regret to say, that her course towards us has been a course of perpetual encroachment. But, Sir, I will not look back upon what is past for the purpose of reviving disturbing recollections."

I should be very glad if the honorable gentleman would show how England derives so highly important benefits from the treaty in a military point of view, or what proof there is that she so considers the matter.

Mr. Dix here entered into some explanation of the advantage, in a military point of view, supposed to have been gained by Great Britain on the northeastern boundary; and, in confirmation of his opinion, read extracts from notes of debates in the British Parliament.

The passages which the honorable member has read, however pertinent they may be to another question, do not touch the question immediately before us. I understand quite well what was said of the heights; but nobody, so far as I know, ever spoke of this supposed military road, or military communication, as of any importance at all, unless it be in a remark, not very intelligible, in an article ascribed to Lord Palmerston.

I was induced to refer to this subject, Sir, by a circumstance which I have not long been apprised of. Lord Palmerston (if he be the author of certain publications ascribed to him) says that all the important points were given up by Lord Ashburton to the United States. I might here state, too, that Lord Palmerston called the whole treaty "the Ashburton capitulation," declaring that it yielded every thing that was of importance to Great Britain, and that all its stipulations were to the advantage of the United States, and to the sacrifice of the interests of England. But it is not on such general, and, I may add, such unjust statements, nor on any off-hand expressions used in debate, though in the roundest terms, that this question must turn. He speaks of this military road, but he entirely misplaces it. The road which runs from New Brunswick to Canada follows the north side of the St. John to the mouth of the Madawaska, and then, turning northwest, follows that stream to Lake Temiscoata, and thence proceeds over a depressed part of the Highlands till it strikes the St. Lawrence one hundred and seventeen miles below Quebec. This is the road which has been always used, and there is no other.

I admit that it is very convenient for the British government to possess territory through which they may enjoy a road; it is of great value as an avenue of communication in time of peace; but as a military communication it is of no value at all. What business can an army ever have there? Besides, it is no gorge, no pass, no narrow defile, to be defended by a fort. If a fort should be built there, an army could, at pleasure, make a *detour* so as to keep out of the reach of its guns. It is very useful, I admit, in time of peace. But does not every body know, military man or not, that unless there is a defile, or some narrow place through which troops must pass, and which a fortification will command, that a mere open road must, in time of war, be in the power of the strongest? If we retained by treaty the territory over which the road is to be constructed, and war came, would not the English take possession of it if they could? Would they be restrained by a regard to the treaty of Washington? I have never yet heard a reason adduced why this communication should be regarded as of the slightest possible advantage in a military point of view.

But the circumstance to which I allude is, that, by a map published with the speech of the honorable member from Missouri, made in the Senate, on the question of ratifying the treaty,* this well-known and long-used road is laid down, prob-

* Mr. Benton.

ably from the same source of error which misled Lord Palmerston, as following the St. John, on its south side, to the mouth of the St. Francis; thence along that river to its source, and thence, by a single bound, over the Highlands to the St. Lawrence, near Quebec. This is all imagination. It is called the "Valley Road." Valley Road indeed! Why, Sir, it is represented as running over the very ridge of the most inaccessible part of the Highlands! It is made to cross abrupt and broken precipices, two thousand feet high! It is, at different points of its imaginary course, from fifty to a hundred miles distant from the real road.

So much, Mr. President, for the great boon of military communication conceded to England. It is nothing more nor less than a common road, along streams and lakes, and over a country in great part rather flat. It then passes the heights to the St. Lawrence. If war breaks out, we shall take it if we can, and if we need it, of which there is not the slightest probability. It will never be protected by fortifications, and never can be. It will be just as easy to take it from England, in case of war, as it would be to keep possession of it, if it were our own.

In regard to the defence of the heights, I shall dispose of that subject in a few words. There is a ridge of highlands which does approach the River St. Lawrence, although it is not true that it overlooks Quebec; on the contrary, the ridge is at the distance of thirty or forty miles.

It is very natural that military men in England, or indeed in any part of Europe, should have attached great importance to these mountains. The great military authority of England, perhaps the highest living military authority, had served in India and on the European continent, and it was natural enough that he should apply European ideas of military defences to America. But they are quite inapplicable. Highlands such as these are not ordinarily found on the great battle-fields of Europe. They are neither Alps nor Pyrenees; they have no passes through them, nor roads over them, and never will have.

Then there was another cause of misconception on this subject in England. In 1839 an *ex parte* survey was made, as I have said, by Colonel Mudge and Mr. Featherstonhaugh, if survey it could be called, of the region in the North of Maine, for the use of the British government. I dare say Colonel Mudge is an intelligent and respectable officer; how much personal attention he gave the subject I do not know. As to Mr. Featherstonhaugh, he has been in our service, and his authority is not worth a straw. These two persons made a report, containing this very singular statement: That in the ridge of highlands nearest to the St. Lawrence there was a great *hiatus* in one particular place, a gap of thirty or forty miles, in which the elevation did not exceed fifty feet. This is certainly the strangest statement that ever was made.* Their whole report gave but one measurement by the barometer, and that measurement stated the height of twelve hundred feet. A survey and map were made the following year by our own commissioners, Messrs. Graham and Talcott, of the Corps of Topographical Engineers, and Professor Renwick, of Columbia College. On this map, the very spot where this gap was said to be situated is dotted over thickly with figures showing heights varying from twelve hundred to two thousand feet, and forming one rough and lofty ridge, marked by abrupt and almost perpendicular precipices. When this map and report of Messrs. Mudge and Featherstonhaugh were published, the British authorities saw that this alleged gap was laid down as an indefensible point, and it was probably on that ground alone that they desired a line east of that ridge, in order that they might guard against access of a hostile power from the United States. But in truth there is no such gap; our engineers proved this, and we quite well understood it when agreeing to the boundary. Any man of common sense, military or not, must therefore now see, that nothing can be more imaginary or unfounded than the idea that any importance attaches to the possession of these heights.

Sir, there are two old and well-known roads to Canada; one by way of Lake Champlain and the Richelieu, to Montreal. This is the route which armies have traversed so often, in different periods of our history. The other leads from the Kennebec River to the sources of the Chaudière and the Du Loup, and so to Quebec. This last was the track of Arnold's march. East of this, there is no practicable communication for troops between Maine and Canada till we get to the Madawaska. We had before us a report from General Wool, while this treaty

* See page 44 of their printed report.

was under negotiation, in which that intelligent officer declares that it is perfectly idle to think of fortifying any point east of this road. East of Arnold's track it is a mountain region, through which no army can possibly pass into Canada. With General Wool was associated, in this examination, Major Graham, whom I have already mentioned. His report to General Wool, made in the year 1838, clearly points out the Kennebec and Chaudière road as the only practicable route for an army between Maine and Quebec. He was subsequently employed as a commissioner in the *ex parte* surveys of the United States. Being an engineer officer of high character for military knowledge and scientific accuracy, his opinion had the weight it ought to have, and which will be readily given to it by all who know him. His subsequent and still more thorough acquaintance with this mountain range, in its whole extent, has only confirmed the judgment which he had previously formed. And, Sir, this avenue to Canada, this practicable avenue, and only practicable avenue east of that by way of Lake Champlain, is left now just as it was found by the treaty. The treaty does not touch it, nor in any manner affect it.

But I must go further. I said that the treaty of Washington was a treaty of equivalents, in which it was expected that each party should give something and receive something. I am now willing to meet any gentleman, be he a military man or not, who will make the assertion, that, in a military point of view, the greatest advantages derived from that treaty are on the side of Great Britain. It was on this point that I wished to say something in reply to an honorable member from New York,* who will have it that in this treaty England supposes that she got the advantage of us. Sir, I do not think the military advantages she obtained by it are worth a rush. But even if they were, if she had obtained advantages of the greatest value, would it not have been fair in the member from New York to state, nevertheless, whether there were not equivalent military advantages obtained, on our side, in other parts of the line? Would it not have been candid and proper in him, when adverting to the military advantages obtained by England, in a communication between New Brunswick and Canada, if such

* Mr. Dickinson.

advantages there were, to have stated, on the other hand, and at the same time, our recovery of Rouse's Point, at the outlet of Lake Champlain? an advantage which overbalanced all others, forty times told. I must be allowed to say, that I certainly never expected that a member from New York, above all other men, should speak of this treaty as conferring military advantages on Great Britain without full equivalents. I listened to it, I confess, with utter astonishment. A distinguished Senator from that State* saw at the time, very clearly, the advantage gained by this treaty to the United States and to New York. He voted willingly for its ratification, and he never will say that Great Britain obtained a balance of advantages in a military point of view.

Why, how is the State of New York affected by this treaty? Sir, is not Rouse's Point perfectly well known, and admitted, by every military man, to be the key of Lake Champlain? It commands every vessel passing up or down the lake, between New York and Canada. It had always been supposed that this point lay some distance south of the parallel of 45°, which was our boundary line with Canada, and therefore was within the United States; and, under this supposition, the United States purchased the land, and commenced the erection of a strong fortress. But a more accurate survey having been made in 1818, by astronomers on both sides, it was found that the parallel of 45° ran south of this fortress, and thus Rouse's Point, with the fort upon it, was found to be in the British dominions. This discovery created, as well it might, a great sensation here. None knows this better than the honorable member from South Carolina,† who was then at the head of the Department of War. As Rouse's Point was no longer ours, we sent our engineers to examine the shores of the lake, to find some other place or places which we might fortify. They made a report on their return, saying that there were two other points some distance south of Rouse's Point, one called Windmill Point, on the east side of the lake, and the other called Stony Point, on the west side, which it became necessary now to fortify, and they gave an estimate of the probable expense. When this treaty was in process of negotiation, we called for the opinion of military men

* Mr. Wright.

† Mr. Calhoun.

respecting the value of Rouse's Point, in order to see whether it was highly desirable to obtain it. We had their report before us, in which it was stated, that the natural and best point for the defence of the outlet of Lake Champlain was Rouse's Point. In fact, any body might see that this was the case who would look at the map. The point projects into the narrowest passage by which the waters of the lake pass into the Richelieu. Any vessel, passing into or out of the lake, must come within point-blank range of the guns of a fortress erected on this point; and it ran out so far that any such vessel must approach the fort, head on, for several miles, so as to be exposed to a raking fire from the battery, before she could possibly bring her broadside to bear upon the fort at all. It was very different with the points farther south. Between them the passage was much wider; so much so, indeed, that a vessel might pass directly between the two, and not be in reach of point-blank shot from either.

Mr. Dickinson of New York here interposed, to ask whether the Dutch line did not give us Rouse's Point.

Certainly not. It gave us a semicircular line, running round the fort, but not including what we had possessed before. And besides, we had rejected the Dutch line, and the whole point now clearly belonged to England. It was all within the British territory.

I was saying that a vessel might pass between Windmill Point and Stony Point, and be without the range of both, till her broadside could be brought to bear upon either of them. The forts would be entirely independent of each other, and, having no communication, could not render each other the least assistance in case of attack. But the military men told us there was no sort of question that Rouse's Point was extremely desirable as a point of military defence. This is plain enough, and I need not spend time to prove it. Of one thing I am certain, that the true road to Canada is by the way of Lake Champlain. That is the old path. I take to myself the credit of having said here, thirty years ago, speaking of the mode of taking Canada, that, when an American woodsman undertakes to fell a tree, he does not begin by lopping off the branches, but strikes his axe at once into the trunk. The trunk, in relation to Canada, is Montreal, and the River St. Lawrence down to Quebec; and so we found in the last war. It is not my purpose to scan the propriety of military measures then adopted, but I suppose it to have been rather accidental and unfortunate that we began the attack in Upper Canada. It would have been better military policy, as I suppose, to have pushed our whole force by the way of Lake Champlain, and made a direct movement on Montreal; and though we might thereby have lost the glories of the battles of the Thames and of Lundy's Lane, and of the sortie from Fort Erie, yet we should have won other laurels of equal, and perhaps greater value, at Montreal. Once successful in this movement, the whole country above would have fallen into our power. Is not this evident to every gentleman?

Rouse's Point is the best means of defending both the ingress into the lake, and the exit from it. And I say now, that on the whole frontier of the State of New York, with the single exception of the Narrows below the city, there is not a point of equal importance. I hope this government will last for ever; but if it does not, and if, in the judgment of Heaven, so great a calamity shall befall us as the rupture of this Union, and the State of New York shall thereby be thrown upon her own defences, I ask, Is there a single point, except the Narrows, the possession of which she will so much desire? No, there is not one. And how did we obtain this advantage for her? The parallel of 45° north was established by the treaty of 1783 as our boundary with Canada in that part of the line. But, as I have stated, that line was found to run south of Rouse's Point. And how did we get back this precious possession? By running a semicircle like that of the King of the Netherlands? No; we went back to the old line, which had always been supposed to be the true line, and the establishment of which gave us not only Rouse's Point, but a strip of land containing some thirty or forty thousand acres between the parallel of 45° and the old line.

The same arrangement gave us a similar advantage in Vermont; and I have never heard that the constituents of my friend near me* made any complaint of the treaty. That State got about sixty or seventy thousand acres, including several villages, which would otherwise have been left on the British side of the

* Mr. Phelps.

line. We received Rouse's Point, and this additional land, as one of the equivalents for the cession of territory made in Maine. And what did we do for New Hampshire? There was an ancient dispute as to which was the northwesternmost head of the Connecticut River. Several streams were found, either of which might be insisted on as the true boundary. But we claimed that which is called Hall's Stream. This had not formerly been allowed; the Dutch award did not give to New Hampshire what she claimed; and Mr. Van Ness, our commissioner, appointed under the treaty of Ghent, after examining the ground, came to the conclusion that we were not entitled to Hall's Stream. I thought that we were so entitled, although I admit that Hall's Stream does not join the Connecticut River till after it has passed the parallel of 45°. By the treaty of Washington this demand was agreed to, and it gave New Hampshire one hundred thousand acres of land. I do not say that we obtained this wrongfully; but I do say that we got that which Mr. Van Ness had doubted our right to. I thought the claim just, however, and the line was established accordingly. And here let me say, once for all, that, if we had gone for arbitration, we should inevitably have lost what the treaty gave to Vermont and New York; because all that was clear matter of cession, and not adjustment of doubtful boundary.

I think that I ought now to relieve the Senate from any further remarks on this northeastern boundary. I say that it was a favorable arrangement, both to Maine and Massachusetts, and that nine tenths of their people are well satisfied with it; and I say also, that it was advantageous to New Hampshire, Vermont, and New York. And I say further, that it gave up no important military point, but, on the contrary, obtained one of the greatest consequence and value. And here I leave that part of the case for the consideration of the Senate and of the country.

Here the Senate adjourned. On the following day, Mr. Webster resumed his speech as follows: —

Yesterday I read from the proceedings in the British Parliament an extract from a despatch of Lord Palmerston to Mr. Fox, in which Lord Palmerston says that the British government, as early as 1840, had perceived that they never could come to a settlement of this controversy with the government of Mr. Van Buren. I do not wish to say whether the fault was more on one side than the other; but I wish to bar, in the first place, any inference of an improper character which may be drawn from that statement of the British Secretary of State for Foreign Affairs. It was not that they looked forward to a change which should bring gentlemen into power more pliable, or more agreeable to the purposes of England. No, Sir, those remarks of Lord Palmerston, whether true or false, were not caused by any peculiar stoutness or stiffness which Mr. Van Buren had ever maintained on our side of the merits of the question. The merits of the boundary question were never discussed by Mr. Van Buren to any extent. The thing that his administration discussed was the formation of a convention of exploration and arbitration to settle the question. A few years before this despatch of Lord Palmerston to Mr. Fox, the two governments, as I have repeatedly said, had agreed how the question should be settled. They had agreed that there should be an exploration. Mr. Van Buren had proposed and urged arbitration also. England had agreed to this, at his request. The governments had agreed to these two principles, therefore, long before the date of that letter of Lord Palmerston; and from the time of that agreement, till near the close of Mr. Van Buren's administration, the whole correspondence turned on the arrangement of details of a convention for arbitration, according to the stipulation of the parties. It was not, therefore, on account of any notion that Mr. Van Buren stood up for American questions better than others. It was because these subordinate questions respecting the convention for arbitration had got into so much complexity, were so embarrassed with projects and counter-projects, had become so difficult and entangled; and because every effort to disentangle them had made the matter worse. On this account alone, Lord Palmerston made the remark. I wish to draw no inference that would be injurious to others, to make no imputation on Mr. Van Buren. But it is necessary to remember, that this dispute had run on for years, and was likely to run on for ever, though the main principles had already been agreed on, namely, exploration and arbitration. It was an endless discussion of details and forms of proceeding, in which the parties receded farther and farther from each other every day.

One thing more, Sir, by way of explanation. I referred yesterday to the report made by General Wool, in respect to the road from Kennebec. In point of fact, the place which General Wool recommended, in 1838, to be fortified, was a few miles farther east, towards the waters of the Penobscot River, than Arnold's route; but, generally, the remark I made was perfectly true, that there has not been a road or passage at any considerable distance east of that line. The honorable member from New York yesterday produced extracts from certain debates in Parliament respecting the importance of the territory ceded to England, in a military point of view. I beg to refer to some others which I hold in my hand, but which I shall not read; the speeches of Sir Charles Napier, Lord Palmerston, Sir Howard Douglass, and others, as an offset to those quoted by the honorable member. But I do not think it of importance to balance those opinions against each other. Some gentlemen appear to entertain one set of opinions, some another; and, for my own part, I candidly admit that, by both the one and the other, facts are overstated. I do not believe, Sir, that any thing, in a military point of view, ceded by us to England, is of any great consequence to us or to her; or that any thing important in that respect was ceded by either party, always excepting Rouse's Point. I do believe it was an object of importance to repossess ourselves of the site of that fortress, and on that point I shall proceed to make a few remarks that escaped me yesterday.

I do not complain here that the member from New York has underrated the importance of that acquisition. He has not spoken of it. But what I do complain of, if complaint it may be called, is, that, when he spoke of cessions made to England by the treaty of Washington, a treaty which proposed to proceed on the ground of mutual concessions, equivalents, and considerations, when referring to such a treaty to show the concessions made to England, he did not consider it necessary to state, on the other hand, the corresponding cessions made by England to us. And I say again, that the cession of Rouse's Point by her must be, and is, considered, by those best capable of appreciating its value, of more importance in a military light than all the cessions we made to England. To show how our government have regarded its importance, let me remind you, that, immediately on the close of the last war, although the country was heavily in debt, there was nothing to which the government addressed itself with more zeal than the fortifying this point, as the natural defence of Lake Champlain. As early as 1816, the government paid twenty or thirty thousand dollars for the site, and went on with the work at an expense of one hundred thousand dollars. But in 1818, the astronomers appointed on both sides found it was on the English side of the boundary. That, of course, terminated our operations. But that is not all. How did our government regard the acquisition by the treaty of Washington? Why, the ink with which that treaty was signed was hardly dry, when the most eminent engineers were despatched to that place, who examined its strength, and proceeded to renew and rebuild it. And no military work, not even the fortifications for the defence of the Narrows, approaching the harbor of New York, has been proceeded with by the government with more zeal. Having said so much, Sir, I will merely add, that if gentlemen desire to obtain more information on this important subject, they may consult the head of the engineer corps, Colonel Totten, and Commodore Morris, who went there by instructions to examine it, and who reported thereon.

And here, Sir, I conclude my remarks on the question of the northeastern boundary.

I now leave it to the country to say, whether this question, this troublesome, and annoying, and dangerous question, which had lasted through the ordinary length of two generations, having been taken up in 1841, was not promptly settled and well settled; whether it was not well settled for Maine and Massachusetts, and well settled for the whole country; and whether, in the opinion of all fair and candid men, the complaint about it which we hear at this day does not arise entirely from a desire that those connected with the accomplishment of a measure so important to the peace of the country should not be allowed to derive too much credit from it.

Mr. President, the destruction of the steamboat "Caroline," in the harbor of Schlosser, by a British force, in December, 1837, and the arrest of Alexander McLeod, a British subject, composing part of that force, four years afterwards, by the authorities of New York, and his trial for an alleged murder committed by him on that occasion, have been subjects of remark, here and elsewhere, at this session of Congress. They are connected subjects, and call, in the first place, for a brief historical narrative.

In the year 1837, a civil commotion, or rebellion, which had broken out in Canada, had been suppressed, and many persons engaged in it had fled to the United States. In the autumn of that year, these persons, associating with themselves many persons of lawless character in the United States, made actual war on Canada, and took possession of Navy Island, belonging to England, in the Niagara River. It may be the safest course to give an account of these occurrences from official sources. Mr. Van Buren thus recites the facts, as the government of the United States understood them, in his message of December, 1838: —

"I had hoped that the respect for the laws and regard for the peace and honor of their own country, which have ever characterized the citizens of the United States, would have prevented any portion of them from using any means to promote insurrection in the territory of a power with which we are at peace, and with which the United States are desirous of maintaining the most friendly relations. I deeply regret, however, to be obliged to inform you that this has not been the case.

"Information has been given to me, derived from official and other sources, that many citizens of the United States have associated together, to make hostile incursions from our territory into Canada, and to aid and abet insurrection there, in violation of the obligations and laws of the United States, and in open disregard of their own duties as citizens. This information has been in part confirmed by a hostile invasion actually made by citizens of the United States, in conjunction with Canadians and others, and accompanied by a forcible seizure of the property of our citizens, and an application thereof to the prosecution of military operations against the authorities and people of Canada. The results of these criminal assaults upon the peace and order of a neighboring country have been, as was to be expected, fatally destructive to the misguided or deluded persons engaged in them, and highly injurious to those in whose behalf they are professed to have been undertaken. The authorities in Canada, from intelligence received of such intended movements among our citizens, have felt themselves obliged to take precautionary measures against them, have actually embodied the militia, and assumed an attitude to repel an invasion, to which they believed the colonies were exposed from the United States. A state of feeling on both sides of the frontier had thus been produced, which called for prompt and vigorous interference."

The following is the British account of the same occur rence: —

"In this state of things, a small band of Canadian refugees, who had taken shelter in the State of New York, formed a league with a number of the citizens of the United States for the purpose of invading the British territory, not to join a party engaged in civil war, because civil war at that time in Canada there was none, but in order to commit, within the British territory, the crimes of robbery, arson, and murder.

"By a neglect on the part of that government,* which seems to admit of but one explanation, the storehouses which contained the arms and ammunition of the State were left unguarded, and were consequently broken open by this gang, who carried off thence, in open day, and in the most public manner, cannon and other implements of war.

"After some days' preparation, these people proceeded, without any interruption from the government or authorities of the State of New York, and under the command of an American citizen, to invade and occupy Navy Island, and part of the British territory; and having engaged the steamboat Caroline, which, for their special service, was cut out of the ice, in which she had been inclosed in the port of Buffalo, they had used her for the purpose of bringing over to Navy Island, from the United States territory, men, arms, ammunition, stores, and provisions.

"The preparations made for this invasion of British territory by a band of men organized, armed, and equipped within the United States, and consisting partly of British subjects and partly of American citizens, had induced the British authorities to station a military force at Chippewa, to repel the threatened invasion, and to defend her Majesty's territory. The commander of that fort, seeing that the Caroline was used as a means *of supply and reinforcement for the invaders*, who had occupied Navy Island, judged that the capture and destruction of that vessel would prevent supplies and reinforcements from passing over to the island, and would, moreover, deprive the force on the island of the means of passing over to the British territory on the mainland."

According to the British account, the expedition sent to capture the Caroline expected to find her at Navy Island; but when the commanding officer came round the point of the island in the night, he found that she was moored to the other shore. This did not deter him from making the capture. In that capture a citizen of the United States by the name of Durfree lost his life;

* New York.

the British authorities pretend, by a chance shot from one of his own party; the American, by a shot from one of the British party.

This transaction took place on the 29th of December, 1837, in the first year of Mr. Van Buren's administration. No sooner was it known here, and made the subject of a communication by Mr. Forsyth to Mr. Fox, than the latter avowed it as an act done by the British authorities, and justified it, as a proper and necessary measure of self-defence. Observe, Sir, if you please, that the Caroline was destroyed in December, 1837, and Mr. Fox's avowal of that destruction as a government act, and his justification of it, were made in January following, so soon as knowledge of the occurrence reached Washington. Now, if the avowal of the British minister, made in the name of his government, was a sufficiently authentic avowal, why, then, from that moment, the government of Great Britain became responsible for the act, and the United States was to look to that government for reparation, or redress, or whatever act or acknowledgment or apology the case called for. If Mr. Fox's letter was proper proof that the destruction of the Caroline was an act of public force, then the government of Great Britain was directly responsible to the government of the United States; and of the British government directly, and the British government only, was satisfaction to be demanded. Nothing was immediately done; the matter was suffered to lie, and grow cool; but it afterwards became a question at what time the United States government did first learn, by sufficient evidence and authority, that the British government had avowed the destruction of the Caroline as its own act. Now, in the first place, there was the direct avowal of Mr. Fox made at the time, and never disapproved. This avowal, and the account of the transaction, reached London in February, 1838. Lord Palmerston thinks that, in conversations with Mr. Stevenson, not long subsequent, he intimated distinctly that the destruction of the vessel would turn out to be justifiable. At all events, it is certain, that, on the 22d day of May, 1838, in an official note to Lord Palmerston, written by instructions from this government, demanding reparation for her destruction, Mr. Stevenson stated, "that the government of the United States did consider that transaction as an outrage upon the United States, and a violation of United

States territory, committed by British troops, planned and executed by the Lieutenant-Governor of Upper Canada." It is clear, then, that the government of the United States so understood the matter, when it gave Mr. Stevenson the instructions on which he made this demand. The administration knew, full well, that the expedition was a public expedition, set on foot by the authorities of Canada, avowed here, immediately, by Mr. Fox, as an act of which the British government took upon itself the responsibility, and never disavowed by that government at any time or in any way.

And now, Sir, why was this aggression on the territory of the United States, why was this indignity, suffered to remain unvindicated and unredressed for three years? Why was no answer made, and none insisted on, to Mr. Stevenson's official and direct demand for reparation? The jealous guardians of national honor, so tenaciously alive to what took place in 1842, what opiate had drugged their patriotism for so many years? Whose fault was it that, up to 1841, the government of Great Britain had been brought to no acknowledgment, no explanation, no apology? This long and unbroken slumber over public outrage and national indignity, who indulged in it? Nay, if the government of the United States thought it had not sufficient evidence that the *outrage* was, as it had declared it to be itself, a public outrage, then it was a *private* outrage, the invasion of our territory, and the murder of an American citizen, without any justification, or pretence of justification; and had it not become high time that such an outrage was redressed?

Sir, there is no escape from this. The administration of Mr. Van Buren knew perfectly well that the destruction of the Caroline was an act of public force, done by the British authorities in Canada. They knew it had never been disavowed at home. The act was a wrongful one on the part of the Canadian forces. They had no right to invade the territory of the United States. It was an aggression for which satisfaction was due, and should have been insisted on immediately, and insisted on perseveringly. But this was not done. The administration slept, and slept on, and would have slept till this time, if it had not been waked by the arrest of McLeod. Being on this side of the line, and making foolish and false boasts of his martial achievements, McLeod was arrested in November, 1840, on the charge of the murder of Durfree, in capturing the Caroline, and committed to prison by the authorities of New York. He was bailed; but violence and mobs overawed the courts, and he was recommitted to jail.

This was an important and very exciting occurrence. Mr. Fox made a demand for his immediate release. The administration of Mr. Van Buren roused itself, and looked round to ascertain its position. Mr. Fox again asserted, that the destruction of the Caroline was an act of public force, done by public authority, and avowed by the English government, as the American government had long before known. To this Mr. Forsyth replied, in a note of December 26th, 1840, thus: "If the destruction of the Caroline was a public act of persons in her Majesty's service, obeying the order of their superior authorities, this fact has not been before communicated to the government of the United States by a person authorized to make the admission." Certainly, Mr. President, it is not easy to reconcile this language with the instructions under which Mr. Stevenson made his demand of May, 1838, and which demand he accompanied with the declaration, that the act was planned and executed by the authorities of Canada. Whether the act of the Governor had or had not been approved at home, the government of the United States, one would think, could hardly need to be informed, in 1840, that that act was committed by persons in her Majesty's service, obeying the order of their superior authorities. Mr. Forsyth adds, very properly, that it will be for the courts to decide on the validity of the defence. It is worthy of remark, that, in this letter of the 26th of December, 1840, Mr. Forsyth complains, that up to that day the government of the United States had not become acquainted with the views and intentions of the government of England respecting the destruction of the Caroline! Now, Mr. President, this was the state of things in the winter of 1840–41, and on the 4th of March, 1841, when General William Henry Harrison became President of the United States.

On the 12th of that same month of March, Mr. Fox wrote to the Department of State a letter, in which, after referring to his original correspondence with Mr. Forsyth, in which he had avowed and justified the capture of the Caroline as an act of necessary defence, he proceeds to say: —

"The undersigned is directed, in the first place, to make known to the government of the United States, that her Majesty's government entirely approve of the course pursued by the undersigned in that correspondence, and of the language adopted by him in the official letters above mentioned.

"And the undersigned is now instructed again to demand from the government of the United States, formally, in the name of the British government, the immediate release of Mr. Alexander McLeod.

"The grounds upon which the British government make this demand upon the government of the United States are these: That the transaction on account of which Mr. McLeod has been arrested, and is to be put upon his trial, was a transaction of a public character, planned and executed by persons duly empowered by her Majesty's colonial authorities to take any steps, and to do any acts, which might be necessary for the defence of her Majesty's territories, and for the protection of her Majesty's subjects; and that, consequently, those subjects of her Majesty who engaged in that transaction were performing an act of public duty, for which they cannot be made personally and individually answerable to the laws and tribunals of any foreign country.

"The transaction may have been, as her Majesty's government are of opinion that it was, a justifiable employment of force for the purpose of defending the British territory from the unprovoked attack of a band of British rebels and American pirates, who, having been permitted to arm and organize themselves within the territory of the United States, had actually invaded and occupied a portion of the territory of her Majesty; or it may have been, as alleged by Mr. Forsyth in his note to the undersigned of the 26th of December, 'a most unjustifiable invasion, in time of peace, of the territory of the United States.' But it is a question essentially of a political and international kind, which can be discussed and settled only between the two governments, and which the courts of justice of the State of New York cannot by possibility have any means of judging, or any right of deciding."

The British government insisted that it must have been known, and was well known, long before, that it had avowed and justified the capture of the Caroline, and taken upon itself the responsibility. Mr. Forsyth, as you have seen, Sir, in his note of December 26th, had said that fact had not been before communicated by a person authorized to make the admission. What, then, was to be done? Here was a new, fresh, and direct avowal of the act by the British government, and a formal demand for McLeod's immediate release. And how did General Harrison's administration treat this? Sir, just as it ought to have treated it. It was not poor and mean enough, in its intercourse with a foreign government, to make any reflections on its predecessor, or appear to strike out a new path for itself. It did not seek to derogate, in the slightest degree, from the propriety of what had been said and done by Mr. Van Buren and Mr. Forsyth, whatever eminent example it might have found for such a course of conduct. No; it rather adopted what Mr. Forsyth had said in December, to wit, that at that time no authentic avowal had been communicated to the United States. But now an avowal had been made, on the authority of the government itself; and General Harrison acted, and rightly acted, on the case made by this avowal. And what opinions did he form, and what course did he pursue, in a crisis, and in regard to transactions, so intimately connected with the peace and honor of the country?

Sir, in the first place, General Harrison was of opinion, that the entering of the United States territory by British troops, for the purpose of capturing or destroying the Caroline, was unjustifiable. That it was an aggression, a violation of the territory of the United States. Not that the British forces might not have destroyed that vessel, if they could have found her on their own side of the line; for she was unlawfully employed, she was assisting to make war on Canada. But she could not be followed into a port of the United States, and there captured. This was an offence against the dignity and sovereignty of this government, for which apology and satisfaction ought long since to have been obtained, and which apology and satisfaction it was not yet too late to demand. This was General Harrison's opinion.

In the next place, and on the other hand, General Harrison was of opinion, that the arrest and detention of McLeod were contrary to the law of nations. McLeod was a soldier acting under the authority of his government, and obeying orders which he was bound to obey. It was absurd to say, that a soldier, who must obey orders or be shot, may still be hanged if he does obey them. Was the President of the United States to turn aside from facing the British lion, and fall on a lamb? Was he to quail before the crown of England, and take vengeance on a private soldier? No, Sir, that was not in character for William Henry Harrison. He held the British government responsible.

He soon died, to the great grief of his country, but in the time of his successor that responsibility was justly appealed to, and satisfactorily fulfilled.

Mr. Fox's letter, written under instructions from Lord Palmerston, was a little peremptory, and some expressions were regarded as not quite courteous and conciliatory. This caused some hesitation; but General Harrison said that he would not cavil at phrases, since, in the main, the British complaint was well founded, and we ought at once to do what we could to place ourselves right.

Sir, the members of the administration were all of one mind on this occasion. General Harrison, himself a man of large general reading and long experience, was decidedly of opinion that McLeod could not be lawfully held to answer in the courts of New York for what had been done by him as a soldier, under superior orders. All the members of the administration were of the same opinion, without doubt or hesitation. I may without impropriety say, that Mr. Crittenden, Mr. Ewing, Mr. Bell, Mr. Badger, and Mr. Granger were not all likely to come to an erroneous conclusion, on this question of public law, after they had given it full consideration and examination.

Mr. Fox's letter was answered; and from that answer I will read an extract.

"Mr. Fox informs the government of the United States that he is instructed to make known to it that the government of her Majesty entirely approve the course pursued by him in his correspondence with Mr. Forsyth in December last, and the language adopted by him on that occasion; and that the government have instructed him 'again to demand from the government of the United States, formally, in the name of the British government, the immediate release of Mr. Alexander McLeod'; that 'the grounds upon which the British government make this demand upon the government of the United States are these: That the transaction on account of which Mr. McLeod has been arrested, and is to be put upon his trial, was a transaction of a public character, planned and executed by persons duly empowered by her Majesty's colonial authorities to take any steps, and to do any acts, which might be necessary for the defence of her Majesty's territories, and for the protection of her Majesty's subjects; and that, consequently, those subjects of her Majesty who engaged in that transaction were performing an act of public duty, for which they cannot be made personally and individually answerable to the laws and tribunals of any foreign country.'

"The President is not certain that he understands precisely the meaning intended by her Majesty's government to be conveyed by the foregoing instruction.

"This doubt has occasioned with the President some hesitation; but he inclines to take it for granted that the main purpose of the instruction was to cause it to be signified to the government of the United States that the attack on the steamboat Caroline was an act of public force, done by the British colonial authorities, and fully recognized by the Queen's government at home; and that, consequently, no individual concerned in that transaction can, according to the just principles of the laws of nations, be held personally answerable, in the ordinary courts of law, as for a private offence; and that, upon this avowal of her Majesty's government, Alexander McLeod, now imprisoned on an indictment for murder, alleged to have been committed in that attack, ought to be released by such proceedings as are usual and are suitable to the case.

"The President adopted the conclusion, that nothing more than this could have been intended to be expressed, from the consideration that her Majesty's government must be fully aware that, in the United States, as in England, persons confined under judicial process can be released from that confinement only by judicial process. In neither country, as the undersigned supposes, can the arm of the executive power interfere, directly or forcibly, to release or deliver the prisoner. His discharge must be sought in a manner conformable to the principles of law, and the proceedings of courts of judicature. If an indictment like that which has been found against Alexander McLeod, and under circumstances like those which belong to his case, were pending against an individual in one of the courts of England, there is no doubt that the law officer of the crown might enter a *nolle prosequi*, or that the prisoner might cause himself to be brought up on *habeas corpus* and discharged, if his ground of discharge should be adjudged sufficient, or that he might prove the same facts, and insist on the same defence or exemption, on his trial.

"All these are legal modes of proceeding, well known to the laws and practice of both countries. But the undersigned does not suppose that, if such a case were to arise in England, the power of the executive government could be exerted in any more direct manner.

"Even in the case of ambassadors and other public ministers, whose right to exemption from arrest is personal, requiring no fact to be ascertained but the mere fact of diplomatic character, and to arrest whom is sometimes made a highly penal offence, if the arrest be actually made, it must be discharged by application to the courts of law.

"It is understood that Alexander McLeod is holden, as well on civil as on criminal process, for acts alleged to have been done by him in the attack on the Caroline, and his defence or ground of acquittal must be the same in both cases. And this strongly illustrates, as the undersigned conceives, the propriety of the foregoing observations; since it is quite clear that the executive government cannot interfere to arrest a civil suit between private parties in any stage of its progress, but that such suit must go on to its regular judicial termination. If, therefore, any course different from such as have been now mentioned was in contemplation of her Majesty's government, something would seem to have been expected from the government of the United States as little conformable to the laws and usages of the English government as to those of the United States, and to which this government cannot accede.

"The government of the United States, therefore, acting upon the presumption which is already adopted, that nothing extraordinary or unusual was expected or requested of it, decided, on the reception of Mr. Fox's note, to take such measures as the occasion and its own duty appeared to require.

"In his note to Mr. Fox of the 26th of December last, Mr. Forsyth, the Secretary of State of the United States, observes, that, 'if the destruction of the Caroline was a public act of persons in her Majesty's service, obeying the order of their superior authorities, this fact has not been before communicated to the government of the United States by a person authorized to make the admission; and it will be for the court, which has taken cognizance of the offence with which Mr. McLeod is charged, to decide upon its validity when legally established before it'; and adds: 'The President deems this a proper occasion to remind the government of her Britannic Majesty that the case of the Caroline has been long since brought to the attention of her Majesty's principal Secretary of State for Foreign Affairs, who, up to this day, has not communicated its decision thereupon. It is hoped that the government of her Majesty will perceive the importance of no longer leaving the government of the United States uninformed of its views and intentions upon a subject which has naturally produced much exasperation, and which has led to such grave consequences.'

"The communication of the fact that the destruction of the Caroline was an act of public force by the British authorities, being formally made to the government of the United States by Mr. Fox's note, the case assumes a different aspect.

"The government of the United States entertains no doubt, that, after this avowal of the transaction as a public transaction, authorized and undertaken by the British authorities, individuals concerned in it ought not, by the principles of public law and the general usage of civilized states, to be holden personally responsible in the ordinary tribunals of law for their participation in it. And the President presumes that it can hardly be necessary to say that the American people, not distrustful of their ability to redress public wrongs by public means, cannot desire the punishment of individuals when the act complained of is declared to have been the act of the government itself.

"Soon after the date of Mr. Fox's note, an instruction was given to the Attorney-General of the United States, from this department, by direction of the President, which fully sets forth the opinions of this government on the subject of Mr. McLeod's imprisonment; a copy of which instruction the undersigned has the honor herewith to inclose.

"The indictment against McLeod is pending in a State court; but his rights, whatever they may be, are no less safe, it is to be presumed, than if he were holden to answer in one of this government.

"He demands immunity from personal responsibility by virtue of the law of nations; and that law, in civilized states, is to be respected in all courts. None is either so high or so low as to escape from its authority in cases to which its rules and principles apply."

And now, Sir, who will deny that this decision was entirely correct? Who will deny that this arrest of McLeod, and this threatening to hang him, were just cause of offence to the British government? Sir, what should we ourselves have thought, in a like case? If United States troops, by the lawful authority of their government, were ordered to pass over the line of boundary for any purpose, retaliation, reprisal, fresh pursuit of an enemy, or any thing else, and the government of the territory invaded, not bringing our government to account, but sleeping three years over the affront, should then snatch up one of our citizens found in its jurisdiction, and who had been one of the force, and proceed to try, condemn, and execute him, Sir, would not the whole country have risen up like one man? Should we have submitted to it for a moment? Suppose that now, by order of the President, and in conformity to law, an American army should enter Canada, or Oregon, for any purpose which the government of the United States thought just and was ready to defend, and the British government, turning away from demanding responsibility or satisfaction from us, should seize an individual soldier, try him, convict him, and execute him. Should we not declare war at once, or make war? Would this be submitted to for a moment? Is there a man, with an American heart in his bosom, who would remain silent, in the face of such an outrage on public law and such an insult to the flag and sovereignty of his country? Who would endure that an American soldier, acting in obedience to lawful authority, as a part of a public military force, should be arrested, tried, and executed as a private murderer? Sir, if we had received such an insult, and atonement had not been instantly made, we should have avenged it at any expense of treasure and of blood. A manly feeling of honor and character, therefore, a sense of justice, and respect for the opinion of the civilized world, a conviction of what would have been our own conduct in a like case, all called on General Harrison to do exactly what he did.

England had assumed her proper responsibility, and what was it? She had made an aggression upon the United States by entering her territory for a belligerent purpose. She had invaded the sanctity of our territorial rights. As to the mere destruction of the vessel, if perpetrated on the Canadian side, it would have been quite justifiable. The persons engaged in that vessel were, it is to be remembered, violating the laws of their own country, as well as the law of nations; some of them suffered for that offence, and I wish all had suffered.

Mr. Allen here desired to know where the proof was of the fact that the Caroline was so engaged? Was there any record of the fact?

Yes, there is proof, abundant proof. The fact that the vessel was so engaged was, I believe, pretty well proved on the trial and conviction of Van Rensselaer. But, besides, there is abundant proof in the Department of State, in the evidence taken in Canada by the authorities there, and sent to Great Britain, and which could be confirmed by any body who lived anywhere from Buffalo down to Schlosser. It was proved by the *res gestæ*. What were the condition and conduct of the Caroline? Mr. Stevenson, making the best case he could for the United States, said that she was cleared out at Buffalo, in the latter part of December, to ply between Buffalo and Schlosser, on the same side of the river, a few miles below. Lord Palmerston, with his usual sarcasm, and with more than a usual occasion for the application of that sarcasm, said, "It was very true she was cleared out; but Mr. Stevenson forgot that she was also 'cut out' of the ice in which she had been laid up for the winter, and that, in departing from Buffalo, instead of going down to Schlosser, she went down to Navy Island"; and his Lordship asked, "What new outbreak of traffic made it necessary to have a steamboat plying, in the depth of winter, between Buffalo and Schlosser, when exactly between those two places, on the shore, there was a very convenient railroad?" I will most respectfully suggest all this to the consideration of the chairman of the Committee on Foreign Relations. And, as further evidence, I will state the entire omission of the government of the United States, during the whole of Mr. Van Buren's administration, to make any demand for reparation for the property destroyed. So far as I remember, such a suggestion was never made. But one thing I do very well remember, and that is, that a person who had some interest in the property came to the city of Washington, and thought of making an application to the government, in the time of Mr. Van Buren, for indemnity. He was told that the sooner he shut his mouth on that subject the better, for he himself, knowing that the purpose to which the vessel was to be applied came within the purview of the statutes of the United States against fitting out hostile expeditions against countries with which the United States were at peace, was liable to prosecution; and he ever afterwards, profiting by this friendly admonition, held his peace. That is another piece of evidence which I respectfully submit to the consideration of the chairman of the Committee on Foreign Relations.

Well, Sir, McLeod's case went on in the court of New York, and I was utterly surprised at the decision of that court on the *habeas corpus*. On the peril and at the risk of my professional reputation, I now say, that the opinion of the court of New York in that case is not a respectable opinion, either on account of the result at which it arrives, or the reasoning on which it proceeds.*

McLeod was tried and acquitted; there being no proof that he had killed Durfree. Congress afterwards passed an act, that,

* This opinion has been ably and learnedly reviewed by Judge Tallmadge, of the Superior Court of the City of New York. Of this review the late Chief Justice Spencer says: "It refutes and overthrows the opinion most amply." Chancellor Kent says of it: "It is conclusive upon every point. I should have been proud if I had been the author of it." This opinion of the Supreme Court of New York is not likely to be received, at home or abroad, as the American understanding of an important principle of public law.

if such cases should arise hereafter, they should be immediately transferred to the courts of the United States. That was a necessary and a proper law. It was requisite, in order to enable the government of the United States to maintain the peace of the country. It was perfectly constitutional; because it is a just and important principle, quite a fundamental principle, indeed, that the judicial power of the general government should be co-extensive with its legislative and executive powers. When the authority and duty of this government are to be judicially discussed and decided, that decision must be in the courts of the United States, or else the tie which holds the government together would become a band of straw. McLeod's acquittal put an end to all question concerning his case; and Congress having passed a law providing for such cases in future, it only remained that a proper explanation and apology, all that a nation of high honor could ask, or a nation of high honor could give, should be obtained for the violation of territorial sovereignty; and that was obtained. It was not obtained in Mr. Van Buren's time, but obtained, concurrently with the settlement of other questions, in 1842.*

Before Mr. Fox's letter was answered, Sir, the President had directed the Attorney-General to proceed to New York, with copies of the official correspondence, and with instructions to signify to the Governor of New York the judgment which had been formed here.† These instructions have been referred to, and they are public. The moment was critical. A mob had arrested judicial proceedings on the frontier. The trial of McLeod was expected to come on immediately at Lockport; and what would be the fate of the prisoner, between the opinions entertained inside of the court-house and lawless violence without, no one could foresee. The instructions were in the spirit of the answer to Mr. Fox's letter. And I now call on the member from New York to furnish authority for his charge, made in his speech the other day, that the government of the United States had "interfered, directly and palpably," with the proceedings of the courts of New York. There is no authority, not a particle, for any such statement. All that was done was made

* See the letter of Mr. Webster to Lord Ashburton, of the 27th of July, 1842, and Lord Ashburton's answer, in the sixth volume.

† See the instructions to Mr. Crittenden, in the sixth volume.

public. He has no other authority for what he said than the public papers; they do not bear him out. To say, on the ground of what is publicly known, that the government of the United States interfered, "directly and palpably," with the proceedings in New York, is wholly to misconceive and mistake the transaction. There was no demand for the delivery of McLeod to the United States; there was no attempt to arrest the proceedings of the New York court. Mr. Fox was told that these proceedings must go on, until they were judicially terminated; that McLeod was in confinement, by judicial process, and could only be released by judicial process under the same authority. All this is plainly stated in the instructions to Mr. Crittenden, and no man who reads that paper can fall into any mistake about it. There was no "direct and palpable" interference with the New York courts, nor any interference at all. The Governor of New York did not think there was, nor did any body else ever think there was, who informed himself of the facts of the case.

Mr. President, the honorable Senator from Ohio* bestowed, I believe, a very considerable degree of attention upon topics connected with the treaty of Washington. It so happened that my engagements did not permit me to be in the Senate during the delivery of any considerable portion of that speech. I was present occasionally, however, and heard some parts of it. I have not been able to find any particular account of the honorable member's remarks. In the only printed speech by him on which I have been able to lay my hands, it is said that he took occasion to speak, in general terms, of various topics, enumerating them, embraced in the treaty of 1842. As I have not seen those remarks, I shall not now undertake to make any further allusion to them. If I should happen to see them hereafter, so far as I may believe that they have not been answered by what I have already said, or may now say, I may, perhaps, deem it worth while to embrace some opportunity of taking such notice of them as they may seem to require.

MR. ALLEN. I will state, for the satisfaction of the Senator, the general substance of what I said on the subject. If he so desires, I will now proceed to do so.

* Mr. Allen.

I think that, upon the whole, when the gentleman shall furnish the public with a copy of his speech, I may, perhaps, have a more proper opportunity to pay attention to it, especially as I have to say something of other speeches, which may at present occupy as much of the time of the Senate as can well be devoted to this subject.

The honorable member from New York, nearest the chair,* made a speech on this subject, of which I propose to take some notice. Before doing so I shall take notice of the "extracts from the speech of Mr. C. J. Ingersoll, in the House of Representatives," which he has borrowed and incorporated into his speech by way of note.

Mr. Dickinson explained that he was not responsible for the statement in the note to his speech, and that he did not make the extracts from Mr. Ingersoll's speech a part of his own. Mr. Webster proceeded.

The passage quoted by the gentleman from New York from the speech of Mr. C. J. Ingersoll is as follows: —

"Out of this controversy arose the arrest of Alexander McLeod. What he† intended to state now consisted of facts not yet generally known, but which would soon be made known, for they were in progress of publication, and he had received them in no confidence, from the best authority. When McLeod was arrested, General Harrison had just died, and Mr. Tyler was not yet at home as his successor. Mr. Webster, who was *de facto* the administration, — Mr. Webster wrote to the Governor of New York, with his own hand, a letter, and sent it by express, marked 'private,' in which the Governor was told that he must release McLeod, or see the magnificent commercial emporium laid in ashes. The brilliant description given by the gentleman from Virginia of the prospective destruction of that city in the case of a war was, in a measure, anticipated on this occasion. McLeod must be released, said the Secretary of State, or New York must be laid in ashes. The Governor asked when this would be done. The reply was, *forthwith*. Do you not see coming on the waves of the sea the Paixhan guns? and if McLeod be not released New York will be destroyed. But, said the Governor, the power of pardon is vested in me, and even if he be convicted, he may be pardoned. O, no, said the Secretary, if you even try him, you will bring destruction on yourselves."

Notwithstanding the circumstantial detail of facts in the fore-

* Mr. Dickinson. † Mr. Ingersoll.

going passage, they are wholly without foundation. It is implied that a correspondence consisting of an exchange of letters took place between me and the Governor of New York. A single letter only, which I shall presently read to the Senate, was written by me; and the entire detail of the supposed contents of the correspondence; the conflagration "of the commercial emporium," the "Paixhan guns," the assertion ascribed to me, that "McLeod must be released or New York must be laid in ashes," the repetition of this remark in a subsequent letter, the intimation of the Governor of New York that he had the pardoning power, and my alleged reply, that, "if you even try McLeod, you will bring destruction on yourselves"; I say, Sir, this entire detail is imaginary, and altogether destitute of foundation in fact.

The following are the circumstances as they actually occurred. When McLeod was arrested, there was a good deal of conversation in Washington and elsewhere about what would happen. It was a subject of very considerable conversation, and certainly of embarrassment to the government. It was hoped and expected by me, and I believe by the President and other members of the Cabinet, that the Governor of New York would see that it was a case in which, if he were invested with authority by the constitution and the laws of the State, he would recommend the entering of a *nolle prosequi* by the prosecuting officer of the State of New York. It was expected that he would do so, and General Harrison one day said to me, that he had received a letter from a friend, in which he was informed that the Governor of New York had made up his mind to take that course, and that he was very glad of it, as it relieved the general government from its embarrassment. It was about the time that the Attorney-General was to proceed to New York to see how the matter stood, or perhaps a day or two after he had left Washington. The case was to be tried within ten days, at Lockport, in the western part of that State. Having received this information, General Harrison directed me to write a note of thanks to the Governor, stating that he thought he had done exactly what was proper, and by so doing had relieved the government from some embarrassment, and the country from some danger of collision with a foreign power. And that is every thing said in that letter, or any other letter written by me to the Governor of the State of New York, marked private. The letter is here if any one wishes to see it, or to hear it read.

Mr. Crittenden suggested that the letter should be read.

Very well. Here it is, I will read it.

"(Private.) "*Department of State,*
Washington, March 17th, 1841.

"MY DEAR SIR,—The President has learned, not directly, but by means of a letter from a friend, that you had expressed a disposition to direct a *nolle prosequi* in the case of the indictment against McLeod, on being informed by this government that the British government has officially avowed the attack on the Caroline as an act done by its own authority. The President directs me to express his thanks for the promptitude with which you appear disposed to perform an act, which he supposes proper for the occasion, and which is calculated to relieve this government from embarrassment, and the country from some danger of collision with a foreign power.

"You will have seen Mr. Crittenden, whom I take this occasion to commend to your kindest regard.

"I have the honor to be, yours, truly,
"DANIEL WEBSTER.

"HIS EXCELLENCY, WM. H. SEWARD,
Governor of New York."

MR. MANGUM. Was that the only letter written?

Yes, the only letter; the only private letter ever written by me to the Governor of New York in the world.

The speech quoted by the gentleman from New York proceeds: "The next step taken by the administration was to appoint a district attorney, who was to be charged with the defence of Alexander McLeod, the gentleman who was lately removed from office, and a fee of five thousand dollars was put into his hands for this purpose." This statement, Sir, is entirely unfounded. The government of the United States had no more to do than the government of France with the employment of Mr. Spencer for the defence of McLeod. They never interfered with his appointment in the slightest degree. It is true, they furnished to Mr. Spencer, as they would have furnished to any other counsel, the official correspondence, to prove that the government of Great Britain avowed the act of the destruction of the Caroline as their own. The speech continues: "Application was afterwards made to the chief justice of the State of New York for the release of McLeod. The judge did not think proper to grant the application. The marshal was about to let him go, when he was told that he must do it at his peril; and that, if McLeod went out of prison, he should go in." I do not know what the marshal had to do with the case. McLeod was in prison under the authority of the State of New York. I do not know how it was possible that the marshal, an officer of the United States, could interfere.

But there are some other matters in the speech to which I must refer. "He would call on the honorable member from Massachusetts* to sustain him in what he was about to say." I do not find that the honorable member from Massachusetts has yet sustained him in these statements, and I rather think he never will. He asserts that I wrote to the Committee on Foreign Affairs of the House on that subject, asking an outfit and a salary for a special minister to England to settle the Oregon question. This statement is as destitute of foundation as those to which I have already alluded. I never wrote such a letter, to the best of my recollection. "These are facts," he says, "which no one will dispute." I dispute them. I say I have no recollection of them at all. I do not believe Mr. Adams has any recollection of any such note being written by me. If I had written such a note, I think I should remember it.

The author of the speech next proceeds to a topic no way connected with what he has been discussing.

Here Mr. Webster read an extract from the speech of Mr. Ingersoll, charging him (Mr. W.) with offering to give Oregon for free trade with England, in a speech made at a public dinner, in Baltimore, May, 1843.

Here by me sits a Senator from Maryland,† who was present at that dinner, and heard my speech; and if I needed a witness beyond my own statement and printed speech, I could readily call upon him. In that speech, I did not mention Oregon, nor allude to it in the remotest degree. The statement that I did so is wholly unfounded in fact. The author of this speech was not there. If he knew any thing about it, he must have acquired

* Mr. Adams.

† Mr. Johnson.

his knowledge from the printed speech; but in that there is not the slightest reference to Oregon. He says further, that my speech at Baltimore contained a strong recommendation of a commercial treaty with England. Why, Sir, a commercial treaty with England to regulate the subjects upon which I was talking at Baltimore, the duties laid on goods by the two countries, was just the thing that I did *not* recommend, and which I there declared the treaty-making power had no right to make, no authority to make. He would represent me as holding out the idea, that the power of laying duties for revenue was a power that could be freely exercised by the President and Senate, as part of the treaty-making power! Why, I hope that I know more of the Constitution than that. The ground I took was just the reverse of that, exactly the reverse. Sir, my correspondence, public and private, with England, at that time, led me to anticipate, before long, some change in the policy of England with respect to certain articles, the produce of this country; some change with respect to the policy of the corn-laws. I suggested in that speech how very important it would be, if things should so turn out, that that great product of ours, Indian corn, of which we raise five times as much as we do of wheat, (principally the product of the West and Southwest, especially of the State of Tennessee, which raises annually I do not know how many millions,) I suggested, I say, how fortunate it would be, if an arrangement could be made by which that article of human food could be freely imported into England. I said that, in the spirit that prevailed, and which I knew prevailed, (for I knew that the topic had been discussed in England,) if an arrangement could be made in some proper manner to produce such a result, it would be a piece of great good fortune. But, then, did I not immediately proceed to say, that it could not be done by treaty? I used the word "arrangement," studiously used it, to avoid the conclusion that it could be done by treaty. I will read what I said:—

"But with regard to the direct intercourse between us and England great interest is excited, many wishes expressed, and strong opinions entertained in favor of an attempt to settle duties on certain articles by treaty or arrangement. I say, gentlemen, by 'arrangement,' and I use that term by design. The Constitution of the United States leaves with Congress the great business of laying duties to support the government.

It has made it the duty of the House of Representatives, the popular branch of the government, to take the lead on such subjects. There have been some few cases in which treaties have been entered into, having the effect to limit duties; but it is not necessary, and that is an important part of the whole subject, it is not necessary to go upon the idea that, if we come to an understanding with foreign governments upon rates of duties, that understanding can be effected only by means of a treaty ratified by the President and two thirds of the Senate, according to the form of the Constitution.

. . . . .

"It is true a treaty is the law of the land. But, then, as the whole business of revenue and general provision for all the wants of the country is undoubtedly a very peculiar business of the House of Representatives or of Congress, I am of opinion, and always have been, that there should be no encroachment upon it by the exercise of the treaty-making power, unless in case of great and evident necessity."

There have been some cases of necessity, like that of the convention with France for the acquisition of Louisiana.* And yet he says that in this speech, in which Oregon was not mentioned at all, in which I repudiated the raising of revenue by treaty, I offered Oregon to England for free trade, and recommended a treaty with her for the purpose of laying duties.

The author of the speech further says: "By this treaty, the good old Bay State, which he loved with filial reverence, was disintegrated, torn asunder." Massachusetts torn asunder! Sir, Massachusetts and Maine owned in common a tract of wild land on the northern and eastern boundary of the latter State. The jurisdiction was exclusively in Maine. The boundary had never been run; and after fifty-nine years of ineffectual attempts, as we have seen, to settle the adverse claims of the United States and Great Britain, all parties concerned, Maine and Massachusetts, and the two national governments, united in the conventional line laid down in the treaty of Washington. By this line Massachusetts, for a just and reasonable equivalent, parted with her interest in a portion of the wild lands on the frontier; and by this step, the author of the speech says, Massachusetts "is disintegrated and torn asunder." Can absurdity go further?

* By the eighth article of this convention, it was stipulated that for twelve years the vessels of France and Spain, laden with the produce of those countries respectively, should be admitted into the port of New Orleans, in the same manner as the ships of the United States coming directly from France or Spain.

Mr. President, I will now take some further notice of what has been said by the member from New York.* I exceedingly regret, that the observations of the gentleman make it my duty to take some notice of them. Our acquaintance is short, but it has not been unpleasant. I have always thought him a man of courteous manners and kind feelings, but it cannot be expected that I shall sit here and listen to statements such as the honorable member has made on this question, and not answer them. I repeat, it gives me great pain to take notice of the gentleman's speech. This controversy is not mine; all can bear witness to that. I have not undertaken to advance, of my own accord, a single word about the treaty of Washington. I am forced, driven to it; and, Sir, when I am driven to the wall, I mean to stand up and make battle, even against the most formidable odds.

The gentleman says that we made a very important concession of territory to England under that treaty. Now, that treaty proposed to be a treaty of concession on both sides. The gentleman states concessions made by the United States, but entirely forgets to state those made on the other side. He takes no notice of the cession of Rouse's Point; or of a strip of land a hundred miles long, on the border of the State of New York. But, Sir, what I wish principally to do now, is to turn to another part of this speech. I before gave the gentleman notice that I would call upon him for the authority upon which he made such a statement, as that an attempt was made at Washington by members of the government to stop the course of justice in New York; and now, if the gentleman is ready with the proofs, I would be glad to have them.

Mr. Dickinson. I will reserve what I have to say until the gentleman has done, when I shall produce it to his satisfaction.

I undertake to say, no authority will be produced, or is producible, that there were attempts made at Washington to interfere with the trial of McLeod. I have already gone over the circumstances as they occurred. It was suggested by the President to Governor Seward, that the President was gratified that he had come to the conclusion to enter a *nolle prosequi* in the case of

* Mr. Dickinson.

McLeod. Was that a palpable interference with judicial authority? Was that a resistance of the ordinary process of law? The government of the United States had nothing at all to do with the trial of McLeod in the New York courts, except to see that he was furnished with the proof of facts necessary to his defence. But I wish to know in what school the gentleman has learned that, if a man is in prison, and his counsel moves to have him brought up on the writ of *habeas corpus*, that step is any resistance of judicial process in favor of the prisoner? It is easy to give to any thing the name of a direct and palpable interference. He may apply the term to the journey of the Attorney-General to Albany, or to any other act or occurrence. But that does not prove it so. To make good his statement he must prove that the government did some act, or acts, which the common sense of men holds to be a palpable and direct interference. I say there was none. He quotes the letter of instructions to the Attorney-General. That proposes no interference. That letter says to the Attorney-General, that, if the case were pending in the courts of the United States, so that the President could have control over it, he would direct the prosecuting officer to enter a *nolle prosequi;* but as it is within the jurisdiction of New York, it is referred to the Governor of that State. That is the substance, in this respect, of the letter which the Attorney-General carried to the Governor of New York, and there was not another act done by authority at Washington in this matter, and I call upon the gentleman at his leisure to produce his authority for his statements.

After a few more remarks upon the use made by Mr. Dickinson of the speech of Mr. Ingersoll, and explanations on this subject between Mr. Webster and Mr. Dickinson, Mr. Webster proceeded as follows: —

I will now allude, Mr. President, as briefly as possible, to some other provisions of the treaty of Washington. The article for the delivery of fugitives from justice has been assailed. It has been said that an innocent woman had been sent back to Scotland, under its provisions. Why, I believe the fact is, that a woman had murdered her husband, or some relative in Scotland, and fled to this country. She was pursued, demanded, and carried back, and from some defect in the testimony, or from some other cause, such as not unfrequently occurs in criminal trials, she was acquitted.* But, Sir, I undertake to say, that the article for the extradition of offenders, contained in the treaty of 1842, if there was nothing else in the treaty of any importance, has of itself been of more value to this country, and is of more value to the progress of civilization, the cause of humanity, and the good understanding between nations, than can be readily computed. What were the state and condition of this country, Sir, on the borders and frontiers, at the time of this treaty? Why, it was the time when the "patriot societies" or "Hunters' Lodges" were in full operation, when companies were formed and officers appointed by secret associations, to carry on the war in Canada; and, as I have said already, the disturbances were so frequent and so threatening, that the United States government despatched General Scott to the frontier, to make a draft on New York for militia in order to preserve the peace of the border. And now, Sir, what was it that repressed these disorders, and restored the peace of the border? Nothing but this agreement between the two governments, that, if those "patriots" and "barn-burners" went from one side to the other to destroy their neighbors' property, trying, all the time, to bring on a war, (for that was their object,) they should be delivered up to be punished. As soon as that provision was agreed to, the disturbances ceased, on the one side and on the other. They were heard of no more. In the formation of this clause of the treaty I had the advantage of consultation with a venerable friend near me, one of the members from Michigan.† He pressed me not to forego the opportunity of introducing some such provision. He examined it; and I will ask him if he knows any other cause for the instantaneous suppression of these border difficulties than this treaty provision?

Mr. Woodbridge rose, and spoke, in reply, as follows: —

"Mr. President, I may not disregard the allusion which the gentleman has done me the honor to make to me, in reference to the inconsiderable part which I deemed it my duty to take in the matter in question. A brief statement of some facts which occurred, and a glance, simply, at the condition of that border country from which I come, will be all that the occasion seems to demand.

* The verdict on the trial was one known to the law of Scotland, though not to our law, namely, "not proven."

† Mr. Woodbridge.

"That part of Canada with which the people of Michigan are brought more immediately in contact, extends from the head of Lake Erie to Point Edwards, at the lower extremity of Lake Huron, a distance of about one hundred miles. Along this intermediate distance, the straits of Detroit and of St. Clair furnish every imaginable facility for the escape of fugitives. For their entire length, the shores of those straits, on either side, exhibit lines of dense and continuous settlement. Their shores are lined, and their smooth surface covered, with boats and vessels of all dimensions and descriptions, from the bark canoe to the steamer of a thousand tons. If the perpetrator of crime can reach a bark canoe or a light skiff, and detach himself from the shore, he may in a few minutes defy pursuit, for he will be within a foreign jurisdiction. In *such* a condition of things, no society can be safe unless there be some power to reclaim fugitives from justice. While your territorial government existed there, and its executive administration, under the control of this national government, was in the hands of my honorable colleague,* a conventional arrangement, informal undoubtedly in its character, was entered into by him with the authorities of Canada, sustained by local legislation on both sides, by which these evils were greatly lessened. When the present State government took the place of the territorial government, this arrangement of necessity ceased; and then the evils alluded to were greatly aggravated, and became eminently dangerous. Shortly before the first session of Congress, at which I attended, after the inauguration of General Harrison, a very aggravated case of crime occurred, and its perpetrators, as usual, escaped into Canada. It was made the subject of an official communication to the State legislature. And soon after my arrival here, I deemed it to be my duty to lay the matter before the Secretary of State, with a view to the adoption of some appropriate convention with Great Britain.

"The honorable Senator, then Secretary of State, was pleased to receive the suggestion favorably; but suggested to me the expediency of obtaining, if practicable, the sense of the Senate on the subject. Accordingly, I afterwards introduced a resolution here, having that object in view, and it was referred to the consideration of the Committee on Foreign Relations, of which an honorable Senator from Virginia,† not now a member of the Senate, was chairman.

"Mr. Rives expressed himself very decidedly in favor of the proposition. But negotiations having been begun, or being about to commence, with Lord Ashburton, it was not deemed expedient, I believe, that it should then be made matter of discussion in the Senate. I had not ceased to feel very earnest solicitude on the subject; and, as the

* General Cass. † Mr. Rives.

negotiation approached its termination, Mr. Webster did me the honor to send to me the *project* of that article of the treaty which relates to the subject. He desired me to consider it and to exhibit it, confidentially perhaps, to such Senators as came from border States, for their consideration, and for such modification of its terms and scope as they might deem expedient. This I did. The form and scope of the article met, I believe, with the approbation of all to whom I showed it. Nor was any modification suggested, except, perhaps, one very immaterial one, suggested by an honorable Senator from New York. Of all this I advised Mr. Webster, and the project became afterwards an article of the treaty, with but little if any variation. I believe I can throw no more light on the subject, Sir. But the honorable Senator, having intimated to me that, in his discussion of the subject, he might perhaps have occasion to refer to the part I took in the matter, I have provided myself with the copy of the message to the legislature of Michigan, of which I had in the beginning made use, and which, in order to show the extent of the evil referred to, and the necessity which existed for some treaty stipulation on the subject, I ask the Secretary to read." *

The extract having been read, Mr. Woodbridge then proceeded: "I have now only to add my entire and unqualified conviction, that no act of the legislative or treaty-making power, that I have ever known, has been more successful in its operation than this article of the treaty; nor could any provision have been attended by more happy consequences to the peace and safety of society in that remote frontier."

After this statement from Mr. Woodbridge, Mr. Webster proceeded as follows: —

I am happy to find that, in its operation, the provision has satisfied those who felt an interest in its adoption. But I may now state, I suppose without offence and without cavil, that since the negotiation of this treaty, containing this article, we have negotiated treaties with other governments of Europe containing similar provisions, and that between other governments of Europe themselves treaties have been negotiated containing that provision, a provision never before known to have existed in any

* The Secretary here read an extract from the message of Mr. Woodbridge, when Governor of Michigan, to the legislature of that State, calling its attention earnestly to the facilities which exist along the interior boundaries of the United States for the escape of fugitives from justice; and saying, that a very recent occurrence, of the most painful and atrocious character, had drawn his own attention to it, and recommending, in strong terms, that the *peculiar* situation of Michigan, in this respect, should be laid before Congress, with a view of urging the expediency of some negotiation on the subject between the United States and England.

of the treaties between European nations. I am happy to see, therefore, that it has shown itself to be useful to the citizens of the United States, for whose benefit it was devised and adopted; that it has proved itself worthy of favor and imitation in the judgment of the most enlightened nations of Europe; and that it has never been complained of by any body, except by murderers, and fugitives, and felons themselves.

Now, Sir, comes the matter of the African squadron, to which I am induced to turn my attention for a moment, out of sincere respect to the member from Arkansas,* who suggested the other day that to that article he had objection. There is no man whose opinions are more independent than those of that gentleman, and no one maintains them with more candor. But, if I understood him, he appears to think that that article gave up the right of search. What does he mean? We never claimed that right, we had consequently no such right to give up. Or does he mean exactly the opposite of what he says, that the treaty yielded to England her claim of such right? No such thing. The arrangement made by this treaty was designed to carry into effect those stipulations in the treaty of Ghent which we thought binding on us, as well as to effect an object important to this country, to the interests of humanity, and to the general cause of civilization throughout the world, without raising the difficulty attending the question of the right of search. The object of it was to accomplish all that was desirable, in a way that should avoid the possibility of subjecting our vessels, under any pretence, to the right of search. I will not dwell on this. But allow me to state the sentiments on this subject of persons in the service of the United States abroad, whose opinions are entitled to respect. A letter has been received at the Department of State, from Mr. Henry Wheaton, our minister at Berlin, in which he expresses his approbation of the arrangement alluded to as particularly satisfactory, and as adapted to secure the desired end, by the only means consistent with our maritime rights. Mr. Wheaton adds the remark, that "the policy of the United States may consequently be said, on this occasion, perhaps for the first time, to have had a most decisive influence on that of Europe." †

* Mr. Sevier.

† See Mr. Wheaton's letter in the Appendix to this Speech, No. I

I am quite willing to rest on this opinion of Mr. Wheaton, as to the propriety and safety, the security and the wisdom, of the article in this treaty respecting the suppression of the African slave trade by a squadron of our own, against any little artillery that may be used against it here. I do not allude to the opinion of the gentleman; I have for him the highest respect. I was thinking of what is said in other comments to which I have referred. But I need not stop here. Upon the appearance of this treaty between the United States and England, the leading states of Europe did, in fact, alter their whole policy on this subject. The treaty of December, 1841, between the Five Powers, had not been ratified by France. There was so much opposition to it in France, on the ground that it gave the right of search to the English cruisers, that the king and M. Guizot, though the treaty was negotiated according to their instructions, did not choose to ratify it. What, then, was done? When this treaty of Washington became known in Europe, the wise men of France and England who wished to do all they could to suppress the African slave trade, and to do it in a manner securing in the highest degree the immunity of the flag of either, and the supremacy of neither, agreed to abandon the quintuple treaty of 1841, the unratified treaty; they gave it up. They adopted the treaty of Washington as their model; and I have now in my hand the convention between France and England, signed in London on the 29th of May, 1845, the articles of which, in respect to the manner of putting an end to the slave trade, embody, exactly, the provisions contained in the treaty of Washington.

Thus it is seen that France has borrowed, from the treaty stipulations between the United States and England, the mode of fulfilling her own duties and accomplishing her own purpose, in perfect accordance with the immunity of her flag. I need hardly say, Sir, that France is the nation which was earliest, and has been most constantly wakeful, in her jealousy of the supremacy of the maritime power of England. She has kept her eye on it, steadily, for centuries. The immunity of flags is a deep principle, it is a sentiment, one may almost say it is a passion, with all the people of France. And France, jealous, quick of perception, thoroughly hostile to any extension of the right of maritime search or visit, under any pretences whatever, has seen, in the example of the treaty of Washington, a mode of fulfilling her duties for the suppression of the African slave trade, without disturbing the most sensitive of all her fears.

Allow me, Sir, to read the eighth and ninth articles of the treaty of Washington, and the first, second, and third articles of the convention between England and France.

Mr. Webster here read the designated articles of the treaty of Washington, and the convention between England and France.*

Mr. President, there is another topic on which I have to say a few words. It has been said that the treaty of Washington, and the negotiations accompanying it, leave the great and interesting question of impressment where they found it. With all humility and modesty, I must beg to express my dissent from that opinion. I must be permitted to say, that the correspondence connected with the negotiation of that treaty, although impressment was not mentioned in the treaty itself, has, in the judgment of the world, or at least of persons of consideration and authority in the world, been regarded as not having left the question of impressment where it found it, but as having placed the true doctrine in opposition to it on a higher and stronger foundation. The letter addressed on that subject from the Department of State to the British plenipotentiary, and his answer, are among the papers. I only wish the letter to be read. It recites the general history of the question between England and the United States. Lord Ashburton had no authority to make stipulations on the subject; but that is a circumstance which I do not regret, because I do not deem the subject as one at all proper for treaty stipulation.

Mr. Webster here read extracts from the letter, and among others this: † —

"In the early disputes between the two governments on this so long contested topic, the distinguished person to whose hands were first intrusted the seals of this department ‡ declared, that 'the simplest rule will be, that the vessel being American shall be evidence that the seamen on board are such.'

"Fifty years' experience, the utter failure of many negotiations, and a careful reconsideration now had of the whole subject, at a moment

* See Appendix to this Speech, No. II.

† See the letter in the sixth volume.

‡ Mr. Jefferson.

when the passions are laid, and no present interest or emergency exists to bias the judgment, have fully convinced this government that this is not only the simplest and best, but the only, rule which can be adopted and observed, consistently with the rights and honor of the United States and the security of their citizens. That rule announces, therefore, what will hereafter be the principle maintained by their government. IN EVERY REGULARLY DOCUMENTED AMERICAN MERCHANT-VESSEL, THE CREW WHO NAVIGATE IT WILL FIND THEIR PROTECTION IN THE FLAG WHICH IS OVER THEM."

This declaration will stand. Not on account of any particular ability displayed in the letter which it concludes; still less on account of the name subscribed to it. But it will stand, because it announces the true principles of public law; because it announces the great doctrine of the equality and independence of nations upon the seas; and because it announces the determination of the government and the people of the United States to uphold those principles, and to maintain that doctrine, through good report and through evil report, for ever. We shall negotiate no more, nor attempt to negotiate more, about impressment. We shall not treat, hereafter, of its limitation to parallels of latitude and longitude. We shall not treat of its allowance or disallowance in broad seas or narrow seas. We shall think no more of stipulating for exemption from its exercise of some of the persons composing crews. Henceforth, the deck of every American vessel is inaccessible for any such purpose. It is protected, guarded, defended, by the declaration which I have read, and that declaration will stand.

Sir, another most important question of maritime law, growing out of the case of the "Creole," and other similar cases, was the subject of a letter to the British plenipotentiary, and of an answer from him. An honorable member from South Carolina * had taken, as is well known, a great interest in the matter involved in that question. He had expressed his opinion of its importance here, and had been sustained by the Senate. Occasion was taken of Lord Ashburton's mission to communicate to him and to his government the opinions which this government entertained; and I would now ask the honorable member if any similar cause of complaint has since arisen.

Mr. Calhoun said he had heard of none.

* Mr. Calhoun.

I trust, Sir, that none will arise hereafter. I refer to the letter to Lord Ashburton on this subject, as containing what the American government regarded as the true principle of the maritime law, and to his very sensible and proper answer.

Mr. President, I have reached the end of these remarks, and the completion of my purpose; and I am now ready, Sir, to put the question to the Senate, and to the country, whether the northeastern boundary has not been fairly and satisfactorily settled; whether proper satisfaction and apology have not been obtained, for an aggression on the soil and territory of the United States; whether proper and safe stipulations have not been entered into, for the fulfilment of the duty of the government, and for meeting the earnest desire of the people, in the suppression of the slave trade; whether, in pursuance of these stipulations, a degree of success in the attainment of that object has not been reached, wholly unknown before; whether crimes disturbing the peace of nations have not been suppressed; whether the safety of the Southern coasting trade has not been secured; whether impressment has not been struck out from the list of contested questions among nations; and finally, and more than all, whether any thing has been done to tarnish the lustre of the American name and character?

Mr. President, my best services, like those of every other good citizen, are due to my country; and I submit them, and their results, in all humility, to her judgment. But standing here, to-day, in the Senate of the United States, and speaking in behalf of the administration of which I formed a part, and in behalf of the two houses of Congress, who sustained that administration, cordially and effectually, in every thing relating to this day's discussion, I am willing to appeal to the public men of the age, whether, in 1842, and in the city of Washington, something was not done for the suppression of crime, for the true exposition of the principles of public law, for the freedom and security of commerce on the ocean, and for the peace of the world?

APPENDIX.

No. I. — Page 143.

Mr. Wheaton to Mr. Webster.

Berlin, November 15, 1842.

Sir, — Your despatch, No. 36, inclosing copy of the treaty recently concluded at Washington, between the United States and Great Britain, has just reached me. I beg leave to congratulate you, Sir, on the happy termination of this arduous negotiation, in which the rights, honor, and interests of our country have been so successfully maintained. The arrangement it contains on the subject of the African slave trade is particularly satisfactory, as adapted to secure the end proposed by the only means consistent with our maritime rights. This arrangement has decided the course of the French government in respect to this matter. Its ambassador in London notified to the conference of the five great powers the final determination of France not to ratify the treaty of December, 1841, and, at the same time, expressed her disposition to fulfil the stipulations of the separate treaties of 1831 and 1834, between her and Great Britain. The treaty of 1841, therefore, now subsists only between four of the great powers by whom it was originally concluded; and as three of these (Austria, Prussia, and Russia) are very little concerned in the navigation of the ocean and the trade in the African seas, and have, besides, taken precautions in the treaty itself to secure their commerce from interruption by the exercise of the right of search in other parts, this compact may now be considered as almost a dead letter.

The policy of the United States may consequently be said, on this occasion, perhaps for the first time, to have had a most decisive influence on that of Europe. This will probably more frequently occur hereafter; and it should be an encouragement to us to cultivate our maritime resources, and to strengthen our naval arm, by which alone we are known and felt among the nations of the earth.

No. II. — Page 145.

Treaty of Washington. — [*Extract.*]

Article VIII. — The parties mutually stipulate, that each shall prepare, equip, and maintain in service, on the coast of Africa, a sufficient and adequate squadron, or naval force of vessels, of suitable numbers and descriptions, to carry in all not less than eighty guns, to enforce, separately and respectively, the laws, rights, and obligations of each of the two countries, for the suppression of the slave trade; the said squadrons to be independent of each other, but the two governments stipulating, nevertheless, to give such orders to the officers commanding their respective forces as shall enable them most effectually to act in concert and coöperation, upon mutual consultation, as exigencies may arise, for the attainment of the true object of this article: copies of all such orders to be communicated by each government to the other respectively.

Article IX. — Whereas, notwithstanding all efforts which may be made on the coast of Africa for suppressing the slave trade, the facilities for carrying on that traffic and avoiding the vigilance of cruisers by the fraudulent use of flags, and other means, are so great, and the temptations for pursuing it, while a market can be found for slaves, so strong, as that the desired result may be long delayed, unless all markets be shut against the purchase of African negroes, the parties to this treaty agree that they will unite in all becoming representations and remonstrances, with any and all powers within whose dominions such markets are allowed to exist; and that they will urge upon all such powers the propriety and duty of closing such markets effectually, at once and for ever.

Convention between her Majesty and the King of the French for the Suppression of the Traffic in Slaves. — [*Extract.*]

Article I. — In order that the flags of her Majesty the Queen of the United Kingdom of Great Britain and Ireland, and of his Majesty the King of the French, may not, contrary to the law of nations and the laws in force in the two countries, be usurped to cover the slave trade, and in order to provide for the more effectual suppression of that traffic, his Majesty the King of the French engages, as soon as may be practicable, to station on the west coast of Africa, from Cape Verd to 16° 30′ south latitude, a naval force of at least twenty-six cruisers, consisting of sailing and steam vessels; and her Majesty the Queen of the United Kingdom of Great Britain and Ireland engages, as soon as may be pracicable, to station on the same part of the west coast of Africa a naval force of not less than twenty-six cruisers, consisting of sailing vessels and steam vessels; and on the east coast of Africa such number of cruisers as her Majesty shall judge sufficient for the prevention of the trade on that coast; which cruisers shall be employed for the purposes above mentioned, in conformity with the following stipulations.

Article II. — The said British and French naval forces shall act in concert for the suppression of the slave trade. It will be their duty to watch strictly every part of the west coast of Africa, within the limits described in Article I., where the slave trade is carried on. For this purpose they shall exercise fully and completely all the powers vested in the crowns of Great Britain and France for the suppression of the slave trade, subject only to the modifications hereinafter mentioned as to British and French ships.

Article III. — The officers of her Majesty the Queen of the United Kingdom of Great Britain and Ireland, and of his Majesty the King of the French, having respectively the command of the squadrons of Great Britain and France, to be employed in carrying out this convention, shall concert together as to the best means of watching strictly the parts of the African coast before described, by selecting and defining the stations, and committing the care thereof to English and French cruisers, jointly or separately, as may be deemed most expedient; provided always, that, in case of a station being specially committed to the charge of cruisers of either nation, the cruisers of the other nation may at any time enter the same for the purpose of exercising the rights respectively belonging to them for the suppression of the slave trade.

ORGANIZATION OF THE VOLUNTEER FORCE.*

Mr. President, — I am not at all surprised at the introduction of this bill. For aught I know, it is a necessary one; but it shows, at all events, that the law which it is intended to amend and improve is but a piece of patchwork. That law was not passed for calling into the service of the United States the militia of the country, nor was it passed in the regular exercise of the power conferred upon Congress for raising and maintaining an army. It was a mixed, an anomalous, an incongruous system, as, I will venture to say, this early occasion for its modification proves it to be, and as will be made abundantly evident before the war with Mexico is ended.

I shall not oppose the progress of this bill. I cannot say it is unconstitutional, though I think it is irregular, inconvenient, and not strictly conformable to the exercise of the constitutional power of Congress. If those who are charged with the conduct of the war, and are answerable for its results, think it necessary, I shall not oppose it. But I will take the occasion now presented, Sir, of the second reading of an important bill respecting the troops called into the service in order to carry on the war, to make a few remarks respecting the war itself, and the condition in which we find ourselves in consequence of that war. The war continues; no man can say definitely when it will end; and no man can say, upon any reasonable estimate, what expense will be incurred before its conclusion.

We have received a very important communication from the President, I mean his message of the 16th of June, setting forth

* Remarks in the Senate, on the 24th of June, 1846, on "A Bill to provide for the Organization of the Volunteer Force brought into the Service of the United States."

his views and opinions, and the views and opinions of the Secretary of the Treasury, with respect to the means and sources of revenue for carrying on the war. Upon this, Sir, as well as upon one or two other subjects connected with this bill, I have a few remarks to make.

The executive is responsible for the conduct of the war, and for the application of the resources put at his disposal by the two houses of Congress for the purpose of prosecuting it. For one, I shall not deny the government any supplies which may be considered necessary. Whatever may be thought of the origin of the war, the fact that war does exist is itself a sufficient reason for granting the means for prosecuting that war with effect. Those who condemn the origin of the war, and those who most earnestly long for its termination, will all agree that the refusal of supplies would make no amends for what some lament, and would not hasten what I hope all desire.

The message of the 16th of June informs the Senate and the country, that, for the fiscal year ending July, 1847, there will be, under the operation of the existing law for raising revenue, a deficiency, if the war continues, of twenty millions of dollars, and suggests the ways and means by which it is expected that this deficiency will be made good. I refer to these suggestions for the purpose of making a few observations upon them.

The object is to provide new sources of revenue, which shall realize an amount, beyond that furnished by the provisions of the existing law, of twenty millions of dollars, between this time and the 1st of July next year. That is the object. The first suggestion in the communication from the executive government is, that five millions and a half may be produced by reducing the rates of duties on certain imported articles, and by laying new taxes on certain other articles now free of all duties; meaning principally, I suppose, by those articles now free, and which are to be taxed, tea and coffee. There is also an intimation or an opinion expressed by the Secretary of the Treasury, that a million of dollars will accrue to the treasury under the operation of the warehouse bill, if that bill should become a law. In the next place, it is estimated that, if the bill for graduating the price of the public lands shall become a law, the augmentation of the sales will so far counterbalance any losses incurred in the reduction of price, as on the whole to produce half a million of dollars more than would otherwise be obtained from that source These several sums put together would leave a balance of twelve million five hundred and eighty thousand dollars still to be provided for, and a provision for this balance is contemplated either by loans or by an authority to the treasury to issue treasury-notes, or both, with a distinct recommendation and preference, however, for the authority to issue treasury-notes.

Now, Sir, with an anxious desire that the country shall be led into no mistaken policy in regard to this very important subject of revenue, a subject always important, and intensely important in time of war, I will take occasion to suggest, in very few words, what occurs to me as important to be considered upon these several topics.

In the first place, there is no doubt that a tax properly laid upon tea and coffee will be productive of a clear positive revenue. But this will depend upon two things; first, upon the amount of the duty; and, secondly, upon the mode of laying it. The first is obviously a matter for consideration; and in regard to the second, I suspect that gentlemen who are desirous of raising revenue by this means will find their calculations fallacious unless they make the duty specific. In my opinion, an *ad valorem* duty will disappoint their hopes of any considerable amount of revenue. If I mistake not, under such a system it will be soon found that teas made up in Canton for the New York market will become wonderfully cheap. A specific rate per pound will undoubtedly make the duty productive of revenue.

I doubt not that treasury-notes may be available for the uses of the government to a considerable extent. I do not mean as revenue or income, but as instruments or facilities for the transfer of balances, and as proper to be used in anticipation of taxes or sources of income. In regard to this I would say, simply, that, if it be the purpose of the government, as has been intimated to us for some time, to resort to the issue of treasury-notes, I think the loss of a single day, especially the loss of a single week, will turn out to be quite inconvenient; that is, if the issue of treasury-notes is considered the best and safest, if they can be used by the treasury under authority of law, before the money in the possession of the government is exhausted.

All I wish to say is, that I earnestly recommend to the Committee on Finance to bring in a bill by itself for the issue of treasury-notes immediately. I believe it has been as usual as otherwise for such laws to originate in the Senate; there is no constitutional impediment to such a course, and I hope that these and other important measures, such as the modifying of taxes and laying new ones, will not be suffered to lag along through Congress in a general omnibus bill. Where the subjects are distinct, they should be kept separated; and where they are simple and plain, they should be acted on promptly.

Having said this much of those two sources of assisting the revenue, the tax upon tea and coffee and the issue of treasury-notes, both of which I admit to be efficient, and probably certain in their operation, I have now to say that other matters, suggested and relied on in the communication I have referred to, I consider conjectural, uncertain, and not fit to be the basis of provisions incumbent on us to make, before we leave our seats here, to place the executive in a proper condition to carry on the war. I suppose the calculation will be that a considerable amount will be secured by a reduction of the duties upon articles already taxed, upon the supposition that the importation will be so much increased as to increase the aggregate receipts. I will not say that this is not a well-founded opinion; I have all proper respect for the source from which it comes; but I will venture to say that it is but an opinion; it hardly amounts to the character of an estimate, for want of certain and positive foundation. We have no experience from which we can derive a satisfactory conviction that such will be the result. If I were responsible, I should not choose to place reliance to any extent upon this plan.

The next increase is to come from the operation of the warehouse system. I consider this equally void of any certain foundation to rest upon. I do not see how a million of money, in addition to the present income, is to be derived from admitting goods into the country, to be carried out again without paying any duty whatever. I really do not conceive that the facility of carrying goods through the country, without the payment of duty, is going to produce us a million of dollars. This is a matter of which I should like to see minute details; I should like to see calculations made by which this result is expected to be accomplished. At present I do not see the practicability of it.

And so in regard to the public lands. It may be that the passage of a graduation bill would so enhance the disposition to buy by reducing the price, as considerably to increase the quantity sold; but that that increase will be so great as to produce an overplus of half a million, or any other sum, notwithstanding the diminution of price, is, I think, a matter of opinion which cannot be relied upon. So that these sources of income appear to me rather too uncertain to be the foundation of any satisfactory provisions; there appears rather too much risk in making mere opinions, not to say conjectures, the basis of legislation for producing revenue for the purposes of government.

The truth is, that, if this war continues, we must have a substantial taxation, or we must incur a public debt. We cannot look to treasury-notes as revenue; if they bear interest, and are payable at a distant day, they become of course a public debt. There must, then, be a substantial tax, or there must be a public debt, if the war continues. Our expenses are very great. I do not say they are unnecessary; I make no imputation of that sort at present. I am not sufficiently acquainted with the particulars; but I stated here some time ago, upon the credit of others, that of which I am perfectly convinced, that our expenses have been half a million of dollars a day. Forty days ago we passed an act declaring that war existed, and authorizing the calling out of fifty thousand volunteers. Well, Sir, I have a full conviction that the military expenditures of the government, the expense of raising, equipping, and transporting the force which has already been called out, will be found to amount to twenty millions, or very nearly that sum, at this moment. Some portions of our warlike preparations are peculiarly expensive, I mean the regiments of mounted volunteers. They are necessary, I suppose, for the nature of the service; but there was a document published here, a communication, I think, from the War Department, when Mr. Poinsett was Secretary, in which it was estimated, if I mistake not, that one regiment of mounted riflemen in regular service cost the government per annum as much as three regiments of infantry, each composed of the same number of men. And there is good reason to believe that these occasional regiments of volunteers will be still more expensive. Almost every circumstance connected with this war is calculated to increase the expense. The vast distance to be traversed makes the cost of transportation very great; and it becomes the duty of Congress to provide for this extraordinary expense. I do not say that the expense ought not to be incurred. I only say that, from the nature of the war, the expense must necessarily be very great. And I take this occasion to say, that I have seen with great pleasure the alacrity with which volunteers have rushed to the public service. A spirit of patriotism and devotion to the country's interest has been manifested of which we may justly be proud.

But upon these sources of revenue let me make another remark, though perhaps it is too obvious to require notice. For one half the deficiency the government proposes to rely on treasury-notes or loans. Well, if this be so, then, of course, I suppose the idea of pressing for the present the independent treasury, or sub-treasury, must be abandoned by every one; for what would be the use of treasury-notes under a sub-treasury plan of finance? The issue of treasury-notes would be perfectly inconsistent with the sub-treasury system. It is quite plain that, if the government, for its own use, is driven to the necessity of issuing paper, it can have no occasion to make provision for locking up its treasures. The sub-treasury system makes it penal to issue or receive any thing but specie. They are, therefore, entirely inconsistent with each other.

With respect to loans, I beseech gentlemen not to deceive themselves. There is money enough in the country, it is true, and the credit of the government will be good if we lay such taxes as will produce revenue; but if gentlemen suppose that a loan is to be contracted in this country for the use of the government, to be paid in specie, in the expectation that that specie is to be locked up, they will find themselves mistaken. Those who hold capital will consent to no such thing. If the government makes a loan, it must be made in the ordinary way, payable by instalments or otherwise, under circumstances that will show that this amount of money is not to be drained from all the operations of the business community. I take it for granted, then, if loans are to be made, the new method of keeping the public money must be abandoned.

And now, Sir, having said this much in relation to the ideas communicated to us respecting the mode of raising revenue, I desire to add, that, in my judgment, the time has come to ask for the object, and character, and purposes for which the war is hereafter to be conducted. The people of this country, while they are willing to pay all needful expenses; while they are desirous of sustaining the glory of the American arms; while they are ready to defend every inch of American territory, and maintain all the essential rights of their country; the people, if I do not misread their desires, now wish to know the specific objects and purposes and ends for which this war is further to be carried on. There is not now a hostile foot within the limits of the United States. Our army, at first an army of observation, then an army of occupation, has become an army of invasion; I will not say unjust invasion; but it is encamped at this moment beyond the limits of the United States, and within the acknowledged territory of Mexico; and, if we may credit the rumors which have recently reached us, a purpose is entertained of marching immediately and directly to the city of Mexico.

The people, as I have said, appear to me to demand, and with great reason, a full, distinct, and comprehensible account of the objects and purposes of this war of invasion. The President, by two messages, one of the 13th of May, and the other of the 16th of June, signifies that he is ready to treat with Mexico upon terms of peace; while it appears, at least as far as we know now, that Mexico is not willing to treat. In regard to this, I must say that, in my judgment, if this be the state of the case, Mexico is acting an entirely unreasonable and senseless part, and the government of the United States, to this extent, is acting a proper one; that is to say, as the war does exist, and the American government is ready to treat, without prescribing terms, so as to show that her terms would be unacceptable, and Mexico declines to treat, why then so far the conduct of the United States is reasonable, and the conduct of Mexico unreasonable and senseless. I would desire on all such occasions, for many reasons, and in this case for two more than the rest to keep our country entirely in the right, and to satisfy every individual in the country that it is in the right, and that it desires nothing wrong; and I would advise, if I were called on to give advice, that this government should tender a formal solemn embassy to Mexico. The two reasons which would influence me are, in the first place, Mexico is weak and we are strong; it is a war, therefore, on her part, against great odds; and, in the next place, Mexico is a neighbor, a weak neighbor, a republic formed upon our own model, who, when she threw off the dominion of old Spain, was influenced throughout mainly by our example. We certainly wished her success; we certainly congratulated her upon her change from a viceroyalty to a republic upon our own model. We wished her well; and I think now that the people of the United States have no desire, it would give them, I think, no pleasure, to do her an injury beyond what is necessary to maintain their own rights. The people of the United States cannot wish to crush the republic of Mexico; it cannot be their desire to break down a neighboring republic; it cannot be their wish to drive her back again to a monarchical form of government, and to render her a mere appanage to some one of the thrones of Europe.

This is not a thought which can find harbor in the generous breasts of the American people. Mexico has been unfortunate; she is unfortunate. I really believe the Mexican people are the worst governed people in Christendom. They have yet to learn the true nature of free institutions. Depressed and ruined by a dominant military power, maintaining an army of forty thousand troops, how can a government, limited in its resources as that of Mexico, flourish? It is impossible. She has been unhappy, too, in the production, or rather the non-production, of men to guide her counsels. I am sorry to say it of a republic, but it is nevertheless true. Mexico has produced few or no really enlightened, patriotic men. I verily believe, and I sadly fear, that history will hereafter record the melancholy truth, that, from the time of the establishment of an independent government, the people of Mexico have been worse governed a great deal than they were under the viceroyalty. No body can wish to see her fall; but Mexico must hear the suggestions of reason. She must listen to terms of peace; this she ought to know. And if her government be not hopelessly stupid and infatuated, they must be aware that this is her true interest. Nothing can exceed, I have always thought, the obstinacy and senselessness manifested by Mexico in refusing for so many years to acknowledge the independence of Texas. A correspondence between this government and Mexico upon that subject took place at a time when I had something to do with the administration, so that my attention was particularly directed to the course of conduct pursued by Mexico, and it struck me as resembling, though it was much more senseless, the conduct of old Spain in attempting for many years to reconquer the people of the Low Countries after they had declared their independence.

Mexico must be taught that it is necessary for her to treat for peace upon considerations which belong to the present state of things. We have just claims against her, claims acknowledged by herself in the most solemn form of treaty stipulations. She ought to make provision for the payment of those claims; in short, she must be brought to justice. I am not one of those who would do her an injustice; but it does appear to me that, if, after all that has occurred, she still persists in refusing to receive an American minister on the ground that it was through the fault of the United States that she lost Texas, she will be acting a very unreasonable part.

As to her enlisting the sympathy of foreign powers, I have not the least belief that any power stands behind Mexico. I have not the least belief of her possessing the assurance of any power, that, if she will hold on in the contest, foreign aid will be sent to her. I think the whole policy of the governments of Europe takes a different turn. I believe that they think, and especially England, that it is for their interest to have Mexico at peace; in a state of active industry, cultivating her resources, multiplying her products, and increasing her ability to purchase from them. I believe that this will soon be the declared policy of the British government, as it is undoubtedly the true policy of all governments. I believe, therefore, that if Mexico rests upon any hope that by and by aid and succor will come from foreign sources, that hope will entirely fail.

The newspapers speak of mediation. I doubt whether there is much truth in that; if, however, any offer of mediation be made by the best friend Mexico has, it must come down to this at last, that she must treat for peace. For one, I would vote for a suspension of hostilities to the end that negotiation might take place; and if I were to advise, I would say, make her an offer of a formal embassy. I would be for keeping ourselves entirely in the right. We can afford to do so; we can lose nothing in dignity by it. It is not stooping on our part, because all the world knows that the contest is very unequal. If she will consent to this, I say meet her in negotiation, and in the mean time suspend military operations. But if she will not do this, if she persists foolishly and senselessly in carrying on the war; if she prefers war to peace, then, of course, she must have war, vigorous war, until she is compelled to adopt a different line of conduct.

THE TARIFF.*

Mr. President, — It will be denied by none, that this subject is important in various respects. The bill before the Senate is one which seriously affects, for good or for evil, the revenue of the country, and this in time of war. It also affects the interests, occupations, and pursuits of a vast number of the people of the United States. I may add, that the great principle on which it is founded as a revenue bill, that is to say, that hereafter all duties of customs shall be levied by an assessment *ad valorem*, is an entirely new and untried principle in this government. I may say, too, in respect to the principal practical measure of this bill, that its rates of imposition, and its distribution of duties upon the several articles of import, are quite new. And I suppose I may add, without offence to any gentleman or any party, what I think must appear evident to all who will examine the bill, that it is not drawn with remarkable care, either for the purpose of securing a just collection of the revenue itself, or for a proper distribution of taxes and assessments on importations, according to the principle of the bill itself.

Mr. President, it appears strange, but after all we must admit the fact, that the appearance of this bill in the Senate, with a prospect of its passage, has struck the people generally with surprise. It has brought about no small degree of alarm. The public expectation was not prepared for it. I do not say that there had not been enough of previous admonition or indication. I speak of the fact, and I think it must be the conviction of every person who hears me, who has observed the development of public sentiment since the introduction of this measure,

* A Speech delivered in the Senate, on the 25th and 27th of July, 1846, on the Bill "to reduce the Duties on Imports, and for other Purposes."

that the country is surprised, greatly surprised, at any probability that it should receive the final sanction of Congress and the President. Now, Sir, it seems to me that, in this state of things, with such a measure before us, at this advanced season of the year, when there is no pressing necessity for immediate action, the true policy is to postpone its further consideration. If this were a measure to raise money to carry on a war, if it were a measure of taxation, to authorize the contracting of loans, the issue of treasury-notes, or any other measure which had for its object the supply of means to meet the necessities of government, why, then the exigencies of the case might be a very just motive for proceeding to its immediate consideration. But there is no man within the hearing of my voice, and I am happy that there are some within its hearing who are not of this chamber,* who will say that the treasury will not be as competent, the ability of the government as great, its arm as well nerved to prosecute the war in which we are engaged three months longer, if this bill should not pass, as if it should. Therefore, it seems to me to be a case for further consideration; and, at the close of the remarks which I propose to submit to the Senate, I shall move the postponement of the measure till the next session of Congress.

As a revenue measure, I have heretofore stated shortly my opinion of it. I think it must deceive the hopes of those who expect to derive from it that measure of abundant revenue which has been stated. There can be, in my judgment, no such extraordinary increase of importations as the executive government seems to anticipate. It is not in the nature of things. The treasury cannot, in my opinion, be supplied at the ratio which has been stated, and is expected, by any probable, I will say possible, augmentation of importations. But then, Sir, when I say this, I am met by very extraordinary language. Those who are supposed to express the sentiments of the executive say, that that is a question with which Congress has nothing to do, nothing at all! That is a question which the administration alone is to consider! *We* need give ourselves no trouble; the administration will take care of itself! Hear the language of the official organ of the government: —

* Referring to Mr. Secretary Walker, who was present, occupying the seat of one of the Senators.

"The opponents of the administration complain that the law cannot be fairly administered; and so that deficit will be enlarged by frauds. Now, in reply to this, we urge that these are matters in which the opposition may, as we think, very properly leave the administration to look out for its own interests, and take care of itself. If the government measure is about to injure the country, to break up the business of men, and throw their affairs into confusion; or if, again, the measure proposed by the government is in itself oppressive, or unjust, or unequal; or if the country want a tariff for protection, instead of a tariff for revenue, then it is very proper for an opposition, speaking in behalf of the country, to demonstrate such to be the case. But our opposition seems to have a most parental and guardian anxiety lest the administration, if left to itself, should hereafter find itself embarrassed for want of funds."

Why, Sir, who is it that writes, who is it that dictates, who is it that sanctions, such presumption, such arrogance, such folly as this? The Congress of the United States nothing to do with the assessment and collection of the revenue, and all the interests connected with revenue? That altogether an affair of the administration? Sir, Congress, it seems, has appropriated at this session some fifty or sixty millions of dollars for military and naval and other purposes; but it is no affair of Congress whether the treasury shall be competent to fulfil these appropriations! We have a public debt; we have issued treasury-notes; but it is no affair of Congress whether the public credit shall be sustained, its obligations redeemed, or these treasury-notes paid; that 's an affair of the administration only! We may trust to the administration to take care of all these things, while it takes care of itself!

Sir, I have great respect, all degree of personal respect, and proper official respect, for the persons composing the administration; but when I am asked, whether the great interests connected with the revenue of this country, the security of the public faith, the means of fulfilling the appropriations of Congress, the means of maintaining armies and navies in time of war, shall be properly provided for; and when I am asked to trust all these great and momentous interests to the responsibility of a respectable President and a respectable Secretary of the Treasury, I pause; I forbear from that degree of confidence and homage. As a member of Congress, constituting a very humble part of the legislative power, but intrusted, constitutionally, with a participation in the duty of levying taxes to pay the public debt, maintain the army and navy, and provide for the general defence, I must be permitted not to defer my conscientious discharge of that duty to the personal and political responsibility of the members of the administration, one or all, however respectable.

Sir, I have said that, in my opinion, there can be no such augmented income from importations as is relied upon. I will not go into this subject at large. It has been discussed satisfactorily, ably, I will say admirably, by gentlemen on this floor who have preceded me. I refer particularly to the incomparable speech of my friend, a member of the Senate from the State of Maine.*

And now, Mr. President, since my attention has been thus called to that speech, and since the honorable member has reminded us that the period of his service within these walls is about to expire, I take this occasion, even in the Senate, and in his own presence, to say, that his retirement will be a serious loss to this government and this country. He has been sixteen or eighteen years in the public service. He has devoted himself especially to studying and comprehending the revenue and the finances of the country; and he understands that subject as well as any gentleman connected with the government since the days of Crawford and Gallatin. Nay, as well as either of those gentlemen ever understood it. I hope he may yet be, I am glad to know that he will be, with us one session more; that we may have the benefit of his advice and assistance in that financial crisis which, in my judgment, is sure to arise if this war continues, and this bill should pass. And I can only say, that, retire when he will, he will carry with him the good wishes of every member of this body, the general esteem and regard of the country, and the cordial attachment of his friends, political and personal.

Those who indulge the hope of an augmentation to the extent stated, from increase of exportations, seem to forget altogether, what is as common a truth as any other, that there can be such a thing as over-production. But it has happened many times within my experience in public life. There may be produced in England and in this country more manufactured arti-

* Mr. Evans.

cles than both countries together, with all that they can sell to the rest of the world, can consume or dispose of, and that creates what is commonly called a "glut" in the market. Such instances have been frequent. That there is an indefinite power of consumption is necessarily assumed by all those who think that an indefinite extent of importation may be expected. The hon orable member from Maine stated with great truth and propriety, that the augmentation of imports, drawing after it, or supposed to draw after it, an augmentation of exports, went upon the ground of an augmented consumption on both sides. Now be it ever remembered that there is a limit to the power of consumption, both on one side and the other. Over-production has happened frequently. It may happen again, and therefore it is that I hold it to be exceedingly uncertain and fallacious to rely for revenue, in time of war, upon a matter so theoretical, as that we shall have a vast augmentation of importations, with capacity to pay for them, and a desire to consume them. I think that, if such an importation should take place, which I do not expect and cannot anticipate, we could not pay for it. Sir, what are our means of paying for the importations of foreign manufactured articles in this country? They are two. They are our exports, in the first place, and they are the earnings of freight, or of navigation, in the second place. By carrying out our exportations, we earn a freight. By bringing foreign commodities home, we earn a freight. Our ability, therefore, to discharge foreign debt incurred by importations, consists in the extent of our exports, and of our earnings of freight. If there be a demand for means beyond these, it must be met by a drain of the common currency of the world, specie, to the extent that we possess it, or so far as may be necessary. I take that to be the undoubted truth.

Well, now I will say a word upon this matter of expected importations, although I do not intend to go at any length into the subject. I beg the attention of the honorable member at the head of the Committee on Finance, and all others, to a consideration which I hope has been well weighed. Has it been considered, or has it not, what will be the loss of revenue for the ensuing quarter, if this bill pass, by debenture and reëxportation? There is in the country a vast quantity of merchandisc, imported at high duties. After the first day of December next, if this bill passes, all such commodities will come in at a greatly reduced duty. It is now all liable to reëxportation and debenture. Take the case of brandies, (and there are many others mentioned in a memorandum furnished to me from a very respectable source in New York, altogether friendly to the government,) and look to probabilities. Brandies now pay one dollar a gallon, having been purchased at fifty cents per gallon; by the present bill, the duty is reduced to one hundred per cent. *ad valorem;* that is to say, to fifty cents. There is, then, fifty cents to be made on every gallon of brandy in the United States, if it can be carried out of the country now, and brought in on the 1st of December next. Such being the case, it will go to Cuba or to Canada, and be returned when December comes. So of carpets, and many other articles. I beg to ask, Sir, whether the amount of losses on these articles, to be incurred in this way, has been considered. I know that there has been a general estimate of the treasury, as to what will be the amount of revenue under this bill, and under the proposed deductions from the rates of the bill of 1842; but I will ask, whether it has been known, and is now known, that on brandies, and on spices, pimento, and articles of that sort, a loss of two or three millions will occur under this tariff? I have in my hand a calculation, from good authority, showing the probability of such a loss.

But all losses of revenue caused by reduction of duties are to be made up, it is expected, by the increased amount of our importations. I will only say, in answer to this view, that we have no means of paying for this expected increase of importation, but by exports and freight. Now, how are we to increase our exports? Not in manufactured goods, which now constitute a considerable part of our exportations, because this bill is an axe laid to the root of that productive tree. It seeks to strike down at once the main interest which sustains these exportations. It is not, therefore, from manufactured goods that we can expect this increase. Well, then, from what can we expect it? Why, we have some national articles of export; cotton, tobacco, and some others of the nature of raw materials, or raw products. Now does any body suppose that twenty, thirty, or forty millions of augmented exportation of cotton and tobacco can possibly take place? Allow me to put the question to those concerned, those practically concerned, in this great interest. As the product of cotton increases, the tendency in the price is downwards; therefore, *non sequitur*, that, if we produce so many more million pounds of cotton, just in that extent do our means of importation increase. The question is, whether there is any reasonable expectation whatever, that we shall so increase our exports of cotton, as that the value of the cotton exported shall amount to twenty, thirty, or forty millions of dollars additional? Does any man believe it?

We are in our policy, as is supposed, falling into a conformity with the proposition offered in the English Parliament for the repeal of the corn laws. We are greatly to increase, it is said, our exportation of wheat and Indian corn to England. On that point it will be more convenient for me to speak in another part of my remarks. But now as to the freight, which, as I have said, constitutes one of our means of paying for foreign commodities; what chance is there for the increase of freight? Why, the effect of this bill is to diminish freights, and to affect the navigating interests of the United States most seriously, most deeply; and therefore it is that all the ship-owners of the United States, without an exception so far as we hear from them, oppose the bill. It is said to be in favor of free trade and against monopoly. But every man connected with trade is against it; and this leads me to ask, and I ask with earnestness, and hope to receive an answer, At whose request, at whose recommendation, for the promotion of what interest, is this measure introduced? Is it for the importing merchants? They all reject it, to a man. Is it for the owners of the navigation of the country? They remonstrate against it. The whole internal industry of the country opposes it. The shipping interest opposes it. The importing interest opposes it. Who is it that calls for it or proposes it? Who asks for it? Has there been one single petition presented in its favor from any quarter of the country? Has a single individual in the United States come up here and told you that his interest would be protected, promoted, and advanced by the passage of a measure like this? Sir, there is an imperative unity of the public voice the other way, altogether the other way. And when we are told that the public requires this, and that the people require it, we are to understand by the public certain political men, who have adopted the shibboleth of party for the public, and certain persons who have symbols, ensigns, and party flags, for the people; and that 's all. I aver, Sir, that is all. I call upon any man who is within these walls to stand up and tell me what public interest, what portion of men of business; who, amongst all those who earn their living on the sea or on the land, in the field of agriculture, or in the workshop of the artisan; who, amongst them all, comes up here and asks for such a measure as this? Not a man. If there are any persons out doors in favor of this bill, why, then, Sir, I can only say that silence is contagious, and its friends out doors are as mute as its friends in doors.

It does appear to me, then, that we are to make this alteration in our whole system of revenue, we are to bring this great change over all the departments of private life, we are to produce unknown effects on all the industrial classes of the community, upon a mere theory, an assumption, which suggests that all the interests of the country are severely taxed to maintain the manufacturers. I must say, Sir, that the notions which prevail in the Treasury Department and in the executive government appear to me to be almost insane. We were told, at the early part of the session, that the taxed portion of the community paid fifty millions to the manufacturers; it has now got up to ninety-four millions! Mr. President, if intelligent men, of patriotic purposes, good intentions, and great respectability in many walks of life, private and public, ever were seized with a monomania, that disease has taken a strong hold of those who come to us with such statements and sentiments as these. How else can we account for such a zeal for over-importation; a zeal which looks for a paradise on earth, if we can only be surrounded with British manufactures without stint and without count? The love of importation has become a sort of passion with those at the head of affairs; an unthinking, headlong passion. I repeat, Sir, there is no public demand or public desire manifested for this bill. Then, since it is not called for by any exigency in the government, (for nobody will deny that the government will go on quite as well without it, if not better,) since it is not called for by any demand of the people, can we justify ourselves, by any one single fact or consideration, for making all the change in the revenue and the business of the country which this bill evidently must introduce?

In submitting my views on this subject to the Senate, I propose, Sir, in the first place, to consider the bill as a measure for making all duties on imported goods *ad valorem* duties.

Secondly, to consider its effects on certain interests supposed to be protected by former and now existing laws.

Thirdly, I propose to consider its effects upon the navigation and commercial interests of the country, a topic of very deep interest, which has not as yet been fully considered in this discussion.

Fourthly, I propose to consider its effect on the great industrial employments and labor of the people.

I must be permitted to say, with great respect for gentlemen on the other side, that I enter upon this discussion under some disadvantages. We do not hear from them. We hear no defence of this bill. An honorable member from South Carolina* has said, that "the bill vindicates itself." That is so far true as this, that if it do not vindicate itself, it is not vindicated at all. Nobody here stands sponsor for it. Nobody here answers the objections which are urged against it. I see on the opposite side, Sir, gentlemen of the highest character in this country and of the longest experience in this government, gentlemen who have debated questions, great and small, for thirty years, gentlemen properly considered as being amongst those from whom selection is to be made for the highest honors in the gift of the people; and yet on this question, as important, I will undertake to say, as any which has been discussed in Congress from the formation of the Constitution, we hear from those gentlemen not a word, not one single word. They hear us patiently. They appear to be attentive and thoughtful. But they have "charactered" in their memories at least one of the precepts of Polonius, "Give thy thoughts no tongue!" They "give their thoughts no tongue." I trust they will remember the next, "nor any unproportioned thought his act." They are obedient to the instructive adage, "Be checked for silence, but never taxed for speech." They do not mean to be taxed for speech, whatever else they may be taxed for.

Now, it is not for me to put it to those gentlemen, it is a consideration which, if it arise at all, must arise in their own bosoms, whether they can stake their reputation on this meas-

* Mr. McDuffie.

ure, indorsed, as it is, by them, and yet make no defence of it? Are they willing that their votes should go forth without their reasons? That they must decide for themselves. But I may well ask this. We are, in the contemplation of the Constitution, all here holding common counsel. We come hither to confer, to exchange ideas, to be instructed and informed, if we may, by an interchange of sentiment. But we have no consultation, no conference, no exchange of ideas. Our friends on the other side will neither adopt our reasons nor offer their own. We speak, but they remain dumb. But if they see grounds upon which they can vote for this bill with propriety and safety, why will they not state those grounds to us? If, to all that is urged against this measure on our side, answers arise spontaneous in their breasts, why not give them audible expression? We state our reasons; we ask for theirs; we get no reply. We say, having offered our own sentiments:

"Si quid novisti rectius istis,
Candidus imperti; si non, his utere mecum."

But they will not impart their clear perceptions to us. The superior light that illuminates their own breasts, and enables them to see that the bill is safe for the country and proper for the occasion, sheds no rays upon us. They are as silent as they will be fifty years hence.

Mr. President, I now proceed to that branch of the subject to which I propose first to call the attention of the Senate. The principle of this bill is to collect all duties and customs by a universal *ad valorem* assessment; not an equal assessment, it is true, but still a system of *ad valorem* duties, entirely. Now that has not been the practice of the government at any time since its organization. In every administration, from that of Washington down, a contrary system has always prevailed. And the desire of those who have successfully formed and administered the laws in this respect has been, uniformly, to carry the principles of specific duties as far and as fast as circumstances allowed. That I take to have been the policy of the government from the first; and it has been the sentiment of all connected with the government, so far as I know. I ought, per haps to make an exception in the case of Mr. Clay. I said here, the other day, that I had never heard a public man advocate a system of *ad valorem* duties. The newspapers say (perhaps correctly) that I was mistaken; that Mr. Clay made remarks favorable to that idea in the year 1842. I was not in the Senate at that time, and I did not know that such sentiments had ever been expressed by him; and if they are correctly reported, I am very sorry that such was the case.

Mr. Crittenden here said, "Will the Senator pardon me while I interrupt him for a moment, in order to offer an explanation? Mr. Clay's remarks had reference solely to home valuation."

Ah! that explains the whole matter, and it is a great relief to my mind. I am very much obliged to the honorable Senator. Mr. Clay's proposition, then, was, "If you will bring the article here, and value it here, independent of the foreign invoice, why then I will take that system of valuation." Well, that proposition and this are wide as the poles apart. That qualification of the principle makes it sensible, at least, and far less objectionable, as a revenue measure. A home valuation, by judges of our own appointment here, is one thing; but a valuation founded on foreign invoices and the statements of foreign cost, and on foreign oaths, is another and quite a different thing. I am glad to find, therefore, that Mr. Clay's authority stands exactly where it should stand on such a question as this, in strict conformity with his knowledge, his experience, and his character.

Sir, in the same year (1842), the present Secretary of State, in a speech in the Senate, reasoned in the strongest language upon the necessity, the absolute necessity, of carrying the principle of specification in laying duties as far as possible. Standing here in his place, Mr. Buchanan said: —

"I am not only opposed to any uniform scale of *ad valorem*, but to any and all *ad valorem* duties whatever, except where, from the nature of the article imported, it is not possible to subject it to a specific duty. Our own severe experience has taught us a lesson on this subject which we ought not soon to forget. I cannot refrain from adverting to some of my reasons for this opinion.

"Our *ad valorem* system has produced great frauds upon the revenue, whilst it has driven the regular American merchant from the business of importing, and placed it almost exclusively in the hands of the agents of British manufacturers. The American importer produces his invoice to the collector, containing the actual price at which the imports were purchased abroad, and he pays the fair and regular duty upon this invoice. Not so the British agent. The foreign manufacturer, in his invoice, reduces the price of the articles which he intends to import into our country to the lowest possible standard which he thinks will enable them to pass through the custom-house without being seized for fraud. And the business has been hitherto managed with so much ingenuity as generally to escape detection. The consequence is, that the British agent passes the goods of his employer through the custom-house, on the payment of a much lower duty than the fair American merchant is compelled to pay. In this manner he is undersold in the market by the foreigner, and thus is driven from the competition, whilst the public revenue is fraudulently reduced.

"Again, *ad valorem* duties deprive the American manufacturer of nearly all the benefits of incidental protection where it is most required. When the business of the country is depressed, as it is at present, and when the price of foreign articles sinks to far less than their cost, your duty sinks in the same proportion, and you are also deprived of revenue at the time when it is most needed.

"Our own experience, therefore, ought to have convinced us that, whenever it is possible, from the nature of the article, we ought to substitute specific for *ad valorem* duties. These continue to be the same upon the same articles, notwithstanding the constant fluctuations in prices. They afford a steady revenue to the country, and an equally steady incidental protection. When commodities are usually sold by weight or by measure, you may always subject them to a specific duty and this ought always to be done.

"Let us, then, abandon the idea of a uniform horizontal scale of *ad valorem* duties; and whether the duties be high or low, let us return to the ancient practice of the government. Let us adopt wise discriminations; and, whenever this can be done, impose specific duties."

Now let me say, Sir, that it is proper for us, before we go on this new and untried system, to consider the opinions of wise and experienced men who have gone before us.

On the 28th of February, 1817, the House of Representatives, on motion of Mr. Ingham of Pennsylvania, resolved, "that the Secretary of the Treasury be directed to report to Congress, at the next session, such measures as may be necessary for the more effectual execution of the laws for the collection of the duties on imported goods, wares, and merchandise."

In pursuance of this resolution, Mr. Crawford, at that time Secretary of the Treasury, addressed the following circular to the collectors of the customs throughout the country.

"[CIRCULAR.]

"*Treasury Department*, *November* 11*th*, 1817.

"SIR,—The House of Representatives having, by resolution, required the Secretary of the Treasury to report to Congress, at the next session, such measures as may be necessary for the more effectual execution of the laws for the collection of the duties on goods, wares, and merchandise, I have to request that you will inform me whether, in the discharge of your official duties, any important defects have been detected in the existing provisions.

"As it is only by experience that any system of revenue can be brought to approximate to a state of perfection, it is important to collect into a general mass the practical experience of the intelligent officers employed in superintending the immediate execution of the system.

"You will therefore have the goodness, in pointing out existing defects, to present to the department the provisions best calculated, in your opinion, to effect the object contemplated by the national legislature.

"An early attention to this subject is requested.

"I am, respectfully, &c.,

"WM. H. CRAWFORD."

In obedience to the resolution of the 28th of February, 1817, Mr. Crawford, at the next session of Congress, after having recommended various new provisions for the prevention of fraud, said:—

"Whatever may be the reliance which ought to be placed in the efficacy of the foregoing provisions, it is certainly prudent to diminish, as far as practicable, the list of articles paying *ad valorem* duties.

"The best examination which circumstances have permitted has resulted in the conviction that the following list of articles, now paying *ad valorem* duties, may be subjected to specific duties."

Then follows the list, amounting to seventy-one in all. Here, then, in answer to the call of the House, as to what measures ought to be adopted by Congress for the greater security of the public revenue, Mr. Crawford, at the end of a series of suggestions, amounting I think to twenty-two, adds, that, after all, the true course is, to go as far as possible on the line of specific duties.

Having received the foregoing intimation of Mr. Crawford's opinion, Mr. Ingham, on the 20th of April, 1818, moved another resolution as follows:—

"*Resolved*, That the Secretary of the Treasury be directed to report to Congress, at their next session, what further improvement it may be practicable to make in the tariff of duties upon imported goods, wares, and merchandise, by charging specific duties upon articles which are now charged with duties *ad valorem*."

In order to gather materials for the execution of this resolution, Mr. Crawford addressed the following circular to the collectors of the customs.

"[CIRCULAR.]

"*Treasury Department, May 25th*, 1818.

"SIR, — As the revenue of the United States is now exclusively derived from imports and tonnage, and from the sale of the public lands, it is extremely important to render both systems as perfect as the nature of human institutions will permit.

"The certainty with which specific duties are collected gives them a decided advantage over duties laid upon the value of the article. It is probable that the most important change which can be made in the system will be the substitution of specific for *ad valorem* duties upon all articles susceptible of that change.

"Sensible of the importance of this change, the House of Representatives, at the close of the last session, adopted a resolution directing the Secretary of the Treasury to 'report to Congress, at their next session, what further improvement it may be practicable to make in the tariff of duties upon imported goods, wares, and merchandise, by charging specific duties upon articles which are now charged with duties *ad valorem*.'

"In complying with this resolution, I must avail myself of the experience which you have acquired in the discharge of your official duties.

"To place this department, as well as the House of Representatives, in a situation to judge of the propriety of making the change upon such articles as you may suppose to be susceptible of it, I will thank you to present them in the form of the statement annexed [not preserved] to this communication, showing the original cost of the article, the expense of freight, commissions, and insurance, the rate of *ad valorem* duty now paid, and its amount in the form of a specific duty, and the specific duty proposed to be laid upon it.

"I am, respectfully, &c.,

"WM. H. CRAWFORD.

"P. S. Is it practicable to subject *cloths* of wool, cotton, or flax, &c., to specific duties, by combining the number of threads in a given extent with the weight of the cloth? It is asserted by some of the English manufacturers to be entirely practicable by the aid of magnifying-glasses constructed for that object."

At the following session of Congress, Mr. Crawford communicated the results of his inquiry, in the following letter to the Speaker of the House of Representatives.

"*Treasury Department, February 8th*, 1819.

"SIR, — In obedience to a resolution of the House of Representatives of the 20th of April, 1818, directing the Secretary of the Treasury 'to report to Congress, at its next session, what further improvement it may be practicable to make in the tariff of duties upon imported goods, wares, and merchandise, by charging specific duties upon articles which are now charged with duties *ad valorem*,' I have the honor to submit the enclosed list of articles, exhibiting the original cost, the freight, insurance, and commissions, where it has been practicable; the present *ad valorem* duty reduced to a specific form; and the specific duty which it is conceived may be imposed upon them, respectively, consistent with the public interest.

"It is probable that this list may be considerably extended, should the subject receive no final disposition during the present session.

"I have the honor to be your most obedient servant,

"WM. H. CRAWFORD.

"To the Honorable the SPEAKER of the House of Representatives."

The articles in this list amount to one hundred and fifty-five in number.*

Now, Sir, what is the great fact that makes *ad valorem* duties unsafe as a general principle of finance? I must confess my utter consternation when I heard, the other day, the honorable chairman of the Committee of Finance † say, that he did not believe that a case of fraudulent under-valuation had ever been made out! Why, it is the notoriety of a thousand such cases, occurring every year in this government, and in all governments where the system of *ad valorem* duties in any degree prevails, and the value is ascertained upon the invoices or proof from abroad; it is the notoriety of a thousand such cases of fraud, that has led to the adoption of this general rule, and raised it even into a principle, as I have shown. My friend from Maine ‡ must have satisfied the honorable chairman and the Senate, as well as every body else, of the number and the notoriety of the cases of fraudulent under-valuation, because he enumerated instances, and hundreds of instances, in which goods have

* State Papers, Finance, Vol. III. pp. 415, 416.

† Mr. Lewis.

‡ Mr. Evans.

been seized and forfeited for under-valuation. The cases are numberless; and, Sir, since this subject has come up, and since persons out doors have heard the declaration of the honorable chairman, my desk has been laboring under the weight of facts communicated from various portions of the commercial community. I will state only a few, out of many. Here is one, and here is the proof:—

"A merchant orders goods to be shipped from France and entered at New Orleans for the Western trade, with the understanding that he is to have them at the foreign cost, with the duties and charges added.

A shipment was made and forwarded to the purchaser, amounting to	6,829.93 francs.
At the same time the invoice forwarded with the goods to New Orleans was, ...	5,258.00 francs.
Difference, ...	1,571.93 francs.

Or, $ 316.94 out of $ 1,300.94.

"The goods were valued, therefore, in the entry, at $ 316.94 less than they were to the purchaser, and the purchaser was actually charged for the duty on this $ 316.94 as paid to the government, amounting to $ 95.10. Both the government and the purchaser were, therefore, cheated out of that sum.

"This transaction occurred in the spring of 1846, and I send you a copy of the correspondence in which these facts are stated, and not denied; but the French house attempts a roundabout justification for putting the foreign cost to the purchasers at a greater amount than the entry invoice.

"J. D."

This transaction occurred this very year. And here, Sir, is another, communicated by a most highly respectable merchant of my acquaintance.

"*Boston, July 17th*, 1846.

"Dear Sir,—I am informed that a respectable house in this city received an invoice of European goods from a foreign house, the amount of which was about $ 2,000, and that, after entering the goods at the custom-house by the invoices, they received another invoice valuing the same goods at about $ 8,000, with a letter stating that the first invoice was to levy duties by, and the second to sell by.

"The consignee here, who is also an importer, not being willing to be a party to the fraud, deposited both invoices at the custom-house, where they were yesterday.

"I have no doubt of the authority from which I received this information, but I do not wish to be quoted for it.

"I have thought you might be pleased to know this fact, as the fraud is so great, and the perpetrator beyond the reach of any penal statutes of this country.

"Your most obedient servant,

——— ———.

"Hon. Daniel Webster, *Washington.*

"P. S. I hear that Mr. Lamson is the consignee."

Sir, one case more. A highly respectable firm in Boston, Messrs. George H. Gray & Co., have for many years been dealers in hardware, and in the habit of making importations of certain articles from the North of Europe. In these articles they found themselves constantly undersold by the dealers in New York. They could not understand the reason of this for a long time, but last spring the secret came to light. They had ordered a small amount of hardware to be sent to them, and in due time the goods came, and two invoices came with them. In one invoice the cost was stated at nine hundred and fifty-eight thalers, in the other at one thousand four hundred and two. And the letter accompanying these invoices says: "You find herewith duplicate invoices of the greatest part of your order, &c. The original I send by Havre packet. *You also find herewith an invoice made up in the manner like* [that which] the most *importers of your country require, perhaps to save some duty.*"

Now, Sir, these original invoices, the false and the true, and the original letter which I have read, are now in my hand, and any gentleman who feels disposed may look at them. Of course, Messrs. Gray & Co. carried both invoices to the custom-house, because they are honorable merchants, and the duties were assessed on the higher invoice. And these gentlemen were no longer at a loss to account for the low price at which this description of merchandise had been selling in the city of New York.

But now, Sir, take, not a single case, but the results of ong experience. I am about to read a letter, not addressed to me, but placed in my hands, from a gentleman well known, I presume, to both the Senators of New York, and to other members, This letter, I think, will startle the honorable chairman. It must open to his mind quite a new view of things.

"*Troy*, *July* 14*th*, 1846.

"Le Grand Cannon, Esq.:

"Sir, — Agreeably to your wish, I avail myself of this opportunity to give you the benefit of my experience in mercantile and manufacturing business, hoping it may tend to an improvement of the bill, now pending in the Senate, for the collection of duties. I hope members of Congress will have the same views of the probable results which I anticipate; which are, that the system of *ad valorem* duties does give the foreign importer and manufacturer a very undue advantage over the American importer. This will be apparent from my own experience, which I give you annexed.

"My brother and myself were brought up in the town of Manchester, and are well acquainted with the manufacturers and manufacturing. At the age of twenty years it appeared very evident to me that we could finish goods and import goods into New York about ten per cent. lower than the American merchant; and, with this conviction, I agreed to come out to New York and dispose of the goods, and leave my brother to finish and forward the goods. The result was equal to our expectations. We imported our goods ten per cent. cheaper than our competitors, and by the *ad valorem* duties we paid nearly five per cent. less duties; so that, in twenty-two years, we made nearly a million dollars, whilst nearly all the American merchants failed.

"Now, I reason, what has been will be; and should the present tariff bill pass, it will give the foreign manufacturer a decided advantage, and tend to reduce the rate of duties lower than is anticipated. And I cannot avoid expressing my decided opinion in favor of specific duties, as then the foreign manufacturer would pay the same duties as the American importer.

"Benj. Marshall."

Can any man gainsay the truth of this? Is there a merchant, foreign or American, in the United States, who will express any contrariety of opinion? Is there a man, high or low, who denies it? I know of none; I have heard of none. Sir, it has been the experience of this government, always, that the *ad valorem* system is open to innumerable frauds. What is the case with England? In her notions favorable to free trade, has she rushed madly into a scheme of *ad valorem* duties? Sir, a system of *ad valorem* duties is not *free* trade, but *fraudulent* trade. Has England countenanced this? Not at all; on the contrary, on every occasion of a revision of the tariff of England, a constant effort has been made, and progress attained in every case, to augment the number of specific duties, and reduce the number of *ad valorem* duties. A gentleman in the other house* has taken pains, which I have also done, though I believe not quite so thoroughly as he has, to go through the items of the British tariff, and see what proportion of duties in that tariff are *ad valorem* and what are specific. Now, Sir, the result of that examination shows, that at this day, in this British tariff, out of seven hundred and fourteen articles, six hundred and eight are subject to specific duties. Every duty that from its nature could be made specific is made specific. Nothing is placed in the list of *ad valorem* articles but such as seem to be incapable of assessment in any other form.

Well, Sir, how do we stand then? We have the experience of our own government; we have the judgment of those most distinguished in the administration of our affairs; we have the production of proof, on this most important point, in hundreds and hundreds of instances, of the danger of the *ad valorem* mode of assessing duties. What is produced in its favor? Every importer of the United States, without exception, is against it. Sir, the administration has not a mercantile friend from here to Penobscot, so far as appears, that will come forward and give his opinion in favor of this system. I undertake to say there is not one. There may be members of the "little Congress," to which the honorable member from Connecticut† referred some days ago, some subordinate officers about the custom-house, influenced by I know not what considerations, who may be found ready to sustain such a system. That I do not deny. But I say that no importing merchant can be found between Penobscot and Richmond, who will give his opinion in favor of it, if he is an honest man, and one who gets his living by importation himself. Well, then, how are we to decide? Against our own experience? Against these thousands of substantiated facts? Against these cases now blushing with recent fraud? Against the example, not only of the English government, but against that of all the Continental governments? for the Zoll Verein carries its specific duties much further even than England. Against all this what have we? Why, we have the recommendation of the President of the United States and the Secre-

* Mr. Seaman.

† Mr. Niles.

tary of the Treasury; highly respectable persons; respectable in private life, respectable, and I may say eminent, in some walks of public life; but, I must add, neither of them trained in the knowledge of commerce, neither of them having had habits of intercourse with practical men of the cities, or men of mercantile business. And yet here, in the first year of their administration, fresh to the duties thrown upon them, they come out with a recommendation of a vast change; they propose a new system, adverse to all our own experience, hostile to every thing that we have ever learned, different from the experience of every other country on the face of the earth, and which stands solely on the responsibility of their own individual opinions! I do not think that this is a fair balance of authority; and since nobody here will uphold it, since nobody here will defend it, it is fair enough for me to say, with entire respect to the head of the government and the Department of the Treasury, that the preponderance of authority is quite overwhelming the other way.

But now, Mr. President, I come to a part of this act, to which I am exceedingly desirous to call the attention, the serious attention, of gentlemen on both sides of the Senate. The eighth and ninth sections of this bill appear to me to be so extraordinary and so objectionable, that I cannot persuade myself that any gentleman, who will take the trouble of reading and studying them, will hazard the revenue of the country upon such provisions. In the first place, allow me to read the ninth section of the bill. Let me repeat, that the danger in the practical operation of the *ad valorem* system arises from the great probability of under-valuation, fraudulent or otherwise, in the foreign market. The thing to be guarded against, therefore, wherever the *ad valorem* system of duty prevails, is fraudulent or accidental under-valuation; and therefore the law now in operation provides specific and adequate penalties in such cases. If there be any fraudulent under-valuation under the existing law, and it be detected, there is a penalty, there is redress. But if I understand aright the legal effect of these provisions, that effect will be (and to that I wish to call the attention of the legal minds of the Senate) to remove all penalties whatsoever from fraudulent under-valuation; because, perhaps, of the opinion of the chairman, that no such case need be provided for, as he thinks none such ever yet happened! There will not be, as it seems to me, the smallest penalty, or the least check to any amount of under-valuation that any body may choose to make. Here is the ninth section of the bill: —

"Sec. 9. *And be it further enacted*, That if, upon the examination of any parcel, package, or quantity of goods, of which entry has been made, the appraisers of the United States shall be of opinion that the same was undervalued by the owner, importer, consignee, or agent, with the intention of defrauding the revenue of the United States, it shall be lawful for the collector, within whose district the same may be entered, the sanction of the Secretary of the Treasury being first obtained, if, in his opinion, the same shall be advisable, to take such goods for the use of the United States. And such collector shall cause such goods to be sold at public auction, within twenty days from the time of taking the same, in the manner prescribed by law for the sale of unclaimed goods; and the proceeds of such sale shall be placed forthwith in the treasury of the United States; and such collector is hereby authorized to pay out of the accruing revenue, to the owner, importer, consignee, or agent of the goods so taken, the value thereof as declared in the entry, and five *per centum* upon such amount in addition thereto; and the said collector shall render to the Secretary of the Treasury, with his accounts of the customs, a statement showing the amount of moneys so paid, the amount of duties chargeable on the goods so taken, and the amount of proceeds paid into the treasury; and this section shall be in force until the first of July, eighteen hundred and forty-eight, unless otherwise directed by Congress."

Sir, there never was such a provision as that on the face of the earth! I pray gentlemen to look to it. Here is a man who comes with a *fraudulent invoice;* it is proved to be fraudulent; the present law punishes him by forfeiting the goods; but what does this law say? It says that the collector may take the goods, sell them, put the proceeds into the treasury, but shall pay him the cost, and five per cent. over! So that the *fraudulent* importer, if found out, shall yet be made safe against loss! He may yet sell his goods to the United States for cost, and five per cent. profit. Now, I am guilty of no misrepresentation. Here are the written words. It is exactly what I state. He comes with his goods, and the collector charges him with a fraudulent invoice. "Very well," he says, "if you say so, take the goods and give me what I allege they cost, with five per cent.

profit. Make the most of it!" Whether he made a good importation or a bad one, the law very kindly provides him with a way to get rid of his goods. There is not a particle of penalty, not a particle of inconvenience to be suffered by him. It is all considerate kindness for one proved guilty of a fraud! On general principles, this section would seem to supersede and abrogate all previously existing provisions, because the enactment is made in relation to the same subject-matter, and covers the cases covered by existing laws, and is nowhere said to be additional, or cumulative; but, on the contrary, the twelfth section declares that all previous laws repugnant to the provisions of this act shall be repealed.

But if this be regarded as a new provision, not intended to repeal existing laws, but designed merely to give a new power to the collector or the Secretary, then it is still more objectionable, because, if viewed in that light, it gives a dispensing power, or an unlimited power of favoritism. It enables the Secretary to excuse, and even to reward, one fraudulent importer, while others, not more fraudulent, forfeit their goods. It seems to be thought that the Secretary may well show favor and kindness in particular cases, though deliberate fraud has been actually perpetrated. This is exactly in the spirit of the serving-man's address to Mr. Justice Shallow:—

"I grant your worship that he is a knave, Sir; but yet, God forbid, Sir, but a knave should have some countenance at his friend's request. An honest man, Sir, is able to speak for himself, when a knave is not. I have served your worship, truly, Sir, this eight years, and if I cannot once or twice in a quarter bear out a knave against an honest man, I have but a very little credit with your worship. The knave is mine honest friend, Sir; therefore, I beseech your worship, let him be countenanced."

Mr. Cameron here rose, and was understood to say, that he really could hardly suppose that such a blunder had been committed in passing the bill. He wished to hear the section again.

I will read it again, "with discretion and due emphasis." Well, now, (continued Mr. W., after reading the section,) the fraudulent importer may himself purchase the goods at auction. He may perhaps buy them at fifty per cent., and make the government pay the full amount! And besides, he thus evades the duty altogether. He gets his goods in free, and has a certainty of being paid all that he rates them at, and five per cent. besides. Now, Sir, our predecessors did not leave the matter in that state. The provision in the seventeenth section of the act of 1842, and the nineteenth section of the same act, are the provisions under existing laws for prevention of under-valuation, in addition to the general penalty of forfeiture, when invoiced frauduleutly.

The eighth section of the bill is still more remarkable. I do not mean to say that there is any purpose in the Treasury Department, or any officer of the government, to give facilities to fraudulent importations. They are not capable of that. Yet I say that this eighth section is open to much fraudulent abuse. See what it is: —

"Sec. 8. *And be it further enacted*, That it shall be lawful for the owner, consignee, or agent of imports which have been actually purchased, on entry of the same, to make such addition in the entry to the cost or value given in the invoice, as in his opinion may raise the same to the true market value of such imports in the principal markets of the country whence the importation shall have been made, or in which the goods imported shall have been originally manufactured or produced, as the case may be; and to add thereto all costs and charges which, under existing laws, would form part of the true value at the port where the same may be entered, upon which the duties should be assessed. And it shall be the duty of the collector within whose district the same may be imported or entered, to cause the dutiable value of such imports to be appraised, estimated, and ascertained in accordance with the provisions of existing laws; and if the appraised value thereof shall exceed by ten *per centum* or more the value so declared on the entry, then, in addition to the duties imposed by law on the same, there shall be levied, collected, and paid a duty of twenty *per centum ad valorem* on such appraised value: *Provided*, nevertheless, that under no circumstances shall the duty be assessed upon an amount less than the invoice value, any law of Congress to the contrary notwithstanding."

By statute of long standing, fraudulent invoices for under-valuation are declared to be grounds of forfeiture of the goods, and the seventeenth section of the law of 1842 goes further, and imposes a personal penalty. Its provision is this: —

"*Provided also*, That in all cases when the actual value to be appraised, estimated, and ascertained, as hereinbefore stated, of any goods, wares, and merchandise imported into the United States, and subject to any *ad valorem* duty, or whereon the duty is regulated by, or directed to be imposed or levied on, the value of the square yard, or other parcel or quantity thereof, shall exceed by ten *per centum*, or more, the invoice value, then, in addition to the duty imposed by law on the same, there shall be levied and collected on the same goods, wares, and merchandise fifty *per centum* of the duty imposed on the same, when fairly invoiced."

Now, the object of the eighth section in this bill appears to be to shield the honest importer from the penalties of under-valuation, where he has actually purchased the goods at a price below the market value; and it permits him, in his entry, to add so much to the value given in the invoice, as, in his opinion, will raise the goods to the market value in the country from which they were imported. Yet see how open to abuse. If the value put upon the goods by the appraisers shall exceed by ten per cent. the value so declared by the importer in the entry, then the goods shall be liable to an additional duty of twenty per cent. *ad valorem*. This is a provision for an entry of goods at a valuation which differs from the invoice. It prescribes no *oath* for the importer to take in regard to the addition which he proposes to make; and in all the revenue laws I can find no oath which a collector is authorized to administer, and which is applicable to such a case. Here is opened a door for fraud, if a purpose to commit fraud exists. An importer may require his foreign correspondents to send him half a dozen invoices of the same goods, graduated all along down to seventy-five per cent. below their value; and on arrival he will use that invoice which shall be ten, twenty, or thirty per cent., or more, under the true value, according to circumstances. If he find the appraisers particularly sharp as to such articles as his, he will add something to the invoice; and, according to this section, if he add enough to bring the goods up within ten per cent. of the value as fixed by the appraisers, he escapes all punishment. Suppose the appraisers find that the goods are undervalued only nine per cent., then they are to be entered at their value, and he escapes all risk. At the same time, if the appraisers let the invoice pass at his own valuation, he saves the duty on nine per cent. of the cost of the goods. Within the limit, therefore, of ten per cent. he can play a fraudulent part with impunity.

Under existing laws he must swear that the invoice produced

is that under which the goods were purchased, that it is the true invoice, and that he has no other. But even now a fraudulent importer has great facilities. He may direct his correspondent abroad to send out such an invoice of such goods, at such a price. Well, with that he goes to the custom-house. There are no sharper eyes in the world than those of the men who bring in goods with fraudulent intent. A man intending to defraud the custom-house, gets an invoice of goods; every body says, and the appraisers say, "Well, this is enormous; these goods could not have cost so little as that!" And the collector meditates a seizure. The moment that this is apprehended, the importer comes again, and says, "O, I know how it must have been! It is all a mistake! Here is the true invoice. My correspondent in Paris made a mistake; he corrected it the very next week, and here is the true invoice." Such cases have occurred; and need I say, that, if the goods had not been arrested in their progress, this second invoice never would have appeared. A man may send a false invoice to-day to his consignee in New York, and the New York merchant may go to the custom-house and swear that that is a true invoice, and that he has received no other; and he may enter his goods and get a permit; but before the sale by auction another invoice arrives; and, as happened in the case in Boston to which I alluded, there is one invoice to enter by, and another to sell by. And the importer has time to come in with his subsequent invoice, if threatened with seizure, to relieve himself of all inconveniences from having made, and being shown to have made, a fraudulent undervaluation.

I leave this part of the case by presenting, in behalf and in the name of the whole American importing community, foreign and domestic, of any reputation at all, in behalf of every American importing merchant, in behalf of that whole body of respectable foreign merchants, French, German, and English, who come and reside here, and import goods from their respective countries and elsewhere, under the protection of our laws; in their behalf, and in behalf of every man of them, so far as I have heard, I present their opinions against the extension of the *ad valorem* system. And I would admonish gentlemen, most seriously, to consider whether the objections which I have now urged are not respectable; whether the opinions I have quoted are not respectable; and whether, after all, they are willing, unnecessarily, suddenly, with no other recommendation than that to which I have alluded, to take a step in the dark, and to place the whole income and means of supplying the treasury upon the untried system of *ad valorem* duties.

And now, Sir, with the leave of the Senate, I shall proceed to consider the effects of this bill upon some of those interests which have been regarded as protected interests.

I shall not argue at length the question, whether the government has committed itself to maintain interests that have grown up under laws such as have been passed for thirty years back. I will not argue the question, whether, looking to the policy indicated by the laws of 1789, 1817, 1824, 1828, 1832, and 1842, there has been ground for the industrious and enterprising people of the United States, engaged in home pursuits, to expect government protection for internal industry. The question is, Do these laws, or do they not, from 1789 till the present time, constantly show and maintain a purpose, a policy, which might naturally induce men to invest property in manufactures, and to commit themselves to those pursuits in life? Without lengthened argument, I shall take this for granted.

But, Sir, before I proceed further with this part of the case, I will take notice of what appears, latterly, to be an attempt, by the republication of opinions and expressions, arguments and speeches of mine, at an earlier and later period of life, to found against me a charge of inconsistency on this subject of the protective policy of the country. Mr. President, if it be an inconsistency to hold an opinion upon a subject at one time and in one state of circumstances, and to hold a different opinion upon the same subject at another time and in a different state of circumstances, I admit the charge. Nay, Sir, I will go further; and in regard to questions which, from their nature, do not depend upon circumstances for their true and just solution, I mean constitutional questions, if it be an inconsistency to hold an opinion to-day, even upon such a question, and on that same question to hold a different opinion a quarter of a century afterwards, upon a more comprehensive view of the whole subject, with a more thorough investigation into the original purposes and objects of that Constitution, and especially after a more thorough exposition of those objects and purposes by those who framed it, and have been trusted to administer it, I should not shrink even from that imputation. I hope I know more of the Constitution of my country than I did when I was twenty years old. I hope I have contemplated its great objects more broadly. I hope I have read with deeper interest the sentiments of the great men who framed it. I hope I have studied with more care the condition of the country when the convention assembled to form it. And yet I do not know that I have much to retract or to change on these points.

But, Sir, I am of the opinion of a very eminent person, who had occasion, not long since, to speak of this topic in another place. Inconsistencies of opinion, arising from changes of circumstances, are often justifiable. But there is one sort of inconsistency which is culpable. It is the inconsistency between a man's conviction and his vote; between his conscience and his conduct. No man shall ever charge me with an inconsistency like that. And now, Sir, allow me to say, that I am quite indifferent, or rather thankful, to those conductors of the public press who think they cannot do better than now and then to spread my poor opinions before the public.

I have said many times, and it is true, that, up to the year 1824, the people of that part of the country to which I belong, being addicted to commerce, having been successful in commerce, their capital being very much engaged in commerce, were averse to entering upon a system of manufacturing operations. Every member in Congress from the State of Massachusetts, with the exception, I think, of one, voted against the act of 1824. But what were we to do? Were we not bound, after 1817 and 1824, to consider that the policy of the country was settled, had become settled, as a policy, to protect the domestic industry of the country by solemn laws? The leading speech* which ushered in the act of 1824 was called a speech for the "American System." The bill was carried principally by the Middle States. Pennsylvania and New York would have it so; and what were we to do? Were we to stand aloof from the occupations which others were pursuing around us? Were we to pick clean teeth on a constitutional doubt which a majority

* That of Mr. Clay.

in the councils of the nation had overruled? No, Sir; we had no option. All that was left us was to fall in with the settled policy of the country; because, if any thing can ever settle the policy of the country, or if any thing can ever settle the practical construction of the Constitution of the country, it must be these repeated decisions of Congress, and enactments of successive laws conformable to these decisions. New England, then, did fall in. She went into manufacturing operations, not from original choice, but from the necessity of the circumstances in which the legislation of the country had placed her. And, for one, I resolved then, and have acted upon the resolution ever since, that, having compelled the Eastern States to go into these pursuits for a livelihood, the country was bound to fulfil the just expectations which it had inspired.

Now, before I go into a consideration of the various articles intended to be protected, and the effect of the law upon the interests connected with these manufactures, I wish to make a remark, which is little more than a repetition, in general terms, of what was said by the honorable member from Connecticut the other day. It is the strangest anomaly that ever was seen in any act of legislation, that there is a uniform tendency in this measure to tax the raw material higher than the manufactured article. It allows bringing in cordage, for instance, for the use of the shipping interest of the United States, at a less rate of duty than you can bring in the raw material. Of course, it is prohibitory of internal labor. It is prohibitory of the internal manufacture; and not in that case only, but in a great many others, as I shall show you.

There seems to be a sedulous purpose of hostility to the manufacturing interests. I speak of the tenor and tendency, and the general spirit of this bill. It does prefer, by its enactments, and in its consequences, foreign labor to domestic labor. It does encourage the labor of foreign artisans over and above, and in preference to, the labor of our own artisans here in the United States. I aver it, and I am going to prove it. Now, if that is made out, is there a man in this chamber who will vote for this bill? And yet we are told from other quarters, that this is a bill of peace, that it will settle a vexed question. Depend upon it, it will settle nothing. It is calculated to raise a degree, I had almost said of resentment, at all events of surprise and indignation, not in one man's breast, but in the breasts of a million of people, now earning their bread, as they think, under laws, and assurances that these laws shall be continued, which enable them to import the raw material and work upon it, and bring their labor into market, as advantageously as the labor of the foreign mechanic. Call you that a bill of peace which disturbs all these expectations? It is not peace; it is any thing but peace.

Sir, there is an article, the growth of which is very interesting to the Western States, being well suited to the fertility of their soil. It is hemp. The manufacture of that article into cordage is essential to the navigating interests of the United States. This is one of the cases which I have mentioned, and with reference to which I wish to read several letters from highly respectable gentlemen.

The first letter is from Mr. Isaac P. Davis, of Boston, who has been a rope-maker for forty years, and whose opinion, on this and other subjects, is entitled to respect.

"*Boston*, *July* 16.

"MY DEAR SIR,—I send you a paper which contains an article on hemp and cordage, by a writer who appears to understand the subject.

"I inclose a statement of the average cost of hemp and cordage in Russia for the last five years; also, the freight to the United States; and the cost of freight for a ton of hemp from Missouri, Kentucky, and Indiana. You will see the advantages Russia cordage will have in our market over our own manufacture.

"Foreign cordage also has the advantage of drawback on shipment to another market. We consume six thousand barrels of tar in the manufacture. Yours truly,

"I. P. DAVIS."

The following is the statement alluded to above:—

Cost of a ton of hemp in Russia, including charges,		$140
Freight per ton,		12
		$152
Cost of a ton of cordage,	$150	
Freight per ton,	8	
		$158

The above are the average prices for five years.

Freight of a ton of hemp from Missouri, Kentucky, or Indiana to Boston,	$21

I add two other important letters, from very respectable persons in the same city.

"*Boston*, *July* 15, 1846.

"SIR, — We wish to call your particular attention to the interest of the cordage manufacture, in settling the tariff question now before the Senate. The bill, as passed by the House, is destructive to the interest of the American, and grants a bounty to the foreign manufacturer of twenty or twenty-five per cent., viz.: —

The difference of duty more on hemp than cordage, . .	5 per cent.
The difference of foreign shipping charges, ...	10 "
The difference of freight more, being charged on hemp, on account of its bulk, than cordage, ...	10 "
Making	25 per cent.

"The foreign manufacturer has another advantage over the domestic, in being enabled to deposit in warehouse, and supply the home market when the price will answer, to secure the export demand, by selling at that price. We wish to have justice at the hands of the government, if not protection, and think a specific duty should be laid on cordage that should be equal to at least twenty per cent. over the duty on hemp, besides the extra expense of importing hemp over cordage.

"And we further think it decidedly for the interest of the country, and of the growers of hemp in this country.

"The foreigner will supply cordage under the House bill which will prevent the produce of hemp finding a market here, as the expense of getting American hemp from the place of raising is now over fifty per cent. of the first cost, while cordage can be brought from Russia, exclusive of duty, at from five to seven per cent.

"We think the domestic manufacturer should be allowed a drawback on cordage made from foreign hemp (which has paid a duty) when exported; or, if this cannot be done, the drawback should not be allowed to the importer of foreign cordage on exportation.

"Soliciting your attention to the foregoing, we are, very respectfully, your obedient servants.

"SEWALL & DAY.

"HON. DANIEL WEBSTER."

"*Boston*, *July* 17, 1846.

"DEAR SIR, — It appears to me so extraordinary that so many of our legislators at Washington cannot, or will not, see the injurious effects the proposed tariff will have throughout our country, if adopted, that I cannot refrain from expressing to you my opinion in regard to it, and particularly to the western sections of the country, for instance, where so much hemp is produced. If this *ad valorem* tariff passes, it will bring Russia again in competition with them; whereas, at the present time, but very little Russian hemp is wanted, and our rope-makers are now using the American hemp, almost entirely, for tarred cordage. If the tariff should be adopted by Congress, we shall be able to import Russian tarred cordage cheaper than we can import the same weight in hemp, inasmuch as there is an export duty on hemp in Russia, and many expenses in preparing it to pass inspection if imported, while on cordage there is no export duty of any consequence, a mere trifle, and the yarns are spun in the interior in winter at a cheap rate, of mixed qualities of hemp, not inspected, sent to market on bobbins, from which the rope-makers take the yarns and tar and twist them into ropes of various sizes for exportation, and cheaper than they can ship the same weight in hemp. Thus you see that this tariff will not only affect the Western hemp-growers very injuriously, but it will in a great degree destroy the manufacture of hemp in this country.

"There are many other articles I could mention that would be a general injury to the country by an *ad valorem* tariff, but you, no doubt, are aware of it, and therefore I desist from further observations, excepting that it is astonishing and extraordinary that the government at Washington will not profit by the experience and experiments of the governments of Europe, who have tried *ad valorem* tariffs, and find they do not answer at all, and have resorted to specific tariffs on almost every thing of importance.

"It is now so late in the season, and your duties have been so arduous, that I presume you will not call the attention of Congress to the injurious effects these *reciprocal* treaties have on the commerce of this country.

"I remain, dear Sir, your obedient servant,

"James Harris.

"Hon. Daniel Webster."

What answer is to be made to all this? Is it the result of intention, or of culpable ignorance? Are those who framed this bill determined, of purpose, to break down the manufactures of the country, or are they only indifferent and utterly reckless in all that relates to them?

There is, Sir, another article, very important to the shipping interest, as well as the manufacturing interest, and grown into importance lately, the fate of which is still more striking. Formerly it was not of much consequence, but lately it has become so. It is the article of linseed and of linseed oil. Now, this is a case of very great interest. So important is it, that I shall read to the Senate letters from mercantile men, who say that, if this bill passes, one third of all the trade and shipping between the United States and Calcutta will be cut off and destroyed. Let us see how that stands. Years ago, and when I first remember to have been conversant with commercial men, and was living in the midst of a navigating people, there was a considerable export of the article of flaxseed from the United States to Ireland and England. It is well known that Ireland, a great seat of the linen manufacturers, a country that raises and manufactures so much flax, does not raise its own flaxseed; and the reason of that is, I suppose, that the flax must be pulled before the seed has ripened; if not, the fibre becomes so hard that it does not answer the purpose of fine manufacture, and can be used only for the coarser fabrics. In our Middle and Northern States flax is raised for both purposes. It is suffered to ripen, and the seed is saved and exported to Ireland, or was formerly, whilst the fibre is manufactured into those coarse goods which answer for household purposes, and the flax was spun by our mothers and sisters, and their assistants, in times past. But now this is greatly changed. Linseed oil has become an article of great importance and vastly extensive use. It is manufactured in this country chiefly from linseed imported from abroad, and, as I suppose, mainly in that immature state in which it would not vegetate. Here it is used for the manufacture of linseed oil, and has become a very important matter, not only to the manufacturers of the article here, who have invested large sums of money in the erection of mills, but also to the navigating interest, as touching very seriously the employment of all those vessels of the United States which carry on the trade between us and India. In the first place, let me give you a statement in respect to the establishments for the manufacture of this article.

At the last census, there were eight hundred and forty linseed-oil mills in the United States, and they now number from one thousand to twelve hundred, moved by water or steam.

They consume from twenty bushels of seed daily up to eight hundred, according to their capacity. Taking the daily consumption at only ten bushels each, they will consume in a year three millions of bushels. The whole annual export of flaxseed does not exceed thirty thousand bushels (that is, the matured seed to Ireland), which is only one bushel out of every *hundred* of the crop, the remaining ninety-nine bushels being consumed in making oil.

Present duty on linseed oil, per gallon, ...	25 cents.
Proposed duty, 20 per cent. *ad valorem*, or only, per gallon,	7 "
Being a reduction of	18 cents.

Present import of linseed oil, 200,000 gallons, duty 25 cents,	$ 50,000
Same import, at proposed rate of 7 cents, ...	14,000
Loss in duty, ...	$ 36,000

It will require an increased import of five hundred thousand gallons of oil to get the same amount of duty that we now do, if the duty is reduced as proposed; and this can only be done by destroying our own mills, and stopping the growth of seed in this country. The imports of linseed are about four hundred thousand bushels, paying a freight of one hundred and twenty thousand dollars. The cake is shipped to England, and pays a freight of forty thousand dollars per annum to our packet-ships.

A gentleman engaged in this manufacture writes to me thus: —

"From our own mill we send forty thousand barrels of cake to London yearly.

"England imports three and a half millions of bushels of *linseed entirely free of duty*. She imposes a prohibitory duty on linseed oil, and does not import a single gallon. She has capital, machinery, coals, and wages much cheaper than ourselves, and her millers get double the price for their oil-cake that ours do.

"We consume in our mill nine hundred tons of coals yearly.

"No monopoly is asked or expected; but our opinion is, that a duty of twelve and a half or fifteen cents a gallon on oil, in lieu of the present rate of twenty-five cents, with seed free or at five cents duty, will be for the best interests of our farmers, millers, and consumers, and give more revenue than the rates proposed by Mr. McKay in his new bill."

See, then, with what care this interest is protected by the bill on our table! I may not stop here. I have alluded to the effect of this measure upon the commerce and the freight of the country. Here is a letter from one of the most respectable merchants in Boston, formerly a sea-captain.

"*Boston, July* 13, 1846.

"DEAR SIR, — This will introduce to you Mr. N. Sturtevant, a respectable merchant of this place, largely interested in the manufacture of oil from linseed.

"If the tariff passes in the shape it came from the House of Representatives, it will destroy more than one third of our Calcutta trade.

"With great respect, your obedient servant,

"BENJAMIN RICH.

"HON. DANIEL WEBSTER."

And here is another letter, from a mercantile friend of mine in the same city.

"*Boston, July* 13, 1846.

"SIR, — I beg leave to introduce to your acquaintance the bearer of the present, Mr. Noah Sturtevant, one of our largest linseed-oil manufacturers, and who proceeds to Washington upon business relating to the new tariff as affecting the articles of linseed and linseed oil.

"A large proportion of the tonnage now employed in the Calcutta trade with this country is occupied in carrying linseed. With the proposed change in the tariff upon this article, this trade would be broken up.

"Referring to Mr. Sturtevant for further particulars, I remain, Sir, with much respect, your very obedient servant.

"ROBERT G. SHAW.

"HON. DANIEL WEBSTER, *in Washington*."

But, Mr. President, there is a curious specimen of legislative history connected with the duty laid on linseed by this bill. In the twenty per cent. schedule is "flaxseed"; in the ten per cent. schedule is "hempseed, linseed, rapeseed." Originally it stood "flaxseed, linseed, hempseed, rapeseed," in the ten per cent. schedule. Opposition was made to this in the other house, on the ground that flaxseed was not sufficiently protected. *Flaxseed* was therefore carried into the twenty per cent. schedule, leaving its synonyme *linseed* behind in the lower schedule!

I proceed, Sir, to another article in regard to which the advantage is given against the American manufacturer. It is copper. I presented this subject to the consideration of the Senate the other day, and will do no more now than read the statement of persons most concerned in it in the United States, as embodied in their petition to the Senate.

"The undersigned, manufacturers of copper, and others interested in the trade to countries whence this article is obtained, having seen that a bill is now before Congress imposing a duty of five per cent. on raw copper, whilst copper sheathing is to be admitted free, beg leave to submit to your consideration a few remarks upon the effect and impolicy of the proposed measure.

"In order to present the subject in a clear and intelligible manner, we shall endeavor to show the origin of the copper used in the United States, the nature of the trade by which the raw material is obtained, the effect the proposed duty will have upon this trade, and its disastrous consequences upon the manufacturing interests of the country."

Do you see, Sir, you tax the raw material, and let England send in her manufactured article free? This presses on every interest. If our people cannot manufacture raw copper, they cannot import it. We lose the freight of it in that degree, and of course the employment of our ships. This, accordingly, affects the manufacturer of copper here, affects the exports, and affects directly the employment of our ships. For what? Sir, for what purpose? The petition goes on:—

"The consumption of copper in the United States is about thirteen millions of pounds annually. It is obtained,—

	Pounds.
From Chili, in pigs, ...	6,500,000
From England, in sheets, ...	3,500,000
From England, in cakes, ...	500,000
From mines in the United States, . . .	500,000
Old copper, from various sources, . . .	1,500,000
In all, ...	12,500,000

"It will be seen that nearly all the pig or raw copper imported is obtained from Chili (erroneously called *Peruvian copper* in this country), and that England supplies us, in refined copper and copper sheathing, with more than one fourth of all the copper consumed in the United States.

"The trade between the United States and the west coast of South America, embracing Chili, Bolivia, and Peru, is of the annual value of about one million five hundred thousand dollars. The principal articles of export are domestic cottons. Of these, ten or twelve millions of yards are sent annually, constituting more than half the entire value of all our exports to those countries; and as the value of the raw copper obtained in return bears the same relative proportion to all our imports thence, it may be truly said that we *exchange*, in our trade with Chili, ten or twelve millions of yards of cottons for six or seven millions of pounds of copper.

"One of the causes, perhaps the chief cause, enabling us to compete with the English cotton manufacturers in that market has been, that we have made our principal returns in copper, and they have made theirs in the precious metals, usually the least profitable articles of commerce, as is well known to all practical merchants. Without domestic cottons for outward, and without copper for return cargoes, this trade must be abandoned. In the bill referred to, it is proposed to levy a duty of five per cent. on raw copper, and to admit copper sheathing free. Under the present law, where both are free of duty, the American manufacturer has to contend, unaided by government, against the low price of labor, abundance of capital, and cheapness of fuel, enjoyed by the English and Welsh manufacturer. The large imports of copper sheathing from England show the competition against which we contend, and against which we have hitherto sustained ourselves without any protective duty on this important article. But if, in addition to the advantages already enjoyed in England and Wales, the raw material may be taxed here, and copper sheathing be admitted free, we are in effect called upon to pay a bounty to the foreign manufacturer equivalent to the duty levied on the raw material. England now supplies us with more than half the copper sheathing we require; but with this new advantage of five per cent. she will furnish all.

"A large portion of the copper we import from England is made from ores or pig copper obtained in Chili; and if the proposed duty on raw copper be exacted, nearly all that we now get from Chili will be sent to England, and, being there manufactured into sheathing, will be sent to the United States; thus giving to English vessels the benefit of transporting, and to English manufacturers the profits of refining and rolling the raw material, besides depriving us of our best market for the sale or exchange of our domestic cottons.

"It is estimated that the capital now invested in copper manufactures in the United States is about one million and a half of dollars, embracing five refining and rolling mills, and employing a large number of workmen. Hitherto these establishments have struggled, unaided by government, against the superior advantages of English and Welsh manufacturers; and we now only ask for them a continuance of the same freedom of competition. We ask no privileges or special protection. If the bill referred to become a law, these must be closed, or continued under ruinous disadvantages.

"The navigating interests thank you for competition, but let it be a state of competition. Do not proceed in carrying out duties in such sort as to put down the whole American product, using none but the manufactures of England for the sheathing of your vessels."

I will read another paragraph from the petition:—

"We have thus shown what will be the effects of the proposed duty; the impolicy of the principle involved is not less obvious. Without entering into the hackneyed question of free trade and protective duties, we may freely aver that it is not the intention of Congress to tax the citizens of the United States for the benefit of foreigners; and yet such is the operation of this duty. We tax a raw material, which we want for manufacturing purposes, and we charge our manufacturers with that tax, if at the same time we allow foreigners to manufacture that material and send it to us free of duty. This is a bounty to foreigners, and a tax upon ourselves. What would be said of the policy of England, were she to tax raw cotton and admit cotton manufactures free of duty?"

There is another article, white-lead, with respect to which the same policy is observed; and on that subject I have received the following statements from a very intelligent and respectable quarter in New York:—

"The capital invested in the manufacture of white-lead in the United States amounts to upwards of two million three hundred and fifty thousand dollars. About one thousand men as laborers are employed in the business, and forty-two million pounds, or six hundred thousand pigs, of lead, all of which is the produce of the Missouri and Illinois mines, in the fabric. The present duty is four cents per pound, the proposed duty is twenty per cent., which will be equal to one cent, or at most to one cent and one fifth, per pound. The white-lead manufactured in the United States is *not inferior* to that of any other country, and has attained its present goodness within the last three years, owing principally to the encouragement given by the tariff of 1842, which has induced the investment of large additional capital in the manufacture of the article, thereby creating great competition amongst the manufacturers.

"The price of pure lead in oil in 1820, at which time there were but two factories in the country, was fourteen cents per pound. Since that time it has been gradually declining in price, and is now worth only six and a half cents.

"Perhaps there is no article imported into this country in favor of which there is so strong a prejudice as that of English white-lead; for, notwithstanding the duty of four cents, considerable quantities are yearly imported and sold at a profit to the English manufacturer. If, with the present duty, the American manufacturer can merely sustain himself against the prejudice existing in favor of the foreign article, should the duty be reduced to one cent per pound, what but total ruin must to him be the consequence?

"We think the foregoing facts could not have been known to the framers of the bill now before the Senate, and that the Senate will see the justice of transferring it to the schedule of articles under the *forty*, or at least the *thirty* per cent. duty."

Mr. President, there is one manufacture just beginning amongst us, of such an interesting character to the labor of the country, and the agricultural interests, that I beg to call the particular attention of the Senate to it. It is that article which they call *mousseline de laine*, a woollen fabric just commenced in this country, and whose early life is to be crushed by this bill. It has been a matter of immense import for some years past. Now I wish to state the facts connected with one of the establishments just set up for the manufacture of this article. There was no manufacture of this article before the tariff of 1842. After the tariff of 1842 was enacted, it began in several of the Middle and Eastern States. Among the rest, within a few months, or at least within the year, a manufactory of this kind has been attempted to be established at Manchester, New Hampshire, near the residence of my honorable friend from that State, on my right.* It proceeds on the basis of a large capital. Those concerned ask for no new protection. They can maintain themselves under the tariff of 1842. But what will be the consequence, if this mischievous measure is to prevail? I have a statement from the agent conducting that establishment, an intelligent and respectable gentleman, every way worthy of credit and reliance; and I beg leave to refer to it, for the especial consideration of the gentlemen from Ohio and Pennsylvania. He says that, before there was any expectation that this bill would pass, they had sent agents into Ohio and the western part of Pennsylvania to buy wool; that they proposed to buy annually from three hundred thousand to five hundred thousand dollars worth of wool in those States, and perhaps in the western part of New York. I suppose that is of some importance to the

* Mr. Cilley.

wool-growers of Ohio, Pennsylvania, and New York. When the news reached New Hampshire that this bill, as it now stands here, had passed the House of Representatives, these agents were directed not to buy another pound; and they never will buy another pound until they know that this bill cannot pass. This is an eminent instance in which home manufactures aid agriculture. It well deserves the attention of all wool-growers. When will the Western farmers sell as much wheat annually to England, as shall equal their loss, by this bill, in the article of wool alone?

Mr. President, here is another petition, or a paper in the form of a petition, respecting another raw material. It furnishes another small, but striking exemplification of the nature of the bill. Hear what the persons concerned in this manufacture say: —

"*New York, July* 13, 1846.

"Dear Sir, — The subscribers, manufacturers of brimstone, respectfully ask the liberty to call your attention to the following facts.

"About four years ago, they commenced the manufacture or refining of brimstone. Previous to that time, all the brimstone used in making gunpowder, and for other purposes, in this country, was imported from Europe, chiefly from France and England, and the price was about seventy-five dollars a ton.

"Since the introduction of the manufacture as above mentioned, the price has been very much reduced, and is now, and has been for more than a year past, a fraction less than forty dollars a ton.

"The tariff of 1842 admits crude brimstone free of duty, and levies a duty of twenty-five per cent. upon refined. Mr. McKay's bill lays a duty of fifteen per cent. on crude, and only twenty per cent. upon refined brimstone.

"The quantity of crude imported into the country is not large, and the amount of revenue which can be raised from it will be more than counterbalanced by the increased price which government will be obliged to pay for its annual purchases of brimstone for the Ordnance and Navy Departments.

"Should McKay's bill become a law without amendment, the manufacture in this country must be abandoned, because the advantage in low rate of wages, interest, and so forth, enjoyed by the European manufacturer, will enable him to undersell the American in his own market.

"In view of the national importance of the manufacture of this indispensable munition of war, the undersigned respectfully and earnestly solicit you to use your influence to have the article of crude brimstone taken from schedule E, and placed on schedule H, of the proposed tariff, so as to be admitted, as at present, free of duty.

"Very respectfully, your obedient servants,

"JEFFRIES & CATTERFIELD.

"Hon. DANIEL WEBSTER."

Thus we see a reduction in the price of this article of thirty-five dollars a ton, in consequence of the tariff of 1842, and the manufacture of which will now be totally destroyed by this bill.

I shall read another letter, relating to an article connected with that topic, which was alluded to, and very handsomely discussed, yesterday, by my friend from Rhode Island.* It is a very curious specimen of legislation with reference to an article of some importance, sulphuric acid: —

"*Boston*, *July* 9, 1846.

"SIR, — I have works in Newton for the manufacture of sulphuric acid, or oil of vitriol, the most extensive works of the kind in the country, and knowing you would wish to be put in possession of the bearing of the proposed tariff of Mr. McKay upon the different interests it affects, I take the liberty of showing the operation of it upon the article that I manufacture, and the obvious design of some one to strike a blow at this business. By this tariff, acids of various kinds, such as muriatic, nitric, and others, used for chemical or medicinal purposes, or for manufacturing, or in the fine arts, are charged with a duty of twenty per cent., unless otherwise provided for.

"As an exception to other acids, sulphuric acid, or oil of vitriol, is particularly specified, and is charged with a duty of ten per cent., and the material from which this is made, sulphur, which has been heretofore free, is charged with a duty of fifteen per cent. I have been at a loss to know the reason for singling out this acid in the way it has been, for it is evident that it has been particularly dwelt upon in constructing this tariff; and for the want of any information in the matter, I cannot avoid the suspicion that it has been arranged by the representation of those specially interested to crush the manufacture in this country.

"During the past year the supply of bleaching powders has been very short, so much so as to drive some of the bleachers into making a substitute, called bleaching liquor; and I am informed that the substitute is

* Mr. Simmons.

preferred by those who have used it, on account of its doing the work fully as well, and being much cheaper than the powders.

"The manufacture of bleaching powders has also been carried on in this country during the last ten years to a considerable extent, with a duty of one cent per pound on the imported, which is more than twenty per cent. And therefore I do not believe the article has yet been made to be profitable to manufacturers; yet the manufacture in this country of the powders, and more particularly of the liquor, is a cause of alarm to the foreign manufacturers.

"Sulphuric acid enters largely into the cost of making bleaching powders and bleaching liquor; and it is evident that the foreign maker of bleaching powders could not better attain his end than by raising the cost of making sulphuric acid in this country, at the same time that he gets a reduction of duty on his powder.

"As I have formed this opinion, I have thought proper to communicate it.

"I am, Sir, with high respect, your obedient servant,

"GEORGE GARDNER.

"Hon. DANIEL WEBSTER."

Here, then, on the one hand, the foreign agent prays for and urges the passage of Mr. McKay's bill; and, on the other, the American manufacturer implores us to stick to the tariff of 1842, reject Mr. McKay's bill, and suffer him to go on and get an honest living, as heretofore. They have a directly opposite interest; and as it is no matter of revenue of any considerable amount, how are we to interpret the fact, that the former is so obviously protected at the expense of the latter? How is it that, in this contest, the foreign manufacturer obtains the preference? Are the suspicions of this gentleman, whom I know to be a highly respectable man of business, entirely unreasonable? He says there must have been some one at work, having an interest foreign and hostile to the interest of the American producer of this article, and similar articles; and judge you, whether that be not the case. It is plain and manifest that it is an English provision, favorable to English labor, and prejudicial to American labor.

I am admonished that it is high time to leave these various articles; I will not call them minor articles, because they are all important. There are many more to which I might have directed the attention of the Senate. There are the articles of skins and pelts, of which nothing is said here, but which affect a great many hundred persons employed. The same thing takes place in regard to them. The raw material is taxed higher than the manufactured articles. Now, I want somebody to show if the result of this bill be not to benefit the foreign manufacturer and laborer, at the sacrifice of our own manufacturer and laborer. I wish somebody to show where there is one case in which discrimination has been resorted to, and in which it has been in favor of the American laborer or the American manufacturer. Everywhere it is the other way.

Sir, the honorable member from Connecticut* spoke, the other day, of a "petty Congress" of subordinate persons, brought together from about the custom-houses and the great marts of importation, and of the evident proofs that this bill was prepared in that "petty Congress." Mr. President, I know nothing of that; but I say, not willingly, but from a sense of duty, that the long series of provisions contained in this bill, in which discrimination is obviously made *against* the American manufacturer, and *in favor* of the foreign manufacturer, gives rise to very awkward suspicions. If there has been, in truth, such a "petty Congress" as has been mentioned, for whose benefit were its deliberations carried on? What interest, whose interest, was its "petty Senate," and its "petty House of Representatives," assiduously seeking to promote?

But I now go from these interests to articles of more prominence, and perhaps greater importance; and I wish to say, that in discussing the effects of this tariff upon the industrial labor of the country, with the single exception which I have named in regard to the new manufacture of *mousseline de laine*, I make no particular comment on this bill, in regard to the great interests of that part of the country with which I am connected. I leave that to the consideration of others. I will not permit myself to be supposed to be influenced, on these topics, by the interests of manufacturers around me, and amongst whom I live, and for whose prosperity and happiness I never can feel unconcerned. Driven from her original and chosen pursuit, to which she had been enthusiastically addicted, commerce, and compelled to enter upon the field of manufactures, twenty-two years ago, if it be now the pleasure of this government, if it be the sense

* Mr. Niles.

of the American people, if the South, and the Middle, and the West say so, New England *can go back, and still live.* You can distress her, you can cripple her, you can cramp her, but you cannot annihilate her industry, her self-respect, her capacity to take care of herself. A country of workingmen who are able, if necessity calls for it, to work fourteen hours a day, may bid defiance to all tariffs, and all miserable, false, partial legislation. They stand upon the strength of their own character, resolution, and capacity; and by this strength and that capacity they will maintain themselves, do what you please. Not, Sir, that there is one house in New England, at this moment, in which the proceedings of this day are not looked for with intensest interest. No man rises in the morning but to see the newspaper. No woman retires at night without inquiring of her husband the progress of this great measure in Washington. They ask about it in the streets. They ask about it in the schools. They ask about it in the shoemakers' shops, the machine-shops, the tailors' shops, the saddlers' shops, and, in short, in the shops of all artisans and handicrafts. They ask about it everywhere. And they will take whatever answer comes as men should take it; and they will feel as men should feel when they hear it. I therefore leave, Sir, to the Senate, all these considerations. I will not suffer myself to be subjected to the temptation of being led away by causes which might be supposed to influence me, and turning from them, therefore, I proceed to the consideration of other subjects, in which, so far as New England is concerned, if she have any interest at all, it is in favor of this bill, and against protected interests. Does she mean the less to exercise her power, little or great, or whatever it may be, in favor of those whose interests are menaced by this bill? No, Sir; never.

I am now about to speak of the iron interest and the coal interest; great interests, in which several of the States are concerned, but which, by way of eminence, men are accustomed to call the great Pennsylvanian interests; and so they are. Massachusetts is a purchaser of Pennsylvania coal, and she is a purchaser of Pennsylvania iron. She is one of the best purchasers of these articles from her Pennsylvania friends. She will, to the extent of her power, maintain a just system for the preservation of these great interests, precisely as if they were her own. And,

Sir, I do not fear that I am running any hazard at all when I say, that this feeling of Massachusetts towards Pennsylvania is entirely reciprocated by Pennsylvania towards Massachusetts. I hear it whispered about these halls, that there might come some *specific* for the case of Pennsylvania: that there might be an amendment moved to soothe her on the subject of iron and coal, leaving all the rest of the country to the desolation of this bill. But, Sir, no such thing can take place. Pennsylvania would not degrade herself by accepting such a boon. Pennsylvania stands, and her representatives here stand, pledged and instructed to the tariff of 1842. But I take this occasion to say for myself, that I am now arguing against this bill, this particular bill, and I have not said, and I shall not say now, what other provisions it might be advisable for the houses of Congress to adopt. But I have not the least fear in the world, Sir, that Pennsylvania is going to bend her proud neck, to take a boon from those who are inflicting this severe measure of discomfort and distress upon the country; that she will just take a sop to herself and turn her back upon her friends. There is not a Pennsylvanian who would consent to such a degrading, debasing, discreditable act of selfishness. Now let us proceed to consider these important subjects of the iron trade and coal trade of Pennsylvania.

It is well known that Pennsylvania is very rich in mineral wealth. Next to England, Pennsylvania, considering her connection east with the Atlantic and west with the Mississippi, and then considering her soil and mineral productions, is perhaps the richest spot on the face of the globe. She has greater means of supporting population than any country I know of in the world, except it be the south end of the island of Great Britain. For thirty years, the making of iron in Pennsylvania has been a considerable business. The present duty on iron, by the law of 1842, is $25 per ton for plain bar-iron. The proposed duty is thirty per cent. *ad valorem* on the imported article. Now, the price of iron at Liverpool at this moment is £8, or $40, per ton. The amount of duty, therefore, proposed by the bill, that is to say, a duty of thirty per cent. *ad valorem*, would be $12.50, or one half the present duty.

I will read the clause of the bill with respect to iron, for it is worthy of being read:—

"Iron, in bars, blooms, bolts, loops, pigs, rods, slabs, or other form not otherwise provided for, thirty per cent."

Here we see, then, that the same *ad valorem* duty is assessed on iron as a raw material, and on all its successive stages of manufacture. There are proprietors in Pennsylvania who hold great estates in iron mountains, which are called "royalties." They sell the ore at so much a ton in the earth. This, as a raw material, is protected in the bill by a duty of thirty per cent. *ad valorem.* But the duty, being still the same thirty per cent. *ad valorem,* only rises on the article in different stages of its manufacture, as the value of the manufactured article progressively rises. American labor, therefore, gets no protection over foreign labor. As the manufacture of iron advances from one degree to another, it calls, in each successive step, for a higher degree of labor. But the bill makes no discrimination in favor of this labor. English labor, in advancing the manufacture of its higher stages, is as much regarded and protected as American labor. But as labor is higher here than in England, (and long may it continue so,) if there be not a discriminating protection, the work must of course fall into foreign hands, and the loss fall on the American laborers. The question, therefore, is one which touches the interest of the American worker in iron to the quick; and it will be understood by the man who works at the furnace, at the forge, at the mill, and in all the still more advanced and finer operations.

But now let us look to the act of 1842, and see its careful enumeration and specific assessment of duties on iron, and on articles of iron manufacture. It reads thus.

Mr. Webster here read at length the first six paragraphs of the fourth section of the act of the 30th of August, 1842, by which specific duties are laid upon imported iron, in every form of the unmanufactured or manufactured article.

Here we see *labor* protected. The duties are specific, and they are enhanced more and more as labor constitutes more and more of the value of the article. This is the spirit of the act of 1842. No such spirit is manifested in this bill.

Let me now, Mr. President, after reading this long legal enactment, direct the attention of the Senate to the amount of capital invested in the iron interests at this time in Pennsylvania.

			Annual Product. Tons.
Furnaces up to 1842,	Charcoal,	206	173,369
	Anthracite,	7	16,487
		213	189,856
Furnaces since 1842,	Charcoal,	67	75,200
	Anthracite,	36	103,000
		316	368,056

Increased product of old furnaces,	37,971
Product of new furnaces,	178,200
	216,171

This prodigious increase of the business has, of course, called for a large investment and employment of capital, which, after much reflection, is estimated at forty-seven dollars per ton for every ton of pig metal manufactured by charcoal, and twenty-five dollars per ton for every ton manufactured by anthracite. This would give, for seventy-five thousand two hundred tons of the former, a capital of $ 3,534,400, and for one hundred and three thousand tons of the latter, a capital of $ 2,575,000; making together the enormous sum of $ 6,109,400 invested in furnaces alone since 1842. The aggregate capital, therefore, would be calculated upon the same estimate: —

	Tons.	Capital.
Charcoal furnaces previous to 1842,	173,369	$ 8,148,343
Anthracite furnaces previous to 1842,	16,487	412,175
		8,560,518
New,	75,200 103,000	6,109,400
	368,056	$ 14,669,918

These 368,056 tons, at $ 30 per ton, would be worth	$ 11,040,680		
It is probable that one half of this metal is converted into bar, hoop, sheet, and boiler iron, and nails, at a cost of at least $ 50 per ton more,	9,201,400	Capital for conversion at $20 per ton,	3,680,560
The other half into castings at $ 20 per ton,	3,680,560	Do. at $ 10,	1,840,280
	$ 23,922,640		$ 20,190,758

And where does this enormous sum of money go, and how is

it expended? All in labor and agricultural products. For of what material is iron composed? Coal, limestone, iron ores, sand, and fire-clay, almost worthless unless converted into iron. The number of men employed in producing the above iron would be, in the charcoal operations, one man to every twenty tons, and in the anthracite, one man to every twenty-four tons of pig metal. This includes all the miners of coal and limestone, wood-choppers, and laborers of every kind. Upon this estimate there would be employed, in charcoal, twelve thousand four hundred and twenty-eight; in anthracite, four thousand nine hundred and seventy-eight; in all, seventeen thousand four hundred and six. Allowing a wife and four children as sustained by each laborer, we have a population of eighty-seven thousand and thirty. To which if we add the labor employed in its conversion into bars, hoops, sheets, boiler-plate, nails, castings, railway iron, and so forth, which would more than double those *directly* dependent, we should have one hundred and seventy-four thousand and sixty men, women, and children. But when we look still further, at the labor created by this business in railways, canals, and so forth, both that of man and horse, who can estimate it?

We see thus what the iron interest of Pennsylvania is. The inquiry now is, Can this interest survive, and hope to enjoy moderate prosperity, under the provisions of this bill? The people of the State of Pennsylvania ask the government to suspend execution of the sentence pronounced against them till the question shall be fairly considered.

Notwithstanding the acknowledged richness of the Pennsylvania mines, and notwithstanding the great improvements which have been made in the State in the means of transportation for heavy articles, there are yet disadvantages of a serious nature to be overcome. Her mountains abound with the best of iron ore, but then they are in the interior. They are remote from tide-water. The largest regions of iron production are a hundred and fifty miles from the navigable arms of the sea. The case is far different in Wales and Scotland, the furnaces in those countries being almost immediately contiguous to navigation. Hence their products are sent all over the world at less cost. English and Scotch iron may be brought to New York and Boston at one half the cost of bringing iron from the principal iron-works in Pennsylvania to the same markets.

Freight on iron from Wales and Scotland to New York and Boston may be stated, on an average, at from one dollar and fifty cents to two dollars and fifty cents per ton. But the average cost of transportation from the principal establishments in Pennsylvania to the same market is from three dollars to five dollars and a half per ton. When the tariff of 1842 went into operation, the English iron was uncommonly low, say £ 4 10*s.* per ton. With an *ad valorem* duty of thirty per cent., as proposed by this act, and the usual freights, the article could have been offered here at thirty-two or thirty-three dollars. Could Pennsylvania have stood this competition? It is plain that she could not, and that her iron-works must have stopped but for the helping hand of that act. I observe in the English Mining Journal of January last the following statement: —

> "It will be remembered that in 1842 the amount of pig metal exported from Glasgow alone was seventy thousand tons; and it is a painful fact, that since 1842 the exportation of pig iron has all but ceased. Under these circumstances, we are at a loss to conceive how our surplus iron is to be disposed of."

On this English statement, an intelligent friend of mine remarks thus: —

> "What will be the effect of this over-trading and surplus stock if it can be exported here under a thirty per cent. *ad valorem* duty? which is no duty whatever, for at the time it is most needed it is *lowest.* Specific duties are the only check which we have upon fraud and perjury? Abandon them, and you have effectually prostrated the trade, and placed us entirely in the hands of unscrupulous foreigners. But let us see how this *ad valorem* duty will work. In June, 1824, bar iron in England was £ 7 per ton, and in January, 1825, the price was £ 14 per ton, and it fell the same year to £ 10. In 1826 and 1827 the highest quotation was £ 9, while in 1832 it fell to £ 4 15*s.* In June, 1844, the price was £ 6; in April, £ 9 15*s.*; in July, £ 7 15*s.*; in October, £ 8 15*s.*; and in December, £ 10. Thus it will be seen that in 1832 thirty per cent. duty would have produced $ 6.84 per ton, while in December, 1844, it would have been $ 14.40, and in January, 1825, $ 20.16."

Sir, in my opinion, we have before us at this moment the general question, Shall we give efficient protection to the American production of iron? If we say we will, then it is clear this bill ought not to pass. If it should pass, leaving iron, with all its manufactures and ramifications, at thirty per cent. *ad valorem*, they might just as well be put at five per cent. The trade would as soon have it so, as I understand. The manufacture declined under the old "Compromise Act." It rose in 1842, and the labor of persons employed rose in proportion. That law was certainly hailed in Pennsylvania as being conformable to all her views and opinions. Now, Sir, let us come to a conclusion. Let us decide, once for all. I am for protecting the domestic iron interests of the United States. Are you? If you are, reject this bill. If you are not, say so, and pass the bill; and let every man along the branches and up to the sources of the Susquehanna and the Schuylkill, and every man beyond the Alleghanies, in Pennsylvania, and every man in Maryland, Tennessee, Virginia, and every other State in which iron is produced, understand you. Let us have no more fighting under false colors. Enough of that. If you favor the domestic manufacture of iron, reject the bill. If you wish to destroy that domestic manufacture, pass the bill.

Closely connected with the iron interest is that of coal; and therefore it is necessary to see how that great interest is likely to fare.

Pennsylvania produces of anthracite coal alone two million five hundred thousand tons annually. The capital invested in these anthracite mines, and the several railroads connected with them, in all the coal-fields, is near forty million dollars. In the Schuylkill region alone, including the cost of the Reading Railroad and Schuylkill Canal, the investment amounts to twenty-six million eight hundred thousand dollars. The increase of product of the Schuylkill region, under the Compromise Act, from 1837 to 1842, was only thirty-two thousand tons. In the succeeding three years, that is to say, from 1842 to 1845, that increase amounted to no less than five hundred and sixty thousand. The price of labor, of course, became greatly advanced; but the price of coal fell from $ 5.50 per ton to $ 3.37. A pretty good proof this that prices may fall in consequence of protection.

And here, Sir, I wish to advert to a general fact, worthy to be recollected in all our political economy. The increase in the investments of capital in great works of this kind tends to reduce the profits on that capital. That is a necessary result.

But then it has exactly the reverse action upon labor; for the more that capital is invested in these great operations, the greater is the call for labor, and therefore the ratio is here the other way, and the rates of labor increase as the profits of capital are diminished. Well, is there any thing *undemocratic* and unpopular in such a system as that? a system that causes a diminution of profits to the capitalist and an increase of remuneration to the hand of labor.

But the serious inquiry now is, whether Pennsylvania coal, with the degree of protection which this bill proposes, can maintain competition with the coal of Nova Scotia and New Brunswick? That is a matter of commercial calculation and of figures. The present duty on coal is $1.75 per ton. This bill puts the duty at thirty per cent. *ad valorem*, which is equal to forty-two cents per ton at present prices; that is to say, it is now proposed to reduce the duty on coal by the difference of $ 1.33 in every ton; a sum almost equal to the price of coal in Nova Scotia.

Nova Scotia coal, on board the vessel in the harbors of that Province, costs $1.50 per ton. If to this we add the duty at thirty per cent., the aggregate will be $1.95. Coal, therefore, on board vessels in Nova Scotia, costing $1.95 per ton, is free to proceed to any part of the United States. The freight of coal from Nova Scotia to Boston, I am informed, is now $ 2.25 per ton. So that the cost of a ton of Nova Scotia coal at Boston, duties included, will be $ 4.20.

The cost of coal on board the vessel at Philadelphia is said to be $ 3.50; $ 2.00 being the price at the mines, and $ 1.50 the cost of land transportation. Adding freight from Philadelphia to Boston, at $1.75 per ton, the Pennsylvania coal will cost in Boston $ 5.25. The Nova Scotia coal is cheaper, therefore, by the difference between $ 4.20 and $ 5.25. This difference of twenty per cent. is of course a serious matter, and is likely to be entirely fatal to the home article. One cannot say how soon it may come about, but there would seem to be no doubt, that, in the end, the coal from the Provinces must take the place of that from Pennsylvania under such a tariff as this. It will be seen, if this statement of costs and prices be accurate, that the rate of duty proposed by this bill is no protection whatever. The foreign article might as well come in free. The coal of Pennsylvania, like her iron, is far in the interior, and although it is brought to navigable waters by one of the noblest of works for land transportation, yet the charge is heavy. As will be seen by the statements which I have already made, the freight of coal from Pottsville to tide-water is equal to the cost of the article on board the vessel at Nova Scotia. Land transportation of heavy articles over long distances is necessarily expensive, notwithstanding the means of conveyance may be highly improved. The cheaper transport by sea is seen in many striking instances.

New England is not a limestone country. There is very little of her surface that can be called limestone land east of the Green Mountains. On the other hand, great portions of the Middle States and some portions of the Southern States have lime in abundance. Yet lime from Maine finds its way to the cities along the Southern coast, and sometimes, I believe, even to New Orleans. This is because, although Maine is not what can be called a limestone country, she yet happens to have one vast quarry upon the very edge of salt water.

It is said that there are mines at Wilkesbarre, from which coal may be placed on board of boats in the rivers at the Nova Scotia price; that is to say $1.50 per ton, or even lower, say $1.00; and in these boats it may reach tide-water by inland navigation. Yet the distance is great, and the expense so large, that the article only holds competition with the Pottsville coal. Distance is comparatively of little moment in conveyance by sea. I think I have heard it stated that manufactures of iron, such as nails, may be brought from Massachusetts into Market Street, Philadelphia, for less cost of transport than the same articles can be brought to the city from works ten miles off.

For all practical purposes, therefore, we must consider the iron mines of Wales and Scotland, and the coal mines of Nova Scotia, as being close by us. And if we mean to be supplied by our own products, we must act accordingly.

Sir, there is another view of this subject not uninteresting, and very fit to be taken. What is coal? A coarse and raw natural product. What is it which has created its value at the moment it comes to be consumed? Clearly, labor. It is the product of human labor; and that labor, while giving value to coal, has called for contributions from many other branches and varieties of human labor. Coal undug, and still in the mines, at Pottsville, is worth twenty cents per ton. At the place of consumption, at New York or Boston, it is worth $ 5.25 per ton. The difference is the value added to the original material by the hand of man; and to the creation of this value, farmers, merchants, tradesmen, mechanics, ship-builders, sailors, and those employed in the land transportation, have all contributed. To these, therefore, it has given employment. The population of Pottsville is said to consume a million of dollars annually of agricultural products; and another million, probably, in manufactured articles. Thus the miners, the farmers, and the mechanics stand side by side in this great interest. Shall they be protected against injurious foreign competition, or shall they not?

Sir, the calculations which I have submitted have been made from *data* or materials furnished from authentic sources, and I believe they may be relied on.

Mr. Johnson of Maryland here rose and said, that it was now late in the day, and, if the Senator from Massachusetts would yield the floor, he would move that the Senate adjourn.

This motion prevailed, and the Senate here adjourned.

On Monday, the 27th of July, Mr. Webster resumed his argument as follows: —

It is a circumstance a good deal characteristic, Mr. President, of the state of things in which we find ourselves placed, and strongly indicative of that absorbing interest which belongs to the question before us, that I have not the honor, to-day, to address a full Senate. Since the commencement of my observations on Saturday morning, an honorable member from one of the Southern States* has vacated his seat in this body. We perhaps may soon hear from him the reasons which led him to leave the situation which he had occupied with so much usefulness and reputation. I am no otherwise acquainted with those reasons, than as I gather them from a very extraordinary article in the government paper of this morning, or rather of Saturday evening. From that I infer that the honorable member left his seat here from an inability to support the measure of the administration now before us, and from a great unwillingness, on the other hand, to disoblige his party friends and connections by

* Mr. Haywood of North Carolina.

voting against it. Sir, as he has gone, I may speak of him as a man of character and standing, here and at home; a man of learning and attainments, of great courtesy, and of unsurpassed industry and attention in the discharge of his public duties; and, as we all know, as far as we can judge of his course in the Senate, an intelligent and constant friend of the present administration.

Now, Sir, I confess that I am ashamed of my country when I see a gentleman of such character, on his retiring from this place from such a motive, hunted, abused, defamed, according to the degree of abuse and defamation which some writer for the government, in the paper of the government, sees fit to pour out against him. It is a disgrace to the civilization of the age. It is a disgrace to American civilization. It is a disgrace to this government. It is a disgrace to the American press.

Another article of common intelligence is not unworthy of notice, before I proceed to the remaining observations which I intend to submit to the Senate. If we may believe the current reports of the day, the administration of the government is now in possession of official and authentic information that an extraordinary and vigorous effort is making throughout the whole republic of Mexico to sustain herself in the war now carried on against her by the United States. I suppose the government is now informed that Bravo is appointed President of Mexico *ad interim*, and that Paredes, with such forces as he can collect, is marching to the north; and that there is a spirit of united resistance, united action, and of general contribution toward the defence of the country, such as was never manifested before; that the clergy contribute, that the provinces contribute, that individuals contribute, in a manner altogether unknown in Mexico since the time of her revolution. I suppose that the government is at this moment in possession of intelligence to this effect; how well founded the information is they are to judge; but that they have such information, from official sources, I entertain no doubt at all. I refer to it only as affording a new reason why we should do nothing to disturb the just expectations of revenue, or to diminish the necessary income of the treasury.

Now, Sir, as connected with that subject, I will read to the Senate a paper which I had not strength to read on Saturday, and I will make no comment on it, except so far as to describe the character of the gentleman who wrote it, and the character of the gentleman to whom it was addressed. The writer is Edward H. Nichol, Esq., of the city of New York, a merchant of very high character in that city; a gentleman every way friendly to the present administration of the government and to the party now in power; a gentleman who was an administration candidate, very recently, for a seat in the other house of Congress. The letter respects the effect of this bill on six articles of importation, viz. spirits, pepper, pimento, cassia, cloves, and sugar and molasses. It is addressed to Isaac Townsend, Esq., another highly respectable merchant, and of the same political associations. And I will venture to say, that, if the gentlemen connected with the administration of the government had sought amongst all its friends of the mercantile class, throughout the whole country, for the most intelligent and competent gentlemen to give them their opinions and advice on the subject of this tariff bill, they would have found nobody of superior qualifications for that office to Mr. Edward H. Nichol. Having said so much, I will read this letter, and submit it to the Senate without further remark.

" ISAAC TOWNSEND, ESQ.:

" Dear Sir,— In answer to your note under date of the 13th instant, propounding certain questions as regards the present tariff, and the one now proposed and under discussion in the Senate, I answer in the following manner, viz.: —

Spirits. — The duty accruing on spirits of all kinds, under the present tariff, at 85 to 90 cents per gallon, may be estimated at	$1,400,000
to	$1,500,000
The average cost at the different places of production may be estimated at 42 to 45 cents per gallon, on which the *ad valorem* duty, as now proposed, would be 100 per cent., and, estimating the annual importation to be equal to that of the last three or four years, viz. 1,000,000 to 1,500,000 gallons, would yield about	720,000
Difference, ...	$780,000
Pepper. — The annual consumption of pepper may be estimated at 3,500,000 pounds, present duty 5 cents per pound, yielding	$175,000
The average cost at the place of production is $2\frac{1}{4}$ to 3 cents per pound, and proposed duty of 30 per cent *ad valorem* would yield	34,500
Difference, ...	$140,500

Pimento.—The annual consumption of pimento may be estimated at 1,500,000 pounds, and, with the present duty of 5 cents per pound, would yield . . . . $ 75,000

The average cost at the place of production, $3\frac{1}{4}$ to 4 cents per pound, on which the proposed duty of 40 per cent. *ad valorem* would be about 18,000

Difference, ... $ 57,000

Cassia.—The annual consumption of cassia is about 1,000,000 pounds; and, at the present duty of 5 cents per pound, would yield $ 50,000

The average cost at the place of production is 7 cents per pound, and the proposed duty of 30 per cent. *ad valorem* would yield 20,000

Difference, ... $ 30,000

Cloves.—The annual consumption of cloves is about 160,000 pounds; at 8 cents per pound the present duty would yield . . $ 12,800

The cost at the place of production is 13 to 14 cents per pound; at 30 per cent. *ad valorem*, ... 6,400

Difference, ... $ 6,400

Sugar and Molasses.—The annual duty accruing under the present tariff of 85 to 90 per cent. *ad valorem* may be estimated at from $ 3,000,000 to . . . . $ 3,500,000

Whereas the proposed duty, 30 per cent. *ad valorem*, would yield 1,400,000

Say, difference, ... $ 2,100,000

Recapitulation.	Present.	Proposed.	Difference.
Spirits, ...	$ 1,500,000	$ 720,000	$ 780,000
Pepper, ...	175,000	34,500	140,500
Pimento, ...	75,000	18,000	57,000
Cassia, ...	50,000	20,000	30,000
Cloves, ...	12,800	6,400	6,400
Sugar and Molasses, ...	3,500,000	1,400,000	2,100,000
	$ 5,312,800	$ 2,198,900	$ 3,113,900

"You will notice by this hasty sketch which I now hand you, that the difference between the present duty and that now proposed is about three millions one hundred and thirteen thousand nine hundred dollars on the various articles above named. It is to be presumed that there will be a gradual increase of importations; yet a number of years must elapse before it will make up the deficiency. As regards the exportations of foreign merchandise, should the proposed tariff become a law, it is difficult to arrive at any definite conclusion. It is to be presumed, however, that, with the large surplus in the different warehouses now in the Atlantic cities, and the very limited demand we must have previous to the 1st of December, (as no jobber or vender will buy any more than to supply his daily demands,) the exportations will be large, exceeding the ordinary exportations under the present tariff, and may make draughts on the various custom-houses, in debenture, to the extent of $ 800,000 to $ 1,000,000 more than otherwise would be.

"The importers, should the proposed tariff become a law, will very soon begin to ship their goods out of the country; then reimport them, and place them in the warehouses, to remain or be taken out in detached parcels previous to the 1st of December; when whatever then remains will be subject to a low duty. How much better and more just would it be (as was the case when the reduction of the tariff took place in 1830 and 1831) to let all merchandise "not in broken parcels' go to the custom-house on the eve of the 1st of December, and remain, rather than force the merchants to the expense of shipping for the purpose of *evading* the present duties.

"You must be aware, as well as myself, that the importations for the next five months must be extremely limited, and that all the goods that are imported for the next five months will go to the public stores for the benefit of the proposed reductions. Consequently, the government will derive little or no revenue from foreign importations for that period.

"So far as my experience teaches me, I have ever been in favor of specific instead of *ad valorem* duties, believing that the revenue is more securely collected, and extending likewise protection to every honest importer. You will notice that two thirds of the merchandise imported subject to *ad valorem* duties is brought into our city by foreigners. These men come among us possessing no national feeling, and little or no regard for our laws or institutions, and a custom-house oath is but a by-word with them. They locate themselves in by-streets and alleys, subject to no military or jury duty, and pay little or no taxes. They have a branch of their house or workshop in Europe, and however intelligent or adroit our appraisers may be, it is almost impossible to detect them in their falsified invoices.

"Should the proposed tariff become a law, the American merchants will, from necessity, almost cease to be importers, so far as our trade is concerned with Europe. Therefore, let our duties be ascertained by weight and measure, and we shall at least stand a fair and equal chance at the custom-house with these foreign importers.

"If these remarks should be of any service to you, I shall be pleased and gratified, and I remain, respectfully, yours.

"Edward H. Nichol.

"*New York*, *July* 17, 1846."

On Saturday, Mr. President, I submitted remarks, estimates, and calculations upon the subject of iron and coal, and I founded those remarks and estimates on the iron and coal of Pennsylvania for the sake of precision, and to make such calculations an example of the rest. I have now only to say, in that respect, that there are also iron and coal in New York, in Tennessee, in Georgia, in Virginia, in Maryland, all coming in, share and share alike, for the good or for the evil which the new system will produce.

I now proceed, Sir, to say something upon the influence, the necessary influence, which this proposed change in our system will exercise upon the commerce and navigation of the country. I shall do that by exhibiting a series of tables which will speak for themselves; which I know to have been drawn up with great accuracy, founded on the last official communication of the Secretary of the Treasury, so far as revenue is concerned, and on estimates regarding the value of freights, collected from the first mercantile sources in the country. As a general remark on these various papers, and one which they fully confirm, I wish to say, what would naturally be expected to be true, that for some years past, since the favor and protection of the government were given to the internal manufactures of the country, the foreign trade of the country has conformed to that state of things. A change in the business of navigation, and commerce, and freight, consequent upon these internal changes, is quite as striking as these internal changes themselves. The great element of that change is in the nature of the main articles of import, showing a diminution of manufactured articles, and a vast augmentation of raw materials, or articles serving as such. The consequence of this, as will be seen by the tables I am about to exhibit, is a large actual increase of the earnings of the shipping interest on imports; because, as all know, the freight is proportioned to the bulk of the article, and not to its cost. It is the space that the commodity fills in the ship, and not its value, which regulates the rate of freight. Therefore it is, that, though the importations may be greatly augmented in value, from being composed of manufactured articles chiefly, yet the freight is not increased in the same ratio, but may be diminished. That fact is notorious to all who are acquainted with the commerce of the country. It is perfectly understood by all the ship-owners of the United States, and is of itself sufficient to account for the great and important fact, that the navigating interest of the United States, the ship-owners to a man, oppose this change, because the existing system gives more employment to navigation than that which is now attempted to be substituted for it.

A heavy mass or amount, in value, of manufactured articles, as is well known, comes from France and England. Our more various commodities, and our importations of heavy articles, come from round the Capes, and from Brazil and the North of Europe. The tables which I propose to exhibit to the Senate will show the amount of these, respectively, and the change produced in them within the last five years.

Let me first premise, that articles of import into the United States are properly divisible into three classes. First, those articles which come here manufactured, and fit for use or for sale; secondly, articles not manufactured, brought here for consumption as imported, without any manufacture after they arrive; thirdly, those articles which are in the nature of raw materials, and are brought here to undergo a process of manufacture. Let us, then, see the amount of freight derived from these three respective classes of imports.

Net Imports for 1845.

1. *Foreign Manufactured Articles.*

Articles.	Value.	Duties.	Freights.
Silk, ...	$10,840,000	$2,968,000	$36,100
Wool, ...	10,750,000	3,755,000	80,625
Cotton, ...	13,360,000	4,908,000	133,360
Flax, ...	4,893,000	1,263,000	48,930
Iron, ...	4,022,000	1,607,000	120,360
Railroad iron, ...	1,000,000	600,000	96,000
Cigars, ...	1,086,000	305,000	25,000
Brass and other metals, ...	3,690,000	688,000	55,500
Earthen and glass ware, . . .	3,122,000	1,087,000	218,540
Clothing, ready made, ...	1,108,000	449,000	11,080
Hats and bonnets, ...	732,000	256,000	10,980
Leather, boots, and shoes, ...	848,000	242,000	12,720
Paper, ...	276,000	60,000	4,140
Cotton bagging, ...	102,000	56,000	1,530
Other unenumerated articles, . .	3,000,000	250,000	75,000
Total, ...	$58,829,000	$18,494,000	$929,865

2. *Foreign Articles for Consumption.*

Articles.	Value.	Duties.	Freights.
Coffee,	$ 5,380,000	Free.	$ 943,580
Tea,	4,809,000	Free.	343,000
Sugar (proportion of),	2,024,000	$ 1,067,000	375,000
Wines,	1,493,000	1,292,000	111,925
Spirits,	1,095,000	1,554,000	109,500
Fruits and spices,	1,480,000	560,000	124,000
Molasses (proportion of),	1,000,000	300,000	280,000
Salt,	883,000	678,000	247,000
Coal,	188,000	130,000	188,000
Fish,	300,000	50,000	30,000
Beer, ale, and porter,	90,000	19,000	8,000
Other unenumerated articles,	1,500,000	89,000	225,000
Total,	$ 20,242,000	$ 5,739,000	$ 2,985,005

3. *Foreign Articles for Manufacture in the United States.*

Articles.	Value.	Duties.	Freights.
Sugar (proportion of),	$ 2,025,000	$ 1,510,000	$ 562,500
Molasses (proportion of),	2,072,000	591,000	450,000
Iron (proportion of),	2,966,000	1,401,000	415,000
Steel,	750,000	97,000	25,000
Hides and furs,	4,706,000	332,000	610,000
Copper and brass,	1,951,000	Free.	140,000
Mahogany,	248,000	40,000	49,600
Wool,	1,667,000	123,000	330,050
Rags,	416,000	27,000	75,000
Saltpetre,	486,000	Free.	245,000
Hemp,	483,000	173,000	78,000
Indigo,	768,000	53,000	15,000
Dye-stuffs, &c.,	294,000	Free.	190,000
Bristles,	178,000	3,000	4,000
Camphor,	143,000	35,000	3,000
Dye-woods,	337,000	Free.	50,000
Linseed,	369,000	19,000	205,000
Raw silk,	710,000	173,000	12,000
Other unenumerated articles,	2,000,000	100,000	295,000
Total,	$ 22,569,000	$ 4,677,000	$ 3,754,150

Recapitulation.

	Value.	Duties.	Freights.
Foreign manufactured articles,	$ 58,829,000	$ 18,494,000	$ 929,865
Foreign articles for consumption,	20,242,000	5,739,000	2,985,005
Foreign articles for manufacture in this country,	22,569,000	4,677,000	3,754,150
Aggregate,	$ 101,640,000	$ 28,910,000	$ 7,669,020

Now, Sir, I have said that changes have taken place in the foreign trade of the country since the enlargement of the manufacturing system of the United States, which were naturally to be expected. And I think it was suggested the other day by my friend from Vermont, near me,* that a common and great

* Mr. Phelps.

mistake is, that we do not accommodate our legislation to these changing circumstances; and that we think that we can go back to where we were years ago, without disturbing any interests except those immediately affected; whereas, such are the connection and cohesion of all these interests, and so closely are they united, that they become at last mutually dependent on each other, and there is no disturbing one great branch of the system without injury to all the rest.

Here is a table of our trade with South America, and beyond the Capes, with a comparison of that trade in the year 1828 and the present year.

Comparison of our Trade at two different Periods with Places beyond the Cape of Good Hope, and South America.

In 1828.

Names of Places.	Imports.	Domestic Exports.	Tons of Shipping employed.
Dutch East Indies, ...	$ 113,000	$ 83,000	1,454
British East Indies, ...	1,543,000	55,000	2,589
Manilla, ...	60,000	20,000	829
China, ...	5,340,000	230,000	9,900
Buenos Ayres and Montevideo, . .	317,000	94,000	1,363
Brazils, ...	3,009,000	1,505,000	24,482
Other South American ports, . .	1,904,000	1,776,000	8,672
Total, ...	$ 12,286,000	$ 3,763,000	49,289

In 1845.

Names of Places.	Imports.	Domestic Exports.	Tons of Shipping employed.
Dutch East Indies, ...	$ 935,000	$ 98,000	4,900
British East Indies, ...	1,650,000	338,000	10,479
Manilla, ...	725,000	92,000	6,636
China, ...	4,931,000	1,110,000	15,035
Buenos Ayres and Montevideo, . .	1,561,000	640,000	17,300
Brazils, ...	6,883,000	2,409,000	48,550
Other South American ports, . .	8,434,000	2,574,000	19,747
Total, ...	$ 25,119,000	$ 7,261,000	122,647
Increase, ...	104 per cent.	90 per cent.	150 per cent.

This great increase of tonnage employed over the increase in the value of imports, is owing to the present importation of the coarse and bulky articles for manufacture, instead of manufactured silk and cotton goods of China, Manilla, and Calcutta.

To be more particular, I now give a general description of the goods imported from those places in each year.

In 1828:—

	Value.
Manufactured cotton goods,	$ 1,041,000
Manufactured silk goods,	2,627,000
Indigo (which was imported for export),	1,030,000
Hides,	1,040,000
Sugar,	284,000
Copper, in pigs and bars,	650,000
Teas,	1,800,000
Wool,	18,000
Coffee,	1,700,000
Specie,	1,000,000
Unenumerated articles,	1,096,000
	$ 12,286,000

In 1845:—

Manufactured cotton goods,	$ 1,500
Manufactured silk goods,	150,000
Indigo,	660,000
Hides,	3,600,000
Sugar,	419,000
Copper, in pigs and bars,	365,000
Teas,	4,075,000
Wool,	563,000
Coffee,	6,600,000
Saltpetre,	500,000
Linseed,	300,000
Gunny-bags,	110,000
Drugs and dye-stuffs,	150,000
Ginger,	40,000
Cocoa,	170,000
Spices,	15,000
Hemp,	248,000
Specie,	1,200,000
Unenumerated articles,	5,952,500
Total,	$ 25,119,000

It is thus apparent that the increased employment of our tonnage to the amount of one hundred and fifty per cent. in this distant transport has been from the importation of the raw materials for manufacture in our country, and of the increased quantities of coffee and teas; and no doubt increased exportation of our domestic products to those distant places has been promoted by this increase in imports. These domestic products are manufac-

19*

tured cotton and woollen goods, lumber, and articles of furniture, provisions of all kinds, naval stores, cotton, tobacco, ice, candles, and other miscellaneous articles.

I have another table, Mr. President, exhibiting our trade with the North of Europe, presenting the same general result, and, as we have ceased to import hemp to a great extent from Russia, the increase in the tonnage is principally from exportations.

Comparison of our Trade at two different Periods with the North of Europe, viz. Russia, Sweden, Germany, and Holland.

These show a falling off in the imports.	Value.
In the year 1828, ...	$11,214,000
In the year 1845, ...	4,059,000
Decrease of	$7,155,000
And an increase in our domestic exports.	
In the year 1828, ...	$5,085,000
In the year 1845, ...	6,346,000
Increase of	$1,261,000
And an increase in the tonnage employed.	
In 1828, ...	136,100 tons.
In 1845, ...	197,000 tons.
Increase, ...	60,900 tons.

This increase is from the transport of our domestic exports to those places.

It will be interesting to note some of the articles of import from those places, in which that reduction strikingly appears.

Articles Imported.	Value in 1828.	Value in 1845.
Manufactures of cotton and flax, ...	$2,190,000	$165,500
Manufactures of iron and steel, ...	2,204,000	677,000
Manufactures of glass, ...	458,000	128,000
Manufactures of leather, ...	330,000	2,100
Manufactures of sail-cloth, ...	345,000	186,000
Manufactures of linseed oil, ...	130,000	13,000
Manufactures of cordage, ...	145,000	54,000
Unmanufactured hemp, ...	990,000	211,000
Unmanufactured flax, ...	37,000	31,000
Unmanufactured wool, ...	97,000	31,000
Unmanufactured rags, ...	None.	12,000
Total, ...	$6,926,000	$1,510,600

Thus showing a reduction in the manufactured goods, hemp,

and other articles imported from those countries, of more than three fourths of the whole amount.

These facts are certainly of importance in considering the employment of our shipping in the transport coastwise of raw material, such as cotton, flax, hemp, iron, coal, &c., for the manufacture, in our own country, of goods which have taken the place of the foreign manufactured goods imported and consumed by us sixteen years ago.

A very important fact in connection with this part of the subject is, that this distant trade is in our own vessels. It is shared with none. We know that, in the trade between us and England, about a third of the navigation is in the hands of England. But the trade with the North of Europe is on American account, and to our advantage; and to a great extent, also, we pay for the importations by domestic products. We do not now hear of any extraordinary amounts of specie to meet the demands of this trade, because the products of our own industry and our own people, in a manufactured state, are carried out. These remarks might be extended to other tables showing like results; but I am quite desirous of getting through the duty which remains to be performed by me on this occasion, and I shall, therefore, pass this part of the case with a very few additional observations.

It is obvious, Sir, that, for the same reason that the raw material imported for the manufacturer pays a large proportion of freight, articles of export of like nature from our side for the same purpose pay also a large proportion, as every body knows is the case with cotton. This proves that, in every measure concerning the interests of navigation, we should consult rather the great and bulky articles than the small, where the value is great and the bulk diminished.

Now be pleased to notice these results. Fifty-eight millions of dollars in value of manufactured goods imported yield less than one million for freight. Twenty-two millions of dollars brought in articles to be manufactured here yield three millions and three quarters; being very nearly one half of all the freight earned on all our imports. Certainly, this is a most important fact, and worthy of all attention.

We propose, then, Mr. President, in the first place, to diminish and discourage labor and industry at home, by taxing the raw materials which are brought into the country for manufacture. We propose, in the second place, to diminish the earnings of freight very materially, by diminishing the importation of bulky articles, always brought in our own ships. We propose, in the third place, to diminish the amount of exports of our own domestic manufactured goods, by refusing to take in exchange for them raw materials, the products of other countries. This is our present policy! This is our notion of free trade! Surely, Mr. President, this enlightened system cannot fail to attract the admiration of the world!

Now, Sir, one cannot say to what extent this change of system may affect the navigation of the country, but its tendency is, unquestionably, to cripple and cramp the navigating interest. Its tendency is to diminish the demand for tonnage, for navigation, for the carrying trade. I think I might on this occasion, without impropriety, call the attention of the Senator from Maine farthest from me,* a gentleman who here represents a State, if not first, at least among the very first, in regard to the amount of its navigation. The ships of Maine are found in every quarter; beyond the great Capes and in the North Sea. They bring home these raw materials; and every thing that diminishes the consumption of these raw materials in our own country diminishes the chances of employment to every ship-owner in the State of Maine. I will read an extract or two from a letter which I have received on this subject.

" *Baltimore*, 20*th July*, 1846.

" Sir, — I notice that the new tariff bill has in its schedules silk, mahogany, hides, Brazilletto wood, logwood, fustic, Rio Hache wood, Lima wood, sandal-wood, red cedar, pig copper, nitrate of soda or the sal soda of Peru, saltpetre, block, and all sorts of crude woods, and many drugs of bulk, all more or less dutiable, and tea and coffee left free.

" This is curious free trade.

" These are the articles that give our vessels homeward freights, and, being chiefly gross articles of great bulk, they appeal most strongly to be classed in the free list. You know very well that our outward-bound vessels to the English islands can get no sort of return cargo unless they go to Cuba or Porto Rico for sugar or molasses, or else to some salt port, or bring home some sort of wood or hides from St. Thomas or the Main. I speak of small vessels that trade to the West Indies and the Spanish Main.

* Mr. Fairfield.

"Gross, crude articles of this sort aid shipping interests, and assist making up cargoes to Europe of various such articles *if free*, such as logwood particularly, and Brazilletto and Rio Hache wood, in cotton ships, even, for dunnage.

"I call free trade the policy that lets crude articles in free, as in 'old times.'

"As far as I can judge, and being myself engaged in shipping interests, I think this bill very unfriendly to such interests; and as to being a free-trade bill, it is any thing else, as I understand free trade, as to the articles named.

"I am, dear Sir, your friend and fellow-citizen,

"WILLIAM MILES."

I now come, Mr. President, to the last topic on which I propose to trespass on the patience of the Senate; it is the effect of the change proposed by this bill upon the general employment, labor, and industry of the country. And I would beg, Sir, in this view, to ask the reading of a petition which has been lying on my table for some days, but which I have not had an opportunity to present. It is a very short petition from the mechanics and artisans of the city of Boston.* Now, Sir, these petitioners remonstrate against this bill, not in behalf of corporations and great establishments, not in behalf of rich manufacturers, but in behalf of "men who labor with their own hands," whose "only capital is their labor," and "who depend on that labor for their support, and for any thing they may be able to lay up."

Mr. President, he who is the most large and liberal in the tone of his sentiment towards all the interests of all parts of the country; he who most honestly and firmly believes that these interests, though various, are consistent; that they all may well be protected, preserved, and fostered by a wise administration of law under the existing Constitution of the United States; and he who is the most expansive patriot, and wishes well, and equally well, to every part of the country; even he must admit, that, to a great extent, there is a marked division and difference between the plantation States of the South and the masses in the agricultural and manufacturing States of the North. There is a difference growing out of early constitutions, early laws and

* The petition was then read by the Secretary.

habits, and resulting in a different description of labor; and, to some extent, with the most liberal sentiments and feelings, every man who is concerned in enacting laws with candor, justice, and intelligence must pay a proper regard to that distinction. The truth is, that in one part of the country labor is a thing more unconnected with capital than in the other. Labor, as an earning principle, or as an element of society working for itself, with its own hopes of gain, enjoyment, and competence, is a different thing from that labor, which, in the other part of the country, attaches to capital, rises and falls with capital, and is in truth a part of capital. Now, Sir, in considering the general effect of the change sought to be brought about, or likely to be brought about, by this bill, upon the employment of men in this country, regard is properly to be paid to this difference which I have mentioned; yet it is, at the same time, true, that there are forms of labor, especially along the sea-coast and along the rivers, in all the Southern States, which are to be injuriously affected by this bill, as much as the labor of any portion of the Middle or Northern States. The artisan in every State has just the same interest at the South as at the North. And this is at the foundation of all our laws, from 1789 downward, which have in view the protection of American labor. The first purpose, the first object, was the full protection of the labor of these artisans. That subject was gone over the other day by my friend from Maryland,* who presented to the consideration of the Senate the first memorial ever sent to Congress on the subject of protection. It was from the city of Baltimore, and it was in 1789. And from that day to this, Baltimore has been more earnest and steady in her attachment to a system of law which she supposed gave encouragement to her artisans, than almost any other city of the Union. I say, Sir, she has been steady and earnest. If she ever falters for a moment, she in a moment resumes her attitude, and pursues her accustomed course.

Now, Sir, taking the mass of men as they exist amongst us, what is it that constitutes their prosperity? Throughout the country, perhaps more especially at the North, from early laws and habits, there is a distribution of all the property accumulat-

* Mr. Johnson.

ed in one generation among the whole succession of sons and daughters in the next. Property is everywhere distributed as fast as it is accumulated, and not in more than one case out of a hundred is there an accumulation beyond the earnings of one or two generations. The first consequence of this is a great division of property into small parcels, and a considerable equality in the condition of a great portion of the people. The next consequence is, that, out of the whole mass, there is a very small proportion, hardly worthy of being named, that does not pursue some active business for a living. Who is there that lives on his income? How many, out of millions of prosperous people between this place and the British Provinces, and throughout the North and West, are there who live without being engaged in active business? The number is not worth naming. This is therefore a country of labor. I do not mean manual labor entirely. There is a great deal of that; but I mean some sort of employment that requires personal attention, either of oversight or manual performance; some form of active business. That is the character of our people, and that is the condition of our people. Our destiny is labor. Now, what is the first great cause of prosperity with such a people? Simply, *employment.* Why, we have cheap food and cheap clothing, and there is no sort of doubt that these things are very desirable to all persons of moderate circumstances, and laborers. But they are not the first requisites. The first requisite is that which enables men to buy food and clothing, cheap or dear. And if I were to illustrate my opinions on this subject by example, I should take, of all the instances in the world, the present condition of Ireland.

I am not, Mr. President, about to prescribe acts of legislation for Ireland, or principles to the Parliament of Great Britain for the government of Ireland. I am not about to suggest any remedy for the bad state of things which exists in that country; but what that state of things is, and what has produced it, are as plain and visible to my view as a turnpike-road; and I confess that I am astonished that learned and intelligent men have been brought up under certain notions or systems which appear to have so turned their eyes from the true view of the case, that they have been unable to solve the Irish problem. Well, now, what is it? Ireland is an over-peopled country, it is said. It has eight and a half millions of people on an area of thirty-one thousand eight hundred square miles. It is, then, a very dense population; perhaps a thicker population, upon the whole, than England. But why are the people of Ireland not prosperous, contented, and happy? We hear of a potato panic, and a population in Ireland distressed by the high price of potatoes. Why, Sir, the price of potatoes in this city is three times the price of potatoes in Dublin; and at this moment potatoes are twice as dear throughout the United States as throughout Ireland. There are potatoes enough, or food of other kinds, but the people are not able to buy them. And why? That is the stringent question. Why cannot the people of Ireland buy potatoes, or other food? The answer to this question solves the Irish case; and that answer is simply this, the people have not employment. They cannot obtain wages. They cannot earn money. The sum of their social misery lies in these few words. There is no adequate demand for labor. One half, or less than one half, of all the strong and healthy laborers of Ireland are quite enough to fulfil all demand and occupy all employments. Does not this admitted fact explain the whole case? If but half the laborers are employed, or the whole employed but half the time, or, in whatever form of division it be stated, if the result is that there is, in so thickly peopled a country, only half enough of employment for labor and industry, who need be surprised to find poverty and want the consequence? And who can be surprised, then, that other evils, not less to be lamented, should also be found to exist among a people of warm temperament and social habits and tendencies? It would be strange if all these results should not happen.

But, then, this only advances the inquiry to the real question, which is, *Why* are the laboring people of Ireland so destitute of useful and profitable employment? This is a question of the deepest interest to those who are charged with the duty of remedying the evil, if it can be remedied. But it is rather beside any present purpose of mine. It may be said, in general, that Ireland has been unfortunate, as well as badly governed. In the course of two centuries, much the greater part of the soil of Ireland, generally supposed to be as much as nine tenths, has been forfeited to the crown; and by the crown given or sold to persons in England. the heads of opulent families, or others. These new English proprietors are known as absentee landlords. They own a vast portion of the island. The absentee landlord is not a man who has grown up in Ireland, and has gone over to England to spend his income. He may be a man who never saw Ireland in his life. I have heard of families no member of which had visited its Irish estates for half a century, the lands being all the time under "rack-rent," in the hands of "middle-men," and all pressing the peasantry and labor to the dust.

There is a strange idea, at least it seems strange to me, which most respectable men entertain on this subject of Ireland. Mr. McCulloch, so highly distinguished an authority, for example, will insist upon it that there is no evil in Irish absenteeism. He proceeds on the theory, which, he says, admits of no exception, that it is best for a man to buy where he can buy cheapest. Well, that is undoubtedly so, if he have the means of buying. If Irish absenteeism did not diminish the employment of the people of Ireland, and so diminish their means of buying, the argument would hold. But who does not see, that, if the landlord lived in Ireland, consuming for his family and retainers the products of Ireland, it would augment the employment of Ireland? It seems clear to me that residence would not only give general countenance and encouragement to the laboring classes, and benefit both landlord and tenant, by dispensing with the services of middle-men, but that it would also do positive good by producing new demands for labor. From early times the English government has discouraged, in Ireland, every sort of manufacture, except the linen manufacture in the North. It has, on the other hand, encouraged agriculture. It has given bounties on wheat exported. The consequence has come to be this, that the surface of Ireland is cut up into so many tenements and holdings, that every man's labor is confined to such a small quantity of land, that there is not half employment for labor, and the lands are cultivated miserably after all. Mr. McCulloch says that four fifths of the labor of Ireland is laid out upon the land. There is no other source of employment or occupation. This land, being under a "rack-rent," is frequently in little patches, sometimes of not more than a quarter of an acre, merely to raise potatoes, the cheapest kind of food. This is the reason why labor is nothing, and can produce nothing but mere physical living, until the system shall be entirely changed. This constitutes the great difference between the state of things in Europe and America. In Europe the question is, how men can live. With us the question is, how well they can live. Can they live on wholesome food, in commodious and comfortable dwellings? Can they be well clothed, and be able to educate their children? Such questions do not arise to the political economists of Europe. When reasoning on such cases as that of Ireland, the question with them is, how physical being can be kept from death. That is all.

Sir, if I were not overwhelmed with topics, and if I were not conscious of having already occupied the time of the Senate quite too long, I would turn your attention to the contrasts, produced by the very causes which we are now considering, between Ireland and Scotland. The population of Ireland, as I have said, is eight millions and a half, on an area of thirty-one thousand eight hundred square miles. Scotland has a population of less than three millions, and an area of twenty-six thousand square miles, only one third of which is arable.

But, nevertheless, the shipping tonnage of Scotland is four hundred and twenty-nine thousand tons, employing twenty-eight thousand men; while that of Ireland is only one hundred and forty thousand, employing eleven or twelve thousand men. With regard to the agriculture of Scotland, though her climate is not so good, nor her soil so rich, as that of Ireland, yet Scotland is a wheat-growing country, and the prices are high, and all agricultural business active. How has this come about? This great reformation, it is said, has been accomplished within sixty or seventy years; and respectable authorities say that the growth of the manufacturing cities of Glasgow, Paisley, Edinburgh, and the rest, by furnishing a market for the immediate sale of agricultural products, has doubled those products, raised them from a lower to a higher species of production, and changed the whole face of the country. I will not pursue this illustration further. It is enough to say, that Scotland has commerce, manufactures, and a variety of employments for labor. In Ireland there is little of commerce and little of manufactures, four fifths of the whole labor of the country being bestowed on the land. These facts are enough to show why Scotland is the Scotland which we find her, and Ireland the Ireland which we find her.

Now, Sir, no man can deny that the course of things in this

country, for the last twenty or thirty years, has had a wonderful effect in producing a variety of employments. How much employment has been furnished by the canals and railroads, in addition to the great amount of labor, not only in the factories, rendered so odious in some quarters by calling them monopolies and close corporations, but in the workshops, in the warehouses, on the sea and on the land, and in every department of business! There is a great and general activity, and a great variety in the employments of men amongst us; and that is just exactly what our condition ought to be.

The interest of every laboring community requires diversity of occupations, pursuits, and objects of industry. The more that diversity is multiplied or extended, the better. To diversify employment is to increase employment, and to enhance wages. And, Sir, take this great truth; place it on the title-page of every book of political economy intended for the use of the United States; put it in every Farmer's Almanac; let it be the heading of the column in every Mechanic's Magazine; proclaim it everywhere, and make it a proverb, that *where there is work for the hands of men, there will be work for their teeth.* Where there is employment, there will be bread. It is a great blessing to the poor to have cheap food; but greater than that, prior to that, and of still higher value, is the blessing of being able to buy food by honest and respectable employment. Employment feeds, and clothes, and instructs. Employment gives health, sobriety, and morals. Constant employment and well-paid labor produce, in a country like ours, general prosperity, content, and cheerfulness. Thus happy have we seen the country. Thus happy may we long continue to see it.

And now, Sir, with a very few words addressed to particular interests, I shall relieve the Senate. It has appeared to me particularly strange that our friends from the grain-growing States of the Northwest do not take a different view from that which they now entertain of their ultimate, permanent interest. They are grain-growers. They entertain the hope, especially since the repeal of the British corn laws, that they shall be able to produce wheat to a still larger extent, and obtain for their commodity a commensurate price abroad. For myself, I am fully of opinion that there will be a great disappointment in this respect. I do admit, for I have always believed it, that, with the British ports open to the admission of American Indian corn, or maize, there will be a great deal of it sent to Europe, because of the cheapness of the article, and because, when it comes to be known, it will be, I think, well received amongst the laboring classes. But it seems to me that a few facts may be enough to satisfy us that there cannot be a vast augmentation of Western and Southwestern exportations of wheat, on account of any new demand in Europe. In the first place, our agricultural products have done little more than to keep pace with the increase of our own population. In the next place, the agricultural product of England about keeps pace with her augmenting population, from year to year. And in the third place, if we refer to the list of prices, we shall find that wheat is at this moment, after all we have heard of panics and fears of panics, twenty per cent. lower than in former years; and I see by Mr. Brown's price-current of the 3d of this month, that prime flour was $ 5.28 per barrel in Liverpool, or, rather, yielded that return to the exporter from the United States. It does appear to me, Sir, that gentlemen who live on these fertile lands of the West, among the most prosperous and most favored communities, would do exceedingly well to consider whether, in fact, they gain any thing by a supposed augmentation of exportations, whether they profit any thing by an extension of the market abroad, whilst they diminish the demand at home. If, by an importation of British manufactures, we encourage the production of the articles manufactured in Europe rather than in America, and bringing the goods here to the United States, is that not certain to diminish the consumption at home of agricultural products, by diminishing the number of consumers? So that, after all, it comes to this, whether it is better for an agriculturist to have a home market than to have a foreign market!

Well, Sir, allow me to say a word on this subject to gentlemen of some of the Southern States. They will allow me at least to give them tables and calculations. I will not undertake to instruct their reason, but wish to draw their attention to facts. The State of Massachusetts is a great grain-purchasing State. I have here a table of the quantities of grain and some other articles purchased by and consumed in Massachusetts in one year, and it strikes me to be worthy of attention.

Flour, 630,000 bbls. at $ 5.50 per bbl., ...	$ 3,465,000
Corn and other grains, 3,100,000 bushels, at 54c.,	1,674,000
Coal, 180,000 tons, at $ 5.75 per ton, ...	1,035,000
Wool, 7,200,000 lbs., at 33c. per lb., ...	2,376,000
Lumber of all kinds, ...	4,100,000
Lead, ...	1,300,000
Beef, pork, bacon, and lard, ...	3,000,000
	$ 16,950,000

The corn comes chiefly from the eastern shore of Virginia, North Carolina, and Maryland. Where else can these States expect to find a market like this?

Now, Sir, what is the advantage to these corn-growing States of turning our people, the consumers of these articles, out of their workshops, and making agricultural producers of them also? This is a strange policy; where men have already more agricultural products than they can find a market for, to increase the product! On the other hand, where there are more mouths to feed than can be supplied, to increase the number of mouths!

The Northwestern States are destined to be manufacturing States. They have iron and coal. They have a people of laborious habits. They have already capital enough to begin works such as belong to new States and new communities; and when the time comes, and it cannot but come soon, they will see their true interest to be, to feed the Northern and Eastern manufacturers, as far as they may require it, and in the mean time begin to vary their own occupations, by having classes of men amongst them who are not of the now universal agricultural population. The sooner they begin this work the better; and begin it they will, because they are an intelligent and active people, and cannot fail to see in what direction their true interest lies.

Sir, it does not become me to do more than suggest in what the interest of other parts of the country appears to me to consist. Men more competent to judge will decide, and I do not wish to exempt them from an exercise of their judgment. But now, in regard to this manufacture of cotton, I said the other day that I should not take up the New England case. She would be injured, injured to a certain extent, unquestionably; but she would not be injured so much as the new establishments of the South. It appears to me the plainest proposition in the world, that there is nothing which the whole South can so profitably turn its attention to as the manufacture of these coarse cotton fabrics. The South might soon come to undersell New England altogether, because it is a fabric in the value of which the raw material is the most important element. As labor, therefore, forms but a small portion of the article produced in its manufactured state, it requires less capital for machinery and expensive establishments. The raw material being the principal element composing the value gives, of course, an advantage to those who raise the raw material, and who manufacture it just where it is produced. Now I must say, that, at the exhibition here last month or the month before, nothing appeared to me better done than some of these cheap cotton fabrics from Virginia, North Carolina, and Georgia; and I believe, as strongly as I may venture to believe any thing against the opinion of men of more local knowledge, that these manufactures will succeed and prosper, if we let them alone, in the Southern States. And I wish them to prosper. They have arisen in a desire on the part of the Southern people to clothe themselves and their people against New England competition. I conceive it to be for the interest of every community to produce its own clothing; and it strikes me that the effort on the part of the South ought to be encouraged.

But it is time that I relieve the Senate from this discussion. I certainly feel the momentous importance of the subject. I feel that, in the course of my public life, I have never had a more responsible duty to perform, and certainly I never looked forward with more interest to the consequences. If the present system of things be deranged, no man can tell where that derangement is to stop, or what are to be the ultimate results. This, Sir, is a proceeding in which we cannot see the end from the beginning. With respect to the great question of the revenue, I hold that the responsibility of providing revenue for the treasury rests with Congress. I hold that we are not at liberty o devolve that responsibility upon the executive government; and I would ask the administration itself, with all respect, if, now that there seems less prospect than we had hoped of an early termination of this war, if now, within three or four months of the commencement of the next session of Congress, if now with the tried system which we are sure of for the production of adequate revenue, so far as we may expect revenue at all from duties and customs, it would not feel safer itself, after the rejection of this bill, than if it should pass?

Sir, I beseech gentlemen to pause. If I were a friend of the administration, and I do not mean to call myself its enemy, for I have no unfriendly feeling to it, I would beseech it not to make this leap in the dark, in the early part of its career, unnecessarily, in the midst of a war, a war of which no man can see the end, and of which no man can now reckon the expense. I would beseech it to stand firm on established ground, on the system on which our revenue now stands; and to lay aside all propositions for extensive and elementary change.

Having said this, I have discharged my duty. I leave it to the judgment of the Senate. I am not to be seduced, on the one hand, by any disposition to embarrass the administration. I certainly feel none; I hope I have manifested none; and, on the other hand, I am not to be deterred by clamor in the press and elsewhere against those who conscientiously, in matters of the highest interest, fulfil their duty. And, Sir, though a most respectable member of this Senate has been made the object of unmeasured opprobrium, because, on a great question connected with the credit and honor of the government and its revenues in time of war, he could not bring himself to think with the majority of his friends, yet even the consequences which have fallen upon him shall not deter me from the fearless discharge of my duty.

I indicated, at the commencement of my speech, that I should conclude it with a motion to postpone the consideration of this bill to the next session of Congress. Upon reflection, I deem it proper to say, that I have so far changed that purpose as that I shall venture upon one amendment, to see whether a disposition exists in the Senate to take this bill exactly as it is, or whether, in the particular I shall mention, it ought not, in the judgment of the Senate, to be changed. It is that extraordinary provision to which I alluded on Saturday, by which, in cases of undervaluation with intention to defraud, the goods are to be seized and sold, and the importer to be paid the value of the goods as rated in his invoice, and five per cent. over. I now move that that provision be struck out.*

* This motion prevailed.

THE TARIFF.*

AFTER the conclusion of the foregoing argument, and some further discussion, Mr. Clayton submitted the following resolution, which passed the Senate: —

"*Resolved*, That the bill be committed to the Committee on Finance, with instructions to remove the new duties imposed by said bill, in all cases, where any foreign raw material is taxed to the prejudice of any mechanic or manufacturer, so that no other or higher duty shall be collected on any such raw material than is provided by the act of the 30th of August, 1842: and further, so to regulate all the duties imposed by this bill, as to raise a revenue sufficient for the exigencies of the country."

On the following day (28th July), Mr. Lewis, the chairman of the committee, reported back the bill without alteration, and moved that the committee be discharged from the further consideration of the instructions contained in Mr. Clayton's resolution.

A discussion arose on this motion, in the course of which Mr. Webster spoke as follows.

THE question now before the Senate is in one respect a test question, as it has been described by the honorable member from Missouri; † not exactly in the light in which he views it, or in the sense in which he wishes to be understood, but in quite a different sense, in another aspect altogether. We are here, Sir, calling ourselves every day a democratic Congress, and the majority of the body is said to be about to pass a great democratic measure. I suppose, if any meaning is attached to these terms, it is that this is a measure favorable to the masses, favorable to the people, preferring the interests of the

* Remarks in the Senate of the United States, on the 28th of July, 1846.

† Mr. Benton.

masses to the interests of a few, preferring the interests of the great body of the people to those who may be called the possessors of a large amount of wealth. Well, Sir, what sort of a bill does the question now about to be taken show that this "great democratic measure" is? or what sort of a measure is this popular democratic bill? It purports to be an "act reducing the duty on imports, and for other purposes." The title would not describe the bill at all, if it did not indicate that there were other purposes besides the mere reduction of duties; and one of those other purposes is to enhance duties. The true interpretation of the bill, therefore, is, that it is an act for reducing certain duties and enhancing certain other duties on articles of importation.

Now, Sir, let us see whether this is such a bill as is pretended, a bill in favor of the masses, in favor of the people! Just look at the question now submitted to the Senate! This bill does reduce duties, but on what? Why, there may be some articles on which the duties are reduced for the benefit of the middling classes; but the great reduction of duties is on such articles as those of which I read to you yesterday a list from the letter of Mr. Nichol. You reduce the duty on spirits of all kinds to the great extent which I mentioned yesterday. You reduce the duty on spices to the great extent which I mentioned yesterday. You reduce the duty on imported tropical fruits and other fruits. You reduce the duty on ready-made clothing. You reduce the duty on rich and expensive carpets. You reduce the duty on rich cut-glass. You reduce every one of these duties, and you saw that this reduction keeps out of the treasury more than the whole of the duty laid upon certain other articles. But these are your reductions, your main reductions. They are all on articles of luxury, of extreme luxury; spirits, spices, silks, costly carpets, rich cut-glass, ready-made clothing; articles which none of the middling classes are interested in, or in the habit of buying or using. Now it is proposed to see whether you will or will not, by the instructions to your committee, continue the practice of freeing the raw material, upon which all the manufacturing and laboring people of the country earn a living, when they get it. That question is now distinctly put to you, and put to this Senate. On the raw material, which is to come here and furnish employment and occupation to the manufacturers and artisans of the country, you have raised the duty. Perhaps on all these raw materials, but certainly on many of them, as I showed yesterday, you have raised the duty above the standard of that tariff which you say is an obnoxious Whig measure, and for the reduction of whose duties you stand pledged. Now you have been asked to send the bill to your committee, with instructions, in every case where the duty on the raw material, as proposed by this bill, exceeds the duty on the same raw material imposed by the Whig tariff of 1842, to take it off, and you won't do it; you won't do it! No. You indulge in the luxury of taxing the poor man and the laborer! That is the whole tendency, the whole character, the whole effect, of the bill. One may see everywhere in it the desire to revel in the delight of taking away men's employment. That is the character of this bill. And this is the question now before the Senate.

Sir, I had hoped that the honorable gentleman* who spoke yesterday with so much effect on the necessity of protecting the mechanics and laborers, who dwelt with so much emphasis on the very objectionable feature of taxing the raw material, I had hoped that he would have held to his purpose. I say that this bill holds a language that cannot be mistaken, that cannot and will not be misunderstood. It is not a bill for the people. It is not a bill for the masses. It is not a bill to add to the comforts of those in middle life, or of the poor. It is not a bill for employment. It is a bill for the relief of the highest and most luxurious classes of the country, and a bill imposing onerous duties on the great industrious masses, and for taking away the means of living from labor everywhere throughout the land. It cannot be disguised. You cannot mask its features. No man is so blind as not to see what this bill is; and the people will not be so callous, I trust, as not to feel it. In this sense, and in this view, the question now about to be put is a test question. We shall have the voice of the Senate upon it. We shall know who is for raising the duty on various articles to the prejudice, and in many cases to the ruin, of our own countrymen, working here at home as artisans and handicraftsmen, and who is at the same time for reducing the duties on the highest luxuries. That is

* Mr. Benton.

the test, and no man can escape it. No man will escape that test.

Now I shall vote to keep this proposition in the hands of the committee. The committee has not tried whether it can obey the instructions of the Senate. Last night they were instructed to do their duty, and at a very early hour this morning they say they have made up their mind. Was ever the like heard before? The chairman asks to be discharged. I don't believe they were convened on this matter for ten minutes. I doubt whether they have been together at all. What is the difficulty of ascertaining the amount of duty on the general list of raw materials, and reducing the rates of this bill to those of the act of 1842? There is not a gentleman who could not do it in two hours. If they had been disposed, the committee could have obeyed your instructions before meridian this day. I am rather inclined to think, Sir, that they did not fatigue themselves by examining this matter. I am rather inclined to think it was their opinion that the best way was to take a short cut and move to be discharged, in the hope that some occurrence or other would enable them to carry that motion. I do not believe that they have opened a book, or looked at any list of raw materials. I am disposed to think, Mr. President, they are as *raw* on the whole subject as they were yesterday.

I repeat, Sir, that this bill has a face and front, so that, when it is held up to the country, no man need write at the bottom of it whether it is a democratic bill or an aristocratic bill. When it shows to all the laboring portions of this community, that their daily labor and daily bread are directly interfered with; that, wherever it can be done, a tax is laid upon the raw materials upon which they work and earn their living; when they see at the same time, in the next line, the duties on those high classes of luxuries, spirits, silks, expensive carpets, rich cut-glass, and the rest of them, are reduced, will they ask any body to tell them what that bill is? Will they need any one to give a name to it? Sir, it names itself. It has the face and front of an aristocratic bill, oppressive of the poor and working man; and in every respect it corresponds to its face and front.

Some remarks were now made by Mr. McDuffie of South Carolina, in which reference was had to resolutions adopted in Boston in 1820, against the tariff bill commonly known as "Mr. Baldwin's bill," which resolutions, at the request of Mr. McDuffie, were read at the Secretary's table. After some explanations between Mr. Webster and Mr. McDuffie, Mr. Webster continued as follows: —

A word, Sir, about these resolutions of 1820. I remember the state of things very well. The commercial people of New England in 1820 were in a considerable state of alarm. They had business all over the world. They thought that a policy had been begun at Washington which would interfere with their commerce, and it was of that they were afraid. How was this great evil, of which they had become afraid, fastened upon them? By the *minimums* introduced into the tariff law of 1816, by South Carolina, in order to cut off the trade of the United States with India. The *minimum* principle, so odious now, was moved in Congress by a most respectable and distinguished member from South Carolina, not now living.* It was carried by South Carolina, against every vote of Massachusetts. I do not think there was a vote of Massachusetts, not one, in favor of the measure. It is not, then, because the *minimum* principle is bad in itself, that it is now opposed. Why, Sir, *minimum* is now spoken of here as if it were a Pawnee Indian, or one of the Camanches, that eats up and destroys every body and every thing.

Mr. McDuffie. So it does.

Well, bad as it is, it was introduced by South Carolina, against every vote of Massachusetts.

Well, then, in 1820, an eminent member of Congress from Pennsylvania introduced a high protective tariff, bearing, among certain other things, especially upon iron. I refer to Mr. Baldwin, afterwards judge of the Supreme Court. That tariff went to protect every thing out of New England. Thus was New England between the upper and nether mill-stone, between the South Carolina tariff, with its *minimums* on cottons, which cut off the India trade, and the Pennsylvania tariff, which looked mainly to that State. Is it to be wondered at that we were alarmed?

I wish the gentleman had dwelt a little more, in his address to the chair, on the effect of this bill upon the iron and coal of Pennsylvania. But I agree that, whether it be owing to change

* Mr. Lowndes.

of opinion, wrought by circumstances, by a change in the condition of things in the country, or otherwise, I agree, that, in the present state of things, which has existed since 1824, there is no going back from that principle of protection which was then established. The law of 1824 did not pass with the consent of Massachusetts. It received but one vote, I think, from the entire delegation from Massachusetts, in both Houses of Congress. As I said the other day, New England had been addicted to commerce. But she supposed the time had come when she must conform herself to the law of the country, and invest her capital, for her labor was her capital, and employ her industry, in such pursuits as the country had promised to protect and uphold. Now, Sir, if there be any thing inconsistent in that, I admit the inconsistency. I still agree to every word of the resolution of Faneuil Hall of 1820. But in the present state of things there is an essential importance, an absolute moral necessity, for maintaining those habits, pursuits, businesses, and employments into which men entered twenty-two years ago, upon the faith of the declared sentiments and policy of a majority of both houses of Congress.

Now, Sir, in regard to the assessment of duties, the great measure proposed by this bill, I confine myself to the substance of the instructions given to the committee yesterday, and from which it is now proposed to relieve them, that is, raw material. The honorable member says that in most cases this imposition is small, only five per cent. Well, what is that? Why, five per cent. is enough to put an end to a great many of the employments of the United States. If they had not competition from abroad, it would be a different thing. But when you tax the raw material and admit the manufactured article free, or at a lower rate of duty, if any body will go into the manufacture under these circumstances, it will very soon be found that the tax on the raw material of five per cent., which the honorable member from South Carolina considers a small matter, a very small matter, is enough to decide the competition between the American and English manufacturer. England lets in the commodity free. She is full of skill and capital. Money can be got at a much lower rate of interest than here, and labor at less than half price. How, then, can you expect the American manufacturer to be able to compete with England, when, with all these disadvantages against him, you tax his raw material and admit the commodities of his rival at a low rate of duty? How is he to contend, not only against cheaper capital and cheaper labor, but also against a tax on his raw material? He cannot do it. Now the gentleman says, and he has a right to the opinion, that the laboring man will be benefited by the cheaper price of such cotton as he wears. He stated the other day that he thought there would be an importation of ten millions of that sort of cotton. If that should happen, there would be a very singular sight exhibited upon the ocean. For the statistical tables show that, in the course of last year, the United States exported, carried out of the country, and sold, four and a half millions of the same sort of cotton.

MR. McDUFFIE. The coarse article?

Essentially the same. The article costing seven cents a yard in Boston. Now if an article costing six or seven cents in Boston, like the article expected to be imported, is exported in such quantities, is there any reasonable foundation for the opinion that ten millions of the same goods would be imported? This is a matter of opinion. I will not say that the expectation is groundless, because I will always treat the honorable member's opinions with the highest degree of respect. But it appears to me perfectly plain, that the descriptions of articles alluded to by him, since they are exported in such quantities, cannot be expected to be imported to such an extent as he seems inclined to anticipate.

Sir, the honorable member has expressed the opinion, that the farmers, by which term I suppose he means the persons employed in agriculture at the North, (we usually distinguish between farmers and planters,) will be greatly benefited by the bill. He supposes that they are now taxed for the benefit of their neighbors, the mechanics and manufacturers. Now, Sir, the question being asked, the answer will be decisive, Were prices ever lower? Were they ever lower to the farmers than they are now? Is it a well-founded opinion, that manufactured articles could be produced, and brought here from England, below the present rates in this country? The Senator stated a very strong case apparently, the case of the daughter of an Illinois farmer, who was clad in cotton cloth not worth over four or five cents a yard.

And why? And why, Sir? That only advances the discussion one stage. The evident answer to that question is, because there was no market of consumption for the grain on her father's farm. That is the proximate cause. Flour is now two dollars a barrel in Missouri; and under the repeal of the corn laws we have reason to believe that good flour at St. Louis will, as a correspondent in that part of the world writes me, not be above a dollar and a half a barrel. Well, if the gentleman is right in supposing that these agricultural products will rise up to a great price in consequence of any recently occurring event, he may hold very well to the other opinion, that the introduction of English commodities at such a rate of duties as will bring them in here in great quantities should be encouraged. I can only say in respect to this, that in my judgment it is a great fallacy. I do not doubt that the repeal of the corn laws may have a beneficial effect in extending liberal sentiments and a liberal spirit amongst nations. But that it is to relieve the American market of its surplus grain, I do not believe. The people of England will not consume more bread. England is annually increasing her agricultural products. Agriculture is improving. The English landlords are improving their stock with a profusion of expenditure almost incredible in this country. Last year one of these proprietors expended a hundred thousand dollars in draining his estate in order to increase the product of wheat. If you look, Sir, to Pennsylvania, to New York, to Maryland, as well as the New England States, you will find that the farmer looks for remunerating profit in the sale of his products among the mechanics and manufacturers of the towns and villages. Look to the statistics, and you will see how much of agriculture goes with every product of manufacture in the United States. Of that, England herself is an example. An honorable member from Pennsylvania of the other house has gone into that with perfect accuracy and precision, so that I need not dwell on it. I will not extend these remarks. But with regard to my proposition, you must submit to a great loss of revenue on the luxuries I have mentioned, at the same time that you reduce the wages of labor by taxing the raw material. "Look here upon this picture, and on this," and let the country decide.

THE SUB-TREASURY.*

Mr. President, — I shall occupy the attention of the Senate but a few moments on the measure now before it. Before, however, I proceed to do this, I feel it a duty to call the attention of the honorable Senator from Alabama † and the other members of the Senate to what I see stated in the official journal of the last evening in regard to another matter which has lately received the action of this body. And I do so in order to prevent an erroneous impression from going abroad as a matter of fact. I find in "The Union" of last evening the following paragraph: —

"Much has been said of false invoices, as if the importer had only to falsify his invoice, and so pay under the *ad valorem* system as little duty as he chose. The fact is, that the value of the goods taxed is to be settled, not by the importer's invoice, but by competent and skilful appraisers. They are to appraise the goods at their actual market value *in our ports*, in New York or Philadelphia; not at Canton or Manchester. In this point of view, the appraisers, whose duty it will be to understand the state of our markets, will give only such regard to the importer's invoice as it may seem entitled to. They may, if they please, take the invoice as *primâ facie* evidence of the actual cost of the goods, and so approximately of their actual worth in our markets. But it is only *primâ facie* evidence. The appraisers must value the goods upon their own judgment, after all. Yet the importer is obliged to present an invoice; and one provision of the new law goes far towards making this

* Remarks in the Senate of the United States, on the 1st of August, 1846, on the Third Reading of the Bill "to provide for the better Organization of the Treasury, and for the Collection, Safe-keeping, Transfer, and Disbursement of the Public Revenue."

† Mr. Lewis.

invoice a true exponent of the value of the goods; for the law provides, that if the value placed upon the goods by the importer, on entering them at the custom-house, is less by ten per cent. than the value at which they are subsequently appraised, then twenty per cent. *additional* duty upon the appraised value is to be levied and collected."

Now, a more enormous error than this was never put forth to the world. The law of the land, as it now stands, requires that the value fixed upon goods by the United States appraisers shall be the value, not here, but at the place of exportation. This is a fact which all business men well know, and which the chairman of the Committee on Finance will himself confirm.

Mr. Lewis here nodded assent.

Those who indulge themselves so much in remarks (not always very courteous) on the course of others, should be cautious first to understand subjects themselves. Here is an assertion of an alleged fact, while the very opposite is true.

But, not to detain the Senate longer on a matter of this sort, I will make an observation or two on the bill now pending, and, as I presume, soon to become a law.

I have always been opposed to this system of a "constitutional treasury," or "independent treasury," or "sub-treasury," which is the old name for it. The evils of such a system are insurmountable, and of various kinds. But I shall now briefly point out what I consider its evil consequences on the operations of the government, without adverting to its effect on the general business of the country. I shall preface what I have to say with a very short history of this scheme. Owing to an unhappy controversy between a former President of the Union * and the late Bank of the United States, the custody of the national funds was withdrawn from the national bank and committed to certain selected State banks. As soon as the money was deposited in their vaults, the then Secretary of the Treasury † instructed the directors of those banks to be very free and liberal in making discounts to merchants on the money in their vaults. The banks complied with this order, and the result was, that in 1837 they generally stopped payment. In consequence of this state of things, President Van Buren called a special session of Con

* General Jackson. † Mr. Taney.

gress in September, 1837, and this project of the independent treasury was then brought forward for the first time. It failed, however, at that time, and again at a subsequent Congress; but in 1840 it passed into a law. Such, however, was found to be its practical working, that it was not suffered to continue in operation a year, but was repealed in 1841.

Now, there might have been at least some plausible reason for resorting to a new system in the keeping of the public treasure in 1837, for the national bank had ceased to exist, and the State banks had all broken down. The public money must be kept somewhere, and the government thereupon resolved to try "the untried experiment" of keeping the public funds in vaults of its own. For the last five years we have been under a system of which this formed no part. Now the first question which I wish to put to gentlemen who advocate this bill is this: Do they not all admit that the public moneys are now safe? Do they harbor any fear that there will be public defalcations? Is there any apprehension of the loss of the public treasure if this bill shall not be adopted? For my own part, I think the public deposits are perfectly safe where they are. The banks to which they are intrusted have given us the most ample security, and that security for the most part is in stocks of the United States. If our own stock is adequate security, then the banks are in fact for the most part creditors of the United States, instead of being its debtors. They hold more of our stock than they do of our funds. Under such circumstances, none can say that the public money is unsafe, and no danger, therefore, will be incurred in that respect from the postponement, or even the rejection, of this bill. The banks have acted with very great prudence and propriety; they have not indulged in any excess of discounts; but, feeling the responsibility under which they were placed, they have proceeded with discretion, and have ever been ready to accommodate the government in any manner not inconsistent with their duty to the stockholders and to the country. If gentlemen admit that the condition of the public money is at present as safe as we can make it, then what is the benefit which they seek from this bill, or where is the necessity of passing it?

Considering it as a measure of the administration, it appears to me that it is likely, instead of proving of any benefit to the government, only to arrest or thwart the operations of the treasury. To me it is most clear that the bill will become, in its practical effect, a clog on the administration. I refer gentlemen to the twenty-first and twenty-second sections of the bill as it now stands. Let them examine the probable working of these portions of the law, and then say whether the bill will not prove, not only of no assistance to the fiscal operation of the government, but, on the contrary, a great embarrassment.

I can readily understand that, if the amendments which were proposed to the twenty-first section had prevailed, much facility might have resulted to the treasury from the use of treasury drafts, placed in the hands of disbursing officers to be paid out to the creditors of the government. But the Senate, by a large majority, rejected those amendments. In its present state, the bill subtracts from the facility which would otherwise have attended the operation of these treasury drafts. As the law now stands, if a man comes to the treasury with a demand for money, he gets a draft to the desired amount, which he indorses, and which is then a transferable security, and may pass through as many hands as may be necessary or convenient to the holders, and may be kept out just as long as they please. There is an unrestricted circulation of this treasury draft, and it is transferable without any further indorsement. But here, under this bill, it is made the duty of the Secretary of the Treasury to hasten the presentation of all such drafts, and to prescribe a time within which they shall be presented and paid. If the place of payment be near at hand, then they are to be presented immediately, and not to be kept or left outstanding. The amendment made here is just the reverse of the bill. The House bill goes to restrain the circulation of the drafts; our proposition gives it greater facilities. The purposes of the two are in open hostility with each other. It is clear that, if the bill shall stand as it now is, instead of being of any use to the treasury, it will operate as a downright restraint on facilities which it would otherwise enjoy.

Confining my remarks altogether to the character of this bill, considered as an administration measure, I proceed, on the other hand, to consider what will be the disadvantages to the government from its becoming a law. I go on the supposition that the bill is to be executed, not evaded; and I say that, if the specie payments which it enjoins are required *bonâ fide*, it will operate as a great embarrassment to the government should it be placed in a condition in which it would be necessary to negotiate a loan. There is authority for a loan now, and the government has its option between such a measure and the issue of treasury-notes. But if this law shall be carried out, no loan will be possible. And why not? Because the law will demand that eight or ten millions of dollars in hard specie shall be withdrawn from active circulation, some four or five millions of it being locked up in government chests and vaults, and some four or five millions more being constantly *in transitu*, as the payments of the government may require. Then, if the government wants a loan, how is it to be got? The practical mode at present pursued is this. Some large banker takes, for example, two millions of the government loan. But this man cannot furnish the cash unless he finds banks who are willing to take the United States stock and advance him a temporary loan upon it, until, to use the business phrase, he shall be able to "place the money"; that is, shall be able to find persons who will take the stock with the view of holding it and receiving interest upon it. This is the mode now pursued. But what will be the condition of the banks who may be asked by him to advance money upon stock after this bill shall have become a law? How can they possibly do it? The sum they agree to advance must be paid in gold and silver, taken on the instant out of their own vaults and carried across the street to be locked up in the vaults of some government depository. If the bullion remained with the banks, and a credit on their books was all that was required, they might do it; but the specie is instantly called for, and is so much deducted from the basis of their circulation. Their customers will not agree to it, their directors will not agree to it, their stockholders will not agree to it. I say, therefore, if this law is not evaded, but is obeyed *bonâ fide*, any negotiation of a government loan must be out of the question. I put that fact to any man acquainted with business, and ask if he can gainsay it.

I do not mean to go at any length into the embarrassments which this bill must inflict on the mercantile community; but there is one so obvious and prominent that I cannot forbear mentioning it, in connection with another bill which we have recently passed. Those who expect an adequate revenue under the new tariff law look of course for largely augmented importations, and they expect that the duties on these importations are to be paid. This bill says they are to be paid in gold and silver; and I ask, Where is the importer to get his money? The ordinary way is to go to a bank, and say to the directors or the president, I have five thousand dollars of duties to pay to-day. The bank, knowing that he is about to enter his goods, and that it will immediately get the money back from the custom-house, makes no difficulty; but if it knew that the money, instead of coming back into its vaults, was to be lugged off in specie and locked up in a government vault, and that so much was to be taken from the basis of its circulation, it would not be quite so ready to accommodate him; and even the apprehension of a difficulty of this kind is, in the matter of credit and advances, more than half as bad as the thing itself. The apprehended evil creates as great an unwillingness in the banks to advance as the evil itself.

I agree, indeed, that the severity of the pressure will be mitigated by the use of treasury-notes, so long as those treasury-notes remain in circulation; and therefore I say that gentlemen may be assured of one thing: if this sub-treasury system is to be adopted, the system of treasury-notes will be coeval with it in duration. As long as the one stands, the other must be resorted to, for the law would be altogether intolerable without such a relief. And here I say again, what I recently said on the subject of treasury-notes, that I see no reason why treasury-notes should not be issued at once. There seems to prevail an idea at the treasury, that the government should not issue its notes as long as it has a dollar in the treasury, and that they must spend the six millions, or whatever other balance there may be there, before any treasury-note is issued. It was my idea that the government should issue notes while it had money under its keeping, and thereby the government might sustain its credit. But it seems that other notions have prevailed. Now I think that, for the same reason that this bill will create embarrassment in regard to a loan, it will create the same embarrassment in relation to treasury-notes, because it will cast discredit generally upon all securities issued by the government.

And now I will call the attention of the Senate to the condi tion of things as they at present exist, and as they will be. I suppose the warehousing bill is destined to pass into a law. The new tariff has become a law, and it has reduced the duties to be imposed on foreign goods. Of course the imports for this and for the next quarter will be very limited. Men will either not bring in goods at all now, or only for the purpose of taking them out to get the benefit of the drawback, and not to enter them for payment of duty. The receipts, therefore, must be very small. There is another reason why they will fall below the ordinary amount. There is in the country a large quantity of goods which have been brought in, but not consumed. These will be reëxported for drawback, and stored in some neighboring port until the tariff law goes into effect, and then they will be reimported. All this must create a serious loss to the treasury. After the 1st of December a large amount of warehoused goods will be entered for duty; and as the articles exported for debenture will also be returning, the probable receipts of the quarter commencing on the 1st of January must be very large. Yet, as this is the very time when this law begins to demand that all duties shall be paid in specie, just at the time when the amount of importation is at the highest point in the whole year, this demand for gold and silver will look the importing merchant in the face. Do not gentlemen see how serious an inconvenience must be inflicted by such a concurrence of circumstances? It is plain that the government can get no loan at such a time. It will be as much as the banks can do to stand the call that will be made upon them for specie by their own customers, especially if the importations shall be any thing like what is calculated by the Secretary of the Treasury. The prospect of such a demand, and the knowledge beforehand that it may come, will act as strongly against the possibility of a loan as the fact itself. The certain prospect that their specie will be called for, to be locked up in government vaults even for a short time, will induce the banks to curtail their discounts, and must be productive of very great embarrassment, both public and private.

I say, in all seriousness, that this should be entitled "A bill to embarrass the treasury in the disbursement of the public money." Here will be both the tariff and the sub-treasury coming into practical operation at one time. Is not one of them enough to cope with at once? Then we are under the pressure of a public war, a war of which none can see the end; and it is under these circumstances that we have ventured upon an entire change in the collection of revenue, and adopted a system wholly untried. Is it necessary, on the top of this, to introduce another new and untried system in the disbursement of our revenue? Must we have more experiments? a new system of collection and a new system of disbursement? Is this prudent?

But as I promised when I rose to detain the Senate but for a few minutes, I will do no more than put a question or two to gentlemen on the other side.

Will any man say that the public moneys are now unsafe? Does any man apprehend that they are likely to be lost? [A pause.] Nobody will say so.

I put to gentlemen another question. Is there any gentleman here who will say that he believes this law will give any new facilities to the government? [Mr. W. here paused again.] If there is, I should like to hear his voice. I shall be greatly obliged to him to say so now, and not to answer the interrogatory only by crying "Ay" on the passage of this bill. I greatly fear that I shall not hear any other affirmative reply. I doubt if there is one gentleman who will or can answer either of these questions in the affirmative. On the contrary, I leave it to gentlemen who are connected with the administration, and who, from their position, live in habits of daily intercourse with those who conduct the government, to say whether it is not their own candid opinion that this bill, administration bill though it be, will not prove a help, but rather a hinderance, to them in the administration of our fiscal concerns?

The operation of this law on the commercial community, its strange, un-American character, have been so fully exposed by the honorable Senators from Maine and Connecticut* that I will not now enter on that part of the subject. I frankly confess that I did not expect that this sub-treasury scheme would ever be revived. I had heard of "Polk, Dallas, and the tariff of 1842," but I really never did expect to hear of "Polk, Dallas, and the old dead sub-treasury."

* Mr. Evans and Mr. Huntington.

I would move to postpone the further consideration of this bill to the next Congress, but that I do not wish to be voted down. I will therefore simply throw out the suggestion, that it will be for the advantage both of the government and the people that it should be so postponed.

THE MEXICAN WAR.*

MR. PRESIDENT, — If my health had been better, and more time had remained to us, it was my purpose to address the Senate on the bill before us, and also on several topics with which it is connected. This purpose, under existing circumstances, I must necessarily forego. The true origin of the war with Mexico, and the motives and purposes for which it was originally commenced, however ably discussed already, are subjects not yet exhausted. I have been particularly desirous of examining them. I am greatly deceived, Mr. President, if we shall not ere long see facts coming to the light, and circumstances found coinciding and concurring, which will fix on the executive government a more definite and distinct purpose, intended to be effected by the coöperation of others, in bringing on hostilities with Mexico, than has as yet been clearly developed or fully understood.

At present, I should hardly have risen but to lay before the Senate the resolutions of the House of Representatives of Massachusetts, adopted on Thursday last. We have a great deal of commentary and criticism on State resolutions brought here. Those of Michigan particularly have been very sharply and narrowly looked into, to see whether they really mean what they seem to mean. These resolutions of Massachusetts, I hope, are sufficiently distinct and decided. They admit of neither doubt nor cavil, even if doubt or cavil were permissible in such a case.

What the legislature of Massachusetts thinks, it has said,

* Remarks in the Senate of the United States, on the 1st of March, 1847, on the Bill commonly called the "Three Million Bill," by which that sum of money was appropriated for the purpose of discharging any extraordinary expenses which might be incurred in bringing the war to a conclusion.

and said plainly and directly. Mr. President, I have not, before any tribunal, tried my ingenuity at what the lawyers call a special demurrer for many years; and I never tried it here in the Senate. In the business of legislation, and especially in considering State resolutions and the proceedings of public assemblies, it is our duty, of course, to understand every thing according to the common meaning of the words used. Of all occasions, these are the last in which one should stick in the bark, or seek for loopholes, or means of escape; or, in the language of an eminent judge of former times, "hitch and hang on pins and particles." We must take the substance fairly, and as it is, and not hesitate about forms and phrases. When public bodies address us, whether we comply with their wishes or not, we are at least bound to understand them as they mean to be understood; to seek for no subterfuges, and to rely on no far-fetched and subtile difficulties or exceptions. All such attempts will be justly regarded only as so many contrivances resorted to in order to get rid of the responsibility of meeting the public voice directly and manfully, and looking our constituents boldly in the face.

Sir, we are in the midst of a war, not waged at home in defence of our soil, but waged a thousand miles off, and in the heart of the territories of another government. Of that war no one yet sees the end, and no one counts the cost. It is not denied that this war is now prosecuted for the acquisition of territory; at least, if any deny it, others admit it, and all know it to be true.

Under these circumstances, and plainly seeing this purpose to exist, seven or eight of the free States, comprising some of the largest, have remonstrated against the prosecution of the war for such a purpose, in language suited to express their meaning. These remonstrances come here with the distinct and precise object of dissuading us from the further prosecution of the war, for the acquisition of territory by conquest. Before territory is actually obtained, and its future character fixed, they beseech us to give up an object so full of danger. One and all, they protest against the extension of slave territory; one and all, they regard it as the solemn duty of the representatives of the free States to take security, in advance, that no more slave States shall be added to the Union. They demand of us this pledge, this assurance, before the purchase-money is paid, or the bargain concluded. And yet, Mr. President, ingenuity has been taxed to its utmost; criticisms both deep and shallow, and hypercriticisms quite incomprehensible, have all been resorted to, in the hope of showing that we do not understand the people; that their resolutions are not what they seem to be; that they do not require any immediate movement or present opposition; that they only look to some distant future, some emergencies yet to arise; that they only refer to a disposition in regard to territory, after it shall have been acquired and settled; and in one instance, I think, it was said that it did not appear that any thing was required of us for fifty years to come.

Mr. President, I understand all these things very differently. Such is not the voice of the free States, and of other States, as I receive it. Their trumpet gives forth no uncertain sound. Its tones are clear and distinct. I understand that a loud and imperative call is made upon us to act now; to take securities now; to make it certain, now, that no more slave States shall ever be added to this Union.

I will read, Sir, the Massachusetts resolutions: —

"*Resolved unanimously*, That the legislature of Massachusetts views the existence of human slavery within the limits of the United States as a great calamity, an immense moral and political evil, which ought to be abolished as soon as that end can be properly and constitutionally attained; and that its extension should be uniformly and earnestly opposed by all good and patriotic men throughout the Union.

"*Resolved unanimously*, That the people of Massachusetts will strenuously resist the annexation of any new territory to this Union, in which the institution of slavery is to be tolerated or established; and the legislature, in behalf of the people of this Commonwealth, do hereby solemnly protest against the acquisition of any additional territory, without an express provision by Congress that there shall be neither slavery nor involuntary servitude in such territory, otherwise than for the punishment of crime."

Sir, is there any possibility of misunderstanding this? Is there any escape from the meaning of this language? And yet they are hardly more explicit than the resolutions of other legislatures, Michigan, New York, Vermont, and all the rest.

The House of Representatives of Massachusetts is, I believe, the most numerous legislative body in the country. On this occasion it was not full; but among those present there was an entire unanimity. For the resolutions there were two hundred and thirty-two votes; against them, none. Not one man stood up to justify the war upon such grounds as those upon which it has been, from day to day, defended here. Massachusetts, without one dissenting voice, and I thank her for it, and am proud of her for it, has denounced the whole object for which our armies are now traversing the plains of Mexico, or about to plunge into the pestilence of her coasts. The people of Massachusetts are as unanimous as the members of their legislature, and so are her representatives here. I have heard no man in the State, in public or in private life, express a different opinion. If any thing is certain, it is certain that the sentiment of the whole North is utterly opposed to the acquisition of territory, to be formed into new slave-holding States, and, as such, admitted into the Union.

But here, Sir, I cannot but pause. I am arrested by occurrences of this night, which, I confess, fill me with alarm. They are ominous, portentous. Votes which have been just passed by majorities here cannot fail to awaken public attention. Every patriotic American, every man who wishes to preserve the Constitution, ought to ponder them well. I heard, Sir, the honorable member from New York,* and with a great part of his remarks I agreed; I thought they must lead to some useful result. But then what does he come to, after all? He is for acquiring territory under the Wilmot Proviso; but, at any rate, he is for acquiring territory. He will not vote against all territory to form new States, though he is willing to say they ought not to be slave States. Other gentlemen of his party from the Northern and Eastern States vote in the same way, and with the same view. This is called "the policy of the Northern Democracy." I so denominate the party only because it so denominates itself. A gentleman from South Carolina,† if I understood him rightly, said he wanted no new territory; all he desired was equality, and no exclusion; he wished the South to be saved from any thing derogatory; and yet he does not vote against the acquisition of territory. Nor do other Senators from Southern States. They are therefore, in general, in favor

* Mr. Dix. † Mr. Butler.

of new territory and new States, being slave States. This is the policy of the Southern Democracy. Both parties agree, therefore, to carry on the war for territory, though it be not decided now whether the character of newly acquired territory shall be that of freedom or of slavery. This point they are willing to leave for future agitation and future controversy. Gentlemen who are in favor of the Wilmot Proviso are ready, nevertheless, to vote for this bill, though that proviso be struck out. The gentleman from New York is ready to take that course, and his Northern and Eastern friends, who sit round him here in the Senate, are as ready as he is. They all demand acquisition, and maintain the war for that purpose. On the other hand, the other branch of the party votes eagerly and unitedly for territory, the Wilmot Proviso being rejected, because these gentlemen take it for granted that, that proviso being rejected, States formed out of Mexico will necessarily be slave States, and added to this Union as such.

Now, Sir, it has appeared to me from the beginning, that the proposition contained in the amendment which was submitted some days ago by my friend, the honorable member from Georgia,* was the true and the only true policy for us to pursue. That proposition was in these words: —

"*Provided, always*, And it is hereby declared to be the true intent and meaning of Congress in making this appropriation, that the war with Mexico ought not to be prosecuted by this government with any view to the dismemberment of that republic, or to the acquisition by conquest of any portion of her territory; that this government ever desires to maintain and preserve peaceful and friendly relations with all nations; and, particularly with the neighboring republic of Mexico, will always be ready to enter into negotiations, with a view to terminate the present unhappy conflict on terms which shall secure the just rights and preserve inviolate the national honor of the United States and of Mexico; that it is especially desirable, in order to maintain and preserve those amicable relations which ought always to exist between neighboring republics, that the boundary of the State of Texas should be definitively settled, and that provision be made by the republic of Mexico for the prompt and equitable settlement of the just claims of our citizens on that republic."

* Mr. Berrien.

This amendment rejects all desire for the dismemberment of Mexico; it rejects acquisition of territory by conquest; it signifies a wish for the restoration of peace, and a readiness on our part to enter into negotiations, and to treat, not only for peace, but also for boundaries and indemnities. This amendment has been rejected, and now I come to the point: Who has rejected it? By whose votes has this amendment, this very evening, been lost? Sir, it has been lost by the votes of the honorable member from New York and his Northern and Eastern friends. It has been voted down by the "Northern Democracy." If this "Northern Democracy" had supported this amendment, it would have prevailed, and we should then have had no new territory at all, and of course no new slave territory; no new States at all, and of course no new slave States. This is certain and indisputable. If the Senate had said what that resolution proposes, the danger would have been over. But these gentlemen would not vote for it. To a man, they voted against it. Every member of the Senate belonging to the Democratic party, in the Northern States, however warmly he might have declared himself against new slave States, yet refused to vote against all territorial acquisition, a measure proposed and offered as a perfect security against more slave States. They are for acquiring territory; they are for more States; and, for the sake of this, they are willing to run the risk of these new States being slave States, and to meet all the convulsions which the discussion of that momentous question may hereafter produce. Sir, if there be wisdom, or prudence, or consistency, or sound policy, or comprehensive foresight in all this, I cannot see it.

The amendment of the honorable member from Georgia was supported by the votes of twenty-four members of the Senate. Twenty-nine members voted against it. Of these twenty-nine, there were six gentlemen representing Northern and Eastern States; viz. one from Maine, one from New Hampshire, one from Connecticut, two from New York, and one from Pennsylvania. If these six members had voted for the resolution, they would have changed the majority, and there would, from that moment, have been no apprehension of new slave territory or new slave States. Against the resolution, also, we heard the voices of five members from the free States in the Northwest; viz. one from Ohio, two from Indiana, one from Michigan, and one from Illinois.

So it is evident that, if all the Senators from the free States had voted for this amendment, and against the acquisition of territory, such acquisition would have been denounced, in advance, by nearly two thirds of the whole Senate, and the question of more slave States settled for ever. For, let me say to you, Sir, and to the country, that, whenever this question is settled, it must be settled in the Senate. It might have been settled here this night, and settled finally and for ever.

Mr. President, I arraign no men and no parties. I take no judgment into my own hands. But I present this simple statement of facts and consequences to the country; and ask for it, humbly but most earnestly, the serious consideration of the people. Shall we prosecute this war for the purpose of bringing on a controversy which is likely to shake the government to its centre.

And now, Sir, who are the twenty-four members who supported the amendment of the member from Georgia? They are the Whigs of the Senate, Whigs from the North and the South, the East and the West. In their judgment it is due to the best interests of the country, to its safety, to peace and harmony, and to the well-being of the Constitution, to declare at once, to proclaim now, that we desire no new States, nor territory to form new States out of, as the end of conquest. For one, I enter into this declaration with all my heart. We want no extension of territory, we want no accession of new States. The country is already large enough. I do not speak of any cession which may be made in the establishment of boundaries, or of the acquisition of a port or two on the Pacific, for the benefit of navigation and commerce. But I speak of large territories, obtained by conquest, to form States to be annexed to the Union; and I say I am opposed to such acquisition altogether. I am opposed to the prosecution of the war for any such purposes.

Mr. President, I must be indulged here in a short retrospection. In the present posture of things and of parties, we may well look back upon the past. Within a year or two after Texas had achieved its independence, there were those who already spoke of its annexation to the United States. Against that project I felt it to be my duty to take an early and a decided course. Having occasion to address political friends in the city of New York, in March, 1837, I expressed my sentiments as fully and as strongly as I could. From those opinions I have never swerved. From the first I saw nothing, and have seen nothing, but evil and danger to arise to the country from such annexation. The prudence of Mr. Van Buren stifled the project for a time; but in the latter part of the administration of Mr. Tyler it was revived. Sir, the transactions and occurrences from that time onward, till the measure was finally consummated in December, 1845, are matters of history and record. That history and that record can neither be falsified nor erased. There they stand, and must stand for ever; and they proclaim to the whole world, and to all ages, that Texas was brought into this Union, slavery and all, only by means of the aid and active coöperation of those who now call themselves the "Northern Democracy" of the United States; in other words, by those who assert their own right to be regarded as nearest and dearest to the people, among all the public men of the country. Where was the honorable member from New York, where were his Northern and Eastern friends, when Texas was pressing to get into the Union, bringing slaves and slavery with her? Where were they, I ask? Were they standing up like men against slaves and slavery? Was the annexation of a new slave State an object which "Northern Democracy" opposed, or from which it averted its eyes with horror? Sir, the gentleman from New York, and his friends, were counselling and assisting, aiding and abetting, the whole proceeding. Some of them were voting here as eagerly as if the salvation of the country depended on bringing in another slave State. Others of us from the North opposed annexation as far as we could. We remonstrated, we protested, we voted; but the "Northern Democracy" helped to outvote us, to defeat us, to overwhelm us. And they accomplished their purpose. Nay, more. The party in the North which calls itself, by way of distinction and eminence, the "Liberty Party," opposed with all its force the election of the Whig candidate* in 1844, when it had the power of assisting in and securing the election of that candidate, and of preventing Mr. Polk's election; and when it was as clear and visible as the sun at noonday, that Mr. Polk's election would bring slave-holding Texas into the Union. No man can deny this. And in the party

* Mr. Clay.

of this "Northern Democracy," and in this "Liberty Party" too, probably, are those, at this moment, who profess themselves ready to meet all the consequences, to stand the chance of all convulsions, to see the fountains of the great deep broken up, rather than that new slave States should be added to the Union; but who, nevertheless, will not join with us in a declaration against new States of any character, thereby shutting the door for ever against the further admission of slavery.

Here, Sir, is a chapter of political inconsistency which demands the consideration of the country, and is not unlikely to attract the attention of the age. If it be any thing but party attachment, carried, recklessly, to every extent, and party antipathy maddened into insanity, I know not how to describe it.

Sir, I fear we are not yet arrived at the beginning of the end. I pretend to see but little of the future, and that little affords no gratification. All I can scan is contention, strife, and agitation. Before we obtain a perfect right to conquered territory, there must be a cession. A cession can only be made by treaty. No treaty can pass the Senate, till the Constitution is overthrown, without the consent of two thirds of its members. Now who can shut his eyes to the great probability of a successful resistance to any treaty of cession, from one quarter of the Senate or another? Will the North consent to a treaty bringing in territory subject to slavery? Will the South consent to a treaty bringing in territory from which slavery is excluded? Sir, the future is full of difficulties and full of dangers. We are suffering to pass the golden opportunity for securing harmony and the stability of the Constitution. We appear to me to be rushing upon perils headlong, and with our eyes wide open. But I put my trust in Providence, and in that good sense and patriotism of the people, which will yet, I hope, be awakened before it is too late.

THE TEN REGIMENT BILL.*

ALTHOUGH laboring under deep depression,† I still feel it my duty, at as early a moment as I may be able, to address the Senate upon the state of the country, and on the further prosecution of the war. I have listened, Sir, silently, but attentively, to the discussion which has taken place upon this bill, and upon other connected subjects; and it is not my purpose to enter into the historical narrative, or the historical argument which has accompanied its discussion, on the one side or on the other. New events have arisen, bringing new questions; and since the resumption of the discussion upon this measure, two or three days ago, these events have been alluded to, first by the honorable Senator who conducts this bill through the Senate, and again by the Senator before me from South Carolina. By both these honorable members these events have been declared to be well known to all the world, and by one of them‡ it was remarked that there need be no affectation of mystery. Since these statements were made, I have heard the gentleman from South Carolina§ express his views on the question. I have heard him on various and momentous subjects, on many interesting occasions, and I desire to say, Sir, that I never heard him with more unqualified concurrence in every word he uttered. The topics which he discussed were presented, it appears to me, in their just light, and he sustained his views in regard to them with that

* Remarks in the Senate of the United States, on the 17th of March, 1848, on the Bill to raise for a limited time an additional Military Force, commonly called the "Ten Regiment Bill."

† Intelligence had lately been received of the death, in Mexico, of Major Edward Webster, an officer in the Massachusetts Regiment of Volunteers.

‡ Mr. Cass.

§ Mr. Calhoun.

clearness and power of argument which always characterize his efforts in debate. I thank him.

I thank him especially for the manly stand he took upon one point, which has not been so much discussed here as others; I mean the plain, absolute unconstitutionality and illegality of the attempt of the executive to enact laws by executive authority in conquered territories out of the United States. Sir, whether the power exists in the President or not may be inferred by answering another question, Does he wear a crown? That is the only question. If he wears a crown, if he is the king of the country, if we are his subjects, and they who are conquered by the arms of the country become his subjects also and owe him allegiance, why, then, according to well-established principles, until the interference of the legislature, but no longer even then, he may conquer, he may govern, he may impose laws, he may lay taxes, he may assess duties. The king of England has done it, in various cases, from the conquest of Wales and Ireland down to the conquest of the West India Islands, in the war of 1756, and in the wars growing out of the French Revolution. The king of England has done it; done it by royal prerogative; done it in the government of his own subjects, existing in or inhabiting territories not under the protection of English law, but governed by him until Parliament puts them under that protection.

Now, Sir, there was laid before us, at the commencement of the session, a system of legislation for Mexico as for a conquered country. Let us not confound ideas that are in themselves separable and necessarily distinct. It is not the question, whether he who is in an enemy's country at the head of an army may not supply his daily wants; whether he may not, if he choose so to conduct the war, seize the granaries and the herds of the enemy in whose country he is. That is one thing; but the question is here, whether, sitting in the Presidential house, by an act of mere authority, when the country is conquered and subdued, the President of the United States may, by, and of, and through his own power, establish in Mexico a system of civil law. We have read, Sir, and some of us have not forgotten it, in books of authority treating of the law of nations, that, when a country is conquered or ceded, its existing laws are not changed till the competent authority of the conquering power changes them. That I hold to be the universal doctrine of public law. Well, here is a system of levying taxes, repealing old laws, and making new ones, and a system behind that, of which I read with pain and mortification; for I find in this communication of the Secretary, sanctioned by the President, that our brave troops (as they are always called, ten times in every page) were directed to lay hold on all the little municipal treasures, all the little collections for social purposes, that supported the interior, the municipal, what we should call the parish concerns of Mexico! they were directed to seize them all! The War Department issued orders to chase the government of Mexico like a partridge on the mountain, from place to place, to give it no rest for the sole of its foot; and another order issued from the Treasury Department at the same time directed this seizure of all these small and petty sums of public money. I am obliged, therefore, to the gentleman from South Carolina, for having brought this subject to the attention of the Senate.

I am happy in having an opportunity of expressing my repugnance to all the doctrine and all the practice. Where will it lead to? What does the President do with this money? Why, he supports the army! But this money never passes under any appropriation of law. The Constitution of the United States says that the executive power shall have no appropriations for military purposes for more than two years. But here there is a standing appropriation, put at the disposal and discretion of the President of the United States, of all the money he can collect by this system of personal executive legislation over seven millions of people, and that under the Constitution of the United States! If the statement of this case does not attract the attention of the community, in short, if the question is not argued before an American Senate when it is stated, it is beyond my power to illustrate it by any further argument.

Sir, while I rejoice that the honorable member from South Carolina has done so important a service as to put this question in a proper and clear light before the community and the Senate; and while I agree, as I have said, in all that he has uttered on the topics which he has treated; that topic which weighs upon my mind and my conscience more than all the rest is one which he did not treat, and in regard to which I fear I may not expect (would to God that I might!) his concurrence, and the strength of his arm; I mean the object, plain and manifest, original in the inception of this war, not always avowed, but always the real object; the creation of new States on the southern border of the United States, to be formed out of the territory of Mexico, and the people inhabiting that territory. If, after a service of thirty years in these councils, he could have taken a lead; if his convictions of duty, I mean to say, could have allowed him to take a lead and make a stand for the integrity of the United States, even with these large recent accessions, which I am willing to consider as brotherly accessions that I have no disposition to reject, discourage, or discountenance, in the existing circumstances of the case; if, I say, Sir, at the end of our common service, now for thirty years, the honorable member could have seen his line of duty to lie in such a direction that he could take a stand for the integrity of the United States, these United States into whose service he and I entered in early life, with warm and equally warm patriotic affections, the love of a known country, a defined country, an American country; if he had found it consistent with his duty to take such a stand, and I had perished in supporting him in it, I should feel that I had perished in a service eminently connected with the prosperity and true honor of the country.

Mr. President, I am obliged to my friend from Georgia* for having taken that view of some topics in this case, with his usual clearness and ability, which will relieve me from the necessity of discussing those subjects which he has treated. I feel, Sir, the great embarrassment which surrounds me, brought about by those events which have taken place and been adverted to in the Senate. It has been stated by the gentleman already alluded to,† that the whole world knows that a treaty has come hither from Mexico, that it has been acted upon here, and is sent back; that a member of this body, occupying an eminent position in its deliberations and conduct, has been sent out as a minister, with full powers to make explanations; of course, not explanations of what was done in Mexico, but explanations of what has been done here. There has been such a paper here. I allude to none of its particulars, although, fol-

* Mr. Berrien.

† Mr. Cass.

lowing the example of the honorable member from Michigan, who says that all the world knows there is a treaty, I might say that all the world knows, too, exactly what the treaty is; for the details are as well known as the principal fact. I feel, Sir, as I said, a new embarrassment. On the events that have occurred here within three weeks, political friends to some extent differ, and that goes nearer to my heart than any shaft that political adversaries could direct.

The war is odious. Generally speaking, taking the whole country together, the war is odious in a high degree. The country is distressed. A treaty has been offered. It has been here, and it has been sent back. Now I feel, Sir, that there has been manifested throughout the country a very strong desire, for the sake of peace, that this treaty, or any treaty, should be ratified. The business of the country is disorganized and obstructed. Men know not what to calculate upon. The occupations of life are embarrassed. The finances of individuals, as well as of the country, are much deranged, the circumstances of individuals placing them in great exigency and necessity of immediate relief; and there has come up a strong expression in favor of *any* treaty, on *any* terms, if it will bring peace. Now, Sir, I am not for *any* treaty, on *any* terms, though it bring peace. In my judgment, with entire diffidence therein and entire deference to the better judgment of others, this indiscriminate demand of peace, under any circumstances and on any terms, is either an effusion of ecstatic delight at the prospect of getting rid of an abominated war, or else the result of a feeling for which I have not so much respect, that we are to take this, whatever it may be; or, I will rather say, that we are to take whatever may be offered, lest our masters should give us harder terms. It is either an overflow of joy at the prospect of putting an end to the war, or else a proof that men's resolution cools.

I believe, Sir, that the press on all sides, with very few exceptions, perhaps, uniting for once, have for the last three weeks pressed the Senate, by their daily counsels and advice, to take the treaty, whatever it may be. All these considerations, which seem to me to spring from the first impulse, and not from the sober second thought of the people, appear to be designed, I will not say designed, but calculated, as they have been calculated, to press forward the counsels of the Senate; and to induce us to take any bit of parchment, or any bit of paper, which could be called or concluded to be a treaty, to clench it, and confirm it, with our eyes blindfolded; no, Sir, with our eyes dead, sightless as the eyes of a marble statue, to all the future.

On these subjects, Sir, to the extent to which it may be proper for me to discuss them, I wish to declare my sentiments once for all; not going back to the origin of the war, not reëxamining orders of the executive, not pausing to consider, as my honorable friend from Georgia has done, the various stages in the progress of the campaigns, in which it might seem to have been, and I think he has proved that it was, the duty of the executive to consider the propriety of arresting the war. Without attempting any of this sort of discursive dissertation upon the case, I nevertheless desire to express my opinions upon the state of the country, upon the further prosecution of the war, and upon that most important, and, if not vital, most interesting question, the revenue, and the ability of the country, under the existing legislation of Congress, to supply the public demands. An understanding, however, was entered into yesterday, to which I was a party, that the question upon the final passage of this bill should be taken to-day. I do not propose to depart from that understanding. If I had strength, which I have not, and health, which I have not, there is not time, without forcing the Senate into a very late session, to say what I wish to say. I will, therefore, with the permission of the Senate, and I hope not without the concurrence of the honorable member who is at the head of the Finance Committee, postpone what I have further to say upon this subject until the early part of next week, when I understand the loan bill will be before us. This measure is to raise men; that measure is to pay them. The object, therefore, of both is one, the further prosecution of the war with Mexico. What I have to say, then, may as appropriately be said on one bill as the other, and therefore I shall not now detain the Senate; but if an opportunity should be offered, upon the earliest introduction of the loan bill, I shall claim the privilege of expressing myself on the several points to which I have now alluded.

General Cass followed, at considerable length, in defence of the principles on which the war had been conducted. At the conclusion of his speech Mr. Webster made the following remarks: —

I entertain no intention of discussing the general topics introduced in the speech of the honorable gentleman. On one point only I wish to say a few words, and that is with regard to the remarks which he made upon the speech of the honorable member from South Carolina,* and some observations of my own upon this assumed authority by the executive of the United States to levy and collect taxes in Mexico. Now, Sir, when gentlemen of experience and character debate these grave questions, the first thing is to ascertain what these questions are, and to present them truly, according to their character, for discussion. The honorable member from Michigan supposes that this levying of taxes and imposts in the territories of Mexico, by the authority of the President of the United States, is an act of war. It is no such thing.

MR. CASS (in his seat). It is a right of war.

It is neither an act nor a right of war, according to the law of nations. He calls it a contribution. It is no contribution. It is a legislative act; and when the honorable member quoted those portions of the United States Constitution which he thought applicable to the case, he might without impropriety have quoted another passage, which says that all legislative power is vested in the Senate and House of Representatives.

Now, it comes exactly to this: Is the establishment of a code of customs in Mexico an act of war, or an act derived from war, or an act of legislation? Why, clearly, it is the latter. I want to know how the President of the United States can overturn the revenue law of Mexico, and establish a new one in its stead, any more than he can overturn the law of the descent of property, the law of inheritance, the criminal code, or any other portion of Mexican law? A contribution levied upon Mexico! It is no such thing. What is it? It is a code of custom duties, framed here in the Treasury Department, and sent to Mexico, to be exercised upon whom, and upon whose property? Upon the Mexicans? Why, no, Sir. Very little of it upon Mexicans, because it is a law of imposts. It is a law upon those who import goods and merchandise into Mexico, upon all the neutrals of the world, upon all non-combatants; and not only

* Mr. Calhoun.

that, but it is a law levying a duty of imposts upon goods and merchandise carried thither by citizens of the United States; and that the honorable gentleman calls a "contribution"!

MR. CASS. I do.

Well, then, I think he calls things by names which have no more relation to them than black has to white. It is not a contribution at all.

MR. FOOTE. I would ask the honorable gentleman whether he conceives it to be the duty of the government of the United States to protect the revenue officers of Mexico in the collection of duties; or should their proceedings have been superseded by proceedings of a similar kind on the part of the United States? What would he have done in the case?

Just exactly what Congress in its discretion shall think fit to do. What I say is, that it is an exercise of legislative power, and no exercise of military power. If there is any analogy between that and the case mentioned by the honorable gentleman, of the marshals of the French army levying contributions as they marched from city to city, *flagrante bello*, at the head of their forces, I do not understand the logic which makes the comparison. Nor can I perceive any analogy in the cases. When an army marches through an enemy's country, it is supposed to have the right of supporting itself by the strong hand; it has the absolute right of war, whether it choose to exercise it or not, to make plunder and to seize private property. And what is contribution? Why, it is a substitute for the law of pillage, the practice of plunder. When an army approaches a city, the commander of that army asks so much support, so many thousand crowns, such and such provisions; he says he will take them by the strong hand, unless the authorities compound by giving so much money, in consideration of which he will forbear the exercise of that military right.

Let me ask the honorable gentleman another question. A part of this system sanctioned by the President was, that the moneys collected by these levies should be paid over to the military and naval officers. Could they not just as well have been ordered to be brought here, and put into our treasury? Does it make a particle of difference, and is it not a system of revenue established under executive authority in Mexico? and will any man call that military contribution? Let it be shown by any authentic work on national law, by any decided case, by any course of reasoning or argument, that the levying of a permanent system of revenue, in a conquered territory, is exactly the same thing as a temporary or occasional military contribution of a marching army, and then the charge brought against the administration cannot be maintained.

OBJECTS OF THE MEXICAN WAR.*

On the 2d of February, 1848, the treaty called a "treaty of peace, friendship, limits, and settlement, between the United States of America and the Mexican Republic," was signed at Guadalupe Hidalgo. This treaty, with the advice and consent of the Senate, was ratified by the President of the United States on the 16th of March. In the mean time, a bill, introduced into the House of Representatives on the 18th of February, to authorize a loan of sixteen millions of dollars for the purpose of carrying on the war, passed through that house, and was considered in the Senate. Other war measures were considered and adopted by the two houses, after the signature and ratification of the treaty. On the 23d of March, the Sixteen Million Loan Bill being under consideration, Mr. Webster spoke as follows.

Mr. President, — On Friday a bill passed the Senate for raising ten regiments of new troops for the further prosecution of the war against Mexico; and we have been informed that that measure is shortly to be followed, in this branch of the legislature, by a bill to raise twenty regiments of volunteers for the same service. I was desirous of expressing my opinions against the object of these bills, against the supposed necessity which leads to their enactment, and against the general policy which they are apparently designed to promote. Circumstances personal to myself, but beyond my control, compelled me to forego, on that day, the execution of that design. The bill now before the Senate is a measure for raising money to meet the exigencies of the government, and to provide the means, as well

* A Speech delivered in the Senate of the United States, on the 23d of March, 1848, on the Bill from the House of Representatives for raising a Loan of Sixteen Millions of Dollars.

as for other things, for the pay and support of these thirty regiments.

Sir, the scenes through which we have passed, and are passing, here, are various. For a fortnight the world supposes we have been occupied with the ratification of a treaty of peace, and that within these walls, "the world shut out," notes of peace, and hopes of peace, nay, strong assurances of peace, and indications of peace, have been uttered to console and to cheer us. Sir, it has been over and over stated, and is public, that we have ratified a treaty, of course a treaty of peace, and, as the country has been led to suppose, not of an uncertain, empty, and delusive peace, but of real and substantial, a gratifying and an enduring peace, a peace which would stanch the wounds of war, prevent the further flow of human blood, cut off these enormous expenses, and return our friends, and our brothers, and our children, if they be yet living, from the land of slaughter, and the land of still more dismal destruction by climate, to our firesides and our arms.

Hardly have these halcyon notes ceased upon our ears, when, in resumed public session, we are summoned to fresh warlike operations; to create a new army of thirty thousand men for the further prosecution of the war; to carry the war, in the language of the President, still more dreadfully into the vital parts of the enemy, and to press home, by fire and sword, the claims we make, and the grounds which we insist upon, against our fallen, prostrate, I had almost said, our ignoble enemy. If we may judge from the opening speech of the honorable Senator from Michigan, and from other speeches that have been made upon this floor, there has been no time, from the commencement of the war, when it has been more urgently pressed upon us, not only to maintain, but to increase, our military means; not only to continue the war, but to press it still more vigorously than at present.

Pray, what does all this mean? Is it, I ask, confessed, then, is it confessed that we are no nearer a peace than we were when we snatched up this bit of paper called, or miscalled, a treaty, and ratified it? Have we yet to fight it out to the utmost, as if nothing pacific had intervened?

I wish, Sir, to treat the proceedings of this and of every department of the government with the utmost respect. The Constitution of this government, and the exercise of its just powers in the administration of the laws under it, have been the cherished object of all my unimportant life. But, if the subject were not one too deeply interesting, I should say our proceedings here may well enough cause a smile. In the ordinary transaction of the foreign relations of this and of all other governments, the course has been to negotiate first, and to ratify afterwards. This seems to be the natural order of conducting intercourse between foreign states. We have chosen to reverse this order. We ratify first, and negotiate afterwards. We set up a treaty, such as we find it and choose to make it, and then send two ministers plenipotentiary to negotiate thereupon in the capital of the enemy. One would think, Sir, the ordinary course of proceeding much the juster; that to negotiate, to hold intercourse, and come to some arrangement, by authorized agents, and then to submit that arrangement to the sovereign authority to which these agents are responsible, would be always the most desirable method of proceeding. It strikes me that the course we have adopted is strange, is even *grotesque.* So far as I know, it is unprecedented in the history of diplomatic intercourse. Learned gentlemen on the floor of the Senate, interested to defend and protect this course, may, in their extensive reading, have found examples of it. I know of none.

Sir, we are in possession, by military power, of New Mexico and California, countries belonging hitherto to the United States of Mexico. We are informed by the President that it is his purpose to retain them, to consider them as territory fit to be attached to these United States of America; and our military operations and designs now before the Senate are to enforce this claim of the executive of the United States. We are to compel Mexico to agree that the part of her dominions called New Mexico, and that called California, shall be ceded to us. We are in possession, as is said, and she shall yield her title to us. This is the precise object of this new army of thirty thousand men. Sir, it is the identical object, in my judgment, for which the war was originally commenced, for which it has hitherto been prosecuted, and in furtherance of which this treaty is to be used, but as one means to bring about this general result; that general result depending, after all, on our own superior power, and on the necessity of submitting to any terms which we may prescribe to fallen, fallen, fallen Mexico!

Sir, the members composing the other house, the more popular branch of the legislature, have all been elected since, I had almost said, the fatal, I will say the remarkable, events of the 11th and 13th days of May, 1846. The other house has passed a resolution affirming that "the war with Mexico was begun unconstitutionally and unnecessarily by the executive government of the United States." I concur in that sentiment; I hold that to be the most recent and authentic expression of the will and opinion of the majority of the people of the United States.

There is, Sir, another proposition, not so authentically announced hitherto, but, in my judgment, equally true and equally capable of demonstration; and that is, that this war was begun, has been continued, and is now prosecuted, for the great and leading purpose of the acquisition of new territory, out of which to bring new States, with their Mexican population, into this our Union of the United States.

If unavowed at first, this purpose did not remain unavowed long. However often it may be said that we did not go to war for conquest,

> "credat Judæus Apella,
> Non ego,"

yet the moment we get possession of territory we must retain it and make it our own. Now I think that this original object has not been changed, has not been varied. Sir, I think it exists in the eyes of those who originally contemplated it, and who began the war for it, as plain, as attractive to them, and from which they no more avert their eyes now than they did then or have done at any time since. We have compelled a treaty of cession; we know in our consciences that it is compelled. We use it as an instrument and an agency, in conjunction with other instruments and other agencies of a more formidable and destructive character, to enforce the cession of Mexican territory, to acquire territory for new States to be added to this Union. We know, every intelligent man knows, that there is no stronger desire in the breast of a Mexican citizen than to retain the territory which belongs to the republic. We know that the Mexican people will part with it, if part they must, with regret, with pangs of sorrow. That we know; we know it is all forced; and therefore, because we know it must be forced, because we know that (whether the government, which we consider our creature, do or do not agree to it) the Mexican people will never accede to the terms of this treaty but through the impulse of absolute necessity, and the impression made upon them by absolute and irresistible force, therefore we purpose to overwhelm them with another army. We purpose to raise another army of ten thousand regulars and twenty thousand volunteers, and to pour them in and upon the Mexican people.

Now, Sir, I should be happy to agree, notwithstanding all this tocsin, and all this cry of all the Semproniuses in the land, that *their* "voices are still for war," — I should be happy to agree, and substantially I do agree, to the opinion of the Senator from South Carolina. I think I have myself uttered the sentiment, within a fortnight, to the same effect, that, after all, *the war with Mexico is substantially over*, that there can be no more fighting. In the present state of things, my opinion is that the people of this country will not sustain the war. They will not go for its heavy expenses; they will not find any gratification in putting the bayonet to the throats of the Mexican people. For my part, I hope the ten regiment bill will never become a law. Three weeks ago I should have entertained that hope with the utmost confidence; events instruct me to abate my confidence. I still *hope* it will not pass.

And here, I dare say, I shall be called by some a "Mexican Whig." The man who can stand up here and say that he hopes that what the administration projects, and the further prosecution of the war with Mexico requires, may not be carried into effect, must be an enemy to his country, or what gentlemen have considered the same thing, an enemy to the President of the United States, and to his administration and his party. He is a Mexican. Sir, I think very badly of the Mexican character, high and low, out and out; but names do not terrify me. Besides, if I have suffered in this respect, if I have rendered myself subject to the reproaches of these stipendiary presses, these hired abusers of the motives of public men, I have the honor, on this occasion, to be in very respectable company. In the reproachful sense of that term, I don't know a greater Mexican in this body than the honorable Senator from Michigan, the chairman of the Committee on Military Affairs.

Mr. Cass. Will the gentleman be good enough to explain what sort of a Mexican I am?

On the resumption of the bill in the Senate the other day, the gentleman told us that its principal object was to frighten Mexico; it would touch his humanity too much to hurt her! He would frighten her —

Mr. Cass. Does the gentleman affirm that I said that?

Yes; twice.

Mr. Cass. No, Sir, I beg your pardon, I did not say it. I did not say it would touch my humanity to hurt her.

Be it so.

Mr. Cass. Will the honorable Senator allow me to repeat my statement of the object of the bill? I said it was twofold: first, that it would enable us to prosecute the war, if necessary; and, second, that it would show Mexico we were prepared to do so; and thus, by its moral effect, would induce her to ratify the treaty.

The gentleman said, that the principal object of the bill was to frighten Mexico, and that this would be more humane than to harm her.

Mr. Cass. That 's true.

Well, Sir, the remarkable characteristic of that speech, that which makes it so much a Mexican speech, is, that the gentleman spoke it in the hearing of Mexico, as well as in the hearing of this Senate. We are accused here, because what we say is heard by Mexico, and Mexico derives encouragement from what is said here. And yet the honorable member comes forth and tells Mexico that the principal object of the bill is to frighten her! The words have passed along the wires; they are on the Gulf, and are floating away to Vera Cruz; and when they get there, they will signify to Mexico, "After all, ye good Mexicans, my principal object is to frighten you; and to the end that you may not be frightened too much, I have given you this indication of my purpose."

But, Sir, in any view of this case, in any view of the proper policy of this government, to be pursued according to any man's apprehension and judgment, where is the necessity for this augmentation, by regiments, of the military force of the country? I hold in my hand here a note, which I suppose to be substantially correct, of the present military force of the United States. I cannot answer for its entire accuracy, but I believe it to be substantially according to fact. We have twenty-five regiments of regular troops, of various arms; if full, they would amount to 28,960 rank and file, and including officers to 30,296 men. These, with the exception of six or seven hundred men, are now all out of the United States and in field service in Mexico, or *en route* to Mexico. These regiments are not full; casualties and the climate have sadly reduced their numbers. If the recruiting service were now to yield ten thousand men, it would not more than fill up these regiments, so that every brigadier and colonel and captain should have his appropriate and his full command. Here is a call, then, on the country now for the enlistment of ten thousand men, to fill up the regiments in the foreign service of the United States.

I understand, Sir, that there is a report from General Scott; from General Scott, a man who has performed the most brilliant campaign on recent military record, a man who has warred against the enemy, warred against the climate, warred against a thousand unpropitious circumstances, and has carried the flag of his country to the capital of the enemy, honorably, proudly, *humanely*, to his own permanent honor, and the great military credit of his country: General Scott; and where is he? At Puebla! at Puebla, undergoing an inquiry before his inferiors in rank, and other persons without military rank; while the high powers he has exercised, and exercised with so much distinction, are transferred to another, I do not say to one unworthy of them, but to one inferior in rank, station, and experience to himself.

But General Scott reports, as I understand, that, in February, there were twenty thousand regular troops under his command and *en route*, and we have thirty regiments of volunteers for the war. If full, this would make thirty-four thousand men, or, including officers, thirty-five thousand. So that, if the regiments were full, there is at this moment a number of troops, regular and volunteer, of not less than fifty-five or sixty thousand men, including recruits on the way. And with these twenty thousand men in the field, of regular troops, there were also ten thousand volunteers; making, of regulars and volunteers under General Scott, thirty thousand men. The Senator from Michigan knows these things better than I do, but I believe this is very nearly the fact. Now all these troops are regularly officered; there is no deficiency, in the line or in the staff, of officers. They are all full. Where there is any deficiency it consists of men.

Now, Sir, there may be a plausible reason for saying that there is difficulty in recruiting at home for the supply of deficiency in the volunteer regiments. It may be said that volunteers choose to enlist under officers of their own knowledge and selection; they do not incline to enlist as individual volunteers, to join regiments abroad, under officers of whom they know nothing. There may be something in that; but pray what conclusion does it lead to, if not to this, that all these regiments must moulder away, by casualties or disease, until the privates are less in number than the officers themselves.

But, however that may be with respect to volunteers, in regard to recruiting for the regular service, in filling up the regiments by pay and bounties according to existing laws, or new laws, if new ones are necessary, there is no reason on earth why we should now create five hundred new officers, for the purpose of getting ten thousand more men. The officers are already there; in that respect there is no deficiency. All that is wanted is men, and there is place for the men; and I suppose no gentleman, here or elsewhere, thinks that recruiting will go on faster than would be necessary to obtain men to fill up the deficiencies in the regiments abroad.

But now, Sir, what do we want of a greater force than we have in Mexico? I am not saying, What do we want of a force greater than we can supply? but What is the object of bringing these new regiments into the field? What do we propose? There is no army to fight. I suppose there are not five hundred men under arms in any part of Mexico; probably not half that number, except in one place. Mexico is prostrate. It is not the government that resists us. Why, it is notorious that the government of Mexico is on our side, that it is an instrument by which we hope to establish such a peace, and accomplish such a treaty, as we like. As far as I understand the matter, the government of Mexico owes its life and breath and being to the support of our arms, and to the hope, I do not say how inspired, that somehow or other, and at no distant period, she will have the pecuniary means of carrying it on, from our three millions, or our twelve millions, or from some of our other millions.

What do we propose to do, then, with these thirty regiments which it is designed to throw into Mexico? Are we going to cut the throats of her people? Are we to thrust the sword deeper and deeper into the "vital parts" of Mexico? What is it proposed to do? Sir, I can see no object in it; and yet, while we are pressed and urged to adopt this proposition to raise ten and twenty regiments, we are told, and the public is told, and the public believes, that we are on the verge of a safe and an honorable peace. Every one looks every morning for tidings of a confirmed peace, or of confirmed hopes of peace. We gather it from the administration, and from every organ of the administration from Dan to Beersheba. And yet warlike preparations, the incurring of expenses, the imposition of new charges upon the treasury, are pressed here, as if peace were not in all our thoughts, at least not in any of our expectations.

Now, Sir, I propose to hold a plain talk to-day; and I say that, according to my best judgment, the object of the bill is patronage, office, the gratification of friends. This very measure for raising ten regiments creates four or five hundred officers; colonels, subalterns, and not them only, for for all these I feel some respect, but there are also paymasters, contractors, persons engaged in the transportation service, commissaries, even down to sutlers, *et id genus omne*, people who handle the public money without facing the foe, one and all of whom are true descendants, or if not, true representatives, of Ancient Pistol, who said,

> "I shall sutler be
> Unto the camp, and profits will accrue."

Sir, I hope, with no disrespect for the applicants, and the aspirants, and the patriots (and among them are some sincere patriots) who would fight for their country, and those others who are not ready to fight, but who are willing to be paid, with due respect for all of them according to their several degrees and their merits, I hope they will all be disappointed. I hope that, as the pleasant season advances, the whole may find it for their interest to place themselves, of mild mornings, in the cars, and take their destination to their respective places of honorable private occupation and of civil employment. They have my good wishes that they may find the way to their homes from the Avenue and the Capitol, and from the purlieus of the President's house, in good health themselves, and that they may find their families all very happy to receive them.

But, Sir, to speak more seriously, this war was waged for the object of creating new States, on the southern frontier of the United States, out of Mexican territory, and with such population as could be found resident thereupon. I have opposed this object. I am against all accessions of territory to form new States. And this is no matter of sentimentality, which I am to parade before mass meetings or before my constituents at home. It is not a matter with me of declamation, or of regret, or of expressed repugnance. It is a matter of firm, unchangeable purpose. I yield nothing to the force of circumstances that have occurred, or that I can consider as likely to occur. And therefore I say, Sir, that, if I were asked to-day whether, for the sake of peace, I would take a treaty for adding two new States to the Union on our southern border, I would say, *No!* distinctly, No! And I wish every man in the United States to understand that to be my judgment and my purpose.

I said upon our *southern* border, because the present proposition takes that locality. I would say the same of the western, the northeastern, or of any other border. I resist to-day, and for ever, and to the end, any proposition to add any foreign territory, south or west, north or east, to the States of this Union, as they are constituted and held together under the Constitution. I do not want the colonists of England on the north; and as little do I want the population of Mexico on the south. I resist and reject all, and all with equal resolution. Therefore I say, that, if the question were put to me to-day, whether I would take peace under the present state of the country, distressed as it is, during the existence of a war odious as this is, under circumstances so afflictive as now exist to humanity, and so disturbing to the business of those whom I represent, I say still, if it were put to me whether I would have peace, with new States, I would say, No! no! And that because, Sir, in my judgment, there is no necessity of being driven into that dilemma. Other gentlemen think differently. I hold no man's conscience; but I mean to make a clean breast of it myself; and I protest that I see no reason, I believe there is none, why we cannot obtain as safe a peace, as honorable and as prompt a peace, without territory as with it. The two things are separable. There is no necessary connection between them. Mexico does not wish us to take her territory, while she receives our money. Far from it. She yields her assent, if she yields it at all, reluctantly, and we all know it. It is the result of force, and there is no man here who does not know that. And let me say, Sir, that, if this Trist paper shall finally be rejected in Mexico, it is most likely to be because those who under our protection hold the power there cannot persuade the Mexican Congress or people to agree to this cession of territory. The thing most likely to break up what we now expect to take place is the repugnance of the Mexican people to part with their territory. They would prefer to keep their territory, and that we should keep our money; as I prefer we should keep our money, and they their territory. We shall see. I pretend to no powers of prediction. I do not know what may happen. The times are full of strange events. But I think it certain that, if the treaty which has gone to Mexico shall fail to be ratified, it will be because of the aversion of the Mexican Congress, or the Mexican people, to cede the territory, or any part of it, belonging to their republic.

I have said that I would rather have no peace for the present, than have a peace which brings territory for new States; and the reason is, that we shall get peace as soon without territory as with it, more safe, more durable, and vastly more honorable to us, the great republic of the world.

But we hear gentlemen say, We must have some territory, the people demand it. I deny it; at least, I see no proof of it whatever. I do not doubt that there are individuals of an enterprising character, disposed to emigrate, who know nothing about New Mexico but that it is far off, and nothing about California but that it is still farther off, who are tired of the dull pursuits of agriculture and of civil life; that there are hundreds and thousands of such persons to whom whatsoever is new and distant is attractive. They feel the spirit of borderers, and the spirit of a borderer, I take it, is to be tolerably contented with his condition where he is, until somebody goes to regions beyond him; and then he is all eagerness to take up his traps and go still farther than he who has thus got in advance of him. With such men the desire to emigrate is an irresistible passion. At least so thought that sagacious observer of human nature, M. de Talleyrand, when he travelled in this country in 1794.

But I say I do not find anywhere any considerable and respectable body of persons who want more territory, and such territory. Twenty-four of us last year in this house voted against the prosecution of the war for territory, because we did not want it, both Southern and Northern men. I believe the Southern gentlemen who concurred in that vote found themselves, even when they had gone against what might be supposed to be local feelings and partialities, sustained on the general policy of not seeking territory, and by the acquisition of territory bringing into our politics certain embarrassing and embroiling questions and considerations. I do not learn that they suffered from the advocacy of such a sentiment. I believe they were supported in it; and I believe that through the greater part of the South, and even of the Southwest, there is no prevalent opinion in favor of acquiring territory, and such territory, and of the augmentation of our population by such an accession. And such, I need not say, is, if not the undivided, the preponderating sentiment of all the North.

But it is said we must take territory for the sake of peace. We must take territory. It is the will of the President. If we do not now take what he offers, we may fare worse. Mr. Polk will take no less, that he is fixed upon. He is immovable. He — has — put — down — his — foot! Well, Sir, he put it down upon "fifty-four forty," but it did n't stay. I speak of the President, as of all Presidents, without disrespect. I know of no reason why his opinion and his will, his purpose, declared to be final, should control us, any more than our purpose, from equally conscientious motives, and under as high responsibilities, should control him. We think he is firm, and will not be moved. I should be sorry, Sir, very sorry, indeed, that we should entertain more respect for the firmness of the individual at the head of the government than we entertain for our own firmness. He stands out against us. Do we fear to stand out against him? For one, I do not. It appears to me to be a slavish doctrine. For one, I am willing to meet the issue, and go to the people all over this broad land. Shall we take peace without new States, or refuse peace without new States? I will stand upon that, and trust the people. And I do that because I think it right, and because I have no distrust of the people. I am not unwilling to put it to their sovereign decision and arbitration. I hold this to be a question vital, permanent, elementary, in the future prosperity of the country and the maintenance of the Constitution; and I am willing to trust that question to the people. I prefer that it should go to them, because, if what I take to be a great constitutional principle, or what is essential to its maintenance, is to be broken down, let it be the act of the people themselves; it shall never be my act. I, therefore, do not distrust the people. I am willing to take their sentiment, from the Gulf to the British Provinces, and from the ocean to the Missouri: Will you continue the war for territory, to be purchased, after all, at an enormous price, a price a thousand times the value of all its purchases, or take peace, contenting yourselves with the honor we have reaped by the military achievements of the army? Will you take peace without territory, and preserve the integrity of the Constitution of the country? I am entirely willing to stand upon that question. I will therefore take the issue: *Peace, with no new States, keeping our own money ourselves, or war till new States shall be acquired, and vast sums paid.* That is the true issue. I am willing to leave that before the people and to the people, because it is a question for themselves. If they support me and think with me, very well. If otherwise, if they will have territory and add new States to the Union, let them do so; and let them be the artificers of their own fortune, for good or for evil.

But, Sir, we tremble before executive power. The truth cannot be concealed. We tremble before executive power! Mr. Polk will take no less than this. If we do not take this, the king's anger may kindle, and he will give us what is worse.

But now, Sir, who and what is Mr. Polk? I speak of him with no manner of disrespect. I mean, thereby, only to ask who and what is the President of the United States for the current moment. He is in the last year of his administration. Formally, officially, it can only be drawn out till the fourth of March, while really and substantially we know that two short months will, or may, produce events that will render the duration of that official term of very little importance. We are on the eve of a Presidential election. That machinery which is employed to collect public opinion or party opinion will be put in operation two months hence. We shall see its result. It may be that the present incumbent of the Presidential office will be again presented to his party friends and admirers for their suffrages for the next Presidential term. I do not say how probable or improbable this is. Perhaps it is not entirely probable. Suppose this not to be the result, what then? Why, then Mr. Polk becomes as absolutely insignificant as any respectable man among the public men of the United States. Honored in private life, valued for his private character, respectable, never eminent, in public life, he will, from the moment a new star arises, have just as little influence as you or I; and, so far as I am concerned, that certainly is little enough.

Sir, political partisans, and aspirants, and office-seekers are not sunflowers. They do not

> "turn to their god when he sets
> The same look which they turned when he rose."

No, Sir, if the respectable gentleman now at the head of the government be nominated, there will be those who will commend his consistency, who will be bound to maintain it, for the interest of his party friends will require it. It will be done. If otherwise, who is there in the whole length and breadth of the land that will care for the consistency of the present incumbent of the office? There will then be new objects. "Manifest destiny" will have pointed out some other man. Sir, the eulogies are now written, the commendations are already elaborated. I do not say every thing fulsome, but every thing panegyrical, has already been written out, with *blanks* for names, to be filled when the convention shall adjourn. When "manifest destiny" shall be unrolled, all these strong panegyrics, wherever they may light, made beforehand, laid up in pigeon-holes, studied, framed, emblazoned, and embossed, will all come out; and then there will be found to be somebody in the United States whose merits have been strangely overlooked, marked out by Providence, a kind of miracle, while all will wonder that nobody ever thought of him before, as a fit, and the only fit, man to be at the head of this great republic!

I shrink not, therefore, from any thing that I feel to be my duty, from any apprehension of the importance and imposing dignity, and the power of will, ascribed to the present incumbent of office. But I wish we possessed that power of will. I wish we had that firmness. Yes, Sir, I wish we had adherence. I wish we could gather something from the spirit of our brave forces, who have met the enemy under circumstances most adverse and have stood the shock. I wish we could imitate Zachary Taylor in his bivouac on the field of Buena Vista. He said he "would remain for the night; he would feel the enemy in the morning, and try his position." I wish, before we surrender, we could make up *our* minds to "*feel* the enemy, and try his position," and I think we should find him, as Taylor did, under the early sun, on his way to San Luis Potosi. That is my judgment.

But, Sir, I come to the all-absorbing question, more particularly, of the creation of new States.

Some years before I entered public life, Louisiana had been obtained under the treaty with France. Shortly after, Florida was obtained under the treaty with Spain. These two countries were situated on our frontier, and commanded the outlets of the great rivers which flow into the Gulf. As I have had occasion to say, in the first of these instances, the President of the United States* supposed that an amendment of the Constitution was required. He acted upon that supposition. Mr. Madison was Secretary of State, and, upon the suggestion of the President, proposed that the proper amendment to the Constitution should be submitted, to bring Louisiana into the Union. Mr. Madison drew it, and submitted it to Mr. Adams, as I have understood. Mr. Madison did not go upon any general idea that new States might be admitted; he did not proceed to a general amendment of the Constitution in that respect. The amendment which he proposed and submitted to Mr. Adams was a simple declaration, by a new article, that "the Province of Louisiana is hereby declared to be part and parcel of the United States." But public opinion, seeing the great importance of the acquisition, took a turn favorable to the affirmation of the power. The act was acquiesced in, and Louisiana became a part of the Union, without any amendment of the Constitution.

On the example of Louisiana, Florida was admitted.

Now, Sir, I consider those transactions as passed, settled, legalized. There they stand as matters of political history.

* Mr. Jefferson.

They are facts against which it would be idle at this day to contend.

My first agency in matters of this kind was upon the proposition for admitting Texas into this Union. That I thought it my duty to oppose, upon the general ground of opposing all formation of new States out of foreign territory, and, I may add, and I ought to add in justice, of States in which slaves were to be represented in the Congress of the United States. I was opposed to this on the ground of its inequality. It happened to me, Sir, to be called upon to address a political meeting in New York, in 1837, soon after the recognition of Texan independence. I state now, Sir, what I have often stated before, that no man, from the first, has been a more sincere well-wisher to the government and the people of Texas than myself. I looked upon the achievement of their independence in the battle of San Jacinto as an extraordinary, almost a marvellous, incident in the affairs of mankind. I was among the first disposed to acknowledge her independence. But from the first, down to this moment, I have opposed, as far as I was able, the annexation of new States to this Union. I stated my reasons on the occasion now referred to, in language which I have now before me, and which I beg to present to the Senate.

Mr. Webster here read the passage from his speech at Niblo's Saloon, New York, which will be found in the first volume of this work, pages 335 to 337, beginning, "But it cannot be disguised, gentlemen, that a desire, or an intention, is already manifested to annex Texas to the United States."

Well, Sir, for a few years I held a position in the executive administration of the government. I left the Department of State in 1843, in the month of May. Within a month after, another (an intelligent gentleman, for whom I cherished a high respect, and who came to a sad and untimely end) had taken my place, I had occasion to know, not officially, but from circumstances, that the annexation of Texas was taken up by Mr. Tyler's administration as an administration measure. It was pushed, pressed, insisted on; and I believe the honorable gentleman to whom I have referred* had something like a passion for the accomplishment of this purpose. And I am afraid that

* Mr. Upshur.

the President of the United States* at that time suffered his ardent feelings not a little to control his more prudent judgment. At any rate, I saw, in 1843, that annexation had become a purpose of the administration. I was not in Congress nor in public life. But, seeing this state of things, I thought it my duty to admonish the country, so far as I could, of the existence of that purpose. There are gentlemen at the North, many of them, there are gentlemen now in the Capitol, who know, that in the summer of 1843, being fully persuaded that this purpose was embraced with zeal and determination by the executive department of the government of the United States, I thought it my duty, and asked them to concur with me in the attempt, to make that purpose known to the country. I conferred with gentlemen of distinction and influence. I proposed means for exciting public attention to the question of annexation, before it should have become a party question; for I had learned that, when any topic becomes a party question, it is in vain to argue upon it.

But the optimists, and the quietists, and those who said, All things are well, and let all things alone, discouraged, discountenanced, and repressed any such effort. The North, they said, could take care of itself; the country could take care of itself, and would not sustain Mr. Tyler in his project of annexation. When the time should come, they said, the power of the North would be felt, and would be found sufficient to resist and prevent the consummation of the measure. And I could now refer to paragraphs and articles in the most respectable and leading journals of the North, in which it was attempted to produce the impression that there was no danger; there could be no addition of new States, and men need not alarm themselves about that.

I was not in Congress, Sir, when the preliminary resolutions, providing for the annexation of Texas, passed. I only know that, up to a very short period before the passage of those resolutions, the impression in that part of the country of which I have spoken was, that no such measure could be adopted. But I have found in the course of thirty years' experience, that whatever measures the executive government may embrace and push are

* Mr. Tyler.

quite likely to succeed in the end. There is always a giving way somewhere. The executive government acts with uniformity, with steadiness, with entire unity of purpose. And sooner or later, often enough, and, according to my construction of our history, quite too often, it effects its purposes. In this way it becomes the predominating power of the government.

Well, Sir, just before the commencement of the present administration, the resolutions for the annexation of Texas were passed in Congress. Texas complied with the provisions of those resolutions, and was here, or the case was here, on the 22d day of December, 1845, for her final admission into the Union, as one of the States. I took occasion then to say, that I hoped I had shown all proper regard for Texas; that I had been certainly opposed to annexation; that, if I should go over the whole matter again, I should have nothing new to add; that I had acted, all along, under the unanimous declaration of all parties, and of the legislature of Massachusetts; that I thought there must be some limit to the extent of our territories, and that I wished this country should exhibit to the world the example of a powerful republic, without greediness and hunger of empire. And I added, that while I held, with as much faithfulness as any citizen of the country, to all the original arrangements and compromises of the Constitution under which we live, I never could, and I never should, bring myself to be in favor of the admission of any States into the Union as slave-holding States; and I might have added, any States at all, to be formed out of territories not now belonging to us.

Now, as I have said, in all this I acted under the resolutions of the State of Massachusetts, certainly concurrent with my own judgment, so often repeated, and reaffirmed by the unanimous consent of all men of all parties, that I could not well go through the series, pointing out, not only the impolicy, but the unconstitutionality, of such annexation. If a State proposes to come into the Union, and to come in as a slave State, then there is an augmentation of the inequality in the representation of the people; an inequality already existing, with which I do not quarrel, and which I never will attempt to alter, but shall preserve as long as I have a vote to give, or any voice in this government, because it is a part of the original compact. Let it stand. But then there is another consideration of vastly more general importance even than that; more general, because it affects all the States, free and slave-holding; and it is, that, if States formed out of territories thus thinly populated come into the Union, they necessarily and inevitably break up the relation existing between the two branches of the government, and destroy its balance. They break up the intended relation between the Senate and the House of Representatives. If you bring in new States, any State that comes in must have two Senators. She may come in with fifty or sixty thousand people, or more. You may have, from a particular State, more Senators than you have Representatives. Can any thing occur to disfigure and derange the form of government under which we live more sig nally than that? Here would be a Senate bearing no proportion to the people, out of all relation to them, by the addition of new States; from some of them only one Representative, perhaps, and two Senators, whereas the larger States may have ten, fifteen, or even thirty Representatives, and but two Senators. The Senate, augmented by these new Senators coming from States where there are few people, becomes an odious oligarchy. It holds power without any adequate constituency. Sir, it is but "borough-mongering" upon a large scale. Now, I do not depend upon theory; I ask the Senate and the country to look at facts, to see where we were when we made our departure three years ago, and where we now are; and I leave it to the imagination to conjecture where we shall be.

We admitted Texas; one State for the present; but, Sir, if you refer to the resolutions providing for the annexation of Texas, you find a provision that it shall be in the power of Congress hereafter to make four new States out of Texan territory. Present and prospectively, five new States, with ten Senators, may come into the Union out of Texas. Three years ago we did this; we now propose to make two States. Undoubtedly, if we take, as the President recommends, New Mexico and California, there must then be four new Senators. We shall then have provided, in these territories out of the United States along our southern borders, for the creation of States enough to send fourteen Senators into this chamber. Now, what will be the relation between these Senators and the people they represent, or the States from which they come? I do not understand that there is any very accurate census of Texas. It is generally supposed to contain one hundred and fifty thousand persons. I doubt whether it contains above one hundred thousand.

MR. MANGUM. It contains one hundred and forty-nine thousand.

My honorable friend on my left says, a hundred and forty-nine thousand. I put it down, then, one hundred and fifty thousand. Well, Sir, Texas is not destined, probably, to be a country of dense population. We will suppose it to have at the present time a population of near one hundred and fifty thousand. New Mexico may have sixty or seventy thousand inhabitants; say seventy thousand. In California, there are not supposed to be above twenty-five thousand men; but undoubtedly, if this territory should become ours, persons from Oregon, and from our Western States, will find their way to San Francisco, where there is some good land, and we may suppose they will shortly amount to sixty or seventy thousand. We will put them down at seventy thousand. Then the whole territory in this estimate, which is as high as any man puts it, will contain two hundred and ninety thousand persons, and they will send us, whenever we ask for them, fourteen Senators; a population less than that of the State of Vermont, and not the eighth part of that of New York. Fourteen Senators, and not as many people as Vermont! and no more people than New Hampshire! and not so many people as the good State of New Jersey!

But then, Sir, Texas claims to the line of the Rio Grande, and if it be her true line, why then of course she absorbs a considerable part, nay, the greater part, of the population of what is now called New Mexico. I do not argue the question of the true southern or western line of Texas; I only say, that it is apparent to every body who will look at the map, and learn any thing of the matter, that New Mexico cannot be divided by this river, the Rio Grande, which is a shallow, fordable, insignificant stream, creeping along through a narrow valley, at the base of enormous mountains. New Mexico must remain together; it must be a State with its seventy thousand people, and so it will be; and so will California.

But then, Sir, suppose Texas to remain a unit, and but one State for the present; still we shall have three States, Texas, New Mexico, and California. We shall have six Senators, then, for less than three hundred thousand people. We shall have as many Senators for three hundred thousand people in that region as we have for New York, Pennsylvania, and Ohio, with four or five millions of people; and that is what we call an equal representation! Is not this enormous? Have gentlemen considered this? Have they looked at it? Are they willing to look it in the face, and then say they embrace it? I trust, Sir, the people will look at it and consider it. And now let me add, that this disproportion can never be diminished; it must remain for ever. How are you going to diminish it? Why, here is Texas, with a hundred and forty-nine thousand people, with one State. Suppose that population should flow into Texas, where will it go? Not to any dense point, but to be spread over all that region, in places remote from the Gulf, in places remote from what is now the capital of Texas; and therefore, as soon as there are in other portions of Texas people enough within our common construction of the Constitution and our practice in respect to the admission of States, my honorable friend from Texas* will have a new State, and I have no doubt he has chalked it out already.

As to New Mexico, its population is not likely to increase. It is a settled country; the people living along in the bottom of the valley on the sides of a little stream, a garter of land only on one side and the other, filled by coarse landholders and miserable *peons*. It can sustain, not only under this cultivation, but under any cultivation that our American race would ever submit to, no more people than are there now. There will, then, be two Senators for sixty thousand inhabitants in New Mexico to the end of our lives and to the end of the lives of our children.

And how is it with California? We propose to take California, from the forty-second degree of north latitude down to the thirty-second. We propose to take ten degrees along the coast of the Pacific. Scattered along the coast for that great distance are settlements and villages and ports; and in the rear all is wilderness and barrenness, and Indian country. But if, just about San Francisco, and perhaps Monterey, emigrants enough should settle to make up one State, then the people five hun-

* Mr. Rusk.

dred miles off would have another State. And so this disproportion of the Senate to the people will go on, and must go on, and we cannot prevent it.

I say, Sir, that, according to my conscientious conviction, we are now fixing on the Constitution of the United States, and its frame of government, a monstrosity, a disfiguration, an enormity! Sir, I hardly dare trust myself. I don't know but I may be under some delusion. It may be the weakness of my eyes that forms this monstrous apparition. But, if I may trust myself, if I can persuade myself that I am in my right mind, then it does appear to me that we in this Senate have been and are acting, and are likely to be acting hereafter, and immediately, a part which will form the most remarkable epoch in the history of our country. I hold it to be enormous, flagrant, an outrage upon all the principles of popular republican government, and on the elementary provisions of the Constitution under which we live, and which we have sworn to support.

But then, Sir, what relieves the case from this enormity? What is our reliance? Why, it is that we stipulate that these new States shall only be brought in at a suitable time. And pray, what is to constitute the suitableness of time? Who is to judge of it? I tell you, Sir, that suitable time will come when the preponderance of party power here makes it necessary to bring in new States. Be assured it will be a suitable time when votes are wanted in this Senate. We have had some little experience of that. Texas came in at a "suitable time," a *very* suitable time! Texas was finally admitted in December, 1845. My friend near me here, for whom I have a great regard, and whose acquaintance I have cultivated with pleasure,* took his seat in March, 1846, with his colleague. In July, 1846, these two Texan votes turned the balance in the Senate, and overthrew the tariff of 1842, in my judgment the best system of revenue ever established in this country. Gentlemen on the opposite side think otherwise. They think it fortunate. They think that was a suitable time, and they mean to take care that other times shall be equally suitable. I understand it perfectly well. That is the difference of opinion between me and these honorable gentlemen. To their policy, their objects, and their

* Mr. Rusk.

purposes the time was *suitable*, and the aid was efficient and decisive.

Sir, in 1850 perhaps a similar question may be agitated here. It is not likely to be before that time, but agitated it will be then, unless a change in the administration of the government shall take place. According to my apprehension, looking at general results as flowing from our established system of commerce and revenue, in two years from this time we shall probably be engaged in a new revision of our system: in the work of establishing, if we can, a tariff of specific duties; of protecting, if we can, our domestic industry and the manufactures of the country; in the work of preventing, if we can, the overwhelming flood of foreign importations. Suppose that to be part of the future: that would be exactly the "suitable time," if necessary, for two Senators from New Mexico to make their appearance here!

But, again, we hear another halcyon, soothing tone, which quiets none of my alarms, assuages none of my apprehensions, commends me to my nightly rest with no more resignation. And that is, the plea that we may trust the popular branch of the legislature, we may look to the House of Representatives, to the Northern and Middle States and even the sound men of the South, and trust them to take care that States be not admitted sooner than they should be, or for party purposes. I am compelled, by experience, to distrust all such reliances. If we cannot rely on ourselves, when we have the clear constitutional authority competent to carry us through, and the motives intensely powerful, I beg to know how we can rely on others? Have we more reliance on the patriotism, the firmness, of others, than on our own?

Besides, experience shows us that things of this sort may be *sprung* upon Congress and the people. It was so in the case of Texas. It was so in the Twenty-eighth Congress. The members of that Congress were not chosen to decide the question of annexation or no annexation. They came in on other grounds, political and party, and were supported for reasons not connected with that question. What then? The administration sprung upon them the question of annexation. It obtained a *snap* judgment upon it, and carried the measure of annexation. That is indubitable, as I could show by many instances, of which I shall state only one.

Four gentlemen from the State of Connecticut were elected before the question arose, belonging to the dominant party. They had not been here long before they were committed to annexation; and when it was known in Connecticut that annexation was in contemplation, remonstrances, private, public, and legislative, were uttered, in tones that any one could hear who could hear thunder. Did they move them? Not at all. Every one of them voted for annexation! The election came on, and they were turned out, to a man. But what did those care who had had the benefit of their votes? Such agencies, if it be not more proper to call them such instrumentalities, retain respect no longer than they continue to be useful.

Sir, we take New Mexico and California; who is weak enough to suppose that there is an end? Don't we hear it avowed every day, that it would be proper also to take Sonora, Tamaulipas, and other provinces of Northern Mexico? Who thinks that the hunger for dominion will stop here of itself? It is said, to be sure, that our present acquisitions will prove so lean and unsatisfactory, that we shall seek no further. In my judgment, we may as well say of a rapacious animal, that, if he has made one unproductive hunt, he will not try for a better foray.

But further. There are some things one can argue against with temper, and submit to, if overruled, without mortification. There are other things that seem to affect one's consciousness of being a sensible man, and to imply a disposition to impose upon his common sense. And of this class of topics, or pretences, I have never heard of any thing, and I cannot conceive of any thing, more ridiculous in itself, more absurd, and more affrontive to all sober judgment, than the cry that we are getting indemnity by the acquisition of New Mexico and California. I hold they are not worth a dollar; and we pay for them vast sums of money! We have expended, as every body knows, large treasures in the prosecution of the war; and now what is to constitute this indemnity? What do gentlemen mean by it? Let us see a little how this stands. We get a country; we get, in the first instance, a cession, or an acknowledgment of boundary, (I care not which way you state it,) of the country between the Nueces and the Rio Grande. What this country is appears from a publication made by a gentleman in the other house.* He speaks of the country in the following manner: —

"The country from the Nueces to the valley of the Rio Grande is poor, sterile, sandy, and barren, with not a single tree of any size or value on our whole route. The only tree which we saw was the musquit-tree, and very few of these. The musquit is a small tree, resembling an old and decayed peach-tree. The whole country may be truly called a perfect waste, uninhabited and uninhabitable. There is not a drop of running water between the two rivers, except in the two small streams of San Salvador and Santa Gertrudis, and these only contain water in the rainy season. Neither of them had running water when we passed them. The *chaparral* commences within forty or fifty miles of the Rio Grande. This is poor, rocky, and sandy; covered with prickly pear, thistles, and almost every sticking thing, constituting a thick and perfectly impenetrable undergrowth. For any useful or agricultural purpose, the country is not worth a *sous*.

"So far as we were able to form any opinion of this desert upon the other routes which had been travelled, its character, everywhere between the two rivers, is pretty much the same. We learned that the route pursued by General Taylor, south of ours, was through a country similar to that through which we passed; as also was that travelled by General Wool from San Antonio to Presidio on the Rio Grande. From what we both saw and heard, the whole command came to the conclusion which I have already expressed, that it was worth *nothing*. I have no hesitation in saying, that I would not hazard the life of one valuable and useful man for every foot of land between San Patricio and the valley of the Rio Grande. The country is not now, and can never be, of the *slightest value*."

Major Gaines has been there lately. He is a competent observer. He is contradicted by nobody. And so far as that country is concerned, I take it for granted that it is not worth a dollar.

Now of New Mexico, what of that? Forty-nine fiftieths, at least, of the whole of New Mexico, are a barren waste, a desert plain of mountain, with no wood, no timber. Little fagots for lighting a fire are carried thirty or forty miles on mules. There is no fall of rain there as in temperate climates. It is Asiatic in scenery altogether: enormously high mountains, running up some of them ten thousand feet, with narrow valleys

* Major Gaines.

at their bases, through which streams sometimes trickle along. A strip, a garter, winds along, through which runs the Rio Grande, from far away up in the Rocky Mountains to latitude 33°, a distance of three or four hundred miles. There these sixty thousand persons reside. In the mountains on the right and left are streams which, obeying the natural tendency as tributaries, should flow into the Rio Grande, and which, in certain seasons, when rains are abundant, do, some of them, actually reach the Rio Grande; while the greater part always, and all for the greater part of the year, never reach an outlet to the sea, but are absorbed in the sands and desert plains of the country. There is no cultivation there. There is cultivation where there is artificial watering or irrigation, and nowhere else. Men can live only in the narrow valley, and in the gorges of the mountains which rise round it, and not along the course of the streams which lose themselves in the sands.

Now there is no public domain in New Mexico, not a foot of land, to the soil of which we shall obtain title. Not an acre becomes ours when the country becomes ours. More than that, the country is as full of people, such as they are, as it is likely to be. There is not the least thing in it to invite settlement from the fertile valley of the Mississippi. And I undertake to say, there would not be two hundred families of persons who would emigrate from the United States to New Mexico, for agricultural purposes, in fifty years. They could not live there Suppose they were to cultivate the lands; they could only make them productive in a slight degree by irrigation or artificial watering. The people there produce little, and live on little. That is not the characteristic, I take it, of the people of the Eastern or of the Middle States, or of the Valley of the Mississippi. They produce a good deal, and they consume a good deal.

Again, Sir, New Mexico is not like Texas. I have hoped, and I still hope, that Texas will be filled up from among ourselves, not with Spaniards, not with *peons;* that its inhabitants will not be Mexican landlords, with troops of slaves, predial or otherwise.

Mr. Rusk here rose, and said that he disliked to interrupt the Senator, and therefore he had said nothing while he was describing the country between the Nueces and the Rio Grande; but he wished now to say, that, when that country comes to be known, it will be found to be as valuable as any part of Texas. The valley of the Rio Grande is valuable from its source to its mouth. But he did not look upon *that* as indemnity; he claimed that as the *right* of Texas. So far as the Mexican population is concerned, there is a good deal of it in Texas; and it comprises many respectable persons, wealthy, intelligent, and distinguished. A good many are now moving in from New Mexico, and settling in Texas.

I take what I say from Major Gaines. But I am glad to hear that any part of New Mexico is fit for the foot of civilized man. And I am glad, moreover, that there are some persons in New Mexico who are not so blindly attached to their miserable condition as not to make an effort to come out of their country, and get into a better.

Sir, I would, if I had time, call the attention of the Senate to an instructive speech made in the other house by Mr. Smith of Connecticut. He seems to have examined all the authorities, to have conversed with all the travellers, to have corresponded with all our agents. His speech contains communications from all of them; and I commend it to every man in the United States who wishes to know what we are about to acquire by the annexation of New Mexico.

New Mexico is secluded, isolated, a place by itself, in the midst and at the foot of vast mountains, five hundred miles from the settled part of Texas, and as far from anywhere else! It does not belong anywhere! It has no *belongings* about it! At this moment it is absolutely more retired and shut out from communication with the civilized world than Hawaii or any of the other islands of the Pacific sea. In seclusion and remoteness, New Mexico may press hard on the character and condition of Typee. And its people are infinitely less elevated, in morals and condition, than the people of the Sandwich Islands. We had much better have Senators from Oahu. They are far less intelligent than the better class of our Indian neighbors. Commend me to the Cherokees, to the Choctaws; if you please, speak of the Pawnees, of the Snakes, the Flatfeet, of any thing but the *Digging* Indians, and I will be satisfied not to take the people of New Mexico. Have they any notion of our institutions, or of *any* free institutions? Have they any notion of popular government? Not the slightest! Not the slightest on earth! When the question is asked, What will be their constitution? it is farcical to talk of such people making a constitution for themselves. They do not know the meaning of the term, they do not know its import. They know nothing at all about it; and I can tell you, Sir, that when they are made a Territory, and are to be made a State, such a constitution as the executive power of this government may think fit to send them will be sent, and will be adopted. The constitution of our *fellow-citizens* of New Mexico will be framed in the city of Washington.

Now what says in regard to all Mexico Colonel Hardin, that most lamented and distinguished officer, honorably known as a member of the other house, and who has fallen gallantly fighting in the service of his country? Here is his description: —

"The whole country is miserably watered. Large districts have no water at all. The streams are small, and at great distances apart. One day we marched on the road from Monclova to Parras thirty-five miles without water, a pretty severe day's marching for infantry.

"Grass is very scarce, and indeed there is none at all in many regions for miles square. Its place its supplied with prickly pear and thorny bushes. There is not one acre in two hundred, more probably not one in five hundred, of all the land we have seen in Mexico, which can ever be cultivated; the greater portion of it is the most desolate region I could ever have imagined. The pure granite hills of New England are a paradise to it, for they are without the thorny briers and venomous reptiles which infest the barbed barrenness of Mexico. The good land and cultivated spots in Mexico are but dots on the map. Were it not that it takes so very little to support a Mexican, and that the land which is cultivated yields its produce with little labor, it would be surprising how its sparse population is sustained. All the towns we have visited, with perhaps the exception of Parras, are depopulating, as is also the whole country.

"The people are on a par with their land. One in two hundred or five hundred is rich, and lives like a nabob; the rest are *peons*, or servants sold for debt, who work for their masters, and are as subservient as the slaves of the South, and look like Indians, and, indeed, are not more capable of self-government. One man, Jacobus Sanchez, owns three fourths of all the land our column has passed over in Mexico. We are told we have seen the best part of Northern Mexico; if so, the whole of it is not worth much.

"I came to Mexico in favor of getting or taking enough of it to pay the expenses of the war. I now doubt whether all Northern Mexico is worth the expenses of our column of three thousand men. The expenses of the war must be enormous; we have paid enormous prices for every thing, much beyond the usual prices of the country."

There it is. That 's all North Mexico; and New Mexico is not the better part of it.

Sir, there is a recent traveller, not unfriendly to the United States, if we may judge from his work, for he speaks well of us everywhere; an Englishman, named Ruxton. He gives an account of the morals and the manners of the population of New Mexico. And, Mr. President and Senators, I shall take leave to introduce you to these soon to be your respected *fellow-citizens* of New Mexico: —

"It is remarkable that, although existing from the earliest times of the colonization of New Mexico, a period of two centuries, in a state of continual hostility with the numerous savage tribes of Indians who surround their territory, and in constant insecurity of life and property from their attacks, being also far removed from the enervating influences of large cities, and, in their isolated situation, entirely dependent upon their own resources, the inhabitants are totally destitute of those qualities which, for the above reasons, we might naturally have expected to distinguish them, and are as deficient in energy of character and physical courage as they are in all the moral and intellectual qualities. In their social state but one degree removed from the veriest savages, they might take a lesson even from these in morality and the conventional decencies of life. Imposing no restraint on their passions, a shameless and universal concubinage exists, and a total disregard of morality, to which it would be impossible to find a parallel in any country calling itself civilized. A want of honorable principle, and consummate duplicity and treachery, characterize all their dealings. Liars by nature, they are treacherous and faithless to their friends, cowardly and cringing to their enemies; cruel, as all cowards are, they unite savage ferocity with their want of animal courage; as an example of which, their recent massacre of Governor Bent, and other Americans, may be given, one of a hundred instances."

These, Sir, are soon to be our beloved countrymen!

Mr. President, for a good many years I have struggled in opposition to every thing which I thought tended to strengthen the arm of executive power. I think it is growing more and more formidable every day. And I think that by yielding to it in this, as in other instances, we give it a strength which it will be difficult hereafter to resist. I think that it is nothing less than the fear of executive power which induces us to acquiesce in the acquisition of territory; fear, *fear*, and nothing else.

In the little part which I have acted in public life, it has been my purpose to maintain the people of the United States, what the Constitution designed to make them, *one people*, one in interest, one in character, and one in political feeling. If we depart from that, we break it all up. What sympathy can there be between the people of Mexico and California and the inhabitants of the Valley of the Mississippi and the Eastern States in the choice of a President? Do they know the same man? Do they concur in any general constitutional principles? Not at all.

Arbitrary governments may have territories and distant possessions, because arbitrary governments may rule them by different laws and different systems. Russia may rule in the Ukraine and the provinces of the Caucasus and Kamtschatka by different codes, ordinances, or ukases. We can do no such thing. They must be of us, *part* of us, or else strangers.

I think I see that in progress which will disfigure and deform the Constitution. While these territories remain territories, they will be a trouble and an annoyance; they will draw after them vast expenses; they will probably require as many troops as we have maintained during the last twenty years to defend them against the Indian tribes. We must maintain an army at that immense distance. When they shall become States, they will be still more likely to give us trouble.

I think I see a course adopted which is likely to turn the Constitution of the land into a deformed monster, into a curse rather than a blessing; in fact, a frame of an unequal government, not founded on popular representation, not founded on equality, but on the grossest inequality; and I think that this process will go on, or that there is *danger* that it will go on, until this Union shall fall to pieces. I resist it, to-day and always! Whoever falters or whoever flies, I continue the contest!

I know, Sir, that all the portents are discouraging. Would to God I could auspicate good influences! Would to God that those who think with me, and myself, could hope for stronger support! Would that we could stand where we desire to stand I see the signs are sinister. But with few, or alone, my position is fixed. If there were time, I would gladly awaken the country. I believe the country might be awakened, although it may be too late. For myself, supported or unsupported, by the blessing of God, I shall do my duty. I see well enough all the adverse indications. But I am sustained by a deep and a conscientious sense of duty; and while supported by that feeling, and while such great interests are at stake, I defy auguries, and ask no omen but my country's cause!

EXCLUSION OF SLAVERY FROM THE TERRITORIES.*

In the course of the first session of the Thirtieth Congress, a bill passed the House of Representatives to organize a government for the Territory of Oregon. This bill received several amendments on its passage through the Senate, and among them one moved by Mr. Douglass of Illinois, on the 10th of August, by which the eighth section of the law of the 6th of March, 1820, for the admission of Missouri, was revived and adopted, as a part of the bill, and declared to be "in full force, and binding, for the future organization of the territories of the United States, in the same sense and with the same understanding with which it was originally adopted."

This, with some of the other amendments of the Senate, was disagreed to by the House. On the return of the bill to the Senate, a discussion arose, and continued for several days, on the question of agreement or disagreement with the amendments of the House to the Senate's amendments.

The principal subject of this discussion was whether the Senate would recede from the above-mentioned amendment moved by Mr. Douglass, which was finally decided in the affirmative. In these discussions, a considerable portion of which was of a conversational character, Mr. Webster took a leading part; but of most of what was said by him, as by other Senators, no report has been preserved. The session of the Senate at which the last and most animated discussion of this subject took place, nominally on Saturday of the 12th of August, was prolonged till ten o'clock, A. M., of Sunday, the 13th. In the course of the debate on this day Mr. Webster spoke as follows.

I am very little inclined to prolong this debate, and I hope I am utterly disinclined to bring into it any new warmth or ex-

* Remarks made in the Senate of the United States, on the 12th of August, 1848.

citement. I wish to say a few words, however, first, upon the question as it is presented to us, as a parliamentary question; and secondly, upon the general political questions involved in the debate.

As a question of parliamentary proceeding, I understand the case to be this. The House of Representatives sent us a bill for the establishment of a territorial government in Oregon; and no motion has been made in the Senate to strike out any part of that bill. The bill purporting to respect Oregon, simply and alone, has not been the subject of any objection in this branch of the legislature. The Senate has proposed no important amendment to this bill, affecting Oregon itself; and the honorable member from Missouri* was right, entirely right, when he said that the amendment now under consideration had no relation to Oregon. That is perfectly true; and therefore the amendment which the Senate has adopted, and the House has disagreed to, has no connection with the immediate subject before it. The truth is, that it is an amendment by which the Senate wishes to have now a public, legal declaration, not respecting Oregon, but respecting the newly acquired territories of California and New Mexico. It wishes now to make a line of slavery, which shall include those new territories. The amendment says that the line of the "Missouri Compromise" shall be the line to the Pacific, and then goes on to say, in the language of the bill as it now stands, that the Ordinance of 1787 shall be applicable to Oregon; and therefore I say that the amendment proposed is foreign to the immediate object of the bill. It does nothing to modify, restrain, or affect, in any way, the government which we propose to establish over Oregon, or the condition or character of that government, or of the people under it. In a parliamentary view, this is the state of the case.

Now, Sir, this amendment has been attached to this bill by a strong majority of the Senate. That majority had the right, as it had the power, to pass it. The House disagreed to that amendment. If the majority of the Senate, who attached it to the bill, are of opinion that a conference with the House will lead to some adjustment of the question, by which this amendment, or something equivalent to it, may be adopted by the

* Mr. Benton.

House, it is very proper for them to urge a conference. It is very fair, quite parliamentary, and there is not a word to be said against it. But my position is that of one who voted against the amendment, who thinks that it ought not to be attached to this bill; and therefore I naturally vote for the motion to get rid of it, that is, "to recede."

So much for the parliamentary question. Now there are two or three political questions arising in this case, which I wish to state dispassionately; not to argue, but to state. The honorable member from Georgia,* for whom I have great respect, and with whom it is my delight to cultivate personal friendship, has stated, with great propriety, the importance of this question. He has said, that it is a question interesting to the South and to the North, and one which may very well also attract the attention of mankind. He has not stated any part of this too strongly. It is such a question. Without doubt, it is a question which may well attract the attention of mankind. On the subjects involved in this debate, the whole world is not now asleep. It is wide awake; and I agree with the honorable member, that, if what is now proposed to be done by us who resist this amendment is, as he supposes, unjust and injurious to any portion of this community, or against its constitutional rights, that injustice should be presented to the civilized world, and we, who concur in the proceeding, ought to submit ourselves to its rebuke. I am glad that the honorable gentleman proposes to refer this question to the great tribunal of Modern Civilization, as well as the great tribunal of the American People. It is proper. It is a question of magnitude enough, of interest enough, to all the civilized nations of the earth, to call from those who support the one side or the other a statement of the grounds upon which they act.

Now I propose to state as briefly as I can the grounds upon which I proceed, historical and constitutional; and will endeavor to use as few words as possible, so that I may relieve the Senate from hearing me at the earliest possible moment. In the first place, to view the matter historically. This Constitution, founded in 1787, and the government under it, organized in 1789, do recognize the existence of slavery in certain States, then belonging to the Union; and a particular description of slavery.

* Mr. Berrien.

I hope that what I am about to say may be received without any supposition that I intend the slightest disrespect. But this particular description of slavery does not, I believe, now exist in Europe, nor in any other civilized portion of the habitable globe. It is not a predial slavery. It is not analogous to the case of the *predial* slaves, or slaves *glebæ adscripti* of Russia, or Hungary, or other states. It is a peculiar system of personal slavery, by which the person who is called a slave is transferable as a chattel, from hand to hand. I speak of this as a fact; and that is the fact. And I will say further, perhaps other gentlemen may remember the instances, that although slavery, as a system of servitude attached to the earth, exists in various countries of Europe, I am not at the present moment aware of any place on the globe in which this property of man in a human being as a slave, transferable as a chattel, exists, except America. Now, that it existed, in the form in which it still exists, in certain States, at the formation of this Constitution, and that the framers of that instrument, and those who adopted it, agreed that, as far as it existed, it should not be disturbed or interfered with by the new general government, there is no doubt.

The Constitution of the United States recognizes it as an existing fact, an existing relation between the inhabitants of the Southern States. I do not call it an "institution," because that term is not applicable to it; for that seems to imply a voluntary establishment. When I first came here, it was a matter of frequent reproach to England, the mother country, that slavery had been entailed upon the colonies by her, against their consent, and that which is now considered a cherished "institution" was then regarded as, I will not say an *evil*, but an entailment on the Colonies by the policy of the mother country against their wishes. At any rate, it stands upon the Constitution. The Constitution was adopted in 1788, and went into operation in 1789. When it was adopted, the state of the country was this: slavery existed in the Southern States; there was a very large extent of unoccupied territory, the whole Northwestern Territory, which, it was understood, was destined to be formed into States; and it was then determined that no slavery should exist in this territory. I gather now, as a matter of inference from the history of the time and the history of the debates, that the prevailing motives with the North for agreeing to this recognition of the existence of slavery in the Southern States, and giving a representation to those States founded in part upon their slaves, rested on the supposition that no acquisition of territory would be made to form new States on the southern frontier of this country, either by cession or conquest. No one looked to any acquisition of new territory on the southern or southwestern frontier. The exclusion of slavery from the Northwestern Territory and the prospective abolition of the foreign slave trade were generally, the former unanimously, agreed to; and on the basis of these considerations, the South insisted that where slavery existed it should not be interfered with, and that it should have a certain ratio of representation in Congress. And now, Sir, I am one, who, believing such to be the understanding on which the Constitution was framed, mean to abide by it.

There is another principle, equally clear, by which I mean to abide; and that is, that in the Convention, and in the first Congress, when appealed to on the subject by petitions, and all along in the history of this government, it was and has been a conceded point, that slavery in the States in which it exists is a matter of State regulation exclusively, and that Congress has not the least power over it, or right to interfere with it. Therefore I say, that all agitations and attempts to disturb the relations between master and slave, by persons not living in the slave States, are unconstitutional in their spirit, and are, in my opinion, productive of nothing but evil and mischief. I countenance none of them. The manner in which the governments of those States where slavery exists are to regulate it, is for their own consideration, under their responsibility to their constituents, to the general laws of propriety, humanity, and justice, and to God. Associations formed elsewhere, springing from a feeling of humanity, or any other cause, have nothing whatever to do with it, nor right to interfere with it. They have never received any encouragement from me, and they never will. In my opinion, they have done nothing but delay and defeat their own professed objects.

I have now stated, as I understand it, the condition of things upon the adoption of the Constitution of the United States. What has happened since? Sir, it has happened that, above and beyond all contemplation or expectation of the original framers of the Constitution, or the people who adopted it, foreign territory has been acquired by cession, first from France, and then from Spain, on our southern frontier. And what has been the result? Five slave-holding States have been created and added to the Union, bringing ten Senators into this body, (I include Texas, which I consider in the light of a foreign acquisition also,) and up to this hour in which I address you, not one free State has been admitted to the Union from all this acquired territory!

Mr. Berrien (in his seat). Yes, Iowa.

Iowa is not yet in the Union. Her Senators are not here. When she comes in, there will be one to five, one free State to five slave States, formed out of new territories. Now, it seems strange to me that there should be any complaint of injustice exercised by the North toward the South. Northern votes have been necessary, they have been ready, and they have been given, to aid in the admission of these five new slave-holding States. These are facts; and as the gentleman from Georgia has very properly put it as a case in which we are to present ourselves before the world for its judgment, let us now see how we stand. I do not represent the North. I state my own case; and I present the matter in that light in which I am willing, as an individual member of Congress, to be judged by civilized humanity. I say, then, that, according to true history, the slave-holding interest in this country has not been a disfavored interest; it has not been disfavored by the North. The North has concurred to bring in these five slave-holding States out of newly acquired territory, which acquisitions were not at all in the contemplation of the Convention which formed the Constitution, or of the people when they agreed that there should be a representation of three fifths of the slaves in the then existing States.

Mr. President, what is the result of this? We stand here now, at least I do, for one, to say, that, considering there have been already five new slave-holding States formed out of newly acquired territory, and only one non-slaveholding State, at most, I do not feel that I am called on to go further; I do not feel the obligation to yield more. But our friends of the South say, You deprive us of all our rights. We have fought for this territory, and you deny us participation in it. Let us consider this question as it really is; and since the honorable gentleman from Georgia proposes to leave the case to the enlightened and impartial judgment of mankind, and as I agree with him that it is a case proper to be considered by the enlightened part of mankind, let us see how the matter in truth stands. Gentlemen who advocate the case which my honorable friend from Georgia, with so much ability, sustains, declare that we invade their rights, that we deprive them of a participation in the enjoyment of territories acquired by the common services and common exertions of all. Is this true? How deprive? Of what do we deprive them? Why, they say that we deprive them of the privilege of carrying their slaves, as slaves, into the new territories. Well, Sir, what is the amount of that? They say that in this way we deprive them of the opportunity of going into this acquired territory with their property. Their "property"? What do they mean by "property"? We certainly do not deprive them of the privilege of going into these newly acquired territories with all that, in the general estimate of human society, in the general, and common, and universal understanding of mankind, is esteemed property. Not at all. The truth is just this. They have, in their own States, peculiar laws, which create property in persons. They have a system of local legislation on which slavery rests; while every body agrees that it is against natural law, or at least against the common understanding which prevails among men as to what is natural law.

I am not going into metaphysics, for therein I should encounter the honorable member from South Carolina,* and we should find "no end, in wandering mazes lost," until after the time for the adjournment of Congress. The Southern States have peculiar laws, and by those laws there is property in slaves. This is purely local. The real meaning, then, of Southern gentlemen, in making this complaint, is, that they cannot go into the territories of the United States carrying with them their own peculiar local law, a law which creates property in persons. This, according to their own statement, is all the ground of complaint they have. Now here, I think, gentlemen are unjust towards us. How unjust they are, others will judge; generations that will come after us will judge. It will not be contended that this sort of

* Mr. Calhoun.

personal slavery exists by general law. It exists only by local law. I do not mean to deny the validity of that local law where it is established; but I say it is, after all, local law. It is nothing more. And wherever that local law does not extend, property in persons does not exist. Well, Sir, what is now the demand on the part of our Southern friends? They say, "We will carry our local laws with us wherever we go. We insist that Congress does us injustice unless it establishes in the territory in which we wish to go our own local law." This demand I for one resist, and shall resist. It goes upon the idea that there is an inequality, unless persons under this local law, and holding property by authority of that law, can go into new territory and there establish that local law, to the exclusion of the general law. Mr. President, it was a maxim of the civil law, that, between slavery and freedom, freedom should always be presumed, and slavery must always be proved. If any question arose as to the *status* of an individual in Rome, he was presumed to be free until he was proved to be a slave, because slavery is an exception to the general rule. Such, I suppose, is the general law of mankind. An individual is to be presumed to be free, until a law can be produced which creates ownership in his person. I do not dispute the force and validity of the local law, as I have already said; but I say, it is a matter to be proved; and therefore, if individuals go into any part of the earth, it is to be proved that they are not freemen, or else the presumption is that they are.

Now our friends seem to think that an inequality arises from restraining them from going into the territories, unless there be a law provided which shall protect their ownership in persons. The assertion is, that we create an inequality. Is there nothing to be said on the other side in relation to inequality? Sir, from the date of this Constitution, and in the counsels that formed and established this Constitution, and I suppose in all men's judgment since, it is received as a settled truth, that slave labor and free labor do not exist well together. I have before me a declaration of Mr. Mason, in the Convention that formed the Constitution, to that effect. Mr. Mason, as is well known, was a distinguished member from Virginia. He says that the objection to slave labor is, that it puts free white labor in disrepute; that it causes labor to be regarded as derogatory to the character of the free white man, and that the free white man despises to work, to use his expression, where slaves are employed. This is a matter of great interest to the free States, if it be true, as to a great extent it certainly is, that wherever slave labor prevails free white labor is excluded or discouraged. I agree that slave labor does not necessarily exclude free labor totally. There is free white labor in Virginia, Tennessee, and other States, where most of the labor is done by slaves. But it necessarily loses something of its respectability, by the side of, and when associated with, slave labor. Wherever labor is mainly performed by slaves, it is regarded as degrading to freemen. The freemen of the North, therefore, have a deep interest in keeping labor free, exclusively free, in the new territories.

But, Sir, let us look further into this alleged inequality. There is no pretence that Southern people may not go into territory which shall be subject to the Ordinance of 1787. The only restraint is, that they shall not carry slaves thither, and continue that relation. They say this shuts them altogether out. Why, Sir, there can be nothing more inaccurate in point of fact than this statement. I understand that one half the people who settled Illinois are people, or descendants of people, who came from the Southern States. And I suppose that one third of the people of Ohio are those, or descendants of those, who emigrated from the South; and I venture to say, that, in respect to those two States, they are at this day settled by people of Southern origin in as great a proportion as they are by people of Northern origin, according to the general numbers and proportion of people, South and North. There are as many people from the South, in proportion to the whole people of the South, in those States, as there are from the North, in proportion to the whole people of the North. There is, then, no exclusion of Southern people; there is only the exclusion of a peculiar local law. Neither in principle nor in fact is there any inequality.

The question now is, whether it is not competent to Congress, in the exercise of a fair and just discretion, considering that there have been five slave-holding States added to this Union out of foreign acquisitions, and as yet only one free State, to prevent their further increase. That is the question. I see no injustice in it. As to the power of Congress, I have nothing to add to what I said the other day. Congress has full power over the subject. It may establish any such government, and any such laws, in the territories, as in its discretion it may see fit. It is subject, of course, to the rules of justice and propriety; but it is under no constitutional restraints.

I have said that I shall consent to no extension of the area of slavery upon this continent, nor to any increase of slave representation in the other house of Congress. I have now stated my reasons for my conduct and my vote. We of the North have already gone, in this respect, far beyond all that any Southern man could have expected, or did expect, at the time of the adoption of the Constitution. I repeat the statement of the fact of the creation of five new slave-holding States out of newly acquired territory. We have done that which, if those who framed the Constitution had foreseen, they never would have agreed to slave representation. We have yielded thus far; and we have now in the House of Representatives twenty persons voting upon this very question, and upon all other questions, who are there only in virtue of the representation of slaves.

Let me conclude, therefore, by remarking, that, while I am willing to present this as showing my own judgment and position, in regard to this case, and I beg it to be understood that I am speaking for no other than myself, and while I am willing to offer it to the whole world as my own justification, I rest on these propositions: First, That when this Constitution was adopted, nobody looked for any new acquisition of territory to be formed into slave-holding States. Secondly, That the principles of the Constitution prohibited, and were intended to prohibit, and should be construed to prohibit, all interference of the general government with slavery as it existed and as it still exists in the States. And then, looking to the operation of these new acquisitions, which have in this great degree had the effect of strengthening that interest in the South by the addition of these five States, I feel that there is nothing unjust, nothing of which any honest man can complain, if he is intelligent, and I feel that there is nothing with which the civilized world, if they take notice of so humble a person as myself, will reproach me, when I say, as I said the other day, that I have made up my mind, for one, that under no circumstances will I consent to the further extension of the area of slavery in the United States, or to the further increase of slave representation in the House of Representatives.

THE PANAMA RAILROAD.*

I SHOULD regret, Sir, that a measure which I regard as exceedingly important should be disposed of by indefinite postponement. I had hoped that the measure might be allowed to proceed until its details were arranged so that they might be satisfactory to the Senate, and I rise merely to express my opinion in favor of the measure, generally, concurring in it especially for the reasons assigned by the honorable Senator from Missouri.† I think the circumstances of the country call for the adoption of this particular measure. I do not mean to say, Sir, that there may not be several modes of establishing a communication with the Pacific coast that are equally desirable. I am willing to say, on the other hand, that I have regarded the subject of a communication from the Atlantic to the Pacific, by way of Tehuantepec, as preferable, on account of its being nearer to our ports on the Gulf; and I will add, that, if the proposition for a railroad were now before us, connecting the two oceans by that route, and the project had advanced so far that we could pronounce it to be practicable, I should give it my most hearty support. I do not think the view which has been adopted by the Senator from Connecticut ‡ is entirely correct, that the present exigency for a channel of communication will be a very short one. I do not apprehend that there will cease to be an occasion for a great deal of intercourse between the Atlantic and Pacific, and between our own territories on

* Remarks in the Senate, on the 31st of January, 1849, on the Motion submitted by Mr. Allen, of Ohio, to postpone indefinitely the Bill making an appropriation for the transportation of the United States Mails by Railroad across the Isthmus of Panama.

† Mr. Benton. ‡ Mr. Niles.

either side of the continent. I think the progress of things is onward; and, let the speculations and operations in the gold mines go forward more or less rapidly, I think an intercourse is now to be opened for general purposes of trade and commerce between the Atlantic and Pacific.

I have not devoted my attention to the particular provisions or details of this measure. I am not in possession of such estimates as enable me to say whether the limitations so called in the bill now on your table, or the limitation which will be in the same bill if the motion of the Senator from Connecticut prevail, is the best. The bill proposes to authorize the Secretary of the Navy to contract for the transportation of goods and merchandise, munitions of war, and troops, across the isthmus, and to pay for this transportation an annual sum. The bill limits that sum at two hundred and fifty thousand dollars. The Senator from Connecticut moves to substitute one hundred and fifty thousand. Without more information than I have upon this point, I cannot say which would be the proper sum. I understand that the parties who have undertaken the construction of the road estimate its cost at four or five millions of dollars; and they have founded their opinion upon the cost commonly attending the construction of roads in the United States, economically conducted, making, of course, proper allowance for the necessarily augmented expense of a work to be done so far from the resources which are to supply the means. It is known, too, Sir, that a very great reduction for wear and tear is made from the receipts of all railroads, so that the general estimates of income, by reference to any ordinary rule of computation, not allowing for the wear of the road, would be very inadequate to represent the actual state of things that will arise when this road has been completed.

Now, it is evident, Sir, that this proposed road will shorten the distance between the ports of the United States on the Atlantic and the ports of the United States on the Pacific. It is a nearer route probably by not less than ten thousand miles, certainly not less than nine thousand. It will shorten the communication in point of time more than one half, and whatever shortens the time diminishes the cost. If troops are to be conveyed, they are under pay while at sea; if munitions of war or merchandise are to be transported, they ought to reach their destination within as short a time as possible; and in every point of view in which we can make an estimate of this matter, we must all, I think, see that a great, a very great, I am not prepared to say how great a saving, will inure to the United States by adopting the shorter route.

I will state, Sir, that, with respect to other modes of conveyance, I have no doubt that we shall ere long have them across the continent from our own frontier territory on one side to that on the other. I entertain as little doubt that there will be a communication established over the other route through Tehuantepec. I entertain no doubt at all about this; but I do think that there is an exigency, a present want of conveyance, and that this is the readiest, and the only ready, mode of obtaining it. I think there is a prospect, if this project be favored by the government of the United States, from the known enterprise of the respectable gentlemen who have undertaken it, that it will be as sure to be accomplished as any work can possibly be. My honorable friend from Ohio* says that it will be time enough to make this contract when the work is done. In ordinary cases this would be very true; but it must be remembered that this is a very great work, requiring an expenditure of four or five millions of dollars, and it is but reasonable that those who embark their fortunes in it should have some assurance that they will receive the patronage of the government.

Now, in respect to the amount of money to be paid, no man knows less what would be the proper sum to be paid than I do. If it be the pleasure of the Senate and the other branch of Congress, that matter may be left more in the discretion and within the control of Congress hereafter. I do not look upon this as a matter by which a speculation is to be made, on the part of the contractors, out of the treasury of the United States.

Upon the whole, I think the work ought to be commenced as early as practicable, and that it ought to be speedily completed, for the reasons stated by the Senator from Missouri. This plan appears practicable; I think the object is attainable, and I think it is attainable at a reasonable expense, and therefore I am decidedly in favor of the amendment. At the same time, I shall concur in any amendment or alteration, either with the view of re-

* Mr. Allen.

ducing the expense, or limiting still further the Navy Department with respect to the extent to which it will pledge the credit of the United States. I think, as I said before, that the circumstances of the country call for the road, and there is nothing in these circumstances that is likely to make it so short-lived or temporary as some Senators seem to imagine; that there is no probability that this work will not be necessary for a number of years. And I repeat again, if there were a proposition now before us for the other route, and if that proposition were in as advanced a state as this, and if we were to have but one, I would give the preference to the route by Tehuantepec; but I still think that, as this work is practicable, and as a channel of communication is necessary for us, we ought not to hesitate to adopt the one proposed, in order that we may avail ourselves of the advantages which it will furnish, until we shall be able to construct a road through our own territory.

On the 6th of February, the same subject being under debate, Mr. Webster spoke as follows: —

Mr. President, in my opinion, unless this bill shall pass, we shall find ourselves a year hence in exactly the same condition with regard to communication with the western shore of this continent that we now are. And whether we should adopt this bill or not depends upon the general view which we entertain of the necessity, or high utility and expediency, of proceeding as soon as may be to open a communication across the continent somewhere between the Atlantic and the Pacific Oceans. I have no idea, that, without the assistance in advance, so far as any thing is pledged in advance by this bill, this communication will ever be made. I am sure it will not. It requires a very great sum of money. It requires heavy capital, and much credit to raise it. It has to be expended a good way from home, under agencies, some of them sent from this country; some of them found, as well as they may be found, there.

Now let us look at the general aspect of the case, and see whether it be necessary or expedient on the part of the government to encourage and set forward the making of this communication; and then, in the next place, whether the terms proposed in the memorial upon which this bill is founded, or in the amendment proposed, are reasonable.

The basis of the whole, Sir, is our treaty with New Granada, which was ratified by this body, and proclaimed in June, 1848. Looking to the security of a mode of communication across the continent at this isthmus, this government took great pains to obtain the right from the government of New Granada, and by the treaty it is stipulated that whatsoever communication should be made across the isthmus should be open to the government of the United States and citizens of the United States upon as good terms as to the citizens of New Granada itself. This government, looking upon this stipulation as a benefit obtained, a boon conceded by the government of New Granada, as an equivalent for this consideration, entered, on its part, into an engagement to protect, and guaranty, and defend the neutrality of this whole isthmus. This will be seen by reference to the thirty-fifth article of the treaty, which will be found in the volume of the laws of the last session. It is there very distinctly stated. There is no question about it. We are under treaty obligations to maintain the neutrality of this isthmus, and the authority of the government of New Granada over it.

Now, it so happens, that some time before, two or three years previous, the government of New Granada had made a grant to certain citizens of France and England, enabling them to make this railroad and hold an exclusive property in it. One of the terms and conditions of that grant was, that something should be done, or a certain deposit should be made, within a certain period. I believe six hundred thousand francs, or some such large sum, was to be deposited within a certain period. Progress was not made by that company in getting ready the deposit in money, but the charter of the French company had not quite run out when this government ratified the treaty with New Granada. It expired soon afterwards, however, so that no embarrassment arose from that circumstance. The charter reverted to the government of New Granada, because the French company had not made good their deposit. Under these circumstances, Sir, a new contract was entered into by the persons whose names are attached to this memorial. They are not assignees of any French company, as the Senator from Kentucky* suggested, but stand in the place of original gran-

* Mr. Underwood.

tees from the government of New Grenada, and by the terms contained in the grant they have now the privilege of making this railroad across the isthmus, having eight years to do it in.

The honorable Senator from Kentucky thinks that it would have been better if the government of the United States had appeared earlier, and taken upon itself to make this railroad, according to our old-fashioned way of internal improvements. Well, suppose that were so, how does it bear upon the question now before us? We have not the grant. We cannot obtain the grant. It is in the hands of others, and, in my opinion, much better for our purpose than in the possession of the government. At any rate, the only question now before us is the propriety or the expediency, or the impropriety or the inexpediency, of helping forward the making of this road under the grant, the purport of which is exhibited in the memorial now before us. That is the whole question. It was put upon that ground by the honorable Senator from Missouri,* and the only practical question is, Is it worth our while, at this expense and for this purpose, to encourage the making of this road?

Now, Sir, there are two considerations which present themselves. One of them is properly stated in the bill itself. One inducement to government is to provide for the transportation of its own troops, munitions of war, naval stores, and the mails. But it is obvious at once that that is not the only object. Does the government look to nothing but the transportation of its own materials, mails, and troops? Does it not look, as in other extensive undertakings, to a general public accommodation, an accommodation of the people, and convenience to the commerce of the country, not likely to be obtained without this aid? That larger and more general consideration, that consideration of benefit to the trade and commerce of the country, is certainly, if not the greatest, equally great, in my judgment, with any that results from the mere saving of expense in the transportation of troops, munitions of war, and the mails. Well, then, if we have guarantied the neutrality of the isthmus; if we maintain a communication by steamships from the Atlantic ports to this end of the road, at a great expense; if we maintain a communication in like manner from the ports of the Pacific to the

* Mr. Benton.

other end of the road at Panama, at a great expense; the question is one of practical good sense and expediency, whether we shall connect these two lines of water communication by land communication, and whether the terms of the contract now before us are reasonable.

Certainly, it must strike every body, it seems to me, that it is desirable that there should be this passage across the isthmus, since we have expended so much money to get to the isthmus, both on the one side and on the other.

Well, then, what are the terms of the contract? Are they reasonable or unreasonable? I do not intend to say more in this respect than to present to the Senate some few general estimates and statements, which every man's experience will enable him to judge of, and in regard to the correctness of which there can, I think, be very little doubt. The estimated cost of the road, according to Colonel Abert, is five millions of dollars, or thereabouts; that is to say, Colonel Abert begins by stating the average cost of railroads in the New England States at forty-nine or fifty thousand dollars per mile. He allows fifty per cent. additional cost for the nature of the country, the distance of the place, and other causes naturally augmenting the cost of constructing the road. Taking the distance to be fifty-two miles, the result is a cost for one track of $ 3,815,000; another track is half a million more; so that, together, they make $ 4,315,000. Well, then, it is certainly a very low estimate to suppose that the difference between that sum and five millions may be necessary for breakwaters, piers, and improvements in harbors, to render both sides accessible and safe. Then, again, there is the expense for warehouses, a very important item, to be included within this residuum. Taking, then, the aggregate to be not less than five millions of dollars, the question is, whether it is not reasonable to expect this government to contribute such a sum as the proposed substitute contemplates towards the opening of this communication between the two oceans.

Now, Sir, I do not see, I confess, any foundation for such supposed large profits as the honorable member from Kentucky thinks likely to accrue. Here are certain rates of passage and certain rates of freight fixed in this bill. The rates of passage are eight dollars per man or passenger for the first five years;

afterwards a low rate is stipulated. Now, upon any estimate we may make from these rates, what will be the amount of income from passengers a year? As far as we can now judge, how many people per day would be likely to travel over this road? Why, I can well imagine that, at some seasons of the year, there would be a great many passengers; but I suppose that at other seasons, although it would be necessary for the company to keep up the same equipment, and to incur the same expense, there would be very few passengers.

But does any one suppose that, for the next ten years, it will not be a high estimate to calculate that a hundred passengers a day will pass over the road? That would be to suppose that vessels would arrive there with a hundred passengers a day. I have no idea that that number would be conveyed. And as to goods or freights, the Senator from Kentucky supposes that the amount to be conveyed will be about ten thousand tons a year. But suppose the passengers to be a hundred a day, there is eight hundred dollars. Suppose the goods will amount to one hundred tons a day (three times as much in a year as the Senator estimates), that makes another eight hundred dollars, and in the aggregate sixteen hundred dollars a day. Then, if you allow three hundred working days for the year, the amount of the gross receipts will be four hundred and eighty thousand dollars. Well, if this were all clear income, it would be very well; but it will be subject to a very great reduction for the expenses of keeping the road in operation, as in the case of all other railroads. Colonel Abert's estimates make the expenses and repairs equal to one half of the gross receipts; consequently, equal to two hundred and forty thousand dollars a year. The whole amount of clear receipts, then, two hundred and forty thousand dollars, will be less than five per cent. on the capital to be invested.

To take another view of it. Suppose that seventy-five persons a day and seventy-five tons of goods, which is quite as much, perhaps, as may be expected, pass over the road; upon a like estimate, allowing three hundred working days to the year, the result will be an income amounting to a little over three per cent. on the capital. Of course, if you suppose that the passengers will not exceed fifty, it reduces the sum still more, and renders the dividend on the capital not quite two and a half per cent. We cannot, judging from experience, expect that the cost of the road per mile will be less than the sum named. We have built roads over the United States, North and South, at various degrees of cost. The Harlem Railroad, I believe, cost four millions of dollars, being fifty thousand dollars a mile for eighty miles. The Hudson River Railroad, it is said, has cost about fifty thousand dollars a mile.

And now, when we look at the income of this proposed road, we are to take with us one very important consideration. Here is one terminus of the road on the Atlantic, the other on the Pacific; the distance between the two extremities is fifty-two miles, and there is no intermediate trade or traffic. I do not know any road in the country that could sustain itself without some intermediate traffic. It is generally supposed that no railroad in New England could now be sustained upon the through travel alone. It is stated on good authority, that on the road from Worcester to Albany, for the years 1841, 1842, and 1843, the receipts from way-passengers, for one of those years, were greater than the entire receipts from *through*-passengers for the whole three years. And it is those receipts from way-passengers, this intermediate travel and traffic, which enable the road to maintain itself and make a dividend. Now, no one supposes that, for a great length of time, there can be any thing like any way-travel upon this road. There is no town of any importance at the ends, and no adjacent inhabitants. Those who disembark at one extremity of the road will pass over it, and embark at the other extremity of it, and this is all the travel the road will obtain. This is a very important consideration attached to all railroads and canals everywhere. It is a remark that is true of the Erie Canal, in its early history, that the receipts for the business between Albany and Buffalo both ways, for three years, amounted only to two and a half per cent. of the entire receipts for tolls. There is no dispute about this, and the enlarged receipts of the canal have been created, in a great degree, by the growth of the country, and the extension of traffic along the line. The traffic on the Panama route is yet to be created. It is to be produced by the growth and extension of commerce on the coast, and between the Atlantic and Pacific Oceans. Its business is to become profitable, if ever, by the course of trade taking that direction in consequence of the creation of the railroad itself.

Now, Sir, I agree entirely with what has been suggested, that many of these expectations in regard to changing the course of trade, by the establishment of this road, will not be realized. I agree entirely, that for the present there will be much less use for the road than many men of ardent imaginations suppose. I know it is the opinion of gentlemen engaged in the whale-fishery, that their cargoes will not bear the expense of transshipment, and that it will be found cheaper for them to follow the old track around the Cape. Not only is this so, but while they are at sea they are always looking out for the object of their voyage. I remember to have perused, some years ago, an extract from the journal of Commodore Biddle. He was returning from a cruise in the Pacific, and, after having got within the Gulf-stream, he met a "whaler" from Nantucket, outward bound, on a three years' voyage. The man at the masthead of the whaler hailed the Commodore to know *if he had seen any fish.* From the time of their leaving port until they return to it, they keep constantly looking out for their prey; and I am told that this is especially the case on the coast of Brazil, where they meet with the species of the whale called the black whale, and after turning the Cape they look out for sperm whales. So that, besides the expense of transshipment, there is the other consideration, that during all the while they are at sea they are continually in pursuit of the object of their enterprise.

We may reasonably conclude, then, that this railroad will not be used for the transit of the cargoes of whale ships. Experienced merchants do not credit the suggestion that the China trade will ever use the projected railroad. So that, on the whole, it is by no means clear that it is prudent to undertake the making of this road, as a mere speculation. But is there not a higher object, in which the interest of this country is deeply concerned, for which the work should be undertaken and completed? Senators may answer this question on general grounds. For my own part, I have no hesitation, from the consideration of what has already been done, and what may be done. I think it a great object to connect the two oceans, and I myself think the price to be paid is little enough. I think it is by no means too high, and my fears are whether, after all, they will be able to make the road without still further encouragement. Considering, however, the character of the petitioners, we have reason to believe that, with the assurance that this sum will be paid, they may be able to obtain so much more credit and so much greater facility in conducting their operations, that they will be able to complete the work.

There is one other thing to be remembered, that this will be the only way of crossing the isthmus for many years to come. Public attention has been very strongly drawn to this subject. We have now extensive territories on the other side of the continent, and although we do not know whether the immediate object of those who invest their capital in the undertaking will be attained, although we do not know whether they will, for ten years to come, be remunerated for their outlay, still the advantage to the public which must accrue from the direction given to the business of the country which must necessarily be carried through that channel, will be of so decided a character that it ought to be undertaken. Whether the hopes and expectations of those who visit the gold region shall or shall not be realized, the commerce of the country will, nevertheless, be benefited, by having a ready communication between the Atlantic and Pacific coast. I believe, therefore, that the public generally are decidedly in favor of some immediate measure, to be begun *now*, to open a communication which shall so much shorten the distance between the United States on this side of the mountains and the territory of the United States on the other side. It is in this point of view that I think this is precisely the measure that is called for by the judgment of the whole country, and the only practicable measure that has been suggested; and it is for these reasons that I sustain it.

THE CONSTITUTION AND THE UNION.*

On the 25th of January, 1850, Mr. Clay submitted a series of resolutions to the Senate, on the subject of slavery, in connection with the various questions which had arisen in consequence of the acquisition of Mexican territory. These resolutions furnished the occasion of a protracted debate. On Wednesday, the 6th of March, Mr. Walker of Wisconsin engaged in the discussion, but owing to the length of time taken up by repeated interruptions, he was unable to finish his argument. In the mean time it had been generally understood that Mr. Webster would, at an early day, take an opportunity of addressing the Senate on the present aspect of the slavery question, on the dangers to the Union of the existing agitation, and on the terms of honorable adjustment. In the expectation of hearing a speech from him on these all-important topics, an immense audience assembled in the Senate-chamber at an early hour of Thursday, the 7th of March. The floor, the galleries, and the antechambers of the Senate were crowded, and it was with difficulty that the members themselves were able to force their way to their seats.

At twelve o'clock the special order of the day was announced, and the Vice-President stated that Mr. Walker of Wisconsin was entitled to the floor. That gentleman, however, rose and said, —

"Mr. President, this vast audience has not come together to hear me, and there is but one man, in my opinion, who can assemble such an audience. They expect to hear him, and I feel it to be my duty, therefore, as it is my pleasure, to give the floor to the Senator from Massachusetts. I understand it is immaterial to him upon which of these questions he speaks, and therefore I will not move to postpone the special order."

Mr. Webster then rose, and, after making his acknowledgments to the

* A Speech delivered in the Senate of the United States, on the 7th of March, 1850.

Senators from Wisconsin (Mr. Walker) and New York (Mr. Seward) for their courtesy in yielding the floor to him, delivered the following speech, which, in consideration of its character and of the manner in which it was received throughout the country, has been entitled a speech for "the Constitution and the Union." In the pamphlet edition it was dedicated in the following terms to the people of Massachusetts:—

WITH THE HIGHEST RESPECT,

AND THE DEEPEST SENSE OF OBLIGATION

I DEDICATE THIS SPEECH

TO THE

PEOPLE OF MASSACHUSETTS.

"HIS EGO GRATIORA DICTU ALIA ESSE SCIO; SED ME VERA PRO GRATIS LOQUI, ETSI MEUM INGENIUM NON MONERET, NECESSITAS COGIT. VELLEM, EQUIDEM, VOBIS PLACERE; SED MULTO MALO VOS SALVOS ESSE, QUALICUMQUE ERGA ME ANIMO FUTURI ESTIS."

DANIEL WEBSTER.

MR. PRESIDENT, — I wish to speak to-day, not as a Massachusetts man, nor as a Northern man, but as an American, and a member of the Senate of the United States. It is fortunate that there is a Senate of the United States; a body not yet moved from its propriety, not lost to a just sense of its own dignity and its own high responsibilities, and a body to which the country looks, with confidence, for wise, moderate, patriotic, and healing counsels. It is not to be denied that we live in the midst of strong agitations, and are surrounded by very considerable dangers to our institutions and government. The imprisoned winds are let loose. The East, the North, and the stormy South combine to throw the whole sea into commotion, to toss its billows to the skies, and disclose its profoundest depths. I do not affect to regard myself, Mr. President, as holding, or as fit to hold, the helm in this combat with the political elements; but I have a duty to perform, and I mean to perform it with fidelity, not without a sense of existing dangers, but not without hope. I have a part to act, not for my own security or safety, for I am looking out for no fragment upon which to float away from the wreck, if wreck there must be, but for the good of the whole, and the preservation of all; and there is that which will keep me to my duty during this struggle, whether the sun and the stars shall appear, or shall not appear for many days. I speak to-day for the preservation of the Union. "Hear me for my cause." I speak to-day, out of a solicitous and anxious heart, for the restoration to the country of that quiet and that harmony which make the blessings of this Union so rich, and so dear to us all. These are the topics that I propose to myself to discuss; these are the motives, and the sole motives, that influence me in the wish to communicate my opinions to the Senate and the country; and if I can do any thing, however little, for the promotion of these ends, I shall have accomplished all that I expect.

Mr. President, it may not be amiss to recur very briefly to the events which, equally sudden and extraordinary, have brought the country into its present political condition. In May, 1846, the United States declared war against Mexico. Our armies, then on the frontiers, entered the provinces of that republic, met and defeated all her troops, penetrated her mountain passes, and occupied her capital. The marine force of the United States took possession of her forts and her towns, on the Atlantic and on the Pacific. In less than two years a treaty was negotiated, by which Mexico ceded to the United States a vast territory, extending seven or eight hundred miles along the shores of the Pacific, and reaching back over the mountains, and across the desert, until it joins the frontier of the State of Texas. It so happened, in the distracted and feeble condition of the Mexican government, that, before the declaration of war by the United States against Mexico had become known in California, the people of California, under the lead of American officers, overthrew the existing Mexican provincial government, and raised an independent flag. When the news arrived at San Francisco that war had been declared by the United States against Mexico, this independent flag was pulled down, and the stars and stripes of this Union hoisted in its stead. So, Sir, before the war was over, the forces of the United States, military and naval, had possession of San Francisco and Upper California, and a great rush of emigrants from various parts of the world took place into California in 1846 and 1847. But now behold another wonder.

In January of 1848, a party of Mormons made a discovery

of an extraordinarily rich mine of gold, or rather of a great quantity of gold, hardly proper to be called a mine, for it was spread near the surface, on the lower part of the south, or American, branch of the Sacramento. They attempted to conceal their discovery for some time; but soon another discovery of gold, perhaps of greater importance, was made, on another part of the American branch of the Sacramento, and near Sutter's Fort, as it is called. The fame of these discoveries spread far and wide. They inflamed more and more the spirit of emigration towards California, which had already been excited, and adventurers crowded into the country by hundreds, and flocked towards the Bay of San Francisco. This, as I have said, took place in the winter and spring of 1848. The digging commenced in the spring of that year, and from that time to this the work of searching for gold has been prosecuted with a success not heretofore known in the history of this globe. You recollect, Sir, how incredulous at first the American public was at the accounts which reached us of these discoveries; but we all know, now, that these accounts received, and continue to receive, daily confirmation, and down to the present moment I suppose the assurance is as strong, after the experience of these several months, of the existence of deposits of gold apparently inexhaustible in the regions near San Francisco, in California, as it was at any period of the earlier dates of the accounts.

It so happened, Sir, that although, after the return of peace, it became a very important subject for legislative consideration and legislative decision to provide a proper territorial government for California, yet differences of opinion between the two houses of Congress prevented the establishment of any such territorial government at the last session. Under this state of things, the inhabitants of California, already amounting to a considerable number, thought it to be their duty, in the summer of last year, to establish a local government. Under the proclamation of General Riley, the people chose delegates to a convention, and that convention met at Monterey. It formed a constitution for the State of California, which, being referred to the people, was adopted by them in their primary assemblages. Desirous of immediate connection with the United States, its Senators were appointed and representatives cho sen, who have come hither, bringing with them the authentic constitution of the State of California; and they now present themselves, asking, in behalf of their constituents, that it may be admitted into this Union as one of the United States. This constitution, Sir, contains an express prohibition of slavery, or involuntary servitude, in the State of California. It is said, and I suppose truly, that, of the members who composed that convention, some sixteen were natives of, and had been residents in, the slave-holding States, about twenty-two were from the non-slave-holding States, and the remaining ten members were either native Californians or old settlers in that country. This prohibition of slavery, it is said, was inserted with entire unanimity.

It is this circumstance, Sir, the prohibition of slavery, which has contributed to raise, I do not say it has wholly raised, the dispute as to the propriety of the admission of California into the Union under this constitution. It is not to be denied, Mr. President, nobody thinks of denying, that, whatever reasons were assigned at the commencement of the late war with Mexico, it was prosecuted for the purpose of the acquisition of territory, and under the alleged argument that the cession of territory was the only form in which proper compensation could be obtained by the United States from Mexico, for the various claims and demands which the people of this country had against that government. At any rate, it will be found that President Polk's message, at the commencement of the session of December, 1847, avowed that the war was to be prosecuted until some acquisition of territory should be made. As the acquisition was to be south of the line of the United States, in warm climates and countries, it was naturally, I suppose, expected by the South, that whatever acquisitions were made in that region would be added to the slave-holding portion of the United States. Very little of accurate information was possessed of the real physical character, either of California or New Mexico, and events have not turned out as was expected. Both California and New Mexico are likely to come in as free States; and therefore some degree of disappointment and surprise has resulted. In other words, it is obvious that the question which has so long harassed the country, and at some times very seriously alarmed the minds of wise and good men, has come upon us for a fresh discussion; the question of slavery in these United States.

Now, Sir, I propose, perhaps at the expense of some detail and consequent detention of the Senate, to review historically this question, which, partly in consequence of its own importance, and partly, perhaps mostly, in consequence of the manner in which it has been discussed in different portions of the country, has been a source of so much alienation and unkind feeling between them.

We all know, Sir, that slavery has existed in the world from time immemorial. There was slavery, in the earliest periods of history, among the Oriental nations. There was slavery among the Jews; the theocratic government of that people issued no injunction against it. There was slavery among the Greeks; and the ingenious philosophy of the Greeks found, or sought to find, a justification for it exactly upon the grounds which have been assumed for such a justification in this country; that is, a natural and original difference among the races of mankind, and the inferiority of the black or colored race to the white. The Greeks justified their system of slavery upon that idea, precisely. They held the African and some of the Asiatic tribes to be inferior to the white race; but they did not show, I think, by any close process of logic, that, if this were true, the more intelligent and the stronger had therefore a right to subjugate the weaker.

The more manly philosophy and jurisprudence of the Romans placed the justification of slavery on entirely different grounds. The Roman jurists, from the first and down to the fall of the empire, admitted that slavery was against the natural law, by which, as they maintained, all men, of whatsoever clime, color, or capacity, were equal; but they justified slavery, first, upon the ground and authority of the law of nations, arguing, and arguing truly, that at that day the conventional law of nations admitted that captives in war, whose lives, according to the notions of the times, were at the absolute disposal of the captors, might, in exchange for exemption from death, be made slaves for life, and that such servitude might descend to their posterity. The jurists of Rome also maintained, that, by the civil law, there might be servitude or slavery, personal and hereditary; first, by the voluntary act of an individual, who might sell himself into slavery; secondly, by his being reduced into a state of slavery by his creditors, in satisfaction of his debts;

and, thirdly, by being placed in a state of servitude or slavery for crime. At the introduction of Christianity, the Roman world was full of slaves, and I suppose there is to be found no injunction against that relation between man and man in the teachings of the Gospel of Jesus Christ or of any of his Apostles. The object of the instruction imparted to mankind by the founder of Christianity was to touch the heart, purify the soul, and improve the lives of individual men. That object went directly to the first fountain of all the political and social relations of the human race, as well as of all true religious feeling, the individual heart and mind of man.

Now, Sir, upon the general nature and influence of slavery there exists a wide difference of opinion between the northern portion of this country and the southern. It is said on the one side, that, although not the subject of any injunction or direct prohibition in the New Testament, slavery is a wrong; that it is founded merely in the right of the strongest; and that it is an oppression, like unjust wars, like all those conflicts by which a powerful nation subjects a weaker to its will; and that, in its nature, whatever may be said of it in the modifications which have taken place, it is not according to the meek spirit of the Gospel. It is not "kindly affectioned"; it does not "seek another's, and not its own"; it does not "let the oppressed go free." These are sentiments that are cherished, and of late with greatly augmented force, among the people of the Northern States. They have taken hold of the religious sentiment of that part of the country, as they have, more or less, taken hold of the religious feelings of a considerable portion of mankind. The South, upon the other side, having been accustomed to this relation between the two races all their lives, from their birth, having been taught, in general, to treat the subjects of this bondage with care and kindness, and I believe, in general, feeling great kindness for them, have not taken the view of the subject which I have mentioned. There are thousands of religious men, with consciences as tender as any of their brethren at the North, who do not see the unlawfulness of slavery; and there are more thousands, perhaps, that, whatsoever they may think of it in its origin, and as a matter depending upon natural right, yet take things as they are, and, finding slavery to be an established relation of the society in which they live, can see no way in which, let their opinions on the abstract question be what they may, it is in the power of the present generation to relieve themselves from this relation. And candor obliges me to say, that I believe they are just as conscientious, many of them, and the religious people, all of them, as they are at the North who hold different opinions.

The honorable Senator from South Carolina* the other day alluded to the separation of that great religious community, the Methodist Episcopal Church. That separation was brought about by differences of opinion upon this particular subject of slavery. I felt great concern, as that dispute went on, about the result. I was in hopes that the difference of opinion might be adjusted, because I looked upon that religious denomination as one of the great props of religion and morals throughout the whole country, from Maine to Georgia, and westward to our utmost western boundary. The result was against my wishes and against my hopes. I have read all their proceedings and all their arguments; but I have never yet been able to come to the conclusion that there was any real ground for that separation; in other words, that any good could be produced by that separation. I must say I think there was some want of candor and charity. Sir, when a question of this kind seizes on the religious sentiments of mankind, and comes to be discussed in religious assemblies of the clergy and laity, there is always to be expected, or always to be feared, a great degree of excitement. It is in the nature of man, manifested by his whole history, that religious disputes are apt to become warm in proportion to the strength of the convictions which men entertain of the magnitude of the questions at issue. In all such disputes, there will sometimes be found men with whom every thing is absolute; absolutely wrong, or absolutely right. They see the right clearly; they think others ought so to see it, and they are disposed to establish a broad line of distinction between what is right and what is wrong. They are not seldom willing to establish that line upon their own convictions of truth and justice; and are ready to mark and guard it by placing along it a series of dogmas, as lines of

* Mr. Calhoun.

boundary on the earth's surface are marked by posts and stones. There are men who, with clear perceptions, as they think, of their own duty, do not see how too eager a pursuit of one duty may involve them in the violation of others, or how too warm an embracement of one truth may lead to a disregard of other truths equally important. As I heard it stated strongly, not many days ago, these persons are disposed to mount upon some particular duty, as upon a war-horse, and to drive furiously on and upon and over all other duties that may stand in the way. There are men who, in reference to disputes of that sort, are of opinion that human duties may be ascertained with the exactness of mathematics. They deal with morals as with mathematics; and they think what is right may be distinguished from what is wrong with the precision of an algebraic equation. They have, therefore, none too much charity towards others who differ from them. They are apt, too, to think that nothing is good but what is perfect, and that there are no compromises or modifications to be made in consideration of difference of opinion or in deference to other men's judgment. If their perspicacious vision enables them to detect a spot on the face of the sun, they think that a good reason why the sun should be struck down from heaven. They prefer the chance of running into utter darkness to living in heavenly light, if that heavenly light be not absolutely without any imperfection. There are impatient men; too impatient always to give heed to the admonition of St. Paul, that we are not to "do evil that good may come"; too impatient to wait for the slow progress of moral causes in the improvement of mankind. They do not remember that the doctrines and the miracles of Jesus Christ have, in eighteen hundred years, converted only a small portion of the human race; and among the nations that are converted to Christianity, they forget how many vices and crimes, public and private, still prevail, and that many of them, public crimes especially, which are so clearly offences against the Christian religion, pass without exciting particular indignation. Thus wars are waged, and unjust wars. I do not deny that there may be just wars. There certainly are; but it was the remark of an eminent person, not many years ago, on the other side of the Atlantic, that it is one of the greatest reproaches to human nature that wars are sometimes just. The defence of nations sometimes causes a just war against the injustice of other nations. In this state of sentiment upon the general nature of slavery lies the cause of a great part of those unhappy divisions, exasperations, and reproaches which find vent and support in different parts of the Union.

But we must view things as they are. Slavery does exist in the United States. It did exist in the States before the adoption of this Constitution, and at that time. Let us, therefore, consider for a moment what was the state of sentiment, North and South, in regard to slavery, at the time this Constitution was adopted. A remarkable change has taken place since; but what did the wise and great men of all parts of the country think of slavery then? In what estimation did they hold it at the time when this Constitution was adopted? It will be found, Sir, if we will carry ourselves by historical research back to that day, and ascertain men's opinions by authentic records still existing among us, that there was then no diversity of opinion between the North and the South upon the subject of slavery. It will be found that both parts of the country held it equally an evil, a moral and political evil. It will not be found that, either at the North or at the South, there was much, though there was some, invective against slavery as inhuman and cruel. The great ground of objection to it was political; that it weakened the social fabric; that, taking the place of free labor, society became less strong and labor less productive; and therefore we find from all the eminent men of the time the clearest expression of their opinion that slavery is an evil. They ascribed its existence here, not without truth, and not without some acerbity of temper and force of language, to the injurious policy of the mother country, who, to favor the navigator, had entailed these evils upon the Colonies. I need hardly refer, Sir, particularly to the publications of the day. They are matters of history on the record. The eminent men, the most eminent men, and nearly all the conspicuous politicians of the South, held the same sentiments; that slavery was an evil, a blight, a scourge, and a curse. There are no terms of reprobation of slavery so vehement in the North at that day as in the South. The North was not so much excited against it as the South; and the reason is, I suppose, that there was much less of it at the North, and the people did not see, or think they saw, the evils so prominently as they were seen, or thought to be seen, at the South.

Then, Sir, when this Constitution was framed, this was the light in which the Federal Convention viewed it. That body reflected the judgment and sentiments of the great men of the South. A member of the other house, whom I have not the honor to know, has, in a recent speech, collected extracts from these public documents. They prove the truth of what I am saying, and the question then was, how to deal with it, and how to deal with it as an evil. They came to this general result. They thought that slavery could not be continued in the country if the importation of slaves were made to cease, and therefore they provided that, after a certain period, the importation might be prevented by the act of the new government. The period of twenty years was proposed by some gentleman from the North, I think, and many members of the Convention from the South opposed it as being too long. Mr. Madison especially was somewhat warm against it. He said it would bring too much of this mischief into the country to allow the importation of slaves for such a period. Because we must take along with us, in the whole of this discussion, when we are considering the sentiments and opinions in which the constitutional provision originated, that the conviction of all men was, that, if the importation of slaves ceased, the white race would multiply faster than the black race, and that slavery would therefore gradually wear out and expire. It may not be improper here to allude to that, I had almost said, celebrated opinion of Mr. Madison. You observe, Sir, that the term *slave*, or *slavery*, is not used in the Constitution. The Constitution does not require that "fugitive slaves" shall be delivered up. It requires that persons held to service in one State, and escaping into another, shall be delivered up. Mr. Madison opposed the introduction of the term *slave*, or *slavery*, into the Constitution; for he said that he did not wish to see it recognized by the Constitution of the United States of America that there could be property in men.

Now, Sir, all this took place in the Convention in 1787; but connected with this, concurrent and contemporaneous, is another important transaction, not sufficiently attended to. The Convention for framing this Constitution assembled in Philadelphia in May, and sat until September, 1787. During all that time the Congress of the United States was in session at New York. It was a matter of design, as we know, that the Convention should not assemble in the same city where Congress was holding its sessions. Almost all the public men of the country, therefore, of distinction and eminence, were in one or the other of these two assemblies; and I think it happened, in some instances, that the same gentlemen were members of both bodies. If I mistake not, such was the case with Mr. Rufus King, then a member of Congress from Massachusetts. Now, at the very time when the Convention in Philadelphia was framing this Constitution, the Congress in New York was framing the Ordinance of 1787, for the organization and government of the territory northwest of the Ohio. They passed that Ordinance on the 13th of July, 1787, at New York, the very month, perhaps the very day, on which these questions about the importation of slaves and the character of slavery were debated in the Convention at Philadelphia. So far as we can now learn, there was a perfect concurrence of opinion between these two bodies; and it resulted in this Ordinance of 1787, excluding slavery from all the territory over which the Congress of the United States had jurisdiction, and that was all the territory northwest of the Ohio. Three years before, Virginia and other States had made a cession of that great territory to the United States; and a most munificent act it was. I never reflect upon it without a disposition to do honor and justice, and justice would be the highest honor, to Virginia, for the cession of her northwestern territory. I will say, Sir, it is one of her fairest claims to the respect and gratitude of the country, and that, perhaps, it is only second to that other claim which belongs to her; that from her counsels, and from the intelligence and patriotism of her leading statesmen, proceeded the first idea put into practice of the formation of a general constitution of the United States. The Ordinance of 1787 applied to the whole territory over which the Congress of the United States had jurisdiction. It was adopted two years before the Constitution of the United

States went into operation; because the Ordinance took effect immediately on its passage, while the Constitution of the United States, having been framed, was to be sent to the States to be adopted by their Conventions; and then a government was to be organized under it. This Ordinance, then, was in operation and force when the Constitution was adopted, and the government put in motion, in April, 1789.

Mr. President, three things are quite clear as historical truths. One is, that there was an expectation that, on the ceasing of the importation of slaves from Africa, slavery would begin to run out here. That was hoped and expected. Another is, that, as far as there was any power in Congress to prevent the spread of slavery in the United States, that power was executed in the most absolute manner, and to the fullest extent. An honorable member,* whose health does not allow him to be here to-day —

A SENATOR. He is here.

I am very happy to hear that he is; may he long be here, and in the enjoyment of health to serve his country! The honorable member said, the other day, that he considered this Ordinance as the first in the series of measures calculated to enfeeble the South, and deprive them of their just participation in the benefits and privileges of this government. He says, very properly, that it was enacted under the old Confederation, and before this Constitution went into effect; but my present purpose is only to say, Mr. President, that it was established with the entire and unanimous concurrence of the whole South. Why, there it stands! The vote of every State in the Union was unanimous in favor of the Ordinance, with the exception of a single individual vote, and that individual vote was given by a Northern man. This Ordinance prohibiting slavery for ever northwest of the Ohio has the hand and seal of every Southern member in Congress. It was therefore no aggression of the North on the South. The other and third clear historical truth is, that the Convention meant to leave slavery in the States as they found it, entirely under the authority and control of the States themselves.

This was the state of things, Sir, and this the state of opin-

* Mr. Calhoun.

ion, under which those very important matters were arranged, and those three important things done; that is, the establishment of the Constitution of the United States with a recognition of slavery as it existed in the States; the establishment of the ordinance for the government of the Northwestern Territory, prohibiting, to the full extent of all territory owned by the United States, the introduction of slavery into that territory, while leaving to the States all power over slavery in their own limits; and creating a power, in the new government, to put an end to the importation of slaves, after a limited period. There was entire coincidence and concurrence of sentiment between the North and the South, upon all these questions, at the period of the adoption of the Constitution. But opinions, Sir, have changed, greatly changed; changed North and changed South. Slavery is not regarded in the South now as it was then. I see an honorable member of this body paying me the honor of listening to my remarks;* he brings to my mind, Sir, freshly and vividly, what I have learned of his great ancestor, so much distinguished in his day and generation, so worthy to be succeeded by so worthy a grandson, and of the sentiments he expressed in the Convention in Philadelphia.†

Here we may pause. There was, if not an entire unanimity, a general concurrence of sentiment running through the whole community, and especially entertained by the eminent men of all parts of the country. But soon a change began, at the North and the South, and a difference of opinion showed itself; the North growing much more warm and strong against slavery, and the South growing much more warm and strong in its support. Sir, there is no generation of mankind whose opinions are not subject to be influenced by what appear to them to be their present emergent and exigent interests. I impute to the South no particularly selfish view in the change which has come over her. I impute to her certainly no dishonest view. All that has happened has been natural. It has followed those causes which always influence the human mind and operate upon it. What, then, have been the causes which have created so new a feeling in favor of slavery in the South, which have changed the

* Mr. Mason of Virginia.

† See Madison Papers, Vol. III. pp. 1390, 1428, *et seq.*

whole nomenclature of the South on that subject, so that, from being thought and described in the terms I have mentioned and will not repeat, it has now become an institution, a cherished institution, in that quarter; no evil, no scourge, but a great religious, social, and moral blessing, as I think I have heard it latterly spoken of? I suppose this, Sir, is owing to the rapid growth and sudden extension of the COTTON plantations of the South. So far as any motive consistent with honor, justice, and general judgment could act, it was the COTTON interest that gave a new desire to promote slavery, to spread it, and to use its labor. I again say that this change was produced by causes which must always produce like effects. The whole interest of the South became connected, more or less, with the extension of slavery. If we look back to the history of the commerce of this country in the early years of this government, what were our exports? Cotton was hardly, or but to a very limited extent, known. In 1791 the first parcel of cotton of the growth of the United States was exported, and amounted only to 19,200 pounds.* It has gone on increasing rapidly, until the whole crop may now, perhaps, in a season of great product and high prices, amount to a hundred millions of dollars. In the years I have mentioned, there was more of wax, more of indigo, more of rice, more of almost every article of export from the South, than of cotton. When Mr. Jay negotiated the treaty of 1794 with England, it is evident from the twelfth article of the treaty, which was suspended by the Senate, that he did not know that cotton was exported at all from the United States.

Well, Sir, we know what followed. The age of cotton became the golden age of our Southern brethren. It gratified their desire for improvement and accumulation, at the same time that it excited it. The desire grew by what it fed upon, and there soon came to be an eagerness for other territory, a new area or new areas for the cultivation of the cotton crop; and measures leading to this result were brought about rapidly, one after another, under the lead of Southern men at the head of the government, they having a majority in both branches of Congress to

* Seybert's Statistics, p. 92. A small parcel of cotton found its way to Liverpool from the United States in 1784, and was refused admission, on the ground that it could not be the growth of the United States.

accomplish their ends. The honorable member from South Carolina* observed that there has been a majority all along in favor of the North. If that be true, Sir, the North has acted either very liberally and kindly, or very weakly; for they never exercised that majority efficiently five times in the history of the government, when a division or trial of strength arose. Never. Whether they were out-generalled, or whether it was owing to other causes, I shall not stop to consider; but no man acquainted with the history of the Union can deny that the general lead in the politics of the country, for three fourths of the period that has elapsed since the adoption of the Constitution, has been a Southern lead.

In 1802, in pursuit of the idea of opening a new cotton region, the United States obtained a cession from Georgia of the whole of her western territory, now embracing the rich and growing States of Alabama and Mississippi. In 1803 Louisiana was purchased from France, out of which the States of Louisiana, Arkansas, and Missouri have been framed, as slave-holding States. In 1819 the cession of Florida was made, bringing in another region adapted to cultivation by slaves. Sir, the honorable member from South Carolina thought he saw in certain operations of the government, such as the manner of collecting the revenue, and the tendency of measures calculated to promote emigration into the country, what accounts for the more rapid growth of the North than the South. He ascribes that more rapid growth, not to the operation of time, but to the system of government and administration established under this Constitution. That is matter of opinion. To a certain extent it may be true; but it does seem to me that, if any operation of the government can be shown in any degree to have promoted the population, and growth, and wealth of the North, it is much more sure that there are sundry important and distinct operations of the government, about which no man can doubt, tending to promote, and which absolutely have promoted, the increase of the slave interest and the slave territory of the South. It was not time that brought in Louisiana; it was the act of men. It was not time that brought in Florida; it was the act of men. And lastly, Sir, to complete those acts of legislation

* Mr. Calhoun.

which have contributed so much to enlarge the area of the institution of slavery, Texas, great and vast and illimitable Texas, was added to the Union as a slave State in 1845; and that, Sir, pretty much closed the whole chapter, and settled the whole account.

That closed the whole chapter and settled the whole account, because the annexation of Texas, upon the conditions and under the guaranties upon which she was admitted, did not leave within the control of this government an acre of land, capable of being cultivated by slave labor, between this Capitol and the Rio Grande or the Nueces, or whatever is the proper boundary of Texas; not an acre. From that moment, the whole country, from this place to the western boundary of Texas, was fixed, pledged, fastened, decided, to be slave territory for ever, by the solemn guaranties of law. And I now say, Sir, as the proposition upon which I stand this day, and upon the truth and firmness of which I intend to act until it is overthrown, that there is not at this moment within the United States, or any territory of the United States, a single foot of land, the character of which, in regard to its being free territory or slave territory, is not fixed by some law, and some irrepealable law, beyond the power of the action of the government. Is it not so with respect to Texas? It is most manifestly so. The honorable member from South Carolina, at the time of the admission of Texas, held an important post in the executive department of the government; he was Secretary of State. Another eminent person of great activity and adroitness in affairs, I mean the late Secretary of the Treasury,* was a conspicuous member of this body, and took the lead in the business of annexation, in coöperation with the Secretary of State; and I must say that they did their business faithfully and thoroughly; there was no botch left in it. They rounded it off, and made as close joiner-work as ever was exhibited. Resolutions of annexation were brought into Congress, fitly joined together, compact, efficient, conclusive upon the great object which they had in view, and those resolutions passed.

Allow me to read a part of these resolutions. It is the third clause of the second section of the resolution of the 1st of March,

* Mr. Walker.

1845, for the admission of Texas, which applies to this part of the case. That clause is as follows: —

> "New States, of convenient size, not exceeding four in number, in addition to said State of Texas, and having sufficient population, may hereafter, by the consent of said State, be formed out of the territory thereof, which shall be entitled to admission under the provisions of the Federal Constitution. And such States as may be formed out of that portion of said territory lying south of thirty-six degrees thirty minutes north latitude, commonly known as the Missouri Compromise line, shall be admitted into the Union with or without slavery, as the people of each State asking admission may desire; and in such State or States as shall be formed out of said territory north of said Missouri Compromise line, slavery or involuntary servitude (except for crime) shall be prohibited."

Now, what is here stipulated, enacted, and secured? It is, that all Texas south of 36° 30′, which is nearly the whole of it, shall be admitted into the Union as a slave State. It was a slave State, and therefore came in as a slave State; and the guaranty is, that new States shall be made out of it, to the number of four, in addition to the State then in existence and admitted at that time by these resolutions, and that such States as are formed out of that portion of Texas lying south of 36° 30′ may come in as slave States. I know no form of legislation which can strengthen this. I know no mode of recognition that can add a tittle of weight to it. I listened respectfully to the resolutions of my honorable friend from Tennessee.* He proposed to recognize that stipulation with Texas. But any additional recognition would weaken the force of it; because it stands here on the ground of a contract, a thing done for a consideration. It is a law founded on a contract with Texas, and designed to carry that contract into effect. A recognition now, founded not on any consideration or any contract, would not be so strong as it now stands on the face of the resolution. I know no way, I candidly confess, in which this government, acting in good faith, as I trust it always will, can relieve itself from that stipulation and pledge, by any honest course of legislation whatever. And therefore I say again, that, so far as Texas is concerned, in the whole of that State

* Mr. Bell.

south of 36° 30′, which, I suppose, embraces all the territory capable of slave cultivation, there is no land, not an acre, the character of which is not established by law; a law which cannot be repealed without the violation of a contract, and plain disregard of the public faith.

I hope, Sir, it is now apparent that my proposition, so far as it respects Texas, has been maintained, and that the provision in this article is clear and absolute; and it has been well suggested by my friend from Rhode Island,* that that part of Texas which lies north of 36° 30′ of north latitude, and which may be formed into free States, is dependent, in like manner, upon the consent of Texas, herself a slave State.

Now, Sir, how came this? How came it to pass that within these walls, where it is said by the honorable member from South Carolina that the free States have always had a majority, this resolution of annexation, such as I have described it, obtained a majority in both houses of Congress? Sir, it obtained that majority by the great number of Northern votes added to the entire Southern vote, or at least nearly the whole of the Southern vote. The aggregate was made up of Northern and Southern votes. In the House of Representatives there were about eighty Southern votes and about fifty Northern votes for the admission of Texas. In the Senate the vote for the admission of Texas was twenty-seven, and twenty-five against it; and of those twenty-seven votes, constituting the majority, no less than thirteen came from the free States, and four of them were from New England. The whole of these thirteen Senators, constituting within a fraction, you see, one half of all the votes in this body for the admission of this immeasurable extent of slave territory, were sent here by free States.

Sir, there is not so remarkable a chapter in our history of political events, political parties, and political men as is afforded by this admission of a new slave-holding territory, so vast that a bird cannot fly over it in a week. New England, as I have said, with some of her own votes, supported this measure. Three fourths of the votes of liberty-loving Connecticut were given for it in the other house, and one half here. There

* Mr. Greene.

was one vote for it from Maine, but, I am happy to say, not the vote of the honorable member who addressed the Senate the day before yesterday,* and who was then a Representative from Maine in the House of Representatives; but there was one vote from Maine, ay, and there was one vote for it from Massachusetts, given by a gentleman then representing, and now living in, the district in which the prevalence of Free Soil sentiment for a couple of years or so has defeated the choice of any member to represent it in Congress. Sir, that body of Northern and Eastern men who gave those votes at that time are now seen taking upon themselves, in the nomenclature of politics, the appellation of the Northern Democracy. They undertook to wield the destinies of this empire, if I may give that name to a republic, and their policy was, and they persisted in it, to bring into this country and under this government all the territory they could. They did it, in the case of Texas, under pledges, absolute pledges, to the slave interest, and they afterwards lent their aid in bringing in these new conquests, to take their chance for slavery or freedom. My honorable friend from Georgia,† in March, 1847, moved the Senate to declare that the war ought not to be prosecuted for the conquest of territory, or for the dismemberment of Mexico. The whole of the Northern Democracy voted against it. He did not get a vote from them. It suited the patriotic and elevated sentiments of the Northern Democracy to bring in a world from among the mountains and valleys of California and New Mexico, or any other part of Mexico, and then quarrel about it; to bring it in, and then endeavor to put upon it the saving grace of the Wilmot Proviso. There were two eminent and highly respectable gentlemen from the North and East, then leading gentlemen in the Senate, (I refer, and I do so with entire respect, for I entertain for both of those gentlemen, in general, high regard, to Mr. Dix of New York and Mr. Niles of Connecticut,) who both voted for the admission of Texas. They would not have that vote any other way than as it stood; and they would have it as it did stand. I speak of the vote upon the annexation of Texas. Those two gentlemen would have the resolution of annexation just as it is, without amend-

* Mr. Hamlin. † Mr. Berrien.

ment; and they voted for it just as it is, and their eyes were all open to its true character. The honorable member from South Carolina who addressed us the other day was then Secretary of State. His correspondence with Mr. Murphy, the Chargé d'Affaires of the United States in Texas, had been published. That correspondence was all before those gentlemen, and the Secretary had the boldness and candor to avow in that correspondence, that the great object sought by the annexation of Texas was to strengthen the slave interest of the South. Why, Sir, he said so in so many words ——

MR. CALHOUN. Will the honorable Senator permit me to interrupt him for a moment?

Certainly.

MR. CALHOUN. I am very reluctant to interrupt the honorable gentleman; but, upon a point of so much importance, I deem it right to put myself *rectus in curia*. I did not put it upon the ground assumed by the Senator. I put it upon this ground: that Great Britain had announced to this country, in so many words, that her object was to abolish slavery in Texas, and, through Texas, to accomplish the abolition of slavery in the United States and the world. The ground I put it on was, that it would make an exposed frontier, and, if Great Britain succeeded in her object, it would be impossible that that frontier could be secured against the aggressions of the Abolitionists; and that this government was bound, under the guaranties of the Constitution, to protect us against such a state of things.

That comes, I suppose, Sir, to exactly the same thing. It was, that Texas must be obtained for the security of the slave interest of the South.

MR. CALHOUN. Another view is very distinctly given.

That was the object set forth in the correspondence of a worthy gentleman not now living,* who preceded the honorable member from South Carolina in the Department of State. There repose on the files of the Department, as I have occasion to know, strong letters from Mr. Upshur to the United States minister in England, and I believe there are some to the same minister from the honorable Senator himself, asserting to this effect the sentiments of this government; namely, that Great

* Mr. Upshur.

Britain was expected not to interfere to take Texas out of the hands of its then existing government and make it a free country. But my argument, my suggestion, is this; that those gentlemen who composed the Northern Democracy when Texas was brought into the Union saw clearly that it was brought in as a slave country, and brought in for the purpose of being maintained as slave territory, to the Greek Kalends. I rather think the honorable gentleman who was then Secretary of State might, in some of his correspondence with Mr. Murphy, have suggested that it was not expedient to say too much about this object, lest it should create some alarm. At any rate, Mr. Murphy wrote to him that England was anxious to get rid of the constitution of Texas, because it was a constitution establishing slavery; and that what the United States had to do was to aid the people of Texas in upholding their constitution; but that nothing should be said which should offend the fanatical men of the North. But, Sir, the honorable member did avow this object himself, openly, boldly, and manfully; he did not disguise his conduct or his motives.

Mr. Calhoun. Never, never.

What he means he is very apt to say.

Mr. Calhoun. Always, always.

And I honor him for it.

This admission of Texas was in 1845. Then, in 1847, *flagrante bello* between the United States and Mexico, the proposition I have mentioned was brought forward by my friend from Georgia, and the Northern Democracy voted steadily against it. Their remedy was to apply to the acquisitions, after they should come in, the Wilmot Proviso. What follows? These two gentlemen,* worthy and honorable and influential men, (and if they had not been they could not have carried the measure,) these two gentlemen, members of this body, brought in Texas, and by their votes they also prevented the passage of the resolution of the honorable member from Georgia, and then they went home and took the lead in the Free Soil party. And there they stand, Sir! They leave us here, bound

* Messrs. Niles of Connecticut and Dix of New York.

in honor and conscience by the resolutions of annexation; they leave us here, to take the odium of fulfilling the obligations in favor of slavery which they voted us into, or else the greater odium of violating those obligations, while they are at home making capital and rousing speeches for free soil and no slavery. And therefore I say, Sir, that there is not a chapter in our history, respecting public measures and public men, more full of what would create surprise, more full of what does create, in my mind, extreme mortification, than that of the conduct of the Northern Democracy on this subject.

Mr. President, sometimes, when a man is found in a new relation to things around him and to other men, he says the world has changed, and that he has not changed. I believe, Sir, that our self-respect leads us often to make this declaration in regard to ourselves when it is not exactly true. An individual is more apt to change, perhaps, than all the world around him. But, under the present circumstances, and under the responsibility which I know I incur by what I am now stating here, I feel at liberty to recur to the various expressions and statements, made at various times, of my own opinions and resolutions respecting the admission of Texas, and all that has followed. Sir, as early as 1836, or in the early part of 1837, there was conversation and correspondence between myself and some private friends on this project of annexing Texas to the United States; and an honorable gentleman with whom I have had a long acquaintance, a friend of mine, now perhaps in this chamber, I mean General Hamilton, of South Carolina, was privy to that correspondence. I had voted for the recognition of Texan independence, because I believed it to be an existing fact, surprising and astonishing as it was, and I wished well to the new republic; but I manifested from the first utter opposition to bringing her, with her slave territory, into the Union. I happened, in 1837, to make a public address to political friends in New York, and I then stated my sentiments upon the subject. It was the first time that I had occasion to advert to it; and I will ask a friend near me to have the kindness to read an extract from the speech made by me on that occasion. It was delivered in Niblo's Garden, in 1837.

Mr. Greene then read the following extract from the speech of Mr. Webster to which he referred:—

"Gentlemen, we all see that, by whomsoever possessed, Texas is likely to be a slave-holding country; and I frankly avow my entire unwillingness to do any thing which shall extend the slavery of the African race on this continent, or add other slave-holding States to the Union. When I say that I regard slavery in itself as a great moral, social, and political evil, I only use language which has been adopted by distinguished men, themselves citizens of slave-holding States. I shall do nothing, therefore, to favor or encourage its further extension. We have slavery already amongst us. The Constitution found it in the Union; it recognized it, and gave it solemn guaranties. To the full extent of these guaranties we are all bound, in honor, in justice and by the Constitution. All the stipulations contained in the Constitution in favor of the slave-holding States which are already in the Union ought to be fulfilled, and, so far as depends on me, shall be fulfilled, in the fulness of their spirit, and to the exactness of their letter. Slavery, as it exists in the States, is beyond the reach of Congress. It is a concern of the States themselves; they have never submitted it to Congress, and Congress has no rightful power over it. I shall concur, therefore, in no act, no measure, no menace, no indication of purpose, which shall interfere or threaten to interfere with the exclusive authority of the several States over the subject of slavery as it exists within their respective limits. All this appears to me to be matter of plain and imperative duty.

"But when we come to speak of admitting new States, the subject assumes an entirely different aspect. Our rights and our duties are then both different. . . . . .

"I see, therefore, no political necessity for the annexation of Texas to the Union; no advantages to be derived from it; and objections to it of a strong, and, in my judgment, decisive character."

I have nothing, Sir, to add to, or to take from, those sentiments. That speech, the Senate will perceive, was made in 1837. The purpose of immediately annexing Texas at that time was abandoned or postponed; and it was not revived with any vigor for some years. In the mean time it happened that I had become a member of the executive administration, and was for a short period in the Department of State. The annexation of Texas was a subject of conversation, not confidential, with the President and heads of departments, as well as with other public men. No serious attempt was then made, however, to bring it about. I left the Department of State in May, 1843, and shortly after I learned, though by means which were no way connected with official information, that a design had been taken up of bringing Texas, with her slave territory and population, into this Union. I was in Washington at the time, and persons are now here who will remember that we had an arranged meeting for conversation upon it. I went home to Massachusetts and proclaimed the existence of that purpose, but I could get no audience and but little attention. Some did not believe it, and some were too much engaged in their own pursuits to give it any heed. They had gone to their farms or to their merchandise, and it was impossible to arouse any feeling in New England, or in Massachusetts, that should combine the two great political parties against this annexation; and, indeed, there was no hope of bringing the Northern Democracy into that view, for their leaning was all the other way. But, Sir, even with Whigs, and leading Whigs, I am ashamed to say, there was a great indifference towards the admission of Texas, with slave territory, into this Union.

The project went on. I was then out of Congress. The annexation resolutions passed on the 1st of March, 1845; the legislature of Texas complied with the conditions and accepted the guaranties; for the language of the resolution is, that Texas is to come in "upon the conditions and under the guaranties herein prescribed." I was returned to the Senate in March, 1845, and was here in December following, when the acceptance by Texas of the conditions proposed by Congress was communicated to us by the President, and an act for the consummation of the union was laid before the two houses. The connection was then not completed. A final law, doing the deed of annexation ultimately, had not been passed; and when it was put upon its final passage here, I expressed my opposition to it, and recorded my vote in the negative; and there that vote stands, with the observations that I made upon that occasion.* Nor is this the only occasion on which I have expressed myself to the same effect. It has happened that, between 1837 and this time, on various occasions, I have expressed my entire opposition to the admission of slave States, or the acquisition of new slave territories, to be added to the United States. I know, Sir, no change in my own sentiments, or my own pur-

* See the remarks on the Admission of Texas, p. 55 of this volume.

poses, in that respect. I will now ask my friend from Rhode Island to read another extract from a speech of mine made at a Whig Convention in Springfield, Massachusetts, in the month of September, 1847.

Mr. Greene here read the following extract: —

"We hear much just now of a *panacea* for the dangers and evils of slavery and slave annexation, which they call the 'Wilmot Proviso.' That certainly is a just sentiment, but it is not a sentiment to found any new party upon. It is not a sentiment on which Massachusetts Whigs differ. There is not a man in this hall who holds to it more firmly than I do, nor one who adheres to it more than another.

"I feel some little interest in this matter, Sir. Did not I commit myself in 1837 to the whole doctrine, fully, entirely? And I must be permitted to say that I cannot quite consent that more recent discoverers should claim the merit and take out a patent.

"I deny the priority of their invention. Allow me to say, Sir, it is not their thunder. . . . . .

"We are to use the first and the last and every occasion which offers to oppose the extension of slave power.

"But I speak of it here, as in Congress, as a political question, a question for statesmen to act upon. We must so regard it. I certainly do not mean to say that it is less important in a moral point of view, that it is not more important in many other points of view; but as a legislator, or in any official capacity, I must look at it, consider it, and decide it as a matter of political action."

On other occasions, in debates here, I have expressed my determination to vote for no acquisition, or cession, or annexation, north or south, east or west. My opinion has been, that we have territory enough, and that we should follow the Spartan maxim, "Improve, adorn what you have," seek no further. I think that it was in some observations that I made on the three-million loan bill that I avowed this sentiment. In short, Sir, it has been avowed quite as often, in as many places, and before as many assemblies, as any humble opinions of mine ought to be avowed.

But now that, under certain conditions, Texas is in the Union, with all her territory, as a slave State, with a solemn pledge, also, that, if she shall be divided into many States, those States may come in as slave States south of 36° 30′, how are we to deal with this subject? I know no way of honest legislation, when the proper time comes for the enactment, but to carry into effect all that we have stipulated to do. I do not entirely agree with my honorable friend from Tennessee,* that, as soon as the time comes when she is entitled to another representative, we should create a new State. On former occasions, in creating new States out of territories, we have generally gone upon the idea that, when the population of the territory amounts to about sixty thousand, we would consent to its admission as a State. But it is quite a different thing when a State is divided, and two or more States made out of it. It does not follow in such a case that the same rule of apportionment should be applied. That, however, is a matter for the consideration of Congress, when the proper time arrives. I may not then be here; I may have no vote to give on the occasion; but I wish it to be distinctly understood, that, according to my view of the matter, this government is solemnly pledged, by law and contract, to create new States out of Texas, with her consent, when her population shall justify and call for such a proceeding, and, so far as such States are formed out of Texan territory lying south of 36° 30′, to let them come in as slave States. That is the meaning of the contract which our friends, the Northern Democracy, have left us to fulfil; and I, for one, mean to fulfil it, because I will not violate the faith of the government. What I mean to say is, that the time for the admission of new States formed out of Texas, the number of such States, their boundaries, the requisite amount of population, and all other things connected with the admission, are in the free discretion of Congress, except this; to wit, that, when new States formed out of Texas are to be admitted, they have a right, by legal stipulation and contract, to come in as slave States.

Now, as to California and New Mexico, I hold slavery to be excluded from those territories by a law even superior to that which admits and sanctions it in Texas. I mean the law of nature, of physical geography, the law of the formation of the earth. That law settles for ever, with a strength beyond all terms of human enactment, that slavery cannot exist in California or New Mexico. Understand me, Sir; I mean slavery as

* Mr. Bell.

we regard it; the slavery of the colored race as it exists in the Southern States. I shall not discuss the point, but leave it to the learned gentlemen who have undertaken to discuss it; but I suppose there is no slavery of that description in California now. I understand that *peonism*, a sort of penal servitude, exists there, or rather a sort of voluntary sale of a man and his offspring for debt, an arrangement of a peculiar nature known to the law of Mexico. But what I mean to say is, that it is as impossible that African slavery, as we see it among us, should find its way, or be introduced, into California and New Mexico, as any other natural impossibility. California and New Mexico are Asiatic in their formation and scenery. They are composed of vast ridges of mountains, of great height, with broken ridges and deep valleys. The sides of these mountains are entirely barren; their tops capped by perennial snow. There may be in California, now made free by its constitution, and no doubt there are, some tracts of valuable land. But it is not so in New Mexico. Pray, what is the evidence which every gentleman must have obtained on this subject, from information sought by himself or communicated by others? I have inquired and read all I could find, in order to acquire information on this important subject. What is there in New Mexico that could, by any possibility, induce any body to go there with slaves? There are some narrow strips of tillable land on the borders of the rivers; but the rivers themselves dry up before midsummer is gone. All that the people can do in that region is to raise some little articles, some little wheat for their *tortillas*, and that by irrigation. And who expects to see a hundred black men cultivating tobacco, corn, cotton, rice, or any thing else, on lands in New Mexico, made fertile only by irrigation?

I look upon it, therefore, as a fixed fact, to use the current expression of the day, that both California and New Mexico are destined to be free, so far as they are settled at all, which I believe, in regard to New Mexico, will be but partially for a great length of time; free by the arrangement of things ordained by the Power above us. I have therefore to say, in this respect also, that this country is fixed for freedom, to as many persons as shall ever live in it, by a less repealable law than that which attaches to the right of holding slaves in Texas; and I will say further, that, if a resolution or a bill were now before us, to provide a territorial government for New Mexico, I would not vote to put any prohibition into it whatever. Such a prohibition would be idle, as it respects any effect it would have upon the territory; and I would not take pains uselessly to reaffirm an ordinance of nature, nor to reënact the will of God. I would put in no Wilmot Proviso for the mere purpose of a taunt or a reproach. I would put into it no evidence of the votes of superior power, exercised for no purpose but to wound the pride, whether a just and a rational pride, or an irrational pride, of the citizens of the Southern States. I have no such object, no such purpose. They would think it a taunt, an indignity; they would think it to be an act taking away from them what they regard as a proper equality of privilege. Whether they expect to realize any benefit from it or not, they would think it at least a plain theoretic wrong; that something more or less derogatory to their character and their rights had taken place. I propose to inflict no such wound upon any body, unless something essentially important to the country, and efficient to the preservation of liberty and freedom, is to be effected. I repeat, therefore, Sir, and, as I do not propose to address the Senate often on this subject, I repeat it because I wish it to be distinctly understood, that, for the reasons stated, if a proposition were now here to establish a government for New Mexico, and it was moved to insert a provision for a prohibition of slavery, I would not vote for it.

Sir, if we were now making a government for New Mexico, and any body should propose a Wilmot Proviso, I should treat it exactly as Mr. Polk treated that provision for excluding slavery from Oregon. Mr. Polk was known to be in opinion decidedly averse to the Wilmot Proviso; but he felt the necessity of establishing a government for the Territory of Oregon. The proviso was in the bill, but he knew it would be entirely nugatory; and, since it must be entirely nugatory, since it took away no right, no describable, no tangible, no appreciable right of the South, he said he would sign the bill for the sake of enacting a law to form a government in that Territory, and let that entirely useless, and, in that connection, entirely senseless, proviso remain. Sir, we hear occasionally of the annexation of Canada; and if there be any man, any of the Northern Democracy, or any one of the Free Soil party, who supposes it necessary to insert a Wilmot Proviso in a territorial government for New Mexico, that man would of course be of opinion that it is necessary to protect the everlasting snows of Canada from the foot of slavery by the same overspreading wing of an act of Congress. Sir, wherever there is a substantive good to be done, wherever there is a foot of land to be prevented from becoming slave territory, I am ready to assert the principle of the exclusion of slavery. I am pledged to it from the year 1837; I have been pledged to it again and again; and I will perform those pledges; but I will not do a thing unnecessarily that wounds the feelings of others, or that does discredit to my own understanding.

Now, Mr. President, I have established, so far as I proposed to do so, the proposition with which I set out, and upon which I intend to stand or fall; and that is, that the whole territory within the former United States, or in the newly acquired Mexican provinces, has a fixed and settled character, now fixed and settled by law which cannot be repealed; in the case of Texas without a violation of public faith, and by no human power in regard to California or New Mexico; that, therefore, under one or other of these laws, every foot of land in the States or in the Territories has already received a fixed and decided character.

Mr. President, in the excited times in which we live, there is found to exist a state of crimination and recrimination between the North and South. There are lists of grievances produced by each; and those grievances, real or supposed, alienate the minds of one portion of the country from the other, exasperate the feelings, and subdue the sense of fraternal affection, patriotic love, and mutual regard. I shall bestow a little attention, Sir, upon these various grievances existing on the one side and on the other. I begin with complaints of the South. I will not answer, further than I have, the general statements of the honorable Senator from South Carolina, that the North has prospered at the expense of the South in consequence of the manner of administering this government, in the collecting of its revenues, and so forth. These are disputed topics, and I have no inclination to enter into them. But I will allude to other complaints of the South, and especially to one which has in my opinion just foundation; and that is, that there has been found at the North, among individuals and among legislators, a disinclination to perform fully their constitutional duties in regard to the return of persons bound to service who have escaped into the free States. In that respect, the South, in my judgment, is right, and the North is wrong. Every member of every Northern legislature is bound by oath, like every other officer in the country, to support the Constitution of the United States; and the article of the Constitution* which says to these States that they shall deliver up fugitives from service is as binding in honor and conscience as any other article. No man fulfils his duty in any legislature who sets himself to find excuses, evasions, escapes from this constitutional obligation. I have always thought that the Constitution addressed itself to the legislatures of the States or to the States themselves. It says that those persons escaping to other States "shall be delivered up," and I confess I have always been of the opinion that it was an injunction upon the States themselves. When it is said that a person escaping into another State, and coming therefore within the jurisdiction of that State, shall be delivered up, it seems to me the import of the clause is, that the State itself, in obedience to the Constitution, shall cause him to be delivered up. That is my judgment. I have always entertained that opinion, and I entertain it now. But when the subject, some years ago, was before the Supreme Court of the United States, the majority of the judges held that the power to cause fugitives from service to be delivered up was a power to be exercised under the authority of this government. I do not know, on the whole, that it may not have been a fortunate decision. My habit is to respect the result of judicial deliberations and the solemnity of judicial decisions. As it now stands, the business of seeing that these fugitives are delivered up resides in the power of Congress and the national judicature, and my friend at the head of the Judiciary Committee† has a bill on the subject now before the Senate, which, with some amendments to it, I

* Art. IV. Sect. 2, § 2.

† Mr. Mason.

propose to support, with all its provisions, to the fullest extent. And I desire to call the attention of all sober-minded men at the North, of all conscientious men, of all men who are not carried away by some fanatical idea or some false impression, to their constitutional obligations. I put it to all the sober and sound minds at the North as a question of morals and a question of conscience. What right have they, in their legislative capacity or any other capacity, to endeavor to get round this Constitution, or to embarrass the free exercise of the rights secured by the Constitution to the persons whose slaves escape from them? None at all; none at all. Neither in the forum of conscience, nor before the face of the Constitution, are they, in my opinion, justified in such an attempt. Of course it is a matter for their consideration. They probably, in the excitement of the times, have not stopped to consider of this. They have followed what seemed to be the current of thought and of motives, as the occasion arose, and they have neglected to investigate fully the real question, and to consider their constitutional obligations; which, I am sure, if they did consider, they would fulfil with alacrity. I repeat, therefore, Sir, that here is a well-founded ground of complaint against the North, which ought to be removed, which it is now in the power of the different departments of this government to remove; which calls for the enactment of proper laws authorizing the judicature of this government, in the several States, to do all that is necessary for the recapture of fugitive slaves and for their restoration to those who claim them. Wherever I go, and whenever I speak on the subject, and when I speak here I desire to speak to the whole North, I say that the South has been injured in this respect, and has a right to complain; and the North has been too careless of what I think the Constitution peremptorily and emphatically enjoins upon her as a duty.

Complaint has been made against certain resolutions that emanate from legislatures at the North, and are sent here to us, not only on the subject of slavery in this District, but sometimes recommending Congress to consider the means of abolishing slavery in the States. I should be sorry to be called upon to present any resolutions here which could not be referable to any committee or any power in Congress; and therefore I should be unwilling to receive from the legislature of Massachusetts any instructions to present resolutions expressive of any opinion whatever on the subject of slavery, as it exists as the present moment in the States, for two reasons: first, because I do not consider that the legislature of Massachusetts has any thing to do with it; and next, because I do not consider that I, as her representative here, have any thing to do with it. It has become, in my opinion, quite too common; and if the legislatures of the States do not like that opinion, they have a great deal more power to put it down than I have to uphold it; it has become, in my opinion, quite too common a practice for the State legislatures to present resolutions here on all subjects and to instruct us on all subjects. There is no public man that requires instruction more than I do, or who requires information more than I do, or desires it more heartily; but I do not like to have it in too imperative a shape. I took notice, with pleasure, of some remarks made upon this subject, the other day, in the Senate of Massachusetts, by a young man of talent and character, of whom the best hopes may be entertained. I mean Mr. Hillard. He told the Senate of Massachusetts that he would vote for no instructions whatever to be forwarded to members of Congress, nor for any resolutions to be offered expressive of the sense of Massachusetts as to what her members of Congress ought to do. He said that he saw no propriety in one set of public servants giving instructions and reading lectures to another set of public servants. To his own master each of them must stand or fall, and that master is his constituents. I wish these sentiments could become more common. I have never entered into the question, and never shall, as to the binding force of instructions. I will, however, simply say this: if there be any matter pending in this body, while I am a member of it, in which Massachusetts has an interest of her own not adverse to the general interests of the country, I shall pursue her instructions with gladness of heart and with all the efficiency which I can bring to the occasion. But if the question be one which affects her interest, and at the same time equally affects the interests of all the other States, I shall no more regard her particular wishes or instructions than I should regard the wishes of a man who might appoint me an arbitrator or referee to decide some question of important private right between him and his neighbor, and then *instruct* me to decide in his favor. If ever there was a government upon earth it is this government, if ever there was a body upon earth it is this body, which should consider itself as composed by agreement of all, each member appointed by some, but organized by the general consent of all, sitting here, under the solemn obligations of oath and conscience, to do that which they think to be best for the good of the whole.

Then, Sir, there are the Abolition societies, of which I am unwilling to speak, but in regard to which I have very clear notions and opinions. I do not think them useful. I think their operations for the last twenty years have produced nothing good or valuable. At the same time, I believe thousands of their members to be honest and good men, perfectly well-meaning men. They have excited feelings; they think they must do something for the cause of liberty; and, in their sphere of action, they do not see what else they can do than to contribute to an Abolition press, or an Abolition society, or to pay an Abolition lecturer. I do not mean to impute gross motives even to the leaders of these societies, but I am not blind to the consequences of their proceedings. I cannot but see what mischiefs their interference with the South has produced. And is it not plain to every man? Let any gentleman who entertains doubts on this point recur to the debates in the Virginia House of Delegates in 1832, and he will see with what freedom a proposition made by Mr. Jefferson Randolph for the gradual abolition of slavery was discussed in that body. Every one spoke of slavery as he thought; very ignominious and disparaging names and epithets were applied to it. The debates in the House of Delegates on that occasion, I believe, were all published. They were read by every colored man who could read, and to those who could not read, those debates were read by others. At that time Virginia was not unwilling or afraid to discuss this question, and to let that part of her population know as much of the discussion as they could learn. That was in 1832. As has been said by the honorable member from South Carolina, these Abolition societies commenced their course of action in 1835. It is said, I do not know how true it may be, that they sent incendiary publications into the slave States; at any rate, they attempted to arouse, and did arouse, a very strong feeling; in other words, they created great agitation in the North against Southern slavery. Well, what was the result? The bonds of the slaves were bound more firmly than before, their rivets were more strongly fastened. Public opinion, which in Virginia had begun to be exhibited against slavery, and was opening out for the discussion of the question, drew back and shut itself up in its castle. I wish to know whether any body in Virginia can now talk openly as Mr. Randolph, Governor McDowell, and others talked in 1832, and sent their remarks to the press? We all know the fact, and we all know the cause; and every thing that these agitating people have done has been, not to enlarge, but to restrain, not to set free, but to bind faster, the slave population of the South.*

Again, Sir, the violence of the Northern press is complained of. The press violent! Why, Sir, the press is violent everywhere. There are outrageous reproaches in the North against the South, and there are reproaches as vehement in the South against the North. Sir, the extremists of both parts of this country are violent; they mistake loud and violent talk for eloquence and for reason. They think that he who talks loudest reasons best. And this we must expect, when the press is free, as it is here, and I trust always will be; for, with all its licentiousness and all its evil, the entire and absolute freedom of the press is essential to the preservation of government on the basis of a free constitution. Wherever it exists there will be foolish and violent paragraphs in the newspapers, as there are, I am sorry to say, foolish and violent speeches in both houses of Congress. In truth, Sir, I must say that, in my opinion, the vernacular tongue of the country has become greatly vitiated, depraved, and corrupted by the style of our Congressional debates. And if it were possible for those debates to vitiate the principles of the people as much as they have depraved their tastes, I should cry out, "God save the Republic!"

Well, in all this I see no solid grievance, no grievance presented by the South, within the redress of the government, but the single one to which I have referred; and that is, the want of a proper regard to the injunction of the Constitution for the delivery of fugitive slaves.

* See Note at the end of the Speech.

There are also complaints of the North against the South. I need not go over them particularly. The first and gravest is, that the North adopted the Constitution, recognizing the existence of slavery in the States, and recognizing the right, to a certain extent, of the representation of slaves in Congress, under a state of sentiment and expectation which does not now exist; and that, by events, by circumstances, by the eagerness of the South to acquire territory and extend her slave population, the North finds itself, in regard to the relative influence of the South and the North, of the free States and the slave States, where it never did expect to find itself when they agreed to the compact of the Constitution. They complain, therefore, that, instead of slavery being regarded as an evil, as it was then, an evil which all hoped would be extinguished gradually, it is now regarded by the South as an institution to be cherished, and preserved, and extended; an institution which the South has already extended to the utmost of her power by the acquisition of new territory.

Well, then, passing from that, every body in the North reads; and every body reads whatsoever the newspapers contain; and the newspapers, some of them, especially those presses to which I have alluded, are careful to spread about among the people every reproachful sentiment uttered by any Southern man bearing at all against the North; every thing that is calculated to exasperate and to alienate; and there are many such things, as every body will admit, from the South, or some portion of it, which are disseminated among the reading people; and they do exasperate, and alienate, and produce a most mischievous effect upon the public mind at the North. Sir, I would not notice things of this sort appearing in obscure quarters; but one thing has occurred in this debate which struck me very forcibly. An honorable member from Louisiana addressed us the other day on this subject. I suppose there is not a more amiable and worthy gentleman in this chamber, nor a gentleman who would be more slow to give offence to any body, and he did not mean in his remarks to give offence. But what did he say? Why, Sir, he took pains to run a contrast between the slaves of the South and the laboring people of the North, giving the preference, in all points of condition, and comfort, and happiness, to the slaves of the South. The honorable member, doubtless, did not suppose that he gave any offence, or did any injustice. He was merely expressing his opinion. But does he know how remarks of that sort will be received by the laboring people of the North? Why, who are the laboring people of the North? They are the whole North. They are the people who till their own farms with their own hands; freeholders, educated men, independent men. Let me say, Sir, that five sixths of the whole property of the North is in the hands of the laborers of the North; they cultivate their farms, they educate their children, they provide the means of independence. If they are not freeholders, they earn wages; these wages accumulate, are turned into capital, into new freeholds, and small capitalists are created. Such is the case, and such the course of things, among the industrious and frugal. And what can these people think when so respectable and worthy a gentleman as the member from Louisiana undertakes to prove that the absolute ignorance and the abject slavery of the South are more in conformity with the high purposes and destiny of immortal, rational human beings, than the educated, the independent free labor of the North?

There is a more tangible and irritating cause of grievance at the North. Free blacks are constantly employed in the vessels of the North, generally as cooks or stewards. When the vessel arrives at a Southern port, these free colored men are taken on shore, by the police or municipal authority, imprisoned, and kept in prison till the vessel is again ready to sail. This is not only irritating, but exceedingly unjustifiable and oppressive. Mr. Hoar's mission, some time ago, to South Carolina, was a well-intended effort to remove this cause of complaint. The North thinks such imprisonments illegal and unconstitutional; and as the cases occur constantly and frequently, they regard it as a great grievance.

Now, Sir, so far as any of these grievances have their foundation in matters of law, they can be redressed, and ought to be redressed; and so far as they have their foundation in matters of opinion, in sentiment, in mutual crimination and recrimination, all that we can do is to endeavor to allay the agitation, and cultivate a better feeling and more fraternal sentiments between the South and the North.

Mr. President, I should much prefer to have heard from every member on this floor declarations of opinion that this Union could never be dissolved, than the declaration of opinion by any body, that, in any case, under the pressure of any circumstances, such a dissolution was possible. I hear with distress and anguish the word "secession," especially when it falls from the lips of those who are patriotic, and known to the country, and known all over the world, for their political services. Secession! Peaceable secession! Sir, your eyes and mine are never destined to see that miracle. The dismemberment of this vast country without convulsion! The breaking up of the fountains of the great deep without ruffling the surface! Who is so foolish, I beg every body's pardon, as to expect to see any such thing? Sir, he who sees these States, now revolving in harmony around a common centre, and expects to see them quit their places and fly off without convulsion, may look the next hour to see the heavenly bodies rush from their spheres, and jostle against each other in the realms of space, without causing the wreck of the universe. There can be no such thing as a peaceable secession. Peaceable secession is an utter impossibility. Is the great Constitution under which we live, covering this whole country, is it to be thawed and melted away by secession, as the snows on the mountain melt under the influence of a vernal sun, disappear almost unobserved, and run off? No, Sir! No, Sir! I will not state what might produce the disruption of the Union; but, Sir, I see as plainly as I see the sun in heaven what that disruption itself must produce; I see that it must produce war, and such a war as I will not describe, *in its twofold character.*

Peaceable secession! Peaceable secession! The concurrent agreement of all the members of this great republic to separate! A voluntary separation, with alimony on one side and on the other. Why, what would be the result? Where is the line to be drawn? What States are to secede? What is to remain American? What am I to be? An American no longer? Am I to become a sectional man, a local man, a separatist, with no country in common with the gentlemen who sit around me here, or who fill the other house of Congress? Heaven forbid! Where is the flag of the republic to remain? Where is the eagle still to tower? or is he to cower, and shrink, and fall to the ground? Why, Sir, our ancestors, our fathers and our grandfathers, those of them that are yet living amongst us with prolonged lives, would rebuke and reproach us; and our children and our grandchildren would cry out shame upon us, if we of this generation should dishonor these ensigns of the power of the government and the harmony of that Union which is every day felt among us with so much joy and gratitude. What is to become of the army? What is to become of the navy? What is to become of the public lands? How is each of the thirty States to defend itself? I know, although the idea has not been stated distinctly, there is to be, or it is supposed possible that there will be, a Southern Confederacy. I do not mean, when I allude to this statement, that any one seriously contemplates such a state of things. I do not mean to say that it is true, but I have heard it suggested elsewhere, that the idea has been entertained, that, after the dissolution of this Union, a Southern Confederacy might be formed. I am sorry, Sir, that it has ever been thought of, talked of, or dreamed of, in the wildest flights of human imagination. But the idea, so far as it exists, must be of a separation, assigning the slave States to one side and the free States to the other. Sir, I may express myself too strongly, perhaps, but there are impossibilities in the natural as well as in the physical world, and I hold the idea of a separation of these States, those that are free to form one government, and those that are slave-holding to form another, as such an impossibility. We could not separate the States by any such line, if we were to draw it. We could not sit down here to-day and draw a line of separation that would satisfy any five men in the country. There are natural causes that would keep and tie us together, and there are social and domestic relations which we could not break if we would, and which we should not if we could.

Sir, nobody can look over the face of this country at the present moment, nobody can see where its population is the most dense and growing, without being ready to admit, and compelled to admit, that ere long the strength of America will be in the Valley of the Mississippi. Well, now, Sir, I beg to inquire what the wildest enthusiast has to say on the possibility of cutting that river in two, and leaving free States at its source and on its branches, and slave States down near its mouth, each forming a separate government? Pray, Sir, let me say to the people of this country, that these things are worthy of their pondering and of their consideration. Here, Sir, are five millions of freemen in the free States north of the river Ohio. Can any body suppose that this population can be severed, by a line that divides them from the territory of a foreign and an alien government, down somewhere, the Lord knows where, upon the lower banks of the Mississippi? What would become of Missouri? Will she join the *arrondissement* of the slave States? Shall the man from the Yellow Stone and the Platte be connected, in the new republic, with the man who lives on the southern extremity of the Cape of Florida? Sir, I am ashamed to pursue this line of remark. I dislike it, I have an utter disgust for it. I would rather hear of natural blasts and mildews, war, pestilence, and famine, than to hear gentlemen talk of secession. To break up this great government! to dismember this glorious country! to astonish Europe with an act of folly such as Europe for two centuries has never beheld in any government or any people! No, Sir! no, Sir! There will be no secession! Gentlemen are not serious when they talk of secession.

Sir, I hear there is to be a convention held at Nashville. I am bound to believe that, if worthy gentlemen meet at Nashville in convention, their object will be to adopt conciliatory counsels; to advise the South to forbearance and moderation, and to advise the North to forbearance and moderation; and to inculcate principles of brotherly love and affection, and attachment to the Constitution of the country as it now is. I believe, if the convention meet at all, it will be for this purpose; for certainly, if they meet for any purpose hostile to the Union, they have been singularly inappropriate in their selection of a place. I remember, Sir, that, when the treaty of Amiens was concluded between France and England, a sturdy Englishman and a distinguished orator, who regarded the conditions of the peace as ignominious to England, said in the House of Commons, that, if King William could know the terms of that treaty, he would turn in his coffin! Let me commend this saying of Mr. Windham, in all its emphasis and in all its force, to any persons who shall meet at Nashville for the purpose of concerting measures for the overthrow of this Union over the bones of Andrew Jackson!

Sir, I wish now to make two remarks, and hasten to a conclusion. I wish to say, in regard to Texas, that if it should be hereafter, at any time, the pleasure of the government of Texas to cede to the United States a portion, larger or smaller, of her territory which lies adjacent to New Mexico, and north of 36° 30′ of north latitude, to be formed into free States, for a fair equivalent in money or in the payment of her debt, I think it an object well worthy the consideration of Congress, and I shall be happy to concur in it myself, if I should have a connection with the government at that time.

I have one other remark to make. In my observations upon slavery as it has existed in this country, and as it now exists, I have expressed no opinion of the mode of its extinguishment or melioration. I will say, however, though I have nothing to propose, because I do not deem myself so competent as other gentlemen to take any lead on this subject, that if any gentleman from the South shall propose a scheme, to be carried on by this government upon a large scale, for the transportation of free colored people to any colony or any place in the world, I should be quite disposed to incur almost any degree of expense to accomplish that object. Nay, Sir, following an example set more than twenty years ago by a great man,* then a Senator from New York, I would return to Virginia, and through her to the whole South, the money received from the lands and territories ceded by her to this government, for any such purpose as to remove, in whole or in part, or in any way to diminish or deal beneficially with, the free colored population of the Southern States. I have said that I honor Virginia for her cession of this territory. There have been received into the treasury of the United States eighty millions of dollars, the proceeds of the sales of the public lands ceded by her. If the residue should be sold at the same rate, the whole aggregate will exceed two hundred millions of dollars. If Virginia and the South see fit to adopt any proposition to relieve themselves from the free people of color among them, or such as may be made free, they have my full consent that the government shall pay them any sum of money out of the proceeds of that cession which may be adequate to the purpose.

And now, Mr. President, I draw these observations to a

* Mr. Rufus King.

close. I have spoken freely, and I meant to do so. I have sought to make no display. I have sought to enliven the occasion by no animated discussion, nor have I attempted any train of elaborate argument. I have wished only to speak my sentiments, fully and at length, being desirous, once and for all, to let the Senate know, and to let the country know, the opinions and sentiments which I entertain on all these subjects. These opinions are not likely to be suddenly changed. If there be any future service that I can render to the country, consistently with these sentiments and opinions, I shall cheerfully render it. If there be not, I shall still be glad to have had an opportunity to disburden myself from the bottom of my heart, and to make known every political sentiment that therein exists.

And now, Mr. President, instead of speaking of the possibility or utility of secession, instead of dwelling in those caverns of darkness, instead of groping with those ideas so full of all that is horrid and horrible, let us come out into the light of day; let us enjoy the fresh air of Liberty and Union; let us cherish those hopes which belong to us; let us devote ourselves to those great objects that are fit for our consideration and our action; let us raise our conceptions to the magnitude and the importance of the duties that devolve upon us; let our comprehension be as broad as the country for which we act, our aspirations as high as its certain destiny; let us not be pigmies in a case that calls for men. Never did there devolve on any generation of men higher trusts than now devolve upon us, for the preservation of this Constitution and the harmony and peace of all who are destined to live under it. Let us make our generation one of the strongest and brightest links in that golden chain which is destined, I fondly believe, to grapple the people of all the States to this Constitution for ages to come. We have a great, popular, constitutional government, guarded by law and by judicature, and defended by the affections of the whole people. No monarchical throne presses these States together, no iron chain of military power encircles them; they live and stand under a government popular in its form, representative in its character, founded upon principles of equality, and so constructed, we hope, as to last for ever. In all its history it has been beneficent; it has trodden down no man's liberty; it has crushed no State. Its daily respiration is liberty and patriotism; its yet youthful veins are full of enterprise, courage, and honorable love of glory and renown. Large before, the country has now, by recent events, become vastly larger. This republic now extends, with a vast breadth, across the whole continent. The two great seas of the world wash the one and the other shore. We realize, on a mighty scale, the beautiful description of the ornamental border of the buckler of Achilles: —

> "Now, the broad shield complete, the artist crowned
> With his last hand, and poured the ocean round;
> In living silver seemed the waves to roll,
> And beat the buckler's verge, and bound the whole."

NOTE.

Page 358.

Letter from Mr. Webster to the Editors of the National Intelligencer, inclosing Extracts from a Letter of the late Dr. Channing.

Washington, February 15*th*, 1851.

MESSRS. GALES & SEATON: —

Having occasion recently to look over some files of letters written several years ago, I happened to fall on one from the late Rev. Dr. W. E. Channing. It contains passages which I think, coming from such a source, and written at such a time, would be interesting to the country. I have therefore extracted them, and send them to you for publication in your columns. Yours respectfully,

DANIEL WEBSTER.

Boston, May 14*th*, 1828.

MY DEAR SIR: —

I wish to call your attention to a subject of general interest.

A little while ago, Mr. Lundy of Baltimore, the editor of a paper called "The Genius of Universal Emancipation," visited this part of the country, to stir us up to the work of abolishing slavery at the South, and the intention is to organize societies for this purpose. I know few objects into which I should enter with more zeal, but I am aware how cautiously exertions are to be made for it in this part of the country. I know that our Southern brethren interpret every word from this region on the subject of slavery as an expression of hostility. I would ask if they cannot be brought to understand us better, and if we can do any good till we remove their misapprehensions. It seems to me that, before moving in this matter, we ought to say to them distinctly, "We consider slavery as your calamity, not your crime, and we will share with you the burden of putting an end to it. We will consent that the public lands shall be appropriated to this object; or that the general government shall be clothed with power to apply a portion of revenue to it."

I throw out these suggestions merely to illustrate my views. We must first let the Southern States see that we are their *friends* in this affair; that we sympathize with them, and, from principles of patriotism and philanthropy, are willing to share the toil and expense of abolishing slavery, or I fear our interference will avail nothing. I am the more sensitive on this subject from my increased solicitude for the preservation of the Union. I know no public interest so important as this. I ask from the general government hardly any other boon than that it will hold us together, and preserve pacific relations and intercourse among the States. I deprecate every thing which sows discord and exasperates sectional animosities. If it will simply keep us at peace, and will maintain in full power the national courts, for the purpose of settling quietly among citizens of different States questions which might otherwise be settled by arms, I shall be satisfied.

My fear in regard to our efforts against slavery is, that we shall make the case worse by rousing sectional pride and passion for its support, and that we shall only break the country into two great parties, which may shake the foundations of government.

I have written to you because your situation gives you advantages which perhaps no other man enjoys for ascertaining the method, if any can be devised, by which we may operate beneficially and safely in regard to slavery. Appeals will probably be made soon to the people here, and I wish that wise men would save us from the rashness of enthusiasts, and from the perils to which our very virtues expose us.

With great respect, your friend,

WM. E. CHANNING.

HON. DANIEL WEBSTER.

TRIBUTE TO MR. CALHOUN.*

On the morning of the 31st of March, 1850, Mr. Calhoun died at his lodgings in Washington. Although his health had been for some time failing, he gave his attendance in the Senate, and took part in its deliberations, till a short time before his decease. On the 4th of March he appeared in his seat, but not feeling himself equal to the task of addressing the Senate, a speech prepared by him on the existing controversies was read by Mr. Mason of Virginia. On the 7th of March he was again present during the delivery of Mr. Webster's speech, and followed him with a few remarks relative to the acquisition of Texas. On the 13th of March he appeared in the Senate and spoke in public for the last time. On the 1st of April his lamented decease was announced by his colleague, Mr. Butler. On that occasion Mr. Webster made the following remarks.

I hope the Senate will indulge me in adding a very few words to what has been said. My apology for this presumption is the very long acquaintance which has subsisted between Mr. Calhoun and myself. We were of the same age. I made my first entrance into the House of Representatives in May, 1813. I there found Mr. Calhoun. He had already been a member of that body for two or three years. I found him then an active and efficient member of the House, taking a decided part, and exercising a decided influence, in all its deliberations.

From that day to the day of his death, amidst all the strifes of party and politics, there has subsisted between us, always, and without interruption, a great degree of personal kindness.

Differing widely on many great questions respecting our institutions and the government of the country, those differences never interrupted our personal and social intercourse. I have

* Remarks in the Senate, on the 1st of April, 1850, on occasion of the decease of Hon. John Caldwell Calhoun, Senator from South Carolina.

been present at most of the distinguished instances of the exhibition of his talents in debate. I have always heard him with pleasure, often with much instruction, not unfrequently with the highest degree of admiration.

Mr. Calhoun was calculated to be a leader in whatsoever association of political friends he was thrown. He was a man of undoubted genius and of commanding talent. All the country and all the world admit that. His mind was both perceptive and vigorous. It was clear, quick, and strong.

Sir, the eloquence of Mr. Calhoun, or the manner in which he exhibited his sentiments in public bodies, was part of his intellectual character. It grew out of the qualities of his mind. It was plain, strong, terse, condensed, concise; sometimes impassioned, still always severe. Rejecting ornament, not often seeking far for illustration, his power consisted in the plainness of his propositions, in the closeness of his logic, and in the earnestness and energy of his manner. These are the qualities, as I think, which have enabled him through such a long course of years to speak often, and yet always command attention. His demeanor as a Senator is known to us all, is appreciated, venerated, by us all. No man was more respectful to others; no man carried himself with greater decorum, no man with superior dignity. I think there is not one of us, when he last addressed us from his seat in the Senate, his form still erect, with a voice by no means indicating such a degree of physical weakness as did in fact possess him, with clear tones, and an impressive, and, I may say, an imposing manner, who did not feel that he might imagine that we saw before us a Senator of Rome, while Rome survived.

Sir, I have not, in public nor in private life, known a more assiduous person in the discharge of his appropriate duties. I have known no man who wasted less of life in what is called recreation, or employed less of it in any pursuits not connected with the immediate discharge of his duty. He seemed to have no recreation but the pleasure of conversation with his friends. Out of the chambers of Congress, he was either devoting himself to the acquisition of knowledge pertaining to the immediate subject of the duty before him, or else he was indulging in those social interviews in which he so much delighted.

My honorable friend from Kentucky * has spoken in just terms

* Mr. Clay.

of his colloquial talents. They certainly were singular and eminent. There was a charm in his conversation not often equalled. He delighted especially in conversation and intercourse with young men. I suppose that there has been no man among us, who had more winning manners, in such an intercourse and such conversation, with men comparatively young, than Mr. Calhoun. I believe one great power of his character, in general, was his conversational talent. I believe it is that, as well as a consciousness of his high integrity, and the greatest reverence for his talents and ability, that has made him so endeared an object to the people of the State to which he belonged.

Mr. President, he had the basis, the indispensable basis of all high character; and that was unspotted integrity and unimpeached honor. If he had aspirations, they were high, and honorable, and noble. There was nothing grovelling, or low, or meanly selfish, that came near the head or the heart of Mr. Calhoun. Firm in his purpose, perfectly patriotic and honest, as I am sure he was, in the principles that he espoused, and in the measures that he defended, aside from that large regard for the species of distinction that conducted him to eminent stations for the benefit of the republic, I do not believe he had a selfish motive or selfish feeling. However he may have differed from others of us in his political opinions or his political principles, those principles and those opinions will now descend to posterity under the sanction of a great name. He has lived long enough, he has done enough, and he has done it so well, so successfully, so honorably, as to connect himself for all time with the records of his country. He is now an historical character. Those of us who have known him here will find that he has left upon our minds and our hearts a strong and lasting impression of his person, his character, and his public performances, which, while we live, will never be obliterated. We shall hereafter, I am sure, indulge in it as a grateful recollection, that we have lived in his age, that we have been his contemporaries, that we have seen him, and heard him, and known him. We shall delight to speak of him to those who are rising up to fill our places. And, when the time shall come that we ourselves must go, one after another, to our graves, we shall carry with us a deep sense of his genius and character, his honor and integrity, his amiable deportment in private life, and the purity of his exalted patriotism.

TRIBUTE TO MR. ELMORE.*

On the decease of Mr. Calhoun, the Hon. Franklin H. Elmore was appointed his successor by the Governor of South Carolina. On the 6th of May he took his seat in the Senate, but in an infirm state of health. On the 29th of the same month he expired. It again devolved on Mr. Butler to perform the painful duty of announcing the decease of a colleague, on which occasion the following remarks were made by Mr. Webster.

Mr. President, — I sincerely sympathize with the honorable member from South Carolina, whose painful duty it has been, within so short a period, to announce the death of another colleague. I sympathize, Sir, with all the people of South Carolina, by whom, as I know, the gentleman now deceased was greatly respected and loved. I sympathize with that domestic circle to whom his death will be a loss never to be repaired. And, Sir, I feel that the Senate may well be the object of condolence on the death of a gentleman so well known in the other branch of the legislature, of so much experience in the various duties of public and official life in his own State, and who has so recently come into this body with every qualification to render here important public service, and with every prospect of usefulness, except so far as that prospect may have been dimmed by serious apprehensions in regard to his health.

Sir, I had the good fortune to become acquainted with Mr. Elmore ten or twelve years ago, when he was a member, and I may say a leading member, of the House of Representatives. I had formed a very favorable opinion of his character, as a

* Remarks in the Senate of the United States, on the 30th of May, 1850, on occasion of the decease of Hon. Franklin Harper Elmore.

man of integrity and uprightness, of great respectability, and great talent. I regretted his departure from the councils of the nation, because a person with his qualifications and with his habits of business grows every day more useful in our political circles, so long as he remains in the possession of his faculties and in the active performance of his duties. It happened to me, Sir, some years afterwards, and not now many years since, to form a personal and more private acquaintance with the deceased. I had the pleasure of seeing him among his own friends, of cultivating his acquaintance in the midst of those circles of social life in which he was regarded as a treasure and an ornament. I owe, Sir, to him whatever is due for kindness and hospitality, for generous welcome, and for an extension of the civilities and courtesies of life.

I shall cherish his memory with sincere regard as a valuable and able public man, and a gentleman entitled to high estimation in all the relations of life.

FUGITIVE SLAVE BILL.*

Mr. President, — At an early period of the session I turned my attention to the subject of preparing a bill respecting the reclamation of fugitive slaves, or of certain amendments to the existing law on that subject. In pursuance of this purpose, I conferred with some of the most eminent members of the profession, and especially with a high judicial authority, who has had more to do with questions of this kind, I presume, than any other judge in the United States. After these consultations and conferences, as early as in February, I prepared a bill amendatory of the act of 1793, intending, when a proper time came, to lay it before the Senate for its consideration. I now wish to present the bill to the Senate unaltered, and precisely as it was when prepared in February last.

Mr. Dayton. I hope that the paper will be printed.

The bill was then laid on the table and ordered to be printed, as follows: —

A Bill amendatory of "An Act respecting Fugitives from Justice and Persons escaping from the Service of their Masters," approved February 12, 1793.

Be it enacted by the Senate and House of Representatives of the United States of America in Congress assembled, That the provisions of the said act shall extend to the territories of the United States; and that the commissioners who now are, or who may hereafter be, appointed by the Circuit Courts of the United States, or the District Courts where Cir-

* Remarks made on the 3d of June, 1850, in presenting to the Senate "A Bill amendatory of 'An Act respecting Fugitives from Justice and Persons escaping from the Service of their Masters,'" approved February 12, 1793.

cuit Courts are not established, or by the Territorial courts of the United States, all of which courts are authorized and required to appoint one or more commissioners in each county to take acknowledgments of bail and affidavits, and also to take depositions of witnesses in civil causes, and who shall each, or any judge of the United States, on complaint being made on oath to him that a fugitive from labor is believed to be within the State or Territory in which he lives, issue his warrant to the marshal of the United States, or to any other person who shall be willing to serve it, authorizing an arrest of the fugitive, if within the State or Territory, to be brought before him or some other commissioner or judge of the United States court within the State or Territory, that the right of the person claiming the services of such fugitive may be examined. And on the hearing, depositions duly authenticated and parol proof shall be heard to establish the identity of the fugitive and the right of the claimant, and also to show that slavery is established in the State from which the fugitive absconded. And if on such hearing the commissioner or judge shall find the claim to the services of the fugitive, as asserted, sustained by the evidence, he shall make out a certificate of the material facts proved, and of his judgment thereon, which he shall sign, and which shall be conclusive of the right of the claimant or his agent to take the fugitive back to the State from whence he fled. *Provided*, that if the fugitive shall deny that he owes service to the claimant under the laws of the State where he was held, and, after being duly cautioned as to the solemnities and consequences of an oath, shall swear to the same, the commissioner or judge shall forthwith summon a jury of twelve men to try the right of the claimant, who shall be sworn to try the cause according to evidence, and the commissioner or judge shall preside at the trial, and determine the competency of the proof.

Sec. 2. *And be it further enacted*, That the commissioner shall receive ten dollars in each case tried by him as aforesaid, the jurors fifty cents each, and the marshal or other person serving the process shall receive five dollars for serving the warrant on each fugitive, and for mileage and other services the same as are allowed to the marshal for similar services, to be examined and allowed by the commissioner or judge, and paid by the claimant.

THE BOUNDARIES OF TEXAS.*

While the debate was in progress in the Senate of the United States, upon the resolutions of Mr. Clay, a motion was made by Mr. Foote of Mississippi, for a committee of thirteen, to consider and report a comprehensive plan of adjustment of all the matters in controversy on the subject of slavery. This motion prevailed, and a committee was appointed by ballot, composed of the following persons: Messrs. Clay, Bell, Berrien, Bright, Cass, Cooper, Dickinson, Downs, King, Mangum, Mason, Phelps, and Webster. This committee, on the 8th of May, reported by their chairman (Mr. Clay) a bill, the principal provisions of which were the admission of California with the existing boundaries, the establishment of territorial governments for Utah and New Mexico without the Wilmot Proviso, the settlement of the boundary controversy between New Mexico and Texas, the surrender of fugitive slaves, and the prohibition of the slave trade in the District of Columbia.

While this bill was under consideration, a motion was made by Mr. Turney of Tennessee to strike out the thirty-ninth section, which contained a proposal, to be offered to the acceptance of the people of Texas, for the settlement of their boundary controversy with New Mexico. On this motion Mr. Webster spoke as follows: —

I wish to make a few remarks upon this question, considering it a very important one, under all the aspects in which it is presented. This bill contains three leading subjects, the admission of California into the Union, the establishment of territorial governments for New Mexico and Utah, and the settlement of the boundary line between the United States or New Mexico and the State of Texas. I am in favor of each and every one of these subjects, and should be inclined to vote for them,

* Remarks in the Senate of the United States, on the 13th of June, 1850, on a Motion to strike out the thirty-ninth section of "The Compromise Bill," being the section relative to the Boundaries of Texas.

separately or together, as may best suit the convenience or the general judgment of the Senate, my own opinion having been well known from the beginning to be, that it would have been wiser to proceed with California as a separate measure. Here is now before us a bill providing for the three objects. That provision which relates to the establishment of the boundary between the territory of the United States and Texas is under immediate consideration, and the section embracing that part of the bill is now open to amendment. The present motion is, however, to strike out from the bill the whole section; that is, all that respects the United States and Texas.

Now, Sir, it appears to me that we shall have no question more important than this in the course of our deliberations in the Senate. It seems to me that it is one of the most material points connected with this subject, which gives us all so much general anxiety, the disposition of our territories newly acquired from Mexico.

Mr. President, there are different views entertained with respect to the manner in which these territories should be treated, whether a provision should now be made for establishing in New Mexico and Utah territorial governments in the common form, or whether, California being admitted, these territories should not be left for future consideration. I am most anxious, Sir, to take that course in this respect which shall be most conformable to our common practice heretofore, the most suitable to the occasion, and the most likely to produce a speedy settlement of all the various questions.

Now, Sir, before any territorial government can be established for New Mexico, it is clearly necessary that the boundary of New Mexico should be ascertained, or else defined by a provision simultaneous with that which establishes the government. But that is not all. There is evidently something in this case which goes much further. Some gentlemen are of opinion that the Territory of New Mexico should remain as she is until she is prepared to come in as a State. Well, Sir, it strikes me as highly improbable, if not impossible, that she ever can come in as a State, until we define her boundaries and know what really constitutes New Mexico. If we leave her as she is, how is it to be known who her people are? Who are to get together to form her constitution and apply for admission as a State? What is New Mexico? How is she limited and bounded?

Now I understand it to be admitted by gentlemen here, while Texas claims all the country east of the Rio del Norte up to the forty-second degree of north latitude, and while this claim of hers is not admitted, that she has some title or right, or some claim or plausible pretence of title or right, to a portion of the country between the Nueces and the Rio Grande. What portion, and how far to the north does that pretence or claim of right extend? How far above the common track which leads from Austin into Mexico, along the Presidio road? Where are its true limits? This is quite unsettled, and Texas, in the mean time, claims all along the line, not only up to El Paso del Norte, but still further, on to Santa Fé and Taos, and so to the forty-second degree of north latitude, embracing all that lies to the eastward of the Rio del Norte. If that be so, Sir, every body sees that it takes away a great portion of what has usually been considered as New Mexico. The fact is stated to be, and I suppose truly, that Texas has organized her civil government, not only up to El Paso del Norte, but beyond that, and has established civil jurisdiction some sixty or eighty miles above the Paso del Norte, claiming the whole of that country, with the right to establish her civil jurisdiction over the whole of it, just so soon as her own convenience requires it.

Now, I submit it to every one, what will be the state of things in New Mexico if these matters be not immediately adjusted? I should suppose all must see that things cannot remain as they are long, without some interposition by Congress. It is to be remembered that this territory is becoming Texas territory, in point of fact, every day. I understand an honorable member from Texas to say, that, in that part of the country which lies above the line contemplated by the committee, there are many voters who have actually attached themselves to the Texan government; that several hundred votes were cast last year, as in the exercise of municipal and political rights under the jurisdiction of Texas, by persons, many of whom live as far as seventy or eighty miles above the Paso del Norte, and others a little below.

Texas is a State with a regular constitution, a regular executive and legislative and judicial authority, and it is proposed now to leave New Mexico without any government to resist or contest the claims of Texas. How can that be considered a wise and practical mode of settling the question? The power is all on one side. There is now no authority, executive, legislative, or judicial, that can unitedly call itself the government of New Mexico. There are alcaldes, I suppose, in the cities and towns; but where is the political government, the head, the leading authority of New Mexico? Where is there any thing in New Mexico that can say that it represents the territory? There is nothing upon earth that can do so, nothing anywhere that can remonstrate against Texas. There is nothing that can assert its own rights against Texas. Who is there even that can memorialize Congress? There is nobody but individuals, and those individuals very much disposed, according to recent appearances, at least some of them, to attach themselves to Texas, perhaps from a sort of necessity of having some government. Now, Sir, under this aspect of the case, the time seems to me to be far distant when New Mexico will be able to present herself here as a State, proper to be admitted into this Union. Our young and amiable sister, Texas, is, even by her best friends, admitted to be in love with land. She seeks land, and the immensity of her territory as it is does not satisfy her appetite in that respect.

Sir, with respect to all that country that lies beyond the outer settlements of Texas, beyond San Antonio de Bexar, and thence stretching out to the Paso del Norte in a southwestern direction, I presume it is of little importance to whom it belongs, because I do not suppose that there is a more desert, arid section of country on the continent. The honorable Senator from Missouri * made out a pretty good case for what he called the bucolic region of New Mexico, that is, the banks of the Puerco, and, according to him, there were formerly a great number of sheep depastured along the banks of that river. If so, Sir, that was the exception to the general rule. I suppose that no one doubts that, in the whole country from the Nueces to the Rio Grande, and thence along north between the mountains of Guadalupe, and so also beyond the mountains, the land is of but little value to any body. I take it to be true, as was said by my friend from North Carolina † the other day, that the great want of the country is the want of water. It is true, also, that there is almost a total want of tim-

* Mr. Benton. † Mr. Mangum.

ber, although it is possible in that climate to get on somewhat better without fuel than without water. The expedition that went through there last year found many parts in which there is not a drop of water, sometimes for twenty miles, sometimes for thirty miles, sometimes for forty miles, and sometimes for seventy miles. That there are some few spots more favored is true; but it is certain that, throughout that whole region, there is one fatal want of water; and I understand that, even above the Paso del Norte, on the route to Santa Fé and Taos, there are long stretches where the traveller, be he Indian or be he white man, is driven away from the river by the near approach of the mountains, and is obliged to take his course along the plains; and that in one instance there is a distance of ninety miles to be traversed over these plains, in which he does not find a drop of water. Above this, I believe, the land and the climate are somewhat better.

Now I think that it will require all the population that we can secure to New Mexico to make her hereafter either a respectable Territory or a respectable State; and my opinion is, therefore, that this is of the utmost importance; and, to speak out plainly at once, I think this amendment places almost the whole of New Mexico entirely at the sovereign will and pleasure of Texas. I wish to rescue it from the grasp of Texas. I wish to preserve all of it, so that it may hereafter constitute a respectable political community. And I put it to gentlemen, whether they wish this bill to be passed or not; and, even if they have made up their minds to go against it, to say on their consciences whether it is not better to retain this provision in the bill, for the purpose of keeping New Mexico out of the hands of Texas? That is the precise question presented here to-day, and I think the country must take that view of it. What can New Mexico do against Texas, let her right be ever so good? I entertain a strong opinion, though not a decisive one; I am at least strongly inclined to the opinion that her right is good. But then what is right against might? And if this government neglects her, if she will not define her boundaries, and will not say what New Mexico has or what she is, but leaves that to be decided at some indefinite time hereafter, New Mexico will be pretty likely to disappear from the face of the country, — will become Texas. Texas will swallow her up.

Now I fully believe that this could be made a matter of judicial control and decision. Others, whose opinions are entitled to as much respect as mine, gentlemen connected with the government, think otherwise; and therefore, while they think otherwise, that mode of settlement will never be resorted to. The executive government, probably, would not institute a suit without the recommendation of Congress, which could hardly be obtained without much opposition. Certainly it would not be obtained soon; and if a suit were instituted, nobody can tell exactly when it would be terminated. In the mean time there is no reason to suppose that the executive government will take the responsibility of saying what the line between New Mexico and Texas legally is, and of maintaining that line by military force.

Such being the case, I will say that, as a point of practicable wisdom, it is every way just and expedient for Congress now, this day, to decide what are and what shall be the boundaries of New Mexico. For one, I wish that this line had been fixed at the north passage. Such was not the opinion of the committee; and such, as it appears, is not the opinion of the Senate; and, as the line now stands, it goes twenty miles to the north of that passage. Well, I had rather take that a great deal than to leave the whole matter unsettled; and therefore I repeat, that I wish most earnestly to call the attention of gentlemen who may not be in favor of the bill to the question, whether, if the bill is to be passed, it be not in the highest degree important now, in this bill, to settle the question of the boundary of New Mexico.

THE COMPROMISE BILL.*

ON the 3d of June, an amendment to the "Compromise Bill" was offered by Mr. Soulé, one of the Senators from Louisiana, which was substantially a substitute for some of its most important provisions. While this amendment was before the Senate, Mr. Webster made the following remarks, in vindication of some positions taken in his speech of the 7th of March.

ON the 7th of March, Sir, I declared my opinion to be, that there is not a square rod of territory belonging to the United States, the character of which, for slavery or no slavery, is not already fixed by some irrepealable law. I remain of that opinion. This opinion, Sir, has been a good deal canvassed in the country, and it has been the subject of complaints, sometimes respectful and decorous, and sometimes so loud and so empty as to become mere clamor. But I have seen no argument upon any question of law embraced in that opinion which shakes the firmness with which I hold it, or which leads me to doubt the accuracy of my conclusions as to that part of the opinion which regarded the true construction, or, I might with more propriety say, almost the literal meaning, of the resolutions by which Texas was admitted into the Union. I have heard no argument calculated in the slightest degree to alter that opinion. The committee, I believe, with one accord, concurred in it. A great deal of surprise, real or affected, has been expressed in the country at the announcement by me of that opinion, as if there were something new in it. Yet there need have been no surprise, for there was nothing new in it.

* Remarks made in the Senate of the United States, on the 17th of June, 1850.

Other gentlemen have expressed the same opinion more than once; and I myself, in a speech made here on the 23d of March, 1848, expressed the same opinion, almost in the same words; with which nobody here found any fault, at which nobody here cavilled or made question, and nobody in the country.

With respect to the other ground on which my opinion is founded, that is, the high improbability, in point of fact, that African slavery could be introduced and established in any of the territories acquired by us in pursuance of the late treaty with Mexico, I have learned nothing, heard nothing, from that day to this, which has not entirely confirmed that opinion. That being my judgment on this matter, I voted very readily and cheerfully to omit what is called the Wilmot Proviso from these territorial bills, or to keep it out, rather, when a motion was made to introduce it. I did so upon a very full and deep conviction, that no act of Congress, no provision of law, was necessary, in any degree, for that purpose; that there were natural and sufficient reasons and causes excluding for ever African slavery from those regions. That was my judgment, and I acted on it; and it is my judgment still. Those who think differently will, of course, pursue a different line of conduct, in accordance with their own judgments. That was my opinion then, and it has been strengthened by every thing that I have learned since; and I have no more apprehension to-day of the introduction or establishment of African slavery in these territories, than I have of its introduction into and establishment in Massachusetts.

Well, Sir, I have voted not to place in these territorial bills what is called the Wilmot Proviso, and by that vote have signified a disposition to exclude the prohibition, as a thing unnecessary. I am now called upon to vote upon this amendment, moved by the honorable member from Louisiana,* which provides that the States formed out of New Mexico and Utah shall have the right and privilege of making their own constitutions, and of presenting those constitutions to Congress conformably to the Constitution of the United States, with or without a prohibition against slavery, as the people of those Territories, when about to become States, may see fit.

* Mr. Soulé.

I do not see much practical utility in this amendment, I agree. Nevertheless, if I should vote, now that it is presented to me, against it, it might leave me open to the suspicion of intending or wishing to see that accomplished in another way hereafter which I did not choose to see accomplished by the introduction of the Wilmot Proviso. That is to say, it might seem as if, voting against that form of exclusion or prohibition, I might be willing still that there should be a chance hereafter to enforce it in some other way. Now I think that ingenuousness and steadiness of purpose, under these circumstances, compel me to vote for the amendment, and I shall vote for it. I do it exactly on the same grounds that I voted against the introduction of the proviso. And let it be remembered that I am now speaking of New Mexico and Utah, and other territories acquired from Mexico, and of nothing else. I confine myself to these; and as to them, I say that I see no occasion to make a provision against slavery now, or to reserve to ourselves the right of making such provision hereafter. All this rests on the most thorough conviction, that, under the law of nature, there never can be slavery in these territories. This is the foundation of all. And I voted against the proviso, and I vote now in favor of this amendment, for the reason that all restrictions are unnecessary, absolutely unnecessary; and as such restrictions give offence, and create a kind of resentment, as they create a degree of dissatisfaction, and as I desire to avoid all dissatisfaction, as far as I can, by avoiding all measures that cause it, and which are in my judgment wholly unnecessary, I shall vote now as I voted on a former occasion, and shall support the amendment offered by the honorable member from Louisiana. I repeat again, I do it upon the exact grounds upon which I declared, upon the 7th day of March, that I should resist the Wilmot Proviso.

Sir, it does not seem to strike other Senators as it strikes me, but if there be any qualification to that general remark which I made, or the opinion which I expressed on the 7th of March, that every foot of territory of the United States has a fixed character for slavery or no slavery; if there be any qualification to that remark, it has arisen here, from what seems to be an indisposition to define the boundaries of New Mexico; that is all the danger there is. All that is part of Texas was, by the resolutions of 1845, thrown under the general condition of the Texan territory; and let me say to gentlemen, that if, for want of defining the boundaries of New Mexico, by any proceeding or process hereafter, or by any event hereafter, any portion which they or I do not believe to be Texas should be considered to become Texas, then, so far, that qualification of my remark is applicable. And therefore I do feel, as I had occasion to say two or three days ago, that it is of the utmost importance to pass this bill, to the end that there may be a definite boundary fixed now, and fixed for ever, between the territory of New Mexico and Texas, or the limits of New Mexico and the limits of Texas. Here the question lies. If gentlemen wish to act efficiently for their own purposes, here it is, in my poor judgment, that they are called upon to act. And the thing to be done, and done at once, is to fix the boundaries of New Mexico.

Mr. President, when I see gentlemen from my own part of the country, no doubt from motives of the highest character and for most conscientious purposes, not concurring in any of these great questions with myself, I am aware that I am taking on myself an uncommon degree of responsibility. The fact, that gentlemen with whom I have been accustomed to act in the Senate took a different view of their own duties in the same case, naturally led me to reconsider my own course, to reëxamine my own opinions, to rejudge my own judgment. And now, Sir, that I have gone through this process, without prejudice, as I hope, and certainly I have done so under the greatest feeling of regret at being called upon by a sense of duty to take a step which may dissatisfy some to whom I should always be desirous of rendering my public course and every event and action of my public life acceptable, yet I cannot part from my own settled opinions. I leave consequences to themselves. It is a great emergency, a great exigency, that this country is placed in. I shall endeavor to preserve a proper regard to my own consistency. And here let me say, that neither here nor elsewhere has any thing been advanced to show that on this subject I have said or done any thing inconsistent, in the slightest degree, with any speech, or sentiment, or letter, or declaration that I ever delivered in my life; and all would be convinced of this if men would stop to consider and look at real differences and distinctions. But where all is general denunciation, where all is clamor, where all is idle and empty declamation, where there is no search after truth, no honest disposition to inquire whether one opinion is different from the other, why, every body, in that way of proceeding, may be proclaimed to be inconsistent.

Now, Sir, I do not take the trouble to answer things of this sort that appear in the public press. I know it would be useless. Those who are of an unfriendly disposition would not publish my explanations or distinctions if I were to make them. But, Sir, if any gentleman here has any thing to say on this subject, though I throw out no challenge, yet if any gentleman here chooses to undertake the task, and many there possibly are who think it an easy task, to show in what respect any thing that I said in the debate here on the 7th of March, or any thing contained in my letter to the gentlemen of Newburyport, is inconsistent with any recorded opinion of mine since the question of the annexation of Texas arose, in 1837, I will certainly answer him with great respect and courtesy, and shall be content to stand or fall by the judgment of the country.

Sir, my object is peace. My object is reconciliation. My purpose is, not to make up a case for the North, or to make up a case for the South. My object is not to continue useless and irritating controversies. I am against agitators, North and South. I am against local ideas, North and South, and against all narrow and local contests. I am an American, and I know no locality in America; that is my country. My heart, my sentiments, my judgment, demand of me that I shall pursue such a course as shall promote the good, and the harmony, and the union of the whole country. This I shall do, God willing, to the end of the chapter.

CALIFORNIA PUBLIC LANDS AND BOUNDARIES.*

MR. PRESIDENT, the amendment of the honorable member from Louisiana† respects that part of the present bill which proposes the immediate admission of California into the Union as a State; and the amendment is opposed to that immediate admission. It proposes, on the contrary, that the subject shall be referred back to the people of California; that certain conditions and modifications in the constitution of California shall be proposed to them, and that, if the people of California in convention shall accede to such conditions and modifications, then the President of the United States shall issue his proclamation announcing that fact, and thereupon California shall be admitted into the Union as a State.

The question, therefore, is, whether, upon the whole, it would be more advisable, under all the circumstances of the case, to admit California now, or to send her constitution back again, and postpone to some future and indefinite period her admission into the Union? In my opinion, Sir, it is highly expedient to admit California now. In my opinion, it is highly expedient to give her now a proper position in the Union, and to give her such powers as shall enable her to revolve among the other orbs of our system; and I really believe that that is the settled judgment of a great majority of the people of this country. If there be any question growing out of these territorial acquisitions on which there seems to be a general, I will not say a unanimous, public opinion, it is that, under the circumstances, it

* Remarks in the Senate on the 27th of June, 1850, the Amendment moved by Mr. Soulé being under consideration.

† Mr. Soulé.

is expedient and proper to admit California into the Union without further delay. She presents herself here with a sufficient population. She presents a constitution to which, in a general aspect, as a republican constitution, we can make no objection. The case is urgent and pressing. No new State has ever appeared asking for admission into the Union under circumstances so extraordinary and so striking; nor have the oldest of us seen a case presented of so peculiar a character. There is in the history of mankind, within my knowledge, no instance of such an extraordinary rush of people for private enterprise to one point on the earth's surface. It has been represented heretofore, that there are one hundred and fifty thousand people in California.* It would seem that on this very day there are fifty or sixty thousand persons traversing the great plains between Missouri and the Rocky Mountains, all bound to California. Other thousands are passing round Cape Horn; other thousands again crowd, press, fill up, and more than fill up, every conveyance that will take them to and from the Isthmus. So that it may be said, and truly said, that this very year will add a hundred thousand persons to the population of California. It is the most striking occurrence within our generation, or any generation, as far as respects any private enterprise, and the extraordinary rush of people to a given point upon the earth's surface. The capital of the Territory is supposed to contain thirty or forty thousand people; twelve hundred vessels have already been sent thither; three hundred and fifty or four hundred ships have been found riding in the harbor of San Francisco at the same time. In addition to the gold and all its other internal resources, California looks out upon India, and China, and Polynesia to the west, as we look out upon Europe to the east.

Now the question is, What is to be done with California? Sir, five years ago it happened to me to say, in a public discussion, that perhaps the time was not far distant when there would be established beyond the Rocky Mountains, and on the shore of the Western sea, a great Pacific republic, of which San Francisco would be the capital. I am overwhelmed by the appearance of the possible fulfilment of that prophecy so sud-

* This estimate proved, when the census was taken, to be considerably in excess.

denly. And, Sir, *that is the alternative, in my judgment.* I do not think it safe longer to delay the bringing of California into this Union, unless gentlemen are willing to contemplate the other part of that alternative. Other gentlemen have as good means of information of the state of opinion in California as I have; perhaps better. My information is such, at any rate, that I do not think it safe, if we intend to bring her into the Union at all, to defer that measure to another session of Congress, or to any time beyond that which is absolutely necessary for the despatch of the business of her admission. Then, I suppose, such being the general sentiment of the country, that it would also be the general sentiment of this and the other house of Congress; that is, that it is expedient, if there are no insurmountable obstacles, to bring California into the Union at once; and I do not understand the intention of the author of this amendment otherwise than that, if it were not for objections which he has propounded to the Senate, he should be willing to admit California at once. Now the question is, whether those objections are insurmountable or not? If they are, California must be kept out of the Union, let the consequences be what they may. But if they are not insurmountable, then I think, though things may exist which we might wish had been otherwise, it is a case of so much exigency and emergency, that we ought to admit California.

Let us come, then, at once to that point, and see what these objections are which have been suggested by the honorable member from Louisiana. They divide themselves into two classes. He says, in the first place, that, under the constitution of California, and by the bill unamended, there is no sufficient security that the United States will possess, enjoy, control, or have the right to dispose of the public domain or unappropriated lands in California. That is the first objection. The second relates to the boundaries of California, which he says are extravagantly large, in the first place; in the second place, unnatural; and in the third, impolitic and unfit to be made. Now, Sir, he proposes to remedy what he considers the first great deficiency of the bill, by sending back this constitution to California, and obtaining from a convention of that State an agreement, or compact, to the effect that the State of California shall never interfere with the public lands within the State, or with the primary disposal of them; nor shall ever tax them while held by the United States; nor shall tax non-resident proprietors higher than resident proprietors of the lands in that State shall be taxed. These are provisions which are, all of them, in this bill; but then the honorable member's argument is, that, as they are conditions which, from the nature of the case, can never receive the assent of the people of the State of California, because they can never be presented to them unless the constitution is sent back, they are void, and that the assent or consent of California to those conditions is necessary to make them valid and binding. His argument proceeds upon this idea: that, without some such stipulation or compact on the part of the State, the erection of a territory into a State, a political, and, in some respects, sovereign community, does necessarily establish in that sovereign community a control over the public domain; that when California becomes a State, *ipso facto* she will hold, possess, enjoy, and control the public lands; and this result he derives from an argument founded upon the nature of the sovereignty; because, he says, it is the essence of sovereign power to control the public domain.

Sir, we mislead ourselves often by using terms without sufficient accuracy, or terms not customarily found in the Constitution and laws. That the States are sovereign in many respects nobody doubts; that they are sovereign in all respects nobody contends. The term "sovereign" or "sovereignty" does not occur in the Constitution of the United States. The Constitution does not speak of the States as "sovereign States." It does not speak of this government as a "sovereign government." It avoids studiously the application of terms that might admit of different views, and the true idea of the Constitution of the United States, and also of the constitution of every State in the Union, is, that powers are conferred on the legislature, not by general, vague description, but by enumeration. The government of the United States holds no powers which it does not hold as powers enumerated in the Constitution, or as powers necessarily implied; and the same may be said of every State in the Union. The constitution of each State prescribes definitely the powers that shall belong to the government of the State. But if this were a true source of argument in this case, the honorable member would find that this implication arising from sovereignty would just as naturally adhere to the government of the United States as to that of the States. Certainly, many higher branches of sovereignty are in the government of the United States. The United States government makes war, raises armies, maintains navies, enters into alliances, makes treaties, and coins money; none of which acts of sovereignty are performed by a State government. Nevertheless, there are sovereign powers which the State governments do perform. They punish crimes, impose penalties, regulate the tenure of land, and exercise a municipal sovereignty over it.

Let me remark that this question is not new here. I found it in the Senate the first session that I took my seat here. There is a class of notions which run in a sort of periodical orbit. They come back upon us once in fifteen or twenty years. The idea that the sovereignty of a State necessarily carries with it the ownership of the public lands within its limits was rife here twenty years ago. It was discussed, considered, debated, exploded. It went off, and here it is back again, with exactly the same aspect that attended it then.

Sir, in the year 1828 or 1829, in 1828 I think it was, the legislature of Indiana took up this subject, passed these resolutions, and instructed her members of Congress to support them: —

"*Resolved*, That this State, being a sovereign, free, and independent State, has the exclusive right to the soil and eminent domain of all the unappropriated lands within her acknowledged boundaries; which right was reserved for her by the State of Virginia, in the deed of cession of the Northwestern Territory to the United States, being confirmed and established by the Articles of Confederacy and the Constitution of the United States.

"That our Senators in Congress be instructed, and our Representatives requested, to use every exertion in their power, by reason and argument, to induce the United States to acknowledge this vested right of the State, and to place her upon an equal footing with the original States in every respect whatsoever, as well in fact as in name."

One of the gentlemen (Mr. Hendricks) who represented Indiana at that time in the Senate, and who has recently deceased, performed the duty imposed on him by the instructions of the legislature, and brought forward a section, as an amendment to one of the graduation bills introduced by the honorable member from Missouri,* to that effect. In moving his amendment, Mr. Hendricks said: —

"It had become his duty to present to the Senate resolutions of the General Assembly of the State of Indiana, on the subject of the public lands within the limits of that State. These resolutions, said he, are similar in character to those of the State of Louisiana, a few days ago presented by a Senator from that State. They are also, in some degree, similar to the spirit of a memorial of the State of Illinois, recently presented to the Senate by a Senator from that State. In these resolutions, the legislature of Indiana has solemnly declared that the State, being sovereign, free, and independent, has the exclusive right to the soil and eminent domain of all the unappropriated lands within her acknowledged boundaries, and that this right was reserved to her by the State of Virginia in the deed of cession of the Northwestern Territory to the United States; grounds which, if tenable, as I verily believe they are, strongly appeal to the justice and to the pride of the Senators and Representatives of that magnanimous State."

"It is believed that the compact not to interfere with the primary disposal of the soil, and not to tax the lands for a specified period, cannot confer power on the federal government to hold the soil of that State for any other purposes than those pointed out by the Constitution, even if that compact had emanated from authority unquestionably competent to make it, and had been based on policy as unquestionable. There is no disposition to interfere with this compact as long as it has the form of existence in the statute-book. But its validity is questioned, having been made by the people of the Territory before the State was admitted into the Union; and its irrevocable character, as well as the perpetual obligation which it attempts to impose on the people of the State, is believed to be a dereliction from a fundamental principle of our institutions, which asserts the right of every free people to change their constitutions and laws, from time to time, as their wisdom and experience may direct. Nor does it seem to strengthen the pretension of right, to assert that the general government may hold the soil of the State as an individual may hold it; for it is by no means in that character she does hold. She holds as a sovereign, and subjects the soil of the State to the uncontrollable action of her legislative power."

Proceeding upon the ground that the public lands are the property of the State, he proposed to acknowledge that fact by this section in the graduation bill then before the Senate: —

"Sec. 6. *And be it further enacted*, That the public and unappropri-

* Mr. Benton.

ated lands within the limits of the new States shall be, and the same are hereby, ceded and relinquished in full property to the several States in which the same may be, on condition that such State shall not, at any time hereafter, put such lands into market at a lower minimum price than shall be established by law for the sale of public lands in the territories; and on condition that the Indian title to lands within the limits of any State shall hereafter be extinguished at the expense of such State."

On that occasion, Sir, the Senate was addressed much at length in support of the same proposition by a gentleman now holding an eminent station on the bench of the national judiciary,* who was then a member of Congress from Alabama. He maintained the same general idea. He said:—

"I have long entertained the opinion, that the United States cannot hold land in any State of the Union, except for the purposes enumerated in the Constitution; and whatever right they had to the soil while the country remained under territorial governments passed to the States formed over the same territory, on their admission into the Union on an equal footing with the old States."

The honorable member from Louisiana was only following these precedents. The argument of his able and learned speech was founded on the same general idea. Both gentlemen on that occasion, with the honorable member from Louisiana on this, rest their argument on the same supposed maxim of national law, or public law. On that occasion the gentlemen quoted from Vattel exactly what the member from Louisiana quotes now:—

"The general domain of the nation over the lands it inhabits is naturally connected with the empire, for, establishing itself in a vacant country, the nation certainly did not pretend to have the least dependence there on any other power. And how should an independent nation avoid having authority at home? How should it govern itself at its pleasure in the country it inhabits, if it cannot truly and absolutely dispose of it? And how should it have the full and absolute domain of the place in which it has no command? Another's sovereignty, and the right it comprehends, must take away its freedom of disposal."

Nothing is more just than that doctrine of Vattel properly

* Mr. Justice McKinley.

understood. If a nation establishes itself in a country existing *without an ownership*, why, then the vacant lands become its own. But if a number of persons, occupying land that is owned by, or living in a country that is under, another government, establish a political community, it follows of course that by no act of theirs can they divest the original ownership. The United States own this territory. The land is theirs, theirs by acquisition. It belongs to the government of the United States and the people of the United States. Now, if people owning those parts of the country appropriated heretofore to individual uses by the king of Spain, or if people resident there without title, establish a political community, by what process can it be made out that they become entitled to the whole country? The doctrine of Vattel, as I have shown, is only applicable to a case where a nation enters into a country *vacant of ownership;* and if the gentleman whose words I have read had been kind enough to read the whole of the authority from which he quoted, he would have found, I think, exactly the proper distinction. But he left off in the middle of a paragraph from Vattel's work. It goes on thus: —

"The general domain of the nation over the lands she inhabits is naturally connected with the empire; for, in establishing herself in a vacant country, the nation certainly does not intend to possess it in subjection to any other power. And can we suppose an independent nation not vested with the absolute command in her domestic concerns? Thus we have already observed, that, in taking possession of a country, the nation is presumed to take possession of its government at the same time. We shall here proceed further, and show the natural connection of these two rights in an independent nation. How could she govern herself at her own pleasure in the country she inhabits, if she cannot truly and absolutely dispose of it? And how could she have the full and absolute domain of a place where she has not the command? Another's sovereignty, and the right it comprehends, must deprive her of the free disposal of that place. Add to this the eminent domain which constitutes a part of the sovereignty, and you will the better perceive the intimate connection existing between the domain and the sovereignty of the nation. And, accordingly, what is called the *high domain*, which is nothing but the domain of the body of the nation, or of the sovereign who represents it, is everywhere considered as inseparable from the sovereignty. The *useful domain*, or the domain confined to the rights that may belong to an individual in the state, may be separated from the sovereignty, and nothing prevents the possibility of its belonging to a nation in places that are not under her jurisdiction. Thus many sovereigns have fiefs and other possessions in the territories of another prince. In these cases they possess them in the manner of private individuals.

"The sovereignty, united to the domain, establishes the jurisdiction of the nation in her territories, or the country that belongs to her. It is her province, or that of her sovereign, to exercise justice in all the laces under her jurisdiction; to take cognizance of the crimes committed, and the differences that arise in the country."

Now, that is precisely this case. The government of land, in all that belongs to its title, transmission, inheritance, and alienation, belongs to the municipal authority within whose limits it lies. That is unquestionable. But then there is nothing to prevent another sovereign from possessing the *dominium utile*, the useful domain, or any portion of it. This government may as well hold the lands in California as any individual in the United States. The only difference is this, that the government of the United States holds the lands only for one great purpose; that is, to sell. It holds them in trust to sell for the benefit of the government and people of the United States; and every acre, as soon as sold, falls under the dominion of the municipal sovereign, and is subject to all the rules and regulations prescribed by the local government. The only exception is this; that, in regard to the lands of the United States, that is established by law which, in regard to individuals, might be established by contract; namely, that up to a certain period, or for a certain time, those lands thus the property of the United States shall be so far excluded from the municipal sovereignty under which they are placed, as that they shall not be subject to taxation, or, being owned by non-residents, they shall not be taxed higher than if owned by residents. That is the only exception; and it is as competent to be made between an individual and the State where the land lies, as it is to be imposed by act of Congress.

Sir, there are many instances of States holding lands within the sphere of their own government, and without the sphere of their own government. I think I have understood that, with all her sovereignty, the State of New Jersey never possessed any public domain, nor authority over ungranted lands. All fell, in that State, I believe, into the possession of the original proprietors; and so it happened in a great portion of New York. Massachusetts claimed a great portion of the western part of New York, and her title to it was acknowledged. She sold her title to Messrs. Gorham and Phelps, and they sold to the Holland Land Company; and thus near one third of that State, perhaps, was held by individuals or corporations. That was never supposed to be any infringement on the rights of sovereignty of New York. The same thing happened in other States.

Now the question of sovereignty in this case, or its effect, by implication, on the public domain, is one that has been thoroughly considered, and clearly and fully decided. The history of the laws and usages of the country in this particular has been fully developed by the honorable member from Illinois;* and I will not go over the track he has trodden. He has shown the precedents taken together to be one way. There may be exceptions here and there; but the general idea has been, in the creation of a State, that its admission as a State has no effect at all on the property of the United States lying within its limits. But, Sir, it is hardly worth while for me, in this state of the atmosphere, to argue this point much at length, as it is settled and decided by the highest judicial authority of the country, precisely and explicitly.

The case will be found in 3d Howard. The judgment in that case was pronounced by the gentleman to whom I referred as having given an opinion quite the other way when he was a member of Congress. Now, Sir, the Supreme Court of the United States, in 1845, say this, excluding all idea that the title to the lands depends on any contract made with the new State. This is the decision of the court: —

"We therefore think that the United States hold the public lands within the new States by force of the deeds of cession, and the statutes connected with them, and not by any municipal sovereignty which it may be supposed they possess, or have reserved by compact with the new States, for that particular purpose.

"Full power is given to Congress 'to make all needful rules and regulations respecting the territory or other property of the United States.' This authorized the passage of all laws necessary to secure the rights of

* Mr. Douglas.

the United States to the public lands, and to provide for their sale, and to protect them from taxation.

"And all constitutional laws are binding on the people, in the new States and the old ones, whether they consent to be bound by them or not. Every constitutional act of Congress is passed by the will of the people of the United States, expressed through their representatives on the subject-matter of the enactment; and when so passed, it becomes the supreme law of the land, and operates by its own force on the subject-matter, in whatever State or Territory it may happen to be. The proposition, therefore, that such a law cannot operate upon the subject-matter of its enactment without the express consent of the people of the new States where it may happen to be, contains its own refutation, and requires no further examination."

While that decision of the Supreme Court stands, the authority of the United States over the lands lying in the States is based on the law of Congress. The argument of the honorable member from Louisiana is, that, this being a condition, the assent of the other party or side, or the entering into a compact, is indispensable. But this decision of the Supreme Court precisely and exactly overrules all that, as the honorable member will see. If it had happened that the words in this bill were a reservation, or were understood so, his argument would have lost even its apparent force. But it is enough to say that it has been decided directly and distinctly, at every point, that the authority of the United States does so far extend as, by force of itself, *proprio vigore*, to exempt the public lands from taxation, when new States are created in the territory in which the lands lie.

Then, Sir, what has become of all this danger to the public lands? A compact would make our title no better. It is good enough without it; and we need no compact. The language of the decision is explicit; and therefore I think the member from Illinois was entirely right when he proposed the law which he did, the act for the admission of California, omitting all reference to the idea of compact. The third section of this bill was drafted to satisfy doubts. Exceptions had been taken, and it was thought this section would satisfy and remove those exceptions. It was introduced for that laudable and proper purpose; but it stands, according to the decision to which I have referred, just as well without the third section as with it. What is there to overturn the whole current of our history? What is there to show, in this case, that California has any intention of claiming the ownership of the public lands, as a consequence of her State sovereignty? Why, so far from that, the constitution of California acknowledges the right of the United States to those lands. It goes on, in the ninth article, to provide how those lands which may be granted them by the United States shall be disposed of by the legislature. Is not that an express admission that the public lands within her territory belong to the United States? We must proceed according to, or we must regard, the established precedent in this case; and if any thing be established by law, if any thing be settled by the experience of the government, in the course of the various admissions of States, (nearly half of all the existing States now in the Union,) if any thing is settled by the solemn decision of the court of highest judicature in the country, it is that no such thing as an implication of control over the public lands of the United States arises from the creation of a State, founded on any idea that the public domain necessarily adheres to State sovereignty. Such a notion has never prevailed in the counsels of the country.

Now, Sir, I really hope the honorable member from Louisiana will reconsider the subject; that he will look at what has been decided; that, in this important emergency, he will consider whether it is worth his while to stand on technicalities, and whether it is not rather his duty to conform to the usages and practices of the laws and judicature of the country? The honorable member is younger than most of us, but he will allow me to say, that it is very doubtful whether, in his career as a public man, however long it may be, he will arrive at a more important exigency in the affairs of the country than is now before us. He has taken an important part, and a successful part, in some amendments to the bill. He has accomplished that which he and his friends think important in respect to the territorial governments. Will he not now help us to accomplish his own and a higher work? Will he not reconsider his objections to the admission of California, so far as those objections arise to which I have adverted? This is a common case, an ordinary case; every doubt about it is shut up and concluded by solemn decisions, so far as this objection goes, and ought to be withheld from opposition to the admission of California.

Then there is another objection. He says that the boundaries are wrong, extraordinarily large, unnatural, and impolitic. Now, Sir, these are questions in a great measure depending upon the peculiar circumstances of the case, and the situation, soil, surface, and climate of the country. At an early part of the session, I expressed an opinion, which I still hold, that, if the subject were before us now, we could not make a better boundary for California than is made in her constitution. I came to that opinion from my information respecting the formation of the country, and all the circumstances connected with it. The Senator says the territory of California is three times greater than the average extent of the new States of the Union. Well, Sir, suppose it is. We all know that it has more than three times as many mountains, inaccessible and rocky hills, and sandy wastes, as are possessed by any State of the Union. But how much is there of useful land? how much that may be made to contribute to the support of man and of society? These ought to be the questions. Well, with respect to that, I am sure that everybody has become satisfied that, although California may have a very great sea-board, and a large city or two, yet that the agricultural products of the whole surface now are not, and never will be, equal to one half part of those of the State of Illinois; no, nor yet a fourth, or perhaps a tenth part. In the first place, the entire country, extending from the eastern bottom of the Sierra Nevada, as far as the Gila, is a desert of sand. That takes off thirty or forty thousand square miles of the whole territory, and it is a pretty important reduction. Then, look again at the mountains. There is undoubtedly a long valley on the Sacramento and San Joaquin of tolerably good land, and there may be some good land between the coast mountains and the sea; but, on the whole, nobody will say that, in quantity of good land, or of tolerably good land, there is any excess; on the contrary, there is far less than belongs to most of the new States.

Then there is another consideration. If you separate South California from North California, what will be the value of South California by itself? Why, look upon the map and the question will be answered. Suppose we run the line of 36° 30′ from the sea across to New Mexico; what have you? You have mountains, and you have those vast tracts of land east of the mountains; but from the best information I can obtain, and I have consulted what I suppose every one concedes is the best authority, there cannot be at most, within what would constitute the territory of South California, more than five thousand square miles of good land. Beyond that all is desert lands and mountains. I speak now of lands that may be tilled and cultivated. We must, as I have said, look at climate as well as the surface of the land. Gentlemen will please to remember, that, in this part of California, eight months in every year roll on without a drop of rain falling, and there is not within the whole of it any land whatever that can be cultivated *without irrigation.* So small are the streams, when you depart from those two rivers, the Sacramento and the San Joaquin, that they do not supply water for the cultivation of the very small portion of the land that otherwise might be made tillable. What, then, will be the value of this territory? The gentleman from Louisiana contended for the rights of the South in regard to it. Where is there any value in it? Is it any thing more than a mere nominal right, if it be that? Can it be of any use whatever? Could the South make any use of that territory if it were now a territory, and free from any restraint whatever, which they cannot make of it as part of a State? I think, therefore, that it is a dispute where there is no substantial value in the matter contested.

Mr. President, we ought to look to what is the most practicable thing we can do. The member from Louisiana desires to draw across the territory the line of 36° 30′, the boundary commonly called the Missouri Compromise. Now, is that a practicable measure? Does the gentleman, or do his friends, suppose that, either now or hereafter, by this Congress or the next, any such thing can be done? Looking at the fact, in the first place, that this Southern California is part of California, and within her prescribed boundaries, and next, to the known state of opinion in that region, I have yet to learn, (though I have heard it suggested to the contrary,) after some diligent examination of the proceedings of the convention, that there is any disposition or wish, on the part of the people, from Monterey down to San Diego, to remain by themselves, or form a State by themselves. I find that a member of the convention, Mr Carrillo, I think, from San Angeles, in the early part of the debate, having in the excitement of discussion with some northern members suggested such an idea, afterwards withdrew it in the further progress of the debate, as will be found on page 446 of the report. And I see no evidence from the country to the south of 36° 30′ that it is desirous to set up or to have a government for itself, or to be otherwise associated in government than it is. It is also to be remembered, Mr. President, that this Lower California is the old part of California, and has been settled from one hundred and fifty to two hundred years. Its habits are fixed, and, although not a subject to dwell on, it may be fit to refer to it. So far as I see, in the debates in the California convention, the indications of a fixed purpose to exclude slavery from all parts of California, that sentiment was most strongly expressed by persons, members of the convention, coming from this old part, this southern part, the lower part of California; and therefore I do not see that there is any human probability of their consenting to its admission. Is it not better, then, to take this bill as it stands? We have determined the question in regard to the territories, and, taking it as it stands under the constitution of California, within her borders, and looking to the practical, I may say the certain, operation of things, is it not our bounden duty to bring California into the Union?

Mr. President, the idea most urgent and pressing on my mind in all this matter is, that it is our duty to *accomplish something* on the subject of these territories, to accomplish something that will be as satisfactory to all parts of the country as we can make it. I had no hand in introducing these territories into the Union; I have no responsibility, therefore, for the evils that spring out of that act. But here they are upon us. I wish to deal with the subject in the fairest, most expedient, and just manner, and, according to my fixed opinion, there is nothing to be gained by our discussing, or applying, or agitating the vexed matter of slavery over any of these territories. I wish for my part, as an American, or one who desires to carry on and maintain this government, to see a course adopted that will give all the satisfaction we can give, and that will accomplish something towards restoring peace and quiet to the Union.

Mr. President, as has already been said, and as is known to

us all, we have been here six or seven months. We are called upon to make some disposition of these territories. I think that before all, in regard to time, is the question of the admission of California; and I hope, therefore, that we shall have to-day, or when the question is taken, such a vote on the proposition of the Senator from Louisiana as will decide the case, and show that the judgment of the Senate, as it is of the whole country, is, that California should be admitted without further delay than is necessary by the terms of the act.

I hope, therefore, without going into an elaborate professional argument, that the member from Louisiana will see that there is nothing to dispute about; will see that, without any act of Congress, there is no danger that California will undertake to run away with the public lands, or undertake to tax the public lands or non-residents; and therefore, in respect to California, that we may have a vote which shall be decisive, and so far show to the country that, as to this part of the case, it is a determined question.

The next day (28th June) Mr. Webster spoke as follows, on the same subject, in reply to Mr. Soulé: —

I shall occupy but a very brief time, I hope, in the remarks which I shall make in reply to the honorable member from Louisiana, rather by way of an explanation of what I have heretofore said, than as a discussion of the subject anew. The question really between us, as a substantial question, is this, if there be any; namely, whether the assent or agreement of California is necessary, in order to secure to the United States the property in the public lands, or public domain, now belonging to the United States, and lying within the proposed boundaries of California? That is the question. Is it necessary that something further be done on the part of California to make sure the title of the United States, and their possession and enjoyment to and of the public lands? The honorable gentleman holds the affirmative of that proposition, and, with proper deference, I hold the negative. And I stand upon the history of the country, from the period of the admission of the first State where there was public land intended to be disposed of for the benefit of the United States, I mean Ohio, and that was in the year 1803. The honorable member has said, that, though in the act admitting Ohio there is a condition inserted, as there is here, that the public lands shall not be taxed, there is no stipulation by Ohio that the primary disposal of the soil shall not be interfered with; and that either from the consideration that without any such condition the primary disposition of the soil could not be interfered with by the State, or from the fact that a proper provision, applicable to the whole of the Northwestern Territory, had been already inserted in the Ordinance of 1787. I care not which way it be taken. What I mean to say is this: that from the first establishment of States in this Union over territory possessed by the United States, or over limits within which the United States had more or less public land, it has not been regarded as a part of the public law of America that the States, by merely being created States, by any implication arising from their sovereignty, or otherwise, have obtained, or could obtain, any right whatever to the public property of the United States within their limits. Such, I understand, has been the whole history of the country; and such was precisely the decision of the Supreme Court in the case referred to by me yesterday. The honorable member from Louisiana is kind enough to admit that, if this question were to be discussed in a forensic form, if we were now before a court to settle this question as a question of law, that the decision would be against him.

MR. SOULÉ. — Will the Senator allow me to say, that what I stated was, that, if we were in another forum, the authority quoted by the distinguished Senator would carry with it greater weight than it would be entitled to in this body?

Let me ask, why should that authority, if quoted to-day in the Supreme Court, have any greater respect or weight attached to it than if quoted here? The suggestion of the honorable member was, that this is a political question. It is just the question which has been decided in the case referred to. It is no question of expediency, no question of wisdom or folly, of prudence or imprudence in matters of political concern. It is just exactly a question of public law. It turns on the effect of the treaty with Spain of 1798, upon the provisions of the Constitution and the acts of Congress admitting Alabama into the Union. That is a judicial question emphatically, a question of high public law; and is just exactly the same question here to-day that it was when before the Supreme Court. And, however we decide it here, if dispute arises about it, it must go back before the same tribunal to be there again adjudged. It is, therefore, no question of political expediency, as I have said, and no question of what is wise or unwise, but a question of constitutional law; and that question has been decided by the highest tribunal in this government. And it has been decided, as I should have said yesterday, and perhaps did say, not upon any ground of conflict between the sovereign power in this government and the sovereign power in a State government. Not at all. The court rejected that ground. The court proceeded upon the idea, that the local sovereignty necessarily had control over all lands lying within its limits, except so far as it had parted with that control to individuals, and except so far as the United States, by virtue of the constitutional power of Congress, retained control over the public domain lying within such State.

The honorable member has said, with great propriety, that, if we separate the useful domain from the sovereignty, why, then the useful domain may inure to individuals, as well as to governments; and the gentleman will remember that I said the very same thing yesterday, in just so many terms. But, then, the gentleman seems to alarm us by the danger of this construction. He says it would enable this government to grasp all the lands lying within a State, and establish a federal tenantry within that State. I think the grasp of the gentleman's imagination, in this respect, is far wider than any possible grasp of jurisdiction by this government. He must take along with the general proposition the proper limitation; and that is, that the United States hold these public lands within a State only for sale and settlement, or other proper disposal. The language of all our history, of the cessions, the Ordinance, the Constitution, and all the laws, is in accordance with this idea. The United States hold the lands, not to cultivate, not to lease, but simply to sell or dispose of. They protect the lands till sold or disposed of, and there their authority ends; and every acre, when sold, comes under the proper dominion of the local sovereignty.

The honorable member thinks I did him some injustice in omitting to notice what was contained in his amendment in respect to the mines. I certainly did not intend any injustice or any omission. But it struck me that the question was just the same in regard to the mines as in regard to the ordinary lands which the United States obtained from Mexico by the treaty. What is true of one must be true of the other. Whatever was the government right of Mexico, either to the lands or mines, passes to the government of the United States. Whatever right, in lands or mines, had passed from the government of Mexico into private ownership remains in such ownership, exactly as if the sovereignty had never been changed. Now, it is of no sort of consequence to this argument, or the question arising in this case, what were the laws of Mexico, whether derived from Spain, or established by her own sovereignty, after she had been separated from Spain. So far as private rights were vested in lands or mines, they will remain vested, and every thing that still adhered to the sovereignty of Mexico has passed to the United States, to be disposed of as the United States shall think proper. If there be public domain in the mineral lands, the United States will be entitled to hold them and to dispose of them; and if individuals were entitled to hold any part of them, they will be entitled to continue to hold them. The honorable member's amendment proposes that California shall not obstruct or impede any control which the United States may wish to exercise over the mining region. Need we take a bond from California, that she will not interpose her power to obstruct the Constitution and laws of the United States? Any thing done, or to be done, or omitted to be done, by California, can neither enlarge nor diminish the power of the United States over the lands in California. Nothing is clearer, as a general rule, than that the constitutional powers of Congress can no more be enlarged by the assent of States than they can be diminished by their dissent.

The honorable member alludes again to what he considers a possible danger, of great magnitude to the rest of the Union, from the large boundaries assigned to California; since he thinks there may be within these boundaries one, or two, or three millions of people, at some time to come. Pray, Mr. President, will the honorable member allow me to ask if he supposes the division of the territory into two Territories or two States will tend to retard the population of the whole, so that there will not be, in the whole of the two States, as great a population as there would be in one? I did say yesterday, and said truly, that I thought the case a very urgent and important one; that I saw danger, and great danger, likely to arise from further delay in admitting California into the Union. These apprehensions may have been unfounded; but they were real, genuine, and honest. We take from her the income of her ports, we take her commercial revenues, without affording her any thing in return. How long is it likely that such a state of things will be continued, and be satisfactory to the people of California? But, says the honorable member, is it possible that California dreams of secession? No, Mr. President; I hope she does not dream of any thing of that sort; but she thinks of accession. She must come into the Union before she can go out of it. I think that is a plain proposition. The gentleman has stated, truly enough, that there are ties that bind the people of California to the United States. I hope these ties will be found to exist always, and in all their force. I hope, too, that the argument will be applied, as it may be with equal force, in places not so far off as California. I hope these ties will have a prevalence among the people everywhere and always, which will secure their attachment to the Union.

Mr. King. Mr. President, I wish to call the attention of the honorable Senator to that part of the amendment of the Senator from Louisiana, which relates to the taxing of the public lands. Is the honorable Senator prepared to give his opinion with respect to the power vested in the State of California, if brought into the Union without any relinquishment of that right? Does he think that the power to tax the public lands of the United States does not and will not exist in the State of California?

That principle is entirely embraced within the opinion of the Supreme Court. The power of taxing the public domain is completely denied to the States by virtue of the general authority of Congress. And, say the court, "by virtue of that authority which enables them to make rules and regulations with respect to the territory, the new States, without any compact, can neither interfere with the primary disposal of the soil, nor tax the public lands."

Mr. Soulé's amendment was disagreed to by a vote of ayes 19, nays 36.

LAST ILLNESS AND DEATH OF GENERAL TAYLOR.*

On the 9th of July, 1850, the "Compromise Bill" being under discussion, Mr. Butler of South Carolina was addressing the Senate, but gave way to Mr. Webster, who rose and said: —

Mr. President, — I have permission from the member from South Carolina to interrupt the progress of his speech, in order to make a solemn and mournful suggestion to the Senate. The intelligence which within the last few moments has been received indicates that a very great misfortune is now impending over the country. It is supposed by medical advisers and others that the President of the United States cannot live many hours. This intimation comes in a shape so authentic, and through so many channels of communication, and all tending to the same result, that I have thought it my duty to move the Senate to follow the example which has already been set in the other branch of the national legislature.

At half-past eleven o'clock to-day I called at tne President's mansion to inquire after his health. I was informed that he had passed a very bad night; that he was exceedingly ill this morning, but that at that moment he was more easy and more composed. I had hardly reached my seat in the Senate when it was announced to me that the fever had suddenly returned upon him with very alarming symptoms; that appearances of congestion were obvious; and that it was hardly possible his life could be prolonged through the day.

With the permission, therefore, of my honorable friend from

* Remarks in the Senate of the United States, on the 9th and 10th of July, 1850.

South Carolina, who, I am sure, shares those feelings on this occasion which quite disqualify us for the performance of our duties, even in this very important crisis of public affairs, I venture to move the Senate that it do now adjourn.

The Senate accordingly adjourned.

On the next day, July 10th, the following message was received from the Vice-President, Mr. Fillmore: —

"*Washington*, *July* 10, 1850.

"Fellow-citizens of the Senate and of the House of Representatives:

"I have to perform the melancholy duty of announcing to you that it has pleased Almighty God to remove from this life Zachary Taylor, late President of the United States. He deceased last evening, at the hour of half-past ten o'clock, in the midst of his family and surrounded by affectionate friends, calmly and in the full possession of all his faculties. Among his last words were these, which he uttered with emphatic distinctness: 'I have always done my duty; I am ready to die; my only regret is for the friends I leave behind me.'

"Having announced to you, fellow-citizens, this most afflicting bereavement, and assuring you that it has penetrated no heart with deeper grief than mine, it remains for me to say that I propose, this day, at twelve o'clock, in the hall of the House of Representatives, in the presence of both houses of Congress, to take the oath prescribed by the Constitution, to enable me to enter on the execution of the office which this event has devolved on me.

"MILLARD FILLMORE."

Mr. Webster then submitted the following resolutions: —

"*Resolved*, That the two houses will assemble this day in the hall of the House of Representatives, at twelve o'clock, to be present at the administration of the oath prescribed by the Constitution to the late Vice-President of the United States, to enable him to discharge the powers and duties of the office of President of the United States, devolved on him by the death of Zachary Taylor, late President of the United States.

"*Resolved*, That the Secretary of the Senate present the above resolution to the House of Representatives, and ask its concurrence therein."

These resolutions having been unanimously agreed to, Mr. Downs of Louisiana, as one of the Senators of the State of which General Taylor was a citizen, made a feeling address to the Senate on the melancholy event, and concluded by moving the following resolutions: —

"Whereas it has pleased Divine Providence to remove from this life Zachary Taylor, late President of the United States, the Senate, sharing in the general sorrow which this melancholy event must produce, is desirous of manifesting its sensibility on this occasion: Therefore,

"*Resolved*, That a committee, consisting of Messrs. Webster, Cass and King, be appointed on the part of the Senate to meet such committee as may be appointed on the part of the House of Representatives, to consider and report what measures it may be deemed necessary to adopt to show the respect and affection of Congress for the memory of the illustrious deceased, and to make the necessary arrangements for his funeral.

"*Ordered*, That the Secretary of the Senate communicate the foregoing resolution to the House of Representatives."

Mr. Webster then addressed the Senate as follows: —

MR. SECRETARY, — At a time when the great mass of our fellow-citizens are in the enjoyment of an unusual measure of health and prosperity, throughout the whole country, it has pleased Divine Providence to visit the two houses of Congress, and especially this house, with repeated occasions for mourning and lamentation. Since the commencement of the session, we have followed two of our own members to their last home; and we are now called upon, in conjunction with the other branch of the legislature, and in full sympathy with that deep tone of affliction which I am sure is felt throughout the country, to take part in the due solemnities of the funeral of the late President of the United States.

Truly, Sir, was it said in the communication read to us, that a "great man has fallen among us." The late President of the United States, originally a soldier by profession, having gone through a long and splendid career of military service, had, at the close of the late war with Mexico, become so much endeared to the people of the United States, and had inspired them with so high a degree of regard and confidence, that, without solicitation or application, without pursuing any devious paths of policy, or turning a hair's breadth to the right or left from the path of duty, a great, and powerful, and generous people saw fit, by popular vote and voice, to confer upon him the highest civil authority in the nation. We cannot forget that, as in other instances so in this, the public feeling was won and carried away, in some degree, by the *éclat* of military renown. So it has been always, and so it always will be, because high respect for noble deeds in arms has been and always will be, outpoured from the hearts of the members of a popular government.

But it will be a great mistake to suppose that the late President of the United States owed his advancement to high civil trust, or his great acceptableness with the people, to military talent or ability alone. I believe, Sir, that, associated with the highest admiration for those qualities possessed by him, there was spread throughout the community a high degree of confidence and faith in his integrity, and honor, and uprightness as a man. I believe he was especially regarded as both a firm and a mild man in the exercise of authority; and I have observed more than once, in this and in other popular governments, that the prevalent motive with the masses of mankind for conferring high power on individuals is a confidence in their mildness, their paternal, protecting, prudent, and safe character. The people naturally feel safe where they feel themselves to be under the control and protection of sober counsel, of impartial minds, and a general paternal superintendence.

I suppose, Sir, that no case ever happened, in the very best days of the Roman republic, when a man found himself clothed with the highest authority in the state under circumstances more repelling all suspicion of personal application, of pursuing any crooked path in politics, or of having been actuated by sinister views and purposes, than in the case of the worthy, and eminent, and distinguished, and good man whose death we now deplore.

He has left to the people of his country a legacy in this. He has left them a bright example, which addresses itself with peculiar force to the young and rising generation; for it tells them that there is a path to the highest degree of renown, straight onward, steady, without change or deviation.

Mr. Secretary, my friend from Louisiana* has detailed shortly the events in the military career of General Taylor. His service through his life was mostly on the frontier, and always a hard service, often in combat with the tribes of Indians along the frontier for so many thousands of miles. It has been justly remarked, by one of the most eloquent men

* Mr. Downs.

whose voice was ever heard in these houses,* that it is not in Indian wars that heroes are celebrated, but that it is there that they are formed. The hard service, the stern discipline, devolving upon all those who have a great extent of frontier to defend, often, with irregular troops, being called on suddenly to enter into contests with savages, to study the habits of savage life and savage war, in order to foresee and overcome their stratagems, all these things tend to make hardy military character.

For a very short time, Sir, I had a connection with the executive government of this country; and at that time very perilous and embarrassing circumstances existed between the United States and the Indians on the borders, and war was actually carried on between the United States and the Florida tribes. I very well remember that those who took counsel together on that occasion officially, and who were desirous of placing the military command in the safest hands, came to the conclusion, that there was no man in the service more fully uniting the qualities of military ability and great personal prudence than Zachary Taylor; and he was appointed to the command.

Unfortunately, his career at the head of this government was short. For my part, in all that I have seen of him, I have found much to respect and nothing to condemn. The circumstances under which he conducted the government for the short time he was at the head of it have been such as perhaps not to give him a very favorable opportunity of developing his principles and his policy, and carrying them out; but I believe he has left on the minds of the country a strong impression, first, of his absolute honesty and integrity of character; next, of his sound, practical good-sense; and, lastly, of the mildness, kindness, and friendliness of his temper towards all his countrymen.

But he is gone. He is ours no more, except in the force of his example. Sir, I heard with infinite delight the sentiments expressed by my honorable friend from Louisiana who has just resumed his seat, when he earnestly prayed that this event might be used to soften the animosities, to allay party criminations and recriminations, and to restore fellowship and good

* Fisher Ames.

feeling among the various sections of the Union. Mr. Secretary, great as is our loss to-day, if these inestimable and inappreciable blessings shall have been secured to us even by the death of Zachary Taylor, they have not been purchased at too high a price; and if his spirit, from the regions to which he has scended, could see these results flowing from his unexpected and untimely end, if he could see that he had entwined a soldier's laurel around a martyr's crown, he would say exultingly, "Happy am I, that by my death I have done more for that country which I loved and served, than I did or could do by all the devotion and all the efforts that I could make in her behalf during the short span of my earthly existence."

Mr. Secretary, great as this calamity is, we mourn not as those without hope. We have seen one eminent man, and another eminent man, and at last a man in the most eminent station, fall away from the midst of us. But I doubt not there is a Power above us exercising over us that parental care that has guarded our progress for so many years. I have confidence still that the place of the departed will be supplied; that the kind, beneficent favor of Almighty God will still be with us, and that we shall be borne along, and borne upward and upward on the wings of his sustaining providence. May God grant that, in the time that is before us, there may not be wanting to us as wise men, as good men for our counsellors, as he whose funeral obsequies we now propose to celebrate!

THE COMPROMISE MEASURES.*

Mr. President, — It was my purpose, on Tuesday of last week, to follow the honorable member from South Carolina,† who was addressing the Senate on the morning of that day, with what I then had, and now have, to say upon the subject of this bill. But before the honorable member had concluded his remarks, it was announced to us that the late chief magistrate of the United States was dangerously ill, and the Senate was moved to adjourn. The solemn event of the decease of the President took place that evening.

Sir, various and most interesting reflections present themselves to the minds of men, growing out of that occurrence. The chief magistrate of a great republic died suddenly. Recently elected to that office by the spontaneous voice of his fellow-countrymen, possessing in a high degree their confidence and regard, ere yet he had had a fair opportunity to develop the principles of his civil administration, he fell by the stroke of death. Yet, Sir, mixed with the sad thoughts which this event suggests, and the melancholy feeling which spread over the

* A Speech delivered in the Senate of the United States, on the 17th of July, 1850, on the Bill reported by the Committee of Thirteen, commonly called "The Compromise Bill."

The following motto was prefixed to the Speech in the pamphlet edition: —

"Alas! alas! when will this speculating against fact and reason end? What will quiet these panic fears which we entertain of the hostile effect of a conciliatory conduct? Is all authority of course lost when it is not pushed to the extreme?

"All these objections being in fact no more than suspicions, conjectures, divinations, formed in defiance of fact and experience, they did not discourage me from entertaining the idea of conciliatory concession, founded on the principles which I have stated." — Edmund Burke.

† Mr. Butler.

whole country, the real lovers and admirers of our constitutional government, in the midst of their grief and affliction, found something consoling and gratifying. The executive head of a great nation had fallen suddenly; no disturbance arose; no shock was felt in the great and free republic. Credit, public and private, was in no way disturbed, and danger to the community or individuals was nowhere felt. The legislative authority was neither dissolved nor prorogued; nor was there any further interruption or delay in the exercise of the ordinary functions of every branch of the government, than such as was necessary for the indulgence, the proper indulgence, of the grief which afflicted Congress and the country. Sir, for his country General Taylor did not live long enough; but there were circumstances in his death so favorable for his own fame and character, so gratifying to all to whom he was most dear, that he may be said to have died fortunately.

> "That life is long which answers life's great end."

A gallant soldier, able and experienced in his profession, he had achieved all that was to be expected by him in that line of duty. Placed at the head of the government, as I have said, by the free voice of the people, he died in the full possession of the gratitude of his country. He died in the midst of domestic affections and domestic happiness. He died in the consciousness of duty performed. He died here, in the midst of the councils of his country; which country, through us, its organs, has bestowed upon him those simple, but grand and imposing rites, which the republic confers on the most distinguished of her sons.

> "Such honors Ilium to her hero paid,
> And peaceful slept the mighty Hector's shade."

He has run the race destined for him by Providence, and he sleeps with the blessings of his countrymen.

Mr. President, I proceed now to say upon the subject before us what it was my purpose then to have said. I begin by remarking, that the longer we stay in the midst of this agitating subject, the longer the final disposition of it is postponed, the greater will be the intensity of that anxiety which possesses my breast. I wish, Sir, so far as I can, to harmonize opinions. I wish to facilitate some measure of conciliation. I wish to consummate some proposition or other, that shall bring op-

35*

posing sentiments together, and give the country repose. It is not my purpose to-day to compare or contrast measures or plans which have been proposed. A measure was suggested by the President* in his message of 1848. The same measure, substantially, was again recommended by the late President,† in his message of 1849. Then there is before us this proposition of the Committee of Thirteen. I do not regard these as opposite, conflicting, or, to use the language of the day, antagonistical propositions at all. To a certain extent, they all agree. Beyond what was proposed either by Mr. Polk or by the late President, this report of the committee, and the bill now before us, go another step. Their suggestions were, and especially that of the late President, to admit California, and for the present to stop there. The bill before the Senate proposes to admit California, but also to make a proper provision, if the Senate deem the provision proper, for the Territories of New Mexico and Utah. I confess, Sir, my judgment from the first has been, that it was indispensable that Congress should make some provision for these Territories; but I have been indifferent whether the things necessary to be done should be done in one bill or in separate bills, except that, as a matter of expediency, it was and has been my opinion, from the beginning, that it would have been better to have proceeded measure by measure. That was a matter of opinion upon the expediency of the course. I was one of the Committee of Thirteen. Circumstances called me to my home during its deliberations; and the general opinion of the committee at that time seemed to be, and I thought the better opinion, in favor of beginning with California, and then taking up the other measures in their order. Upon further consideration, the committee, very fairly, I doubt not, and in the exercise of their best judgment and discretion, thought fit to unite the three things which are in this bill. Well, Sir, whether singly or together, each and every one of these objects meets my approbation, and they are all, in my judgment, desirable.

In the first place, I think it is a desirable object to admit California. I do not conceal from myself, nor do I wish to conceal from others, that California is before us with some degree

* Mr. Polk. † General Taylor.

of irregularity stamped upon her proceedings. She has not been through the previous process of territorial existence. She has formed her constitution without our consent. But I consider, Sir, that California, from the extraordinary circumstances which have attended her birth and progress to the present moment, entitles herself, by the necessity of the case, to an exemption from the ordinary rules. Who expected to see such a great community spring up in such an incredibly short time? Who expected to see a hundred or a hundred and fifty thousand people engaged in such an employment, with so much activity, and enterprise, and commerce, drawing to themselves the admiration and regard of the whole world, in the period of a few months? Well, Sir, she comes to us with a constitution framed upon republican models, and conformable to the Constitution of the United States; and under these circumstances, still regarding her application as premature and irregular, I am for admitting her, as there has been nothing done which her admission on our part will not cure. She will be lawfully in the Union if we admit her, and therefore I have no hesitation upon that point.

Then, with respect to the Territories, I have been and I am of opinion, that we should not separate, at the end of this session of Congress, without having made a suitable provision for their government. I do not think it safe to allow things to stand as they are. It has been thought that there may be such a thing as admitting California, and stopping there. Well, it is not impossible, in the nature of things, that such a course of policy should be adopted, if it would meet the proper concurrence. But then I have always supposed, Sir, that, if we were now acting upon California as a separate measure, and should, in the prosecution of that measure, admit her into the Union, the inquiry would immediately arise, What is next to be done? I have never supposed that the questions respecting the Territories would thereby be put to rest, even for the present. I have supposed, on the contrary, that the very next thing to be done would be to take up the subject of a government for the Territories, and prosecute that subject until it should be in some manner terminated by Congress, to the exclusion of all ordinary subjects of legislation. I am not authorized to state, Sir, I do not know, the opinion of the honorable members of the Committee on Territories. The honorable member from Illinois, who is at the head of that committee, sits near me, and I take it for granted that he can say whether I am right or not in the opinion, that, if we should this day admit California alone, he would to-morrow feel it his duty to bring in a bill for the government of the Territories, or to make some disposition of them.

MR. DOUGLAS (in a low voice). Does the Senator wish an answer?

I should like to know the honorable member's purpose.

MR. DOUGLAS. Mr. President, if California should be admitted by herself, I should certainly feel it my duty, as the chairman of the Commitee on Territories, to move to take up the subject of the Territories at once, and put them through, and also the Texas boundary question, and to settle them by detail, if they are not settled in the aggregate, together. I can say such is the opinion and determination of a majority of that committee.

Then, Sir, it is as I supposed. We should not get rid of the subject, even for the present, by admitting California alone. Now, Sir, it is not wise to conceal our còndition from ourselves. Suppose we admit California alone. My honorable friend from Illinois brings in, then, a bill for a territorial government for New Mexico and Utah. We must open our eyes to the state of opinion in the two houses respectively, and endeavor to foresee what would be the probable fate of such a bill. If it be a bill containing a prohibition of slavery, we know it could not pass this house. If it be a bill without such prohibition, we know what difficulty it would encounter elsewhere. So that we very little relieve ourselves from the embarrassing circumstances in which we are placed by taking up California and acting upon it alone. I am therefore, Sir, decidedly in favor of passing this bill in the form in which it is upon your table.

But, Sir, if it be the pleasure of the Senate to approve the motion which is shortly to be made for laying this whole measure upon the table, and thereby disposing of this bill, I can only say, for one, that, if this measure be defeated by that proceeding, or any other, I hold myself not only inclined, but bound, to consider any other measures which may be suggested. The case is pressing, and the circumstances of the country are urgent. When have we ever before had any foreign question, any exterior question, if I may say so, that has occupied the consideration of Congress for seven months, and yet been brought to no result? When have we had a subject before us that has paralyzed all the operations of government, that has displaced the regular proceedings of the two houses of Congress, and has left us, at the end of seven months of a session, without the ordinary annual appropriation bills? What is now proposed is, to make a territorial government for New Mexico and Utah, without restriction. I feel authorized to assume, from the circumstances before us, that it is in the power of gentlemen of the South to decide whether this territorial government without restriction, as provided in the bill, shall be established or not. I have voted against restriction for the reasons which I have already given to the Senate, and may repeat; but it now lies with Southern gentlemen to say whether this bill, thus providing for territorial governments without restriction, shall pass or not; and they will decide that question, doubtless, by reference to what is likely to happen if it should not pass.

Now, Sir, I am prepared to say, that, if this measure does not pass, I am ready to support other proper measures that can and will pass. I shall never consent to end this session of Congress until some provision is made for New Mexico. Utah is less important. Let her repose herself upon the borders of the Salt Lake another year, if necessary. But as to New Mexico, situated as she is, with a controversy on her hands with her more powerful neighbor, Texas, I shall never consent to the adjournment of Congress without a provision made for avoiding a collision, and for the settlement of the point in controversy, between that Territory and that State. I have the strongest objection to a premature creation of States. I stated that objection at length in the Senate some two years ago. The bringing in of small States with a representation in the Senate equal to the representation of the largest States in the Union, and with a very small number of people, deranges and disturbs the proper balance between the Senate and the House of Representatives. It converts the Senate into a kind of oligarchy. There may be six, or eight, or ten small States in the Southwest, having as many Senators in Congress as they have Representatives. This objection is founded upon the incongruity which such a case produces in the constitutional relation of the Senate and the House. It disfigures the symmetry of the government; and in this respect it does not make the slightest possible difference, in my estimation, whether they are to be free States or slave States. I am not disposed to convert a Territory that is immature, and not fit to come into the Union on account of want of population, into a State, merely because it will be a free State. That does not weigh with me a hair. But my objection has been and is, as I have stated, or attempted to state, that the admission of States with so small an amount of population deranges the system. It makes the Senate what it was never intended by the Constitution to be. Nevertheless, Sir, as I favor the admission of California, although she presents herself before us with some irregularities in her course of proceeding, so there are greater evils, in my judgment, than the admission of New Mexico as a State now, at once, or than the provision that she shall be admitted in a certain time hereafter. I do not think that so great an evil as it would be to leave New Mexico without a government, without protection, on the very eve of probable hostilities with Texas, so far as I can discern; for, to my mind, there is the highest degree of probability that there will arise collisions, contests, and, for aught I know, bloodshed, if the boundaries of New Mexico are not settled by Congress.

Sir, I know no question so important, connected with all these matters, as this settlement of the Texan boundary. That immediately and intimately, in my judgment, touches the question of the duration of peace and quiet in the country; and I cannot conceive how gentlemen, looking upon that subject in all its aspects, can satisfy themselves with the idea of retiring from their seats here, and leaving it where it is. I should be derelict to my duty if I did not persist, to the last, in bringing it to a decision by the authority of Congress. If a motion be made, as it has been announced is intended, to lay this bill upon the table, and that motion prevails, this measure is at an end. Then there must be a resort to some other measures; and I am disposed to say that, in case of the failure of this bill, I shall be in favor of a bill which shall provide for three things; namely, the admission of California with its present constitution and boundaries, the settlement of the Texan boundary, and the admission of New Mexico as a State. Such a measure will produce a termination of the controversies which now agitate us, and relieve the country from distraction.

Sir, this measure is opposed by the North, or some of the North, and by the South, or some of the South; and it has the remarkable misfortune to encounter resistance by persons the most directly opposed to each other in every matter connected with the subject under consideration. There are those, (I do not speak, of course, of members of Congress, and I do not desire to be understood as making any allusion whatever, in what I may say, to members of this house or of the other,) there are those in the country who say, on the part of the South, that the South by this bill gives up every thing to the North, and that they will fight it to the last; and there are those, on the part of the North, who say, that this bill gives up every thing to the South, and that they will fight it to the last. And really, Sir, strange as it may seem, this disposition to make battle upon the bill, by those who never agreed in any thing before under the light of heaven, has created a sort of fellowship and good feeling between them. One says, Give me your hand, my good fellow; you mean to go against this bill to the death, because it gives up the rights of the South; I mean to go against the bill to the death, because it gives up the rights of the North; let us shake hands and cry out, "Down with the bill!" and then unitedly raise the shout,

> "A day, an hour, of virtuous liberty
> Is worth a whole eternity in bondage!"

Such is the consistency of the opposition to this measure.

Now, Sir, I ascribe nothing but the best and purest motives to any of the gentlemen, on either side of this chamber, or of the other house, who take a view of this subject which differs from my own. I cannot but regret, certainly, that gentlemen who sit around me, and especially my honorable colleague,* and my friends from Massachusetts in the other house, are obliged, by their sense of duty, to oppose a measure which I feel bound by my conscience to support to the utmost of my ability. They are just as high-minded, as patriotic, as pure, and every way as

* Mr. Davis.

well-intentioned as I am; and, Sir, if it was put to vote, and the question were to be decided by a majority, I must confess my friends from Massachusetts would outvote me. But still my own opinions are not in the least degree changed. I feel that every interest of the State, one of whose representatives I am, as well as every great interest of the whole country, requires that this measure, or some measure as healing, composing, and conciliatory as this, should be adopted by Congress before its adjournment. That is my object, and I shall steadily pursue it.

Let us examine this. If I may analyze the matter a little, both in regard to the North and the South, Massachusetts, being a Northern State, may be taken as a representative of Northern interests. What does she gain by this bill? What does she lose by it? If this bill passes, Massachusetts and the North gain the admission of California as a free State, with her present constitution, a very highly desirable object, as I believe, to all the North. She gains, also, the quieting of the New Mexican question and the Texas boundary, which, in my judgment, as I have already said, is the most important of all these questions, because it is the one most immediately menacing evil consequences, if such consequences be not arrested by this or some similar measure. She gains the quiet of New Mexico, and she gains the settlement of the Texas boundary, objects all desirable and most important. More than that, Sir, she gains, and the whole North gains, and the whole country gains, the final adjustment of by far the greater part of all the slavery questions. When I speak of this bill in that connection, I mean also to connect it with the other subjects recommended by the committee; and I say that, if the whole report of that committee could be carried out, one of the greatest of all possible benefits will be secured; that is, the settlement, to an extent of far more than a majority of them all, of the questions connected with slavery which have so long agitated the country. And then, Sir, Massachusetts, and the North, and the whole country, gain the restoration of this government to the ordinary exercise of its functions. The North and the South will see Congress replaced in its position of an active, beneficial, parental legislature for the whole Union. Consider, Sir, what has happened? While it is of the utmost importance that this restoration of Congress to the exercise of its ordinary functions should be accomplished, here we are, seven or eight months from the beginning of the session, hardly able to keep the government alive. All is paralysis. We are nearly brought to a stand. Every thing is suspended upon this one topic, this one idea, as if there were no object in government, no uses in government, no duties of those who administer government, but to settle one question.

Well, Sir, the next inquiry is, What do Massachusetts and the North, the antislavery States, lose by this adjustment? I put the question to every gentleman here, and to every man in the country. They lose the application of what is called the Wilmot Proviso to these Territories, and that is all. There is nothing else that I suppose the whole North are not willing to do, or willing to have done. They wish to get California into the Union and quiet New Mexico; they wish to terminate the dispute about the Texan boundary, cost what it reasonably may. They make no sacrifice in all these. What they sacrifice is this: the application of the Wilmot Proviso to the Territories of New Mexico and Utah; and that is all. Now, what is the importance of that loss, or that sacrifice, in any reasonable man's estimate? Its importance, Sir, depends upon its necessity. If, in any reasonable man's judgment, the necessity of the application of that proviso to New Mexico is apparent, why, then it is important to those who hold that the further extension of slavery is to be resisted, as a matter of principle. But if it be not necessary, if circumstances do not call for it, why, then there is no sacrifice made in refusing or declining to apply the Wilmot Proviso.

Now, Sir, allow me to say, that the Wilmot Proviso is no matter of principle; it is a means to an end; and it cannot be raised to the dignity of a principle. The principle of the North I take to be, that there shall be no further extension of slave territory. Let that be admitted; what then? It does not necessarily follow that in every case you must apply the Wilmot Proviso. If there are other circumstances that are imperative and conclusive, and such as influence and control the judgment of reasonable men, rendering it unnecessary, for the establishment of that principle, to apply a measure which is obnoxious and disagreeable to others, and regarded by them as derogatory to their equality as members of the Union, then, I say, it is neither right, nor patriotic, nor just to apply it.

My honorable colleague admitted the other day, with great propriety and frankness, that if it were certain, or if it could be made certain, that natural causes necessarily exclude slavery from New Mexico, then the restriction ought not to be inserted in the bill. Now, by certainty I suppose my colleague meant not mathematical certainty; I suppose he meant that high probability, that moral certainty, which governs men in all the concerns of life. Our duties to society, our pursuits in life, are all measured by that high probability which is something short of mathematical certainty, but which we are bound to act upon in every daily transaction, either in a public or in a private capacity. The question, therefore, (I address myself to gentlemen of the North,) is this: Is the probability of the exclusion of slavery from New Mexico by natural causes so high, and strong, and conclusive, as that we should act upon it as we act on the same degree of probability applied to other questions, in civil, moral, and social relations? I shall not recur to what I have myself said, heretofore, on this subject; for I suppose my friend from Pennsylvania,* and my friend from Connecticut,† who discussed this matter latterly, have left it proved, and as much demonstrated as any problem of a moral and political character can be demonstrated, that New Mexico is not a country in which slavery exists, or into which it can ever be introduced. If that were not so upon previous evidence, and if now any thing further need be added, we have before us to-day an authentic expression of the will of the inhabitants of that country themselves, who, it is agreed on all hands, have the ultimate right of decision on a subject that concerns themselves alone, and that expression is against slavery.

What is it, then, that is yielded by the North but a mere abstraction, a naked possibility, upon which no man would act? No man would venture a farthing to-day for a great inheritance to be bestowed on him when slavery should be established in New Mexico. Now that there is an authentic declaration upon the subject by the people of New Mexico themselves, what is there that should lead us to hesitate in settling this matter? Why should we proceed upon the ground of adhering to the Wilmot Proviso as an abstract notion? And I must

* Mr. Cooper. † Mr. Smith.

be permitted to say, that, as applied to this case, it is all an abstraction. I do not mean to say that the injunction against slavery in the Ordinance of 1787 was a mere abstraction; on the contrary, it had its uses; but I say the application of that rule to this case is a mere abstraction, and nothing else. It does not affect the state of things in the slightest degree, present or future. Every thing is to be now, and remain hereafter, with or without that restriction, just as it would the other way. It is, therefore, in my judgment, clearly an abstraction.

I am sorry, Sir, very sorry, that my friend from Connecticut,* who has studied this case a great deal more than I have, not only as a member of this body, but while he was a member of the other house, and has demonstrated, beyond the power of any conscientious man's denial, that there can be no slavery in the Territory about which we are speaking, that the South is mistaken in supposing it possible to derive any benefit from it, and that the North is mistaken in supposing that that which they desire to prohibit will ever need any prohibition there; I am sorry to see that my very able friend, having demonstrated the case, did not carry out his own demonstration. The expression of his purpose to vote against this bill followed one of the clearest and strongest demonstrations in its favor that I have heard from the mouth of man. What is the reason of his opposition? Why, the gentleman said he was instructed by the legislature of Connecticut to oppose it; and, on the whole, he did not feel it to be his duty to depart from those instructions.

It has become, Sir, an object of considerable importance in the history of this government, to inquire how far instructions, given *ex parte* and under one state of circumstances, are to govern those who are to act under another state of circumstances, and not upon an *ex parte* hearing, but upon a hearing of the whole matter. The proposition, that a member of this government, in giving a vote to bind all the country, is to take as his instructions the will of a small part of the country, whether in his own State or out of it, is a proposition that is above or below all argument. Where men are sworn to act conscientiously for the good of the whole, according to their own best judgment

* Mr. Smith.

and opinion, if the proposition is asserted that they are, nevertheless, bound to take the individual opinion of a few, and be exclusively bound by that opinion, there is no room for argument; every man's moral perception, without argument, decides on such a proposition. I know, Sir, that, in a popular government like ours, instructions of this sort will be given, and pledges required. It is in the nature of the case. Political men in this country love the people; they love popular applause and promotion, and they are willing to make promises; and, as in other sorts of love, so in this, when the blood burns, the soul prodigally lends the tongue vows. It is especially the case in some States, in which, in electioneering contests, instructions become little constitutions, which men vow to support. These instructions are often given under circumstances very remote from those that exist when the duty comes to be performed; and, I am sorry to say, they are often given on collateral considerations. I will not say when or where, how remotely or how lately; but I am very much inclined to think that we should find, in the history of the country, cases in which instructions are ready to be given, or ready to be withheld, as the support of some little fragment of some sectional party may be, or may not be, obtained thereby.

Sir, it is curious enough to observe how differently this idea, that a member chosen into a public body, to act for the whole country, is bound, nevertheless, by the instructions of those who elected him, which has risen to a sort of rule in some of the American States, is received and treated elsewhere. According to our notions and habits of thinking, it is not only allowable for, but incumbent upon, a member of Congress, to follow the instructions given by his own particular constituents, although his vote affects the interest, the honor, the welfare, the renown, of twenty millions of people. As an instance, Sir, of the various views taken of this subject, as a question of morals, I may refer to what happened in the Chamber of Deputies of France some years ago, perhaps while the honorable member from Michigan* was residing in Paris, but more probably shortly after his return. A gentleman, who was a candidate for the Chamber of Deputies, promised his constituents that on a cer-

* Mr. Cass.

tain measure, expected to come before the Chamber, he would vote as they required. They required him to vote so and so, and he said he would do it. Well, Sir, he was chosen; and when he came to the Chamber to take the oath of office, he was told, Not so fast! Objection was made. The Chamber said he did not come there as a fair man; he did not come as an impartial man, to judge of the interests of the whole country upon the great questions that were to come before the Chamber. He was pledged and trammelled; he had given up his conscience and promised his vote, and therefore did not stand on an equality with other members of that assembly who came unpledged and untrammelled, and bound to exercise their own best judgments. In short, they rejected him; and whoever wishes to see the most beautiful disquisition upon political morals, and the duty of those who represent the people, that I know of since the time of Mr. Burke's speech at Bristol, can be gratified by reading M. Guizot's speech on that occasion. The member came under pledges made to a few to give his vote for them, although it might be against the many, and they held him not to be a worthy representative of France, fit to act on the questions which concerned the interests of the whole kingdom.

I know, Sir, how easily we glide into this habit of following instructions; although I know, also, that members of Congress wish to act conscientiously always, and I believe they wish themselves free from these trammels. But the truth is, that under the doctrine of instructions Congress is not free. To the extent to which this doctrine may at any time prevail in it, the two houses are not deliberative bodies. Congress needs a "Wilmot Proviso," much more than the snow-capped mountains of New Mexico or the salt plains of Utah. If the genius of American liberty, or some angel from a higher sphere, could fly over the land with a scroll bearing words, and with power to give effect to those words, and those words should be, "Be it ordained that neither in the Senate nor in the House of Representatives in Congress assembled shall there be slavery or involuntary servitude, except for crime," it would be a glorious crowning honor to the Constitution of the United States. O thou spirit of Nathan Dane! How couldst thou take so much pains to set men's limbs free in the Territories, and never deign to add even a proviso in favor of the freedom of opinion and conscience in the halls of Congress!

Sir, I am of opinion that every public consideration connected with the interests of the State, one of whose representatives, and the most humble of them all, I am, shows the absolute necessity of settling this question at once, upon fair and reasonable terms; the necessity of judging subjects according to their real merit and importance, and acting accordingly; and that we should not be carried away by fancies of gorgons, hydras, and chimeras dire, to the utter disregard of all that is substantially valuable, important, and essential in the administration of the government. Massachusetts, one of the smallest of the States of the Union, circumscribed within the limits of eight thousand square miles of barren, rocky, and sterile territory, possesses within its limits at this moment nearly a million of people. With the same ratio of population, New York would contain nearly six million people, and Virginia more than seven million. What are the occupations and pursuits of such a population on so small a territory? A very small portion of them live by the tillage of the land. They are engaged in those pursuits which fall under the control, protection, and regulation of the laws of this government. These pursuits are commerce, navigation, the fisheries, and manufactures, every one of which is under the influence of the operation of acts of Congress every day. On none of these subjects does Congress ever pass a law that does not materially affect the happiness, industry, and prosperity of Massachusetts; yes, and of Rhode Island too [looking at the Rhode Island Senators]. Is it not, then, of great importance to all these interests that the government should be carried on regularly? that it should have the power of action, of motion, and legislation? Is it not the greatest calamity, that it should be all paralyzed, hung up, dependent upon one idea, as if there was no object in government, no use in government, no desirable protection from government, and no desirable legislation by government, except what relates to the single topic of slavery?

I cannot conceive that these great interests would be readily surrendered by the business men of the country, the laboring community of the Northern States, to abstractions, to naked possibilities, to idle fears that evils may ensue if a particular abstract measure be not passed. Men must live; to live, they must work. And how is this to be done, if in this way all the business of society is stopped, and every thing is placed in a state of stagnation, and no man can even conjecture when the ordinary march of affairs is to be resumed. Depend upon it, the people of the North wish to see an end put to this state of things. They desire to see a measure of conciliation pass, and to have harmony restored; to be again in the enjoyment of a good government, under the protection and action of good laws; and that their interrupted labors may be profitably resumed, that their daily employment may return, that their daily means of subsistence and education for themselves and their families may be provided. There has not been, in my acquaintance with the people of this country, a moment in which so much alarm has been experienced, so much sinking of the heart felt, at the state of public affairs, in a time of peace, as now. I leave it to others to judge for themselves, who may better know public opinion; but, for my part, I believe it is the conviction of five sixths of the whole North, that questions such as have occupied us here should not be allowed any longer to embarrass the government, and defeat the just hopes of those who support it, and expect to live under its protection and care.

I have alluded to the argument of my friend from Connecticut, because it is the ablest argument on this subject that I have heard; and I have alluded to his intimated vote as illustrating what I consider the evil of instructing men, before a case arises, as to what shall be their conduct upon that case. The honorable member from Connecticut is as independent as any other man, and of course will not understand me to mean any thing personal in what I have said. I take his case merely as an illustration of the folly and absurdity of instructions. Why should a man of his strength of intellect, and while acting for the whole country, be controlled in his judgment by instructions given by others, with little knowledge of the circumstances, and no view of the whole case?

I have now, Mr. President, said what I think the North may gain, and what it may lose. Now let us inquire how it is with the South. In the first place, I think that the South, if all these measures pass, will gain an acceptable and satisfactory mode for the reclamation of fugitive slaves. As to the territorial acquisitions, I am bound in candor to say, taking Maryland as an example, for instance, that Maryland will gain just what Massachusetts loses, and that is nothing at all; because I have not the slightest idea that, by any thing we can do here, any provision could be made by which the territory of New Mexico and Utah could become susceptible of slave labor, and so useful to the South. Now, let me say, Mr. President, with great respect and kindness, that I wish Southern gentlemen should consider this matter calmly and deliberately. There are none in this chamber, certainly, who desire the dissolution of this Union, nor in the other house of Congress. But all the world out of doors is not as wise and patriotic as gentlemen within these walls. I am quite aware that there are those who raise the loudest clamor against the Wilmot Proviso, and other restrictions upon slavery, that would be exceedingly gratified, nevertheless, to have that restriction imposed. I believe there are those scattered all along from here to the Gulf of Mexico who would say, "Let them put on further restrictions; let them push the South a little further, and then we shall know what we have to do." But, again, the Southern States gain what they think important and gratifying; that is, an exemption from a derogatory inequality. They find themselves placed where they wish to be placed, and, as far as the territories are concerned, relieved from what they consider the Wilmot yoke. This appeases a feeling of wounded pride; and they gain, too, the general restoration of peace and harmony in the progress of the government, in the beneficial operations of which they have a full share. One of the evils attendant upon this question is the harsh judgment passed by one portion of the Union upon another, founded, not on the conduct of the North or South generally, but on the conduct of particular persons or associations in each part respectively. Unjust charges are made by one against the other, and these are retaliated by those who are the objects of them. Accusations made by individuals in the North are attributed by the South to the whole North indiscriminately. On the other hand, extravagant individuals at the South utter objectionable sentiments; and these are bruited all over the North as Southern sentiments, and therefore the South is denounced. In the same way, sentiments springing from the Abolitionists of the North, which no man of character and sense approves, are spread in the South; and the whole North are there charged with being Abolitionists, or tinctured with Abolitionism. Now, one side is just as fair and as true as the other. It is a prejudice of which both sides must rid themselves if they ever mean to come together as brethren, enjoying one renown, one destiny, and expecting one and the same destiny hereafter. If we mean to live together, common prudence should teach us to treat each other with respect.

The Nashville Address has been alluded to, and it has been charged upon the whole South, as a syllabus of Southern sentiments. Now, I do not believe a word of this. Far be it from me to impute to the South, generally, the sentiments of the Nashville Convention. That address is a studied disunion argument. It proceeds upon the ground that there must be a separation of the States, first, because the North acts so injuriously to the South that the South must secede; and, secondly, even if it were not so, and a better sense of duty should return to the North, still, such is the diversity of interest, that they cannot be kept together.

Mr. Barnwell (interposing). Will the honorable Senator refer to that portion of the address which contains the sentiment which he declares implies the desire for disunion in any event whatever; for that I understand is the charge against the address?

What I understand about this address is this. I say the argument of the address is, that the States cannot be kept together; because, first, the general disposition of the North is to invade the rights of the South, stating this in general language merely; and then, secondly, even if this were not so, and the North should get into a better temper in that respect, still no permanent peace could be expected, and no union long maintained, on account of the diversity of interests between the different portions of the Union. There is, according to the address, but one condition on which people can live together under the same government; and that is, when interests are entirely identical. An exact identity of interest, according to its notions, is the only security for good government.

Mr. Barnwell. With regard to the first part, the honorable Senator is correct, and I have no doubt at all that it is the character of the address, that, unless a great change be produced in the temper of the

Northern people, and the treatment which they give to us on account of our institutions, no permanent union between us can exist. With regard to the latter part, I contend that the address contains no such sentiment. It states distinctly that, in the position which the different portions of the Union occupy with regard to each other, with the want of that identity of interest between them, it is absolutely essential to the South that its sectional interests should be independent of the control of the North.

And what does that mean but separation?

Mr. Barnwell. Not at all. It means what I have always alleged, that the North has no right to interfere with the institution of slavery. If that interference is stopped, we do not contend that there is any necessity for a dissolution of the Union. But if it is persisted in, then the opinion of the address is, and I believe the opinion of a large portion of the Southern people is, that the Union cannot be made to endure.

It is hardly worth while, as the paper is not before us, for the honorable member from South Carolina and myself to enter into a discussion about this address. If I understand its argument, it is as I expressed it, that, even if the North were better behaved, there is a want of identity of interests between the North and the South which must soon break up the Union. As far as regards the gentleman's remark, that the North must abstain from any interference with the peculiar institutions of the South, why, every sensible man in the North thinks exactly so. I know that the sensible men of the North are of opinion, that the institution of slavery, as it exists in the States, was intended originally to be, has ever been, and now justly is, entirely out of the scope and reach of the legislation of this government; and this every body understands.

But I was saying that I can and shall impute no sentiment of disunion to the South, generally. Why, whom do I sit among? With whom have I been associated here for thirty years? With good Union men from the South. And in this chamber, and in late years, have there not been men from the South who have resisted every thing that threatened danger to the Union? Have there not been men here that, at some risk of losing favor with their constituents, have resisted the Mexican war, the acquisition of territory by arms, nay, men who played for the last stake, and, after the conquest was made, resisted the ratification of the treaty by which these territories were brought under the control of this government? Sir, with these recollections, which do so much honor to the character of these gentlemen, and with these acts, which attest the entire loyalty of the great body of the South to the Union, I shall indulge in no general complaint against them; nor, so far as it comes within the power of my rebuke, will I tolerate it. They have the same interests, they are descended from the same Revolutionary blood, and believe the glory of the country to be as much theirs as ours; and I verily believe they desire to secure as perpetual an attachment to the North as the most intelligent men of the North do to perpetuate such an attachment to the South. I believe that the great masses of the people, both North and South, aside from the influence of agitation, are for the Union and for the Constitution; and God grant that they may remain so, and prevent every thing which may overturn either the one or the other!

I was sorry to hear, because I thought it was quite unjust, that all the folly and madness of the recent expedition to Cuba was chargeable upon the South, generally. The South had nothing more to do with it than Massachusetts, or the city of Boston, or the city of New York. It is unjust to say that such a violation of the law was perpetrated by the South, or found more apology or justification in the general Southern mind, than it found in New York or in Massachusetts.

Mr. Butler (in his seat). Not a bit more.

Now, the Senator from Connecticut told the truth the other day, and I am obliged to him for it. I do not mean that it is unusual for him, but I mean that it is a great deal more unusual, in the course of this debate, to hear the real truth spoken, than to hear ingenious sophisms and empty abstractions. But he told us the truth in respect to these territorial acquisitions; that it was not the North or the South that were the real authors of that conquest, but that it was the party who supported Mr. Polk for the Presidency, and who supported his measures while in the Presidency. The South, undoubtedly, as the party most in favor of the administration, took the lead; and that part of the North that upheld the administration followed, not as little Iulus followed his father, "*non passibus æquis*," but with the same stride as its leaders. And therefore I was glad that my honorable friend from Connecticut, instead of giving us a normal, stereotyped speech against the South, told the truth of these transactions.

There are other topics, which I pass over. I said something formerly about the imprisonment of the black citizens of the North engaged in navigation, who go South, and are there arrested. That is a serious business, and we see that England has complained of it, as violating our treaty with her. I think it is an evil that ought to be redressed; for I never could see any necessity for it, and I am fully persuaded that other means can be taken to relieve the South from alarm without committing an outrage upon those who, at home, are considered as American citizens. At the same time, I am bound to say that I know nothing in the world to prevent any free citizen of Massachusetts, imprisoned under the laws of South Carolina, from trying the question of the constitutionality of that law, by applying at once to any judge of the United States for a writ of *habeas corpus*. I do not think, therefore, that there was any great necessity of making it a matter of public embassy. I think that was rather calculated to inflame feeling than to do good. But I must say, as I have said heretofore, that the gentleman who went from Massachusetts* was one of the most respectable men in the Commonwealth, bearing an excellent character, of excellent temper, and every way entitled to the regard of others to the extent to which he has enjoyed the regard of the people of Massachusetts.

Sir, I was in Boston some month or two ago, and, at a meeting of the people, said, that the public mind of Massachusetts, and the North, was laboring under certain prejudices, and that I would take an occasion, which I did not then enjoy, to state what I supposed these prejudices to be, and how they had arisen. I shall say a few words on the subject now. In the first place, I think that there is no prejudice on the part of the people of Massachusetts or of the North, arising out of any ill-will, or any want of patriotism or good feeling toward the whole country. It all originates in misinformation, false representation, and misapprehensions arising from the laborious

* Mr. Hoar.

efforts that have been made for the last twenty years to pervert the public judgment and irritate the public feeling.

The first of these misapprehensions is an exaggerated sense of the actual evil of the reclamation of fugitive slaves, felt by Massachusetts and the other New England States. What produced that sentiment? The cases do not exist. There has not been a case within the knowledge of this generation, in which a man has been taken back from Massachusetts into slavery by process of law, not one; and yet there are hundreds of people, who read nothing but Abolition newspapers, who suppose that these cases arise weekly; that, as a common thing, men, and sometimes their wives and children, are dragged back from the free soil of Massachusetts into slavery at the South.

Mr. Hale (interposing). Will the honorable Senator allow me to ask him a question? Is he not mistaken in the point of fact in regard to the State of Massachusetts? I recollect something occurring in Massachusetts, not more than three or four years ago, in relation to a man by the name of Pearson, and that there was a large public meeting on the subject in Faneuil Hall.

I will state how that was. That was a case of kidnapping by some one who claimed, or pretended to claim, the negro, and ran away with him by force. What I mean to say is, that there has been no man, under the Constitution and laws of the country, sent back from Massachusetts into slavery, this generation. I have stated before, and I state now, that cases of violent seizure or kidnapping have occurred, and they may occur in any State in the Union, under any provisions of law.

Now, Sir, this prejudice, created by the incessant action on the public mind of Abolition societies, Abolition presses, and Abolition lecturers, has grown very strong. No drum-head, in the longest day's march, was ever more incessantly beaten and smitten, than public sentiment in the North has been, every month, and day, and hour, by the din, and roll, and rub-a-dub of Abolition writers and Abolition lecturers. That it is which has created the prejudice.

Sir, the principle of the restitution of runaway slaves is not objectionable, unless the Constitution is objectionable. If the Constitution is right in that respect, the principle is right, and the law providing for carrying it into effect is right. If that be so, and if there be no abuse of the right under any law of Congress, or any other law, then what is there to complain of?

I not only say, Sir, that there has been no case, so far as I can learn, of the reclamation of a slave by his master, which ended in taking him back to slavery, this generation, but I will add, that, so far as I have been able to go back in my researches, so far as I have been able to hear and learn in that part of the country, there has been no one case of false claim. Who knows in all New England of a single case of false claim having ever been set up to an alleged fugitive from slavery? It may possibly have happened; but I have never known it nor heard of it, although I have made diligent inquiry; nor do I believe there is the slightest danger of it, for all the community are alive to, and would take instant alarm at, any appearance of such a case, and especially at this time. There is no danger of any such violence being perpetrated.

Before I pass from this subject, Sir, I will say that what seems extraordinary is, that this principle of restitution, which has existed in the country for more than two hundred years without complaint, sometimes as a matter of agreement between the North and the South, and sometimes as a matter of comity, should all at once, and after the length of time I have mentioned, become a subject of excitement. I have in my hand a letter from Governor Berkeley, of Virginia, to Governor Winthrop, of Massachusetts, written in the year 1644, more than two hundred years ago, in which he says that a certain gentleman, naming him, had lost some servants, giving their names, whom he supposes to have fled into the jurisdiction of Massachusetts; and the member from Kentucky * will be pleased to learn that it contains a precedent for what he considers to be the proper course of proceeding in such cases. Governor Berkeley states that the gentleman, the owner of the slaves, has made it appear in court that they are his slaves and have run away. He goes on to say, "We expect you to use all kind offices for the restoration to their master of these fugitives, as we constantly exercise the same offices in restoring runaways to you." At that day I do not suppose there were a great many slaves in Massachusetts; but there was an extensive system of

* Mr. Clay.

apprenticeship, and hundreds of persons were bound apprentices in Massachusetts, some of whom would run away. They were as likely to run to Virginia as anywhere else; and in such cases they were returned, upon demand, to their masters. Indeed, it was found necessary in the early laws of Massachusetts to make provision for the seizure and return of runaway apprentices. In all the revisions of our laws, this provision remains; and it is in the Revised Statutes now before me. It provides that runaway apprentices shall be secured upon the application of their masters, or any one on their behalf, and put into jail until they can be sent for by them; and there is no trial by jury in the case, either. I say, therefore, that the exaggerated statement of the danger and mischief arising from this right of reclaiming slaves is a prejudice, produced by the causes I have stated, and one which ought not longer to haunt and terrify the public mind.

With great respect for those who differ from me, I will also state, that I think it is a prejudice to insist with so much earnestness upon the application of the Wilmot Proviso to these Territories of New Mexico and Utah, because of its obvious inapplicability, and the want of all reasonable necessity for making that application in the manner proposed, and as it is deemed offensive and affronting to the South.

Another prejudice against the South is just exactly that which exists in the South against the North, and consists in imputing to a whole portion of the country the extravagances of individuals. I will say only, before I depart from this part of the case, that the State in whose representation I bear a part is a Union State, thoroughly and emphatically; that she is attached to the Union and the Constitution by indissoluble ties; that she connects all her own history from colonial times, her struggle for independence, her efforts for the establishment of this government, and all the benefits and blessings which she has enjoyed under it, in one great attractive whole, to which her affections are constantly and powerfully drawn. All these make up a history in which she has taken a part, and the whole of which she enjoys as a most precious inheritance. She is a State for the Union; she will be for the Union. It is the law of her destiny; it is the law of her situation; it is a law imposed upon her by the recollections of the past, and by every interest for the present and every hope for the future.

Mr. President, it has always seemed to me to be a grateful reflection, that, however short and transient may be the lives of individuals, states may be permanent. The great corporations that embrace the government of mankind, protect their liberties, and secure their happiness, may have something of perpetuity, and, as I might say, of earthly immortality. For my part, Sir, I gratify myself by contemplating what in the future will be the condition of that generous State, which has done me the honor to keep me in the counsels of the country for so many years. I see nothing about her in prospect less than that which encircles her now. I feel that when I, and all those that now hear me, shall have gone to our last home, and afterwards, when mould may have gathered upon our memories, as it will have done upon our tombs, that State, so early to take her part in the great contest of the Revolution, will stand, as she has stood and now stands, like that column which, near her Capitol, perpetuates the memory of the first great battle of the Revolution, firm, erect, and immovable. I believe, Sir, that, if commotion shall shake the country, there will be one rock for ever, as solid as the granite of her hills, for the Union to repose upon. I believe that, if disasters arise, bringing clouds which shall obscure the ensign now over her and over us, there will be one star that will but burn the brighter amid the darkness of that night; and I believe that, if in the remotest ages (I trust they will be infinitely remote) an occasion shall occur when the sternest duties of patriotism are demanded and to be performed, Massachusetts will imitate her own example; and that, as at the breaking out of the Revolution she was the first to offer the outpouring of her blood and her treasure in the struggle for liberty, so she will be hereafter ready, when the emergency arises, to repeat and renew that offer, with a thousand times as many warm hearts, and a thousand times as many strong hands.

And now, Mr. President, to return at last to the principal and important question before us, What are we to do? How are we to bring this emergent and pressing question to an issue and an end? Here have we been seven and a half months, disputing about points which, in my judgment, are of no practical importance to one or the other part of the country. Are we to dwell for ever upon a single topic, a single idea? Are we to forget all the purposes for which governments are instituted, and continue everlastingly to dispute about that which is of no essential consequence? I think, Sir, the country calls upon us loudly and imperatively to settle this question. I think that the whole world is looking to see whether this great popular government can get through such a crisis. We are the observed of all observers. It is not to be disputed or doubted, that the eyes of all Christendom are upon us. We have stood through many trials. Can we not stand through this, which takes so much the character of a sectional controversy? Can we stand that? There is no inquiring man in all Europe who does not ask himself that question every day, when he reads the intelligence of the morning. Can this country, with one set of interests at the South, and another set of interests at the North, and these interests supposed, but falsely supposed, to be at variance; can this people see what is so evident to the whole world beside, that this Union is their main hope and greatest benefit, and that their interests in every part are entirely compatible? Can they see, and will they feel, that their prosperity, their respectability among the nations of the earth, and their happiness at home, depend upon the maintenance of their Union and their Constitution? That is the question. I agree that local divisions are apt to warp the understandings of men, and to excite a belligerent feeling between section and section. It is natural, in times of irritation, for one part of the country to say, If you do that, I will do this, and so get up a feeling of hostility and defiance. Then comes belligerent legislation, and then an appeal to arms. The question is, whether we have the true patriotism, the Americanism, necessary to carry us through such a trial. The whole world is looking towards us with extreme anxiety. For myself, I propose, Sir, to abide by the principles and the purposes which I have avowed. I shall stand by the Union, and by all who stand by it. I shall do justice to the whole country, according to the best of my ability, in all I say, and act for the good of the whole country in all I do. I mean to stand upon the Constitution. I need no other platform. I shall know but one country. The ends I aim at shall be my country's, my God's, and Truth's. I was born an American: I will live an American; I shall die an American; and I intend to perform the duties incumbent upon me in that character to the end of my career. I mean to do this, with absolute disregard of personal consequences. What are personal consequences? What is the individual man, with all the good or evil that may betide him, in comparison with the good or evil which may befall a great country in a crisis like this, and in the midst of great transactions which concern that country's fate? Let the consequences be what they will, I am careless. No man can suffer too much, and no man can fall too soon, if he suffer or if he fall in defence of the liberties and Constitution of his country.

LEGAL ARGUMENTS

AND

SPEECHES TO THE JURY.

DEFENCE OF THE KENNISTONS.*

INTRODUCTORY NOTE.†

THE trial of Levi and Laban Kenniston for highway robbery on the person of Major Elijah Putnam Goodridge, in Newbury, in the county of Essex, on the 19th of December, 1816, was one of the most remarkable trials ever had in Massachusetts. It was remarkable not so much for the dramatic character of its incidents, as for the unwearied pertinacity of the principal actor in the grossest falsehood and perjury. It was a trial awful in its instructions, and painfully interesting in the mystery which still hangs like a shroud around the motives of Mr. Goodridge.

A brief statement of the facts will fully exhibit the remarkable power of Mr. Webster in unmasking the hypocrisy which, for a long time, not only imposed upon the whole community, but misled by its subtlety the entire body of the Essex Bar.

Major Goodridge was a young man of good education and respectable connections; of fine personal appearance, gentlemanly deportment, and good character. His place of business was Bangor, Maine, and at the time of the alleged robbery he was on his way to Boston, travelling in a one-horse sleigh, alone, with a considerable sum of money. Before leaving home he procured a pair of pistols, which he discharged and loaded daily, as he said, in some unfrequented piece of woods, for he did not wish it to be known that he was armed. He said, moreover, that he took the precaution to put a private mark upon every piece of money in his possession, so as to be able to identify it if he should be robbed. His somewhat singular reason for these preliminary measures was, that he had heard of a robbery in Maine, not long before.

* An Argument addressed to the Jury, at the Term of the Supreme Judicial Court of Massachusetts held at Ipswich in April, 1817.

† The following account of this celebrated case was furnished by Stephen W. Marston, Esq., of Newburyport, who, together with Samuel L. Knapp, Esq., of the same place, was associated with Mr. Webster in the defence of the Kennistons.

When he arrived at Exeter, New Hampshire, he procured nine balls, and then, for the first time, made no secret of having pistols. At this place he left his sleigh, obtained a saddle, and started for Newburyport on horseback, late in the afternoon of the 19th of December, passing the Essex Merrimack Bridge a few minutes before nine o'clock. On the brow of the hill, a short distance from the bridge, is the place of the robbery, in full view of several houses, on a great thoroughfare, where people are constantly passing, and where the mail-coach and two wagons were known to have passed within a few minutes of the time of the alleged robbery.

The Major's story was as follows. Three men suddenly appeared before him, one of whom seized the bridle of his horse, presented a pistol, and demanded his money. The Major, pretending to be getting his money, seized a pistol from his portmanteau with his right hand, grasped the ruffian at his horse's head with his left, and both discharged their pistols at the same instant, the ball of his adversary passing through the Major's hand. The three robbers then pulled him from his horse, dragged him over the frozen ground and over the fence, beating him till he was senseless, and robbed him of about seventeen hundred dollars in gold and paper money, and left him with his gold watch and all his papers in the field. Recovering in about half an hour, he went back to the bridge, passed several houses without calling, and, at the toll-house, accused the first person he met with, a female, of robbing him; and so continued charging various people about him with the robbery. After some time a lantern was procured, and himself with others started for the place of the robbery, where were found his watch, papers, penknife, and other articles. He represented to them that the robbers had bruised his head, stamped upon his breast, and stabbed him in several places. Physicians were called, and he appeared to be insane. The next day he went to Newburyport, and was confined to his bed for several weeks. A reward of three hundred dollars, soon increased by voluntary subscription to one thousand, was offered for the detection of the robbers and the recovery of the money. As soon as the Major was able to leave his bed, he went to Danvers, consulted his friends there, and the result of his deliberations and inquiries was the arrest of the Kennistons, who were found in an obscure part of the town of Newmarket, New Hampshire, their place of residence. In their house the Major found some pieces of his marked gold, deposited under a pork-barrel in the cellar; he also found there a ten-dollar note, which he identified as his own.

This was proof indeed of the fact of the robbery, which seemed for a time effectually fastened upon the Kennistons. But one circumstance after another came to light in regard to the transaction, until some people felt doubts creeping over their minds as to the truthfulness of the

Major's story. These were few in number, it is true, but such an intimation, coming from any respectable source, was enough to startle the Major and his friends from their apathy, and incited them to renewed efforts to probe this dark and mysterious transaction to its depths. The result was a determination to search the house of Mr. Pearson, the toll-gatherer at the bridge; but here nothing was found. They then procured the services of an old conjurer of Danvers, Swimmington by name, and under his direction, with witch-hazel and metallic rods, renewed their search upon Mr. Pearson's premises, this time discovering the Major's gold and paper wrappers. Mr. Pearson was arrested, carried to Newburyport, examined before two magistrates, and discharged at once. This operation proved most unpropitious to the Major's plans. So great was the indignation of Mr. Pearson's friends, for he was a respectable man, that they lost all control over themselves, and after the examination, detaching the horses from his sleigh, they drew him home themselves.

It now became more necessary than ever that some one should be found who might be connected with the Kennistons in the robbery, for the circumstances in relation to these men were such, that the public could not believe that they had committed the daring deed, though the evidence was incontestable that they had received a portion of the spoils. The next step, therefore, was to arrest one Taber of Boston, who had formerly lived in Portland, and whom Goodridge said he had seen in Alfred on his way up, and from whom he pretended to have obtained information in regard to the Kennistons. In Taber's house were found a number of the marked wrappers which the Major had put round his gold before leaving home. Taber was likewise brought to Newburyport, examined, and bound over for trial with the Kennistons.

Notwithstanding all this accumulation of evidence, the public were not satisfied. It seemed to be necessary that somebody living near the bridge should be connected with the transaction, and Mr. Joseph Jackman was fastened upon as that unfortunate man, he having left Newbury for New York very soon after the alleged robbery. Thither Goodridge immediately proceeded, found Jackman, who was living there with his brother, searched the house, and in the garret, among some old rubbish, found a large number of his marked wrappers! The Major's touch was magical, and underneath his fingers gold and bank-notes grew in plenty. Jackman was arrested and lodged in "the Tombs," while Good ridge returned to Boston, got a requisition from the Governor, and had him brought in irons to Ipswich, where the Supreme Judicial Court was then in session. The grand jury had risen, but he was examined before a magistrate, and ordered to recognize to appear at the next term; which he did, and was discharged. An indictment had been found against the Kennistons and Taber, and the time of trial had arrived. Nothwithstanding the doubts and suspicions which had been excited by the conduct of Goodridge, yet the evidence against the Kennistons, Taber, and Jackman was so overwhelming, that almost every one felt sure of their conviction. To such an extent did this opinion prevail, that no eminent member of the Essex Bar was willing to undertake their defence. Under these circumstances, two or three individuals, who had been early convinced that the Major's stories were false from beginning to end, determined, the day before the trial, to send to Suffolk for counsel. Mr. Webster had just then removed to Boston from Portsmouth; his services were engaged, and late in the night preceding the day of trial he arrived at Ipswich, having had no opportunity to examine the witnesses, and but little time for consultation. The indictment against Taber was *nol prossed*, and the trial of the Kennistons commenced. Mr. Webster, as senior counsel, conducted the defence with a degree of ability, boldness, tact, and legal learning which had rarely been witnessed in Essex County, and, notwithstanding the accumulated mass of evidence against the Kennistons, they were acquitted.

At the next term of the Supreme Judicial Court, Jackman was indicted and tried, but the jury did not agree, though the Hon. William Prescott had been employed to assist the prosecuting officer. Jackman was again tried at the next term of the court, at this time defended by Mr. Webster, and acquitted.

The criminal prosecutions growing out of this affair being thus ended, Mr. Pearson commenced an action against Goodridge for malicious prosecution, laying his damages at $2,000, which sum the jury awarded him without leaving their seats. In this case, also, Mr. Webster was counsel for the plaintiff; and time had brought forth so many new facts, and the evidence was so clear and overwhelming against Goodridge, that the public became satisfied that *he was his own robber!* He was surrendered by his bail, committed to jail, took the poor debtors' oath, and soon after left the Commonwealth, and has not resided here since. It is understood that he finally settled in Norfolk, Virginia, where he still lives. The public rarely stop to consider how much they are indebted to men like Mr. Webster for laying bare the villany of such a deep-laid and diabolical plot. But for him there is no doubt the Kennistons and Jackman would have been convicted of highway robbery, though innocent.

The following report of Mr. Webster's speech is quite imperfect; a mere skeleton, affording but a very inadequate idea of the argument which was actually addressed by him to the jury.

Gentlemen of the Jury, — It is true that the offence charged in the indictment in this case is not capital; but perhaps this can hardly be considered as favorable to the defendants. To those who are guilty, and without hope of escape, no doubt the lightness of the penalty of transgression gives consolation. But if the defendants are innocent, it is more natural for them to be thinking upon what they have lost by that alteration of the law which has left highway robbery no longer capital, than upon what the guilty might gain by it. They have lost those great privileges in their trial, which the law allows, in capital cases, for the protection of innocence against unfounded accusation. They have lost the right of being previously furnished with a copy of the indictment, and a list of the government witnesses. They have lost the right of peremptory challenge; and, notwithstanding the prejudices which they know have been excited against them, they must show legal cause of challenge, in each individual case, or else take the jury as they find it. They have lost the benefit of assignment of counsel by the court. They have lost the benefit of the Commonwealth's process to bring in witnesses in their behalf. When to these circumstances it is added that they are strangers, almost wholly without friends, and without the means for preparing their defence, it is evident they must take their trial under great disadvantages.

But without dwelling on these considerations, I proceed, Gentlemen of the Jury, to ask your attention to those circumstances which cannot but cast doubts on the story of the prosecutor.

In the first place, it is impossible to believe that a robbery of this sort could have been committed by three or four men without previous arrangement and concert, and of course without the knowledge of the fact that Goodridge would be there, and that he had money. They did not go on the highway, in such a place, in a cold December's night, for the general purpose of attacking the first passenger, running the chance of his being somebody who had money. It is not easy to believe that a gang of robbers existed, that they acted systematically, communicating intelligence to one another, and meeting and dispersing as occasion required, and that this gang had their head-quarters in such a place as Newburyport. No town is more distinguished for the general correctness of the habits of its citizens; and it is of such a size that every man in it may be known to all the rest.

The pursuits, occupations, and habits of every person within it are within the observation of his neighbors. A suspicious stranger would be instantly observed, and all his movements could be easily traced. This is not the place to be the general rendezvous of a gang of robbers. Offenders of this sort hang on the skirts of large towns. From the commission of their crimes they hasten into the crowd, and hide themselves in the populousness of great cities.

If it be wholly improbable that a gang existed in such a place for the purpose of general plunder, the next inquiry is, Is there any reason to think that there was a special or particular combination, for the single purpose of robbing the prosecutor? Now it is material to observe, that not only is there no evidence of any such combination, but also, that circumstances existed which render it next to impossible that the defendants could have been parties to such a combination, or even that they could have any knowledge of the existence of any such man as Goodridge, or that any person, with money, was expected to come from the eastward, and to be near Essex Bridge, at or about nine o'clock, the evening when the robbery is said to have been committed.

One of the defendants had been for some weeks in Newburyport, the other passed the bridge from New Hampshire at twelve o'clock on the 19th of December, 1816. At this time, Goodridge had not yet arrived at Exeter, twelve or fourteen miles from the bridge. How, then, could either of the defendants know that he was coming? Besides, he says that nobody, as far as he is aware, knew on the road that he had money, and nothing happened till he reached Exeter, according to his account, from which it might be conjectured that such was the case. Here, as he relates it, it became known that he had pistols; and he must wish you to infer that the plan to rob him was laid here, at Exeter, by some of the persons who inferred that he had money from his being armed. Who were these persons? Certainly not the defendants, or either of them. Certainly not Taber. Certainly not Jackman. Were they persons of suspicious characters? Was he in a house of a suspicious character? On this point he gives us no information. He has either not taken the pains to inquire, or he chooses not to communicate the result of his inquiries. Yet nothing could be more important, since he seems compelled to lay the scene of the plot against him at Exeter, than to know who the persons were that he saw, or who saw him, at that place. On the face of the facts now proved, nothing could be more improbable than that the plan of robbery was concerted at Exeter. If so, why should those who concerted it send forward to Newburyport to engage the defendants, especially as they did not know that they were there? What should induce any persons so suddenly to apply to the defendants to assist in a robbery? There was nothing in their personal character or previous history that should induce this.

Nor was there time for all this. If the prosecutor had not lingered on the road, for reasons not yet discovered, he must have been in Newburyport long before the time at which he states the robbery to have been committed. How, then, could any one expect to leave Exeter, come to Newburyport, fifteen miles, there look out for and find out assistants for a highway robbery, and get back two miles to a convenient place for the commission of the crime? That any body should have undertaken to act thus is wholly improbable; and, in point of fact, there is not the least proof of any body's travelling, that afternoon, from Exeter to Newburyport, or of any person who was at the tavern at Exeter having left it that afternoon. In all probability, nothing of this sort could have taken place without being capable of detection and proof. In every particular, the prosecutor has wholly failed to show the least probability of a plan to rob him having been laid at Exeter.

But how comes it that Goodridge was near or quite four hours and a half in travelling a distance which might have been travelled in two hours or two hours and a half. He says he missed his way, and went the Salisbury road. But some of the jury know that this could not have delayed him more than five or ten minutes. He ought to be able to give some better account of this delay.

Failing, as he seems to do, to create any belief that a plan to rob him was arranged at Exeter, the prosecutor goes back to Alfred, and says he saw there a man whom Taber resembles. But Taber is proved to have been at that time, and at the time of the robbery, in Boston. This is proved beyond question. It is so certain, that the Solicitor-General has *nol prossed* the indictment against him.

There is an end, then, of all pretence of the adoption of a scheme of robbery at Alfred. This leaves the prosecutor altogether unable to point out any manner in which it should become known that he had money, or in which a design to rob him should originate.

It is next to be considered whether the prosecutor's story is either natural or consistent. But, on the threshold of the inquiry, every one puts the question, What motive had the prosecutor to be guilty of the abominable conduct of feigning a robbery? It is difficult to assign motives. The jury do not know enough of his character or circumstances. Such things have happened, and may happen again. Suppose he owed money in Boston, and had it not to pay? Who knows how high he might estimate the value of a plausible apology? Some men have also a whimsical ambition of distinction. There is no end to the variety of modes in which human vanity exhibits itself. A story of this nature excites the public sympathy. It attracts general attention. It causes the name of the prosecutor to be celebrated as a man who has been attacked, and, after a manly resistance, overcome by robbers, and who has renewed his resistance as soon as returning life and sensation enabled him, and, after a second conflict, has been quite subdued, beaten and bruised out of all sense and sensation, and finally left for dead on the field. It is not easy to say how far such motives, trifling and ridiculous as most men would think them, might influence the prosecutor, when connected with any expectation of favor or indulgence, if he wanted such, from his creditors. It is to be remembered that he probably did not see all the consequences of his conduct, if his robbery be a pretence. He might not intend to prosecute any body. But he probably found, and indeed there is evidence to show, that it was necessary for him to do something to find out the authors of the alleged robbery. He manifested no particular zeal on this subject. He was in no haste. He appears rather to have been pressed by others to do that which, if he had really been robbed, we should suppose he would have been most earnest to do, the earliest moment.

But could he so seriously wound himself? Could he or would he shoot a pistol-bullet through his hand, in order to render the robbery probable, and to obtain belief in his story? All exhibitions are subject to accidents. Whether they are serious or farcical, they may, in some particulars, not proceed exactly as they are designed to do. If we knew that this shot through the hand, if made by himself, must have been intentionally made by himself, it would be a circumstance of greater weight. The bullet went through the sleeve of his coat. He might have intended it should go through nothing else. It is quite certain he did not receive the wound in the way he described. He says he was pulling or thrusting aside the robber's pistol, and while his hand was on it, it was fired, and the contents passed through his hand. This could not have been so, because no part of the contents went through the hand, except the ball. There was powder on the sleeve of his coat, and from the appearance one would think the pistol to have been three or four feet from the hand when fired. The fact of the pistol-bullet being fired through the hand, is doubtless a circumstance of importance. It may not be easy to account for it; but it is to be weighed with other circumstances.

It is most extraordinary, that, in the whole case, the prosecutor should prove hardly any fact in any way but by his own oath. He chooses to trust every thing on his own credit with the jury. Had he the money with him which he mentions? If so, his clerks or persons connected with him in business must have known it; yet no witness is produced. Nothing can be more important than to prove that he had the money. Yet he does not prove it. Why should he leave this essential fact without further support? He is not surprised with this defence, he knew what it would be. He knew that nothing could be more important than to prove that, in truth, he did possess the money which he says he lost; yet he does not prove it. All that he saw, and all that he did, and every thing that occurred to him until the alleged robbery, rests solely on his own credit. He does not see fit to corroborate any fact by the testimony of any witness. So he went to New York to arrest Jackman. He did arrest him. He swears positively that he found in his possession papers which he lost at the time of the robbery; yet he neither produces the papers themselves, nor the persons who assisted in the search.

In like manner, he represents his intercourse with Taber at Boston. Taber, he says, made certain confessions. They made a bargain for a disclosure or confession on one side, and a reward on the other. But no one heard these confessions except Goodridge himself. Taber now confronts him, and pronounces this part of his story to be wholly false; and there is nobody who can support the prosecutor.

A jury cannot too seriously reflect on this part of the case. There are many most important allegations of fact, which, if true, could easily be shown by other witnesses, and yet are not so shown.

How came Mr. Goodridge to set out from Bangor, armed in this formal and formidable manner? How came he to be so apprehensive of a robbery? The reason he gives is completely ridiculous. As the foundation of his alarm, he tells a story of a robbery which he had heard of, but which, as far as appears, no one else ever heard of; and the story itself is so perfectly absurd, it is difficult to resist the belief that it was the product of his imagination at the moment. He seems to have been a little too confident that an attempt would be made to rob him. The manner in which he carried his money, as he says, indicated a strong expectation of this sort. His gold he wrapped in a cambric cloth, put it into a shot bag, and then into a portmanteau. One parcel of bills, of a hundred dollars in amount, he put into his pocket-book; another, of somewhat more than a thousand dollars, he carried next his person, underneath all his clothes. Having disposed of his money in this way, and armed himself with two good pistols, he set out from Bangor. The jury will judge whether this extraordinary care of his money, and this formal arming of himself to defend it, are not circumstances of a very suspicious character.

He stated that he did not travel in the night; that he would not so much expose himself to robbers. He said that, when he came near Alfred, he did not go into the village, but stopped a few miles short, because night was coming on, and he would not trust himself and his money out at night. He represents himself to have observed this rule constantly and invariably until he got to Exeter. Yet, when the time came for the robbery, he was found out at night. He left Exeter about sunset, intending to go to Newburyport, fifteen miles distant, that evening. When he is asked how this should happen, he says he had no fear of robbers after he left the District of Maine. He thought himself quite safe when he arrived at Exeter. Yet he told the jury, that at Exeter he thought it necessary to load his pistol afresh. He asked for a private room at the inn. He told the persons in attendance that he wished such a room for the purpose of changing his clothes. He charged them not to suffer him to be interrupted. But he now testifies that his object was not to change his dress, but to put new loading into his pistols. What sort of a story is this?

He says he now felt himself out of all danger from robbers, and was therefore willing to travel at night. At the same time, he thought himself in very great danger from robbers, and therefore took the utmost pains to keep his pistols well loaded and in good order. To account for the pains he took about loading his pistols at Exeter, he says it was his invariable practice, every day after he left Bangor, to discharge and load again one or both of his pistols; that he never missed doing this; that he avoided doing it at the inns, lest he should create suspicion, but that he did it, while alone, on the road, every day.

How far this is probable the jury will judge. It will be observed that he gave up his habits of caution as he approached the place of the robbery. He then loaded his pistols at the tavern, where persons might and did see him; and he then also travelled in the night. He passed the bridge over Merrimack River a few minutes before nine o'clock. He was now at a part of his progress where he was within the observation of other witnesses, and something could be known of him besides what he told of himself. Immediately after him passed the two persons with their wagons, Shaw and Keyser. Close upon them followed the mail-coach. Now, these wagons and the mail must have passed within three rods, at most, of Goodridge, at the very time of the robbery. They must have been very near the spot, the very moment of the attack; and if he was under the robbers' hands as long as he represents, or if they staid on the spot long enough to do half what he says they did, they must have been there when the wagons and the stage passed. At any rate, it is next to impossible, by any computation of time, to put these carriages so far from the spot, that the drivers should not have heard the cry of murder, which he says he raised, or the report of the two pistols, which he says were discharged. In three quarters of an hour, or an hour, he returned, and repassed the bridge.

The jury will next naturally look to the appearances exhibited on the field after the robbery. The portmanteau was there. The witnesses say, that the straps which fastened it to the saddle had been neither cut nor broken. They were carefully unbuckled. This was very considerate for robbers. It had been opened, and its contents were scattered about the field. The pocket-book, too, had been opened, and many papers it contained found on the ground. Nothing valuable was lost but money. The robbers did not think it well to go off at once with the portmanteau and the pocket-book. The place was so secure, so remote, so unfrequented; they were so far from the highway, at least one full rod; there were so few persons passing, probably not more than four or five then in the road, within hearing of the pistols and the cries of Goodridge; there being, too, not above five or six dwelling-houses, full of people, within the hearing of the report of a pistol; these circumstances were all so favorable to their safety, that the robbers sat down to look over the prosecutor's papers, carefully examined the contents of his pocket-book and portmanteau, and took only the things which they needed! There was money belonging to other persons. The robbers did not take it. They found out it was not the prosecutor's, and left it. It may be said to be favorable to the prosecutor's story, that the money which did not belong to him, and the plunder of which would seem to be the most probable inducement he could have to feign a robbery, was not taken. But the jury will consider whether this circumstance does not bear quite as strongly the other way, and whether they can believe that robbers could have left this money, either from accident or design.

The robbers, by Goodridge's account, were extremely careful to search his person. Having found money in his portmanteau and in his pocket-book, they still forthwith stripped him to the skin, and searched until they found the sum which had been so carefully deposited under his clothes. Was it likely, that, having found money in the places where it is ordinarily carried, robbers should proceed to search for more, where they had no reason to suppose more would be found? Goodridge says that no person knew of his having put his bank-notes in that situation. On the first attack, however, they proceeded to open one garment after another, until they penetrated to the treasure, which was beneath them all.

The testimony of Mr. Howard is material. He examined Goodridge's pistol, which was found on the spot, and thinks it had not been fired at all. If this be so, it would follow that the wound through the hand was not made by this pistol; but then, as the pistol is now discharged, if it had not been fired, he is not correct in swearing that he fired it at the robbers, nor could it have been loaded at Exeter, as he testified.

In the whole case, there is nothing, perhaps, more deserving consideration, than the prosecutor's statement of the violence which the robbers used towards him. He says he was struck with a heavy club, on the back part of his head. He fell senseless to the ground. Three or four rough-handed villains then dragged him to the fence, and through it or over it, with such force as to break one of the boards. They then plundered his money. Presently he came to his senses; perceived his situation; saw one of the robbers sitting or standing near; he valiantly sprung upon, and would have overcome him, but the ruffian called out for his comrades, who returned, and all together they renewed their attack upon, subdued him, and redoubled their violence. They struck him heavy blows; they threw him violently to the ground; they kicked him in the side; they choked him; one of them, to use his own words, jumped upon his breast. They left him only when they supposed they had killed him. He went back to Pearson's, at the bridge, in a state of delirium, and it was several hours before his recollection came to him. This is his account. Now, in point of fact, it is certain that on no part of his person was there the least mark of this beating and wounding. The blow on the head, which brought him senseless to the ground, neither broke the skin, nor caused any tumor, nor left any mark whatever. He fell from his horse on the frozen ground, without any appearance of injury. He was drawn through or over the fence with such force as to break the rail, but not so as to leave any wound or scratch on him. A second time he is knocked down, kicked, stamped upon, choked, and in every way abused and beaten till sense had departed, and the breath of life hardly remained; and yet no wound, bruise, discoloration, or mark of injury was found to result from all this. Except the wound in his hand, and a few slight punctures in his left arm, apparently made with his own penknife, which was found open on the spot, there was no wound or mark which the surgeons, upon repeated examinations, could anywhere discover. This is a story not to be believed. No matter who tells it, it is so impossible to be true, that all belief is set at defiance. No man can believe it. All this tale of blows which left no marks, and of wounds which could not be discovered, must be the work of imagination. If the jury can believe that he was robbed, it is impossible they can believe his account of the manner of it.

With respect, next, to delirium. The jury have heard the physicians. Two of them have no doubt it was all feigned. Dr. Spofford spoke in a more guarded manner, but it was very evident his opinion agreed with theirs. In the height of his raving, the physician who was present said to others, that he could find nothing the matter with the man, and that his pulse was perfectly regular. But consider the facts which Dr. Balch testifies. He suspected the whole of this illness and delirium to be feigned. He wished to ascertain the truth. While he or others were present, Goodridge appeared to be in the greatest pains and agony from his wounds. He could not turn himself in bed, nor be turned by others, without infinite distress. His mind, too, was as much disordered as his body. He was constantly raving about robbery and murder. At length the physicians and others withdrew, and left him alone in the room. Dr. Balch returned softly to the door, which he had left partly open, and there he had a full view of his patient, unobserved by him. Goodridge was then very quiet. His incoherent exclamations had ceased. Dr. Balch saw him turn over without inconvenience. Pretty soon he sat up in bed, and adjusted his neckcloth and his hair. Then, hearing footsteps on the staircase, he instantly sunk into the bed again; his pains all returned, and he cried out against robbers and murderers as loud as ever. Now, these facts are all sworn to by an intelligent witness, who cannot be mistaken in them; a respectable physician, whose veracity or accuracy is in no way impeached or questioned. After this, it is difficult to retain any good opinion of the prosecutor. Robbed or not robbed, this was his conduct; and such conduct necessarily takes away all claim to sympathy and respect. The jury will consider whether it does not also take away all right to be believed in any thing. For if they should be of opinion that in any one point he has intentionally misrepresented facts, he can be believed in nothing. No man is to be convicted on the testimony of a witness whom the jury has found wilfully violating the truth in any particular.

The next part of the case is the conduct of the prosecutor in attempting to find out the robbers, after he had recovered from his illness. He suspected Mr. Pearson, a very honest, respectable man, who keeps the tavern at the bridge. He searched his house and premises. He sent for a conjurer to come, with his metallic rods and witch-hazel, to find the stolen money. Goodridge says now, that he thought he should find it, if the conjurer's instruments were properly prepared. He professes to have full faith in the art. Was this folly, or fraud, or a strange mixture of both? Pretty soon after the last search, gold pieces were actually found near Mr. Pearson's house, in the manner stated by the female witness. How came they there? Did the robber deposit them there? That is not possible. Did he accidentally leave them there? Why should not a robber take as good care of his money as others? It is certain, too, that the gold pieces were not put there at the time of the robbery, because the ground was then bare; but when these pieces were found, there were several inches of snow below them. When Goodridge searched here with his conjurer, he was on this spot, alone and unobserved, as he thought. Whether he did not, at that time, drop his gold into the snow, the jury will judge. When he came to this search, he proposed something very ridiculous. He proposed that all persons about to assist in the search should be examined, to see that they had nothing which they could put into Pearson's possession, for the purpose of being found there. But how was this examination to be made? Why, truly, Goodridge proposed that every man should examine himself, and that, among others, he would examine himself, till he was satisfied he had nothing in his pockets which he could leave at Pearson's, with the fraudulent design of being afterwards found there, as evidence against Pearson. What construction would be given to such conduct?

As to Jackman, Goodridge went to New York and arrested him. In his room he says he found paper coverings of gold, with his own figures on them, and pieces of an old and useless receipt, which he can identify, and which he had in his possession at the time of the robbery. He found these things lying on the floor in Jackman's room. What should induce the robbers, when they left all other papers, to take this receipt? And what should induce Jackman to carry it to New York, and keep it, with the coverings of the gold, in a situation where it was likely to be found, and used as evidence against him?

There is no end to the series of improbabilities growing out of the prosecutor's story.

One thing especially deserves notice. Wherever Goodridge searches, he always finds something; and what he finds, he always can identify and swear to, as being his. The thing found has always some marks by which he knows it. Yet he never finds much. He never finds the mass of his lost treasure. He finds just enough to be evidence, and no more.

These are the circumstances which tend to raise doubts of the truth of the prosecutor's relation. It is for the jury to say, whether it would be safe to convict any man for this robbery until these doubts shall be cleared up. No doubt they are to judge him candidly; but they are not to make every thing yield to a regard to his reputation, or a desire to vindicate him from the suspicion of a fraudulent prosecution.

He stands like other witnesses, except that he is a very interested witness; and he must hope for credit, if at all, from the consistency and general probability of the facts to which he testifies. The jury will not convict the prisoners to save the prosecutor from disgrace. He has had every opportunity of making out his case. If any person in the State could have corroborated any part of his story, that person he could have produced. He has had the benefit of full time, and good counsel, and of the Commonwealth's process, to bring in his witnesses. More than all, he has had an opportunity of telling his own story, with the simplicity that belongs to truth, if it were true, and the frankness and earnestness of an honest man, if he be such. It is for the jury to say, under their oaths, how he has acquitted himself in these particulars, and whether he has left their minds free from doubt as to the truth of his narration.

But if Goodridge were really robbed, is there satisfactory evidence that the defendants had a hand in the commission of this offence? The evidence relied on is the finding of the money in their house. It appears that these defendants lived together, and, with a sister, constituted one family. Their father lived in another part of the same house, and with his wife constituted another and distinct family. In this house, some six weeks after the robbery, the prosecutor made a search; and the result has been stated by the witnesses. Now, if the money had been passed or used by the defendants it might have been conclusive. If found about their persons, it might have been very strong proof. But, under the circumstances of this case, the mere finding of money in their house, and that only in places where the prosecutor had previously been, is no evidence at all. With respect to the gold pieces, it is certainly true that they were found in Goodridge's track. They were found only where he had been, and might have put them.

When the sheriff was in the house and Goodridge in the cellar, gold was found in the cellar. When the sheriff was up stairs and Goodridge in the rooms below, the sheriff was called down to look for money where Goodridge directed, and there money was found. As to the bank-note, the evidence is not quite so clear. Mr. Leavitt says he found a note in a drawer in a room in which none of the party had before been; that he thought it an uncurrent or counterfeit note, and not a part of Goodridge's money, and left it where he found it, without further notice. An hour or two afterward, Upton perceived a note in the same drawer, Goodridge being then with or near him, and called to Leavitt. Leavitt told him that he had discovered that note before, but that it could not be Goodridge's. It was then examined. Leavitt says he looked at it, and saw writing on the back of it. Upton says he looked at it, and saw writing on the back of it. He says also that it was shown to Goodridge, who examined it in the same way that he and Leavitt examined it. None of the party at this time suspected it to be Goodridge's. It was then put into Leavitt's pocket-book, where it remained till evening, when it was taken out at the tavern; and then it turns out to be, plainly and clearly, one of Goodridge's notes, and has the name of "James Poor, Bangor," in Goodridge's own handwriting, on the back of it. The first thing that strikes one in this account is, Why was not this discovery made at the time? Goodridge was looking for notes, as well as gold. He was looking for Boston notes, for such he had lost. He was looking for ten-dollar notes, for such he had lost. He was looking for notes which he could recognize and identify. He would, therefore, naturally be particularly attentive to any writing or marks upon such as he might find. Under these circumstances, a note is found in the house of the supposed robbers. It is a Boston note, it is a ten-dollar note, it has writing on the back of it; that writing is the name of his town and the name of one of his neighbors; more than all, that writing is his own handwriting! Notwithstanding all this, neither Goodridge, nor Upton, nor the sheriff, examined it so as to see whether it was Goodridge's money. Notwithstanding it so fully resembled, in all points, the money they were looking for, and notwithstanding they also saw writing on the back of it, which, they must know, if they read it, would probably have shown where it came from, neither of them did so far examine it as to see any proof of its being Goodridge's.

This is hardly to be believed. It must be a pretty strong faith in the prosecutor that could credit this story. In every part of it, it is improbable and absurd. It is much more easy to believe that the note was changed. There might have been, and there probably was, an uncurrent or counterfeit note found in the drawer by Leavitt. He certainly did not at the time think it to be Goodridge's, and he left it in the drawer where he found it. Before he saw it again, the prosecutor had been in that room, and was in or near it when the sheriff was again called in, and asked to put that bill in his pocket-book. How do the jury know that this was the same note which Leavitt had before seen? Or suppose it was. Leavitt carried it to Coffin's; in the evening he produced it, and, after having been handed about for some time among the company, it turns out to be Goodridge's note, and to have upon it infallible marks of identity. How do the jury know that a sleight of hand had not changed the note at Coffin's? It is sufficient to say, the note might have been changed. It is not certain that this is the note which Leavitt first found in the drawer, and this not being certain, it is not proof against the defendants.

Is it not extremely improbable, if the defendants are guilty, that they should deposit the money in the places where it was found? Why should they put it in small parcels in so many places, for no end but to multiply the chances of detection? Why, especially, should they put a doubloon in their father's pocket-book? There is no evidence, nor any ground of suspicion, that the father knew of the money being in his pocket-book. He swears he did not know it. His general character is unimpeached, and there is nothing against his credit. The inquiry at Stratham was calculated to elicit the truth; and, after all, there is not the slightest reason to suspect that he knew that the doubloon was in his pocket-book. What could possibly induce the defendants to place it there? No man can conjecture a reason. On the other hand, if this is a fraudulent proceeding on the part of the prosecutor, this circumstance could be explained. He did not know that the pocket-book, and the garment in which it was found, did not belong to one of the defendants. He was as likely, therefore, to place it there as elsewhere. It is very material to consider that nothing was found in that part of the house which belonged to the defendants. Every thing was discovered in the father's apartments. They were not found, therefore, in the possession of the defendants, any more than if they had been discovered in any other house in the neighborhood. The two tenements, it is true, were under the same roof; but they were not on that account the same tenements. They were as distinct as any other houses. Now, how should it happen that the several parcels of money should all be found in the father's possession? He is not suspected, certainly there is no reason to suspect him, of having had any hand either in the commission of the robbery or the concealing of the goods. He swears he had no knowledge of any part of this money being in his house. It is not easy to imagine how it came there, unless it be supposed to have been put there by some one who did not know what part of the house belonged to the defendants and what part did not.

The witnesses on the part of the prosecution have testified that the defendants, when arrested, manifested great agitation and alarm; paleness overspread their faces, and drops of sweat stood on their temples. This satisfied the witnesses of the defendants' guilt, and they now state the circumstances as being indubitable proof. This argument manifests, in those who use it, an equal want of sense and sensibility. It is precisely fitted to the feeling and the intellect of a bum-bailiff. In a court of justice it deserves nothing but contempt. Is there nothing that can agitate the frame or excite the blood but the consciousness of guilt? If the defendants were innocent, would they not feel indignation at this unjust accusation? If they saw an attempt to produce false evidence against them, would they not be angry? And, seeing the production of such evidence, might they not feel fear and alarm? And have indignation, and anger, and terror, no power to affect the human countenance or the human frame?

Miserable, miserable, indeed, is the reasoning which would infer any man's guilt from his agitation when he found himself accused of a heinous offence; when he saw evidence which he might know to be false and fraudulent brought against him; when his house was filled, from the garret to the cellar, by those whom he might esteem as false witnesses; and when he himself, instead of being at liberty to observe their conduct and watch their motions, was a prisoner in close custody in his own house, with the fists of a catch-poll clenched upon his throat.

The defendants were at Newburyport the afternoon and evening of the robbery. For the greater part of the time they show where they were, and what they were doing. Their proof, it is true, does not apply to every moment. But when it is considered that, from the moment of their arrest, they have been in close prison, perhaps they have shown as much as could be expected. Few men, when called on afterwards, can remember, and fewer still can prove, how they have passed every half-hour of an evening. At a reasonable hour they both came to the house where Laban had lodged the night before. Nothing suspicious was observed in their manner or conversation. Is it probable they would thus come unconcernedly into the company of others, from a field of robbery, and, as they must have supposed, of murder, before they could have ascertained whether the stain of blood was not on their garments? They remained in the place a part of the next day. The town was alarmed; a strict inquiry was made of all strangers, and of the defendants among others. Nothing suspicious was discovered. They avoided no inquiry, nor did they leave the town in any haste. The jury has had an opportunity of seeing the defendants. Does their general appearance indicate that hardihood which would enable them to act this cool, unconcerned part? Is it not more likely they would have fled?

From the time of the robbery to the arrest, five or six weeks, the defendants were engaged in their usual occupations. They are not found to have passed a dollar of money to any body. They continued their ordinary habits of labor. No man saw money about them, nor any circumstance that might lead to a suspicion that they had money. Nothing occurred tending in any degree to excite suspicion against them. When arrested, and when all this array of evidence was brought against them, and when they could hope in nothing but their innocence, immunity was offered them again if they would confess. They were pressed, and urged, and allured, by every motive which could be set before them, to acknowledge their participation in the offence, and to bring out their accomplices. They steadily protested that they could confess nothing because they knew nothing. In defiance of all the discoveries made in their house, they have trusted to their innocence. On that, and on the candor and discernment of an enlightened jury, they still rely.

If the jury are satisfied that there is the highest improbability that these persons could have had any previous knowledge of Goodridge, or been concerned in any previous concert to rob him; if their conduct that evening and the next day was marked by no circumstances of suspicion; if from that moment until their arrest nothing appeared against them; if they neither passed money, nor are found to have had money; if the manner of the search of their house, and the circumstances attending it, excite strong suspicions of unfair and fraudulent practices; if, in the hour of their utmost peril, no promises of safety could draw from the defendants any confession affecting themselves or others, it will be for the jury to say whether they can pronounce them guilty.

THE DARTMOUTH COLLEGE CASE.*

THE action, The Trustees of Dartmouth College *vs.* William H. Woodward, was commenced in the Court of Common Pleas, Grafton County, State of New Hampshire, February term, 1817. The declaration was trover for the books of record, original charter, common seal, and other corporate property of the College. The conversion was alleged to have been made on the 7th day of October, 1816. The proper pleas were filed, and by consent the cause was carried directly to the Superior Court of New Hampshire, by appeal, and entered at the May term, 1817. The general issue was pleaded by the defendant, and joined by the plaintiffs. The facts in the case were then agreed upon by the parties, and drawn up in the form of a special verdict, reciting the charter of the College and the acts of the legislature of the State, passed June and December, 1816, by which the said corporation of Dartmouth College was *enlarged* and *improved*, and the said charter *amended.*

The question made in the case was, whether those acts of the legislature were valid and binding upon the corporation, without their acceptance or assent, and not repugnant to the Constitution of the United States. If so, the verdict found for the defendants; otherwise, it found for the plaintiffs.

The cause was continued to the September term of the court in Rockingham County, where it was argued; and at the November term of the same year, in Grafton County, the opinion of the court was delivered by Chief Justice Richardson, in favor of the validity and constitutionality of the acts of the legislature; and judgment was accordingly entered for the defendant on the special verdict.

Thereupon a writ of error was sued out by the original plaintiffs, to remove the cause to the Supreme Court of the United States; where it

* Argument before the Supreme Court of the United States, at Washington, on the 10th of March, 1818.

was entered at the term of the court holden at Washington on the first Monday of February, 1818.

The cause came on for argument on the 10th day of March, 1818, before all the judges. It was argued by Mr. Webster and Mr. Hopkinson for the plaintiffs in error, and by Mr. Holmes and the Attorney-General (Wirt) for the defendant in error.

At the term of the court holden in February, 1819, the opinion of the judges was delivered by Chief Justice Marshall, declaring the acts of the legislature unconstitutional and invalid, and reversing the judgment of the State court. The court, with the exception of Mr. Justice Duvall, were unanimous.

The following was the argument of Mr. Webster for the plaintiffs in error.

The general question is, whether the acts of the legislature of New Hampshire of the 27th of June, and of the 18th and 26th of December, 1816, are valid and binding on the plaintiffs, *without their acceptance or assent.*

The charter of 1769 created and established a corporation, to consist of twelve persons, and no more; to be called the "Trustees of Dartmouth College." The preamble to the charter recites, that it is granted on the application and request of the Rev. Eleazer Wheelock: That Dr. Wheelock, about the year 1754, established a charity school, at his own expense, and on his own estate and plantation: That for several years, through the assistance of well-disposed persons in America, granted at his solicitation, he had clothed, maintained, and educated a number of native Indians, and employed them afterwards as missionaries and schoolmasters among the savage tribes: That, his design promising to be useful, he had constituted the Rev. Mr. Whitaker to be his attorney, with power to solicit contributions, in England, for the further extension and carrying on of his undertaking; and that he had requested the Earl of Dartmouth, Baron Smith, Mr. Thornton, and other gentlemen, to receive such sums as might be contributed, in England, towards supporting his school, and to be trustees thereof, for his charity; which these persons had agreed to do: That thereupon Dr. Wheelock had executed to them a deed of trust, in pursuance of such agreement between him and them, and, for divers good reasons, had referred it to these persons to determine the place in which the school should be finally established: And, to enable them to form a proper decision on this subject, had laid before them the several offers which had been made to him by the several governments in America, in order to induce him to settle and establish his school within the limits of such governments for their own emolument, and the increase of learning in their respective places, as well as for the furtherance of his general original design: And inasmuch as a number of the proprietors of lands in New Hampshire, animated by the example of the Governor himself and others, and in consideration that, without any impediment to its original design, the school might be enlarged and improved, to promote learning among the English, and to supply ministers to the people of that Province, had promised large tracts of land, provided the school should be established in that Province, the persons before mentioned, having weighed the reasons in favor of the several places proposed, had given the preference to this Province, and these offers: That Dr. Wheelock therefore represented the necessity of a legal incorporation, and proposed that certain gentlemen in America, whom he had already named and appointed in his will to be trustees of his charity after his decease, should compose the corporation. Upon this recital, and in consideration of the laudable original design of Dr. Wheelock, and willing that the best means of education be established in New Hampshire, for the benefit of the Province, the king granted the charter, by the advice of his Provincial Council.

The substance of the facts thus recited is, that Dr. Wheelock had founded a charity, on funds owned and procured by himself; that he was at that time the sole dispenser and sole administrator, as well as the legal owner, of these funds; that he had made his will, devising this property in trust, to continue the existence and uses of the school, and appointed trustees; that, in this state of things, he had been invited to fix his school, permanently, in New Hampshire, and to extend the design of it to the education of the youth of that Province; that before he removed his school, or accepted this invitation, which his friends in England had advised him to accept, he applied for a charter, to be granted, not to whomsoever the king or government of the Province should please, but to such persons as he named and appointed, namely, the persons whom he had already appointed to be the future trustees of his charity by his will.

The charter, or letters patent, then proceed to create such a corporation, and to appoint twelve persons to constitute it, by the name of the "Trustees of Dartmouth College"; to have perpetual existence, as such corporation, and with power to hold and dispose of lands and goods, for the use of the college, with all the ordinary powers of corporations. They are in their discretion to apply the funds and property of the college to the support of the president, tutors, ministers, and other officers of the college, and such missionaries and schoolmasters as they may see fit to employ among the Indians. There are to be twelve trustees for ever, *and no more;* and they are to have the right of filling vacancies occurring in their own body. The Rev. Mr. Wheelock is declared to be the founder of the college, and is, by the charter, appointed first president, with power to appoint a successor by his last will. All proper powers of government, superintendence, and visitation are vested in the trustees. They are to appoint and remove all officers at their discretion; to fix their salaries, and assign their duties; and to make all ordinances, orders, and laws for the government of the students. To the end that the persons who had acted as depositaries of the contributions in England, and who had also been contributors themselves, might be satisfied of the good use of their contributions, the president was annually, or when required, to transmit to them an account of the progress of the institution and the disbursements of its funds, so long as they should continue to act in that trust. These letters patent are to be good and effectual, in law, *against the king, his heirs and successors for ever*, without further grant or confirmation; and the trustees are to hold all and singular these privileges, advantages, liberties, and immunities to them and to their successors for ever.

No funds are given to the college by this charter. A corporate existence and capacity are given to the trustees, with the privileges and immunities which have been mentioned, to enable the founder and his associates the better to manage the funds which they themselves had contributed, and such others as they might afterwards obtain.

After the institution thus created and constituted had existed, uninterruptedly and usefully, nearly fifty years, the legislature of New Hampshire passed the acts in question.

The first act makes the twelve trustees under the charter, and nine other individuals, to be appointed by the Governor and Council, a corporation, by a new name; and to this new corporation transfers all the *property*, *rights*, *powers*, *liberties*, *and privileges* of the old corporation; with further power to establish new colleges and an institute, and to apply all or any part of the funds to these purposes; subject to the power and control of a board of twenty-five overseers, to be appointed by the Governor and Council.

The second act makes further provisions for executing the objects of the first, and the last act authorizes the defendant, the treasurer of the plaintiffs, to retain and hold their property, against their will.

If these acts are valid, the old corporation is abolished, and a new one created. The first act does, in fact, if it can have any effect, create a new corporation, and transfer to it all the property and franchises of the old. The two corporations are not the same, in any thing which essentially belongs to the existence of a corporation. They have different names, and different powers, rights, and duties. Their organization is wholly different. The powers of the corporation are not vested in the same, or similar hands. In one, the trustees are twelve, and no more. In the other, they are twenty-one. In one, the power is in a single board. In the other, it is divided between two boards. Although the act professes to include the old trustees in the new corporation, yet that was without their assent, and against their remonstrance; and no person can be compelled to be a member of such a corporation against his will. It was neither expected nor intended that they should be members of the new corporation. The act itself treats the old corporation as at an end, and, going on the ground that all its functions have ceased, it provides for the first meeting and organization of the new corporation. It expressly provides, also, that the new corporation shall have and hold all the property of the old; a provision which would be quite unnecessary upon any other ground, than that the old corporation was dissolved. But if it could be contended that the effect of these acts was not entirely to abolish the old corporation, yet it is manifest that they impair and invade the rights, property, and powers of the trustees under the charter, as a corporation, and the legal rights, privileges, and immunities which belong to them, as individual members of the corporation.

The twelve trustees were the *sole* legal owners of all the property acquired under the charter. By the acts, others are admitted, against *their* will, to be joint owners. The twelve individuals who are trustees were possessed of all the franchises and immunities conferred by the charter. By the acts, *nine* other trustees and *twenty-five* overseers are admitted, against their will, to divide these franchises and immunities with them.

If, either as a corporation or as individuals, they have any legal rights, this forcible intrusion of others violates those rights, as manifestly as an entire and complete ouster and dispossession. These acts alter the whole constitution of the corporation. They affect the rights of the whole body as a corporation, and the rights of the individuals who compose it. They revoke corporate powers and franchises. They alienate and transfer the property of the college to others. By the charter, the trustees had a right to fill vacancies in their own number. This is now taken away. They were to consist of twelve, and, by express provision, of no more. This is altered. They and their successors, appointed by themselves, were for ever to hold the property. The legislature has found successors for them, before their seats are vacant. The powers and privileges which the twelve were to exercise exclusively, are now to be exercised by others. By one of the acts, they are subjected to heavy penalties if they exercise their offices, or any of those powers and privileges granted them by charter, and which they had exercised for fifty years. They are to be punished for not accepting the new grant, and taking its benefits. This, it must be confessed, is rather a summary mode of settling a question of constitutional right. Not only are new trustees forced into the corporation, but new trusts and uses are created. The college is turned into a university. Power is given to create new colleges, and, to authorize any diversion of the funds which may be agreeable to the new boards, sufficient latitude is given by the undefined power of establishing an institute. To these new colleges, and this institute, the funds contributed by the founder, Dr. Wheelock, and by the original donors, the Earl of Dartmouth and others, are to be applied, in plain and manifest disregard of the uses to which they were given.

The president, one of the old trustees, had a right to his office, salary, and emoluments, subject to the twelve trustees alone. His title to these is now changed, and he is made accountable to new masters. So also all the professors and tutors. If the legislature can at pleasure make these alterations and changes in the rights and privileges of the plaintiffs, it may, with equal propriety, abolish these rights and privileges altogether. The same power which can do any part of this work can accomplish the whole. And, indeed, the argument on which these acts have been hitherto defended goes altogether on the ground, that this is such a corporation as the legislature may abolish at pleasure; and that its members have no *rights*, *liberties*, *franchises*, *property*, *or privileges*, which the legislature may not revoke, annul, alienate, or transfer to others, whenever it sees fit.

It will be contended by the plaintiffs, that these acts are not valid and binding on them, without their assent, —

1. Because they are against common right, and the Constitution of New Hampshire.

2. Because they are repugnant to the Constitution of the United States.

I am aware of the limits which bound the jurisdiction of the court in this case, and that on this record nothing can be decided but the single question, whether these acts are repugnant to the Constitution of the United States. Yet it may assist in forming an opinion of their true nature and character to compare them with those fundamental principles introduced into the State governments for the purpose of limiting the exercise of the legislative power, and which the Constitution of New Hampshire expresses with great fulness and accuracy.

It is not too much to assert, that the legislature of New Hampshire would not have been competent to pass the acts in question, and to make them binding on the plaintiffs without their assent, even if there had been, in the Constitution of New Hampshire, or of the United States, no special restriction on their power, because these acts are not the exercise of a power properly legislative.* Their effect and object are to take away, from one, rights, property, and franchises, and to grant them to another. This is not the exercise of a legislative power. To justify the taking away of vested rights there must be a forfeiture,

* Calder et ux. *v* Bull, 3 Dallas, 386.

to adjudge upon and declare which is the proper province of the judiciary. Attainder and confiscation are acts of sovereign power, not acts of legislation. The British Parliament, among other unlimited powers, claims that of altering and vacating charters; not as an act of ordinary legislation, but of uncontrolled authority. It is theoretically omnipotent. Yet, in modern times, it has very rarely attempted the exercise of this power. In a celebrated instance, those who asserted this power in Parliament vindicated its exercise only in a case in which it could be shown, 1st. That the charter in question was a charter of political power; 2d. That there was a great and overruling state necessity, justifying the violation of the charter; 3d. That the charter had been abused and justly forfeited.* The bill affecting this charter did not pass. Its history is well known. The act which afterwards did pass, passed *with the assent of the corporation*. Even in the worst times, this power of Parliament to repeal and rescind charters has not often been exercised. The illegal proceedings in the reign of Charles the Second were under color of law. Judgments of forfeiture were obtained in the courts. Such was the case of the *quo warranto* against the city of London, and the proceedings by which the charter of Massachusetts was vacated.

The legislature of New Hampshire has no more power over the rights of the plaintiffs than existed somewhere, in some department of government, before the Revolution. The British Parliament could not have annulled or revoked this grant as an act of ordinary legislation. If it had done it at all, it could only have been in virtue of that sovereign power, called omnipotent, which does not belong to any legislature in the United States. The legislature of New Hampshire has the same power over this charter which belonged to the king who granted it, and no more. By the law of England, the power to create corporations is a part of the royal prerogative.† By the Revolution, this power may be considered as having devolved on the legislature of the State, and it has accordingly been exercised by the legislature. But the king cannot abolish a corporation, or new-model it, or alter its powers, without its assent. This

* Annual Register, 1784, p. 160; Parl. Reg. 1783; Mr. Burke's Speech on Mr. Fox's East India Bill, Burke's Works, Vol. II. p. 414, 417 467 468, 486.
† 1 Black. 472, 473.

is the acknowledged and well-known doctrine of the common law. "Whatever might have been the notion in former times," says Lord Mansfield, "it is most certain now that the corporations of the universities are lay corporations; and that the crown cannot take away from them any rights that have been formerly subsisting in them under old charters or prescriptive usage." * After forfeiture duly found, the king may regrant the franchises; but a grant of franchises already granted, and of which no forfeiture has been found, is void.

Corporate franchises can only be forfeited by trial and judgment.† In case of a new charter or grant to an existing corporation, it may accept or reject it as it pleases. ‡ It may accept such part of the grant as it chooses, and reject the rest.§ In the very nature of things, a charter cannot be forced upon any body. No one can be compelled to accept a grant; and without acceptance the grant is necessarily void. ‖ It cannot be pretented that the legislature, as successor to the king in this part of his prerogative, has any power to revoke, vacate, or alter this charter. If, therefore, the legislature has not this power by any specific grant contained in the constitution; nor as included in its ordinary legislative powers; nor by reason of its succession to the prerogatives of the crown in this particular, on what ground would the authority to pass these acts rest, even if there were no prohibitory clauses in the constitution and the Bill of Rights?

But there *are* prohibitions in the constitution and Bill of Rights of New Hampshire, introduced for the purpose of limiting the legislative power and protecting the rights and property of the citizens. One prohibition is "that no person shall be deprived of his property, immunities, or privileges, put out of the protection of the law, or deprived of his life, liberty, or estate, but by judgment of his peers or the law of the land."

In the opinion, however, which was given in the court below, it is denied that the trustees under the charter had any

* 3 Burr. 1656. † King *v.* Pasmore, 3 Term Rep. 244.

‡ King *v.* Vice-Chancellor of Cambridge, 3 Burr. 1656; 3 Term Rep. 240 —Lord Kenyon

§ 3 Burr. 1661, and King *v.* Pasmore, *ubi supra.*

‖ Ellis *v.* Marshall, 2 Mass. Rep. 277; 1 Kyd on Corporations, 65, 66.

property, immunity, liberty, or privilege in this corporation, within the meaning of this prohibition in the Bill of Rights. It is said that it is a public corporation and public property; that the trustees have no greater interest in it than any other individuals; that it is not private property, which they can sell or transmit to their heirs, and that therefore they have no interest in it; that their office is a public trust, like that of the Governor or a judge, and that they have no more concern in the property of the college than the Governor in the property of the State, or than the judges in the fines which they impose on the culprits at their bar; that it is nothing to them whether their powers shall be extended or lessened, any more than it is to their honors whether their jurisdiction shall be enlarged or diminished. It is necessary, therefore, to inquire into the true nature and character of the corporation which was created by the charter of 1769.

There are divers sorts of corporations; and it may be safely admitted that the legislature has more power over some than others.* Some corporations are for government and political arrangement; such, for example, as cities, counties, and towns in New England. These may be changed and modified as public convenience may require, due regard being always had to the rights of property. Of such corporations, all who live within the limits are of course obliged to be members, and to submit to the duties which the law imposes on them as such. Other civil corporations are for the advancement of trade and business, such as banks, insurance companies, and the like. These are created, not by general law, but usually by grant. Their constitution is special. It is such as the legislature sees fit to give, and the grantees to accept.

The corporation in question is not a civil, although it is a lay corporation. It is an eleemosynary corporation. It is a private charity, originally founded and endowed by an individual, with a charter obtained for it at his request, for the better administration of his charity. "The eleemosynary sort of corporations are such as are constituted for the perpetual distributions of the free alms or bounty of the founder of them, to such persons as he has directed. Of this are all hospitals for the

* 1 Wooddeson, 474; 1 Black. 467.

maintenance of the poor, sick, and impotent; and all colleges both in our universities and out of them." * Eleemosynary corporations are for the management of private property, according to the will of the donors. They are private corporations. A college is as much a private corporation as a hospital; especially a college founded, as this was, by private bounty. A college is a charity. "The establishment of learning," says Lord Hardwicke, "is a charity, and so considered in the statute of Elizabeth. A devise to a college, for their benefit, is a laudable charity, and deserves encouragement." †

The legal signification of *a charity* is derived chiefly from the statute 43 Eliz. ch. 4. "Those purposes," says Sir William Grant, "are considered *charitable* which that statute enumerates." ‡ Colleges are enumerated as charities in that statute. The government, in these cases, lends its aid to perpetuate the beneficent intention of the donor, by granting a charter under which his private charity shall continue to be dispensed after his death. This is done either by incorporating the objects of the charity, as, for instance, the scholars in a college or the poor in a hospital, or by incorporating those who are to be governors or trustees of the charity. § In cases of the first sort, the founder is, by the common law, visitor. In early times it became a maxim, that he who gave the property might regulate it in future. *Cujus est dare, ejus est disponere.* This right of visitation descended from the founder to his heir as a right of property, and precisely as his other property went to his heir; and in default of heirs it went to the king, as all other property goes to the king for the want of heirs. The right of visitation arises from the property. It grows out of the endowment. The founder may, if he please, part with it at the time when he establishes the charity, and may vest it in others. Therefore, if he chooses that governors, trustees, or overseers should be appointed in the charter, he may cause it to be done, and his power of visitation may be transferred to them, instead of descending to his heirs. The persons thus assigned or appointed by the founder will be visitors, with all the powers of the founder, in exclusion of his heir. ‖ The right of visitation, then, accrues to them, as a matter of property, by the gift, transfer, or

* 1 Black. 471.
† 1 Ves. 537.
‡ 9 Ves. Jun. 405.
§ 1 Wood. 474.
‖ 1 Black. 471.

appointment of the founder. This is a private right, which they can assert in all legal modes, and in which they have the same protection of the law as in all other rights. As visitors they may make rules, ordinances, and statutes, and alter and repeal them, as far as permitted so to do by the charter.* Al though the charter proceeds from the crown or the government, it is considered as the will of the donor. It is obtained at his request. He imposes it as the rule which is to prevail in the dispensation of his bounty in all future times. The king or government which grants the charter is not thereby the founder, but he who furnishes the funds. The gift of the revenues is the foundation.†

The leading case on this subject is Phillips *v.* Bury.‡ This was an ejectment brought to recover the rectory-house, &c. of Exeter College in Oxford. The question was whether the plaintiff or defendant was legal rector. Exeter College was founded by an individual, and incorporated by a charter granted by Queen Elizabeth. The controversy turned upon the power of the visitor, and, in the discussion of the cause, the nature of college charters and corporations was very fully considered. Lord Holt's judgment, copied from his own manuscript, is found in 2 Term Reports, 346. The following is an extract:—

"That we may the better apprehend the nature of a visitor, we are to consider that there are in law two sorts of corporations aggregate; such as are for public government, and such as are for private charity. Those that are for the public government of a town, city, mystery, or the like, being for public advantage, are to be governed according to the laws of the land. If they make any particular private laws and constitutions, the validity and justice of them is examinable in the king's courts. Of these there are no particular private founders, and consequently no particular visitor; there are no patrons of these; therefore, if no provision be in the charter how the succession shall continue, the law supplieth the defect of that constitution, and saith it shall be by election; as mayor, aldermen, common council, and the like. But *private* and particular corporations for charity, founded and endowed by private persons, are subject to the private government of those who erect them; and therefore, if there be no visitor appointed by the found-

* 2 Term Rep. 350, 351.

† 1 Black. 480.

‡ 1 Lord Raymond, 5; Comb. 265; Holt, 715; 1 Shower, 360; 4 Mod. 106, Skinn. 447.

er, the law appoints the founder and his heirs to be visitors, who are to act and proceed according to the particular laws and constitutions assigned them by the founder. It is now admitted on all hands that the founder is patron, and, as founder, is visitor, if no particular visitor be assigned; so that patronage and visitation are necessary consequents one upon another. For this visitatorial power was not introduced by any canons or constitutions ecclesiastical (as was said by a learned gentleman whom I have in my eye, in his argument of this case); it is an appointment of law. It ariseth from the property which the founder had in the lands assigned to support the charity; and as he is the author of the charity, the law gives him and his heirs a visitatorial power, that is, an authority to inspect the actions and regulate the behavior of the members that partake of the charity. For it is fit the members that are endowed, and that have the charity bestowed upon them, should not be left to themselves, but pursue the intent and design of him that bestowed it upon them. *Now indeed, where the poor, or those that receive the charity, are not incorporated, but there are certain trustees who dispose of the charity, there is no visitor, because the interest of the revenue is not vested in the poor that have the benefit of the charity, but they are subject to the orders and directions of the trustees.* But where they who are to enjoy the benefit of the charity are incorporated, there to prevent all perverting of the charity, or to compose differences that may happen among them, there is by law a visitatorial power; and it being a creature of the founder's own, it is reason that he and his heirs should have that power, unless by the founder it is vested in some other. Now there is no manner of difference beween a college and a hospital, except only in degree. A hospital is for those that are poor, and mean, and low, and sickly; a college is for another sort of indigent persons; but it hath another intent, to study in and breed up persons in the world that have no otherwise to live; but still it is as much within the reasons as hospitals. And if in a hospital the master and poor are incorporated, it is a college having a common seal to act by, although it hath not the name of a college (which always supposeth a corporation), because it is of an inferior degree; and in the one case and in the other there must be a visitor, either the founder and his heirs or one appointed by him; and both are eleemosynary."

Lord Holt concludes his whole argument by again repeating, that that college was a *private corporation*, and that the founder had a right to appoint a visitor, and to give him such power as he saw fit.*

* 1 Lord Raymond, 9.

The learned Bishop Stillingfleet's argument in the same cause, as a member of the House of Lords, when it was there heard, exhibits very clearly the nature of colleges and similar corporations. It is to the following effect. "That this absolute and conclusive power of visitors is no more than the law hath appointed in other cases, upon commissions of charitable uses: that the common law, and not any ecclesiastical canons, do place the power of visitation in the founder and his heirs, *unless he settle it upon others:* that although corporations for public government be subject to the courts of Westminster Hall, which have no particular or special visitors, yet corporations for charity, founded and endowed by private persons, are subject to the rule and government of those that erect them; but where the persons to whom the charity is given are not incorporated, there is no such visitatorial power, because the interest of the revenue is not invested in them; but where they are, the right of visitation ariseth from the foundation, and the founder may convey *it to whom and in what manner he pleases; and the visitor acts as founder, and by the same authority which he had, and consequently is no more accountable than he had been:* that the king by his charter can make a society to be incorporated so as to have the rights belonging to persons, as to legal capacities: that colleges, although founded by private persons, are yet incorporated by the king's charter; but although the kings by their charter made the colleges to be such in law, that is, to be legal corporations, yet they left to the particular founders authority to appoint what statutes they thought fit for the regulation of them. And not only the statutes, but the appointment of visitors, was left to them, and the manner of government, and the several conditions on which any persons were to be made or continue partakers of their bounty." *

These opinions received the sanction of the House of Lords, and they seem to be settled and undoubted law. Where there is a charter, vesting proper powers in trustees, or governors, they are visitors; and there is no control in any body else; except only that the courts of equity or of law will interfere so far as to preserve the revenues and prevent the perversion of the funds, and to keep the visitors within their prescribed bounds. "If

* 1 Burn's Eccles. Law, 443, Appendix, No. 3.

there be a charter with proper powers, the charity must be regulated in the manner prescribed by the charter. There is no ground for the controlling interposition of the courts of chancery. The interposition of the courts, therefore, in those instances in which the charities were founded on charters or by act of Parliament, and a visitor or governor and trustees appointed, must be referred to the general jurisdiction of the courts in all cases in which a trust conferred appears to have been abused, and not to an original right to direct the management of the charity, or the conduct of the governors or trustees." * "The original of all *visitatorial* power is the property of the donor, and the power every one has to dispose, direct, and regulate his own property; like the case of patronage; *cujus est dare*, &c. Therefore, if either the crown or the subject creates an eleemosynary foundation, and vests the charity in the persons who are to receive the benefit of it, since a contest might arise about the government of it, the law allows the founder or his heirs, or the person specially appointed by him to be visitor, to determine concerning his own creature. If the charity is not vested in the persons who are to partake, but in trustees for their benefit, no visitor can arise by implication, but the trustees have that power." †

"There is nothing better established," says Lord Commissioner Eyre, "than that this court does not entertain a general jurisdiction, or regulate and control charities *established by charter*. There the establishment is fixed and determined; and the court has no power to vary it. If the governors established for the regulation of it are not those who have the management of the revenue, this court has no jurisdiction, and if it is ever so much abused, as far as it respects the jurisdiction of this court it is without remedy; but if those established as governors have also the management of the revenues, this court does assume a jurisdiction of necessity, so far as they are to be considered as trustees of the revenue." ‡

"The foundations of colleges," says Lord Mansfield, "are to be considered in two views; namely, as they are *corporations* and

* 2 Fonb. 205, 206.

† Green *v*. Rutherforth, 1 Ves. 472, per Lord Hardwicke.

‡ Attorney-General *v*. Foundling Hospital, 2 Ves. Jun. 47. See also 2 Kyd on Corporations, 195; Cooper's Equity Pleading, 292.

as they are *eleemosynary*. As eleemosynary, they are the creatures of the founder; he may delegate his power, either generally or specially; he may prescribe particular modes and manners, as to the exercise of part of it. If he makes a general visitor (as by the general words *visitator sit*), the person so constituted has all incidental power; but he may be restrained as to particular instances. The founder may appoint a special visitor for a particular purpose, and no further. The founder may make a general visitor; and yet appoint an inferior particular power, to be executed without going to the visitor in the first instance." * And even if the king be founder, if he grant a charter, incorporating trustees and governors, *they are visitors*, and the king cannot visit.† A subsequent donation, or ingrafted fellowship, falls under the same general visitatorial power, if not otherwise specially provided.‡

In New England, and perhaps throughout the United States, eleemosynary corporations have been generally established in the latter mode; that is, by incorporating governors, or trustees, and vesting in them the right of visitation. Small variations may have been in some instances adopted; as in the case of Harvard College, where some power of inspection is given to the overseers, but not, strictly speaking, a visitatorial power, which still belongs, it is apprehended, to the fellows or members of the corporation. In general, there are many donors. A charter is obtained, comprising them all, or some of them, and such others as they choose to include, with the right of appointing successors. They are thus the visitors of their own charity, and appoint others, such as they may see fit, to exercise the same office in time to come. All such corporations are private. The case before the court is clearly that of an eleemosynary corporation. It is, in the strictest legal sense, a private charity. In King *v.* St. Catherine's Hall, § that college is called a private eleemosynary lay corporation. It was endowed by a private founder, and incorporated by letters patent. And in the same manner was Dartmouth College founded and incorporated. Dr. Wheelock is declared by the charter to be its founder. It

* St. John's College, Cambridge, *v.* Todington, 1 Burr. 200.
† Attorney-General *v.* Middleton, 2 Ves. 328.
‡ Green *v.* Rutherforth, *ubi supra*; St. John's College *v.* Todington *ubi supra*
§ 4 Term Rep. 233.

was established by him, on funds contributed and collected by himself.

As such founder, he had a right of visitation, which he assigned to the trustees, and they received it by his consent and appointment, and held it under the charter.* He appointed these trustees visitors, and in that respect to take place of his heir; as he might have appointed devisees, to take his estate instead of his heir. Little, probably, did he think at that time, that the legislature would ever take away this property and these privileges, and give them to others. Little did he suppose that this charter secured to him and his successors no legal rights. Little did the other donors think so. If they had, the college would have been, what the university is now, a thing upon paper, existing only in name.

The numerous academies in New England have been established substantially in the same manner. They hold their property by the same tenure, and no other. Nor has Harvard College any surer title than Dartmouth College. It may to-day have more friends; but to-morrow it may have more enemies. Its legal rights are the same. So also of Yale College; and, indeed, of all the others. When the legislature gives to these institutions, it may and does accompany its grants with such conditions as it pleases. The grant of lands by the legislature of New Hampshire to Dartmouth College, in 1789, was accompanied with various conditions. When donations are made, by the legislature or others, to a charity already existing, without any condition, or the specification of any new use, the donation follows the nature of the charity. Hence the doctrine, that all eleemosynary corporations are private bodies. They are founded by private persons, and on private property. The public cannot be charitable in these institutions. It is not the money of the public, but of private persons, which is dispensed. It may be public, that is general, in its uses and advantages; and the State may very laudably add contributions of its own to the funds; but it is still private in the tenure of the property, and in the right of administering the funds.

If the doctrine laid down by Lord Holt, and the House of Lords, in Phillips *v.* Bury, and recognized and established in

* Black. *ubi supra.*

all the other cases, be correct, the property of this college was private property; it was vested in the trustees by the charter, and to be administered by them, according to the will of the founder and donors, as expressed in the charter. They were also visitors of the charity, in the most ample sense. They had, therefore, as they contend, privileges, property, and immunities, within the true meaning of the Bill of Rights. They had rights, and still have them, which they can assert against the legislature, as well as against other wrong-doers. It makes no difference, that the estate is holden for certain trusts. The legal estate is still theirs. They have a right in the property, and they have a right of visiting and superintending the trust; and this is an object of legal protection, as much as any other right. The charter declares that the powers conferred on the trustees are "privileges, advantages, liberties, and immunities"; and that they shall be for ever holden by them and their successors. The New Hampshire Bill of Rights declares that no one shall be deprived of his "property, privileges, or immunities," but by judgment of his peers, or the law of the land. The argument on the other side is, that, although these terms may mean something in the Bill of Rights, they mean nothing in this charter. But they are terms of legal signification, and very properly used in the charter. They are equivalent with *franchises.* Blackstone says that *franchise* and *liberty* are used as synonymous terms. And after enumerating other liberties and franchises, he says: "It is likewise a franchise for a number of persons to be incorporated and subsist as a body politic, with a power to maintain perpetual succession and do other corporate acts; and each individual member of such a corporation is also said to have a franchise or freedom." *

Liberties is the term used in Magna Charta as including franchises, privileges, immunities, and all the rights which belong to that class. Professor Sullivan says, the term signifies the "*privileges* that some of the subjects, whether single persons or bodies corporate, have above others by the lawful grant of the king; as the chattels of felons or outlaws, and the lands *and privileges of corporations.*" †

The privilege, then, of being a member of a corporation,

* 2 Black. Com. 37.

† Sull. 41st Lect.

under a lawful grant, and of exercising the rights and powers of such member, is such a privilege, *liberty*, or *franchise*, as has been the object of legal protection, and the subject of a legal interest, from the time of Magna Charta to the present moment. The plaintiffs have such an interest in this corporation, individually, as they could assert and maintain in a court of law, not as agents of the public, but in their own right. Each trustee has a *franchise*, and if he be disturbed in the enjoyment of it, he would have redress, on appealing to the law, as promptly as for any other injury. If the other trustees should conspire against any one of them to prevent his equal right and voice in the appointment of a president or professor, or in the passing of any statute or ordinance of the college, he would be entitled to his action, for depriving him of his franchise. It makes no difference, that this property is to be holden and administered, and these franchises exercised, for the purpose of diffusing learning. No principle and no case establishes any such distinction. The public may be benefited by the use of this property. But this does not change the nature of the property, or the rights of the owners. The object of the charter may be public good; so it is in all other corporations; and this would as well justify the resumption or violation of the grant in any other case as in this. In the case of an advowson, the use is public, and the right cannot be turned to any private benefit or emolument. It is nevertheless a legal private right, and the *property* of the owner, as emphatically as his freehold. The rights and privileges of trustees, visitors, or governors of incorporated colleges, stand on the same foundation. They are so considered, both by Lord Holt and Lord Hardwicke.*

To contend that the rights of the plaintiffs may be taken away, because they derive from them no pecuniary benefit or private emolument, or because they cannot be transmitted to their heirs, or would not be assets to pay their debts, is taking an extremely narrow view of the subject. According to this notion, the case would be different, if, in the charter, they had stipulated for a commission on the disbursement of the funds; and they have ceased to have any interest in the property, because they have undertaken to administer it gratuitously.

* Phillips *v.* Bury, and Green *v.* Rutherforth, *ubi supra* See also 2 Black. 21.

It cannot be necessary to say much in refutation of the idea, that there cannot be a legal interest, or ownership, in any thing which does not yield a pecuniary profit; as if the law regarded no rights but the rights of money, and of visible, tangible property. Of what nature are all rights of suffrage? No elector has a particular personal interest; but each has a legal right, to be exercised at his own discretion, and it cannot be taken away from him. The exercise of this right directly and very materially affects the public; much more so than the exercise of the privileges of a trustee of this college. Consequences of the utmost magnitude may sometimes depend on the exercise of the right of suffrage by one or a few electors. Nobody was ever yet heard to contend, however, that on that account the public might take away the right, or impair it. This notion appears to be borrowed from no better source than the repudiated doctrine of the three judges in the Aylesbury case.* That was an action against a returning officer for refusing the plaintiff's vote, in the election of a member of Parliament. Three of the judges of the King's Bench held, that the action could not be maintained, because, among other objections, "it was not any matter of profit, either *in presenti*, or *in futuro*." It would not enrich the plaintiff *in presenti*, nor would it *in futuro* go to his heirs, or answer to pay his debts. But Lord Holt and the House of Lords were of another opinion. The judgment of the three judges was reversed, and the doctrine they held, having been exploded for a century, seems now for the first time to be revived.

Individuals have a right to use their own property for purposes of benevolence, either towards the public, or towards other individuals. They have a right to exercise this benevolence in such lawful manner as they may choose; and when the government has induced and excited it, by contracting to give perpetuity to the stipulated manner of exercising it, it is not law, but violence, to rescind this contract, and seize on the property. Whether the State will grant these franchises, and under what conditions it will grant them, it decides for itself. But when once granted, the constitution holds them to be sacred, till forfeited for just cause.

* Ashby *v.* White, 2 Lord Raymond, 938.

That all property, of which the use may be beneficial to the public, belongs therefore to the public, is quite a new doctrine. It has no precedent, and is supported by no known principle. Dr. Wheelock might have answered his purposes, in this case, by executing a private deed of trust. He might have conveyed his property to trustees, for precisely such uses as are described in this charter. Indeed, it appears that he had contemplated the establishing of his school in that manner, and had made his will, and devised the property to the same persons who were afterwards appointed trustees in the charter. Many literary and other charitable institutions are founded in that manner, and the trust is renewed, and conferred on other persons, from time to time, as occasion may require. In such a case, no lawyer would or could say, that the legislature might divest the trustees, constituted by deed or will, seize upon the property, and give it to other persons, for other purposes. And does the granting of a charter, which is only done to perpetuate the trust in a more convenient manner, make any difference? Does or can this change the nature of the charity, and turn it into a public political corporation? Happily, we are not without authority on this point. It has been considered and adjudged. Lord Hardwicke says, in so many words, "The charter of the crown cannot make a charity more or less public, but only more permanent than it would otherwise be." *

The granting of the corporation is but making the trust perpetual, and does not alter the nature of the charity. The very object sought in obtaining such charter, and in giving property to such a corporation, is to make and keep it private property, and to clothe it with all the security and inviolability of private property. The intent is, that there shall be a legal private ownership, and that the legal owners shall maintain and protect the property, for the benefit of those for whose use it was designed. Who ever endowed the public? Who ever appointed a legislature to administer his charity? Or who ever heard, before, that a gift to a college, or a hospital, or an asylum, was, in reality, nothing but a gift to the State?

The State of Vermont is a principal donor to Dartmouth College. The lands given lie in that State. This appears in

* Attorney-General *v.* Pearce, 2 Atk. 87.

the special verdict. Is Vermont to be considered as having intended a gift to the State of New Hampshire in this case, as, it has been said, is to be the reasonable construction of all donations to the college? The legislature of New Hampshire affects to represent the public, and therefore claims a right to control all property destined to public use. What hinders Vermont from considering herself equally the representative of the public, and from resuming her grants, at her own pleasure? Her right to do so is less doubtful than the power of New Hampshire to pass the laws in question.

In University *v.* Foy,* the Supreme Court of North Carolina pronounced unconstitutional and void a law repealing a grant to the University of North Carolina, although that university was originally erected and endowed by a statute of the State. That case was a grant of lands, and the court decided that it could not be resumed. This is the grant of a power and capacity to hold lands. Where is the difference of the cases, upon principle?

In Terrett *v.* Taylor † this court decided that a legislative grant or confirmation of lands, for the purposes of moral and religious instruction, could no more be rescinded than other grants. The nature of the use was not holden to make any difference. A grant to a parish or church, for the purposes which have been mentioned, cannot be distinguished, in respect to the title it confers, from a grant to a college for the promotion of piety and learning. To the same purpose may be cited the case of Pawlett *v.* Clark. The State of Vermont, by statute, in 1794, granted to the respective towns in that State certain glebe lands lying within those towns for the sole use and support of religious worship. In 1799, an act was passed to repeal the act of 1794; but this court declared, that the act of 1794, "so far as it granted the glebes to the towns, could not afterwards be repealed by the legislature, so as to divest the rights of the towns under the grant." ‡

It will be for the other side to show that the nature of the use decides the question whether the legislature has power to resume its grants. It will be for those who maintain such a doctrine to show the principles and cases upon which it rests. It will be for them also to fix the limits and boundaries of their

* 2 Haywood's Rep. † 9 Cranch, 43. ‡ 9 Cranch, 292.

doctrine, and to show what are and what are not such uses as to give the legislature this power of resumption and revocation. And to furnish an answer to the cases cited, it will be for them further to show that a grant for the use and support of religious worship stands on other ground than a grant for the promotion of piety and learning.

I hope enough has been said to show that the trustees possessed vested liberties, privileges, and immunities, under this charter; and that such liberties, privileges, and immunities, being once lawfully obtained and vested, are as inviolable as any vested rights of property whatever. Rights to do certain acts, such, for instance, as the visitation and superintendence of a college and the appointment of its officers, may surely be vested rights, to all legal intents, as completely as the right to possess property. A late learned judge of this court has said, "When I say that a *right* is vested in a citizen, I mean that he has the power to do *certain actions*, or to possess *certain things*, according to the law of the land." *

If such be the true nature of the plaintiffs' interests under this charter, what are the articles in the New Hampshire Bill of Rights which these acts infringe?

They infringe the second article; which says, that the citizens of the State have a right to hold and possess property. The plaintiffs had a legal property in this charter; and they had acquired property under it. The acts deprive them of both. They impair and take away the charter; and they appropriate the property to new uses, against their consent. The plaintiffs cannot now hold the property acquired by themselves, and which this article says they have a right to hold.

They infringe the twentieth article. By that article it is declared that, in questions of property, there is a right to trial. The plaintiffs are divested, without trial or judgment.

They infringe the twenty-third article. It is therein declared that no retrospective laws shall be passed. This article bears directly on the case. These acts must be deemed to be retrospective, within the settled construction of that term. What a retrospective law is, has been decided, on the construction of this very article, in the Circuit Court for the First Circuit. The

* 3 Dallas, 394.

learned judge of that circuit says: "Every statute which takes away or impairs vested rights, acquired under existing laws, must be deemed retrospective." * That all such laws are retrospective was decided also in the case of Dash *v.* Van Kleek,† where a most learned judge quotes this article from the constitution of New Hampshire, with manifest approbation, as a plain and clear expression of those fundamental and unalterable principles of justice, which must lie at the foundation of every free and just system of laws. Can any man deny that the plaintiffs had rights, under the charter, which were legally vested, and that by these acts those rights are impaired?

"It is a principle in the English law," says Chief Justice Kent, in the case last cited, "as ancient as the law itself, that a statute, even of its omnipotent Parliament, is not to have a retrospective effect. *Nova constitutio futuris formam imponere debet, et non præteritis.*‡ The maxim in Bracton was taken from the civil law, for we find in that system the same principle, expressed substantially in the same words, that the lawgiver cannot alter his mind to the prejudice of a vested right. *Nemo potest mutare concilium suum in alterius injuriam.*§ This maxim of Papinian is general in its terms, but Dr. Taylor ‖ applies it directly as a restriction upon the lawgiver, and a declaration in the Code leaves no doubt as to the sense of the civil law. *Leges et constitutiones futuris certum est dare formam negotiis, non ad facta præterita revocari, nisi nominatim, et de præterito tempore, et adhuc pendentibus negotiis cautum sit.*¶ This passage, according to the best interpretation of the civilians, relates not merely to future suits, but to future, as contradistinguished from past, contracts and vested rights.** It is indeed admitted that the prince may enact a retrospective law, provided it be done *expressly;* for the will of the prince under the despotism of the Roman emperors was paramount to every obligation. Great latitude was anciently allowed to legislative expositions of statutes; for the separation of the judicial from the legislative power was not then distinctly known or prescribed. The prince was in the habit of interpreting his own laws for particular

* Society *v.* Wheeler, 2 Gal. 103.

† 7 Johnson's Rep. 477.

‡ Bracton, Lib. 4, fol. 228. 2d Inst. 292.

§ Dig. 50. 17. 75.

‖ Elements of the Civil Law, p. 168.

¶ Cod. 1. 14. 7.

** Perezii Prælect. h. t.

occasions. This was called the *Interlocutio Principis;* and this, according to Huber's definition, was, *quando principes inter partes loquuntur et jus dicunt.** No correct civilian, and especially no proud admirer of the ancient republic (if any such then existed), could have reflected on this interference with private rights and pending suits without disgust and indignation; and we are rather surprised to find that, under the violent and arbitrary genius of the Roman government, the principle before us should have been acknowledged and obeyed to the extent in which we find it. The fact shows that it must be founded in the clearest justice. Our case is happily very different from that of the subjects of Justinian. With us the power of the lawgiver is limited and defined; the judicial is regarded as a distinct, independent power; private rights are better understood and more exalted in public estimation, as well as secured by provisions dictated by the spirit of freedom, and unknown to the civil law. Our constitutions do not admit the power assumed by the Roman prince, and the principle we are considering is now to be regarded as sacred."

These acts infringe also the thirty-seventh article of the constitution of New Hampshire; which says, that the powers of government shall be kept separate. By these acts, the legislature assumes to exercise a judicial power. It declares a forfeiture, and resumes franchises, once granted, without trial or hearing.

If the constitution be not altogether waste-paper, it has restrained the power of the legislature in these particulars. If it has any meaning, it is that the legislature shall pass no act directly and manifestly impairing private property and private privileges. It shall not judge by act. It shall not decide by act. It shall not deprive by act. But it shall leave all these things to be tried and adjudged by the law of the land.

The fifteenth article has been referred to before. It declares that no one shall be "deprived of his property, immunities, or privileges, but by the judgment of his peers or the law of the land." Notwithstanding the light in which the learned judges in New Hampshire viewed the rights of the plaintiffs under the charter, and which has been before adverted to, it is found to be admitted in their opinion, that those rights are privileges within

* Prælect. Juris Civ., Vol. II. p. 545.

the meaning of this fifteenth article of the Bill of Rights. Having quoted that article, they say: "That the right to manage the affairs of this college is a privilege, within the meaning of this clause of the Bill of Rights, is not to be doubted." In my humble opinion, this surrenders the point. To resist the effect of this admission, however, the learned judges add: "But how a privilege can be protected from the operation of the law of the land by a clause in the constitution, declaring that it shall not be taken away but by the law of the land, is not very easily understood." This answer goes on the ground, that the acts in question are laws of the land, within the meaning of the constitution. If they be so, the argument drawn from this article is fully answered. If they be not so, it being admitted that the plaintiffs' rights are "privileges," within the meaning of the article, the argument is not answered, and the article is infringed by the acts.

Are, then, these acts of the legislature, which affect only particular persons and their particular privileges, laws of the land? Let this question be answered by the text of Blackstone. "And first it (i. e. law) is a *rule:* not a transient, sudden order from a superior to or concerning a particular person; but something permanent, uniform, and universal. Therefore a particular act of the legislature to confiscate the goods of Titius, or to attaint him of high treason, does not enter into the idea of a municipal law; for the operation of this act is spent upon Titius only, and has no relation to the community in general; it is rather a sentence than a law." * Lord Coke is equally decisive and emphatic. Citing and commenting on the celebrated twenty-ninth chapter of Magna Charta, he says: "No man shall be disseized, &c., unless it be by the lawful judgment, that is, verdict of equals, or by the law of the land, that is (to speak it once for all), by the due course and process of law." † Have the plaintiffs lost their franchises by "due course and process of law"? On the contrary, are not these acts "particular acts of the legislature, which have no relation to the community in general, and which are rather sentences than laws"?

By the law of the land is most clearly intended the general law; a law which hears before it condemns; which proceeds

* 1 Black. Com. 44.

† Coke, 2 Inst. 46.

upon inquiry, and renders judgment only after trial. The meaning is, that every citizen shall hold his life, liberty, property, and immunities under the protection of the general rules which govern society. Every thing which may pass under the form of an enactment is not therefore to be considered the law of the land. If this were so, acts of attainder, bills of pains and penalties, acts of confiscation, acts reversing judgments, and acts directly transferring one man's estate to another, legislative judgments, decrees, and forfeitures in all possible forms, would be the law of the land.

Such a strange construction would render constitutional provisions of the highest importance completely inoperative and void. It would tend directly to establish the union of all powers in the legislature. There would be no general, permanent law for courts to administer or men to live under. The administration of justice would be an empty form, an idle ceremony. Judges would sit to execute legislative judgments and decrees; not to declare the law or to administer the justice of the country. "Is that the law of the land," said Mr. Burke, "upon which, if a man go to Westminster Hall, and ask counsel by what title or tenure he holds his privilege or estate *according to the law of the land*, he should be told, that the law of the land is not yet known; that no decision or decree has been made in his case; that when a decree shall be passed, he will then know *what the law of the land is?* Will this be said to be the law of the land, by any lawyer who has a rag of a gown left upon his back, or a wig with one tie upon his head?"

That the power of electing and appointing the officers of this college is not only a right of the trustees as a corporation, generally, and in the aggregate, but that each individual trustee has also his own individual franchise in such right of election and appointment, is according to the language of all the authorities. Lord Holt says: "It is agreeable to reason and the rules of law, that a franchise should be vested in the corporation aggregate, and yet the benefit of it to redound to the particular members, and to be enjoyed by them in their private capacity. Where the privilege of election is used by particular persons, *it is a particular right, vested in every particular man.*" *

* 2 Lord Raymond, 952.

It is also to be considered, that the president and professors of this college have rights to be affected by these acts. Their interest is similar to that of fellows in the English colleges; because they derive their living, wholly or in part, from the founder's bounty. The president is one of the trustees or corporators. The professors are not necessarily members of the corporation; but they are appointed by the trustees, are removable only by them, and have fixed salaries payable out of the general funds of the college. Both president and professors have freeholds in their offices; subject only to be removed by the trustees, as their legal visitors, for good cause. All the authorities speak of fellowships in colleges as freeholds, notwithstanding the fellows may be liable to be suspended or removed, for misbehavior, by their constituted visitors.

Nothing could have been less expected, in this age, than that there should have been an attempt, by acts of the legislature, to take away these college livings, the inadequate but the only support of literary men who have devoted their lives to the instruction of youth. The president and professors were appointed by the twelve trustees. They were accountable to nobody else, and could be removed by nobody else. They accepted their offices on this tenure. Yet the legislature has appointed other persons, with power to remove these officers and to deprive them of their livings; and those other persons have exercised that power. No description of private property has been regarded as more sacred than college livings. They are the estates and freeholds of a most deserving class of men; of scholars who have consented to forego the advantages of professional and public employments, and to devote themselves to science and literature and the instruction of youth in the quiet retreats of academic life. Whether to dispossess and oust them; to deprive them of their office, and to turn them out of their livings; to do this, not by the power of their legal visitors or governors, but by acts of the legislature, and to do it without forfeiture and without fault; whether all this be not in the highest degree an indefensible and arbitrary proceeding, is a question of which there would seem to be but one side fit for a lawyer or a scholar to espouse.

Of all the attempts of James the Second to overturn the law, and the rights of his subjects, none was esteemed more arbitrary or tyrannical than his attack on Magdalen College, Oxford; and yet that attempt was nothing but to put out one president and put in another. The president of that college, according to the charter and statutes, is to be chosen by the fellows, who are the corporators. There being a vacancy, the king chose to take the appointment out of the hands of the fellows, the legal electors of a president, into his own hands. He therefore sent down his mandate, commanding the fellows to admit for president a person of his nomination; and, inasmuch as this was directly against the charter and constitution of the college, he was pleased to add a *non obstante* clause of sufficiently comprehensive import. The fellows were commanded to admit the person mentioned in the mandate, "any statute, custom, or constitution to the contrary notwithstanding, wherewith we are graciously pleased to dispense, in this behalf." The fellows refused obedience to this mandate, and Dr. Hough, a man of independence and character, was chosen president by the fellows, according to the charter and statutes. The king then assumed the power, in virtue of his prerogative, to send down certain commissioners to turn him out; which was done accordingly; and Parker, a creature suited to the times, put in his place. Because the president, who was rightfully and legally elected, *would not deliver the keys, the doors were broken open.* "The nation as well as the university," says Bishop Burnet,* "looked on all these proceedings with just indignation. It was thought an open piece of robbery and burglary when men, authorized by no legal commission, came and forcibly turned men out of their possession and freehold." Mr. Hume, although a man of different temper, and of other sentiments, in some respects, than Dr. Burnet, speaks of this arbitrary attempt of prerogative in terms not less decisive. "The president, and all the fellows," says he, "except two, who complied, were expelled the college, and Parker was put in possession of the office. This act of violence, of all those which were committed during the reign of James, is perhaps the most illegal and arbitrary. When the dispensing power was the most strenuously insisted on by court lawyers, it had still been allowed that the statutes which regard private property could not legally be in-

* History of his own Times, Vol. III. p. 119.

fringed by that prerogative. Yet, in this instance, it appeared that even these were not now secure from invasion. The privileges of a college are attacked; men are illegally dispossessed of their property for adhering to their duty, to their oaths, and to their religion."

This measure King James lived to repent, after repentance was too late. When the charter of London was restored, and other measures of violence were retracted, to avert the impending revolution, the expelled president and fellows of Magdalen College were permitted to resume their rights. It is evident that this was regarded as an arbitrary interference with private property. Yet private property was no otherwise attacked than as a person was appointed to administer and enjoy the revenues of a college in a manner and by persons not authorized by the constitution of the college. A majority of the members of the corporation would not comply with the king's wishes. A minority would. The object was therefore to make this minority a majority. To this end the king's commissioners were directed to interfere in the case, and they united with the two complying fellows, and expelled the rest; and thus effected a change in the government of the college. The language in which Mr. Hume and all other writers speak of this abortive attempt of oppression, shows that colleges were esteemed to be, as they truly are, private corporations, and the property and privileges which belong to them *private* property and *private* privileges. Court lawyers were found to justify the king in dispensing with the laws; that is, in assuming and exercising a legislative authority. But no lawyer, not even a court lawyer, in the reign of King James the Second, as far as appears, was found to say that, even by this high authority, he could infringe the franchises of the fellows of a college, and take away their livings. Mr. Hume gives the reason; it is, that such franchises were regarded, in a most emphatic sense, *as private property.**

If it could be made to appear that the trustees and the president and professors held their offices and franchises during the pleasure of the legislature, and that the property holden belonged to the State, then indeed the legislature have done no

* See a full account of this case in State Trials, 4th ed., Vol. IV. p. 262.

more than they had a right to do. But this is not so. The charter is a charter of privileges and immunities; and these are holden by the trustees expressly against the State for ever.

It is admitted that the State, by its courts of law, can enforce the will of the donor, and compel a faithful execution of the trust. The plaintiffs claim no exemption from legal responsibility. They hold themselves at all times answerable to the law of the land, for their conduct in the trust committed to them. They ask only to hold the property of which they are owners, and the franchises which belong to them, until they shall be found, by due course and process of law, to have forfeited them.

It can make no difference whether the legislature exercise the power it has assumed by removing the trustees and the president and professors, directly and by name, or by appointing others to expel them. The principle is the same, and in point of fact the result has been the same. If the entire franchise cannot be taken away, neither can it be essentially impaired. If the trustees are legal owners of the property, they are sole owners. If they are visitors, they are sole visitors. No one will be found to say, that, if the legislature may do what it has done, it may not do any thing and every thing which it may choose to do, relative to the property of the corporation, and the privileges of its members and officers.

If the view which has been taken of this question be at all correct, this was an eleemosynary corporation, a private charity. The property was private property. The trustees were visitors, and the right to hold the charter, administer the funds, and visit and govern the college, was a franchise and privilege, solemnly granted to them. The use being public in no way diminishes their legal estate in the property, or their title to the franchise. There is no principle, nor any case, which declares that a gift to such a corporation is a gift to the public. The acts in question violate property. They take away privileges, immunities, and franchises. They deny to the trustees the protection of the law; and they are retrospective in their operation. In all which respects they are against the constitution of New Hampshire.

The plaintiffs contend, in the second place, that the acts in question are repugnant to the tenth section of the first article of the Constitution of the United States. The material words of that section are: "No State shall pass any bill of attainder, *ex post facto* law, or law impairing the obligation of contracts."

The object of these most important provisions in the national constitution has often been discussed, both here and elsewhere. It is exhibited with great clearness and force by one of the distinguished persons who framed that instrument. "Bills of attainder, *ex post facto* laws, and laws impairing the obligation of contracts, are contrary to the first principles of the social compact, and to every principle of sound legislation. The two former are expressly prohibited by the declarations prefixed to some of the State constitutions, and all of them are prohibited by the spirit and scope of these fundamental charters. Our own experience has taught us, nevertheless, that additional fences against these dangers ought not to be omitted. Very properly, therefore, have the convention added this constitutional bulwark, in favor of personal security and private rights; and I am much deceived, if they have not, in so doing, as faithfully consulted the genuine sentiments as the undoubted interests of their constituents. The sober people of America are weary of the fluctuating policy which has directed the public councils. They have seen with regret, and with indignation, that sudden changes, and legislative interferences in cases affecting personal rights, become jobs in the hands of enterprising and influential speculators, and snares to the more industrious and less informed part of the community. They have seen, too, that one legislative interference is but the link of a long chain of repetitions; every subsequent interference being naturally produced by the effects of the preceding." *

It has already been decided in this court, that a *grant* is a contract, within the meaning of this provision; and that a grant by a State is also a contract, as much as the grant of an individual. In the case of Fletcher *v.* Peck † this court says: "A contract is a compact between two or more parties, and is either executory or executed. An executory contract is one in which a party binds himself to do, or not to do, a particular thing; such was the law under which the conveyance was made by the government. A contract executed is one in which the object

* The Federalist, No. 44, by Mr. Madison.

† 6 Cranch, 87.

of contract is performed; and this, says Blackstone, differs in nothing from a grant. The contract between Georgia and the purchasers was executed by the grant. A contract executed, as well as one which is executory, contains obligations binding on the parties. A grant, in its own nature, amounts to an extinguishment of the right of the grantor, and implies a contract not to reassert that right. If, under a fair construction of the Constitution, grants are comprehended under the term contracts, is a grant from the State excluded from the operation of the provision? Is the clause to be considered as inhibiting the State from impairing the obligation of contracts between two individuals, but as excluding from that inhibition contracts made with itself? The words themselves contain no such distinction. They are general, and are applicable to contracts of every description. If contracts made with the State are to be exempted from their operation, the exception must arise from the character of the contracting party, not from the words which are employed. Whatever respect might have been felt for the State sovereignties, it is not to be disguised that the framers of the Constitution viewed with some apprehension the violent acts which might grow out of the feelings of the moment; and that the people of the United States, in adopting that instrument, have manifested a determination to shield themselves and their property from the effects of those sudden and strong passions to which men are exposed. The restrictions on the legislative power of the States are obviously founded in this sentiment; and the Constitution of the United States contains what may be deemed a bill of rights for the people of each State."

It has also been decided, that a grant by a State before the Revolution is as much to be protected as a grant since.* But the case of Terrett *v.* Taylor, before cited, is of all others most pertinent to the present argument. Indeed, the judgment of the court in that case seems to leave little to be argued or decided in this. "A private corporation," say the court, "created by the legislature, may lose its franchises by a *misuser* or a *nonuser* of them; and they may be resumed by the government under a judicial judgment upon a *quo warranto* to ascertain and enforce the forfeiture. This is the common law of the land, and is a

* New Jersey *v.* Wilson, 7 Cranch, 164.

tacit condition annexed to the creation of every such corporation. Upon a change of government, too, it may be admitted, that such exclusive privileges attached to a private corporation as are inconsistent with the new government may be abolished. In respect, also, to *public* corporations which exist only for public purposes, such as counties, towns, cities, and so forth, the legislature may, under proper limitations, have a right to change, modify, enlarge, or restrain them, securing, however, the property for the uses of those for whom and at whose expense it was originally purchased. But that the legislature can repeal statutes creating private corporations, or confirming to them property already acquired under the faith of previous laws, and by such repeal can vest the property of such corporations exclusively in the State, or dispose of the same to such purposes as they please, without the consent or default of the corporators, we are not prepared to admit; and we think ourselves standing upon the principles of natural justice, upon the fundamental laws of every free government, upon the spirit and letter of the Constitution of the United States, and upon the decisions of most respectable judicial tribunals, in resisting such a doctrine."

This court, then, does not admit the doctrine, that a legislature can repeal statutes creating private corporations. If it cannot repeal them altogether, of course it cannot repeal any part of them, or impair them, or essentially alter them, without the consent of the corporators. If, therefore, it has been shown that this college is to be regarded as a private charity, this case is embraced within the very terms of that decision. A grant of corporate powers and privileges is as much a contract as a grant of land. What proves all charters of this sort to be contracts is, that they must be accepted to give them force and effect. If they are not accepted, they are void. And in the case of an existing corporation, if a new charter is given it, it may even accept part and reject the rest. In Rex *v.* Vice-Chancellor of Cambridge,* Lord Mansfield says: "There is a vast deal of difference between a new charter granted to a new corporation, (who must take it as it is given,) and a new charter given to a corporation already in being, and acting either under a former charter or under prescriptive usage. The latter, a corporation

* 3 Burr. 1656.

already existing, are not obliged to accept the new charter *in toto*, and to receive either all or none of it; they may act partly under it, and partly under their old charter or prescription. The validity of these new charters must turn upon the acceptance of them." In the same case Mr. Justice Wilmot says: "It is the concurrence and acceptance of the university that gives the force to the charter of the crown." In the King *v.* Pasmore,* Lord Kenyon observes: "Some things are clear: when a corporation exists capable of discharging its functions, the crown cannot obtrude another charter upon them; they may either accept or reject it." †

In all cases relative to charters, the acceptance of them is uniformly alleged in the pleadings. This shows the general understanding of the law, that they are grants or contracts; and that parties are necessary to give them force and validity. In King *v.* Dr. Askew, ‡ it is said: "The crown cannot oblige a man to be a corporator, without his consent; he shall not be subject to the inconveniences of it, without accepting it and assenting to it." These terms, "acceptance" and "assent," are the very language of contract. In Ellis *v.* Marshall, § it was expressly adjudged that the naming of the defendant among others, in an act of incorporation, did not of itself make him a corporator; and that his assent was necessary to that end. The court speak of the act of incorporation as a grant, and observe: "That a man may refuse a grant, whether from the government or an individual, seems to be a principle too clear to require the support of authorities." But Justice Buller, in King *v.* Pasmore, furnishes, if possible, a still more direct and explicit authority. Speaking of a corporation for government, he says: "I do not know how to reason on this point better than in the manner urged by one of the relator's counsel; who considered the grant of incorporation to be a compact between the crown and a certain number of the subjects, the latter of whom undertake, in consideration of the privileges which are bestowed, to exert themselves for the good government of the place." This language applies with peculiar propriety and force to the case before the court. It was in consequence of the "privileges bestowed," that Dr. Wheelock and his associates undertook

* 3 Term Rep. 240.

† See also 1 Kyd on Corp. 65.

‡ 4 Burr. 2200.

§ 2 Mass. Rep. 269.

to exert themselves for the instruction and education of youth in this college; and it was on the same consideration that the founder endowed it with his property.

And because charters of incorporation are of the nature of contracts, they cannot be altered or varied but by consent of the original parties. If a charter be granted by the king, it may be altered by a new charter granted by the king, and accepted by the corporators. But if the first charter be granted by Parliament, the consent of Parliament must be obtained to any alteration. In King *v.* Miller,* Lord Kenyon says: "Where a corporation takes its rise from the king's charter, the king by granting, and the corporation by accepting another charter, may alter it, because it is done with the consent of all the parties who are competent to consent to the alteration." †

There are, in this case, all the essential constituent parts of a contract. There is something to be contracted about, there are parties, and there are plain terms in which the agreement of the parties on the subject of the contract is expressed. There are mutual considerations and inducements. The charter recites, that the founder, on his part, has agreed to establish his seminary in New Hampshire, and to enlarge it beyond its original design, among other things, for the benefit of that Province; and thereupon a charter is given to him and his associates, designated by himself, promising and assuring to them, under the plighted faith of the State, the right of governing the college and administering its concerns in the manner provided in the charter. There is a complete and perfect grant to them of all the power of superintendence, visitation, and government. Is not this a contract? If lands or money had been granted to him and his associates, for the same purposes, such grant could not be rescinded. And is there any difference, in legal contemplation, between a grant of corporate franchises and a grant of tangible property? No such difference is recognized in any decided case, nor does it exist in the common apprehension of mankind.

It is therefore contended, that this case falls within the true meaning of this provision of the Constitution, as expounded in the decisions of this court; that the charter of 1769 is a con-

* 6 Term Rep. 277.
† See also Ex parte Bolton School, 2 Brown's Ch. Rep. 662.

tract, a stipulation or agreement, mutual in its considerations, express and formal in its terms, and of a most binding and solemn nature. That the acts in question impair this contract, has already been sufficiently shown. They repeal and abrogate its most essential parts.

A single observation may not be improper on the opinion of the court of New Hampshire, which has been published. The learned judges who delivered that opinion have viewed this question in a very different light from that in which the plaintiffs have endeavored to exhibit it. After some general remarks, they assume that this college is a public corporation; and on this basis their judgment rests. Whether all colleges are not regarded as private and eleemosynary corporations, by all law writers and all judicial decisions; whether this college was not founded by Dr. Wheelock; whether the charter was not granted at his request, the better to execute a trust, which he had already created; whether he and his associates did not become visitors, by the charter; and whether Dartmouth College be not, therefore, in the strictest sense, a private charity, are questions which the learned judges do not appear to have discussed.

It is admitted in that opinion, that, if it be a private corporation, its rights stand on the same ground as those of an individual. The great question, therefore, to be decided is, To which class of corporations do colleges thus founded belong? And the plaintiffs have endeavored to satisfy the court, that, according to the well-settled principles and uniform decisions of law, they are private, eleemosynary corporations.

Much has heretofore been said on the necessity of admitting such a power in the legislature as has been assumed in this case. Many cases of possible evil have been imagined, which might otherwise be without remedy. Abuses, it is contended, might arise in the management of such institutions, which the ordinary courts of law would be unable to correct. But this is only another instance of that habit of supposing extreme cases and then of reasoning from them, which is the constant refuge of those who are obliged to defend a cause, which, upon its merits, is indefensible. It would be sufficient to say in answer, that it is not pretended that there was here any such case of necessity. But a still more satisfactory answer is, that the apprehension of danger is groundless, and therefore the whole argument fails. Experience has not taught us that there is danger of great evils or of great inconvenience from this source. Hitherto, neither in our own country nor elsewhere have such cases of necessity occurred. The judicial establishments of the State are presumed to be competent to prevent abuses and violations of trust, in cases of this kind, as well as in all others. If they be not, they are imperfect, and their amendment would be a most proper subject for legislative wisdom. Under the government and protection of the general laws of the land, these institutions have always been found safe, as well as useful. They go on, with the progress of society, accommodating themselves easily, without sudden change or violence, to the alterations which take place in its condition, and in the knowledge, the habits, and pursuits of men. The English colleges were founded in Catholic ages. Their religion was reformed with the general reformation of the nation; and they are suited perfectly well to the purpose of educating the Protestant youth of modern times. Dartmouth College was established under a charter granted by the Provincial government; but a better constitution for a college, or one more adapted to the condition of things under the present government, in all material respects, could not now be framed. Nothing in it was found to need alteration at the Revolution. The wise men of that day saw in it one of the best hopes of future times, and commended it as it was, with parental care, to the protection and guardianship of the government of the State. A charter of more liberal sentiments, of wiser provisions, drawn with more care, or in a better spirit, could not be expected at any time or from any source. The college needed no change in its organization or government. That which it did need was the kindness, the patronage, the bounty of the legislature; not a mock elevation to the character of a university, without the solid benefit of a shilling's donation to sustain the character; not the swelling and empty authority of establishing institutes and other colleges. This unsubstantial pageantry would seem to have been in derision of the scanty endowment and limited means of an unobtrusive, but useful and growing seminary. Least of all was there a necessity, or pretence of necessity, to infringe its legal rights, violate its franchises and privileges, and pour upon it these overwhelming streams of litigation

But this argument from necessity would equally apply in all other cases. If it be well founded, it would prove, that, whenever any inconvenience or evil is experienced from the restrictions imposed on the legislature by the Constitution, these restrictions ought to be disregarded. It is enough to say, that the people have thought otherwise. They have, most wisely, chosen to take the risk of occasional inconvenience from the want of power, in order that there might be a settled limit to its exercise, and a permanent security against its abuse. They have imposed prohibitions and restraints; and they have not rendered these altogether vain and nugatory by conferring the power of dispensation. If inconvenience should arise which the legislature cannot remedy under the power conferred upon it, it is not answerable for such inconvenience. That which it cannot do within the limits prescribed to it, it cannot do at all. No legislature in this country is able, and may the time never come when it shall be able, to apply to itself the memorable expression of a Roman pontiff: "*Licet hoc* DE JURE *non possumus, volumus tamen* DE PLENITUDINE POTESTATIS."

The case before the court is not of ordinary importance, nor of every-day occurrence. It affects not this college only, but every college, and all the literary institutions of the country. They have flourished hitherto, and have become in a high degree respectable and useful to the community. They have all a common principle of existence, the inviolability of their charters. It will be a dangerous, a most dangerous experiment, to hold these institutions subject to the rise and fall of popular parties, and the fluctuations of political opinions. If the franchise may be at any time taken away, or impaired, the property also may be taken away, or its use perverted. Benefactors will have no certainty of effecting the object of their bounty; and learned men will be deterred from devoting themselves to the service of such institutions, from the precarious title of their offices. Colleges and halls will be deserted by all better spirits, and become a theatre for the contentions of politics. Party and faction will be cherished in the places consecrated to piety and learning. These consequences are neither remote nor possible only. They are certain and immediate.

When the court in North Carolina declared the law of the State, which repealed a grant to its university, unconstitutional and void, the legislature had the candor and the wisdom to repeal the law. This example, so honorable to the State which exhibited it, is most fit to be followed on this occasion. And there is good reason to hope that a State, which has hitherto been so much distinguished for temperate counsels, cautious legislation, and regard to law, will not fail to adopt a course which will accord with her highest and best interests, and in no small degree elevate her reputation.

It was for many and obvious reasons most anxiously desired that the question of the power of the legislature over this charter should have been finally decided in the State court. An earnest hope was entertained that the judges of the court might have viewed the case in a light favorable to the rights of the trustees. That hope has failed. It is here that those rights are now to be maintained, or they are prostrated for ever. *Omnia alia perfugia bonorum, subsidia, consilia, auxilia, jura ceciderunt. Quem enim alium appellem? quem obtester? quem implorem? Nisi hoc loco, nisi apud vos, nisi per vos, judices, salutem nostram, quæ spe exigua extremaque pendet, tenuerimus; nihil est præterea quo confugere possimus.*

DEFENCE OF JUDGE JAMES PRESCOTT.*

A PETITION having been presented to the House of Representatives of the Commonwealth of Massachusetts, praying an inquiry into the official conduct of James Prescott, Esquire, Judge of Probate of Wills for the County of Middlesex, and charging him with misconduct and maleadministration in office; and having been referred to a committee, who reported a statement of facts, together with resolutions setting forth that the said Prescott ought to be impeached therefor, at the bar of the Senate of the Commonwealth; on the 2d day of February, 1821, an order was passed accordingly, and the Senate demanded to take measures for his impeachment and appearance to answer thereto. A committee was thereupon appointed to prepare and report articles of impeachment; and John Glen King, Levi Lincoln, William Baylies, Warren Dutton, Samuel P. P. Fay, Lemuel Shaw, and Sherman Leland, Esquires, were appointed managers. Fifteen articles of impeachment were exhibited and read.

The articles substantially charged him with holding probate courts for transacting business at other times than those authorized by law, demanding and taking illegal fees, and acting as counsel, and receiving fees as such, in cases pending in his own court, before him, as judge.

After receiving the respondent's answer to the articles of impeachment, and hearing the evidence in support of and against the same, Messrs. Leland, Shaw, and Dutton argued the case in behalf of the managers. Mr. Hoar then opened the argument on the part of the respondent; Mr. Blake followed, and was succeeded by Mr. Webster, who spoke as follows.

MR. PRESIDENT, — I agree with the honorable managers in the importance which they have attributed to this proceeding. They

* Argument on the Impeachment of James Prescott, before the Senate of Massachusetts, on the 24th of April, 1821.

have, I think, not at all overrated that importance, nor ascribed to the occasion a solemnity which does not belong to it. Perhaps, however, I differ from them in regard to the causes which give interest and importance to this trial, and to the parties likely to be most lastingly and deeply affected by its progress and result. The respondent has as deep a stake, no doubt, in this trial, as he can well have in any thing which does not affect life. Regard for reputation, love of honorable character, affection for those who must suffer with him, if he suffers, and who will feel your sentence of conviction, if you should pronounce one, fall on their own heads, as it falls on his, cannot but excite in his breast an anxiety, which nothing could well increase, and nothing but a consciousness of upright intention could enable him to endure. Yet, Sir, a few years will carry him far beyond the reach of the consequences of this trial. Those same years will bear away, also, in their rapid flight, those who prosecute and those who judge him. But the community remains. The Commonwealth, we trust, will be perpetual. She is yet in her youth, as a free and independent State, and, by analogy to the life of individuals, may be said to be in that period of her existence when principles of action are adopted and character is formed. The honorable respondent will not be the principal sufferer, if he should here fall a victim to charges of undefined and undefinable offences, to loose notions of constitutional law, or novel rules of evidence. By the nature of moral retribution, the evil of such a course would fall most heavily on the State which should pursue it, by shaking its character for justice, and impairing its principles of constitutional liberty. This, Sir, is the first interesting and important impeachment which has arisen under the constitution of the Commonwealth. The decision now to be made cannot but affect subsequent cases. Governments necessarily are more or less regardful of precedents, on interesting public trials, and as, on the present occasion, all who act any part here have naturally considered what has been done and what rules and principles have governed, in similar cases, in other communities, so those who shall come after us will look back to this trial. And I most devoutly hope they may be able to regard it as a safe and useful example, fit to instruct and guide them in their own duty; an example full of wisdom and of moderation; an example of cautious and temperate justice;

an example of law and principle successfully opposed to temporary excitement; an example indicating in all those who bear a leading part in the proceedings a spirit fitted for a judicial trial, and proper for men who act with an enlightened and firm regard to the permanent interests of public constitutional liberty. To preserve the respondent in the office which he fills, or to deprive him of it, may be an object of little interest to the public. But on what principles he is to be so preserved or deprived is an inquiry in the highest degree important, and in which the public has a deep and lasting interest.

The provision which the constitutions of this and other States have made, for trying impeachments before the Senate, is obviously adopted from an analogy to the English constitution. It was perceived, however, and could hardly fail to be perceived, that the resemblance was not strong between the tribunals clothed with the power of trying impeachments in this country and the English House of Lords. This last is not only a branch of the legislature, but a standing judicature. It has jurisdiction to revise the judgments of all other courts. It is accustomed to the daily exercise of judicial power, and has acquired the habit and character which such exercise confers. There is a presumption, therefore, that it will try impeachments as it tries other causes, and that the common rules of evidence, and the forms of proceeding, so essential to the rights of the accused, which prevail in other cases, will prevail also in cases of impeachment. In the construction of our American governments, although the power of judging on impeachments could probably be nowhere so well deposited as with the Senate, yet it could not but be perceived beforehand that this high act of judicature was to be trusted to the hands of those who did not ordinarily perform judicial functions; but who occasionally only, and on such occasions, moreover, as were generally likely to be attended with some excitement, took upon themselves the duty of judges. It must, nevertheless, be confessed, that few evils have been as yet found to result from this arrangement. Although in the various States of the Union there have been several impeachments, there have been fewer convictions, and fewer still in which there is just reason to suppose injustice has taken place. From the experience of the past, I trust we may form favorable anticipations of the future, and that the judgment which this court shall now pronounce, and the rules and principles which shall guide that judgment, will be such as shall secure to the community a rigorous and unrelenting censorship over maleadministration in office, and to individuals entire protection against prejudice, excitement, and injustice.

The respondent is impeached for various instances of alleged misconduct in his office, as Judge of Probate for the County of Middlesex. In order that we may understand the duties which he is charged with violating, it is necessary to inquire into the origin and nature of these duties, and to examine the legal history of the Commonwealth in regard to the officers who, from time to time, have executed and performed these duties. It is now two centuries since our ancestors established a colony here. They brought with them, of course, the general notions with regard to property, the administration of justice, and the peculiar powers and duties of different tribunals, which they had formed in the country which they left; and these notions and general ideas they adopted in practice, with such modifications as circumstances rendered necessary. In England, they had been accustomed to see the jurisdiction over wills and administrations exercised in the spiritual courts, by the bishops or their ordinaries. Here, there were no such courts. Still it was a necessary jurisdiction, to be exercised by some tribunal, and in the early history of the colony it was exercised by the same magistrates, or some of them, on whom the other portions of judicial power were conferred. Wills were proved and administrations granted by the county magistrates, essentially in the same manner as in England by the bishops or their delegates. It seems that any two magistrates, with the clerk of the county court, might prove a will, and cause it to be recorded in the county court, and might grant administrations in like manner.*

At length, by the act of 1685,† it was expressly declared that the county court, in cases of probate of wills and the granting of administrations, should have the same power and authority *as the ordinary in England.*

* Ancient Charters, 204. † Ibid. 205.

By the provincial charter of 1692, all power and jurisdiction in the probate of wills and granting administration was conferred on the Governor and Council. The executive thus became supreme ordinary, and by the provisions of the statutes was to exercise the same power and authority as were exercised by the ordinary in England.

At this time no statute had regulated fees in the probate office; and yet it is not probable that business was done there at that time without fees, any more than at later periods. We must look, therefore, for some other authority than a statute permission for the establishment and regulation of fees in this office. And as the Governor and Council possessed the general power of the courts in England, it is material to inquire into the authority and practice of those courts in this particular. There can be no doubt that, in the English courts, fees, in cases of probate and administration, were, from early times, in most cases regulated by custom and the authority and direction of the courts themselves, without statute provisions. A table of fees, established in 1597, in the time of Archbishop Whitgift, may be seen in Burn's Ecclesiastical Law.*

This table sets forth a long list of charges and fees of office accruing in the administration of estates, such as for "administration," which probably means decreeing administration, "commission," which is the letter of administration, "interlocutory decree," "examination of account," "respite of inventory," "caveat," "citation," "quietus," and many others. At this time there was no statute which established the fees of office in cases of administration, except one single provision in the statute of 21 Hen. VIII. ch. 5, which enacted, that for granting administration on goods under forty pounds, the judge should receive no more than two shillings and sixpence. It appears from the preamble of that statute, that no previous law was existing on the subject, and the grievance recited is, that the bishops and their ordinaries demanded and received greater fees for the probation of testaments, and other things thereunto belonging, than had been aforetime usual and accustomed. The preamble recites also, that an act of Henry the Fifth had ordained that no ordinary should take, for the probation of tes-

* Vol. II. p. 266.

taments or other things to the same belonging, any more than was accustomed and used in the time of King Edward the Third, *which act did endure but to the next Parliament by reason that the said ordinaries did then promise to reform and amend their exactions;* but, inasmuch as the evil was still continued and aggravated, the act proceeded to limit and fix fees of office for the probate of wills, and for other services respecting testate estates, and contains the single provision above mentioned, and no more, respecting administrations on intestate estates.

It is entirely clear and certain, that the fees of bishops and their ordinaries did not have their origin in the grant or provision of any act of Parliament. Such acts were passed only to restrain and limit the amount, and to prevent exaction and extortion. The right to demand and receive fees rested on the general principle of a right to compensation for services rendered; and, in the absence of statute limitations, the amount was ascertained by the practice and usage of the courts, being reasonable and proper. Hence it happened in England that different fees were paid, and probably still are, in the different dioceses, according to the usage of different courts, and the time when their tables of fees were respectively established. "In the several dioceses there are tables of fees, different, as it seemeth, in the several charges, in proportion to the difference of times wherein they have been established." * This is precisely what has happened, and what, whether we are allowed to prove it or not, every member of this court knows now exists, in relation to the different counties of this Commonwealth.

It is most material to the respondent's case to understand clearly on what ground it is that, as Judge of Probate, he had a right to receive fees for services performed in his office There is a difference of opinion, in matter of law, in this respect, between the managers and ourselves, wide enough, in my judgment, to extend over the whole case. If the House of Representatives be right in the legal doctrine which their managers have introduced here, I agree at once that the case is against the respondent, unless, indeed, an indulgence may be allowed to his infirmity in not understanding the law as it is now as-

* 2 Burn, 269.

serted. I will proceed to state the question now at issue between the managers and us, as clearly as I may be able. The managers contend, that all fees of office in such offices as the respondent's arise only from the express grant of the legislature, and that none can be claimed where such grant is not shown. We, on the other hand, humbly submit that the right, in such offices, to receive fees, is the general right to receive reasonable compensation for services rendered and labor performed, and is no otherwise affected by statute than as the amount of fees is or may be thereby limited.

It is certain that judges of probate in this State are required to perform many acts (such, for instance, as granting guardianship to persons *non compotes mentis*), for which no fees are specifically established by the statute. One of the learned managers has expressly advanced the proposition, that for such services the judge is entitled to receive no fees whatever. He contends that the law presumes him to be adequately paid, on a sort of average, for all services by him performed, by the fees specially provided for some. On the contrary, we very humbly insist, that in all such cases the judge has a right to receive a just and reasonable fee of office for the service performed; the amount to be settled on proper principles, and, as well as in any way, by analogy to similar services, for which the amount of fees is fixed by statute. The statute, for example, establishes the fee for a grant of guardianship over minors. It establishes none for guardianship over persons *non compotes mentis*. The precise difference between the learned managers and us is, that they contend that, in the last case, the judge is entitled to receive no fee at all; while we think that he has a right to receive, in such case, a reasonable fee, and that what is reasonable may fairly be determined by reference to what the law allows him in the case of guardianship over minors.

I rejoice, Sir, in behalf of my client, that we have here a plain, intelligible question of law to be discussed and decided. This is a question in which neither prerogative nor discretion has aught to do. It is not to be decided by reasons of state, or those political considerations which we have heard so often, but so indefinitely, and in my judgment so alarmingly, referred to, and relied on, in the opening speeches of more than one of the learned managers. It may possibly happen, Sir, to the learned managers to share the fortunes of the gods in Homer's battles. While they keep themselves in the high atmosphere of prerogative and political discretion, and assail the respondent from the clouds, the advantage in the controversy may remain entirely with them. When they descend, however, to an equal field of mortal combat, and consent to contend with mortal weapons, *cominus ense*, it is probable they may sometimes get, as well as give, a wound. On the present question, we meet the learned managers on equal terms and fair ground, and we are willing that our client's fate should abide the result. The managers have advanced a plain and intelligible proposition, as being the law of the land. If they make it out, they show a good case against the respondent; if they fail so to do, then their case, so far as it rests on this proposition, fails also. Let, then, the proposition be examined.

The proposition is, as before stated, that for services which the law requires judges of probate to perform, but for which there is no particular fee established or provided by statute, they can receive no fee whatever.

In the first place, let it be remarked, that, of the various duties and services required of judges of probate, some grow out of the very nature of their office, and are incidental to it, or arise by common law; others were imposed by statutes passed before the establishment of any fee bill whatever, and others, again, by statutes passed since. The statute commonly called the fee bill was passed for the regulation of fees in other courts, and other offices, as well as of the judges and registers of probate. It imposes no duty whatever on any officer. It treats only of existing duties, and of those no farther than to limit fees. It declares that "the fees of the several persons hereafter mentioned, for the services respectively annexed to their names, shall be as follows," and so forth. The statute then proceeds to enumerate, among other things, certain services of the judges of probate; but it is acknowledged that it does not enumerate or set forth all the services which the law calls on them to perform.

In our opinion, Sir, this is simply a restraining statute. It fixes the amount of fees in the cases mentioned, leaving every thing else as it stood before. I have already stated, that, in

England, fees in the ecclesiastical courts, for probate of wills, and granting administrations, were of earlier date than any statute respecting them, and their amount ascertained by usage and the authority of the courts themselves. "The rule is," says Dr. Burn, "the known and established custom of every place, being reasonable." *

And if the reasonableness of the fee be disputed, it may be tried by jury, whether the fee be reasonable.† If this be so, then clearly there exists a right to some fee, independent of a particular statute; for if there be no right to any fee at all, why refer to a jury to decide what fee would be reasonable? But the law is still more express on this point. "Fees are certain perquisites allowed to officers in the administration of justice, as a recompense for their labor and trouble; ascertained either by acts of Parliament or by ancient usage, which gives them an equal sanction with an act of Parliament." "All such fees as have been allowed by courts of justice to their officers, as a recompense for their labor and attendance, are established fees; and the parties cannot be deprived of them without an act of Parliament." ‡

I may add, that fees are recoverable, in an action of *assumpsit*, as for work and labor performed. The doctrine contended for on the other side is contradicted, in so many words, by a well-settled rule; namely, that if an office be erected for the public good, though no fee is annexed to it, it is a good office; and the party, for the labor and pains which he takes in executing it, may maintain a *quantum meruit*, if not as a fee, yet as a compensation for his trouble.§

The universal practice, Sir, has corresponded with these rules of law. Almost every officer in the Commonwealth, whose compensation consists in fees of office, renders services not enumerated in the fee bill, and is paid for those services; and this through no indulgence or abuse, but with great propriety and justice. Allow me to mention one instance, which may be taken as a sample of many. Some thousands of dollars are paid every year to the clerks of the several Courts of Common

* 4 Burn's Ecclesiastical Law, 267.
† 1 Salkeld, 333.
‡ Coke, Lit. 368; Prec. Chan. 551; Jacob's Law Dict., "Fees."
§ Moore, 808; Jac., "Fees," (A. E.); Hard. 355; Salk. 333.

Pleas in this State, for certified copies of papers and records remaining in their offices. The fee bill neither authorizes the taking of any such fee, nor limits its amount, nor mentions it in any way. There are other instances, equally clear and strong, and they show us that all the courts of justice, and all the officers concerned in its administration, have understood the law as the respondent has understood it; and that the notion of the learned managers derives as little support from practice, as it does from reason or authority. The learned managers have produced no one opinion of any writer, no decision of any court, and, as I think, no shadow of reason, to sustain themselves in the extraordinary ground which they have taken; ground, I admit, essential to be maintained by them, but which the respondent could devoutly wish they had taken somewhat more of pains to examine, before, on the strength of it, they had brought him to this bar. I submit it, Sir, to the judgment of this court, and to the judgment of every judge and every lawyer in the land, whether the law be not, that officers paid by fees have a right to such fees, for services rendered, on the general principle of compensation for work and labor performed; the amount to be ascertained by the statute, in cases in which the statute has made a regulation; and, in other cases, by analogy to the services which are especially provided for, and by a consideration of what is just and reasonable in the case. With all my respect, Sir, for the learned managers, it would be mere affectation if I were to express myself with any diffidence on this part of the case, or should leave the topic with the avowal of any other feeling than surprise, that a judge of the land should be impeached and prosecuted upon the foundation of such opinions as have in this particular been advanced.

Before I proceed further, Sir, I wish to take notice of a point, perhaps not entirely essential to the case. The respondent, in his answer, has stated that the jurisdiction of judges of probate consists of two parts, commonly called the amicable or voluntary and the contentious jurisdiction. One of the learned managers has said, that this distinction can by no means be allowed, and has proceeded to state, if I rightly understood him, that the voluntary jurisdiction of the English ecclesiastical courts has not, in any part of it, devolved on, and been granted to, the judges of probate here. As it is not perhaps material for the present discussion to ascertain precisely what is the true distinction between the voluntary and the contentious jurisdiction of the ecclesiastical courts, as understood in England, I shall content myself with reading a single authority on the sub ject. Dr. Burn says: "Voluntary jurisdiction is exercised in matters which require no judicial proceeding, as in granting probate of wills, letters of administration, sequestration of vacant benefices, institution, and such like; contentious jurisdiction is where there is an action or judicial process, and consisteth in the hearing and determining of causes between party and party." *

It can be now at once seen, Sir, whether any part of the jurisdiction exercised by judges of probate in this State be *voluntary*, within this definition of the distinction between voluntary and contentious.

After these observations, Sir, on the general nature and origin of fees accruing in the probate offices, I shall proceed to a consideration of the charges contained in these articles.

And the first inquiry is, whether any misconduct or maleadministration in office is sufficiently charged upon the respondent in any of them. To decide this question, it is necessary to inquire, what is the law governing impeachments; and by what rule questions arising in such proceedings are to be determined. My learned colleague, who has immediately preceded me, has gone very extensively into this part of the case. I have little to add, and shall not detain you by repetition. I take it, Sir, that this is a court; that the respondent is brought here to be tried; that you are his judges; and that the rule of your decision is to be found in the constitution and the law. If this be not so, my time is misspent in speaking here, and yours also in listening to me. Upon any topics of expediency or policy; upon a question of what may be best, upon the whole; upon a great part of those considerations with which the leading manager opened his case, I have not one word to say. If this be a court, and the respondent on his trial before it; if he is to be tried, and can only be tried for some offence known to the constitution and the law; and if evidence against him can be produced only according to the ordinary rules, then, indeed, coun-

* Vol. I. p. 292.

sel may possibly be of service to him. But if other considerations, such as have been plainly announced, are to prevail, and that were known, counsel owe no duty to their client which could compel them to a totally fruitless effort for his defence. I take it for granted, however, Sir, that this court feels itself bound by the constitution and the law; and I shall therefore proceed to inquire whether these articles, or any of them, are sustained by the constitution and the law.

I take it to be clear, that an impeachment is a prosecution for the violation of existing laws; and that the offence, in cases of impeachment, must be set forth substantially in the same manner as in indictments. I say *substantially*, for there may be in indictments certain technical requisitions, which are not necessary to be regarded in impeachments. The constitution has given this body the power of trying impeachments, without defining what an impeachment is, and therefore necessarily introducing, with the term itself, its usual and received definition, and the character and incidents which belong to it. An impeachment, it is well known, is a judicial proceeding. It is a *trial*, and conviction in that trial is to be followed by forfeiture and punishment. Hence the authorities instruct us, that the rules of proceeding are substantially the same as prevail in other criminal proceedings.* There is, on this occasion, no manner of discretion in this court, any more than there is, in other cases, in a judge or a juror. It is all a question of law and evidence. Nor is there, in regard to the evidence, any more latitude than on trials for murder, or any other crime, in the courts of law. Rules of evidence are rules of law, and their observance on this occasion can no more be dispensed with than any other rule of law. Whatever may be imagined to the contrary, it will commonly be found, that a disregard of the ordinary rules of evidence is but the harbinger of injustice. Tribunals which do not regard those rules seldom regard any other; and those who think they may make free with what the law has ordained respecting evidence, generally find an apology for making free also with what it has ordained respecting other things. They who admit or reject evidence according to no other rule than their own good pleasure, generally decide every thing else by the same rule.

* 2 Wooddeson, 611; 4 Bl. Comm. 259; 1 H. P. C. 150; 1 Chitty's Criminal Law, 169.

This being, then, a judicial proceeding, the first requisite is, that the respondent's offence *should be fully and plainly, substantially and formally, described to him.* This is the express requisition of the constitution. Whatever is necessary to be proved must be alleged; and it must be alleged with ordinary and reasonable certainty. I have already said, that there may be necessary in indictments certain technical niceties, which are not necessary in cases of impeachments. There are, for example, certain things necessary to be stated, in strictness, in indictments, which, nevertheless, it is not necessary to prove precisely as stated. For instance, an indictment must set forth, among other things, the particular day when the offence is alleged to have been committed; but it need not be proved to have been committed on that particular day. It has been holden, in the case of an impeachment, that it is sufficient to state the commission of the offence to have been on or about a particular day. Such was the decision in Lord Winton's case, as may be seen in 4 Hatsell's Precedents, 297. In that case, the respondent, being convicted, made a motion to arrest the judgment, on the ground that "the impeachment was insufficient, for that the time of committing the high treason is not therein laid with sufficient certainty." The principal facts charged in that case were laid to be committed "on or about the months of September, October, or November last"; and the taking of Preston, and the battle there, which are among the acts of treason, were laid to be done "about the 9th, 10th, 11th, 12th, or 13th of November last."

A question was put to the judges, "Whether in indictment for treason or felony it be necessary to allege some certain day upon which the fact is supposed to be committed; or, if it be only alleged in an indictment that the crime was committed on or about a certain day, whether that would be sufficient." And the judges answered, that it is necessary that there be a certain day laid in the indictment, and that to allege that the fact was committed on or about a certain day would not be sufficient. The judges were next asked whether, if a certain day be alleged in an indictment, it be necessary, on the trial, to prove the fact to be committed on that day; and they answered, that it is not necessary. And thereupon the Lords resolved, that the impeachment was sufficiently certain in point of time. This case furnishes a good illustration of the rule, which I think is reasonable and well founded, that whatever is to be proved must be stated, and that no more need be stated.

In the next place, the matter of the charge must be the breach of some known and standing law; the violation of some positive duty. If our constitutions of government have not secured this, they have done very little indeed for the security of civil liberty. "There are two points," said a distinguished statesman, "on which the whole of the liberty of every individual depends; one, the trial by jury; the other, a maxim arising out of the elements of justice itself, that no man shall, under any pretence whatever, be tried upon any thing but a known law." These two great points our constitutions have endeavored to establish; and the constitution of this Commonwealth, in particular, has provisions on this subject as full and ample as can be expressed in the language in which that constitution is written.

Allow me then, Sir, on these rules and principles, to inquire into the legal sufficiency of the charges contained in the first article.

And first, as to the illegality of the time or place of holding the court, I beg to know what there is stated in the article to show that illegality. What fact is alleged on which the managers now rely? Not one. Illegality itself is not a fact, but an inference of law, drawn by the managers, on facts known or supposed by them, but not stated in the charge, nor until the present moment made known to any body else. We hear them now contending, that these courts were illegal for the following reasons, which they say are true, as facts, viz.: —

1. That the register was absent;
2. That the register had no notice to be present;
3. That parties had not notice to be present.

Now, not one of these is stated in the article. No one fact or circumstance now relied on as making a case against the defendant is stated in the charge. Was he not entitled to know, I beg to ask, what was to be proved against him? If it was to be contended that persons were absent from those courts who ought to have been present, or that parties had no notice who were entitled to receive notice, ought not the respondent to be informed, that he might encounter evidence by evidence, and be prepared to disprove what would be attempted to be proved?

This charge, Sir, I maintain, is wholly and entirely insufficient. It is a mere nullity. If it were an indictment in the courts of law, it would be quashed, not for want of formality or technical accuracy, but for want of substance in the charge. I venture to say, there is not a court in the country, from the highest to the lowest, in which such a charge would be thought sufficient to warrant a judgment.

The next charge in this article is for receiving illegal fees for services performed. I contend that this also is substantially defective, in not setting out what sum, in certain, the defendant has received as illegal fees. It is material to his defence that he should be informed, more particularly than he here is, of the charge against him. If it be merely stated, that for divers services respecting one administration he received a certain sum, and for divers others respecting another, another certain sum, and that these sums were too large (which is the form of accusation adopted in this case), he cannot know for what service, or on what particular item, he is charged with having received illegal fees. The legal and the illegal are mixed up together, and he is only told that in the aggregate he has received too much. In some of these cases, there is a number of items or particulars in which fees are charged and received; but in the articles these items or particulars are not stated, and he is left to conjecture, out of ten, or it may be twenty, particular cases, which one it is that the proof is expected to apply to.

My colleague has referred to the cases, in which it has been adjudged, that, in prosecutions against officers for the alleged taking of illegal fees, this general manner of statement is insufficient. It is somewhat remarkable, that ancient acts of Parliament should have been passed expressly for the purpose of protecting officers exercising jurisdiction over wills and administration against prosecutions in this form; which were justly deemed oppressive. The statute 25 Ed. III. ch. 9, after reciting "that the king's justices do take indictments of ordinaries, and of their officers, of extortion, or oppressions, and impeach them, without putting in certain wherein, whereof, or in what manner, they have done extortion," proceeds to enact, "that his justices shall not from henceforth impeach the ordinaries, nor their officers, because of such indictments of general extortions or oppressions, unless they say, and put in certain, in what thing, and of what, and in what manner, the said ordinaries or their officers have done extortions or oppressions."

The charge in this case ought to have stated the precise act for which the fee was taken, and the amount of the fee received. The court could then see whether it were illegal. Whereas the article, after reciting certain services performed by the respondent, some of which are mentioned in the fee bill, and others are not, alleges that for the business aforesaid the respondent demanded and received other and greater fees than are by law allowed. Does this mean that he received excessive fees for every service, or was the whole excess charged on one service? Was the excess taken on those particular services for which a specific fee is given by the statute, or was it taken for those services not mentioned in the fee bill at all? But further, the article proceeds to state, that afterwards, during and upon the settlement of said estate, the respondent did demand and receive divers sums, as fees of office, other and greater than are by law allowed; without stating at all what services were rendered, for which these fees were taken! It is simply a general allegation, that the respondent received from an administrator, in the settlement of an estate, excessive fees; without stating in any manner whatever what the excess was, or even what services were performed?

I beg leave to ask, Sir, of the learned managers, whether they will, as lawyers, express an opinion before this court that this mode of accusation is sufficient? Do they find any precedent for it, or any principle to warrant it? If they mean to say, that proceedings in cases of impeachment are not subject to rule; that the general principles applicable to other criminal proceedings do not apply; this is an intelligible, though it may be an alarming, course of argument. If, on the other hand, they admit that a prosecution by impeachment is to be governed by the general rules applicable to other criminal prosecutions; that the constitution is to control it; and that it is a judicial proceeding; and if they recur, as they have already frequently done, to the law relative to indictments for doctrines and maxims applicable to this proceeding; I again ask them, and I hope in their reply they will not evade an answer, will they, as lawyers, before a tribunal constituted as this, say that, in their opinion, this mode of charging the respondent is constitutional and legal? Standing in the situation they do, and before such a court, will they say that, in their opinion, the respondent is not, constitutionally and legally, entitled to require a more particular statement of his supposed offences? I think, Sir, that candor and justice to the respondent require that the learned managers should express, on this occasion, such opinions on matters of law as they would be willing, as lawyers, here and elsewhere to avow and defend. I must, therefore, even yet again, entreat them to say, in the course of their reply, whether they maintain that this mode of allegation would be sufficient in an indictment; and if not, whether they maintain that in an impeachment it is less necessary that the defendant be informed of the facts intended to be proved against him, than it is in an indictment. The learned managers may possibly answer me, that it is their business only to argue these questions, and the business of the court to decide them. I cannot think, however, that they will be satisfied with such a reply. Under the circumstances in which he is placed, the respondent thinks that the very respectable gentlemen who prosecute him, in behalf of the House of Representatives, owe a sort of duty, even to him. It is far from his wish, however, to interfere with their own sense of their duty. They must judge for themselves on what grounds they ask his conviction from this court. Yet he has a right to ask, and he does most earnestly ask, and would repeatedly and again and again ask, that they will state those grounds plainly and distinctly. For he trusts that, if there be a responsibility, even beyond the immediate occasion, for opinions and sentiments here advanced, they will be entirely willing, as professional men, to meet it.

I now submit to this court, whether the supposed offences of taking illegal fees, as charged in this article, are set forth legally and sufficiently, either by the common rules of proceeding in criminal cases, or according to the constitution of the State.

As to the manner of stating the offence in this article, I mean the allegation that the respondent refused to give, on request, an account of items of fees received, it appears to me to be substantially right, and I have no remarks to make upon it. The question upon that will be, whether the fact is proved.

All the objections which have been made to the first article apply equally to the second; with this further observation, that for the services mentioned in this article the fee bill makes no provision at all. The same objections apply also to the third, fourth, and fifth articles.

It seems to us, Sir, that all these charges for receiving illegal fees, without setting out, in particular, what service was done, and what was the amount of excess, are insufficient to be the foundation of a judgment against the respondent. And especially does this hold of the charge of receiving fees for services not specified in the fee bill; it not being stated what he would be properly entitled to in such cases by usage and the practice of the courts, and there being no allegation that the sum received was an unreasonable compensation for the services performed. In this respect, the articles consider that to be settled by positive law which is not so settled. The second article, for example, alleges that the respondent demanded and received, for certain letters of guardianship granted by him over persons *non compotes mentis*, "other and greater fees than are by law allowed therefor." This supposes, then, that *some* fees are allowed by law therefor; yet this is the very case in which it has been contended by the managers that no fee whatever was due; there being none mentioned in the fee bill. Between the words of the article and the tenor of the argument there appears to me to be no small hostility. Both cannot be right. They cannot stand together. There should be either a new argument to support the article, or a new article to meet the argument.

Having made these observations on the legal sufficiency of all the articles which charge the respondent with holding unlawful courts, and demanding and receiving unlawful fees, before proceeding to those which advance charges of a different nature against him, allow me to advert to the evidence which has been given on these first five articles respectively; and to consider what unlawful act has been *proved* against the respondent in relation to the matters contained in them.

In the first place, it is proved that the respondent held a special probate court at Groton, on the 14th of October, 1816; and at such court granted letters of administration to one Tarbell. This court the register did not attend. With respect to parties concerned in the business then and there to be transacted, they all had notice, as far as appears; and no one has ever been heard to complain on that account.

It has now been contended, Sir, by the learned managers, that this court was holden unlawfully, because not holden at a time previously fixed by law. They maintain that judges of probate can exercise no jurisdiction, except at certain *terms*, when their court is to be holden.

On the contrary, the respondent has supposed, and has acted on the supposition, that he might lawfully hold his court, for the transaction of ordinary business, at such time and place as he might think proper; giving due and proper notice to all parties concerned. He supposes he might so have done, independently of the provisions of any statute; and he supposes, moreover, that he was authorized so to do by the express provision of the statute of 1806.

The first inquiry, then, is, whether the probate courts in this Commonwealth be not courts which may be considered as always open, and authorized at all times to receive applications and transact business, upon due notice to all parties; or whether, on the contrary, their jurisdiction can only be exercised in term, or at such stated periods and times as may be fixed by law. It is true, that the common law courts have usually fixed terms, and can exercise their powers only during the continuance of these terms. In England, the termination as well as the beginning of the term is fixed by law. With us, the first day only is fixed, and the courts, having commenced on the day fixed by law, remain in session as long as the convenience of the occasion requires.

In early ages, the whole year was one continued term. After the introduction of Christianity among the western nations of Europe, the governments ordained that their courts should be always open for the administration of justice; for the purpose, among other things, of showing their disapprobation of the heathen governments, by whom the *dies fasti et nefasti* were carefully, and, as they thought, superstitiously regarded. In the course of time, however, the Church interfered, and succeeded in rescuing certain seasons of the year which it deemed holy time, such as Christmas and Easter, from the agitations of forensic discussion. The necessities of rural labor afterwards added the harvest months to the number of the vacations. The vacations were thus carved out of the year, and what was left was term. Thus, even with regard to the common law courts, the provisions respecting terms were made, not so much for creating terms as for creating vacations. And for this reason it probably is, that as well the termination as the commencement of the term is established by law.

In respect to the spiritual courts, no such positive regulations, as far as I can learn, appear to have been made. Their jurisdiction is one which seems necessarily to require more or less of occasional, as well as stated exercise. The bishop's jurisdiction over wills and administrations was not local, but personal. Hence he might exercise it, not only when he pleased, but where he pleased; within the limits of his diocese or without. He might grant letters of administration, for instance, while without the local limits over which his jurisdiction extends, because it is a personal authority which the law appoints him to exercise. "The power of granting probates is not local, but is annexed to the person of the archbishop or bishop; and therefore a bishop, or the commissary of a bishop, while absent from his diocese, may grant probate of wills respecting property within the same; or if an archbishop or bishop of a province or see in Ireland happens to be in England, he may grant probate of wills relative to effects within his province or diocese." *

Notwithstanding this, however, the canons ordain that the ordinaries shall appoint proper places and times for the keeping of their courts; such as shall be convenient for those who are to make their appearance there. This is for the benefit of suitors. The object is, that there may be some certain times and places when and where persons having business to be transacted may expect to find the judge; and it by no means necessarily takes away the power of transacting business at other times and places. The ordaining of such a rule plainly shows, that before it was made these judges held their courts when and where they pleased, and only when and where they pleased.

If we recur again to the history of this Commonwealth, we shall find that what necessity or convenience had established in

* Toller, 66; 4 Burn, 285.

England, the same necessity or convenience soon established here. By the Colony charter no provision was made for a court for the probate of wills and granting administrations. In 1639 it was ordained that there should be records kept of all wills, administrations, and inventories.* In 1649 an act was passed requiring wills to be proved at the *county court* which should next be after thirty days from the death of the party; and that administration should be there taken.†

These county courts were courts of common law jurisdiction, and were holden at stated terms. But experience seems soon to have shown that, from the nature of probate jurisdiction, its exercise could not be conveniently confined to stated terms; for in 1652 an act was passed *authorizing two magistrates, with the recorder of the county court, to allow and approve of wills, and grant administrations; the clerk to cause the will or administration to be recorded.*‡ The reason of passing this act is obvious. The county court consisted of many magistrates. They assembled to form a court only at stated terms. On this court the law had conferred the powers of probate of wills and granting administrations; and, like other business, it could of course only be transacted at stated terms. This was found to be an inconvenience, and the law which I have cited was passed to remedy it. So that, instead of confining the exercise of the jurisdiction of these courts to stated terms, we find the law has done exactly the contrary. Not only the analogy which they bear to other courts of similar jurisdiction, but our own history, and the early enactments of the Colonial legislature, all conspire to refute the notions which have been advanced, I cannot but think somewhat incautiously advanced, on this occasion.

The provisions of the constitution requiring judges of probate to hold their courts on certain fixed days is perfectly and strictly consistent, nevertheless, with the occasional exercise of their powers at other times. The law has had two objects in this respect; distinct, indeed, but consistent. One is, that there should be certain fixed days when it should be the duty of the judges to attend to the business of their offices and the applications of suitors; the other, that they might, when occasion required, perform such duties and attend to such applications on

* Ancient Charters, 43. † Ibid. 204. ‡ Ibid. 204.

other days. The learned managers seem to have regarded these provisions of law as repugnant, whereas they appear to us to consist perfectly well together.

If it were possible, Sir, that we were still mistaken in all this, there is yet the provision of the special law of 1806, which would seem to put an end to this part of the case. This statute has been already stated; its terms are express, and its object plain beyond all doubt or ambiguity. Not only does this act of itself afford the most complete justification to the respondent in this case, but it proves also that either the legislature or the learned managers have misunderstood the requisition of the constitution in regard to fixed days for holding probate courts. My colleagues have put this part of the argument beyond the power of any answer. I leave it where they left it.

With respect to notice to parties, I have already said that it is not at all proved, or pretended to be proved, that there was any person entitled to notice who did not receive it. It would be absurd and preposterous now to call on the respondent to give positive proof of notice to all persons concerned. As it was his duty to give such notice, it is to be presumed he did give it until the contrary appear. Besides, as no omission to give notice is stated in the article as a fact rendering the court illegal, how is he expected to come here prepared to prove notice?

I have little to add, Sir, to what my learned colleague who immediately preceded me has said respecting the necessity of the register's attending these special courts. One of the learned managers has said that the statute of 1806, which requires notice to parties, requires notice also to the register. I see no sort of reason for such a construction of the act. The words are, that the judge may appoint such times and places for holding his court as he shall deem expedient, giving public notice thereof, or notifying all concerned; and have no relation to the officers of the court. Neither the register, nor the crier, nor the door-keeper is, I should imagine, within this province; and yet I suppose one to be as much within it as the other.

The presence of the register cannot be essential to the existence of the court, any more than the presence of the clerk is essential to the existence of any other court. Like other courts, the court of probate has its clerk, called a register, but he is no more part of the court than the clerk of the Supreme Judicial Court is a component part of that court.

No provision appears to have been made by the Province laws for the appointment of a register. The ordinary, having the whole power over the subject of the probate of wills and granting administrations, might allow a clerk or register to his surrogate or not, at his pleasure. It was necessary, of course, that records should be kept, but this might be done by the judge himself, as some other magistrates keep their own records. There are certain statutes which speak of the register's office, but which seem only to mean the place where the records are kept. They contain no provision for the appointment of such an officer, nor any description of his duties.* It appears, as I am informed by the Suffolk probate records, that a register was appointed by the Governor, by virtue of his power as Supreme Ordinary, immediately after the issuing of the Provincial charter. The first provision made by him for this officer, if I mistake not, is contained in the statute of 1784,† and the duties of the officer are well described in that act. He is to be the register of wills and letters of administration, and to be *keeper* of the records. His signature or assent is necessary to the validity of no act whatever. He is to record official papers, and to keep the records and documents which belong to the office.

It is quite manifest, from the laws made under the charter as well as those enacted since the adoption of the present government, that the presence of the register has not been essential to the existence of a legal probate court. The proof of this is, that certain acts or things, by these statutes, may be done by the judge without the register. By 6 Geo. I. ch. 3, it is provided, that persons to take an inventory of one deceased shall be appointed and sworn by the judge of probate, *if the estate be in the town where he dwells, or within ten miles thereof;* otherwise, by a justice of the peace.‡ By 4 Geo. II. ch. 3, appraisers are to be sworn by the judge, if the estate be within ten miles of his dwelling-house. § By the act of March, 1784, when a minor lives more than ten miles *from the judge's dwelling-house*, his choice may be certified to the judge by a justice of the peace. These several laws plainly contemplate the performance of certain acts by the judge, not at probate courts

* 4 Will. and Mary, ch. 2.
† Massachusetts Laws, Vol. I. p. 155.
‡ Province Laws, p. 222.
§ Ibid. p. 286.

holden at stated times, and without the presence or assistance of the register.

And now, Sir, I have finally to remark, on the subject of holding these special courts, the respondent is proved to have followed the practice which he found established in the office when he was appointed to it. The existence of this practice is proved beyond all doubt or controversy by the evidence of Dr. Prescott.

As to the holding of special courts, therefore, the respondent rests his justification on what he conceives to be the general principle of law, on the express provision of the statute, and the usage which has been proved to exist before and at the time when he came into the office.

The charge, Mr. President, in the first article, of taking illegal fees, has been fully considered by other counsel. I need not detain the court by further comment. It is true that, for what is called a set of administration papers, the respondent received in this case five dollars and fifty-eight cents. It is true, also, that for the same business done at a stated court the fees would have been but three dollars and sixty cents. The reason for this difference is fully stated in the respondent's answer. But it is also true, that the usual sum at stated courts, namely, three dollars and sixty cents, is made up by the insertion of fees for sundry services not specified in the fee bill. Indeed, the learned managers have not, as has been so often before observed, even told us what would have been the precise amount of legal fees in this case. They appear to be marvellously shy of figures. If the court adopt the opinion of the learned managers, that no fees are due where none are specially provided, and that for receiving fees in such cases an officer is impeachable, then there is no doubt that the respondent may be impeached and convicted for his conduct in regard to every administration which he has granted for fifteen years; and there is as little doubt that, on that ground, any judge of probate in the Commonwealth is impeachable; as must be well known to every member of this court, whether they suffer it to be proved here or not.

It is utterly impossible to know by this article itself in what it was intended to charge the respondent with having received illegal fees. Was it for the order of notice? But the statute allows no fee for that. Was it for granting administration? But it is not stated whether it was a litigated case or not, and therefore it cannot be known what he might lawfully receive.

It is not denied, however, that every paper executed by the judge in this case, and every service performed by him, were proper and necessary for the occasion. Even the learned managers have not contended that any thing could have been dispensed with. If, therefore, the amount did not exceed the usual sum, it would seem past all controversy, that the respondent stood justified, if he is right in the general grounds which have been assumed. This question, then, is as to the right to the additional two dollars. This, I apprehend, stands on precisely the same ground as his right to fees for services not set down in the fee bill, namely, on the ground of a *quantum meruit*, or reasonable compensation for labor performed. This special court was holden expressly for the benefit of Tarbell, and at his instance and request. He is charged only with the necessary and unavoidable expenses of the court; expenses which must be borne either by the judge himself, or by the party for whose benefit they were incurred. It was not so much an extraordinary compensation to the judge, but a reïmbursement of expenses actually incurred by him. Here again he is found only to have followed the established practice of the office. He has done no more than his predecessor had done. It is clearly proved, that that predecessor did habitually hold these special courts on request, and that the necessary expenses of proceeding therein before him did exceed those of similar proceedings at the stated courts. There can be no complaint, in this case, of the *amount.* If he had a right to receive any thing, it must be conceded he did not receive too much. A practice of this sort may lead to inconvenience; possibly to abuse; but it did not originate with the respondent, nor does it appear that abuse has followed it in his hands. If he were authorized to hold these special courts, and if they were *necessarily* attended with some augmentation of expense, it would seem perfectly reasonable that those for whom the expense was incurred should defray it. The books teach us, that "an officer who takes a reward, which has been usual in certain cases, for the more diligent or expeditious performance of his duty, cannot be said to be guilty of extortion; for otherwise it would be impossible, in many cases, to have the law executed with success." * These sums were paid voluntarily. The respondent in no proper sense demanded them. He did not refuse to do his official duty till they were paid. So of those sums paid for services not mentioned in the fee bill. Several of these things might have been done by the party himself, or his counsel; such as drawing petition, bond, and so forth. Yet it was usual to have these papers prepared at the probate office, and to pay for them, together with the other expenses. This being the usual course of things, and the party complying with it without objection, and paying voluntarily, there can be no reason, I think, to call it extortion. When the party applied, in this case, for administration papers, he must be supposed to have applied for what was usual. He received what every body else had received for fifteen years, and he paid for what he received at the customary rates, without objection. It ought to be considered, therefore, as a voluntary payment.

In this respect the present case differs from that cited from Coke. There the party refused to do an official act, till an illegal sum was paid. It was an act which the party had a right to have performed, to have it *then* performed, and to have it performed for a stated fee. Refusing to do his duty in this respect till other fees were paid, the officer doubtless was guilty of extortion. But in this case the money was paid voluntarily, for services rendered voluntarily. Most of the services were not, strictly speaking, official services. As before observed, the petition, bond, and so forth, might have been prepared elsewhere, if the party had so chosen. If he had so chosen, and had produced those papers, regularly prepared and executed, and the judge had then refused him a grant of administration, until he had, nevertheless, purchased a set of these papers out of the probate office, then this case would have resembled the one quoted. As the facts are, I think there is no resemblance.

I have thus far endeavored to show that the respondent's conduct, in relation to fees, was legal. If we have failed in this, the next question is, whether his conduct be so clearly illegal as to satisfy the court that it must have proceeded from corrupt motives. And it is to this part of our case that we supposed the evidence of what had been usual in other courts, and

* Bac. Abr., "Extortion."

thought to be legal by other judges, would be strictly applicable and highly important.

It was certainly our belief, that, as the respondent is accused of receiving illegal and excessive fees, in cases where fees are not limited by any positive law, the usage and practice of other judges in similar cases, known to the whole Commonwealth, and continued for many years, would be evidence on which the respondent might rely to rebut the accusation of intentional wrong. We have shown to this tribunal, that in an indictment on this same statute, in the Supreme Judicial Court, evidence of this sort was admitted, and the defendant acquitted on the strength of it. We had supposed it a plain dictate of common sense, that, where a judge was accused of acting contrary to law, he might show, if he could, that he acted honestly, though mistakenly, and to this end he might show that other judges had understood the law in the same way as he had understood it. And if he were able to show, not only that one judge, but many, and indeed all judges, had uniformly understood the law as he himself had, it would amount to a full defence. The learned managers have opposed the introduction of this evidence; and have prevailed on this court to reject it. Setting out with the proposition, that, by law, the respondent could receive no fees where none are expressly provided by statute, they have followed up this doctrine to the conclusion, that, if fees have been taken in any such case by the respondent, he must be convicted, although he should be able to show, as he is able to show, that every court and every judge in the State have supposed the law to be otherwise than the managers now assert it, and have uniformly acted upon that supposition. I am not, Sir, about to enter into another discussion on this point. I am persuaded it would be fruitless. The questions which we proposed to put to the witnesses are in writing, and therefore cannot easily be misrepresented. The court has, on the objection of the managers, overruled these questions, and shut out the evidence. As a matter decided in the cause, and for the purposes of the cause, we must, of course, submit to the decision. Still the question recurs, If the known usage and practice of the courts offered no rule or guide by which the respondent was to direct his conduct in relation to fees for services not enumerated in the fee bill, what rule was to direct him? What is the law which he has broken? We ask for the rule which ought to have governed his conduct and has not governed it; we receive for answer nothing intelligible but this, that where the statute has not expressly given fees, no fees are due, and it is illegal and impeachable to receive them. If the court should be of that opinion, a case is made out against the respondent. If it should not be of that opinion, as we trust it will not, then we submit that no case has been made out against him on this charge.

As to the charge of having refused to give Tarbell an account of items or particulars of the fees demanded, it is enough to say the charge is not proved. On his cross-examination the witness would not state that he asked for items or particulars. He appears simply to have wished a general voucher, to show what sums he had paid for expenses in the probate office, and to have been told that such voucher was not necessary, as the sums would be of course allowed in his account.

I now ask, Sir, where is the proof of corruption, in relation to any of the matters charged in this first article? Where is the moral turpitude, which alone ought to subject the respondent to punishment? Is there any thing in the case which looks like injustice or oppression? As to the special courts, holden for the convenience of the party, no injury arose from them to any body. The witness himself says they were a great accommodation to him, and saved the estate much money. One learned manager has said that these courts may lead to inconvenience and abuse. He has taxed his ingenuity to conjecture, rather than to show, what possible evils might hereafter arise from them. Yet he does this with the statute open before him, which expressly authorizes these courts, and the repeal of which would seem to be the proper remedy to relieve him from his apprehensions.

On the whole, Sir, I trust that the respondent has been able to give a satisfactory answer to every thing contained in the first article; that he is not only not legally proved to be guilty but that his conduct was in all respects unblamable and inoffensive; and that he will go from this trial, not only acquitted of the charges in the article, but also without having suffered in his reputation from the investigation which it has occasioned.

Mr. President, the remarks which have been made on the first article are generally applicable to the four succeeding, and render it unnecessary to comment on those articles, separately and particularly.

The sixth article turns out to be so little supported by any proof, that I do not deem it necessary to add to what has been said upon it. The testimony of Dr. Prescott, and the date of the letter produced, set this long-forgotten occurrence in its true light.

The seventh article appears to me to be a mere nullity. It charges no official misconduct whatever. The learned managers, I suppose, are of the same opinion, otherwise they would have been content with our admission of the article as it stands, and not have contended so ardently for the privilege of proving what was not stated. I have found myself, Sir, more than once mistaken, in the course of this trial, but have not felt more sensible of my own mistakes, on any occasion, than when I found myself wrong in supposing that neither the learned managers, nor any other lawyers, could be found to contend, that in a criminal case more could be proved against a defendant than had been stated; and that it was not enough for such defendant to admit the truth of the facts in the written allegation against him, precisely as they stood, and to demand the judgment of the court thereon. The constitution says that every man's offence shall be *fully and plainly*, *substantially and formally*, described and set forth. The learned managers seem so to construe this provision, as that, nevertheless, if facts be not alleged which show any offence at all to have been committed, still other facts may be found, under the words *unlawfully and corruptly*, which shall amount to an offence.

This seventh article charges the respondent with no misbehavior as a judge. The only offence imputed to him is one which he is said to have committed as an attorney. These overshadowing words, "unlawfully and corruptly," beneath the protection of which the learned managers have sought to shelter themselves, are applied to the respondent's conduct simply as an attorney at law, and not as judge of probate. It is proved, in point of fact, that the respondent performed certain merely clerical labor for a guardian, for which he was paid a reasonable and moderate compensation. The sum thus paid him was allowed, and as we suppose justly allowed, in the subsequent settlement of the guardian's account.

The eighth, ninth, tenth, eleventh, thirteenth, and fourteenth articles have been fully considered by my colleagues, and I will not detain the court by adding any thing to what they have said.

It is the twelfth of these articles, Sir, on which the learned managers seem most confidently to rely. Whatever becomes of the rest of the case, here, at least, there is thought to be a tenable ground. Here is one verdant spot, where impeachment can flourish; a sort of oasis, smiling amid the general desolation which the law and the evidence have spread round the residue of these charges.

I confess, Sir, that I approach the consideration of this article not without some apprehension. But that apprehension arises from nothing in the real nature of the charge, or in the evidence by which it is supported. My apprehension and alarm arise from this; that in a criminal trial, on a most solemn and important occasion, so much weight should be given to mere coloring and declamation, under the form of a criminal accusation. In my judgment, Sir, there is serious cause of alarm, when, in a court of this character, accusations are brought forward so exceedingly loose and indefinite, and arguments are urged in support of them so little resembling what we are accustomed to hear in the ordinary courts of criminal jurisdiction.

The offence in this article, whatever it be, instead of being charged and stated in ordinary legal language, is thrown into the form of a narrative. A story taken from the mouth of a heated, angry, and now contradicted witness, is written down at large, with every imaginable circumstance of aggravation likely to strike undistinguishing minds; and this story, thus told, is the very form in which the article is brought. Here we have, in the article itself, a narrative of all the evidence; we have a dialogue between the parties, and are favored so far as to be shown, by marks of quotation, what sentiments and sentences belong to the respective parties in that dialogue. All convenient epithets and expletives are inserted in this dialogue. We find the "urgent and repeated" demand of the respondent for fees. We perceive, also, that he is made to lead the conversation, on all occasions. He proposed to advise and instruct;

he proposed to allow the sum in the account; and it was, again, on his proposal so to insert it, that it was paid. He is represented as wanting in manners and decorum, as well as in official integrity. It is said he overheard a conversation; and that therefore he prepared to give his advice, before it was asked. In short, Sir, this article contains whatever is most likely to cause the respondent to be convicted before he is heard. I do most solemnly protest against this mode of bringing forward criminal charges. I put it to the feeling of every honorable man, whether he does not instinctively revolt from such a proceeding? In a government so much under the dominion of public opinion, and in a case in which public feeling is so easily excited, I appeal to every man of an honorable and independent mind, whether it be not the height of injustice to send forth charges against a public officer, accompanied with all these circumstances of aggravation and exasperation? Here the evidence, as yet altogether *ex parte*, the story told by a willing, if not a prejudiced witness, goes forth with the charge, embodied in the charge itself, without any distinction whatever between what is meant to be charged as an offence, and the evidence which is to support the charge. For my own part, Sir, I can conceive of nothing more unjust. Would it be tolerated for one moment in a court of law, I beg to ask, that a prosecutor, departing from all the usual forms of accusation, should tell his own story, in his own way, mix up his evidence with his charges, and his own inferences with his evidence, so that the accusation, the evidence, and the argument should all go together? A judge would well deserve impeachment and conviction who should suffer such an indictment to proceed.

In this case, the whole matter might have been stated in five lines. It is simply this, and nothing more; namely, that the respondent, wishing, as an attorney, to obtain certain fees from a guardian, promised, if they were paid, to allow them in the guardianship account, as judge; and being paid, he did so allow them. This is the whole substance and essence of the charge.

Notwithstanding our entire confidence in this court, we cannot but know that the respondent comes to his trial on this article under the greatest disadvantages. There is not a member of the court, nor a reading man in the community, who has not read this charge, and thereby seen at once the accusation, and the evidence which was to support it. The whole story is told, with all the minute circumstances, and no ground is left for the reservation of opinion, or whereupon charity itself can withhold its condemnation. Far be it from me, Sir, to impute this to design. I know not the cause; but, so far as the respondent is concerned, I know it would have been just as fair and favorable to him, if the original *ex parte* affidavit, upon which the article was founded, had been headed as No. 12, and inserted among the articles of impeachment. This, Sir, is the true ground of the alarm which I feel, in regard to this charge; an alarm, I confess, not diminished by perceiving that this article is so great a favorite with the learned managers; for when obliged to give up one and another of their accusations, they have asked us, with an air of confidence and exultation, whether we expect them to give up the twelfth article also.

I will now, Sir, with your permission, proceed to consider whether this article states any legal offence. Stripped of every thing but what is material, it appears to me to amount to no more than this, viz.: 1. That the respondent gave professional advice to a guardian, about the concerns of his ward, and received fees for it. 2. That he allowed those fees in the guardianship account. If this be the substance of the article, then the question follows the division which I have mentioned, and is, 1. Whether he had a right to give such advice, and to be paid for it; and, 2. Whether he had a right to allow the sum so paid in the guardian's account. I think these are the only questions to be considered. It cannot be material, certainly, whether Ware, the guardian, paid the fee willingly or unwillingly. It is certain that the respondent received it. If he had no right to it, then he must take the consequences; if he had a right to it, then there was nothing wrong but Ware's want of promptitude in paying it. Nor is it of any importance, supposing him to be right in allowing this fee in the guardian's account, whether he interlined the charge in an account already drawn out, or had the account drawn over, that it might be inserted. Here, again, we find a circumstance of no moment in itself set forth so as to be prominent and striking, in this charge, and likely to produce an effect. It is said that the sum was allowed by interlineation; as if the respondent had committed one crime to hide another, and had been guilty of forgery to cover up extortion. Sir, not only for the sake of the respondent, but for the sake of all justice, and in behalf of all impartiality and candor, I cannot too often or too earnestly express my extreme regret at the manner in which this charge is made. On a paper not yet finished and recorded, what harm to make an alteration, if it be of a thing in itself proper to be done? Is it not done every day, in every court? Not only affidavits, processes, and other legal papers, but also minutes, decrees, and judgments of the court, before they are recorded, are constantly altered by interlineation, by the court itself, or its order. The paper was in this case before the judge. It had not been recorded. If any new claim had then been produced, fit to be allowed, it was proper to allow it, and certainly not criminal to insert the allowance by interlineation.

If, Sir, the substance of every thing done by the respondent in this case is lawful, then there never can justly be a criminal conviction founded on the mere manner of doing it; even though the manner were believed to be as improper and indecorous as Ware would represent it. There is, therefore, no real inquiry in this case, as I can perceive, but whether the respondent had a right to give advice, and to be paid for it; and whether he had a right to allow it in the account.

And, in the first place, Sir, had the respondent a right to give professional advice to this guardian respecting the estate of his ward?

It has frequently, perhaps as often as otherwise, happened, that judges of probate have been practising lawyers. The statute-book shows that it has all along been supposed that this might be the case. There are acts which declare that in particular, specified cases, such as appeals from their own judgments, they shall not act as counsel; implying, of course, that in other cases they are expected so to act, if they see fit. Until the law of 1818, there was nothing to prevent them from being counsel for executors, administrators, and guardians, as well as any other clients. My colleague who first addressed the court has fully explained the history and state of the law in this particular. There being, then, no positive prohibition, is there any thing in the nature of the case that prevents, or should prevent, in all cases, a judge of probate from rendering professional assistance to executors, administrators, or guardians. I say in all cases, and supposing no fraudulent or collusive intention. The legislature has now passed a law on this subject, which is perhaps very well as a general rule, and now, of course, binding in all cases. But it can hardly be contended that, before the passing of this law, a judge of probate could in no case give professional advice to persons of this character. I admit, most readily, Sir, that, if a case of collusion or fraud were proved, it would deserve impeachment. If the judge and the guardian conspired to cheat the ward, a criminal conviction would be the just reward of both. They would go into utter disgrace together, and nobody would inquire which was the unjust judge, and which the fraudulent guardian; "which was the justice, and which was the thief." But in a case of fair and honest character, where the guardian needed professional advice and the judge was competent to give it, I see no legal objection. No doubt, a man of caution and delicacy would generally be unwilling to render professional services upon the value of which he might be afterwards called upon officially to form an opinion. He would not choose to be under the necessity of judging upon his own claim. Still, there would seem to be no legal incompatibility. He must take care only to judge right. In various other cases, judges of probate are or may be called on to make allowances for moneys paid to themselves. It is so in all cases of official fees. It might be so, also, in the case of a private debt due from the estate of a ward to a judge of probate. If, in this very case, there had been a previous debt due from Ware's ward to the respondent, might he not have asked Ware to pay it? Nay, might he not have "demanded" it? Might he not even have ventured to make an "urgent and repeated request" for it? And if he had been so fortunate as to obtain it, might he not have allowed it in Ware's guardianship account? And although he had been presumptuous enough to insert it, by interlineation, among other articles in the account, before it was finally allowed and passed, instead of drawing off a new account, would even this have been regarded as flagrant injustice or high enormity? Now, I maintain, Sir, that the respondent had in this case a right to give professional advice, and a right to be paid for it;

and until paid his claim was a debt due him from the ward's estate, which he might treat like any other debt. He might receive it as a debt, and then, as a debt paid, allow it in the guardian's account.

As before observed, the first question is, whether he could rightfully give this advice. It was certainly a case in which it was proper for the guardian to take legal advice of somebody. The occasion called for it, and we find the estate to have been essentially benefited by it. It is among the clearest duties of those who act in situations of trust to take legal advice whenever it is necessary. If they do not, and loss ensues, they themselves, and not those whom they represent, must bear that loss. There can be no clearer ground on which to make executors, administrators, and guardians personally liable for losses which happen to estates under their care, than negligence in not obtaining legal advice when necessary and proper. If, instead of giving this fee to the respondent, the guardian had given it to any other professional man, would any body have thought it improper? I presume no one would. Then, what was there in the respondent's situation which rendered it improper for him to give the advice? It concerned no matter that could come before him. It was wholly independent of any proceeding that had arisen, or could arise, in his court. It interfered in no way with his judicial duty, any more than it would have done to give the same advice to the ward himself, before the guardianship. He had, then, as good right to give this advice to the guardian as he would have had to give it to the ward.

And, Sir, in the second place, I think it plain that, if he had a right to give the advice, and to be paid for it, he had not only the right, but was bound, to allow it in the guardian's account. This article is attempted to be supported altogether by accumulating circumstances, no one of which bears resemblance to any thing like a legal offence. Is the respondent to be convicted for having given the advice? "No," it is said, "not that alone, but he demanded a fee for it." Is he to be convicted, then, for giving advice, and for demanding a fee for it, it not being denied that it was a fit occasion for somebody's advice? "No, not convicted for that alone, but he insisted on a fee, and was urgent and pressing for it." If he had a right to the fee, might he not insist upon it, and be urgent for it, till he got it, without a violation of law? "But then he promised to allow it in the guardian's account, and obtained it by means of this promise, and did afterwards allow it." But if it ought to be paid, and the guardian paid it, ought it not to be allowed in his account, and could it be improper for the respondent to say he should so allow it, and actually so to allow it? "But did he not allow it by interlineation?" What sort of interlineation? The account was before him, unrecorded; this came forward as a new charge; and for convenience, and to save labor, it was inserted among other charges, without making a copy of the paper; and this is all the interlineation there is in the case.

I now ask you, Sir, I put it to every member of this court, upon his oath and his conscience, to say to which of these circumstances the guilt attaches. Where is the crime? If this charge had been carried to the account without interlineation, would the respondent have been guiltless? If not, then the interlineation does not constitute his guilt. If the fee had been paid to some one else, and then allowed, in the same manner it was allowed, would the respondent have been guiltless? If so, then the crime is not in the manner of allowing the charge. If the guardian had urged and pressed for the respondent's advice, and in receiving it had paid for it willingly and cheerfully, and it had been properly allowed in the account, would the respondent then have been guiltless? If so, then his mere giving advice, and taking fees for it of a guardian, does not constitute his crime. In this manner, Sir, this article may be analyzed, and it will be found that no one part of it contains the criminal matter, and if there be crime in no one part, there can be no crime in the whole. It is not a case of right acts done with wrong motives, which sometimes may show misconduct, all taken together, although each circumstance may be of itself indifferent. Here is official corruption complained of. We ask in what it consists. We demand to know the legal offence which has been committed. A narrative is rehearsed to us, and we are told that the result of that must be conviction; but on what legal grounds, or for what describable legal reason, I am yet at a loss to understand.

The article mentions another circumstance, which, whether true or false, must exceedingly prejudice the respondent, and yet has no just bearing on the case. It is said the respondent told Ware, that, if he would pay this fee, the "overseers need know nothing about it." Now, Sir, what had the overseers to do with this? No more than the town crier. Those parts of the account which consisted of expenses incurred in their neighborhood were properly enough, though not necessarily, subjected to their examination. They had an interest in having the account right, and their approbation was a convenient voucher. But what had they to do with the propriety of the guardian's taking legal advice, for the benefit of his ward? They could not judge of it, nor were they to approve or disapprove his charge for obtaining such advice. Why, then, I ask, Sir, was this observation about the overseers introduced, not only as evidence, but into the body of the charge itself, as making a part of that charge? What part of any known legal offence does that observation, or others like it, constitute? Nevertheless, Sir, this has had its effect, and in my opinion a most unjust effect.

I will now, Sir, beg leave to make a few remarks on the evidence adduced in support of this article. Of those facts which I have thought alone material, there is no doubt; about them there is no dispute. It is true, that the respondent gave the advice, and received the fee, and allowed it in the account. If this be guilt, he is guilty. As to every thing else in the articles, as to all those allegations which go to degrade the respondent, and in some measure affect his reputation as a man of honor and delicacy, they rest on Ware, and on Ware alone. Now, Sir, I only ask for the respondent the common advantages allowed to persons on trial for alleged offences. I only entreat for him from this court the observance of those rules which prevail on all other occasions, in respect to the construction to be given to evidence, and the allowances which particular considerations render proper.

It is proved that this witness has had a recent misunderstanding with the respondent, and that he comes forward only since that misunderstanding to bring this matter into public notice. Threats of vengeance, for another supposed injury, he has been proved to have uttered more than once. This consideration alone should lead the court to receive his evidence with great caution, when he is not swearing to a substantial fact, in which he might be contradicted, but to the manner of a transaction.

Here is peculiar room for misrepresentation, and coloring, either from mistake or design. What a public officer does can be proved; but the mere manner in which he does it, every word he may say, every gesture he may make, cannot ordinarily be proved; and when a witness comes forth who pretends to remember them, whether he speaks truth or falsehood, it is most difficult to contradict him. It is in such a case, therefore, that a prejudiced witness should be received with the utmost caution and distrust.

There is, Sir, another circumstance of great weight. This is a very stale complaint. It is now nearly six years since this transaction took place. Why has it not been complained of before? There is no new discovery. All that is known now was known then. If Ware thought of it then, as he thinks of it now, why did he not complain then? What has caused his honest indignation so long to slumber? Has it not evidently been roused only by a quarrel with the respondent?

Let me ask, Sir, what a grand jury would say to a prosecutor, who, with the full knowledge of all the facts, should have slept over a supposed injury for six years, and should then come forward to prefer an indictment? What would they say especially if they found him apparently stimulated by recent resentment, and prosecuting, for one supposed ancient injury, with the heat and passion excited by another supposed recent injury? Sir, they would justly look on his evidence with suspicion, and would undoubtedly throw out his bill. Justice would demand it; and in my humble opinion justice demands nothing less on the present occasion.

But, Sir, there is one rule of a more positive nature, which I think applicable to the case; and that is, that a witness detected in one misrepresentation is to be credited in nothing. This rule is obviously founded in the plainest reason, and it would be totally unsafe to disregard it. Now if there be any one part of Ware's testimony more essential than all the rest, as to its effect in giving a bad appearance to the respondent's conduct, it is that in which he testifies that the respondent volunteered in the case, and offered his advice before it was asked. This is a most material part of the whole story; it is indispensable to the keeping of the picture which the learned managers have drawn. And yet, Sir, in this particular Ware is distinctly and positively contradicted by Grout. Now if we were in a court of law, a jury would be instructed, that, if they believed Ware had wilfully deviated from the truth in this respect, nothing which rested solely on his credit would be received as proved. We ask for the respondent, in this, as in other cases, only the common protection of the law. We require only that those rules which have governed other trials may govern his; and according to these rules, I submit to the court that it cannot and ought not to convict the respondent, even if the facts sworn to would, if proved, warrant a conviction, upon the sole testimony of this witness. Even if we were sure that there were no other direct departure from the truth, yet in the whole of his narrative, and the whole of his manner, we see, I think, indications of great animosity and prejudice. If the whole of this transaction were to be recited by a friendly or a candid witness, I do not believe it would strike any body as extraordinary. Any mode of telling this story which shall confine the narrative to the essential facts, will leave it, in my humble opinion, if not a strictly proper, yet by no means an illegal or impeachable transaction. Let it be remembered that a great part of his story is such as cannot be contradicted, though it be false, inasmuch as it relates to alleged conversations between him and the respondent when nobody else was present. Wherever the natural means exist of contradicting or qualifying his testimony, there it is accomplished. Whatever circumstance can be found bearing on it shows that it is in a greater or less degree incorrect. For example, Ware would represent that it was an important part of this arrangement to keep the payment of the fee from the knowledge of the overseers. This was the reason why the charge was to be inserted in the existing account, by interlineation. Yet the evidence is, that a complete copy of this very interlined account was carried home by Ware, where the overseers could see it, and would of course perceive exactly what had been done. This is utterly inconsistent with any purpose of secrecy or concealment.

Making just and reasonable allowances for the considerations which I have mentioned, I ask, is any case proved, by the rules of law, against the respondent? And further, Sir, taking the facts only which are satisfactorily established, and supposing the respondent's conduct to have been wrong, is it clearly shown to have been intentionally wrong? If he ought not to have given the advice, is it any thing more than an error of judgment? Can this court have so little charity for human nature, as to believe that a man of respectable standing could act corruptly for so paltry an object? Even although they should judge his conduct improper, do they believe it to have originated in corrupt motives? For my own part, Sir, notwithstanding all that prejudices and prepossession may have done, and all that the most extraordinary manner of presenting this charge may have done, I will not believe, till the annunciation of its judgment shall compel me, that this court will ever convict the respondent upon this article.

I now beg leave to call the attention of the court to one or two considerations of a general nature, and which appear to me to have an important bearing on the merits of this whole cause. The first is this, that from the day when the respondent was appointed judge of probate, down to the period at which these articles of impeachment close, from the year 1805 to 1821, there is not a single case, with the exception of that alleged by Ware, in which it is even pretended that any secrecy was designed or attempted by the respondent; there is not a single case in which he is even accused of having wished to keep any thing out of sight, or to conceal any fact in his administration, any charge which he had made, or any fee which he had taken. The evidence on which you are to judge him is evidence furnished by himself; and instead of being obliged to seek for testimony in sources beyond the respondent's control, it is his own avowed actions, his public administration, and the records of his office, which the managers of the prosecution alone have been able to produce. And yet he is charged with having acted wilfully and corruptly; as if it were possible that a magistrate, in a high and responsible station, with the eyes of the community upon him, should, for near twenty years, pursue a course of corrupt and wilful maleadministration, of which every act and every instance were formally and publicly put on record by himself, and laid open in the face of the community. Is this agreeable to the laws of human nature? Why, Sir, if the respondent has so long been pursuing a course of conscious, and wilful, and corrupt maleadministration, why do we discover none of the usual and natural traces of such a course, some attempt at concealment, some effort at secrecy? And in all the numberless cases in which he had opportunity and temptation, why is not even a suspicion thrown out, that he has attempted to draw a veil of privacy over his alleged extortions? Is it in reason that you should be obliged to go to his own records for the proof of his pretended crimes? And can you, with even the color of probability, appeal to a course of action unsuspiciously pursued in the face of Heaven, to support an accusation of offences in their very nature private, concealed, and hidden?

Another consideration of a general nature to which I earnestly ask the attention of this honorable court is this, that after all these accusations which have been brought together against the respondent, in all these articles of impeachment, and with all the industry and zeal with which the matter of them has been furnished to the honorable managers, he is not accused, nor suspected, of the crime most likely to bring an unjust judge to the bar of this court. Show me the unjust judgment he has rendered, the illegal order he has given, the corrupt decree he has uttered, the act of oppression he has committed. What, Sir, a magistrate, charged with a long and deliberate perseverance in wilful and corrupt administration, accused of extortion, thought capable of accepting the miserable bribe of a few cents or a few dollars for illegal and unconstitutional acts, and that, too, in an office presenting every day the most abundant opportunities, and, if the respondent were of the character pretended, the most irresistible temptation, to acts of lucrative injustice; and yet not one instance of a corrupt, illegal, or oppressive judgment! I do ask the permission of this honorable court, and of every member of it, to put this to his own conscience. I will ask him, if he can now name a more able and upright magistrate, as shown in all his proceedings and judgments, in all the offices of probate in the State; one whose records are more regularly and properly kept, whose administration is more prompt, correct, and legal, whose competency to the duties is more complete, whose discharge of them is more punctual. I put this earnestly, Sir to the conscience of every member of this honorable court. I appeal more especially to my honorable friend,* intrusted with a share of the management of this prosecution, and who has

* Hon. S. P. P. Fay.

been for twenty years an inhabitant of the county of Middlesex. I will appeal to him, Sir, and I will ask him whether, if he knew that this night his wife should be left a widow and his children fatherless, there is a magistrate in the State in whose protection he had rather they should be left, than in that of the respondent? Forgetting for a moment that he is a prosecutor, and remembering only that he is a citizen of the same county, a member of the same profession, with an acquaintance of twenty years standing, I will ask him if he will say that he believes there is a county in the State in which the office of judge of probate has been better administered for twenty years, than it has been in the county of Middlesex by this respondent. And yet, Sir, you are asked to disgrace him. You are asked to fix on him the stigma of a corrupt and unjust judge, and condemn him to wear it through life.

Mr. President, the case is closed! The fate of the respondent is in your hands. It is for you now to say, whether, from the law and the facts as they have appeared before you, you will proceed to disgrace and disfranchise him. If your duty calls on you to convict him, let justice be done, and convict him; but, I adjure you, let it be a clear, undoubted case. Let it be so for his sake, for you are robbing him of that for which, with all your high powers, you can yield him no compensation; let it be so for your own sakes, for the responsibility of this day's judgment is one which you must carry with you through life. For myself, I am willing here to relinquish the character of an advocate, and to express opinions by which I am prepared to be bound as a citizen and a man. And I say upon my honor and conscience, that I see not how, with the law and constitution for your guides, you can pronounce the respondent guilty. I declare that I have seen no case of wilful and corrupt official misconduct, set forth according to the requisitions of the constitution, and proved according to the common rules of evidence. I see many things imprudent and ill-judged; many things that I could wish had been otherwise; but corruption and crime I do not see.

Sir, the prejudices of the day will soon be forgotten; the passions, if any there be, which have excited or favored this prosecution will subside; but the consequence of the judgment you are about to render will outlive both them and you. The respondent is now brought, a single, unprotected individual, to this formidable bar of judgment, to stand against the power and authority of the State. I know you can crush him, as he stands before you, and clothed as you are with the sovereignty of the State. You have the power "to change his countenance and to send him away." Nor do I remind you, that your judgment is to be rejudged by the community; and, as you have summoned him for trial to this high tribunal, that you are soon to descend yourselves from these seats of justice, and stand before the higher tribunal of the world. I would not fail so much in respect to this honorable court as to hint that it could pronounce a sentence which the community will reverse. No, Sir, it is not the world's revision which I would call on you to regard; but that of your own consciences, when years have gone by and you shall look back on the sentence you are about to render. If you send away the respondent, condemned and sentenced, from your bar, you are yet to meet him in the world on which you cast him out. You will be called to behold him a disgrace to his family, a sorrow and a shame to his children, a living fountain of grief and agony to himself.

If you shall then be able to behold him only as an unjust judge, whom vengeance has overtaken and justice has blasted, you will be able to look upon him, not without pity, but yet without remorse. But if, on the other hand, you shall see, whenever and wherever you meet him, a victim of prejudice or of passion, a sacrifice to a transient excitement; if you shall see in him a man for whose condemnation any provision of the constitution has been violated or any principle of law broken down, then will he be able, humble and low as may be his condition, then will he be able to turn the current of compassion backward, and to look with pity on those who have been his judges. If you are about to visit this respondent with a judgment which shall blast his house; if the bosoms of the innocent and the amiable are to be made to bleed under your infliction, I beseech you to be able to state clear and strong grounds for your proceeding. Prejudice and excitement are transitory, and will pass away. Political expediency, in matters of judicature, is a false and hollow principle, and will never satisfy the conscience of him who is fearful that he may have given a hasty judgment. I earnestly entreat you, for your own sakes, to possess yourselves of solid reasons, founded in truth and justice, for the judgment you pronounce, which you can carry with you till you go down into your graves; reasons which it will require no argument to revive, no sophistry, no excitement, no regard to popular favor, to render satisfactory to your consciences; reasons which you can appeal to in every crisis of your lives, and which shall be able to assure you, in your own great extremity, that you have not judged a fellow-creature without mercy.

Sir, I have done with the case of this individual, and now leave it in your hands. But I would yet once more appeal to you as public men; as statesmen; as men of enlightened minds, capable of a large view of things, and of foreseeing the remote consequences of important transactions; and, as such, I would most earnestly implore you to consider fully of the judgment you may pronounce. You are about to give a construction to constitutional provisions which may adhere to that instrument for ages, either for good or evil. I may perhaps overrate the importance of this occasion to the public welfare; but I confess it does appear to me that, if this body give its sanction to some of the principles which have been advanced on this occasion, then there is a power in the State above the constitution and the law; a power essentially arbitrary and despotic, the exercise of which may be most dangerous. If impeachment be not under the rule of the constitution and the laws, then may we tremble, not only for those who may be impeached, but for all others. If the full benefit of every constitutional provision be not extended to the respondent, his case becomes the case of all the people of the Commonwealth. The constitution is their constitution. They have made it for their own protection, and for his among the rest. They are not eager for his conviction. They desire not his ruin. If he be condemned, without having his offences set forth in the manner which they, by their constitution, have prescribed, and in the manner which they, by their laws, have ordained, then not only is he condemned unjustly, but the rights of the whole people are disregarded. For the sake of the people themselves, therefore, I would resist all attempts to convict by straining the laws or getting over their prohibitions. I hold up before him the broad shield of the constitution; if through that he be pierced and fall, he will be but one sufferer in a common catastrophe.

END OF VOLUME FIFTH.